Facilitation Techniques in Therapeutic Recreation

Second Edition

Facilitation Techniques in Therapeutic Recreation

Second Edition

John Dattilo
Penn State University
&
Alexis McKenney
Florida International University

Venture Publishing, Inc.
State College, PA

Production: George Lauer and Richard Yocum
Cover Design: StepUp Communications, Inc.
Cover Painting: CHRISTINA'S WORLD, 1948 tempera © Andrew Wyeth
Digital Image © The Museum of Modern Art/Licensed by SCALA/Art Resource, NY

Library of Congress Catalogue Card Number 2011929716
ISBN-10: 1-892132-93-1
ISBN-13: 978-1-892132-93-2

For our mothers, Gloria Dattilo and Tish McMahan,
who inspire us with their gentle fortitude;
and our fathers, Martin Dattilo and Ron McKenney,
who comfort us with loving memories.

Table of Contents

Chapter 1 *John Dattilo*

Chapter 2 *Diane Groff and John Dattilo*

Chapter 3 *Alexis McKenney and John Dattilo*

Chapter 4   *Ellen Broach and John Dattilo*

Chapter 5   *Ellen Broach and John Dattilo*

Chapter 6   *Mary Ann Devine*

Chapter 7 *John Dattilo and Richard Williams*

Chapter 8 *Alexis McKenney and John Dattilo*

Chapter 9 *Travis Meckley, John Dattilo, and Sharon Malley*

Chapter 10   *John Dattilo and Ijnanyah Wingate*

Chapter 11   *Sara Tosado, John Dattilo, and Christine Sausser*

Chapter 12   *Sarah Brownlee and John Dattilo*

Chapter 13   *Lourdes Martinez-Cox, John Dattilo, and Kathleen Sheldon*

Chapter 14   *Lynne Cory, Alexis McKenney, and Stephanie Marsden*

Chapter 15   *Ellen Broach and Sarah Richardson*

Chapter 19 *Alexis McKenney and John Dattilo*

Preface

Several years ago, we assembled a task force to identify competencies for students to acquire during their undergraduate studies in therapeutic recreation (TR). The task force was composed of approximately a dozen professionals with experience in TR. We reviewed relevant documents produced by professional organizations including the American Therapeutic Recreation (TR) Association, the Council on TR Certification, the Pew Health Professions Commission, the National Recreation and Parks Association, and the National TR Society.

After the task force determined competencies, we identified textbooks which addressed the competencies. Although some texts were identified to be helpful, no text was found that presented adequate material on competencies associated with facilitation techniques frequently used by TR specialists. Therefore, I agreed to spearhead an effort to alleviate the problem of the absence of a text presenting facilitation techniques to TR specialists.

During the 1990s, The Department of Recreation and Leisure Studies at the University of Georgia was fortunate to be supported by training grants funded by the U.S. Department of Education's Office of Special Education to produce leaders with doctoral and master's degrees. I worked with these students to develop skills required of an educator that extend beyond oral presentation to include skills associated with written presentation. Therefore, I collaborated with students to produce manuscripts designed to enhance TR services. One particular writing venture was development of a document which contained information about facilitation techniques relevant to TR.

Ultimately, we generated a product that could contribute to the body of literature in our field while simultaneously working to enhance each contributor's writing skills. I worked closely with each author trying to ensure that the material presented contained sufficient detail to educate a naive reader. In addition, based on the needs of the field and educational principles, we identified specific sections contained in every chapter to provide a level of consistency to the reader.

Although the chapters included in this book cover a variety of facilitation techniques used by TR specialists, the text clearly is not exhaustive. The competencies generated by the task force became the basis for identification of possible topics while individual expertise and interest guided the actual selection of the techniques presented in the book.

Since publication of the first edition of the book, most of the authors have taken teaching and research positions at universities across the country. Over the years, we have received positive feedback about the usefulness of the book and encouragement to update and expand this text from colleagues preparing students to become TR specialists and practitioners currently engaged in service delivery. To respond to these requests, Lexi McKenney, who was a major contributor to the first edition, agreed to help me work with the authors to produce this 2nd edition. We hope that this book helps contribute to the education of TR specialists and ultimately to improving the lives of people with disabilities.

– J. D.

About Using *Christina's World* on the Cover of this Book

In the painting on the cover of this book, Christina Olson is making her way back from the garden to the farm house in Maine. Christina has cerebral palsy. I chose to use this painting for the cover of the book for several reasons but primarily because I like to use the picture as a metaphor. For me, the picture is a metaphor for therapeutic recreation (TR) specialists using facilitation techniques with people who have disabilities.

The metaphor involves Christina, who is positioned prominently on the bottom left corner of the painting, representing people with disabilities trying to achieve a goal. In this particular case, Christina has the goal of going home, going to the farm house located in the upper right corner of the picture. The farm house represents the goal that we TR specialists have for the people we serve, that is to help individuals experience meaningful and enjoyable leisure.

Christina is the predominant figure in the painting and this reflects how in TR it is important that we have the individuals we serve utmost in our minds, have them drive what we do, and have them be the focus of our services. Although Christina is quite striking, what most impresses me is how much of the painting is consumed by the open field. I interpret the field as the environment and our society and the challenges they create for people with disabilities attempting to experience leisure.

Therefore, for Christina to achieve her goal of returning home she must traverse the field. Her passing through the field symbolizes people with disabilities navigating through life. Facilitation techniques, some of which are presented in the book, allow TR specialists to assist people on their journey to develop knowledge and skills that create a sense of self-determination and connectedness that empower them to experience enjoyment and leisure.

On January 16, 2009, Andrew Wyeth, the man who painted this wonderful picture and so many more, died at his home in Philadelphia at the age of 91. According to Hillary Holland, a spokesperson for the Brandywine River Museum, Andrew Wyeth is well known for his portrayal of the hidden melancholy of the people and landscapes of Pennsylvania's Brandywine Valley and coastal Maine. Wyeth's wife, Betsy, was a strong influence on his career and was the person who introduced him to Christina Olson. Andrew Wyeth befriended Christina and her brother and moved in with them for a time to create a series of studies of the house, its environment, and its occupants. *Christina's World* is one of the paintings he created during that time.

Acknowledgements

Appreciation is extended to all the authors of the chapters contained in this book. The authors of these chapters are quite an amazing group of individuals; many of whom are highly regarded in our field or emerging onto the scene. Several talented people created the figures for this text including Diane Burnet, Michael Gardner, Susan Shu-Chih Huang, and Beaumie Kim–thanks to all of you!

Chapter 1
The Age of Enlightenment for Therapeutic Recreation

John Dattilo

He (Aristotle) concluded that . . .
happiness derives from dedication to the goal of living a good life,
and that such a life entails a never-ending quest for knowledge and wisdom

–James O'Toole

Introduction

As I look into a dictionary to find the word *light*, I read that light is that which makes it possible to see. On first inspection, this definition seems simple enough. I begin to think about my experiences camping and how a flashlight is invaluable when attempting to play an engaging game of gin rummy with my brother, Larry, after the sun has gone down. However, I remember how when that same flashlight is pointed directly at my eyes, that light makes it impossible for me to see. I conclude then that the value of light is dependent on how it is used. Light is not inherently helpful; rather, it is the way it is applied that transforms it into something useful. I am reminded of the story of the man looking for his keys.

A woman is walking down a street when she sees a man on his hands and knees searching through his front lawn. The woman stops and asks the man what he is doing. The man stops his search, looks up, and while shielding his eyes from the bright sun he explains to the woman that he has lost his keys. The woman watches the man who continues to intently search through the grass. She then asks the man where he last saw his keys. The man stops and, once again, shields his eyes from the light as he further explains to the woman that he last saw his keys in his kitchen. Puzzled, the woman asks the man why he is looking for his keys in his front yard when he last saw his keys in the kitchen. The man replies that the light is much better out here.

So, light alone does not do us much good unless we know how to use it. Information has many similarities to light in that information is not inherently useful, but when effectively applied, information becomes useful. When professionals acquire information and use it in an effective manner, these individuals are said to be enlightened.

The purpose of this introductory chapter to this book is to describe how therapeutic recreation (TR) specialists can become more enlightened so that we can enlighten individuals who participate in our programs. The message "to become enlightened so that we may enlighten" is divided into the following three sections: become, enlightened, and enlighten.

Become

Returning to the dictionary, the word *become* is defined as to undergo change or development. If we are to become enlightened we must be willing to change. Henry David Thoreau's words are relevant here, "Things do not change, we do." If TR specialists want to become enlightened, we must be willing to make changes in the manner in which we deliver services. Returning to the analogy of "light," I reflect on my belief that light can help us find our way if, at times, we are willing to change. A story about my oldest son, David, perhaps will illustrate this belief.

> When David turned one year of age, he began attending a play group which met for a few hours each week on campus. Each day, when he and I departed, we drove out of the driveway of our home and turned onto the road we were headed directly into the sun. As the sun shown brightly into his eyes he began to cry. We then approached an intersection and turned; the sun no longer shown into his eyes and David was once more content. However, each time we turned into the sun he cried until the next turn. Needless to say, on those stretches when we were driving into the sun, I tended to have a bit heavier foot on the gas pedal. I tried several approaches to remedy this situation from giving David sunglasses to tinting the car windows, but nothing we did seemed to make a difference. Then, one day, I pulled out of the driveway and onto the street and . . . and . . . nothing! I was facing forward in my typical cringed position and I did not hear any crying. Quickly I turned to see what had happened, and there was little David with a big grin covering his eyes with his hands. Finally, David had learned to make a change in his behavior; by covering his eyes he solved the problem.

To become something requires that an individual undergo change or development. Development implies growth and a movement forward. TR specialists must be willing to change and develop so that we can become enlightened.

Enlightened

When people are enlightened, they experience freedom from ignorance and misinformation. As TR specialists are aware, freedom is a fundamental aspect of the leisure experience. What appears most important in regards to freedom is the perception by individuals that they are free. The French novelist, Antoine de Saint-Exupéry once wrote that "I know but one freedom and that is the freedom of the mind." Freedom of the mind equates to freedom from ignorance.

Contained in his influential book titled *The Rights of Man*, the American political philosopher, Thomas Paine, wrote that "Ignorance is of a peculiar nature; once dispelled, it is impossible to reestablish it. It is not originally a thing of itself, but is only the absence of knowledge." I believe this quote helps to focus our attention on the power of knowledge and the value of becoming enlightened. But a question may arise in your mind as, "What can we do to become enlightened?" I imagine that there are many ways to become enlightened; however, I have chosen to briefly discuss the following four strategies:

- Listen
- Read
- Evaluate
- Research

Listen

I have realized over the years that much can be learned by listening to people. As a practitioner, I learned to listen to what people with disabilities said they wanted for their leisure. When teaching others to work with people with disabilities, I have tried to instill in them the importance of listening. As I have taught students to become TR specialists and watched them interact with participants, I provided them with advice given by William Shakespeare: "Give every man thine ear, but few thy voice."

The suggestion by Shakespeare can be a lesson for all of us. It seems to me that a way to become enlightened is to listen to what other people are saying. Not focusing on what we are going to say but rather taking time to listen to people allows us to be more effective practitioners. We can listen to what participants are trying to tell us, what advice our colleagues are trying to give us, and what guidance our supervisors are trying to share with us. An experience I had after watching some of my eager and enthusiastic students interact with some youth with developmental disabilities may help illustrate my point.

> After observing my students dominating their conversations with the participants, I called a meeting. I had a three-part message I shared with them on that day. Although I might have used more gentle words, the basic message I conveyed to them concerning their interactions with the participants was: sit down, shut up, and listen.

I have repeated that message several times over the years because listening is critical to conveying to others that you care about them. Have you ever shared a conversation with someone who, after the person finished telling a story and it was your turn to speak, appeared to be thinking about what he or she was going to say next? If you happened to take a breath this person would verbally jump in with yet another anecdote. If this interaction continued for any length of time, how did this exchange make you feel? I think it is helpful to remember that feeling as we interact with our participants when they are trying to tell us something. An analogy comes to mind.

A young boy sits near a large boulder at the ocean's edge. In his hand he has a small squirt gun. After filling the gun, he takes aim at the boulder and fires. Much to his dismay, the water careens off the face of the boulder without moving the large rock. It seems that the boulder is not really interested in the boy or his feeble attempt at contact; the boulder stays rigid and apparently unchanged. His interest in the boulder wanes and he glances away from the boulder and spies a rock lying on the ground. As he walks toward the rock a wave comes in and moves the rock about. The boy marvels at the way the rock responds to the oceans advances by tumbling in different directions. It seems as if the rock is just waiting for the ocean to come to it and touch it; the rock changes constantly based on the movements of the ocean. To the boy the boulder was just not listening to him, but the rock surely listened to the ocean.

When working with people with disabilities, do we hold fast to what we have learned initially or do we listen, reflect on what others say, and then decide whether or not to modify the way we deliver our services? It seems to me that simply closing our mouths and opening our ears are actions that help us become enlightened.

Listening and this book. When developing this book, we listened to many people with disabilities about how they felt about different facilitation techniques. We heard from TR specialists and other therapists across the globe engaged in the systematic application of various facilitation techniques. We also listened to each other since the cumulative experience of the authors implementing these facilitation techniques is extensive. In addition, we listened to the feedback given to us by practitioners and students alike after they examined various drafts and the first edition of this text. We learned a great deal from these people and became more enlightened from our efforts.

Read

Many studies have examined variables that could contribute to school achievement. There appears to be only one variable shown to consistently predict a child's success in school—reading. If adults read to children at a very young age and then encourage and support children to read, these children are more successful in school. The words of the American psychologist, B. F. Skinner, come to mind, "We shouldn't teach great books; we should teach a love of reading."

Although we were *required* to read during our formal education, some of us associate our learning with a structured classroom and a teacher telling us what is important rather than reading assigned literature. Unfortunately, by the time some of us are in college, much of our effort is devoted to figuring out the least amount of reading we could get away with doing. To become enlightened, it is imperative that we attempt to keep abreast of new information by reading. After spending time in a library, Robert Fulghum, in his book, *Uh-Oh* wrote the following:

> . . . I had an overwhelming bad news/good news feeling.
> Knowledge and the number of books that contained it were infinite
> - I could <u>never</u> read them <u>all</u>. And as I read one, ten more were
> written somewhere. That was the bad news. The good news was
> that the knowledge and the books that contained it were infinite. I
> would <u>never</u> run out of things to learn. Knowledge was infinite in
> every direction I turned.

Today, more than ever, research on people with disabilities is being conducted and published in journals. Textbooks are being written that attempt to synthesize and integrate this research into practice. The importance of professionals staying abreast of recent innovations became clearer to me through the following experience.

> Many years ago, we began searching for a pediatrician. On one
> interview, we spoke with a physician about a variety of issues.
> When we spoke, he thoughtfully answered our questions. On
> several occasions, he stated his position and then would reach into
> a stack of journals on his desk, pull one out, turn to a page, and
> show us specific studies, tables, and diagrams which supported the
> way he intended to care for our child. Needless to say, he was our
> pediatrician for years; choosing him was one of the best decisions
> we ever made.

TR specialists practicing today are much more fortunate than their predecessors. We now have a growing body of knowledge that expands as studies and other writings are published in the *Therapeutic Recreation Journal*, the *Annual in Therapeutic Recreation*, the *Journal of Recreation Therapy*, and a wide range of journals in related fields. TR is a relatively new and identified by many as an "emerging profession." The initial training of many therapists may have been limited by the lack of research and written application regarding interventions and facilitation techniques expected to be used by TR specialists today. However, many professionals agree, such as Bruce Thyer and his student, Laura Myers, who, in an article about ethical treatment of social work clients, stated that ". . . there are many treatments that have been empirically validated through research, and efforts are being made to identify these procedures and educate clinicians about their existence." Since interventions and facilitation techniques are a critical aspect of TR services, having access to written documentation that can be read, interpreted, and applied is essential to practitioners.

    Over the years, as we have solicited input from a variety of practitioners, educators, and students, the one area that they express to learn more about are facilitation techniques. In the past, TR specialists have been expected to learn most facilitation techniques on the job. Unfortunately, the lyrics sung by the Lynyrd Skynyrd Band applied to many of us: ". . . I know a little, I know a little bout it. . . but baby, I can guess the rest." When it comes to enhancing the lives of people with disabilities, this approach is unacceptable.

Reading and this book. This book contains 19 chapters, each of which is devoted to presenting a specific facilitation technique. An **introduction** is provided in each of the chapters to familiarize the reader with the particular facilitation technique. The introductions contain a preview of what major topics will be presented in the chapter.

Each chapter provides **definitions** of terms relevant to the facilitation technique. As we were developing this book, it became obvious to us that much confusion associated with the facilitation techniques was a direct result of the lack of clarity of terms used to describe the technique and associated procedures. Therefore, in each chapter we provide definitions of relevant terms that we found to be most useful and we use these terms consistently throughout the chapter.

> For example, what is meant by the phrase "facilitation technique?" To begin, the word "facilitation" or "facilitate" in the dictionary is defined as to free from difficulties or obstacles, to make easier, aid or assist. In addition, a "technique" is a systematic procedure by which a complex scientific task is accomplished. Putting these words together we arrive at the definition of a "facilitation technique" as a systematic procedure by which individuals are empowered to overcome difficulties or obstacles. And according to Judy Voelkl, Terry Kinney. and Jeff Witman (2004), appropriate selection and purposeful application of these facilitation techniques is essential to successful outcomes for TR interventions.

Every chapter provides a **description** of the specific facilitation technique. These descriptions are intended to help the reader learn about important considerations when implementing such a technique. Hopefully, by reading this book, current and future TR specialists will become more enlightened.

Evaluate

Although listening and reading are two important ways to become enlightened, TR specialists must also continually evaluate what they do and make necessary adjustments to enhance the services they deliver. Usually, it is easy to spot professionals who are engaged in continuous evaluation of their actions; likewise, individuals who choose not to evaluate their actions are noticeable. Have you ever examined an agency's recreation activity bulletin board and learned that the activities posted have been offered the same way for the past several years? Or have you watched a teacher lecture who may not be that interesting, who continues to use notes that are old, yellowed, and outdated? Often, individuals associated with these actions are in need of an evaluation of their services.

I am often impressed when I see TR specialists providing effective, innovative services. Experience can be a wonderful teacher; however, I think it is useful to consider that twenty years of experience can be one year of experience twenty times. Some experienced professionals may have been engaged in fairly ineffective service delivery for many years. Unless we continuously evaluate what we do, years of experience may not be very useful. I believe that we must continuously listen to those around us, read relevant literature, and strive to evaluate what we do.

Evaluation and this book. Implied in evaluation is a retrospective examination of what has occurred. Although, the information presented in this section has focused on the evaluation of the individual professional, much insight can be gained in examining a particular facilitation technique retrospectively. Therefore, a brief history of the facilitation technique is provided in each chapter.

To help readers visualize implementation of facilitation techniques, **case studies** are included in each chapter. The case studies provide a brief description of the participants followed by a more detailed depiction of the application of a specific facilitation technique by practitioners who have been involved in continuous evaluation of their services. An examination of participants responses to the facilitation techniques are presented to assist readers in becoming enlightened.

Research

The author of *Research in Education*, John Best, stated: "Evaluation seeks conclusions leading to recommendations and decisions; research seeks conclusions leading to new truths." As previously mentioned, TR specialists who continuously evaluate their actions are able to examine what they do, and based on this examination, make recommendations and decisions regarding the way they deliver services. Although evaluation is an important aspect of becoming enlightened, it is not a sufficient one.

The difficulty with relying only on clinical experience and evaluation to help make decisions about practice is that, although participants may achieve therapeutic goals and objectives after they engage in TR programs, it is not clear if these services actually accounted for the improvement. Many other explanations for participants' progress could be provided, such as they matured, other therapies impacted their behavior, their health improved, or they made advances in other areas of their lives. In addition, relying on clinical experience alone does not allow us to become aware of the effects of many new procedures and techniques that are being tested.

Rigorous research studies that hold other variables constant can provide additional support when determining if a specific service achieves desired results. Again, I would like to use a relevant quote from my colleague, Bruce Thyer, who wrote:

> Clients should be offered as a first choice treatment, interventions with some significant degree of empirical support, where such knowledge exists, and only provided other treatments after such first choice treatments have been given a legitimate trial and been shown not to be efficacious.

True professionals base what they do in practice on what has been done in research. In 2002, Cawley and colleagues noted that there is a gap between research and practice and this is troubling since many practitioners do not use the knowledge produced by research. In her suggestion to mental health professionals, Leslie Tutty explained that to provide the most effective treatment available, professionals must keep ". . . current on the research on treatment effectiveness for their particular client populations." Also, after conducting a critical review of empirical research in 2008, Betsy Botts and her colleagues made the following conclusions:

By promoting interventions that lack a scientific research base, vendors and educational decision makers who purchase and institute unproven products are potentially harming the students whom they desire to help by keeping them away from involvement in clinically proven programs. In the absence of proving product efficacy in the form of quality, replicable peer-reviewed research, American educators should not allocate public funds on unproven, though promising interventions. Instead funds should be allocated for research of the programs in question. The need exists for high-quality research adhering to standards set by current professional organizations with the purpose of enabling parents and educators to make wise decisions on the allocation of time, efforts, and financial resources.

Therefore, to become enlightened means that some of us must develop theories and conduct rigorous research while all of us must be consumers of these theories and associated research. It seems to me that if we want TR to be viewed as a profession we would do well to listen to the following words of Daniel Schon from his book *The Reflective Practitioner*:

Professional activity consists in instrumental problem solving made rigorous by the application of specific theory and technique . . . only the *professions* practice rigorously technical problem solving based on specialized scientific knowledge.

Research and this book. Each chapter contains a section on **theoretical foundations**, which identifies various theories or explanations intended to clarify the connection between the facilitation techniques and participants' change in behavior. The theories help to explain the possible way in which the facilitation techniques work. Kinney and colleagues reported that for an intervention to be considered a facilitation technique it should be firmly based on one or several theories.

In addition, in the section of the chapters devoted to **effectiveness** a sampling of different research studies examining effects of facilitation techniques are described. These investigations help to document the effectiveness of some techniques and bring into question the value of others. Philips and Knopman noted that studies on effectiveness investigate the delivery and impact of an intervention as it is implemented in the everyday operation of health care systems. In 2007, *New York Times* columnist, Kate Murphy, interviewed JoAnn Manson, a professor at Harvard's School of Public Health, who stated: "We know lifestyle interventions can be very powerful. But we need to provide scientific evidence on how to incorporate that knowledge into practice."

Although reading the numerous studies presented in this section may seem laborious, this amount of material was included to allow readers the opportunity to evaluate the degree of empirical support for the facilitation technique. These studies may help to determine the effectiveness of the facilitation techniques used by TR specialists and, ultimately, the legitimacy of the profession.

Finally, in addition to the research that has been conducted to examine effects of the various facilitation techniques described in this text, we have reviewed studies examining perceived importance of these facilitation techniques in the delivery of TR services. For example, in 2004, Kinney and colleagues surveyed 306 Certified Therapeutic Recreation Specialists regarding the importance of various techniques used in practice and, in addition to other findings the authors reported that when educating TR specialists:

> The majority of respondents also indicated that greater emphasis should be placed on teaching facilitation techniques as opposed to other modalities. What is important to note is that these are skills and knowledge that the practitioners in current TR practice felt that TR clinicians should possess at entry level.

Enlighten

Turning again to the dictionary, I find that the word *enlighten* is defined as to furnish knowledge to instruct. An important aspect of the role of TR specialists is to teach participants ways they might experience leisure and improve their physical, cognitive, emotional, and social skills. If leisure is such a desired condition and our services are designed to achieve therapeutic outcomes, why then are some people not motivated to learn, play, or participate in recreation activities? After talking with many participants and practitioners over the years and considering my experiences, I have come to the conclusion that this is an important question to try to answer when providing TR services.

One explanation for why some people are not motivated to learn, play, or participate in recreation activities may be found when examining how learning is viewed by individuals and our society. I have learned a great deal by watching young children play. Most all children are born curious and spend a great deal of their waking hours engaged in exploration. They explore so that they learn about the world and themselves. This is why when children's disabilities inhibit their exploration, it is important that early intervention programs be provided for these children to create an environment which is conducive to their exploration.

Children who are curious, who engage in inquiry, and who are intrinsically motivated to explore the world around them are said to be autonomous. In his book, *Why We Do What We Do*, Edward Deci stated that:

> To be autonomous means to act in accord with one's self - it means feeling free and volitional in one's actions. When autonomous, people are fully willing to do what they are doing, and they embrace the activity with a guise of interest.

Children are naturally motivated to explore, play, and learn new things. That is to say, children engage in learning activities for the pure enjoyment of learning, not for some external reward. As a result, once children learn a few words, they use these words to learn more. For example:

> One day I was wrestling with my boys, David and Steven, when Steven was just learning to talk. My primary goal was to keep David, who weighed twice as much as Steven, from landing on Steven. As a result, I positioned myself on all fours over Steven and kept David somewhere on my back. In the midst of the excitement I looked down at Steven and I leaned forward and kissed his check. He looked up at me with his eyes open wide and said "Daddy, why kiss?" Searching for an appropriate response I told him because I loved him. He then asked "Daddy, why love?" Again, I struggled for a response and explained that I loved him because he was my son. He then responded by saying "Daddy, why son?" Although this question was not as easy, I was determined to respond with a comment that would satisfy him. In fact, in an attempt to not curb his curiosity and his intrinsically motivated verbal explorations, I often challenge myself to continue to answer each of Steven's inquiries until he is satisfied and turns his attention to other matters.

If children are inherently motivated to learn, play, and participate in recreation activities, why are some participants not motivated? Well, one possible explanation is that the natural activities of learning and play so inherent in a child's life have been institutionalized. That is, many people have designated schools or other similar institutions as the place where a person's learning occurs and, more specifically to leisure, recreation agencies have been identified as the place where recreation skills are developed.

To facilitate group learning, many schools and formalized recreation programs encourage students and participants to conform to rules that often stifle exploration. Frequently, these agencies place students and participants in a responder role, requiring them to wait to be asked a question rather than to initiate inquiry. Quickly, grades, trophies, prizes, and other consequences associated with external rewards are assigned as indicators of learning and successful participation. These external rewards can tend to undermine the intrinsic motivation previously associated with learning and spontaneous participation in recreation activities. Rather than being focused on stimulating curiosity, some professionals spend much of their time attempting to control the participants or students. For example, in their book, *A Social Psychology of Leisure,* my friends and colleagues, Roger Mannell and Douglas Kleiber, stated that:

> When people are rewarded for listening to music, playing games or volunteering, their behavior can become overjustified, that is, they may begin to attribute their participation to extrinsic motives. Research has suggested that such overjustification can be dangerous. The introduction of extrinsic rewards tends to undermine people's experience of self-determination . . .

To enlighten people who receive our services we might consider the issue of motivation as it relates to leisure participation. Perhaps, rather than asking the question:

"How can we motivate participants?" we might want to ask: "How can we develop an environment in which they will motivate themselves?" Providing flexible and responsive environments which encourage exploration and autonomy, rather than ones that are rigid and controlling and tend to undermine intrinsic motivation associated with learning and recreation participation, may be one way we can enlighten our participants.

Resistance to Enlightenment

Up to this point, I have described how TR specialists might become enlightened so that we can enlighten participants. If you agree that it is important for TR specialists to become enlightened, then you may have a nagging question similar to mine. A question which is directly linked to the development of this book and a question that I would like to address before concluding this chapter is: "Why do some TR specialists resist becoming enlightened?"

In an attempt to address why we might be resistant to becoming enlightened, I would like to present what I call the *Yin-Yang of an Emerging Professional*. If we are associated with an *emerging profession*, we are considered to be *emerging professionals*. We must participate in a balancing act to gain the confidence of participants and become enlightened.

On the one hand, we are thrust into a position as TR specialists where we experience the pressure to be competent professionals providing effective services. We are expected to know what is best for participants and it is assumed that our knowledge and skill development occurred primarily prior to our practice. This aspect of being an emerging professional is related to us being required to address current problems. However, if we only engage in behaviors which allow us to address the present, all too soon our services will become outdated. The words of Virginia Buysse and her colleagues in 2003 addressed this idea:

> Prior to entering the workforce, pre-service students . . . are
> expected to know how to apply research-based knowledge to the
> problems of everyday practice, often with little understanding
> about how to participate in and evaluate research and with
> relatively few opportunities for supportive, reflective research-
> based experiences in the field.

On the other hand, if we are to be enlightened, we place value on listening and reading, and we recognize the need to evaluate our actions and consume our research. Therefore, we must be unsure of what is best and be open to new information that may change the way we deliver services. Our growth, knowledge, and skill development occurs primarily while we are delivering services. By engaging in actions that encourage us to become enlightened, we stay abreast of innovative approaches which will allow us to continue to effectively address problems in the future.

It is challenging to become enlightened. At times, we might lose sight of this aspect of our professional identity and find ourselves responding only to the immediate demands of the agency, participants, and other concerned parties. It takes effort and confidence to admit that we are exploring better ways to deliver services while we are delivering effective services. The challenge of admitting that we do not know something reminds me of what Jerry Seinfeld said about bookstores in his book *Seinlanguage*.

> A bookstore is a "smarter than you" store. And that's why people are intimidated - because to walk into a bookstore, you have to admit there's something you don't know. And the worst part is, you don't even know where it is. You go in the bookstore and you have to ask people, "Where is this? Where is that? Not only do I lack knowledge, I don't even know where to get it." So just to walk into a bookstore you're admitting to the world, "I'm not too bright." It's pretty impressive, really.

Similar to entering a bookstore, we may be intimidated in our work place to admit there are things we do not know. This intimidation may be more obvious to TR specialists than to some other more established professionals because often we must defend what we do and how we do it. Being associated with an emerging profession can be a source of concern since others may doubt our legitimacy; thus, we must continuously educate others about the value of our services. Conversely, being associated with an emerging profession can be a source of excitement since we are in a position to have a significant impact on a profession which is in its early stages of development.

Resistance to enlightenment and this book. Clearly, for TR specialists to effectively provide some facilitation techniques described in this text, such as adventure therapy, aquatic therapy, and therapeutic horseback riding, additional training and certification is needed. However, to help readers feel more confident in their ability to implement facilitation techniques described in each chapter, simple introductory **intervention implementation exercises** have been developed and can be completed by the reader.

Conclusion

Now is the time that we can become enlightened so that we can enlighten people with disabilities. Collectively, we can make this be the age of enlightenment for TR. To become enlightened we can listen to others, read professional journals and texts, evaluate our actions, and consume research. As we become enlightened, we are better able to enlighten others. Creating an environment that encourages participants to be motivated to learn and experience leisure is one way we can enlighten participants. Finding a balance between the demands of competence and the need for research in our professional lives may help us avoid resisting enlightenment.

Conclusions and this book. A conclusion is provided in each chapter to summarize and synthesize the major ideas presented. The conclusions bring closure to the chapter and identify to the reader the most salient points addressed. Discussion questions are also provided to challenge readers to retain various aspects of the chapter. Finally, a list of resources and references are contained in each chapter so that readers can pursue additional resources and readings associated with each facilitation technique.

The book was written to be a resource for TR professionals and students so that they can gain insight into some of the facilitation techniques used by TR specialists. The facilitation techniques provided in this edition are not intended to be comprehensive; rather, we attempt to present those techniques that many of the authors implemented while delivering TR services.

Given the body of knowledge associated with TR and the various facilitation techniques described in this book, the words of my friend and colleague, Dan Dustin, come to mind: "Not one of us is free from responsibility for making the future." I hope you find this text to be helpful in delivering services and, thus, allow you to contribute to improving the future for people with disabilities.

Chapter 2
Adventure Therapy

Diane Groff and John Dattilo

*You can learn more about a person in an hour's
worth of play than in a day of conversation.*

–Plato

Introduction

Adventure therapy is an action-centered approach to treatment that is used within
the field of therapeutic recreation (TR). As opposed to other, more traditional forms
of therapy, adventure therapy encourages individuals to become mentally and
physically engaged in adventure activities. The unfamiliar nature of these activities,
combined with the sense of community developed during participation in activities,
creates a climate in which individuals can challenge their current perceptions and
behaviors, and affords them an opportunity to modify those behaviors.

This chapter is designed to introduce the reader to adventure therapy. To achieve
this purpose, a definition and description of adventure therapy is offered. After a brief
account of its history, the theoretical foundations of adventure therapy are provided
as a means to explore the underlying concepts of adventure therapy. A review of
related literature reveals the effectiveness of adventure therapy, while a case study is
presented as an example of the potential impact of adventure therapy. Finally, in an
attempt to enhance the reader's understanding of adventure therapy, a list of professional resources and intervention implementation exercises are provided.

Definitions

Adventure therapy lacks a clear, consistent definition partly because it is typically
subsumed under the larger category of adventure programming, which also lacks a
clear definition (Itin, 2001). To clarify this situation, the following phrases are defined:

- Adventure Programming
- Adventure Activities
- Adventure Therapy

Adventure Programming

In various settings, adventure programming may be referred to as experiential education, outdoor recreation, adventure recreation, wilderness therapy, and adventure

therapy. For the purposes of this chapter, adventure programming will refer to adventure activities designed to promote interpersonal and intrapersonal change within individuals and groups (Priest, 1990).

Adventure Activities

Adventure activities have uncertain outcomes. Adventure activities typically include activities such as camping, games, initiatives (group problem-solving activities), backpacking, rock climbing, canoeing, and ropes courses.

Adventure Therapy

Adventure therapy refers to the subset of adventure programs that focus on the use of adventure activities to accomplish treatment-related goals. This form of therapy may occur in either wilderness settings or facility-based settings (Gass, 1993). Adventure therapy conducted in wilderness settings generally refers to small-group, multiple-day interventions conducted in remote areas away from modern conveniences such as electricity, buildings, appliances, and stores.

Wilderness settings create effective settings for therapy because they place individuals in unfamiliar environment that offers opportunities for reflection and the development of supportive relationships (Russell, 2001a). Wilderness settings can be particularly powerful in promoting healing and personal growth because they foster the development of physical and emotional survival skills needed to cope in this new environment (Werhen & Groff, 2005). Conversely, facility-based adventure therapy occurs at or close to a facility that provides therapeutic interventions and uses the out-of-doors near or around the facility.

According to Gass (1993) adventure therapy varies according to: (a) the specific needs of the client; (b) the complexity of the client's therapeutic issue(s); (c) the background training and therapeutic expertise of the adventure therapist; (d) the length of time the adventure therapist has to work with the client; (e) the context the client came from and will return to after the adventure experience; (f) the presence of aftercare or follow-up treatment following the adventure experience; (g) the availability of adventure experience(s); and (h) the therapist's ability/limitations in using adventure experiences in his or her treatment approaches. Regardless of the setting or degree of the intervention, adventure therapy is defined as:

> An active approach to psychotherapy for people seeking behavioral change, either voluntarily or through some court-ordered coercion, that utilizes adventure activities, be they group games and initiatives or wilderness expeditions (with some form of real or perceived risk), as the primary therapeutic medium to bring about change (Gillis, 1995, p. 5).

Given that there are many components to this definition, it may be helpful to provide an explanation of the various portions of the definition. These components are:

- Active approach
- People seeking change
- Activities involving risk
- Adventure as the primary medium

Active approach. The phrase "an active approach to psychotherapy" describes the psychological treatment of mental, emotional, physical, or nervous disorders. In addition, it implies some sense of action or movement, as opposed to more passive and traditional verbally based therapy.

People seeking change. According to Gillis (1995), the individuals who may benefit from adventure therapy include those who have psychiatric disorders, been adjudicated, chemical dependencies, and physical disabilities. However, any individual who has treatment-related goals could benefit from adventure therapy. Programs have also been conducted with individuals with acquired brain injuries, breast cancer, stroke, multiple sclerosis, muscular dystrophy, Alzheimer's disease, spina bifida, behavioral disorders, and mental disabilities (Sugarman, 2005). In general, adventure therapy is appropriate for any person with treatment-related goals.

Due to the vulnerability of the populations served, practitioners need to be knowledgeable of and adhere to state laws governing some adventure therapy services (Werhen & Groff, 2005). State laws that apply to adventure therapy may fall under the auspice of counseling, therapy, or adolescent development. It is critical that practitioners understand this connection and be aware of the ethical and legal standards of practice adopted by professional associations and state law. Although there is not one set of guidelines governing all adventure therapy, organizations such as the Association of Experiential Education, the National Association of Therapeutic Schools and Programs, and National Association of Therapeutic Wilderness Camps have guidelines specifying desired professional conduct.

Activities involving risk. According to Project Adventure, adventure activities include any new experience that elicits excitement (Schoel, Prouty, & Radcliffe, 1988). The excitement inherent in adventure activities arises from the perceived risk and fun individuals often anticipate and experience.

Although not an exhaustive list, adventure activities include games, initiatives, ropes courses, wilderness camping, and adventure sports such as rock climbing, rafting, canoeing, and backpacking. The phrase "real and perceived risk" refers to the element of uncertainty inherent in each activity.

Real risks are inherent in every adventure activity and may include equipment failure, insect bites, encounters with animals, and inclement weather. Real risks cannot be eliminated from activities in adventure therapy (similar to not being able to eliminate the real risk from driving a car or walking across the street). It is critical, however, that all of the real risks associated with adventure therapy be managed.

The implementation of staff training and the implementation of a thorough risk-management plan are needed before adventure activities begin. Staff training is critical prior to the implementation of adventure programs. Effective staff training includes key elements such as: knowledge of physical and psychological symptoms of treatment groups served, management, effective intervention techniques, leadership and group dynamics, technical skills needed to lead adventure activities, and helping skills needed to effectively process the experience (Rosol, 2000). Components of a risk-management plan may include information about the proper use of equipment, technical training required of leaders, an emergency plan of action, and rescue procedures.

In addition to the real risks encountered during adventure therapy, participants are likely to experience feelings of perceived risk. Perceived risk represents feelings of uncertainty or apprehension participants are likely to experience as they climb a rock face, hike a trail, or walk across a wire suspended 50 feet above the ground. Real and perceived risks are critical to the success of adventure therapy and are discussed in more detail when a description of adventure therapy is presented.

Adventure as the primary medium. Since the primary goal of therapy is change, adventure therapy focuses on modifying a person's perceptions and/or behaviors. The perceptions that may be enhanced during adventure therapy include such perceptions as locus of control, self-concept, perceived competence, self-efficacy, and self-esteem. Behaviors targeted for modification may include aggressive behaviors, inappropriate social interactions, and truant behaviors.

Summary

Adventure therapy is an active approach. The unfamiliar nature of adventure activities creates an environment that challenges participants to change or modify dysfunctional perceptions and behaviors. Although the setting, duration, and adventure activities utilized within programs may vary, the nature of these experiences provides TR specialists with a useful technique to facilitate change.

Descriptions

Although providing a definition helps to clarify what adventure therapy is, it does little to explain how adventure therapy produces change. In an effort to delineate components of adventure therapy that help facilitate the growth of individuals, a more detailed description of adventure experiences and adventure therapy are provided. The following items are explored:

- The Adventure Experience Paradigm
- Components of Adventure Therapy
- Metaphoric Learning

Adventure Experience Paradigm

Martin and Priest (1986) developed an adventure experience paradigm based on the works of Ellis (1973), Csikszentmihalyi (1975), and Mortlock (1984). Martin and Priest proposed that the degree of risk associated with adventure experiences and the competence individuals bring to the adventure result in five possible conditions. These conditions include:

- Exploration and experimentation
- Adventure
- Peak adventure
- Misadventure
- Devastation and disaster

The conditions of *exploration and experimentation* result when risks are low and competence is high. When an individual's competence is only slightly greater than the risk involved in an activity, the condition of *adventure* occurs. If the risk is relatively equally matched with one's competence, a *peak adventure* is believed to happen. When the risk rises slightly above one's competence a *misadventure* is said to occur. Finally, when an individual's competence is low and the risks are high, *devastation and disaster* may result.

The adventure experience paradigm is based on the premise that the interplay between an individual's perception of risk and competence creates varying degrees of challenge. Facilitated adventure experiences, such as those found in adventure therapy, occur when an individual's perceived competence in an area matches the risk encountered in an activity. The trained professional is therefore responsible for creating a learning environment that facilitates the match of challenge and skill.

For example, an individual may approach a rock climb with an inflated sense of competence and reduced respect for the risk inherent in the activity. The arrogant attitude of the individual may be detrimental to the progress of the group as well as the safety of the individual. To enhance the learning opportunity available through the experience, and to help the individual understand problems associated with her attitude, the facilitator could have the individual climb a route that was slightly beyond her actual ability in the hopes that she will not be able to, or have difficulty completing the climb. When debriefing the activity, the facilitator could suggest that the individual and the group reflect on the rock-climbing experience and highlight the benefits of accurately representing one's strengths and weaknesses. Conversely, another individual in the group may approach the same rock climb with an inflated perception of risk and limited perception of competence. The facilitator could then structure the experience so that the individual receives the help and instruction necessary for him to complete the climb. After successfully completing the climb, the facilitator could suggest that the individual reflect upon the skills he demonstrated during the climb compared to his initial estimation of his abilities.

Each category within the adventure experience paradigm has the potential to create a learning situation. Priest (1990) acknowledged that due to the need to manage risks associated with adventure experiences, the most appropriate opportunities for learning occur in the categories of exploration and experimentation, adventure, peak adventure, and misadventure.

The intent of facilitated adventure experiences, such as adventure therapy, is to assist participants to slowly shift perceptions of competence toward what is realistic (Priest, 1990). The next portion of this section provides a more in-depth understanding of the components of adventure therapy that facilitate individual growth and development.

Components of the Adventure Experience

The process of adventure therapy allows individuals to capitalize on opportunities to reduce perceived limitations that stifle growth and development (Nadler, 1993). Nadler identified the components of adventure that influence this opportunity as:

- The participant
- Disequilibrium
- Novel setting
- Cooperative environment
- Unique problem-solving situations
- Feelings of accomplishment
- Processing the experience
- Generalization and transfer

Participants. Consistent with a participant-centered approach to TR, the individual represents the centerpiece of adventure therapy. Participants' anticipation of the experience causes a sense of internal stimulation and sets the stage for learning.

Disequilibrium. Participants' feelings of stimulation create a state of disequilibrium. Disequilibrium occurs when individuals' previously held beliefs regarding a situation do not apply to the current situation. This internal conflict motivates individuals to either change or modify their beliefs and perceptions in an effort to reduce the discomfort disequilibrium produces.

Novel setting. The reason most individuals experience disequilibrium during adventure therapy is due to the novel setting in which they are placed. Settings in which adventure therapy occurs typically are novel because they are conducted in an unfamiliar area such as wilderness areas, a ropes course (see Figure 2.1), and trails, and/or involve unfamiliar activities, such as rock climbing, camping, and initiatives. The diversity of people who form a group can also create an unfamiliar social environment. The unique physical and social environments present in adventure therapy helps individuals reduce preexisting thoughts and behaviors that may stifle growth and development.

Cooperative environment. Adventure therapy is conducted in a cooperative environment that emphasizes interdependence among group members and cultivates group cohesion. The cooperative environment is generated primarily from establishing group and individual goals. An enhanced cooperative environment develops though as ample time is provided for individuals so that they may communicate with one another.

Unique problem solving. The cooperative environment is stimulated by the unique problem-solving situations presented during most adventure activities. Since most individuals who participate in adventure activities have little previous experience with these activities, they are often forced to rely on their physical, cognitive, and emotional skills to accomplish tasks. In addition, the facilitator will introduce the activity in such a way that it focuses the group's attention on specific components of

Figure 2.1

the activity that have opportunities for learning. The facilitator structures activities so that they become increasingly difficult for group members and the groups by creating challenges that involve unique problem-solving situations.

Feelings of accomplishment. Increasingly more difficult challenges afford individuals and the group an opportunity to continually develop and refine various skills. This mastery-learning situation encourages the group to work together, and leads to feelings of accomplishment. Successfully completing an unfamiliar task can lead to increased self-esteem, improved self-perception, more effective problem-solving, and pride.

Processing the experience. Feelings of accomplishment are further enhanced by verbally processing the experience with participants. Although participants are encouraged to express their thoughts and feelings regarding adventure activities throughout the program, upon completion of an activity the facilitator poses questions, and/or provides comments that encourage the individual and group to reflect on the experience. This process is commonly referred to as *debriefing*. During the debriefing, participants are encouraged to share their reflections and express their thoughts and feelings.

Generalization and transfer. Thoughtful reflection on the experience helps individuals become more aware of their thoughts, feelings, actions, and consequences associated with them. Increased awareness of one's actions facilitates the ability to generalize and transfer the learning to other aspects of life. The generalization and transfer of learning is a critical component of adventure therapy that assists participants in changing dysfunctional thoughts and inappropriate behaviors that may have necessitated their therapy. One key ingredient in the successful generalization and transference of learning are the metaphors used during adventure activities.

Metaphoric Learning

Adventure therapy relies heavily on metaphors to help enhance learning opportunities that occur during participation in adventure activities (Hirsch & Gillis, 2004). Gillis (1995) defined a *metaphoric story* as a symbolic way of experiencing reality, where one thing, such as an adventure experience, is conceived as representing another situation in a person or group's actual lives, their reality. Typically, metaphors are presented at the beginning of activities and are used to provide a framework for the activity. This framework provides a group structure where individuals derive meaning that extend beyond the activity itself.

Metaphoric learning occurs as the group, or individuals, discover that strategies required to complete adventure activities are similar to strategies they could employ when faced with similar challenges. Kimball and Bacon (1993) identified three types of transference-enhancing strategies that could be incorporated into adventure therapy:

- Spontaneous metaphoric transference
- Analogous transference
- Structured metaphoric transference

Spontaneous metaphoric transference. *Spontaneous metaphoric transfer* is when an individual independently discovers important connections between an activity and his or her daily life.

> As an example of spontaneous metaphoric transfer, consider Darissa who has just completed a difficult route on a rock climb (see Figure 2.2). Without the help of the group or facilitator she may exclaim at the end of the climb, "*Wow, I never would have believed that I could have completed that climb! When I started, I felt as helpless as I did when I wanted to try out for the band, but didn't believe that I was good enough. Only this time, I tried as hard as I could and completed the climb. I guess that just shows me that I will never know how capable I am unless I try the activity first.*"

Analogous transference. *Analogous transference* that involves verbal and social learning (modeling) techniques employed to help participants retrospectively understand the importance of the experience. Analogous transference occurs frequently in adventure therapy.

> For example, Darissa may have completed the same difficult climb above and, although elated at her success, thought nothing more about it. While debriefing the activity, the facilitator may ask her to recall a situation in which she felt similar feelings to the ones

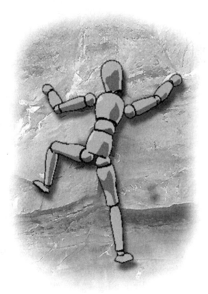

Figure 2.2

experienced during the climb. At that time, she may recall her experience with not trying out for the band due to her feelings of inadequacy. The facilitator may then ask Darissa to envision trying out for the band again, only this time picture utilizing the information she learned about herself during the climb. After considerable thought, the individual might proclaim, *"This time I can see myself trying out for the band and not feeling so scared. I guess that just like during the climb, I'll never know how good it feels to reach the top of anything if I don't at least give it a try."*

Structured metaphoric transference. Another common type of metaphoric learning used in adventure therapy involves structured metaphoric transference. *Structured metaphoric transference* occurs when the therapist purposefully frames a particular activity so the group's attention is focused on a certain aspect of the activity in an attempt to increase the chance for spontaneous discovery of a metaphor. The next section contains examples of following strategies:

For example, a common element of a ropes challenge course is the wall. A wall is typically a 10–12 feet tall, 6 feet wide, wooden structure with a platform built onto the back of it. The group's objective is to get every member of the group safely up and over the wall without using any props. If a group of individuals with chemical dependencies was attempting the activity, the facilitator could focus the group's attention to a particular element of the wall using the following metaphoric story:

We all face challenges in our everyday lives that can appear to be insurmountable. In fact, we may wake up each day not knowing how to face the challenges we think the day will bring. We may look at a challenge and see no way around it. When we face a challenge there are several ways we can respond. We could simply walk away from the challenge and pretend it doesn't exist or pretend that the challenge isn't really important. This solution may leave us feeling bad about ourselves and we may use alcohol or drugs to numb our pain. However, we may look at the challenge and figure out a way to get over the obstacle. Often, we rely on the help of friends and relatives to find the resources we need to overcome a challenge. The objective of this activity is to find a way to get your entire group up and over the wall, without the use of any outside props. It's up to the group to determine how you will face this obstacle. Will you turn away from the challenge before attempting it, or will you pool your resources and find a way to overcome this challenge?

There are several factors associated with metaphoric learning that are useful to consider. Three factors include:

- Isomorphism
- Narratives
- Reflective teams

Isomorphism. A key factor in determining if experiences are metaphoric is the degree of isomorphism between the metaphor situation and real-life situation (Bacon, 1983). *Isomorphism* refers to the overlapping structure between the two situations. In the aforementioned example, the metaphor may work well with individuals who experience chemical dependencies, but may not work particularly well with individuals who do not have problems facing challenging situations.

Narratives. Luckner and Nadler (1995) described metaphoric transference as a way to increase participants' understanding of how an adventure-based event relates to their lives. The authors reported that individuals are continuously in an active state of learning by interpreting information in an effort to make sense of their lives. To learn new information, people must be actively involved in a process of invention, rather than in a passive accumulation of ideas.

Luckner and Nadler explained that a *narrative* (story) is a sequential telling of events related to a specific theme. The narrative is also a foundation metaphor that helps people to organize, remember, and understand life experiences. The narrative helps participants organize and recall the information for transference to other life experiences. Outdoor adventure experiences help participants become aware of and produce accounts of the experiences that give meaning to their lives. Subsequently, reflection upon the major themes that compose one's life story helps an individual interpret and negotiate other life experiences.

Reflective teams. In addition to individual processing, Luckner and Nadler discussed the use of *reflective teams* to help expand or develop a story. A reflective team includes designated individuals that watch a participant in an activity. The participant and the team create stories about the activity experience that results in the entire group expanding the story. To encourage long-term benefits of adventure therapy, it is important for a participant to discover that strategies used to complete adventure activities successfully are similar to strategies that they could employ when faced with similar challenges in various aspects of real life.

Summary

The degree of perceived risk and competence participants bring to adventure activities has the potential to create a myriad of opportunities for learning. Practitioners responsible for facilitating adventure experiences attempt to accurately match an individual's perceived competence with the perceived risk activities in an attempt to maximize this learning potential. Once a cooperative and nurturing learning environment is created, the unique problem-solving situations presented during adventure therapy afford participants opportunities for mastery, which often lead to enhanced feelings of accomplishment and self-esteem. The act of processing these experiences helps participants realize that the lessons they have learned from adventure therapy generalize and transfer to everyday life.

History

The processes that have contributed to the success of adventure therapy have evolved over time. In an attempt to more fully understand adventure therapy it may be helpful to briefly review its history. Berman and Davis-Berman (1995) traced the roots of adventure therapy to three distinct movements:

- Tent Therapy
- Therapeutic Camping
- Outward Bound

Tent Therapy

As early as 1901, the first *tent therapy* program was developed for people receiving psychiatric services at state hospitals. The program involved having participants live in tents for the summer. Although there is no research on effects of tent therapy, staff and participants reported positive effects of the program. Unfortunately, these reported benefits diminished as participants returned to the hospital when cold weather arrived.

The second outdoor approach to therapy began 10 years later when Camp Ahmek was established to provide children with opportunities for recreation and socialization (Berman & Davis-Berman, 1995). This camping experience used the group process in a natural environment to facilitate change. The third, and perhaps the largest influence on adventure therapy, occurred during WWII.

Therapeutic Camping

Kurt Hahn initiated the idea of using adventure programming to improve the survival rate of sailors whose ships were being torpedoed and sunk by German U-boats (Priest, 1995). Most of the sailors were not dying from the explosions, but rather from being thrown overboard and drowning. What concerned the Navy and Kurt Hahn was that regardless of their superior physical condition, the younger sailors were more likely to drown than the older sailors.

Hahn and others theorized that the young sailors were dying because they lacked the experience to cope with stressful situations (Greene & Thompson, 1990). As a result, Hahn developed a program that used *therapeutic camping* as a means to teach sailors how to prepare and deal with hardships they could face. The program emphasized developing leadership skills, self-concept, confidence, and risk-taking by enhancing an individual's skills related to communication, cooperation, trust, and teamwork. The training that began in 1941 resulted in development of Outward Bound.

Outward Bound

The ideas and philosophy of *Outward Bound* grew in popularity during the 1960s when adventure-based programs were developed for adjudicated youth. By the 1970s, the number of programs utilizing adventure therapy was in the thousands. By the 1980s, the number of schools, colleges, youth services, recreation departments, social services, correctional facilities, hospitals, and vocational programs that adopted the use of adventure therapy prompted a surge in popularity (Kimball & Bacon, 1993).

Today, Outward Bound is an international organization that has several branches. The Outward Bound Wilderness program offers an array of wilderness courses throughout the United States. The Expeditionary Learning Schools Outward Bound offer courses designed to enhance individual self-reliance, confidence, teamwork, and environmental stewardship. Outward Bound Discovery courses cater to the needs of delinquent youth and helping them develop the skills needed to reintegrate into society.

Summary

Although adventure therapy has existed for over 100 years, it was during the 1960s that the use of adventure therapy grew in popularity. The popularity of this intervention has permitted identification of components of adventure therapy that may contribute to its success; however, the theoretical foundations governing the use of adventure therapy are still being investigated. What follows is an exploration of the theoretical foundations of adventure therapy.

Theoretical Foundations

Gillis (1995) reported that no one theory appears to be adequate to explain the changes that can occur when participating in adventure experiences. Instead, a variety of social-psychological theories help account for effects of adventure-based therapy. The following theories will be reviewed:

- Self-Perception
- Self-Efficacy
- Explanatory Style
- Social Identity

Self-Perception

Self-concept is a widely researched topic within the field of adventure therapy (Klint, 1990). The term *self-concept* generally refers to an individual's beliefs about his or her personal qualities (Smith & Mackie, 1995). The self-perception theory developed by Darryl Bem (1967) suggests that we obtain much of the information that we use when developing perceptions of ourselves when we observe our behaviors.

For example, if Anton stops to help someone who has fallen during a road race, he may believe that he is a nice person. In another example, if Marika is doing well when learning to water ski for the first time, she may begin to realize that she is coordinated and athletic. The more accessible information is to an individual, the more likely it will be used when developing self-concept (Bem, 1967).

Self-perception theory enhances our understanding of adventure therapy for several reasons. This theory helps explain why the action-oriented nature of adventure therapy is effective. Easley (1991) described the experiential nature of adventure therapy as an awareness or consciousness that survives after the education and restructuring and rethinking about the event occurs. Adventure therapy offers individuals ample opportunities to observe their own behavior because it is a very active "lived" experience. These lived experiences result in concrete, immediate, and observable information that typically has definitive consequences.

For example, lack of group cooperation during an activity is very likely to stop the group from accomplishing its goal. The therapist and participants can subsequently use this information to examine behavioral patterns and beliefs and help participants change their self-concept.

Through adventure experiences, participants receive clear representations of what actions and behaviors are likely to result in what consequences. This may help individuals recognize inappropriate behaviors and provide them with mental representations of how to correct and modify that behavior in the future.

Kimball and Bacon (1993) reported that action-centered therapies, such as adventure therapy, can be particularly effective with adolescents. Most adolescents find that they prefer quick, direct, and concrete forms of communication as opposed to a more reflective, introspective communication. Adolescent culture generally deemphasizes and places little value on cognitive, language-oriented styles of communication.

Adventure therapy attempts to "meet youth on their own turf" by deemphasizing the need for language skills and replacing them with "lived experiences." Therefore, adventure therapy may be a particularly productive environment for adolescents to reflect on and reconsider their self-perceptions since the action orientation of the activity provides them with additional information they can use to define themselves.

Self-Efficacy

Self-efficacy refers to individuals' beliefs that they are capable of successfully accomplishing tasks that test their abilities (Smith & Mackie, 1995). In general, most people want to view themselves in a positive way and feel as if they have skills and abilities that are valued. Feelings of self-efficacy originate from the internal and external information individuals receive about their abilities and ultimately play a role in their motivation to engage in certain behaviors.

Bandura's (1977) self-efficacy theory suggests that information gained through actual experience regarding one's skills and abilities tends to be the most influential in determining feelings of self-efficacy. In addition, performance accomplishments that an individual perceives as important will generalize to other situations more readily.

Adventure therapy can increase a person's self-efficacy for several reasons. First, the unfamiliar environment and perceived risks associated with adventure activities tend to increase the magnitude of the event. Therefore, experiences gained during adventure therapy are likely to be highly valued by individuals, and subsequently, used as a source of information for individuals when evaluating their skills and abilities.

Since adventure therapy typically involves a series of events such as brief, activity, debrief; brief, activity, debrief, participants have numerous opportunities to modify their behavior and develop skills required of the activity. This sequencing of events allows individuals opportunities to master their environment (Kimball & Bacon, 1993). When individuals successfully resolve stressful, challenging situations that initially appeared to be beyond their capabilities, they are likely to feel an increased sense of self-worth and potency.

Second, the unfamiliar environment where therapy occurs can disarm individuals so that they feel less resistant to change. New and unique experiences do not allow individuals to enter the situation with preconceived notions about what they are, or are not, able to accomplish and can limit the amount of self-destructive behavior in which they engage. Experiencing unfamiliar environments may also enhance feelings of self-efficacy.

For example, it would be difficult for Olivia to deny that she can be responsible for others after she successfully helped a peer on a rock climb and was accountable for the safety of that person during the climb.

Explanatory Style: Learned Helplessness and Learned Optimism

Explanatory style captures the way individuals explain why events occur (Seligman, 2006). One explanatory style is identified as *learned helplessness* or the belief that whatever one does will not matter (Seligman, 1975). *Learned optimism* on the other hand, describes individuals who believe that setbacks are temporary occasions that are the result of circumstances, bad luck, or outside influences (Seligman, 2006). Individuals who possess a high degree of optimism will try harder to persevere through negative life events and are less depressed by these experiences (Seligman, 2006).

Repeated personal experiences in which people feel as if they have no control over the situation may result in feelings of helplessness (Seligman, 1975). Learned helplessness occurs when a person generalizes his or her feelings of helplessness in one situation to other aspects of that person's life. Learned helplessness eventually decreases motivation to engage in new activities and undermines attempts made to master situations (Smith & Mackie, 1995). Smith and Mackie reported that if an individual generalizes feelings of helplessness to most areas of life, these feelings may contribute to clinical depression which can be characterized by negative moods, low self-esteem, pessimism, as well as a disruption of thinking, sleeping, eating, and activity patterns.

Given that most adventure programs operate under the philosophy of "challenge by choice," adventure therapy may help to reduce a person's feelings of lack of control and learned helplessness (Gass, 1993). Challenge by choice allows individuals to decide for themselves if, and to what degree, they would like to participate in activities. If people repeatedly refuse to participate in activities, they are encouraged to reflect upon why they did not want to participate and what consequences would likely occur given their decision. By conducting programs within a challenge by choice philosophy, adventure therapy may help individuals regain a sense of control, which was lost while they experienced learned helplessness.

It is important that individuals who are experiencing negative life events develop and maintain an optimistic outlook so that they can make sense of their situation and develop the skills needed to overcome difficult situations (Seligman, 2002). The difficulties experienced during adventure activities can help individuals develop the "psychological resiliency" needed to adopt an optimistic explanatory style (Neill & Dias, 2001). Due to the difficult challenges and failures experienced during adventure activities, individuals have an opportunity to learn how to fail.

The supportive environment of the group can allow individuals to recover from the experience of failing and improve their capacity to face future hardships. Thus challenge and social support work together to create opportunities to work through personal hardship, recover from experiences, and experience personal growth. If individuals feel that they have control over situations and can overcome negative life experiences they may take on a more optimistic explanatory style, more easily confront difficult situations in the future, and become happier individuals.

Social Identity

One of the most fundamental needs of individuals is to feel a sense of belonging (Smith & Mackie, 1995). Feeling a sense of unconditional regard and social support is thus critical for personal growth and development (Russell & Phillips-Miller, 2002). Being identified as part of a group also helps people to establish a sense of *connectedness* with others and provides them with information that they can use to define themselves. Ultimately, group memberships can influence our thoughts, feelings, and actions and, therefore, provide a "social identity."

Group interaction among members in small groups during adventure activities can help lead to behavioral change (Gass, 1993). Since one's personality and sense of identity is largely influenced by involvement and interaction with others, Kimball and Bacon (1993) theorized that structured group experiences help to reshape an individual's perceptions of the self.

In most adventure experiences, conflict will arise within the group due to participation in planned stressful situations. Since the impending consequences of an individual's actions are likely to have an effect on all members of the group, an individual's response to this situation is likely to be monitored and evaluated by all members of the group. When situations such as this arise, guided group discussions, or debriefings, can be used to resolve the problem. Within a safe group environment, observations of individual or group performance can be used to evaluate and encourage modification of dysfunctional behaviors.

The genuine community built during adventure activities can help to create a sense of mutual dependence and trust between members. Since adventure activities require a commitment from each of its members to accomplish a task, individuals have an opportunity to experience how it feels to know their actions influence others, and realize their actions can be significant.

Summary

Although each adventure experience carries the potential for participants to learn, experiences that closely match an individual's perceived competence with the degree of perceived risk are more likely to result in an environment conducive to learning (Csikszentmihalyi, 1993). Based on self-perception theory (Bem, 1967), once a conducive environment to learning is created, the experiential nature of adventure therapy can help people enhance their feelings of self-efficacy (Bandura, 1977) and reduce feelings of helplessness (Seligman, 1975). In addition, the opportunity for structured group experiences that adventure therapy provides (Kimball & Bacon, 1993) can help individuals improve self-perception and develop an optimistic explanatory style that leads to increased happiness. However, research demonstrating the ability of adventure therapy to generate consistent outcomes is ongoing. The following section will elaborate on research related to adventure therapy.

Effectiveness

Although there are many studies that have examined effects of adventure therapy, conclusive findings are lacking due to a shortage of well-designed, meaningful, and applicable studies (Neill, 2003). In the early 1980s, Ewert conducted a review of more than 50 studies on self-concept and other psychological outcomes related to "wilderness and adventure education." He concluded that although Outward Bound programs may positively enhance an individual's self-concept, self-esteem, physical ability, and social interaction, little is known about the type of programs that create change such as length of program, activity mix, and instructional staff. The same situation applies today.

Subjective impressions of program outcomes and individual research studies support the efficacy of adventure therapy, but failure to conduct well-organized, definitive, and controlled research on adventure therapy limits our understanding of its effectiveness (Neill, 2003). Rather than review the numerous individual research studies focused on adventure therapy, this review will focus on key meta-analyses and longitudinal studies that have been conducted in recent years.

One of the most effective ways to statistically synthesize results of many individual studies and summarize the magnitude of change that occurs across and within programs is to conduct a meta-analysis. Meta-analyses allow a researcher to examine the common effect of a treatment from studies that may or may not have used similar instruments and methodology. There have been several meta-analyses of adventure therapy outcomes in recent years such as those completed by Cason and Gillis (1994). Hans (2000) and Hattie, Marsh, Neill, and Richards (1997) and several pertinent longitudinal studies and reviews conducted by Russell (2001b, 2002) as well as Russell and Hendee (2000).

Russell (2001b, 2002) completed a longitudinal assessment of outcomes associated with outdoor behavioral healthcare (OBH). Based on the responses of youth and parents he reported that clients enrolled in an outdoor behavioral healthcare program improved their well-being, as evidenced by reduced scores on the Youth Outcome Questionnaire (Y-OQ). Parental assessment mirrored these positive outcomes.

The authors conducted a longitudinal analysis of outcomes to determine if these scores were sustained over time. An initial analysis of youth scores on the Y-OQ at 3 and 6 months revealed maintenance of positive behaviors; however, parents reported a slight deterioration in their child's behaviors indicating that they believed outcomes were not fully maintained over time. A random sample of the data set revealed that clients did, however, maintain outcomes from treatment and had continued to improve emotionally and behaviorally 1 year postparticipation in the OBH program. The authors concluded that OBH treatment can effectively address the behavioral problems of youth; however, these outcomes may be challenged over time. Practitioners were encouraged to continue to find ways to maintain improvements experienced during treatment.

Because self-concept is the most frequently studied construct in adventure therapy research, **Hans (2000)** attempted to replicate effects found in the meta-analyses conducted by Cason and Gillis (1994) and Hattie and colleagues (1997). A meta-analysis of 24 studies that included 1,632 participants was completed. Hans demonstrated a slightly higher effect on self-concept compared to the two previous meta-analyses. This indicates that participants across all studies shifted toward more internal self-regulation because of participation in adventure programs. Hans reported that two moderator variables (program goal and daily duration) influenced these effects. Larger effects were observed in therapeutically oriented programs and in residential treatment programs of longer duration.

Russell and Hendee (2000) completed a national survey of outdoor behavioral healthcare programs. OBH programs encompass clinically supervised adventure and wilderness-based outdoor therapy designed to help adolescents change destructive, dysfunctional, or problematic behaviors. This area of interest is governed by the OBH Industry Council (OBHIC) formed in 1996.

One key accomplishment of the OBHIC was to establish standards that met insurance and state agency requirements for reimbursement of services (Russell & Hendee, 2000). Standards required for co-payments and reimbursement include the development of individual treatment plans, supervision of clinical staff, regular medical check-ups of clients, appropriate backup procedures governing wilderness operations, and regulated daily caloric intake of participants. The authors concluded from a review of the literature that wilderness programs governed under these guidelines provided consistent evidence to support that OBH helps clients gain a heightened self-concept, and suggested that the development of self refers to several important clinical outcomes such as self-esteem, locus of control, and self-concept. In addition to self-concept, social skills are consistently impacted by OBH.

Deficiencies in social skills may promote delinquent behavior because individuals lack the skills needed to develop close interpersonal relationships; thus, leading to isolation, apathy, defensiveness, aggressiveness, and lack of respect for others. Outdoor behavioral healthcare can positively affect social skills by teaching individuals how to function in an interdependent community, to develop interpersonal communication skills, and to develop cooperative behaviors. Lastly, the authors suggest that OBH can positively influence substance abuse and recidivism, although additional research must be conducted before definitive outcomes can be assured.

Hattie and colleagues (1997) reviewed 96 studies via a meta-analysis of research pertaining to adventure programs. The researchers grouped 40 major outcomes observed into six categories: leadership, self-concept, academic, personality, interpersonal, and "adventuresomeness." Results indicated a mild effect comparable to traditional classroom-based programs but not nearly as effective as overall psychotherapy (Casey & Berman, 1985). Follow-up effects of adventure programs appeared to be more positive. Long-term effects were greater than traditional classroom based programs indicating greater transfer and maintenance of learning over time.

The authors noted that the effects were largely determined from studies conducted with adult businessmen and women or students. The studies conducted with delinquent youth or clinical populations were generally even higher than noted earlier, indicating that the aforementioned results are increasingly relevant for the latter populations. Effects were also greater for wilderness versus adventure programs and programs of longer duration (those lasting more than 20 days). The individual effects noted are primarily associated with self-regulation such as independence, decision-making, assertiveness, self-understanding, confidence, self-efficacy, and internal locus of control. Finally, there were substantial effects on leadership, personality, and adventuresomeness but the authors report that these were less sustainable over time.

Cason and Gillis (1994) conducted a meta-analysis of 43 adventure-based research studies in which adolescents served as subjects. The findings revealed over 235 effect sizes describing 19 outcome measures. Effect sizes represent the amount of change participants experienced at the conclusion of each study and the outcome measure represents the areas where change occurred. The 19 outcome measures were grouped into seven categories: self-concept, behavioral assessment by others, attitude surveys, locus of control, clinical scales, grades, and school attendance. The highest effect sizes occurred in clinical scales, grades, school attendance, and attitude surveys. The authors speculated that the large clinical scale effect sizes may be due to the fact that the clinical scales were used primarily with people receiving residential services, and because the adventure experiences with these individuals may be more intense than with participants residing in the community.

Programs of moderate to extended duration (1–10 months) accounted for the greatest difference in effect sizes, suggesting that adventure programs that are longer in duration may be more effective. Younger adolescents tended to benefit more from participation than older adolescents regardless of the population served, such as adjudicated youth, individuals with emotional or physical disabilities, at-risk adolescents, and youth without disabilities. Research studies rated by the authors as being less rigorous (such as those having no control group or random assignment of participants) accounted for a large portion of the effect sizes. This finding suggests that perhaps some of the positive results reported in the less rigorous studies may have been due to chance. These results suggest that adventure therapy may have a positive effect on adolescent's self-concept, behaviors, attitudes, locus of control, clinical scales, grades, and school attendance; however, more rigorous research is needed to address issues regarding consistent outcomes and mechanisms that create change.

Summary

A considerable amount of research has been conducted to investigate effects of adventure therapy. The application of meta-analyses and longitudinal surveys in recent years provides evidence to support adventure therapy as an empirically based facilitation technique. The two consistently substantiated treatment outcomes are improved self-concept and internal locus of control.

The literature suggests that these outcomes are gained from involvement in long-term residential programs and therapeutically oriented programs (as opposed to education, development, or prevention programs). Although some preliminary evidence supports use of adventure therapy as a means to improve an individual's body image, leadership, academic performance, rate of recidivism, substance abuse, and depression, additional experimental research conducted with large samples with varying diagnoses is needed to support these initial contentions and to determine how and under what conditions these effects will be delivered consistently.

Case Study

Steve

Steve was a 15-year-old in the eighth grade living at home with both parents. Steve had a history of alcohol and drug abuse including the use of marijuana and cocaine. Steve's father had a reported history of alcohol abuse. In conjunction with his drinking, Steve's father admitted to physically abusing his wife and son when he felt angry. Steve's mother confirmed that her husband had physically abused her and Steve; however, she had never filed any reports with local authorities regarding this behavior. Steve's mother did not report a history of alcohol or drug abuse, although she admitted that she occasionally reprimanded Steve physically when she got frustrated with the family situation.

Although Steve had never been arrested or received any treatment for his alcohol and drug abuse, he was referred to a residential adolescent treatment program by the school system due his negative attitude and frequent school absences. His parents agreed to his participation in the program. Upon admission to the treatment facility Steve displayed lethargic behavior and had a flat affect as evidenced by his monotone voice and unwillingness to smile or maintain eye contact with the staff or other residents. When Steve did interact with others it was often in an angry and combative way. After several days of observation by the staff, Steve was referred to the adventure therapy program. Steve's treatment goals were related to his diagnosis of mild depression, which resulted from his lack of trust in others and himself, and his inability to communicate with others openly and honestly regarding his family and his addictions.

Adventure Therapy for Steve

The adventure therapy program consisted of three 1-week phases. Phase I included daily, 4-hour-long adventure therapy sessions conducted on the ropes course and individual therapy by other members of the interdisciplinary team. Phase II consisted of a week-long wilderness camping trip which included backpacking, rock climbing, canoeing, and a 24-hour solo experience in which the individual was required to spend 24 hours alone. Phase III was conducted for 1 week at the treatment facility and included discharge planning and treatment by the interdisciplinary team.

During the first week on the ropes course, Steve chose not to participate in the activities with the group, stating that "these activities are childish and stupid." During the periods in which Steve chose not to participate the facilitators instructed Steve to consider if there were any ways in which he could help the group, even if he choose not to fully participate. Steve commonly responded that he could not think of any role he could assume. On day 3 of the program, group members confronted Steve because they had grown tired of Steve refusing to participate. When confronted, Steve admitted that he was not participating because he was not sure that he could accomplish the tasks the other group members were completing. With the help of the TR specialists, the group implemented a "full value contract," which stated that from that point forward all members of the group would assume some role during each activity unless there were health reasons as to why an individual should not participate in an activity. All members of the group agreed to abide by the contract for the remainder of the program.

For the remainder of the day, Steve reluctantly, yet fully, participated in every activity that the group attempted. However, Steve encountered a major problem on the final event of the day—the "wild woozy." The "wild woozy" is a two-person event in which individuals walk along two opposing cables suspended several feet off the ground. The object of the activity is for the pair to support each other, as the cable grows progressively further apart, for as long as possible. It is important to note that everyone will fall off the cable into the arms of group members who are walking beside the pair at some point along the cable. Individuals who are able to trust their partner and lean into each other with their full weight are likely to go the greatest distance. When Steve attempted the wild woozy with his partner, he deliberately fell into the arms of the group after only a few steps. When confronted with his attempt, Steve stated that he was satisfied, and had tried his hardest. His partner, however, was very angry with Steve and confronted him with his meager attempt at the activity. After an emotional and lengthy debriefing, Steve admitted that due to his lack of trust in himself and others he typically did not attempt difficult activities, or would purposefully fail at an early stage in the activity. Because this was a two-person effort, where one person will only accomplish what the other person is capable of doing, Steve's partner in the wild woozy helped him to realize that his meager attempt at the activity had robbed him from feelings of success. When questioned about the event later that evening, Steve stated, "I disappointed myself, but it felt good to finally talk about that stuff. I had been holding it in for a long time."

Steve's behavior improved slightly during the remainder of the first week; however, the greatest change in his attitude came during the extended wilderness camping trip. From the outset of the trip, Steve was challenged to take on leadership roles such as being the sweeper. The sweeper is responsible for watching over everyone from the back of the group. Steve eagerly approached this responsibility and received a great deal of verbal support for his efforts from the staff and his peers. Steve was given the role of the sweeper on one particularly long hike up to the rock site. One member began to fall far behind the rest of the group because he was developing blisters on his feet. Steve stayed with this person for a long time, but eventually grew angry and left his role as the sweeper to catch up with the rest of the group. When Steve arrived at camp without the other member, the group confronted him to ask why he arrived alone. Steve admitted that he had left his responsibility as sweeper because he was anxious over being so far behind. Steve had not anticipated the extent to which the rest of the group would condemn him for his decision. That evening as the group processed the day the other members of the group told Steve that they no longer trusted him.

The next day during the rock climbing activity, Steve could not find anyone who was willing to belay him or to be belayed by him. As Steve sat and watched the activities, he grew increasingly frustrated and angry. Steve made several attempts to rejoin the group, but they would not respond to his efforts. During lunch, the facilitators confronted Steve about the morning's activities. Steve admitted that he was used to not trusting himself and others, but he was not accustomed to not being trusted by others. The facilitators encouraged Steve to confront the group about his feelings. Steve agreed to do so. After a lengthy discussion, one member of the group agreed to partner up with Steve for the afternoon. Steve's attitude and behaviors changed drastically after that day. For the remainder of the week, Steve was more willing to assist others as well as accept help from others

Once he returned to the facility, Steve talked about how the adventure activities related to the situations he would encounter upon his return home. Steve realized that to be successful in school and at home he would have to rely more on others and allow himself to receive help from others. Steve developed a list of potential resources he could turn to when he felt as if he needed help with a situation. Steve included his mother on the list because he recognized that she would be there to support him; however, he was not willing to rely on his father for help. In addition, Steve made plans to become more involved in the community youth programs operated in his neighborhood.

At the time of his 2-month follow-up, Steve had improved his attendance at school and was maintaining his grades. He reported that he was continuing to be involved in the community youth program and had helped to organize and lead one camping trip for the organization. The group was currently raising money for a skiing trip in the winter. Steve did admit to drinking alcohol over the past 2 months, although he stated that he had not used any drugs. Steve's relationship with his father remained strained. Steve reported that he was growing comfortable talking to his mother and he trusted that she would be there for him.

Summary

Steve's diagnosis of depression stemmed from his inability to trust himself and others, and communicate his feelings to others. The adventure therapy program continually challenged Steve to confront those issues. Through his experiences on the wild woozy and rock climbing, Steve was able to begin to understand the extent to which his inability to trust himself and others was affecting his life. By transferring this learning to other aspects of his life, he made adjustments in his perceptions and behaviors and successfully resolved his problems at home.

Intervention Implementation Exercises

The following sequence of games and initiatives are intended to provide participants with a preliminary understanding of activities pursued in adventure therapy. A large open space, preferably in a gymnasium or outside in grassy area, should be secured for these activities. Leadership of the activities can be assumed by the instructor or members of the group. The activities are adapted from activities presented in *Silver Bullets* (Rohnke, 1984), *Cowstails and Cobras* (Rohnke, 1989), *Quick Silver* (Rohnke & Butler, 1995), *The New Games Book* (Fluegelman, 1976), and *Teamwork and Teamplay* (Cain & Jolliff, 1998). The activities are divided into the following categories:

- Acquaintance Activities
- Communication Activities
- Initiatives

Acquaintance Activities

Toss a Name. This activity is a circle game played in groups of 8 to 10 people. A leader begins the game by saying his or her first name before tossing a ball to the person on his or her right or left. The participants are then asked to continue passing the ball in the same direction after stating their name. When the leader again receives the ball, he or she calls out someone's name in the circle and tosses the ball to him or her. That person calls another individual's name and tosses the ball to them and so on. The leader allows the participants to continue tossing the ball until the participants are familiar with each other's names. The leader then adds an additional ball. The additional ball increases the frequency of names being called and the activity level of the game.

Communication Activities

All Aboard. The intent of this activity is to have the entire group simultaneously stand on a platform, which is raised approximately 2 feet off the ground (Note: 12 to 15 adults can usually fit on a 2' x 2' platform). If a raised platform is not available, the leader may place a piece of plywood on the ground. However, close observation is necessary to ensure that all participants have their feet off the ground. A participant must have both feet off the ground to be counted as on the platform. In addition, the entire group must hold their balanced pose for at least 5 seconds.

Blindfold Shapes. This activity is played in a group of any size. Participants are asked to form a circle, put on blindfolds (or close their eyes), and are given a 75 to 150" rope. Participants are asked to make a distinct square, triangle, pentagon, and other shapes while they keep at least one hand on the rope at all times. When participants agree that the shape is completed, they remove their blindfolds. The activity is repeated using various shapes. If the task becomes easy for participants, the rules may be changed by not allowing conversation during the activity.

Willow. To organize this activity, participants are arranged shoulder to shoulder standing in a circle surrounding one participant who is in the middle of the circle at arm's-length from other participants. Participants in the circle assume a balanced position, placing one leg in front of the other with knees slightly bent. Their hands are flexed with palms facing the center of the circle, while their arms are extended and elbows slightly bent. This position will absorb the fall of the participant in the center. When a ready position has been achieved by all in the circle, the participant in the center prepares for the fall by standing with feet together, body straight and stiff, and arms crossed over his or her chest. The person in the center leans toward the circle and is moved back and forth around the group. The circle of participants should gently perform a controlled, rocking movement.

Trust. This is an active game to enhance group trust. To play, one participant stands at one end of a field or large room with hands flexed, palms out, and arms extended. This person is either blindfolded or has agreed to keep his or her eyes closed. The participant is then asked to jog toward the other end of the space at a steady pace. The rest of the participants are spread out, facing the jogger's approach to keep the jogger from hitting the wall or other barriers. If there is a group of greater than 12 participants, the leader may choose to have 2–3 joggers concurrently. Trust can be broken by inattentive spotters. In addition, spotters should be as quiet as possible to assure the jogger's maximum participation and concentration.

Initiatives

Balloon Train. To play, participants line up front to back, and are directed to place a balloon between each participant. The participants are then asked to move the entire group across an area partially obstructed with obstacles without letting any balloons hit the floor. Some examples of obstacles could be a rolled up mat, a balance beam, large hoop, or milk crates. To increase the level of difficulty, participants can be prohibited from hugging the players in front of them. Variation of the rules for when the balloon hits the ground include starting over, having the two participants who dropped the balloon go to the front or end of the line and replace the balloon, have the group determine how to pick up the balloon and replace it without losing other balloons, or create new rules.

Summary

The aforementioned games and initiatives are a few examples of the numerous activities designed for use in adventure therapy. For other activities the reader is encouraged to examine the books identified in the introduction of this section. Additionally, individuals interested in expanding their repertoire of activities and leadership skills should seek training from a reputable organization. The agency resource list provided at the end of the chapter is intended to help identify organizations which provide training and workshops on adventure programs.

Conclusion

Adventure therapy can be an effective way to help individuals discover, understand, and modify dysfunctional attitudes and behaviors. The effectiveness of this mode of therapy is largely derived from the unfamiliar, challenging, action-oriented activities that force individuals outside of their "comfort zone." With the help of skilled facilitators, individuals are encouraged to reflect upon these experiences and how they relate to issues individuals experience in their lives. As the quote that opened this chapter suggests, adventure therapy capitalizes on its playful atmosphere to create a rich learning environment from which individuals can learn and grow.

Discussion Questions

1. What is the difference between adventure programming and adventure therapy?
2. How does the adventure experience paradigm explain how perceived risk and competence in an adventure experience result in different conditions?
3. What are the eight components of adventure therapy?
4. How might participants transfer the knowledge they gain through adventure therapy to other aspects of their life?
5. According to Luckner and Nadler (1995), how can life narratives be used to process adventure experiences?
6. What were the contributions each of the three historical adventure therapy movements made to adventure therapy?
7. How does understanding the self-perception theory enhance our understanding of adventure therapy?
8. How could adventure therapy address an individual's perception of helplessness and promote self-efficacy?
9. Why might a cooperative adventure experience be more beneficial than a disability awareness program to increase acceptance and social interaction of individuals with disabilities?
10. Identify the outcomes of adventure therapy that Cason and Gillis (1994) found in their meta-analysis of adventure-based research studies with adolescents.

Resources

Agency and Web-Based Resources

Adventure Therapy Web. A web-based resource for an online discussion group and articles related to adventure therapy. http://leegillis.com/AT/ (Retrieved July 23, 2007).

Association of Experiential Education. 2885 Aurora Avenue, Suite #28, Boulder, CO 80303-2252, (303) 440-8844. Premier organization servicing individuals in adventure recreation. Hosts an annual international conference as well as regional conferences. Has a professional interest group exclusively related to adventure therapy. Excellent resource for books and training, as well as contacts with other professionals.

Outdoor Education Research and Evaluation Center. A web-based resource that focuses on outdoor education and methods, such as residential camping, experiential education, environmental education, and adventure therapy. The multi-disciplinary site emphasizes an international perspective. http://wilderdom.com/adventuretherapy.html (Retrieved July 23, 2007).

Project Adventure. P.O. Box 100, Hamilton, MA 01936, (508) 468-7605. Offers extensive training at all levels, as well as an excellent resource for equipment and books.

Wilderness & Protected Area Research Center. College of Natural Resources, University of Idaho, Room 18a. Moscow, ID 83844-1139, (208) 885-7911. A research center that focuses on the human dimensions of wilderness ecosystems. Provides considerable online references to research related to wilderness and adventure therapy. http://www.cnr.uidaho.edu/wrc/ (Retrieved July 23, 2007).

Wilderness Therapy Treatment Network. A charitable nonprofit consumer protection site designed to provide parents, and professionals with relevant research, health and safety information and a program referral network. http://www.wilderness-therapy.org/ (Retrieved July 23, 2007).

Material Resources

Cain, J., & Jolliff, B. (1998). *Teamwork and teamplay*. Dubuque, IA: Kendall/Hunt.
Davis-Berman, J., & Berman, D. S. (1994). *Wilderness therapy: Foundations, theory and research*. Dubuque, IA: Kendall/Hunt.
Fluegelman, A. (1976). *The new games book*. San Francisco: The Headlands Press.
Gass, M. A. (Ed.). (1993). *Adventure therapy: Therapeutic applications of adventure programming*. Dubuque, IA: Kendall/Hunt.
Gass, M. (1995). *Book of metaphors II*. Dubuque, IA: Wm. C. Brown Publishers.
Hirsch, J., & Gillis, H. L. (2004). *Developing metaphors for group activities*. [DVD/CD].
Nadler, R. S., & Luckner, J. L. (1992). *Processing the adventure experience: Theory and practice*. Dubuque, IA: Kendall/Hunt.

Priest, S., & Gass, M. A. (1997). *Effective leadership in adventure programming*. Champaign, IL: Kendall/Hunt.

Priest, S., Gass, M., & Gillis, L. (2003). *The essential elements of facilitation. Skills for enhancing client learning and change*. Seattle, WA: Tarrak Publications.

Rohnke, K. (1984). *Silver bullets: A guide to initiative problems, adventure games, stunts and trust activities*. Hamilton, MA: Project Adventure.

Rohnke, K. (1989). *Cowstails and cobras II: A guide to games, initiatives, ropes courses and adventure curriculum*. Dubuque, IA: Kendall/Hunt.

Rohnke, K., & Butler, S. (1995). *Quicksilver: Adventure games, initiative problems, trust activities and a guide to effective leadership*. Dubuque, IA: Kendall/Hunt.

Schoel, J., Prouty, D., & Radcliff, P. (1995). *Islands of healing: A guide to adventure based counseling* (2nd Ed.). Dubuque, IA: Kendall/Hunt.

References

Bacon, S. (1983). *The conscious use of metaphor in Outward Bound*. Denver: Colorado Outward Bound School.

Bandura, A. (1977). Self-efficacy: Toward a unifying theory of behavioral change. *Psychological Review, 84*, 191–215.

Bem, D. J. (1967). Self-perception: An alternative interpretation of cognitive dissonance phenomena. *Psychological Review, 74*, 183–200.

Berman, D. S., & Davis-Berman, J. (1995). Adventure as psychotherapy: A mental health perspective. *Leisurability, 22*(4), 21–28.

Cason, D., & Gillis, L. (1994). A meta-analysis of outdoor adventure programming with adolescents. *Journal of Experiential Education, 17*(1), 40–47.

Casey, R. J., & Berman, J. S. (1985). The outcomes of psychotherapy with children. *Psychological Bulleting, 98*, 388–400.

Csikszentmihalyi, M. (1975). *Beyond boredom and anxiety*. San Francisco: Jossey-Bass.

Csikszentmihalyi, M. (1993). *The evolving self*. New York: HarperCollins Publishing.

Easley, A. T. (1991). Programmed, non-clinical skill development benefits of leisure activities. In B. Driver, P. Brown, & G. Peterson (Eds.), *Benefits of leisure* (pp. 145–160). State College, PA: Venture Publishing, Inc.

Ellis, M. J. (1973). *Why people play*. Englewood Cliffs, NJ: Prentice-Hall.

Gass, M. A. (Ed.). (1993). *Adventure therapy: Therapeutic applications of adventure programming*. Dubuque, IA: Kendall/Hunt.

Gillis, H. L. (1995). If I conduct outdoor pursuits with clinical populations, am I an adventure therapist? *Leisurability, 22*(4), 5–15.

Greene, J. H., & Thompson, D. (1990). Outward Bound USA. In J. C. Miles & S. Priest (Eds.), *Adventure Education* (pp. 5–9). State College, PA: Venture Publishing, Inc.

Hans, T. (2000). A meta-analysis of the effects of adventure programming on locus of control. *Journal of Contemporary Psychotherapy, 30*(1), 33–60.

Hattie, J. M., Marsh, H. W., Neill, J. T., & Richards, G. E. (1997). Adventure education and Outward Bound: Out-of class experiences that make a lasting difference. *Review of Educational Research, 67*, 43–87.

Hirsch, J., & Gillis, H. L. (2004). *Developing metaphors for group activities*. [DVD/CD].

Itin, C. M. (2001). Adventure therapy: Critical questions. *Journal of Experiential Education, 24*(2), 80–84.

Kimball, R. O., & Bacon, S. B. (1993). The wilderness challenge model. In M. A. Gass (Ed.), *Adventure therapy: Therapeutic applications of adventure programming* (pp. 11–41). Dubuque, IA: Kendall/Hunt.

Klint, K. A. (1990). New directions for inquiry into self-concept and adventure experiences. In J. C. Miles & S. Priest (Eds.), *Adventure Education* (pp. 163–172). State College, PA: Venture Publishing, Inc.

Luckner, J. L., & Nadler, R. S. (1995). Processing adventure experiences: It's the story that counts. *Therapeutic Recreation Journal, 29*(3), 175–183.

Martin, P., & Priest, S. (1986). Understanding the adventure experience. *Journal of Adventure Education, 3*(1), 18–21.

Mortlock, R. G. (1984). *The adventure alternative*. Cumbria, United Kingdom: Cicerone.

Nadler, R. S. (1993). Therapeutic process of change. In M. A. Gass (Ed.), *Adventure therapy: Therapeutic applications of adventure programming* (pp. 57–69). Dubuque, IA: Kendall/Hunt.

Neill, J. T. (2003). Reviewing and benchmarking Adventure Therapy outcomes: Applications of meta-analysis. *Journal of Experiential Education, 25*(3), 316–321.

Neill, J. T., & Dias, K. L. (2001). *Social support helps people grow*. Durham, NH: University of New Hampshire.

Priest, S. (1990). The semantics of adventure education. In J. C. Miles & S. Priest (Eds.), *Adventure Education* (pp. 113–117). State College, PA: Venture Publishing, Inc.

Priest, S. (1995). Editorial. *Leisurability, 22*(4), 3–4.

Rosol, M. (2000). Wilderness therapy for youth-at-risk. *Parks and Recreation, 35*(9), 42–60.

Russell, K. C. (2001a). Exploring how the wilderness therapy process relates to outcomes. *Journal of Experiential Education, 23*(3),170–176.

Russell, K. C. (2001b). Assessment of treatment outcomes in outdoor behavioral healthcare. (Idaho Forest, Wildlife, and Range Experiment Station Re. No. 27). Moscow, ID: University of Idaho.

Russell, K. C. (2002). *Longitudinal assessment of treatment outcomes in outdoor behavioral healthcare*. (Idaho Forest, Wildlife, and Range Experiment Station Rep. No. 28). Moscow, ID: University of Idaho.

Russell, K. C., & Hendee, J. C. (2000) *Outdoor behavioral healthcare: definitions, common practices, and a nationwide survey of programs* (Idaho Forest, Wildlife, and Range Experiment Station Rep. No. 26). Moscow, ID: University of Idaho.

Russell, K. C., & Phillips-Miller, D. (2002). Perspectives on the wilderness therapy process and its relation to outcome. *Child and Youth Care Forum, 31*(6), 415–437.

Schoel, J., Prouty, D., & Radcliffe, P. (1988). *Islands of healing: A guide to adventure based counseling*. Hamilton, MA: Project Adventure, Inc.

Seligman, M. E. P. (1975). *Helplessness: On depression, development, and death*. San Francisco: Freeman.

Seligman, M. E. P. (2002). *Authentic happiness: Using the new positive psychology to realize your potential for lasting fulfillment*. New York: Free Press.

Seligman, M. E. P. (2006). *Learned optimism: How to change your mind and your life*. New York: Vintage Books.

Smith, E., & Mackie, D. (1995). *Social psychology*. New York: Worth Publishers.

Sugerman, D. (2005). "I am more than my cancer:" An exploratory examination of adventure programming and cancer survivors. *Journal of Experiential Education, 28*(1), 72–83.

Werhan, P., & Groff, D. (2005). The wilderness therapy trail. *Parks and Recreation, 40*(11), 24–29.

Chapter 3
Anger Management

Alexis McKenney and John Dattilo

*Speak when you are angry and you will make
the best speech you will ever regret.*

—Ambrose Bierce

Introduction

People are not born with an understanding of how to channel anger properly; rather, it must be learned (Golant & Crane, 1987). Although anger is a common emotion, if expressed inappropriately, or experienced for prolonged periods of time, it can become problematic (Hagiliassis, Gulbenkoglu, DiMarco, Young, & Hudson, 2005). This chapter is designed to introduce the reader to a cognitive-behavioral approach to helping people develop anger-coping strategies. After definitions of anger, aggression, violence, and cognitive behavior therapy are offered, the components of anger are explored. Theoretical foundations for a cognitive-behavioral approach to anger management are presented, as well as various studies in which anger management programs were tested. A case study is provided as an example of the potential effectiveness of a cognitive-behavioral anger management program. Finally, a list of professional resources and anger management interventions are provided.

Definitions

To treat anger effectively, it is important to understand the relationship between anger, aggression, and violence. This section includes definitions of:

- Anger
- Aggression
- Cognitive-Behavioral Interventions

In addition, descriptions of cognitive-behavioral interventions used to help people effectively cope with feelings of anger are explained.

Anger

Anger is a state of emotion that involves a range of feelings from aggravation to rage (Spielberger, 1991) and is a natural response to a situation in which a person might feel threatened or treated unfairly, or is confronting a potentially harmful situation (Reilly, Shopshire, Durazzo & Campbell, 2002). According to Novaco (1975), anger's dimensions include a range of behavioral and physiological symptoms. Behavioral symptoms may include grinding teeth or raised voices. Physiological symptoms may include tensed muscles or perspiration. Anger is expressed meta-phorically with such statements as "I'm fit to be tied" or "I can feel my blood boil."

Aggression

Anger is often the precursor to unwarranted physical aggression, or through passive means, such as insults, sarcasm, or intimidation (Hagiliassis, et al., 2005). According to Lochman and Lenhart (1993), aggression is the "exhibition of deliberate actions directed towards other people or objects, with some intention to destroy or injure the target" (p. 785). Aggression is perhaps the most common reason for referrals of children to clinical mental health services and accounts for more than one-third of referrals to outpatient services (Lipman & Offord, 2006).

   Violence is a manifestation of aggression and can be defined as a symptom demonstrated by "hostile outbursts" (Madow, 1972). The World Health Organization lists three types of violence including self-directed, interpersonal, and collective. *Self-directed violence* identifies the victim and perpetrator as the same individual. *Interpersonal violence* is violent behaviors between individuals. This can include domestic violence, violence in schools or the workplace, and elder abuse. *Collective violence* is violence for social, political, or economical reasons by a group.

Cognitive-Behavioral Interventions

The provision of interventions early in childhood increases the likelihood of reducing current problem behaviors and preventing future issues (Lipman & Offord, 2006). The premise of cognitive-behavioral interventions is that both learning and thinking play an important role in acquisition and maintenance of behavior (Hart & Morgan, 1993). According to Hart and Morgan, cognitive-behavioral interventions are de-signed to preserve the best of clinical behavioral interventions while recognizing the cognitive experiences of the individual. Therefore, the cognitive-behavioral model supports both behavioral and cognitive theories of treatment. Cognitive-behavioral interventions have been used in the treatment of psychological problems such as depression, anxiety, and anger. Hart and Morgan outlined six general characteristics of cognitive-behavioral interventions that include:

- Cognitive and behavior therapies are combined
- Cognition is legitimate
- Cognition is similar to behaviors
- Cognition mediates behaviors
- Cognition is related to behaviors
- Behavioral techniques alter behavior and cognition

Cognitive and behavior therapies are combined. Cognitive-behavioral interventions are designed to combine cognitive and behavior therapies. *Cognitive* interventions are based on the argument that distorted thinking is common in all psychological difficulties (Beck, 1995). Cognitive therapists believe distorted thinking is at the core of negative feelings and behaviors and, therefore, seek to change the manner in which a person conceptualizes things (Reber, 1988). *Behavior* therapy is based on a belief that behavior is determined by events external to the learner (Good & Brophy, 1990). Consequently, behaviorists argue a person's negative behaviors can be attributed to environmental reasons rather than distortions in thinking and, furthermore, often result in the acquisition of poor social skills. Combined, cognitive-behavioral interventions focus on distorted thinking and social deficits (Dodge, 1986) by helping individuals to identify and refocus illogical thoughts with the use of behavioral treatment methods.

Cognition is legitimate. A person's thoughts should be viewed as legitimate by therapists.

> For example, in a sports program, Jimmy may inaccurately believe he cannot catch balls or believe that others view him as always unable to catch a ball. Consequently, Jimmy may frequently refuse to participate in sports or quit once engaged. Although Jimmy's thinking may be illogical, his thoughts are logical to him.

Cognition is similar to behaviors. The same methods used for studying a person's behavior should be applied to the study of cognition. One method of studying a person's behavior is by observing and recording the frequency of a particular behavior within a given time (Dattilo & Murphy, 1987).

> For example, a TR specialist may ask Jimmy how he feels before, during, and after activities, as well as recording the number of times Jimmy catches or drops a ball.

Cognition mediates behavior. Cognition mediates behavior by influencing a person's decision to behave in a particular manner. Consequently, cognition is an appropriate target for intervention and can be altered to produce a behavior change.

> For example, once Jimmy's illogical thoughts are identified and documented, the therapist can begin to help Jimmy to recognize when these thoughts are occurring and how they may be influencing his confidence and decision whether to continue participating in sports.

Cognition is related to behavior. Cognition and behavior are believed to be functionally related, therefore, it can be argued that changing one will change the other.

> For example, once Jimmy understands that he does not always drop the ball, nor do others believe he always drops the ball, he will be less likely to refuse to participate in sports or quit activities in which he is already engaged.

Behavioral techniques alter behavioral cognition. Last, if cognition is related to behavior, then applying behavioral techniques such as positive reinforcement will change cognitive events to alter behaviors. Positive reinforcement, which is "the presentation or delivery of a consequence that makes a behavior occur more often in the future" (Dattilo & Murphy, 1987, p. 51), is a behavioral technique that can be used to influence Jimmy's participation.

> For example, Jimmy may be given verbal praise and asked to discuss what he was thinking and how he felt every time he caught a ball. Consequently, Jimmy will begin to learn that he is capable of catching a ball and that his peers are witnessing his success.

Summary

Anger often results in a feeling of extreme discomfort. Feelings of anger may prompt an individual to commit aggressive or violent acts. Individuals who have difficulty controlling or appropriately expressing their anger often demonstrate negative behaviors. One approach to treating individuals who exhibit difficulties controlling anger is cognitive-behavioral interventions. Cognitive-behavioral interventions combine behavior and cognitive therapies to help individuals improve their behavior through the identification of distorted thoughts and social deficits and applying behavioral techniques.

Descriptions

If anger is an emotional manifestation of displeasure, then it is understandable why violence continues to be a primary societal concern. As a society experiences increasing crime rates, low rates of unemployment, and environmental concerns, it is likely that people will continue to experience the unrest that sometimes leads to aggressive acts.

To better understand the aggression and violence often precipitated by anger, it is helpful to explore the complexities of the emotion. One way to analyze such complexities is through a review of the components of anger. In addition, an examination of cognitive-behavioral training as an approach to treating anger may provide the TR specialist with helpful insights into treatment possibilities. The next section contains descriptions of the following:

- Components of Anger
- Examples of Cognitive-Behavioral Interventions

Components of Anger

To learn coping strategies, it may be useful for individuals to explore components of anger. According to Seligman (1993), anger consists of three components:

- Thought
- Bodily reaction
- Attack

Thought. Seligman (1993) described a thought of anger as so "discreet" that a person may not be aware of its presence. "Often, events get out of hand so quickly you will not be conscious of this thought" (p. 120). An angry thought is one of feeling trespassed.

> For example, Cecilia may refer to a peer in her thoughts as "always cheating" during TR groups. Cecilia may feel that her peer's cheating is unfair to her because she does not win as a result. Feeling trespassed, Cecilia may react without being aware of the thought that provoked the reaction.

Bodily reaction. A bodily reaction to anger is when one's nervous system and muscles prepare for assault. A bodily reaction to anger involves muscles tensing, blood pressure rising, digestive processes halting, and brain processes preparing for an attack.

> For example, Cecilia may experience her fists clenching and heart racing each time she perceives a peer as cheating during games.

Attack. The attack response associated with anger is aimed at stopping the trespass through lashing out. Seligman (1993) argued that while some individuals may react physically, a socialized individual may attack verbally, and a well-socialized individual can probably control the attack.

> For Cecilia, who experiences problems managing her anger, the attack may involve attempting to punch or yell at the peer who has elicited the angry reaction.

Examples of Cognitive-Behavioral Interventions

Based on the cognitive-behavioral model, programs have been developed to improve social behaviors of children and adolescents identified as angry and aggressive. Although the programs described in this section were primarily designed as school-based prevention programs for children (Lochman, Dunn, & Klimes-Dougan, 1993), they have been used in correctional settings (Goldstein, Glick, Reiner, Zimmerman, Coultry, & Gold, 1986) as well. Furthermore, similar cognitive-behavioral programs have been developed for residential and day treatment programs for individuals with psychiatric disorders (Barfield & Hutchinson, 1990). The programs described in this section of the chapter are the:

- Anger Control Program
- Anger Coping Programs
- ZIPPER Strategy

Anger Control Program. One example of a program designed for decreasing inappropriate social skills is the *Anger Control Program* (Lochman, Nelson, & Sims, 1981). People's behavioral responses are influenced by their cognitive, emotional, and physical state. In other words, people are apt to react differently depending on what they are thinking about at the time of the incident or how they feel emotionally and physically at that time.

> For example, Carlos may be thinking about an incident that made him angry before he arrived to an art group, causing him to feel physically tense. When paint is accidentally spilled on his painting (see Figure 3.1), Carlos reacts aggressively toward the peer who spilled the paint, even though the true source of anger is associated with the incident that happened before the painting group began.

These cognitive, emotional, and physical states are influenced by the person's reinforcement history, self-esteem, and physiological arousal. A person's *reinforcement history* includes how the person has traditionally been rewarded or punished by people such as relatives, teachers, supervisors, or peers for exhibiting particular behaviors (Lochman et al., 1981).

> For example, if Carlos has repeatedly been rewarded by his mother for punching people whom he perceives to have attacked him, he may be more likely to react aggressively if paint is accidentally spilled on his painting.

Self-esteem is the degree to which one values oneself (Reber, 1988).

> Therefore, Carlos may react aggressively because of feeling that his painting was destined to be destroyed because no one thought it was pretty anyway.

Figure 3.1

Physiological arousal may cause an individual's muscles to tense or blood pressure to rise (Lochman et al., 1981).

> Consequently, Carlos, who was already feeling tense, may experience a rise in blood pressure and a further tensing of muscles.

The stimulus event is considered to be an external event that prompts a person to cognitively process what is occurring.

> For example, when Carlos is called a "klutz," he can perceive the label as either a simple joke or a threat to his self-esteem.

The way in which he perceives the situation is what is identified as critical to the therapeutic process. For example, if a person is feeling threatened the person will choose to (a) respond aggressively; (b) passively accept or ignore the threat; (c) withdraw and avoid further contact with the threat; or (d) cope with the situation assertively. Although any one of these options may be helpful in a given situation, Lochman and colleagues (1981) suggested that effective communication skills might help the individual use the fourth option that is generally viewed as preferable. The consequences received by the individual will determine whether the results are punishing or reinforcing.

To assist individuals in learning to cope with situations assertively, Lochman, Nelson, and Sims (1981) created the Anger Control Program. The program includes 12 sessions of discussions, modeling, and behavioral rehearsal. *Discussions* involve a group of participants talking with one another and the program facilitator about their reactions to anger-provoking situations (see Figure 3.2). When participants or the facilitator demonstrate appropriate reactions to anger-provoking situations, this is

Figure 3.2

termed *modeling*. *Behavioral rehearsal* includes planned or spontaneous forms of role-play designed to create anger-provoking situations.

Each session in the Anger Control Program contains one or two goals. For example, the goal for the third session is "Problem identification. Learn which specific aspects of a situation create a problem, and lead to anger arousal" (Lochman et al., 1981, p. 147). To accomplish this goal, the facilitator may lead a discussion that prompts participants to explore a situation that frequently causes problems among the group. Consequently, the group can discuss what creates the problem, how they feel when the situation occurs, how it can lead to anger arousal, and how the problem can be effectively confronted.

Anger Coping Programs. The first program described is a follow-up to the Anger Control Program designed for aggressive fourth and fifth graders (Lochman & Lenhart, 1993). The Anger Coping Program includes 18 sessions with goals, objectives, and exercises for each session. The primary objectives of the program include: (a) improve perspective-taking ability, (b) increase ability to notice physiological indications of anger, (c) improve problem-solving ability in social situations, and (d) increase children's repertoire of strategies for dealing with difficult confrontations.

The purpose of the program is to teach people to think about difficult situations before reacting to these situations. Role-plays and peer interactions are included to increase the chance that the skills will be generalized. Role-play is important because it can contribute to healthy adaptation and resolution of stressful or anxiety-producing events that occur during childhood (Levenson & Herman, 1991). Although the program was designed for educational settings, it can be adapted for any setting in which a child is provided treatment.

The second Anger Control Program described was designed for individuals who have sustained a traumatic brain injury (TBI). According to Campbell (2000), these individuals may experience temporary or permanent impairments in not only cognitive and physical functioning, but social and/or behavioral functioning as well. The purpose of this program was to teach individuals who have sustained a TBI the following skills as they move through the program: (a) identifying anger, (b) reacting to anger, (c) recognizing the boiling point, (d) coping with stress and anger, (e) discussing assertive reactions, (f) modeling assertive behavior, (g) role-playing assertive behavior, and (h) processing feelings.

ZIPPER Strategy. Another example of a cognitive-behavioral approach to anger management is the ZIPPER Strategy presented by Wilkening and Gazitt (1991). ZIPPER is a mnemonic created to help children remember how to handle an anger-provoking situation. The mnemonic stands for the following: **z**ip your mouth, **i**dentify the problem, **p**ause, **p**ut yourself in charge, **e**xplore choices, and **r**eset.

Before the start of the ZIPPER Strategy, participants are interviewed, offered a rationale for participation, and asked to commit to learning the strategy (Smith, Siegel, O'Connor, & Thomas, 1994). Once participants sign an agreement to learn the strategy, they participate in five training sessions. Examples of anger-management activities include practicing appropriate responses with external guidance, thinking out loud, and learning role-modeling techniques (Wilkening & Gazitt, 1991).

Summary

While many TR specialists utilize aspects of cognitive-behavioral interventions in their practice, further training is required to conduct cognitive-behavioral groups. Such training includes a graduate degree focused in psychology, counseling, or social work, and any applicable national and/or state certifications (National Association of Cognitive-Behavioral Therapists). TR specialists would benefit from requesting advice of a current cognitive-behavioral therapist or co-treating interventions.

When people feel angry, they may find it difficult to articulate what defines the experience. To better understand anger, it is helpful to identify its complexities. An awareness of the intricacy of anger is important to the TR specialist interested in including an anger control program within TR services. One approach to understanding anger is to explore its components (Seligman, 1993). By exploring the various ways in which an individual may experience anger, the TR specialist is better equipped to address similar issues with participants. With these issues explored, the foundation is laid for the implementation of a cognitive-behavioral intervention for the management of anger. Examples of cognitive-behavioral interventions include the Anger Control Program, Anger Coping Programs, and the ZIPPER Strategy.

History

The history of cognitive-behavioral interventions can be traced to the early work of behavior and cognitive theorists (Meichenbaum, 1993). Cognitive-behavioral interventions primarily emerged in the 1960s out of a growing dissatisfaction with the behavioral approach to psychotherapy. Meichenbaum (1993) argued that research was supporting the belief that how the individual perceived the relationship between behavior and critical events influences an individual's behavior. The role of individual perceptions was demonstrated in an experiment conducted by Lazarus (1966), who found that what people were told about a stressful event had a significant influence on their behavior and physiological responses.

> For instance, if Darian were told that an accident shown in a film was a dramatization rather than an actual accident, he would demonstrate different patterns of responses.

Lazarus's experiment, however, did not prompt changes in psychotherapy until the writings of social learning theorists became prevalent. Social learning theorists emphasize the role of mediated self-regulatory processes in behavior change. The way in which individuals set goals, solve problems, and make decisions are viewed as appropriate for treatment interventions. Individuals are taught to recognize that they reacted to situations because of previously established beliefs. A person's beliefs, however, are not viewed by all professionals as reality-based but rather as devices sometimes used to maintain self-esteem or achieve interpersonal goals. According to Meichenbaum (1993), by the 1970s and 1980s, cognitive-behavioral therapists began to argue that decision making may sometimes be influenced by cognitively distorted beliefs. Consequently, cognitive-behavioral therapists were now teaching individuals strategies for identifying and exploring the reality of their thoughts.

Theoretical Foundations

Cognitive-behavioral interventions combine tenets put forth by behavior and cognitive theorists (Meichenbaum, 1993). Behavior theorists use "conditioning" as a means of shaping behavior with the use of punishments and rewards (Good & Brophy, 1990). Arguing that cognitions play a role in behavior change, cognitive therapists expanded the idea of behaviorism to include the way in which an individual cognitively processes a situation. Cognitive-behavioral interventions have been designed to treat social deficits such as anger and aggression (Lochman & Lenhart, 1993). This section contains theories associated with the following two models:

- Behavioral
- Cognitive

Behavioral Model

The term *behaviorism* was first used by John B. Watson in 1913 to describe the scientific study of behavior (Good & Brophy, 1990). Watson argued that psychology should only be concerned with overt behavior rather than subjective experiences (Austin, 1997). Behaviorists focus on overt behaviors; those behaviors that are readily observable. Conversely, covert behaviors are internally experienced by an individual. The behavioral theory stipulates that normal and abnormal behavior is learned; therefore, a person's maladaptive behavior can be changed through a teaching-learning process that uses reinforcement to increase behaviors and extinction and punishment to decrease behaviors (Good & Brophy, 1990).

Cognitive Model

In the last few decades, there has been a shift from a strictly behavioral orientation for treating anger-related disorders toward a greater interest in human cognition (Hart & Morgan, 1993). One major impetus for the growth of cognitive interventions was the growing dissatisfaction with using a strictly behavioral approach to therapy (Meichenbaum, 1993). The shift toward cognitive therapy can be seen in early studies conducted by Beck (1964), who demonstrated that individuals who are depressed can feel better if their negative or distorted thinking is altered.

Since its inception, cognitive treatment strategies have been used to treat a variety of psychological conditions ranging from depression to anger and aggression. Beck (1995) reported cognitive theory holds that a person's behaviors and feelings are influenced by how that person perceives an event; therefore, people can address psychological difficulties by learning to alter their thoughts. These thoughts are referred to as *automatic thoughts* and are hypothesized to be automatic because they involuntarily surface. Automatic thoughts are those thoughts that prompt people to construe events a particular way and stem from *core beliefs*. Core beliefs spring from an individual's self-perception and view of others and the environment, and are generally viewed as absolute truths by the individual.

For example, Bobby may believe that he is incompetent because he felt too "dumb" to understand the instructions to a model-building kit. In this example, Bobby's automatic thought was that he was not smart enough to understand written instructions. This automatic thought stemmed from Bobby's core belief that he is incompetent.

Summary

Cognitive-behavioral treatment is a primary orientation of psychotherapy and is unique in that it is derived from the behavioral and cognitive models of behavior (Roth & Fonagy, 2005). The behavioral model is based on the argument that behavior is determined by external events (Good & Brophy, 1990). Cognitive theorists consider how an individual cognitively processes a situation (Beck, 1995). Because dysfunctional thinking is central to negative behaviors and emotions, cognitive-behavioral interventions are used to change the manner in which a person conceptualizes situations.

Effectiveness

People who are aggressive tend to lack the skills needed to enact an appropriate strategy when perceiving others to have hostile intentions. Whether the person will continue to display this behavior will depend on the consequences that follow. Cognitive-behavioral treatment programs are designed to enhance the generalization of the intervention by underscoring the idea that different contexts will have different consequences (Lochman et al., 1993). Cognitive-behavioral interventions are designed to help individuals reduce angry and aggressive behavior. Interventions designed to treat children who are aggressive, youth who demonstrate behavioral problems, individuals with disabilities, and adult offenders have been found promising.

In response to studies demonstrating that aggressive behaviors can limit academic success and increase chances of a youth dropping out of school, **Cobb, Sample, Alwell, and Johns (2005)** synthesized findings from research on effective interventions for youth who demonstrated aggressive behavior. Based on a review of literature and subsequent meta-analysis of 16 studies that involved 791 youth with behavioral disorders, attention deficit hyperactivity disorders, and learning disabilities, the authors concluded that cognitive-behavioral interventions were effective in reducing aggressive behavior and the likelihood of dropping out of school. Findings from this review highlight areas of need, such as anger control curricula, cognitive-behavioral training, self-management skills training, and alternative social response training.

Hagiliassis and colleagues (2005) randomly assigned 29 individuals with various levels of intellectual disability and/or complex communication needs, who experienced difficulties in anger control to a 9-week (2 hr/wk) anger management program or a waiting-list control group. The program used a combination of a 4-step problem-solving intervention and assertiveness skills training. There was significant improvement in self-reported anger levels of the intervention group compared to the control group and relative to their pre-intervention scores. When checked 4 months following the intervention, participants continued to demonstrate higher self-reported anger levels than those who were in the comparison group.

Herrmann and McWhirter (2003) examined effects of the Student Created Aggression Replacement Education (SCARE) program with 207 youth at-risk for anger in 7th–9th grades (149 boys and 58 girls). The SCARE program is an anger and aggression management program designed to lower aggression. Participants were randomly assigned to treatment and control groups. Measures were taken before and after participants received the SCARE program. Participants in the program demonstrated significantly lower levels of anger and aggression and a slightly higher level of anger control. After 1 year, participants continued to score lower on measures of aggressive and violent attitudes. The authors concluded that the SCARE program is an effective tool for preventing aggression in youth.

Willner, Jones, Tams, and Green (2002) randomly assigned 14 individuals diagnosed with learning disabilities who were candidates for anger management to a treatment or a waiting-list control group. The anger management intervention (9 wks; 1 x wk; 2-hr sessions) included brainstorming, role-playing, and homework exercises to address managing anger. Session topics included relaxation techniques, aims and rules for the group, triggers that evoke anger, physiological and behavioral components of anger, behavioral and cognitive strategies to avoid build-up of anger and for coping with anger-provoking situations, and acceptable ways of displaying anger. Participants who received the intervention showed a decrease in their anger levels. Also, participants demonstrated further improvement compared to their pre-intervention scores 3 months post-intervention.

Valliant, Ennis, and Raven-Brooks (1995) investigated effects of a cognitive-behavioral intervention for anger management (6 wks, 1 x wk, 2 hr) with 44 adult male incarcerated offenders and 26 adult male probationary offenders. The authors hypothesized that the program would have more positive effects on probationary offenders than incarcerated offenders because probationary offenders would have a more authentic desire to control their anger. Before and after the intervention, participants completed a self-esteem inventory and a hostility inventory. The hostility inventory measured assault, verbal and indirect hostility, irritability, negativism, resentment, suspicion, and guilt. Contrary to the hypothesis that probationary offenders would be more motivated to improve, probationary offenders demonstrated higher levels of guilt. The authors suggested that an increase in feelings of remorse can be viewed as a positive result of treatment. Another positive effect was found with incarcerated offenders who demonstrated lower levels of verbal hostility and resentment. Caution was suggested, however, in interpreting the results. Lower levels of verbal hostility may have been achieved as an adaptive response that represented inmates' desire to complete their sentences with less conflict and interference from authority, rather than to make a lifelong change.

Smith and colleagues (1994) studied effects of a cognitive-behavioral intervention using the ZIPPER Strategy to treat angry and aggressive children (ages 10–11). A multiple baseline design was used across three students to investigate effects of a cognitive-behavioral program (6 sessions, 30 min) in decreasing noncompliance, blaming, bullying, threatening, verbal assaults, and destruction of property. Behavior was observed and recorded on sheets tallying frequency of physical self-cues and correct self-statements displayed during role-play activities. All three participants applied the ZIPPER Strategy as evidenced by their use of self-statements and physical self-cues. Participants displayed a considerable decrease in aggressive and angry behavior. Low levels of aggressive and angry behavior were maintained after the intervention ended. Anecdotal data supported the intervention with two teachers, one resource teacher, and one paraprofessional who reported seeing improvements.

Cognitive-behavioral interventions have been successful in reducing aggressive behavior in adolescents with behavior disorders (Etscheidt, 1991; Feindler et al., 1986). In one study conducted by **Etscheidt (1991)**, 30 adolescents (24 male, 6 female, ages 12–18) were diagnosed as chronically disruptive as evidenced by frequent aggressive, impulsive, and acting-out behaviors. The study was designed to determine: (a) whether fewer aggressive behaviors would be exhibited by participants receiving the intervention, and (b) whether the intervention would be more effective with a positive consequence (incentive). Participants were assigned to one of three groups: (a) a 12-session cognitive-behavioral intervention adapted from the Anger Control Program (Lochman et al., 1981), (b) the same training program plus a positive consequence for using skills imparted, or (c) the control group. Effects were measured by behavioral observations and teacher ratings. Behavior was observed during a 3-week pre-training period and a 3-week post-training period. Aggressive behaviors were recorded and totaled for each participant as negative physical acts, negative interpersonal actions, or destructive behavior. A rating scale was administered by teachers during pre-training and again 10 weeks later during post-training. Both treatment groups displayed more self-control and fewer aggressive behaviors at post-treatment than the control group. Behavioral observations and teacher ratings revealed a decrease in attacking or attempting to attack another with intent to inflict pain, a decrease in class disruptions, and a decrease in destruction of property. No significant differences were found between the two treatment groups. It appears the cognitive-behavioral intervention was effective in reducing aggressive behavior and increasing self-control during the course of treatment. Also, the addition of an incentive program did not appear to substantially improve program effectiveness.

In a study with 21 male adolescents (ages 13–18) who were institutionalized with psychiatric diagnoses, **Feindler, Ecton, Kingsley, and Dubey (1986)** evaluated effects of a cognitive-behavioral intervention (8 wks, 12 sessions) in reducing anger and aggressive behavior. Participants were assigned to a treatment group or a waiting-list control group. To assess change, participants were videotaped and rated on measures of impulsivity and self-control. Daily records of acting-out behavior were used as well. Once pre-assessment measures and baseline recordings of rule violations were completed, the anger-training program was initiated. After the intervention, all participants completed a post-test and data on acting-out behavior were recorded for 3 weeks post-treatment. The cognitive-behavioral intervention reduced anger and aggressive acting-out behavior in participants receiving the training program. Participation in the intervention resulted in a decrease in impulsivity ratings, improvement in ratings of self-control, increased use of more appropriate anger control techniques when confronted with anger-provoking stimuli, and a decrease in restrictions for acting-out behavior.

In a study with 20 boys identified as aggressive (ages 9–11), **Lochman and Curry (1986)** compared effects of two cognitive-behavioral anger-coping interventions to determine if a lack of focus (passive off-task behavior) and on-task behavior could be influenced by including additional sessions in interpersonal problem-solving or impersonal tasks. Participants were assigned to an anger-coping (AC) intervention with interpersonal problem-solving skills, or an anger-coping program plus self-instruction (AC-SIT) intervention that involved completing skill booklets and sequencing matching sheets designed to teach children to internalize self-statements. The authors hypothesized that the AC-SIT condition would result in greater reductions over the AC condition in passive off-task behaviors identified as aggressive. Both groups engaged in 12 sessions (1 hr each) designed to help participants identify problems, generate solutions, and practice self-statements ("Stop! Think! What should I do?") with discussion and role-plays. The AC-SIT group participated in the same program in addition to six self-instruction sessions. Program effectiveness was measured via behavioral observations completed by parents, pupils, and teachers. Although support was not found for the hypothesis, an overall trend revealing a reduction in off-task passive behavior was associated with AC-SIT. This conclusion was drawn because 3% of boys in the AC group demonstrated a decrease in passive-off task behavior compared to 13% in the AC-SIT group.

Based on the cognitive-behavioral model, **Lochman and colleagues (1981)** used the Anger Coping Program to examine the relationship between self-esteem and social problem-solving skills, as well as changes in disruptive and aggressive behaviors in class during a school year. Seventy-six males (grades 4–6) were identified by teachers as the most aggressive and disruptive students and were assigned to one of four conditions: (a) anger-coping; (b) anger-coping plus goal setting; (c) minimal treatment goal setting; and (d) untreated control. Participants who initially demonstrated the highest rates of off-task behavior displayed greatest improvement in classroom behavior as measured by teacher ratings of aggression. Those participants whose parental ratings of aggression were the lowest were those individuals who had initially displayed the poorest problem-solving skills. As a result, the authors contended that interventions based on problem solving improved the behavior of participants with the poorest problem-solving skills. Similarly, self-esteem appeared to mediate participants' responses to treatment conditions. Participants with highest levels of self-esteem displayed greatest reductions in aggression. Aggressive participants with the best initial problem-solving skills in untreated conditions who displayed the greatest improvement were those who had highest levels of self-esteem and problem-solving skills. Conversely, those who became more disruptive as the year progressed were those with lower levels of self-esteem and problem-solving skills. The authors argued that self-esteem and cognitive problem-solving skills partially mediated changes in aggressive and disruptive behavior. In conclusion, the cognitive-behavioral treatment conditions produced the greatest reduction in aggressive and disruptive behavior. Furthermore, those exposed to the anger-coping plus goal-setting treatment condition demonstrated enhanced generalization over the anger-coping group when assessed at follow-up. Although not successful with all participants, the authors concluded that self-esteem and problem-solving skills may be related to degree of improvement in aggressive individuals exposed to a cognitive-behavioral intervention.

Summary

Existing research moderately indicates that anger management is an empirically supported facilitation technique. Nevertheless, cognitive-behavioral anger management interventions show promise in treating youth demonstrating social-cognitive deficits, children who are noncompliant, aggressive, youth who demonstrate behavioral problems, male offenders, and people with disabilities.

Case Study

Chris

Chris was a 10-year-old boy in fourth grade residing in a long-term psychiatric treatment facility for children and adolescents. Chris has a primary diagnosis of attention deficit hyperactivity disorder. Associated problem areas were listed as impulsivity and oppositional defiance. Chris lived with his mother and younger brother prior to being admitted to the facility. Chris's father left the family 6 months prior to Chris's admission. Although Chris was reported as being intermittently explosive by both his mother and teacher, Chris's mother speculated that the recent deterioration in Chris's behavior had occurred as a result of his father's departure. Chris's mother described him as increasingly violent at home and at school. Chris was suspended the day before being admitted to the treatment facility for punching an 8-year-old girl on the bus. Chris's mother also reported that she had to stop Chris from attacking his brother with a knife 1 week prior to the incident on the bus.

This was Chris's second admission to a psychiatric treatment facility within a 2-month period. Chris was in a short-term treatment facility for 1 week 2 months prior to his admission to long-term treatment. His parents agreed to his participation in the children's therapeutic program that consisted of group therapy, TR, play therapy, and school. Upon admission to the facility, Chris displayed agitated and violent behavior. Chris reacted in a hostile manner toward peers who approached him. Chris was restrained after throwing a chair and then physically attacking a peer during free time in the hall his second day in the facility. After 2 weeks, Chris had been recorded as being restrained six times for aggressive behaviors. Two of the times he was restrained occurred during TR, one during school time, and one in play therapy.

Anger Management for Chris

Chris was referred to the children's TR specialist for the anger management program. The anger management program included the ZIPPER Strategy offered in six sessions. Because of the difficulty Chris had with interacting calmly in group activities, he was interviewed alone to determine situations where he had trouble controlling his aggression. From the interview, it was determined that Chris frequently became angry when he felt his peers treated him like he was "stupid." Chris stated that he often felt this way during physical education classes and recess at school. When feeling angry, Chris typically reacted by physically attacking whoever he felt was teasing him or whoever was in closest proximity to him. After completing the interview, the

TR specialist explained the ZIPPER Strategy to Chris. Chris agreed to participate in the program and signed a contract outlining what was expected of him behaviorally, as well as what the program would involve.

At the start of the second session, Chris appeared excited about coming to the group. He sat quietly while the TR specialist pretended to be Chris playing checkers with a peer (Lori). The TR specialist explained that Lori laughed at Chris when he missed a jump. The TR specialist thought of ZIPPER and explained how she would think through each letter. The TR specialist gave Chris a paper describing the ZIPPER Strategy. Chris laughed when he saw the picture of lips. The TR specialist agreed that the picture was funny, then asked Chris if he thought a picture of lips might help him remember what to do. Chris laughed and made a motion of zipping his mouth shut.

Chris arrived at the third session appearing angry. When asked if he was angry, he said that he was and that he did not "want to be here for this group." After further questioning, Chris explained that he was angry because he missed recess time because he fought with a peer. The TR specialist reminded Chris that the anger management program would help him learn to stay out of fights, which meant he would be able to go to the playground with his peers. Chris agreed to continue, and remained for the entire session.

Chris was asked to practice the ZIPPER Strategy with what caused the fight with Lori earlier that day. Once the situation was explained, and the strategy was reviewed, the TR specialist reenacted the situation following the steps of ZIPPER. Chris then attempted to demonstrate the physical cues he was taught. The TR specialist said, "I'm angry, but I know I can use ZIPPER. Z stands for **z**ip my lips." Chris successfully demonstrated "stop" with his hands and zipping his lips with his fingers. Next, the TR specialist said, "I need to **i**dentify what the problem is." Chris hesitated, began to scowl, and then smiled and pointed proudly to his temple. The TR specialist complimented Chris and went on to say, "I need to **p**ause and **p**ut myself in control." Then Chris yelled out, "I don't remember, I quit!" and ran out of the room. After 15 minutes, a staff member returned with Chris, and he agreed to continue. The TR specialist quickly reviewed what Chris had successfully completed up to that point, and then had him repeat after her what to do at the next step: "Stay cool. Don't get angry. I have a better way to handle this. I'm in control." The TR specialist then said, "Next, I need to **e**xplore better ways to handle the problem." With help from the TR specialist and peers, Chris named two other things he could have done, including finding a staff member or calmly telling a peer what made him angry. Last, the TR specialist said, "I **r**eset by returning to playing calmly on the playground with peers."

During the fourth session, Chris was prompted to demonstrate use of the strategy by thinking aloud while practicing the physical cues used in the third session. Chris became frustrated midway through and threatened to leave. However, Chris agreed to stay and try again after another peer took a turn. After two peers went through the strategy, Chris continued and completed the strategy. During the fifth session Chris practiced the strategy; however, he did so by whispering the verbal cues rather than saying them aloud. Chris completed the entire strategy without quitting and needed only one prompt to help him remember that **e** stood for explore.

Since Chris had difficulty with the last session, he repeated the session on the following day. Chris became angry when he tried to model the physical cues without saying the steps. He appeared as though he were going to physically attack the TR specialist but stopped and instead ran out of the room. When he returned the next day, he talked about his frustration and how he could have better handled his anger. The TR specialist identified that Chris had stopped himself from physically attacking the subject of his anger. After Chris successfully modeled the ZIPPER Strategy, he agreed to continue using it now that he had completed the program. The group then discussed how the ZIPPER Strategy could be used in other places. Chris said that he planned to use it in school when he feels others are laughing at him.

The ZIPPER Strategy was presented in a 2-week period. During the first week, Chris was required to sit quietly away from his peers for 5 minutes on nine occasions and was placed in four therapeutic holds for aggressive behavior. During the second week of the program, Chris was required to sit quietly away from his peers for 5 minutes on seven occasions and was placed in two therapeutic holds. For the 3 weeks following the program, Chris was required to sit away from his peers for 5 minutes on three occasions, and was placed in two therapeutic holds. During processing of activities, Chris was able to describe parts of the ZIPPER Strategy that he used when he felt angry. Chris appeared proud of the positive feedback that he received from staff and peers.

At a 1-month follow-up, Chris's attendance at school in the facility had improved and he was passing all of his classes. His teacher reported that he was consistently demonstrating the ability to calm down in situations where he had reacted aggressively in the past. Chris reported that he did not always remember what to do but now asked for staff assistance when this occurred. Chris also spoke of feeling good because he was receiving fewer reprimands, which meant he was allowed to go to more activities than when he started the program.

Summary

Chris's diagnosis of attention deficit hyperactivity disorder occurred based on his inability to remain focused on activities and control his aggressive impulses. The anger management program helped Chris to develop anger control skills. Through his experiences in the program, Chris understood how his anger and aggressive impulses caused him difficulties at home, school, and in recreation activities. By applying what he learned to other situations, Chris stayed focused long enough when frustrated so that he could calmly resolve problems.

Intervention Implementation Exercises

The following intervention exercises are adapted from the ZIPPER Strategy; a cognitive-behavioral intervention (Wilkening & Gazitt, 1991). Exercises relevant to the strategy are presented:

- Get Started
- Introduce ZIPPER
- Promote Cognitive Modeling
- Practice with Help
- Practice Self-Instruction
- Fade Self-Instruction
- Commit to Using the Strategy

Get Started

Conduct interviews with participants to determine typical situations where aggression is a problem. For example:

1. Can you think of a time when you were so angry that you wanted to hit something or someone? (Yes, Karen laughed at me when I tripped while trying to kick the soccer ball yesterday.)
2. What did you do when she laughed? (I kicked the ball away from the group and ran to the TR specialist and told her I wasn't going to play anymore.)
3. How did the TR specialist react to you kicking the soccer ball away from the group? (I had to sit in a chair away from friends.)
4. Do you think you made a good or a bad choice when you kicked the ball away from the group? (A bad choice.)
5. If I told you that I could teach you to make better choices the next time someone made you angry, would you want to learn how? (Yes.)
6. I want to teach you something that I call ZIPPER. It's a word that stands for a series of steps that you can follow the next time someone makes you angry. Would you be willing to learn those steps in the next few days? (Yes.)
7. Great! Learning the steps to ZIPPER and then following those steps when you are angry is going to be hard work. So when you start using ZIPPER, instead of kicking the soccer ball away from the group or acting aggressively in other ways, I'd like to do something special for you. Can you think of something that you'd really like as a reward for all your hard work? (Yes, to play basketball.)

At this time, a contract is made between the participant and interviewer outlining the agreement discussed.

Introduce ZIPPER

Describe ZIPPER steps to participants using cue cards and picture prompts. Give children a ZIPPER handout with the following information: The Zipper Strategy: **Z**—zip your mouth, **I**—identify the problem, **P**—put off what you want to do, **P**—put yourself in control, **E**—explore other solutions, and **R**—return to what you were doing. Provide a list of statements to be used as self-cues.

Z "Stop," hand motions "stop," take a deep breath, and fingers running across mouth like **zipper.**

I   Take a deep breath, put finger to temple, and *identify* problem.

P   **Pause**, take a deep breath, "I may find a better way to handle this," and "Don't get angry."

P   **Put** yourself in control, "stay cool!" put hands on hip, turn thumbs up, and "I'm in control."

E   "What can I do?" shrug shoulders, and **explore** other options.

R   "I've made it!" and **return** to activity.

Promote Cognitive Modeling

Conduct cognitive modeling with the trainer using "thinking aloud" procedure to model use of verbal and physical cues in strategy. Choose a scenario previously identified by a participant as aggression producing such as:

> "Watch me while I pretend to be a person who is playing soccer. Bobby laughs at me when I trip while trying to kick the soccer ball. But I remember I have a new plan to handle this situation. I think of ZIPPER.
>
> "**Z** stands for **z**ip your mouth. (Model physical cues using open hand for stop and finger motion across lips for being quiet.) Yes, if I zip my lips and stay quiet for a minute, I can give myself time to think about what to do.
>
> "I remember that the **I** stands for **i**dentify the problem. The problem is I don't like it when people make fun of me. But I remember I should take a deep breath and think about my plan. (Model physical cues of taking a deep breath and putting finger to temple to signify thinking.) Okay, now I'm ready to control the situation.
>
> "The **P**s are for **p**ause and **p**ut yourself in charge. I'll find a better way to deal with this. (Model the act of counting down from 10.) I won't get angry. I'll tell myself to 'stay cool.' I'm in control now. (Model the use of "thumbs up" to represent successful self-control.)
>
> "Next I'll do the **E** step. What can I do about the laughing? Let me **e**xplore the choices. First, I can ask the person to please stop calling me names. If I do that, he just might stop. Then, I'll ignore it if it happens again. That way he might get tired of trying to make me mad and just quit. Maybe I'll even ask someone (e.g., TR specialist) to help me deal with this. If Bobby stops calling me names, I'll try to make friends. Then he won't want to call me names anymore. You know, I could make a lot of new friends this way.
>
> "My last step is **R** for **r**eset. Yes, I made it. I didn't lose my temper. I'm not in trouble. I can go right on with my playing soccer. If I keep using the ZIPPER strategy, I might even get all my points for good behavior in TR groups."

Practice with Help

Conduct practice of strategy steps with the TR specialist providing verbal cues while the participant models physical response. Choose a scenario based on the types of conflict situations elicited from the participant. Record the number of cues that the participant remembers.

State the following: "Let's review the steps to the ZIPPER. I am going to pretend that someone has just laughed at me. Instead of getting angry and kicking the ball away from the group, I'm going to follow the steps of ZIPPER. While I think out loud, you show me the physical cues I taught you to remember. (Have children take turns.) Someone just laughed at me. I'm angry, but I know I can use ZIPPER.

Z   **Z**ip my lips. (Child demonstrates "stop" signal with hand, deep breath, puts fingers to lips, fingers "zipping" lips.)

I   I need to **i**dentify what the problem is. (Child takes a deep breath and puts finger to temple.)

P   I need to **p**ause. (Child hesitates before speaking.)

P   I need to **p**ut myself in control. (Child verbalizes, "Stay cool. Don't get angry. I have a better way to handle this. I'm in control.")

E   I need to **e**xplore better ways to handle the problem. (Child shrugs shoulders and verbalizes possible solutions.)

R   I **r**eset by returning to the activity so I can continue playing.

Practice Self-Instruction

Participants demonstrate use of the strategy by thinking aloud and demonstrating physical cues. Provide prompts only as needed. Provide reinforcement and corrective feedback. Continue to record the number of cues the participant remembers.

Fade Self-Instruction

Participants whisper verbal cues while modeling physical cues. Provide corrective feedback as in previous days. Continue to record participant performance.

Commit to Using the Strategy

Conduct practice session with participants thinking steps by themselves. Participants should not move lips or say steps aloud, but should model use of appropriate physical cues. Record performance and obtain commitment for future use of strategy.

State the following: "If you remember to use ZIPPER in TR groups, school, in the hall, or at home, what good things do you think will happen to you?"

Review the positive benefits of maintaining the strategy use across time and in different settings. Some benefits that might apply to individual children include earning points or other reinforcement for good behavior, having more friends, getting better grades, feeling better about themselves, etc.

State the following: "You have worked very hard to learn and practice the ZIPPER Strategy. Do you think you can remember to use it when you have a problem in TR groups, school, or at home? How about in the hall and (name other settings where children have reported problems)? Will you try hard to use ZIPPER whenever you need to? You were terrific!"

Summary

The ZIPPER strategy can be implemented as an anger management intervention technique. Although other anger management techniques have been presented within this chapter, the cognitive-behaviorally based ZIPPER strategy provides a systematic method of anger management. Successful anger management interventions can be facilitated for participants by implementing the technique of the ZIPPER strategy utilizing its system of cues as described in this section of the chapter.

Conclusion

This chapter is designed to introduce the reader to a cognitive-behavioral approach to helping people learn to manage their anger. The cognitive-behavioral approach was designed to combine behavioral and cognitive models (Hart & Morgan, 1993). The behavioral model is based on the argument that behavior is determined by external events (Good & Brophy, 1990) while the cognitive model is centered on how an individual cognitively processes a situation (Beck, 1995). This chapter presents an in-depth description of anger management as it relates to TR. The chapter includes related definitions, a description of the strategies, theoretical foundations, effectiveness studies, a case study, and professional resources and references.

Discussion Questions

1. How is anger related to aggression and violence?
2. What are the three components of anger according to Seligman (1993)?
3. How can the three components be experienced by a participant in a TR activity?
4. What three activities comprise the Anger Control Program according to Lochman and colleagues (1981)?
5. How do these three activities associated with the Anger Control Program differ?
6. What are the primary objectives of the Anger Coping Program according to Lochman and Lenhart (1993)?
7. What does the mnemonic ZIPPER stand for?
8. What are the seven exercises used for the ZIPPER Strategy?
9. What were the results of the anger management program in which the case study, "Chris," participated?
10. What are the primary findings of studies conducted using cognitive-behavioral interventions to treat anger?

Resources

Agency Resources

The Louis de la Parte Florida Mental Health Institute. 13301 North 30th Street, Tampa, FL 33612. Offers a curriculum for teaching children and adolescents appropriate ways to express anger. Internet: http://home.fmhi.usf.edu/

National Institute of Mental Health. Public Information and Communications Branch, 6001 Executive Boulevard, Room 8184, MSC 9663, Bethesda, MD 20892-9663. Internet: http://www.nimh.nih.gov/nimhhome/index.cfm

The Center for Mental Health Services. U.S. Department of Health and Human Services. P.O. Box 42557, Washington, DC, 20015. Provides information and services designed to help improve and increase the quality and range of treatment and support services to individuals experiencing mental health problems. Internet: http://mentalhealth.samhsa.gov/cmhs/

Material Resources

Chapman, G. (2007). *Anger: Handling a powerful emotion in a healthy way.* Chicago, IL: Northfield Publishing.
DiGiuseppe, R., & Tafrate, R. C. (2006). *Understanding anger disorders.* New York: Oxford University Press.
Fein, M. L. (1993). *I.A.M. A common sense guide to coping with anger. Integrative anger management.* Westport, CT: Praeger.
Hankin, G. (1988). *Prescription for anger. Coping with angry feelings and angry people.* Beaverton, OR: Princess Publishing.
Kendall, P. (1990). *Child and adolescent behavior therapy: Cognitive-behavioral procedures.* New York: Guilford Press.
Lochman, J. E., Lampron, L. B., Gemmer, T. V., & Harris, R. (1987). Anger coping interventions for aggressive children: Guide to implementation in school settings. In P. A. Keller & S. R. Heyman (Eds.), *Innovations in clinical practice: A source book* (pp. 339–356). Sarasota, FL: Professional Resource Exchange.
McKay, M., Davis, M., & Fanning, P. (2007). *Thoughts and feelings: Taking control of your moods and your life.* Oakland, CA: New Harbinger Publications.
Quick, J., Hernandez, F. M., Earl, M., & Friedman, R. M. (1980). *Appropriate anger expression curriculum.* Tampa, FL: Florida Mental Health Institute.
Reilly, P. M., Shopshire, M. S., Durazzo, T. C., & Campbell, T. A. (2002). *Anger management for substance abuse and mental health patients: A cognitive behavioral therapy manual and participant workbook.* Rockville, MD: National Clearinghouse for Alcohol and Drug Information.

References

Austin, D. (1997). *Therapeutic recreation: Processes and techniques.* Champaign, IL: Sagamore.

Barfield, C. K., & Hutchinson, M. A. (1990). Observations on adolescent anger and an anger control group in residential and day treatment. *Residential Treatment for Children & Youth, 7,* 45–60.

Beck, A. T. (1964). Thinking and depression: II. Theory and therapy. *Archives of General Psychiatry, 10,* 561–571.

Beck, J. S. (1995). *Cognitive therapy: Basics and beyond.* New York: Guilford Press.

Campbell, M. (2000). *Rehabilitation for therapeutic brain injury: Physical therapy practice in context.* Churchill Livingston, NY: Harcourt Publisher Limited.

Cobb, B., Sample, P., Alwell, M., & Johns, N. (2005). *The effects of cognitive behavioral interventions on dropout for youth with disabilities.* Paper presented at 2004 Annual Council for Exceptional Children Conference. New Orleans, LA.

Dattilo, J., & Murphy, W. D. (1987). *Behavior modification in therapeutic recreation.* State College, PA: Venture Publishing, Inc.

Dodge, K. A. (1986). A social information processing model of social competence in children. In M. Perlumutter (Ed.), *Cognitive perspectives on children's social and behavioral development* (pp. 77–125). Hillsdale, NJ: Erlbaum.

Etscheidt, S. (1991). Reducing aggressive behavior and improving self-concept: A cognitive-behavioral training program for behaviorally disordered adolescents. *Behavioral Disorders, 16,* 107–115.

Feindler, E. L., Ecton, R. B., Kingsley, D., & Dubey, D. R. (1986). Group anger control training for institutionalized psychiatric male adolescents. *Behavior Therapy, 17,* 109–123.

Golant, M., & Crane, B. (1987). *Sometimes it's o.k. to be angry!* New York: Tom Doherty Associates.

Goldstein, A. P., Glick, B., Reiner, S., Zimmerman, D., Coultry, T. M., & Gold, D. (1986). Aggression replacement training: A comprehensive intervention for the acting-out delinquent. *Journal of Correctional Education, 37,* 120–126.

Good, T. L., & Brophy, J. E. (1990). *Educational psychology. A realistic approach.* White Plains, NY: Longman.

Hagiliassis, N., Gulbenkoglu, H., DiMarco, M., Young, S., & Hudson, A. (2005). The anger management project: A group intervention for anger in people with physical and multiple disabilities. *Journal of Intellectual & Developmental Disability, 30,* 86–96.

Hart, J. H., & Morgan, J. R. (1993). In A. J. Finch, W. M. Nelson, & E. S. Ott (Eds.), *Cognitive-behavioral procedures with children and adolescents: A practical guide* (pp. 1–19). Needham Heights, MA: Allyn and Bacon.

Herrmann, D. S., & McWhirter, J. J. (2003). Anger and aggression in young adolescents: An experimental evaluation of the SCARE program. *Education and Treatment of Children, 26,* 273–203.

Lazarus, R.S. (1966). *Psychological stress and the coping process.* New York: McGraw-Hill.

Levenson, R. L., Jr., & Herman, J. (1991). The use of role playing as a technique in the psychotherapy of children. *Psychotherapy, 28,* 660–666.

Lipman, E. L, & Offord, M. H. (2006). Conduct disorder in girls. In S. Roman & M. Seeman (Eds.), *Women's mental health: A life cycle approach* (pp. 93–107). Philadelphia: Lippincott, Williams & Wilkins.

Lochman, J. E., & Curry, J. F. (1986). Effects of social problem-solving training and self-instruction training with aggressive boys. *Journal of Clinical Child Psychology, 15,* 159–164.

Lochman, J. E., Dunn, S. E., & Klimes-Dougan, B. (1993). An intervention and consultation model from a social cognitive perspective: A description of the Anger Coping Program. *School Psychology Review, 22,* 458–471.

Lochman, J. E., & Lenhart, L. A. (1993). Anger coping intervention for aggressive children: Conceptual models for outcome effects. *Clinical Psychology Review, 13,* 785–805.

Lochman, J. E., Nelson, W. M., & Sims, J. P. (1981). A cognitive behavioral program for use with aggressive children. *Journal of Clinical Child Psychology, 10,* 146–148.

Madow, L. (1972). *Anger: How to recognize and cope with it.* New York: Macmillan Publishing Company.

Meichenbaum, D. (1993). Changing conceptions of cognitive behavior modification: Retrospect and prospect. *Journal of Consulting and Clinical Psychology, 61,* 202–204.

National Association of Cognitive-Behavioral Therapists. (n.d.) *Certification in cognitive-behavioral therapy.* Retrieved July 31, 2008, from http://www.nacbt.org/certifications.htm

Novaco, R. W. (1975). *Anger control: The development and evaluation of an experimental treatment.* Lexington, MA: D. C. Heath and Company.

Reber, A. S. (1988). *Dictionary of psychology.* New York: Penguin Books.

Reilly, P. M., Shopshire, M. S., Durazzo, T. C., & Campbell, T. A. (2002). *Anger management for substance abuse and mental health patients: A cognitive behavioral therapy manual and participant workbook.* Rockville, MD: National Clearinghouse for Alcohol and Drug Information.

Roth, A., & Fonagy, P. (2005). *What works for whom? A critical review of psych therapy research* (2nd ed.). New York: Guilford.

Seligman, M. (1993). *What you can change . . . And what you can't.* New York: Ballantine Books.

Smith, S. W., Siegel, E. M., O'Connor, A. M., & Thomas, S. B. (1994). Effects of cognitive-behavioral training on angry behavior and aggression of three elementary-aged students. *Behavioral Disorders, 19,* 126–135.

Spielberger, C. D. (1991). *State-Trait Anger Expression Inventory: Revised Research edition professional manual.* Odessa, FL: Psychological Assessment Resources.

Valliant, P. M., Ennis, L. P., & Raven-Brooks, L. (1995). A cognitive-behavior therapy model for anger management with adult offenders. *Journal of Offender Rehabilitation, 22,* 77–93.

Wilkening, P., & Gazitt, N. (1991). *The ZIPPER strategy.* Unpublished manuscript, University of Florida, Department of Special Education, Gainesville, FL.

Willner, P., Jones, J., Tams, R., & Green, G. (2002). A randomized controlled trial of the efficacy of a cognitive-behavioral anger management group for clients with learning disabilities. *Journal of Applied Research in Intellectual Disabilties, 15,* 224–235.

World Health Organization. (n.d.). *Definition and typology of violence.* Retrieved July 31, 2008, from http://www.who.int/violenceprevention/approach/definition/en/index.html

Chapter 4
Aquatic Therapy

Ellen Broach and John Dattilo

*The water is your friend. You don't have to fight with water, just
share the same spirit as the water, and it will help you move.*
— Aleksandr Popov

Introduction

Activity in the water provides experiences of fun and challenge for many people.
Water allows individuals to experience movement that can be performed on land
with difficulty, if at all. Many people gain a sense of achievement as they learn to
understand and control the different forces acting on their bodies in the water. For
some people with disabilities, water may be the only environment in which they can
achieve physical independence (Campion, 1985).

Aquatic therapy, a method of treatment that is conducted in an inherently
freeing environment, facilitates not only physical benefits but psychological and
leisure ones as well. The aquatic environment has potential of meeting goals that
promote health and well-being as deemed essential by Brundtland (2002) and Chan
(2007) of the World Health Organization. The resulting trend is to promote the
transfer of medical treatment efficiently into the community setting and to build
health maintenance as a lifestyle.

This chapter is written to assist those who wish to expand their knowledge of
the effective use of water and swimming as a therapeutic medium. Aquatic therapy
is defined and a description of treatment strategies is presented. A brief history is
followed by an explanation of water physics and biologic processes as the theoretical
foundation of aquatic therapy follows a brief history. In addition, a review of the
literature and two case studies are included in this chapter so that the reader can understand why aquatic therapy interventions can be beneficial. This chapter concludes
with activity ideas and professional resources that a Therapeutic Recreation (TR)
Specialist can use to improve participants' land-based physical and psychological
functioning while they gain independence in the water.

Definition

Aquatic therapy includes passive or active exercise and swimming as modalities
for habilitation or rehabilitation. TR specialists can use aquatic therapy to promote
psychological and physiological improvements while facilitating independence in
swimming and water exercise (Broach & Dattilo, 1996). In addition, TR specialists

who have the training may use aquatic therapy to encourage participants to achieve independent leisure participation, improve their functioning, and enhance their happiness and subsequent life satisfaction and longevity (Ostir, Mardides, Black, & Goodwin, 2000).

General Considerations

Aquatic therapy is delivered in various settings. In the past, aquatic therapy has been provided most often in residential centers as a part of individual rehabilitation. The trend showing a reduction in hospital lengths of stay has resulted in many individuals not having the opportunity to take full advantage of TR services during hospitalization (Carter & O'Morrow, 2006).

Much of the long-term process of rehabilitation can occur in aquatic therapy programs within the community (Coffey & Broach, 2000). As a result, the range of TR services needed in the community is expanding to include services, such as aquatic therapy, that are designed to help participants achieve treatment goals (Becker & Cole, 2004).

Physicians and insurance companies are acknowledging benefits of aquatic therapy and referrals to aquatic programs are increasing (Bintzler, 2006). Some physicians and people in need of treatment are searching for alternatives to expensive outpatient care due to decreases in insurance reimbursement and rising healthcare costs (Cardenas et al., 2001).

Visitors to an aquatic therapy intervention will notice the sound of laughter as a difference from many other treatment venues. Aquatic therapy can result in an increase in participants' functional ability while participating in an enjoyable activity (Broach, Dattilo, & McKenney, 2007). In addition to providing an enjoyable experience, aquatic therapy provides an opportunity for participants to experience themselves in new ways while learning to move their bodies in an efficient manner. Aquatic therapy encourages people to be active; however, movement should occur without pain. The phrase "no pain, no gain" does not apply! Also, aquatic therapy encourages inclusion into individuals' communities (Cole & Becker, 2004).

Regardless of which aquatic therapy intervention is used, it is important to include an analysis of mental adjustment and subsequent instruction in techniques to improve comfort in the water. Similar to other forms of exercise, aquatic therapy requires learning to appreciate effects of buoyancy, turbulence, and weight of the water while acquiring a degree of breathing and head control. Mental adjustment through maintaining balance when in the water involves teaching a participant to roll from back to front while floating in a horizontal position and then recovering to a vertical position. These mental adjustment skills tend to increase the ability to participate in an aquatic therapy program.

Additional guidelines for aquatic rehabilitation include factors related to depth of water, unilateral or bilateral movements, speed of movement, and body position for stability. A participant who has difficulty standing can perform exercises more easily in deeper water. Therefore, it is helpful if a participant progresses from deeper to shallow depths for lower extremity activity. Movement progresses from one extremity (unilateral) to bilateral movements.

As an example, asymmetric bilateral movements (e.g., moving the right hip into flexion or shoulder into flexion while simultaneously moving the left hip or shoulder into extension) are generally less difficult than symmetric bilateral movements (e.g., both hips moving into flexion at the same time).

A participant should progress from the slower, less water-resisted movements to faster movements where resistance dramatically increases. Finally, participants' stability is affected by their standing position in the water. While there are certain positions that have greater stability than others in the water, participants have a tendency to utilize the least stable position. Therefore, it is important that TR specialists instruct the participants in positions of stability.

For instance, the position with the greatest stability is the sitting position with shoulders at the surface of the water with arms extended. As participants gain stability they can stand chest deep with legs spread in a triangle position and then progress to the stick position with legs shoulder width or less apart.

Key considerations when conducting aquatic therapy programs include:

- Assessment
- Groups
- Contraindications and Precautions

Assessment

When considering aquatic therapy, an understanding of the differences between land and water movement is essential. Often, the same exercises used on land will work different muscles when used in water. Thus, different outcomes will be achieved. Aquatic therapy techniques are based on principles governing buoyancy, turbulence, resistance, and balance.

Specific interventions of aquatic therapy are usually based on a land assessment; however, when in the water the effects of buoyancy of water on movement are considered.

For example, an individual who has limited independent shoulder range on land may be able to obtain greater range of motion in the water due to buoyancy.

Therefore, a water assessment and the baseline measure for assessment of progress will be different than on land.

In addition to land-based assessment, assessment of participants in the water can provide information regarding their perceptions related to the water such as their comfort in the water, their attitude regarding therapy in the water and previous water history. Assessment of the actual physical characteristics of the person can include a person's body shape, buoyancy, and contraindications (why participation may be inadvisable). When documenting participation in aquatic therapy, it is important to include: length of treatment, water temperature, water depths, exercises, progressions in exercises, improvements in participants' condition and activity level, any effects of the activity, and number of people present during treatment.

Groups

Working with groups can increase motivation, socialization, and the ability to work longer with more concentration (Broach, et al., in press). Group interactions and support may increase confidence, fellowship, self-empowerment, buffer stress, extroversion, adherence, and decrease a negative focus on oneself (Fredrickson, Tugade, Waugh, & Larkin, 2003). Some aquatic therapy techniques, such as Watsu and Bad Ragaz, are not suitable for group work due to the space and the need for one-to-one therapy; however, when small groups are possible, they can be beneficial for participants as well as an efficient use of time for the TR specialist.

Although classes in aquatic therapy are typically designed to increase physical challenges associated with participation, individuals with varying abilities can participate in the same group. Appropriate exercises for groups may include sitting exercises, resistive exercises, balancing exercises, standing exercises, gait exercises, exercises with flotation dumbbells, lower extremity and upper extremity kickboard exercises, deep-water exercises, and swimming exercises.

Contraindications and Precautions

A TR specialist conducting aquatic therapy must be aware of contraindications and precautions associated with water activity, understand the pathology of the disease or condition, and be prepared to apply aquatic therapy principles. Water activity is contraindicated for individuals with open wounds, bowel incontinence, diseases transmissible by water, hepatitis-A, certain skin conditions, open tracheotomies (until healed), uncontrolled seizures, and unstable blood pressure. In addition, TR specialists conducting aquatic therapy must closely monitor participants with cardiac conditions, high/low blood pressure, loss of sensation, epilepsy, body temperature regulation problems, urinary tract infections, bladder incontinence, fear of the water, intravenous lines, vital lung capacity of less than one-third of nominal for the individual, and those who are subject to fatigue.

Descriptions

Aquatic approaches to treatment have been used for participants with a variety of conditions. The following section describes some specific techniques that are popular aquatic therapy interventions used by TR specialists. Since there are numerous aquatic therapy techniques that are used to achieve functional outcomes, the following information provides only a sampling of the more common techniques and is not meant to be comprehensive.

Formal instruction in the following techniques is needed for TR specialists to provide effective services. Aquatic Therapy and Rehabilitation Industry Certification

(ATRIC) through the International Council for Aquatic Therapy and Rehabilitation Industry, Aquatic Exercise Association instructor certification, Arthritis Aquatic instructor certification, and Multiple Sclerosis instructor certification, in addition to basic aquatic therapy training, are recommended for TR specialists providing aquatic therapy services. Aquatic therapy may include various interventions such as:

- Swimming
- Halliwick
- Dolan
- Sensory-Integration through Movement
- Aquatic PNF
- Bad Ragaz
- Watsu
- Ai Chi
- Task-Type Training Approach

Swimming

Swimming not only has an important role in maintenance of health and general fitness, it forms part of many rehabilitative water programs (Campion, 1990). Swimming can be adapted to each participant's needs and capabilities while facilitating normal patterns of movement. Swimming can involve all the muscle groups and encourage social integration. Although swimming promotes stretching, muscular strength, and endurance (see Figure 4.1), each participant must be assessed to ascertain the appropriateness of each stroke. See Table 4.1 on p. 74, adapted from Campion (1990), for movement patterns involved for each stroke used in documenting of performance. Individuals who utilize swimming as an aquatic therapy tool should be trained in aquatic therapy and possess instructor certifications in swimming.

Figure 4.1

Table 4.1

MOVEMENT PATTERN	STROKES
Hip flexion/extension	Breast stroke kick, side stroke kick, flutter kick
Hip abduction/adduction	Breast stroke kick, scissors kick
Hip internal/external rotation	Back stroke, side stroke, breast stroke kick
Ankle planter-flexion	All strokes
Ankle dorsi-flexion	Kick phase of strokes
Shoulder flexion/extension	All strokes
Shoulder abduction	Elementary back stroke
Elbow flexion/extension	Most strokes
Forearm and wrist flexion/extension	All strokes
Pronation/supination of wrist	Sculling
Wrist flexion/extension	Sculling
Hand flexion/extension	All strokes

When using swimming as an aquatic therapy intervention, knowledge of which muscles are involved in various strokes should be considered for purposes of increasing muscular strength and endurance, increasing range of motion, improving proprioception (sense of movement/position of a body part) and neuromuscular facilitation, and when preparing for possible contraindications (not recommended).

> For example, certain lower extremity movements may be contraindicated for an individual who has had a total hip replacement. For a person who has an anterior (front) incision, external rotation and extension (stretching out) of a lower extremity is contraindicated. A lateral (side) incision means that abduction (movement of body part toward body), flexion (bending or flexing the body part) and internal rotation (inward turning or movement of body parts) are threats, and a posterior (behind) incision means that flexion is a threat. As a general rule, exposing individuals to strong resistance in the water should be avoided for participants who have had hip replacements.

Although swimming can be used as an aquatic therapy intervention, there are specific methods of teaching swimming that can be used to improve function. Two of these methods, Halliwick and Dolan, are described in the next two sections.

Halliwick

The Halliwick method reflects the holistic approach that brings together the elements of a sequential instructional technique and its use as an aquatic therapy technique. This section highlights the Halliwick method and the progression of instruction.

The Halliwick method of teaching water independence was developed by James Macmillan in 1949. The procedure emphasizes physical benefits and provision of a recreation skill that encourages friendships, equality, self-confidence, and improved mood (Getz, Hutzler, & Vermeer, 2006). The method begins by teaching comfort and balance rather than swimming strokes to assist in orientation to the water. Flotation aides are not used since they alter body position and can be potentially unsafe.

Rather, Halliwick requires a one-to-one ratio of participant to a trained instructor. Many activities are presented in a game format in which participants increase awareness of water properties and ways to control their balance.

It has been emphasized by TR specialists using this method in aquatic therapy that the Halliwick method naturally incorporates neurodevelopmental treatment (Shanda, 1996). Neurodevelopmental treatment is a popular system of treatment used primarily with individuals who have neurological disabilities such as cerebral palsy (Accardo & Whitman, 1996) and head injuries.

With this treatment, attempts are made to decrease occurrence of primitive reflexes that have not dissipated. The process of teaching swimming using the Halliwick method naturally incorporates proper postural and balance reactions that are facilitated with neurodevelopmental treatment (Accardo & Whitman, 1996). Specific handling techniques used with the Halliwick method encourage participants to achieve independent movement in the water.

Halliwick teaching is based on a 10-Point Program. Through the 10 points the TR specialist facilitates a process of development through mental adjustment, balance control, and movement which leads to independence in the water. These three concepts—mental adjustment, balance control, and movement—are the essential components of motor learning. Halliwick incorporates four phases of instruction, which include:

- Mental adjustment
- Rotational control
- Inhibition
- Facilitation with progressive steps (10 points) of instruction

Table 4.2

PHASE	POINTS
Mental Adjustment	1. Relaxation and Breath Control 2. Disengagement
Rotational Control	3. Transverse (Vertical) Rotational Control 4. Sagittal Rotational Control 5. Logitudinal (Lateral) Rotational Control 6. Combined Rotational Control
Inhibition	7. Upthrust/Mental Inversion 8. Balance is Stillness
Facilitation	9. Turbulent Gliding 10. Simple Progression or Swimming

Mental adjustment. Mental adjustment involves recognition of buoyancy and rotational control of the body in the water. Two things a person encounters when entering the water are problems with balance and posture. Therefore, mental adjustment involves maintaining balance in a vertical position, controlling breathing, and activities that result in a gradual removal of the therapist's support.

Rotational control. Rotational control involves use of arms or legs to restore balance in the water. A wide range of activities are used to move the participant in different postures while maintaining balance. Balance is achieved as the participant gains control of rotation from a vertical position into the supine position and to the standing position again. Further rotational control is called "lateral rotation control," which involves a 360-degree rotation in a horizontal position.

Inhibition. Inhibition involves holding a desired position in the water. The instructor teaches the participant to hold a posture during events in the pool that might cause currents or turbulence. This inhibition instruction can occur while a participant is standing, squatting, or in a supine position.

Facilitation. Facilitation is the ability to create a controlled movement through the water such as swimming. This includes turbulent gliding when the participant is taught to maintain a balanced position while first being moved passively through the water, then using gentle movements, and then finally progressing to a backstroke.

Dolan

The Dolan method was developed by Mary Dolan, Aquatic Director of Therapeutic Recreation Services in Cincinnati, Ohio. The method was developed to teach individuals with autism how to swim by attaching Styrofoam floats to their back and putting swim fins on their feet. By physically patterning the desired movement and praising the participant, individuals are shown how to move their arms and legs effectively. As participants progress, the flotation devices, and eventually the fins, are removed. Since it is possible that participants may be fearful due to lack of an understanding of the environment, the procedure provides positive reinforcement while being firm and requiring the participant to try.

According to Dolan (1996), because people with autism have difficulty processing incoming sensory stimuli and imitating motor movements, an intrusive method is used that requires participants to push beyond their current level of performance. The process involves feeling one's body in the water rather than relying on verbal instruction and imitation.

Taking participants into deep water with flotation enables them to feel effects of buoyancy and freedom of movement. Fins assist participants in feeling effects of movement in the water. The instructor initiates movement through hands-on patterning. The deep water often decreases self-stimulation behaviors because participants' hands must be used to gain control in the water. Because participants are unable to stand, they become focused on the instructor and the swimming process.

Sensory Integration through Movement

TR specialists can use movement in the water to facilitate sensory integration. The method is characterized by an informal but carefully planned progression of activities that result in successful movement experiences (Buis & Schane, 1980) to meet a participant's functional objectives.

As sensory integration is facilitated, participants develop body awareness (including image and functions); spatial awareness (including laterality/directionality such as right, left, up, down, forward, backward, sideways); pathways; levels (high, medium, low); relationships (over, under, in, out, around, together, beside); experience with central part movements (bending, stretching, twisting, pushing, pulling, kicking); and, finally, practice with locomotor movements (walking, running, jumping, hopping, climbing). According to Buis and Schane (1980), the objective of sensory integration may embody improvements associated with the following systems including:

- Vestibular
- Proprioceptive
- Tactile
- Visual
- Auditory
- Bilateral integration

Vestibular. Vestibular activity promotes improved balance, equilibrium, and posture (Buis & Schane, 1980).

> To encourage vestibular stimulation, TR specialists may turn participants in circles with flotation, pull participants through water in all directions, or sit participants on a kickboard. The participant may also be instructed to jump from the side of the pool, somersault under the water, push off the side of the pool using legs with varied speed forward, backward, and sideways. In addition, pre-swim skills of blowing bubbles while sitting, walking, and jumping are essential for improved swimming posture.

Proprioceptive. The proprioceptive system includes sensations from muscles, tendons, and joints, and gives information about the position of body parts and how they are moving (Accardo & Whitman, 1996).

> Activities that can be used to stimulate the proprioceptive system include instructing participant to push or pull hands or objects (such as kickboards) through the water; engage in tug-of-war or push-of-war; play people-to-people; march with floats in hands to create drag; bear weight with hands with legs floating; lift self out of pool using arms; going in front, inside, outside, around, under, and on top of hula hoops; and, holding a balloon between two participants using various body parts. The proprioceptive system can be facilitated by putting water in balls for ball games, manually cueing correct movements, or by using ankle or wrist weights during exercise or ambulation.

Tactile. The tactile system uses sense of touch for body awareness and motor planning (Accardo & Whitman, 1996). It is helpful to consider that some participants may experience tactile defensiveness. Therefore, the TR specialist may teach with nonthreatening stimuli and use deep pressure when touching.

> To address tactile sensitivity, the instructor can have participants use various textured toys, put on and take off clothes in the water, paint self with brush, pour water on body parts, or blow on arms as long as possible while under the water.

Visual. Since eye muscle control and visual sensory input provides information about body orientation in space (Buis & Schane, 1980), activities that promote eye-hand coordination may be beneficial.

> The TR specialist may encourage participants to throw objects at a target, catch, swim through hoops or legs of others, pour water into containers, follow an obstacle course, blow balls through a straw then without straws, and find letters, shapes, numbers and colors under water.

Auditory. Auditory perception is the ability of the brain to interpret information that enters the body through the ears (Accardo & Whitman, 1996). The auditory system provides participants with the ability to understand what is said.

> The auditory stimuli provided during activities may be enhanced by starting or stopping activities with a bell or whistle, giving step-by-step directions, or choosing a different sound to symbolize movements the participant may make.

Bilateral integration. Bilateral integration is the ability to use both sides of the body together in a coordinated manner (Buis & Schane, 1980). This includes the ability to "cross the midline" of the body.

> To improve bilateral integration, the TR specialist may choose to use activities that include carrying objects with hands together under water; passing ball to individuals on either side with both hands (see Figure 4.2); swimming strokes such as the breaststroke and elementary backstroke; using a stick held horizontally between two hands to hit a beach ball; reaching across midline to hit a ball; sitting in an inner tube and propelling oneself with hands and legs together; holding a ball between one's feet while floating on one's back or while jumping in the pool; using a line on pool bottom to jump from one side to the other sideways, forward, and back; and also, flapping arms like a chicken with short wings, then long wings, then one wing.

Figure 4.2

Aquatic PNF

Aquatic PNF is a form of active aquatic therapy modeled after principles and movement patterns of Proprioceptive Neuromuscular Facilitation (PNF). The term proprioceptive refers to receiving stimulation within tissues of the body and neuromuscular is a term used to denote nerves and muscles. Proprioceptive neuromuscular facilitation describes methods used to promote or hasten response of neuromuscular mechanisms through stimulation of proprioceptors (Morris, 2004). Through stimulation of neuromuscular mechanisms, Aquatic PNF can help individuals with neuromuscular disorders make progress toward achieving typical movement patterns. Aquatic PNF can be provided in either a hands-on or hands-off manner.

> The participant is verbally, visually, and/or tactilely instructed in a series of functional, spiral and diagonal, mass movement patterns while standing, sitting, kneeling, or lying in the water. The patterns may be performed actively or with assistance or resistance provided by the therapist (Jamison & Ogden, 1994).

Bad Ragaz

Bad Ragaz was developed for use in the water in the town of Bad Ragaz, Switzerland (Boyle, 1981). This technique uses water properties to enhance movement patterns that include normal movements.

> Patterns that are spiral and diagonal in character duplicate gross motor movements used in everyday activities such as sitting, standing, walking, reaching, swimming, tennis, golf, baseball, and soccer.

The TR specialist stimulates movements through stimulation of participant's proprioceptive system through stretching, providing resistance, and prompting (Accardo & Whitman, 1996).

Some people with disabilities may have a deficient neuromuscular mechanism that limits their movement causing weakness and poor coordination. To address this problem, Bad Ragaz can be used because it is a method that incorporates principles of proprioceptive neuromuscular facilitation (PNF).

When using this one-on-one therapy, the participant must lie in a supine or prone position in the water with a flotation collar around the neck, belt around the buttocks, and ankle floats if necessary. The TR specialist is positioned either between participant's legs or at participant's head. The TR specialist uses properties of water to handle and instruct participants in certain movements.

When using Bad Ragaz, the TR specialist must not only control participant's position but also his or her own position in the water. If the water is above waist level, the TR specialist both loses stability and must work against the water's buoyancy. The individual patterns are documented in books by Skinner and Thomson (1983) and Davis and Harrison (1988). Application of Bad Ragaz includes the following patterns of exercise:

- Isometric
- Isotonic
- Isokinetic
- Passive

Isometric. Isometric patterns are designed to increase strength and stability. An increase in strength and stability occurs with isometric patterns when participants hold a position while being moved through the water.

Isotonic. Isotonic patterns involve graded resistance controlled by the specialist. The therapist increases resistance by pushing or pulling participants through the water in direction of movement while participants hold a certain position.

Isokinetic. Isokinetic techniques involve graded resistance. Participants control resistance. The specialist stabilizes the body part while participants determine resistance by their speed of movement.

Passive. Using passive techniques, participants are slowly moved through stretching muscle groups. The exercises are intended to facilitate trunk elongation, upper and lower limb stretching, relaxation, and decreasing tone.

Watsu

Watsu combines gentle stretching, joint movement, and deep relaxation while rocking and floating participants in warm water. The procedure uses rhythmical, rotational movements to assist in tension reduction and relaxation. Emphasis is on stretching meridians that correspond to points used in acupuncture. According to the originator of Watsu, Dull (2004), Watsu has been noted to have an important psychological as

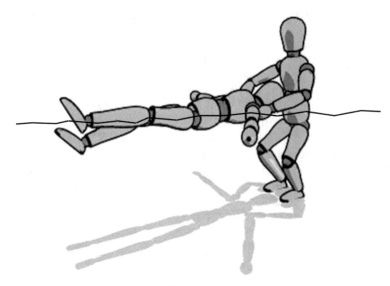

Figure 4.3

well as physical impact. Dull stated that the "free flowing" nature of Watsu is used to promote self-awareness of muscle tension and works to release tension.

Due to the physiological responses of immersion in warm water, participants can often tolerate extensive stretching and soft tissue manipulation that are difficult to tolerate on land. Movement used in Watsu can be beneficial, in that it works to decrease tension in the spine musculature (see Figure 4.3).

Watsu is designed to decrease muscle guarding and tension that occur in land activities due to fear of falling or pain, plasticity, tone, stress, anxiety, and to improve posture, range of motion, breathing pattern, energy, and body awareness (Dull, 2004). Therefore, Watsu may be indicated for individuals with chronic or acute pain, neuromuscular disorders, head injury, spinal cord injury, increased plasticity, chronic fatigue, hyperactivity, depression, or people who are victims of abuse.

Precautions specific to Watsu include range of motion contraindications, pain with joint range of motion, frequent ear infections, and excessive vertigo or vestibular disorder. However, Latourette (1995) stated that these contraindications can usually be addressed with modifications. She added that if Watsu is used as emotional therapy, it should be used in conjunction with a psychological treatment session.

Ai Chi

Ai Chi, developed in Japan by Jun Konno, is a water exercise and relaxation progression program designed to increase relaxation, range of motion, and mobility (Konno & Sova, 1996). Ai Chi combines T'ai Chi concepts with Shiatsu and Watsu techniques. It is performed standing in shoulder-deep water using a combination of deep breathing and slow, full movements of lower and upper extremities and torso. Specifically, progression begins with deep breathing, followed by incorporating upper extremity movement, with trunk movements, and lower extremity movement.

Task-Type Training Approach

The Task-type Training Approach (TTTA) involves a set of principles that guide therapists as they design treatment programs for reducing participants' disabilities. While the TTTA was first described as a way to teach functional activities to people who sustained a stroke, the principles have been extended to include treatment of individuals with various disabilities or limitations, particularly those involving neurologic dysfunction (Morris, 2004).

The TTTA is best described as a task-oriented approach because it emphasizes functional skills performed in functional positions. Participants are encouraged to be active in their skill development, an important characteristic of task-oriented rehabilitation. Equipment to address functional movement might include a tennis racket, golf club, a boat paddle or oar, or a ball. According to Morris (2004), the seven general principles of TTTA are as follows:

- Work in the most shallow water that participants can tolerate.
- Practice functional activities resembling land function activities.
- Remove external stabilization as participant gains functional skills.
- Work in vertical positions such as sitting and standing while encouraging contractions of the muscles with appropriate force in proper sequence.
- Encourage quick, reciprocal movement.
- Encourage active problem solving of movements.
- Gradually increase the difficulty of the functional activity.

Summary

Aquatic therapy is an intervention that can occur in a variety of settings. To show the impact of an aquatic therapy intervention, continuous assessments of an individual's physical ability and mental adjustment in the water is important. TR specialists practicing aquatic therapy should utilize a combination of some of the above techniques and/or others to meet the functional goals of participants while encouraging independence in the water environment.

History

Aquatic therapy has been used for many years and has been a topic of study by various authors (Campion, 1990). Aquatics have been recorded as being used for therapeutic purposes by Greeks, Romans, Egyptians, Hindus, Japanese, and Chinese. According to Campion (1985), the Greeks were the first to appreciate the relationship of water to physical and psychological health when they developed areas near springs for bathing and leisure activity. Campion stated that some of the baths were used solely for therapy around 330 A.D. by the Roman Empire to treat paralysis, arthritis, sports injuries, and burns. She further explained that with the decline of the Roman Empire came the decline of the use of baths. In addition, because of a decrease in the standards in hygiene and morals, according to early Christians, the use of public baths was banned.

The lack of the use of water for therapy lasted through medieval times until the fifteenth century, when physicians slowly increased use of water for therapy. Advances in aquatic therapy continued in Europe, but did not make progress in the United States until the nineteenth century. With World War I and II, increases in the use of water for exercise and maintenance of fitness occurred in the United States. Today, the value of aquatic therapy is gaining recognition as more practitioners learn from research on effects of aquatic therapy.

Theoretical Foundations

Hurley and Turner (1991) suggested that for many individuals with disabilities, buoyancy as well as increased resistance and warmth of water creates an environment for exercise that is more conducive to achieving treatment goals than exercise conducted on land. For Hurley and Turner's suggestion to be understood, knowledge of the properties of water is essential. A number of laws of hydrodynamics and the effects of immersion in warm water are important in understanding activity in the water. Aquatic immersion has profound effects that allow water to be used with therapeutic efficacy for individual with musculoskeletal and neurological problems, cardiopulmonary diseases, psychological impairments, and numerous other conditions. Therefore, the following factors to understand prior to taking an individual into the water are discussed in the next section:

- Buoyancy
- Hydrostatic Pressure
- Center of Buoyancy and Center of Gravity
- Viscosity
- Refraction
- Turbulence
- Warm Water
- General Biologic Effects of Immersion

Buoyancy

There are several principles that are associated with buoyancy. The following principles are presented:

- Archimedes' principle
- Relative density

Archimedes' principle (Giancoli, 1985). Archimedes discovered the principle of buoyancy around 250 B.C. Buoyancy is the force opposing gravity that results in a feeling of weightlessness when immersed in water. In aquatic therapy, this principle can be used with people who are medically limited in weight bearing. Level of buoyancy varies depending on how deep a person is immersed.

Relative density. Relative density is the ratio of the mass of an object to the mass of a volume of water (Giancoli, 1985). The relative density of water is 1.0. Therefore, if a body has a relative density of less than 1.0, it will float, since the weight of the object is less than the weight of the displaced water. If the weight of the body is greater than 1.0, it will sink. If a body is equal to 1.0, it will float just below the water's surface. The relative density of humans varies with age.

> For example, an infant or young child may have a density of .86, resulting in flotation. In adolescence, the relative density of the body increases to approximately .97, resulting in a decrease in flotation. In later life, there is a return of the body towards .86 and easier floatation.

However, some individuals with disabilities may not conform to the relative density norms. Factors affecting individual buoyancy may include fear of water, causing muscle contraction, spasticity, impaired lung capacity, flaccid limbs, and amputations.

> For instance, an individual with spina bifida or muscular dystrophy may have less density in the lower extremities than the arms. Additionally, an individual who has had a spinal cord injury may have altered density in the affected limbs, depending on whether limbs are flaccid or have associated spasticity.

Application to aquatic therapy. Treatment implications regarding Archimedes principle and relative density include less weight bearing when standing in water which is approximately 10% of the person's weight at neck depth, 25% at chest, 50% at waist (see Figure 4.4). Reduced weight bearing results in less joint stress, less effort in movement if movements are slow, less guarded movement resulting in relaxation and better performance, and less stress associated with movement. Due to buoyancy effects of water, movements can be assisted, resisted and/or buoyancy supported. Buoyancy may be used to assist movement when the limb is moved towards the water surface, and may be used to resist movement when the limb is moved away from the surface to a vertical position.

Hydrostatic Pressure

Hydrostatic pressure is the pressure exerted by molecules upon an immersed body (Becker, 2004). According to Pascal's Law, the fluid pressure is equal at a given depth and increases with depth.

> For example, if a round balloon is placed under the water surface the sides of the balloon will be equally compressed because water pressure is the same on all sides.

However, hydrostatic pressure increases and decreases with the density of the fluid. For instance, saltwater molecules will exert greater pressure on an individual than fresh water, which is less dense.

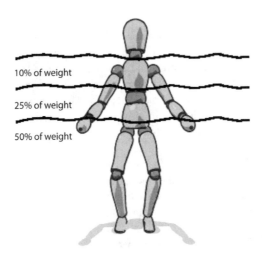

Figure 4.4

Application to aquatic therapy. Because of hydrostatic pressure, vital capacity of participants is important to consider. Vital capacity is the maximum amount of air that can be exhaled after maximum inhalation. Vital capacity is measured in cubic centimeters (cc) of air exhaled. The effect on vital capacity is evident in resistance found with breathing against the weight of water.

Skinner and Thomson (1983) suggested that an individual with a vital capacity of less than 1000 cm³ (in an adult male) should be observed closely when participating in aquatic therapy. The equal pressure of water being felt in all directions may decrease hypersensitivity or tactile defensiveness. Edema (swelling) is reduced and circulation improved if exercises are performed below the surface of water.

Center of Buoyancy and Center of Gravity

The center of buoyancy in a human is generally mid-chest around the zyphoid process and moves depending on the individuals muscle tone or flaccidity. Center of Gravity is located posterior to the mid-sagittal plane at the level of the second sacral vertebra (S-2). When both centers are aligned no rotation occurs to a body floating in the water. When not aligned, rotational forces come into play on a body. An object will reach a stable equilibrium when center of gravity and buoyancy is in the same vertical line. When a body is displaced a new center of buoyancy (thus rotation) occurs (Becker, 2004).

Application to aquatic therapy. A hemiplegic floating prone or supine may roll toward side of spasticity. To alleviate the roll, the participant can turn head away, abduct unaffected arm, put unaffected leg under affected leg, and or bring affected arm to midline. A person who has edema will roll away from affected side. To bring center back towards mid-chest the individual may need to turn his or her head away and/or abduct affected arm.

Viscosity

Viscosity concerns the amount of cohesion of molecules of the same type of matter, or adhesion to other matter (e.g., water molecules' attraction to water molecules and water molecules' attraction to a swimmer in the water) (Skinner & Thomson, 1983). The adhesive force between a body and water is greater than cohesive force of the water. The property of adhesion is why the walls of a glass remain wet after pouring out water. Viscosity acts as a resistance to movement as the molecules of water tend to adhere to the body's surface moving through it.

Application to aquatic therapy. The characteristics of viscosity account for the increased resistance in water that further increases with speed of movement. Since increased resistance allows greater response time to maintain balance, participants may experience less fear of falling in the water than on land. Less fear frequently results in a decrease in tenseness and an increase in relaxation. In addition, due to adhesion, when individuals exit the water they carry water with them (Latourette, 1995). It is useful for the TR specialist to consider viscosity when a participant exits the water with a reminder that they "may feel a little heavy at first."

Refraction

Becker (1997) described refraction as the bending of light as it passes from one medium to another. The denseness of the medium and the angle of the light beam govern the amount of bending. Because water presents resistance to the speed of light, the light passing from the air to water medium will actually bend away from one's perception of the ray when crossing the boundary.

Application to aquatic therapy. Because of refraction, participants may experience difficulty with determining pool depth and their body position. These difficulties may result in participants experiencing an increase in visual and perceptual problems (see Figure 4.5).

Turbulence

Becker (2004) stated that turbulence creates uneven patterns of water movement that may establish patterns of low pressure areas called *eddies* following in the wake of an object moving through a fluid. With increased speed, eddies occur, creating a low-pressure area that has a suction effect. This eddy can be used to pull a body through the water such as is seen when baby ducks follow the mother duck through the water. However, if the movement is reversed, turbulence and resistance are increased. Turbulence lessens the streamlined flow and causes a rise in friction in the fluid.

Application to aquatic therapy. The eddy may be used in aquatic therapy to assist the participant in swimming or ambulating by walking in front of the participant in the direction they are going. Turbulence may be used to work on balance with some participants. The TR specialist may push the water around the participant to cause turbulence, or the participant may be asked to quickly reverse directions

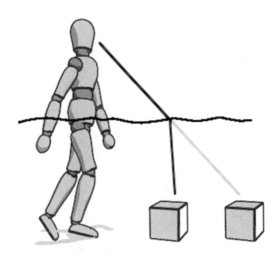

Figure 4.5

when walking. In these two situations, the challenge for participants to maintain their balance is increased.

Warm Water

Conductivity of heat through water is 25 times greater than through air. Therefore, the rate of heat gain or loss is greater in the water compared to land. According to Skinner and Thomson (1983), increased circulation to arms and legs and blood supply to muscles occurs due to the dilation of blood vessels from exposure to warm water. Increased circulation improves the condition of the skin. When warm blood reaches muscles there is an increase in muscle temperature resulting in easier contraction, less stress and spasticity, and consequentially, improved movement.

In addition to warming muscles and blood, a person's heart rate accelerates with increased temperature and exertion (Becker, 2004). However, Davis and Harrison (1988) noted that while there is an initial rise in blood pressure with entry into water, during immersion when arteries dilate, there is a consequential drop in blood pressure. Therefore, a person's heart rate will be 10–15 beats per minute lower with water exercise than land exercise even when exercising at the same metabolic rate. In addition, a rise in body temperature increases a person's metabolism (the physical and chemical processes that occur in the body involving the distribution of nutrients). With this increase in general metabolic rate (the amount of energy expended in a given period) there is an increase in the demand for oxygen and in the production of carbon dioxide, causing an increase in respiratory (breathing) rate.

Application to aquatic therapy. When effects of warm water are combined with effects of buoyancy, including weightlessness and movement with less effort, individuals experience a greater range of movement (Davis & Harrison, 1988).

For example, an individual who is obese and has difficulty with movement on land can move easier, with more support (due to hydrostatic pressure), and with less discomfort in the pool.

This ease of movement can increase a person's confidence when attempting additional movements. As a result of improved movement, a person's muscles become less fatigued; however, since generalized fatigue may be greater in warm water as a result of the ability to work harder, continuous monitoring of participants receiving aquatic therapy is advised.

General Biologic Effects of Immersion

Immersion into an aquatic environment results in physiological changes in the body. Implications to the following systems are discussed:

- Circulatory
- Pulmonary
- Musculoskeletal
- Renal

Circulatory System. Since hydrostatic pressure is greater than venous pressure, blood is displaced upward through a one-way system first into the thighs, then to the abdominal cavity, and finally to great vessels of the chest cavity and into the heart (Becker, 2004). Central venous pressure begins to rise with immersion to the xiphoid and cardiac volume increases 27% to 30% with immersion to the neck.

The healthy cardiac response to this stretching of the myocardium is to contract with greater strength (Weston, O'Hare, Evans, & Corall, 1987). This stretch effect of the heart that results in an average of a 35% increase in stroke volume is commonly referred to as *Starling's Law*. As cardiac filling and stroke volume increase with immersion, heart rate drops from around 12% to 15% because of the increase in stroke efficiency. This drop, and an eventual decrease in blood pressure, is variable and dependent on water temperature.

Pulmonary System. Pulmonary blood flow increases with increased central blood volume and pressure. Vital capacity decreases about 10% when immersed in water up to the neck (Arborelius, Balldin, Lila, & Lundgren, 1972). Fifty to sixty percent of vital capacity reduction is due to increased thoracic blood volume. Forty to fifty percent of reduction is due to hydrostatic forces counteracting inspiratory musculature, especially the diaphragm. This combined effect is to change pulmonary function, increase work of breathing to about 60% with submersion to the neck, and increase respiration rate.

Musculoskeletal System. Immersion affects the musculoskeletal system. One effect of hydrostatic pressure is that blood supply to muscles and skin is significantly increased (Balldin et al., 1971). Immersion at only 36 inches of water depth results in pressure that exceeds average diastolic pressure. This improves oxygen delivery to muscles and improves removal of lactate and other metabolic end products. This immersion decreases pooling and edema in extremities.

Water immersion can increase muscle relaxation as a result of improved blood supply and neutral warmth of water. The buoyancy effect decreases joint compression force. Becker (2004) contended that effects of buoyancy and water resistance make possible higher level of energy expenditure without excessive strain on lower extremity joints.

Renal System. Epstein (1992) found that flow of blood to the kidneys increases immediately upon immersion. With immersion up to the neck, sodium excretion increases up to 10 times normal. Water is carried with the sodium which leads to a diuretic effect. Dieresis increases with time spent in the water and depth of water. Increase in central blood volume also stimulates volume receptors which causes an increase in anti-diuretic hormone also leading to dieresis. Individuals who are immersed in the water for long periods are advised to drink fluids often, and empty leg bags (when appropriate) prior to entering the water.

Summary. The theoretical basis for aquatic therapy includes laws of hydrodynamics and effects of immersion in water, especially warm water. TR specialists are advised to apply each aquatic therapy intervention with knowledge of principles of water physics and physiologic effects. Articulation of these principles can enhance participants' understanding and performance in aquatic therapy.

Effectiveness

According to Broach and Dattilo (1996), aquatic therapy appears to be an intervention that can be used by TR specialists to promote functional improvement while facilitating independence in swimming and water exercise. Broach and Dattilo reviewed research that suggested aquatic therapy can result in physiological improvements for individuals with multiple sclerosis, cystic fibrosis, arthritis, orthopedic impairments, cerebral palsy, and asthma. The authors also reviewed articles that identified psychological benefits of participants as a result of aquatic therapy interventions including improved mood, enhanced self-esteem and body image, and decreased anxiety and depression. The following paragraphs summarize their findings as well as recent findings associated with effects of aquatic therapy on:

- Physical
- Psychological
- Leisure Functioning

Physical Implications

Aquatic therapy has been used to:

- Decrease pain
- Prevent bone loss
- Improve motor performance
- Increase strength
- Increase endurance
- Improved fitness
- Improve pulmonary (lung) functioning

Studies examining efficacy of aquatic therapy relative to these dependent variables are reviewed in the next section.

Decrease pain. Wyatt and colleagues (2001) compared effects of aquatic and traditional exercise programs on functional status and subjective pain levels of 46 persons (ages 45–70) with knee osteoarthritis who participated in either a land exercise group or aquatic intervention group. Pre- and post-test measurements included Subjective Pain Scale, knee range of motion (ROM), thigh girth, and time for a 1-mile walk. Both exercise groups showed a significant increase in all measurements between pre- and post-tests. There were no significant differences between the aquatic exercise group and the land-based exercise group pertaining to knee ROM, thigh girth, and time for a 1-mile walk; however, subjective pain levels were significantly less in the aquatic group when compared with the land-based group. While both aquatic and land-based exercise programs are beneficial to people with osteoarthritis, water-based interventions appear to be more effective in decreasing pain.

    Templeton and colleagues (1996) similarly examined the relationship of subjective pain levels, range of motion, and functional status assistance of 13 participants with rheumatic disease who participated in aquatic exercise. Active joint motion, Functional Status Index scores of assistance and difficulty and pain were taken prior to and following 8 weeks of aquatic therapy. Results showed a significant difference between pre- and post-means pain, active joint motion, and Functional Status Index scores on assistance and difficulty. Pain and active joint motion were negatively correlated and need for assistance and pain, assistance and difficulty, and pain and difficulty were positively correlated. Decreased pain and difficulty experienced in performing daily tasks contributed significantly (94%) to overall increased functional status and active joint motion for select joints. Although findings support use of aquatic therapy to reduce pain and difficulty with tasks while increasing joint flexibility and functional ability, the research design limits generalization.

    Guillemin and colleagues (1994) assessed effects of spring water treatment on chronic low-back pain by comparing a randomly selected group of 50 participants in an aquatic therapy program to a randomly selected group of 52 individuals not receiving aquatic therapy. After 3 weeks (6 x week), participants in the aquatic therapy group reported a reduction in their daily duration of pain, pain intensity, and drug consumption, and showed significant improvement over the control group in their spine mobility immediately after the intervention and 9 months later. The authors concluded that aquatic therapy may have positive short-term and moderate long-term effects on chronic lower back pain.

Woods (1989) investigated effects of aquatic therapy using exercise and modified swimming strokes on strength, range of motion, and pain in 18 individuals with lumbar back pain (6 wks, 3 x wk, $\leq$ 1-hr sessions). While no change was reported in pain levels, a significant improvement in functional ability was found. Because no statistical relationship existed between self-reports of pain and functional capacity for participants, Woods cautioned that reliance on pain reports alone to determine readiness for resumption of occupational or leisure activities may be misleading.

Langridge and Phillips (1988) monitored subjective pain levels and quality of life of 27 participants receiving aquatic therapy. Overall results of a pain questionnaire showed participants perceived less pain after participation. Ninety-six percent of participants showed a statistically significant improvement in their quality of life and 67% showed a decrease in private medical cost. No participants demonstrated an increase in number of drugs taken for back pain, and 44% showed a decrease in amount of drugs taken. The positive results could have been influenced by peer support found in the group approach, and participants' ability to take control by helping themselves through water exercise rather than depending on skilled practitioners in a clinic. While caution is advised in interpreting results of the above studies due to use of non-experimental designs, findings are helpful to when considering use of aquatic therapy interventions for individuals with chronic pain.

Prevent bone loss. Tsukahara and colleagues (1994) found similar results regarding bone densities and swimming. The study was cross-sectional of 97 Japanese post-menopausal women to determine improvement in lumbar area spine bone mineral densities (BMD). BMD was examined because individuals with osteoporosis (a rheumatic disease with complications that may include pain, stiffness, muscle weakness, and joint complications) have decreased bone density. The veteran group of 27 exercisers who had participated in the program for 3 years had higher BMD scores than the scores of the 40 participants involved in the program for 1 month and had higher scores than the 30 non-exercisers.

Benedict and Freeman (1993) used a nonrandomized control group study, including four groups, with BMD tests recorded for each. The first group included 42 female and 31 male volunteers, who were all regular participants in a 6-hour per week swimming and aquatic aerobics program for 10 years. The study also included two volunteer control groups comprised of 58 women and 15 men who attended senior centers for activities (not including swimming), and a group of 10 women and 2 men who neither attended a senior center nor swam. The swimmers' bone densities of the hip and spine were significantly higher than those of the senior center attendees who did not participate in water exercise or swimming.

Improve motor performance. Broach and Dattilo (2001) conducted a replication and extension of the above noted study by Broach and colleagues (1998) to examine effects of aquatic therapy gross motor activity and fatigue. This single subject multiple-probe design across participants was used with four adults with relapsing-remitting Multiple Sclerosis (ages 30–53). This study incorporated two gross motor dependent measures used by Broach and colleagues (1998): walking up and down stairs and rotations on a bicycle. Broach and Dattilo extended this study by including measurements of rotations on an upper ergometer and of fatigue. This study supports previous findings that participation in aquatic therapy by individuals improves gross motor behaviors. Mixed results prevent conclusions regarding effect of AT on mental fatigue.

Broach, Groff, Dattilo, Yaffe, and Gast (1998) examined effects of an aquatic therapy program (3 x wk, 1-hr sessions) on physical behavior in selected daily activities of three adults with multiple sclerosis using a single subject multiple baseline design. Participants demonstrated variable but improved behavior for vacuuming, riding a bicycle, and climbing stairs. Results indicated improvements in gross motor upper extremity and lower extremity activity for the three participants. In addition, Broach, Groff, and Dattilo (1997) administered a fatigue questionnaire and a daily leisure activity log. Results indicated decreased perception of physical and mental fatigue over the course of the aquatic therapy program. The daily leisure activity log showed that duration of activity participation, number of community-based activities, and activity with others increased over the duration of the study.

Increase strength. Broach and Dattilo (2003) examined effects of an aquatic therapy exercise program on strength of four adults with relapsing-remitting multiple sclerosis. A single subject, multiple-probe design across participants was used to collect data. Measures of upper and lower extremities of quadriceps, hamstrings, hip flexion, biceps, triceps, and shoulder abduction strength. Results have implications to strength and perceived activity experience, since the intervention was identified by all participants as being a positive experience and all individuals either maintained or improved strength. Maintenance of strength over time is an important outcome of activity interventions for individuals with multiple sclerosis.

Gehlsen, Grigsby, and Winant (1984) examined effects of a 10-week aquatic program (3 x week, 60-min sessions) on ten adults with multiple sclerosis who were ambulatory and in remission. Measurements were made on strength and fatigue in the knee flexor and extensor muscles, and upper extremities. There was a significant difference in strength for knee extensor muscles for pretrial to mid-trial with no significant improvement after mid-trial. For the upper extremities, a significant increase was seen from pre- to mid-trial to post-tests in all strength measurements. Although results were mixed, strength was improved. Mixed results and use of a non-experimental design associated with this study, and absence of other studies assessing effects of aquatic therapy on strength, indicate a need for further research.

Increase endurance. Broach and colleagues (1997) used a single-subject, multiple-baseline design to examine effects of a 10-week aquatic therapy program (3 x wk, 1-hr sessions) using swimming on the endurance and vital capacity of four people with spinal cord injury. While no changes were found in vital capacity, scores from the Cooper Swim Test, used to assess participants' cardio-respiratory endurance, showed improved endurance across participants. Although generalization is limited without replication, results implied that swimming might improve health of people with spinal cord injuries.

Routi, Troup, and Berger (1994) examined effects of a water exercise program on muscular endurance and aerobic work capacity of older adults (age > 50 years) by comparing performance of 12 participants in a water exercise group and 10 participants in a control group. Participants were tested before and after a 12-week water exercise program (3 x wk, 30-min sessions). Training effects were significantly greater for the water exercise group as compared to the control group on all dependent measures. Individuals recovering from physical injury or muscular disease may employ water exercises with expectations of improving aerobic work capacity and muscular endurance.

Although efficacy of aquatic therapy on cardiovascular endurance has received more attention in the literature than other physical implications, there are few studies examining benefits specific to individuals with disabilities. For example, **Edlund, French, Herbst, Ruttenberg, Ruhling, and Adams (1986)** compared effects of a 12-week swimming therapy program (3 x wk, 1-hr sessions) on strength, endurance, and pulmonary function of 21 children with cystic fibrosis. Nine boys and three girls (ages 7–14) residing in a children's hospital voluntarily participated and were randomly assigned to an experimental group and six girls and five boys were randomly assigned to a control group. Although a significant improvement was found in their clinical state of the disease, the children in the swimming therapy program did not significantly improve their pulmonary function. They did, however, show a statistically significant improvement over the control group in endurance.

Wright and Cowden (1986) examined effects of swim training on 25 individuals with mental retardation in a nonrandomized, pre-, post-test, control group study with one group (mean age 16) who participated in a 10-week training program (2 x wk, 1-hr sessions), and another group of 25 individuals, who were in a control group (mean age 15) and who adhered to normal daily activities. Results showed that the program contributed to a significant increase in cardiovascular endurance and self-concept for participants in the experimental group when compared to the control group.

Improve fitness. Wang and colleagues (2007) used a pre-post random assignment trial with a convenience sample to examine effects of aquatic exercise on physical fitness (flexibility, strength, and aerobic fitness) and self-reported physical functioning and pain in adults with osteoarthritis of the hip or knee. Participants were recruited from community sources and randomly assigned to a 12-week aquatic program or a non-exercise control condition. Data for 38 participants were collected at baseline, week 6, and week 12. Instruments used included a standard goniometer, a handheld dynamometer, the 6-minute walk test, the multidimensional Health Assessment Questionnaire, and a visual analogue scale for pain. There was statistically significant improvement in knee and hip flexibility, strength, and aerobic fitness associated with aquatic exercise, but there was no observed effect on self-reported physical functioning and pain. The exercise adherence rate was 81–87% and no exercise-related adverse effects were observed or reported. While the program did not offer pain relief or self-reported improvements in physical functioning, beneficial short-term effects were found.

Driver, O'Connor, Lox, and Rees (2004) evaluated effects of an aquatics program on fitness parameters of individuals who sustained brain injuries that included cardiovascular endurance, body composition, muscular endurance, and flexibility. A pre- post-test randomized group design was used with eight male and eight female outpatients (ages 35–44) who were above level six on the Ranchos Los Amigos Scale or who had their injury more than 1 year. The sample was randomly assigned to an 8-week aquatic exercise program (3 x wk, 1-hr sessions) or a control group that involved participating in an 8-week vocational rehabilitation class. There was an improvement in all fitness components for the treatment group compared to the control group. Significant differences existed for elbow flexion, lower back range of motion, and grip strength. Finally, increases in fitness were reported to have a positive impact on the exercise groups functional ability and skills in activities of daily living.

Improve pulmonary functioning. To determine effects of aquatic interventions on children with neuromotor impairments, **Getz, Hutzler, and Vermeer (2006)** conducted a review of the literature of 11 articles. Most participants (n=173) in the reviewed articles were children and adolescents with cerebral palsy (63%), and the second most prevalent condition was muscular dystrophy (33%). Authors from seven of the articles reported improvement in body functions, seven reported improvement in activity level, and two of four examined participation level reported change. Only one article included a randomized control study (Dorval, Tereault, & Caron, 1996), two used a quasi-experimental single subject design (Hutzler, Chacham, Bergman & Szeinberg, 1998; Hutzler, Chacham, Bergman, & Reches, 1998), and the remaining articles did not use control groups (3 articles) or were case reports (5 articles). Authors of ten articles reported durations of interventions from 6 weeks to 2 years (1–2 x wk, 30-min sessions). The most common interventions were identified as the Halliwick method (4 studies) and adapted swimming (3 studies) with only one study specifying the exact swimming routine. While authors of five articles reported improvement in body functions (vital capacity, range of motion, strength) and in various activities (gait, gross motor function, manual skills), only one showed statistically significant results in vital capacity (Hutzler et al., 1998). The authors concluded that effectiveness reported in eight of the eleven articles should not be regarded as evidence-based; however, there is evidence to suggest that aquatic therapy might improve respiratory function. Further research of is needed to assess functional, activity, and participation outcomes from aquatic interventions for children with neuromotor impairments.

Only one study was found that examined pulmonary effects of a 10-week aquatic (3 x wk) to a non-aquatic respiratory program on older adults **(Ide, Belini, & Caromano, 2005)**. The authors contended that aging leads to physiological altera-tions that result in adverse social and financial effects and prevention interventions are less expensive and socially more desirable than other therapeutic interventions. Respiratory muscle strength was measured in 81 participants (ages 60–65), 59 of whom completed the program. Participants were randomly assigned to one of three groups, including: (a) an aquatic respiratory exercise group, (b) a group that partici-pated in the same program on land, and (c) a control group who did not participate in exercise. A significant improvement in the inspiratory muscle strength in the aquatic group compared to the control group was found. There was no significant difference in expiratory vital capacity. Results of this research suggest that there are beneficial effects in inspiration through aquatic exercise.

To further examine effects of swimming on children with asthma, **Bar-Or and Inbar (1992)** conducted a literature review to explore effects of swimming on children with asthma. The review suggested that swimming induces less severe broncho constriction than other active activities (e.g., Holmer, Stein, Saltin, Ekblom, & Astrand, 1974). Although reasons for this protective effect of swimming are not clear, the authors cited experimental evidence (e.g., Inbar, Dotan, Dlin, Neuman, & Bar-Or, 1980) implying that positive effects may result, in part, from the high-humidity air at water level, which reduces respiratory heat loss and possible absorption of airway mucus. Although it is possible that negative effects of swimming on individuals with asthma such as the "diving reflex" which is a response to immersion of the face in water, in particular water containing chlorine and its derivatives, especially when air re-circulating occurs (Penny, 1983), Bar-Or and Inbar concluded that swimming was less asthma-inducing than other physically active leisure activities and found swimming to be the most suitable exercise therapy for children with asthma.

The impact of aquatic therapy on pulmonary functioning has been studied primarily as it relates to children with asthma. For example, **Huang, Veiga, Sila, Reed, and Hines (1989)** examined effects of swimming training on 45 children with asthma (ages 6–12) who were randomly assigned to swimming training (3 x wk, 1-hr sessions) or a control group. Pulmonary function, school absenteeism, emergency room visits, hospitalizations, days requiring daily medications, and days of wheezing both during the swimming sessions and for a period of 1 year after the final swimming session were significantly different when compared to data collected 1 year prior to the swim class and to the control group.

In their assessment of the physiologic and clinical effects of exercise in children with cystic fibrosis, **Edlund and colleagues (1986)** (detailed in the section on endurance) found no change in pulmonary function, but reported that sputum production during chest physical-therapy decreased when participants were involved in the program. The exercise associated with the swimming apparently helped to clear the lungs of sputum and a swimming program (at least 3 x wk) appears to be a way to improve the clinical status and quality of life of a person with cystic fibrosis.

Zach, Purrer, and Oberwaldner (1981) examined effects of swimming therapy on forced expiration and sputum clearance of 11 individuals with cystic fibrosis (mean age 10.7) who participated in a 7-week swimming therapy program (17 x 1-hr sessions). Although there was a significant improvement in lung capacity, 10 weeks after the end of the training most scores returned to pre-swimming levels. Even though the authors contend that swimming can assist in mucus clearance and improve ventilatory function in children with cystic fibrosis, the lack of a control group limits interpretation of results.

Another population that has been examined in relation to pulmonary function includes people with muscular dystrophy. **Adams and Chandler (1974)** investigated effects of an 11-month swimming and breathing exercise program (2 x wk, 30-min sessions) on three 11-year-old children. After 4 months, each participant improved in vital capacity. The authors stated that a regular program of therapy could result in increased vital capacity with supervised treatment. Further investigation of methods of maintaining vital capacity is needed for children with muscular dystrophy due to the lack of studies in general, and more specifically, due to the non-experimental design and small number of participants used in this study.

Summary. There are numerous studies that examine physical effects of aquatic therapy. Extant research strongly indicates that aquatic therapy is an empirically supported facilitation technique when used to decrease pain, prevent bone loss, increase strength and endurance, and improve pulmonary function.

Psychological Implications

Although some psychological benefits of aquatics therapy for people without disabilities—primarily college students and older adults—are reported in the literature, there is a lack of research documenting the psychological benefits of aquatic therapy for individuals with disabilities. Some ways psychological enhancement has occurred via aquatic therapy include:

- Improve body image
- Decrease depression
- Enhance mood
- Decrease anxiety

Improve body image. Smith and Michel (2006) used a quasi-experimental, pretest/post-test design convenience sample to examine effects of an aquatic program on perception of body image, participation in health-promoting behaviors, barriers to health-promoting participation, level of physical discomfort, and mobility. Participants included 40 non-exercising pregnant women who were at least 19 weeks gestation. Participants selected an assignment to participate in either the 6-week exercise group (3 x wk, 1-hr session) or non-exercise group. Both groups completed self-report measures and underwent a mobility assessment. The control group was instructed to continue their normal activities of daily living. Women who had participated in the aquatic exercise program reported significantly less physical discomfort, improved mobility, and improved body image and health-promoting behaviors as compared to those in the control group. Therefore, aquatic exercise during pregnancy may enhance physical functioning, decrease maternal discomfort, improve maternal body image, and improve health-promoting behaviors.

    Benedict and Freeman (1993), who observed older adults swimming, noted the impact of aquatic therapy on body image. In this study (detailed in the preventing bone loss section), the researchers assessed body image by projective drawings and the use of a semantic differential survey. Although there was no significant difference in the projective drawings, a significantly improved body image of swimmers was observed as measured by the semantic differential when compared to the control group, who did not participate in water exercise.

Decrease depression. Reduction in depression, noted as a benefit in the literature of aquatic therapy (Skinner & Thomson, 1983), has mixed support. For example, in the previously described non-experimental study by **Benedict and Freeman (1993)**, morale and depression scales were administered. Although results showed that swimmers reported higher morale than the control group, there was no significant difference in level of depression between swimmers and the control group.

In a related study, **Stein and Motta (1992)** compared effects of anaerobic weight training to aerobic swimming on depression and self-concept. Ninety-eight individuals with disabilities (mean age 20) were randomly assigned to a structured 14-week swimming for fitness aerobic class (2 x wk, 50-min sessions), a structured 14-week progressive resistance weight training (2 x wk, 50-min sessions), or a control group that did not exercise. Significant improvement occurred in both experimental groups in self-concept and depression, when compared to the control. In the case of individuals with disabilities who are unable to withstand land-based weight training, water exercise might be an option to enhance self-esteem and decrease depression.

Weiss and Jamieson (1989) conducted a study to evaluate effects of aquatic exercise on subjective depression of 88 women (ages 21–75, majority 45–64). The length of time in the program ranged from 8 weeks to 5 years. All 21 participants who reported symptoms of depression when beginning the class reported fewer depressed feelings, with 91% attributing aquatic therapy as a contributing factor to their improved emotional state. It appeared that this particular program was effective in dissipating the depression-related symptoms. In addition, the women viewed the program as a support group, made new friends in the classes, and found it helpful to converse with others in the group about health, humor, and feelings.

Enhance mood. Assiss and colleagues (2006) compared deep water running to land-based exercises in six women with fibromyalgia. Participants were randomly assigned to either deep water running in a warmed pool or land-based exercises of treadmill walking or jogging (15 wks, 3 x wk, 1-hr sessions). Both groups improved significantly by week 15 when compared to baseline, however only the deep water running group identified fewer limitations to usual activities due to emotional problems.

To examine further the complex relationship between exercise and mental health across cultures, **Berger and Owen (1993)** studied 15 swimmers participating in a 12-week swim program (1 x wk, 90-min sessions) and 15 non-swimmers in a control group from Czechoslovakia and 20 swimmers and 28 non-swimmers from a large, metropolitan college in the United States participating in a 14-week swim program (2 x wk, 50-min sessions). Participants were involved in either a beginning swimming course or a lecture control course. Swimmers from the United States and Czechoslovakia showed significant improvement in reducing tension, depression, anger, and confusion. Results indicated that students felt better after enrolling in the swimming course than before they began the course. This study provides additional support for the belief that swimming positively influences mood across cultures.

Berger and Owen (1992) examined swimming classes and yoga to determine if aerobic exercise improved mood by employing a pre- post-test control-group design with 87 college student volunteers enrolled in two swimming classes (2 x wk, 40-min sessions), a yoga course (1 x wk, 80-min sessions), and a lecture control-group course (3 x wk, 50-min sessions). A significant reduction in anger, confusion, tension, and depression was reported for the swimming and yoga groups when compared to the control group, indicating that aerobic exercise and exercise below one's target heart rate may enhance mood. Perhaps swimming and Hatha yoga are effective in altering mood since they facilitate deep, rhythmical, diaphragmatic breathing (a common element in many stress reduction techniques). Lap swimming and Hatha yoga may influence mood by stretching and relaxing large muscle groups. This study has implications for individuals with disabilities, because some people have difficulty performing land-based aerobic activity, and the water environment may be one of few environments that a person could perform aerobic activity independently (Campion, 1985). These speculations call for further research.

Decrease anxiety. **Parker and Smith (2003)** conducted a quasi-experimental study of six non-exercisers and nine exercisers (ages 19–36, mean 30) participating in a 6-week prenatal aquatic aerobics class to examine differences in reported stress-management behaviors between the two groups pre- and post-intervention. Both groups completed the Health Promotion Lifestyle Profile (Walker et al., 1987) pre- and post-sessions. The instrument contains six sub-scales including stress management. There were no differences in stress management between exercising and non-exercising groups. Aquatic aerobic participants reported significantly higher levels of participation in health promoting stress-management activities and less psychological stress at post-test than the non-exercising group. It seems that aquatic aerobic exercise can play a role in reducing psychological stress in pregnancy.

Summary. There is limited research examining psychological effects of aquatic therapy. Existing research moderately indicates that aquatic therapy is an empirically supported facilitation technique. Although the studies do not include individuals with disabilities, results have implications for people who receive TR services. Since many people with disabilities are unable to participate actively in land-based aerobic activity (Campion, 1985), it may be useful to consider additional benefits from aquatic therapy beyond physiological ones, and to examine psychological benefits such as improved mood.

Leisure Functioning Implications

Aquatic therapy may enhance functional ability that encompasses all areas of life and help to develop a life-long leisure activity that can be enjoyed with other people (Peganoff, 1984). Campion (1985) emphasized that once a person is independent in the water, opportunities for socialization increase. There is, however, limited research on effects of aquatic therapy on a person's leisure lifestyle. Nevertheless, many authors have emphasized the importance of transitioning the person with a disability from residential environments into recreational programs in the community to achieve psychosocial and functional benefits (e.g., Slade & Simmons-Grab, 1987). Although not data-based, there are numerous reports of the benefits of using recreational activity, community reentry, or family training in aquatic therapy to meet goals and to facilitate continued participation (e.g., McNamara, 1994).

In a literature review that included examination of effects of aquatic interventions on children with neuromotor impairments detailed in the physical outcome section, **Getz and colleagues (2006)** examined four studies that involved measuring the influence of aquatic therapy on participation outcomes. Researchers reported improvement in communication skills and social interactions (e.g., Bumin, Uyanik, Yilmaz, Kayihan, & Topcu, 2003) and self-esteem (Peganoff, 1984). Two additional studies (Dorval et al., 1996; Hutzler et al., 1998) reported no statistical differences in self-esteem. Finally, two of the studies (Peganoff, 1984; Hutzler et al., 1998) reported that positive results in participation outcomes were attributed to attainment of independent swimming. Results may suggest that aquatic therapy programs can be designed to achieve independent aquatic performance and participation outcomes.

Getz and colleagues (2006) examined effects of an aquatic intervention with land-based interventions on social function, perceived competence, and social acceptance in children with cerebral palsy. Twenty-two children (17 males) with spastic diplegia participated in the study, with 12 children assigned to the aquatic therapy group using the Halliwick Method and 10 assigned to the land exercise program. Both groups participated for 4 months (2 x wk, 30-min sessions). Social function was measured using the Pediatric Evaluation of Disability Inventory social function domain. Perceived competence and social acceptance were measured using the Pictorial Scale of Perceived Competence and Social Acceptance for Children with CP scale. Although there were no significant differences between groups for physical competence or social function, significant differences were found between groups in social acceptance in favor of the aquatic group. Significant differences were found between pre- and post-test scores in social function in the aquatic group but not the land exercise group. Therefore, the aquatic intervention may have had a positive effect on perceived social acceptance and social function as reported by caregivers.

Beaudouin and Keller (1994) described a program developed by a TR practitioner designed to improve functional abilities, facilitate psychosocial adjustment, and ultimately lead to independent participation in community recreation programs. Assessments were conducted on participants' psychosocial and physical skills such as endurance, strength, and flexibility, as well as their personal interests and functional needs. The program involved the use of water exercises and swimming to meet treatment goals, which generally included moving from individual to group sessions. Although no data were reported on the effectiveness of the program, the authors reported that insurance companies provided 85% reimbursement for treatment, which was attributed to organized and continuous communication with physicians and case managers. The authors stated that successful intervention and documentation strengthened the reputation of the program with physicians and third-party payers. Beaudouin and Keller's article, and articles describing efficacy-based research, provide information on how aquatic therapy can promote leisure functioning.

Summary. There is limited research examining leisure implications of aquatic therapy. Although a benefit of aquatic therapy could be the potential for independence in the aquatic activity after functional goals have been met, there has been little discussion concerning implications of interventions on leisure involvement. TR specialists can address leisure implications by including leisure-related dependent variables in aquatic therapy research such as satisfaction, enjoyment, intrinsic motivation, and self-determination.

Overall Summary

Based on this literature review, there is evidence to support the contention that aquatic therapy could be used by TR specialists who seek to facilitate improved physical and psychological functioning of participants. Existing research strongly indicates that aquatic therapy is an empirically supported facilitation technique when used to influence physical functioning, moderately indicates that aquatic therapy is an empirically supported facilitation technique when used to influence psychological functioning, and is not an empirically supported facilitation technique when used to influence leisure functioning.

Case Studies

Sasha

Peganoff (1984) presented a case study to exemplify use of swimming as a leisure activity that incorporates therapeutic goals for individuals with disabilities. The participant was a 12-year-old girl, Sasha, with spastic right hemiparesis (significant reduction in strength on one side of the body) who participated in an 8-week swimming program (2 x wk, 45-min sessions). The treatment goals included improving: (a) range of motion; (b) functional use and coordination of the right upper extremity; (c) bilateral integration; (d) balance and equilibrium skills; and (e) self-image. The participant showed a 15-degree increase in shoulder flexion and a 10-degree increase in shoulder abduction of the right upper extremity. She began using her right upper extremity during activities of daily living at home. Although the participant refused to swim with others initially, after learning how to swim at the beginner level, she continued the activity in her free time in the presence of family and peers. According to Peganoff, this skill acquisition also resulted in an increase in incidence of satisfaction and compliance with the program as compared to her traditional therapy. Thus, for Sasha, treatment goals achieved through instruction in basic swim strokes were enhanced by incorporating a new leisure skill of interest.

Charlie

In another case study, Johnson (1988) described a 62-year-old man, Charlie, who was diagnosed with amyotrophic lateral sclerosis (ALS) 3 years prior to this aquatic therapy intervention. Upon entering the program, Charlie had respiratory weakness, poor lower extremity muscle strength, and fair to good upper extremity strength. A 10-week aquatic therapy program was prescribed for Charlie (2 x wk, 45-min sessions) to facilitate an increase in strength, flexibility, and conditioning, as well as promote recreation and socialization. Charlie improved from not being able to swim, to swimming 26 lengths of a 20-yard pool with an adapted vest and minimal assistance. Johnson concluded that aquatic therapy for Charlie not only increased endurance and strength, but improved reported energy level and happiness in daily activity as a result of utilizing a challenging leisure activity. According to Johnson, an aquatic therapy program may provide a person who has ALS with a realistic alternative for maintaining physical fitness or continuing with rehabilitation goals while participating in an affordable leisure activity.

Summary

These actual case studies provide a description of outcomes related to aquatic therapy interventions. The outcomes include improved physical abilities as well as leisure-related goals of enjoyment, self-determined activity, and satisfaction. While these case studies used swimming as an aquatic therapy intervention, other aquatic therapy interventions may include additional techniques described in this chapter.

Intervention Implementation Exercises

The following includes four categories of exercises for practical application of aquatic therapy techniques:

- Handling Techniques
- Activities for Mental Adjustment
- Activities for Rotational Control
- Activities for Maintaining Balance

A warm pool (86–93 degrees) is recommended for these exercises. Some of these activities are adapted from Campion (1985). First, handling techniques for aquatic therapy instruction are included so the TR specialist can reassure a participant's safety while facilitating her independent movement. Second, sample activities to assist a participant's adjustment to the water are presented. Third, activities that facilitate lateral, supine, and vertical rotation to enhance a participant's controlled movement in the water are included. Finally, two simple activities that facilitate balance reactions and increase a participant's control of movement in the water are presented.

Handling Techniques

The Halliwick method requires the instructor to use various holds that encourage freedom of movement when teaching the participant such as:

- Vertical holds
- Horizontal holds
- Circle game holds

Vertical holds. In the vertical position, participant's hands rest on instructor's hands without gripping. Gripping causes tension and should be discouraged. As participant requires less support, the instructor may hold participant at the waist for activities such as blowing balls across the water. For example, when practicing jumps facing the instructor, participant places hands on instructor's hands while jumping and blowing across the pool (facing hold). For activities such as riding the bicycle, the swimmer has back to instructor, who supports hands on hands, from behind (rear hold).

Horizontal holds. When a participant is in a supine lying position, the instructor's hands are placed so that the swimmer places their back on the instructor's hand(s), which are at the level of the lungs (supine hold). To relax the participant, the instructor uses an activity called "wriggling around the rocks." Here, the instructor's hands are placed on either side of participant's waist, and moves the person through the water in a zigzag fashion while in a supine position (zigzag hold).

Circle game holds. When games are played in circles, participant and instructor alternate. Holds used depend on participant's comfort. For inexperienced participants, the short arm hold is used with the swimmer's flexed arm resting on the instructor's forearms. For more experienced swimmers, the long arm hold is used while hands are placed on hands with arms fully extended (extended and short arm holds).

The following includes aquatic therapy methods using the Halliwick method of instruction to achieve functional goals. More games and descriptions may be found in books published by the Association of Swimming Therapy (1992) and Margaret Campion, located in the resource list. The following activities are divided into three of four phases of the Halliwick method using holds described in the previous section. These phases include mental adjustment, rotation control, and inhibition.

Activities for Mental Adjustment

There are a variety of aquatic therapy activities that can be complete that facilitate mental adjustment. In this section the following activities are described:

- Blowing balls or eggs
- Taking giant and mini steps

Blowing Balls or Eggs. To blow plastic balls or eggs, the instructor uses a facing or rear hold with support at the waist, while participant is instructed to blow the ball or plastic egg to the therapist or across the pool, while keeping arms forward and keeping the ball or egg in front.

Taking Giant and Mini Steps. To play giant steps, the instructor uses a facing or back hold, while participant is instructed to walk like a giant, using big steps across the pool. For mini steps, participant is instructed to take steps that are as small as possible. A greater degree of balance control may be required when working in small steps.

Activities for Rotational Control

To achieve rotational control it is helpful to engage participants in enjoyable activities in the water. This section highlights the following activities that can be used to achieve rotational control:

- Bells
- Bicycling
- Passing the ball
- Rolling from arm to arm
- Swaying like a tree

Bells. In the bell activity, vertical rotation is practiced in a circle formation using a short or long arm hold with participant and therapist in alternating positions. The participant is instructed to bend knees to the chest and put head back slowly, and then move their head forward and blow. If necessary, facilitation and or control of the participant's body can be provided through the instructor's supporting arm.

Participant can then imitate the wind, sun, and rain. First, participant is asked to blow like the wind toward the middle of the circle. When the instructor states that the sun comes out, participant is asked to put head back and lie out in the sun. Finally, participant is encouraged to make rain by kicking legs.

This activity can also be done in a line formation. When the group walks forward, participants let their legs go behind them, and blow. Then the instructor walks backwards, and participants are instructed to put their knees to their chests, put their heads back, and to extend their bodies lengthwise. The instructions are repeated as the line moves back and forwards. If necessary the swinging movement can be facilitated by the arms of the instructor.

Bicycling, motor boating, or truck driving. Using a rear short arm hold, participant is instructed to bend knees in a position similar to pedaling a bicycle to encourage rotational control. Participant can guide the direction of movement by turning head, body, or arms in the direction they desire. They can pretend their legs are the propellers on a motor boat or the engine of a truck. Participants can hold a round disc to represent a steering wheel and steer in the direction they want to go.

Passing the ball. Passing the ball is used to encourage lateral rotation in a vertical plain as well as crossing midline. This is a circle activity where participants are in front of each instructor, supported at the waist. Participants are asked to pass a ring or ball with their right hand to the participant on their left, look at that person, and then turn their head back to face the inside of the circle. This exercise can be done in a horizontal position with participants supported in a supine hold for lateral rotation in a horizontal plane. To increase an understanding of buoyancy and up-thrust, participants can pass a ball under the water. Differently sized balls can provide variety in the degree of resistance when pushing the ball under water.

Rolling from arm to arm. This game encourages lateral rotation in a vertical or horizontal plane. Rolling from arm to arm begins with participants in front of the instructor facing the circle. Participants are instructed to turn around and face the instructor and then turn and face the circle again. This activity can be done with the participant in a supine position. Participants lie supine with feet toward the center of a circle while the instructor supports participant at the scapula. Each participant is instructed to roll around the circle from instructor to instructor. This can also be done in a vertical position from instructor to instructor. Participants are instructed to face the instructor with hands placed on instructor's shoulders. Participants are asked to take their right hands off the instructor's shoulder and put them in towards the middle of the circle. Participants continue to swing their hands back toward the next instructor's shoulder. Each participant lets go with the left hand, then grips next instructor's right shoulder with it. This rotation is repeated until participant completes the circle. Participant is then asked to perform the above in the opposite direction.

Swaying like a tree in the wind. For lateral rotation in a horizontal plane and relaxation, participant is supported in a supine position, held at the waist. Participant is instructed to lie still and imitate a tree in the wind blowing from side to side. The instructor walks backward, swaying the swimmer from side to side with swimmer in a supine position. If the instructor turns participant's front toward direction of the sway, an additional abdominal stretch and hip extension will occur. Rotating participant's back toward direction of the sway may decrease extension.

Activities for Maintaining Balance

The water is a conducive environment to work on balance, especially when turbulence is created. The following activities can be used to encourage participants to maintain their balance:

- Balancing with turbulence
- Gliding in turbulence

Balancing with turbulence. An activity that facilitates balance with turbulence is to create turbulence around the swimmer while standing, squatting with shoulders under the water and while lying in a supine position. Participant is instructed to maintain a position of stability in all planes.

Gliding in turbulence. Participant floats in a supine position and is moved through water and turbulence created by the instructor. The instructor initiates the turbulence under participant's scapulae (shoulder blades) while walking backwards, causing participant to move.

Summary

The exercises are designed to improve the TR specialist's handling techniques and to increase participants' comfort in the water. For those interested in pursuing a specialty in aquatic therapy, advanced course work is required. Representatives from American Therapeutic Recreation Association and National Therapeutic Recreation Society can provide information about relevant courses and workshops.

Conclusion

Aquatic therapy includes passive and active exercise and swimming to facilitate physical, psychological, and/or leisure outcomes. The water properties of buoyancy and resistance in addition to a warm-water environment provide participants with opportunities for unique and enhanced movement experiences that result in the ability for some participants to achieve treatment goals not possible in land-based activities. While the TR specialist must be knowledgeable of specific aquatic therapy techniques, the properties of the water, indications, contraindications, and efficacy research are considered to maximize treatment outcomes.

Discussion Questions

1. What is aquatic therapy?
2. What are six physical benefits of aquatic therapy?
3. Why can swimming be considered a beneficial medium of aquatic therapy?
4. Why is it important to know what muscle groups are involved in an aquatic therapy intervention?
5. What are general guidelines for aquatic therapy interventions?
6. Why are flotation devices not used with the Halliwick method of instruction?
7. What are the four principles of instruction using the Halliwick method?
8. What is the Dolan method? How is it different from other methods of teaching swimming?
9. Sensory integration includes what six systems discussed in this chapter?
10. What is Watsu?
11. What are six contraindications to aquatic therapy?
12. What is Archimedes' principle?
13. What is an application of Archimedes' principle to aquatic therapy?
14. Describe two possible benefits of hydrodynamic pressure for participants in aquatic therapy?
15. What are three benefits of using warm water in aquatic therapy?
16. What are three potential leisure benefits of aquatic therapy?
17. What are effects of aquatic immersion on the circulatory system?
18. What are effects of immersion on the musculoskeletal system?

Resources

Agency Resources

American Therapeutic Recreation Association Aquatic Therapy Network. http://www.atra-tr.org

Aquatic Therapy and Rehabilitation Institute. http://www.atri.org/
International Council for Aquatic Therapy and Rehabilitation Industry Certification: http://www.icatric.org/mainasp/default.asp

Material Resources

Carter, M. J., Dolan, M. A., & LeConey, S. P. (1994). *Designing instructional swim programs for individuals with disabilities*. Reston, VA: American Alliance for Health, Physical Education, Recreation and Dance.

Melzack, R. (1983). *Pain measurement and assessment*. New York: Raven Press.

References

Adams, M. A., & Chandler, L. S. (1974). Effects of physical therapy program on vital capacity of participants with muscular dystrophy. *Physical Therapy, 54*, 494–496.

Accardo, P. J., & Whitman, B. Y., (1996). *Dictionary of developmental disabilities terminology*. Baltimore: Paul H. Brookes.

Arborelius, M., Balldin, U. I., Lila, B., & Lundgren, C. E. (1972). Regional lung function in man during immersion with the head above water. *Aerospace Medicine, 43*, 707–707.

Assiss, M. R., Silva, L. E., Alves, A. M. B., Pessanha, A. P., Valim,V., et al. (2006). A randomized controlled trial of deep water running: Clinical effectiveness of aquatic exercise to treat fibromyalgia. *Arthritis Care and Research, 55*(1), 57–65.

Association of Swimming Therapy (1992). *Swimming for people with disabilities*. London, United Kingdom: Bedford Row.

Balldin, U. I., et al. (1971). Changes in the elimination of 133 xenon from the anterior tibia muscle in man induced by immersion in water and by shifts in body position. *Aerospace Medicine, 42*, 489–493.

Bar-Or, O., & Inbar, O. (1992). Swimming and asthma: Benefits and deleterious effects. *Sports Medicine, 14*, 397–405.

Beaudouin, M., & Keller, J. (1994). Aquatic solutions: A continuum of services for individuals with physical disabilities in the community. *Therapeutic Recreation Journal, 28*, 193–202.

Becker, B. E. (1997). Aquatic physics. In R. Routi, D. Morris, & A. J. Cole (Eds.), *Aquatic rehabilitation* (pp. 15–23). Philadelphia: Raven Publishers.

Becker, B. E. (2004). Biophysiologic Aspects of Hydrotherapy. In B. E. Becker & A. J. Cole (Eds.), *Comprehensive aquatic therapy* (2nd ed., pp. 19–56). Philadelphia: Butterworth-Heinemann.

Becker, B. E., & Cole, A. J. (2004). *Comprehensive aquatic therapy*. Newton, MA: Butterworth-Heinemann.

Benedict, A., & Freeman, R. (1993). The effect of aquatic exercise on aged persons' bone density, body image and morale. *Activities, Adaptation & Aging, 17*, 67–85.

Berger, B., & Owen, D. (1992). Mood alteration with yoga and swimming: Aerobic exercise may not be necessary. *Perceptual and Motor Skills, 75*, 1331–1343.

Berger, B., Owen, D., & Man, F. (1993). A brief review of the literature and examination of the acute mood benefits of exercise in Czechoslovakian and United States swimmers. *International Journal of Sport Psychology, 24*, 130–150.

Bintzler, S. (2006, November). Water works wonders. *Park and Recreation Magazine*. Retrieved April 3rd, 2007, from http://www.nrpa.org/content/default. aspx?documentId=4936

Boyle, A. (1981). The Bad Ragaz ring method. *Physiotherapy, 67*, 265–268.

Broach, E., & Dattilo, J. (1996). Aquatic therapy: A viable therapeutic recreation option. *Therapeutic Recreation Journal, 30*, 213–239.

Broach, E., & Dattilo, J. (2001). Effects of aquatic therapy on adults with multiple sclerosis. *Therapeutic Recreation Journal, 35*, 141–154.

Broach, E., & Dattilo, J. (2003). The effect of aquatic therapy on strength of adults with multiple sclerosis. *Therapeutic Recreation Journal, 37*, 224–239.

Broach, E., Dattilo, J., & McKenney, A. (2007). Effects of aquatic therapy on perceived fun or enjoyment experiences of participants with multiple sclerosis. *Therapeutic Recreation Journal, 41*, 179–200.

Broach, E., Groff, D., & Dattilo, J. (1997). The effects of swimming therapy on individuals with spinal cord injury. *Therapeutic Recreation Journal, 21*, 159–172.

Broach, E., Groff, D., Dattilo, J., Yaffe, R., & Gast, D. (1998). The effects of aquatic therapy on the physical behavior of people with multiple sclerosis. *ATRA Annual.*

Brundtland, G. H. (2002). WHO Conference on Health and Disability. Retrieved March 1st, 2007, from http://www.who.int/director-general/speeches/2002/english/20020418_disabilitytrieste.html

Buis, J. M., & Schane, C. S. (1980). Movement exploration as a technique for teaching pre-swimming skills to students with developmental delays. *Practical Pointers, 4*(8), 1–110.

Bumin, G., Uyanik, M., Yilmaz, I., Kayihan, H., & Topcu, M. (2003). Hydrotherapy for Rett syndrome. *Journal of Rehabilitation Medicine, 35*, 44–45.

Campion, M. R. (1990). *Adult hydrotherapy.* Oxford, United Kingdom: Heinemann Medical Books.

Campion, M. R. (1985). *Hydrotherapy in pediatrics.* Oxford, United Kingdom: Heinemann Medical Books.

Cardenas, D. D., Haselkorn, J. K, McElligott, J. M., & Gnatz, S. M. (2001). A bibliography of cost-effectiveness practices in physical medicine and rehabilitation: AAPM&R white paper. *Archives of Physical Medicine and Rehabilitation, 82*, 711–719.

Carter, M. J., & O'Morrow, G. S. (2006). *Effective management in therapeutic recreation service.* State College, PA: Venture Publishing, Inc.

Chan, M. (2007). Public health in the 21st century: Optimism in the midst of unprecedented challenges. Retrieved April 3rd, 2007, from http://www.who.int/dg/speeches/2007/030407_whd2007/en/index.html

Coffey, F., & Broach, E. (2000). Certified therapeutic recreation specialist. In Norton, C., & Jamison, L. (Eds), *A team approach to the aquatic continuum of care,* (pp. 145–158). Boston: Butterworth-Heinneman Publishing.

Cole, A., & Becker, B. (2004). *Comprehensive aquatic therapy* (2nd ed.). Philadelphia: Butterworth-Heinemann Publishing.

Davis, B. C., & Harrison, R. A. (1988). *Hydrotherapy in practice.* New York: Churchill Livingston.

Dolan, M. (1996). *The Dolan method.* Paper presentation at the Aquatic Recreation Therapy Institute. National Recreation and Park Association. Kansas City, MO.

Dorval, G., Tereault, S., & Caron, C. (1996). Impact of aquatic programmes on adolescents with cerebral palsy. *Occupational Therapy International, 3*, 241–261.

Driver, S., O'Connor, J., Lox, C., & Rees, K. (2004). Evaluation of an aquatics program on fitness parameters of individuals with a brain injury. *Brain Injury, 18*, 847–859.

Dull, H. (2004). *Watsu: Freeing the body in water.* Victoria, BC: Trafford.

Edlund, L. D., French, R. W., Herbst, J. J., Ruttenberg, H. D., Ruhling, R. O., & Adams, T. D. (1986). Effects of a swimming program on children with cystic fibrosis. *American Journal of Diseases in Children, 140,* 80–83.

Epstein, M. (1992). Renal effects of head-out of water immersion in humans: a 15 year update. *Physiological Review, 72,* 563–621.

Fredrickson, B. L., Tugade, M., Waugh, C., & Larkin, G. (2003). What good are positive emotions in crises? A prospective study of resilience and emotions following the terrorist attacks on the United States on September 11th, 2001. *Journal of Personality and Social Psychology, 84,* 365–376.

Gehlsen, G., Grigsby, S., & Winant, D. (1984). Effects on an aquatic fitness program on the muscular strength and endurance of participants with multiple sclerosis. *Physical Therapy, 64,* 653–657.

Getz, M., Hutzler, Y., & Vermeer, A. (2006). Effects of aquatic interventions in children with neuromotor impairments: A systematic review of the literature. *Clinical Rehabilitation, 20,* 927–936.

Giancoli, D. C. (1985). *Physics: Principles with applications* (2nd ed.). Englewood Cliffs, NJ: Prentice Hall.

Guillemin, F., Constant, F., Collin, J. F., & Boulange, M. (1994). Short- and long-term effect of spa therapy in chronic low back pain. *British Journal of Rheumatology, 33,* 148–151.

Holmer, I., Stein, E., Saltin, B., Ekblom, B., & Astrand, P. (1974). Hemodynamic and respiratory responses compared in swimming and running. *Journal of Applied Physiology, 37,* 149–154.

Huang, S., Veiga, R., Sila, U., Reed, E., & Hines, S. (1989). The effect of swimming in asthmatic children: Participants in a swimming program in the city of Baltimore. *Journal of Asthma, 26,* 117–121.

Hutzler, Y., Chacham, A., Bergman, U., & Szeinberg, A. (1998). Effects of movement and swimming program on vital capacity and water orientation skills of children with cerebral palsy. *Developmental Medicine & Child Neurology, 40,* 176–181.

Hutzler, Y., Chacham, A., Bergman, U., & Reches, I. (1998). Effects of a movement swimming program on water orientation skills and self concept of kindergarten children with cerebral palsy. *Perceptual Motor Skills, 86,* 111–118.

Hurley, E., & Turner, C. (1991). Neurology and aquatic therapy. *Clinical Management, 11*(1), 26–30.

Ide, M. R., Belini, M. A., & Caromano, F. A. (2005). Effects of an aquatic versus non-aquatic respiratory exercise program on the respiratory muscle strength in healthy aged persons. *Clinics, 60,* 151–158.

Inbar, O., Dotan, R., Dlin, R., Neuman, I., & Bar-Or, O. (1980). Breathing dry or humid air and exercise-induced asthma during swimming. *European Journal of Applied Physiology, 44,* 43–50.

Jamison, L., & Ogden, D. (1994). *Aquatic Therapy: Using PNF Patterns.* San Antonio, TX: Therapy Skill Builders.

Johnson, C. R. (1988). Aquatic therapy for an ALS participant. *The American Journal of Occupational Therapy, 42,* 115–120.

Konno, J., & Sova, R. (1996). *Ai Chi: Flowing aquatic energy*. Port Washington, WI: DSL, Ltd.

Langridge, J. C., & Phillips, D. (1988). Group hydrotherapy exercises for chronic back pain sufferers. *Physiotherapy, 74*, 269–273.

Latourette, D. (1995, November). *Aquatic therapy*. Presented at the ATRA Aquatic Therapy Workshop, Atlanta, GA.

McNamara, S. (1994). Marketing aquatic therapy. *Rehab Management, 5*, 67–70.

Morris, D. M. (2004). Aquatic rehabilitation for the treatment of neurologic disorders. In A. J. Cole & B. E. Becker (Eds.) (2nd ed.): *Comprehensive Aquatic Therapy* (pp. 151–176). Boston: Butterworth-Heinemann.

Ostir, G. V., Mardides, K. S., Black, S. A., & Goodwin, J. S. (2000). Emotional well being predicts subsequent functional independence and survival. *Journal of the American Geriatrics Society, 48*(5), 590–592.

Peganoff, S. A. (1984). The use of aquatics with cerebral palsied adolescents. *The American Journal of Occupational Therapy, 38*, 469–473.

Parker, K. M., & Smith, S. A. (2003). Aquatic aerobic exercise as a means of stress reduction during pregnancy. *Journal of Perinatal Education, 12*, 6–17.

Penny, P. (1983). Swimming pool wheezing. *British Medical Journal, 278*, 442–461.

Routi, R. G., Troup, J. T., & Berger, R. A. (1994). The effects of nonswimming water exercises on older adults. *Journal of Sports Physical Therapy, 19*, 140–144.

Shanda, L. (1996, October). *Halliwick*. Presented at the NRPA Aquatic Recreation Therapy Institute, Kansas City, MO.

Skinner, A. T., & Thomson, A. M. (Eds.). (1983). *Duffield's exercise in the water* (3rd ed.). Philadelphia: Bailliere Tindall.

Slade, C., & Simmons-Grab, D. (1987). Therapeutic swimming as a community based program. *Cognitive Rehabilitation, 5*(2), 18–20.

Smith, S. A., & Michel, Y. (2006). A pilot study on the effects of aquatic exercises on discomforts of pregnancy. *Journal of Obstetric, Gynecologic, & Neonatal Nursing, 35*, 315–323.

Stein, P. N., & Motta, R. W. (1992). Effects of aerobic and nonaerobic exercise on depression and self-concept. *Perceptual and Motor Skills, 74*, 79–89.

Templeton, M. S., Booth, D. L., O'Kelly, W. D. (1996). Effects of aquatic therapy on joint flexibility and functional ability in subjects with rheumatic disease. *Journal of Orthopedic Sports Physical Therapy, 23*, 376–381.

Tsukahara, N., Toda, A., Goto, J., & Ezawa, I. (1994). Cross-sectional and longitudinal studies on the effect of water exercise in controlling bone loss in Japanese postmenopausal women. *Journal of Nutrition and Science Vitaminology, 40*, 37–47.

Walker S. N., Seghrist K. R., & Pender, N. J. (1987). The health-promoting lifestyle profile: Development and psychometric properties. *Nursing Research, 36*, 76–81.

Wang, T. J., Belza B., Thompson F. E., Whitney, J. D., & Bennett K. (2007). Effects of aquatic exercise on flexibility, strength and aerobic fitness in adults with osteoarthritis of the hip or knee. *Journal of Advanced Nursing, 57*, 141–152.

Weston, C. F., O'Hare, J. P., Evans, J. M., & Corall, R. J. M. (1987). Haemodynamic changes in man during immersion in water at different temperatures. *Clinical Science, 73*, 613–616.

Weiss, C. R., & Jamieson, N. B. (1989). Women, subjective depression, and water exercise. *Health Care for Women International, 10,* 75–88.

Woods, D. A. (1989). Rehabilitation aquatics for low back injury: Functional gains or pain reduction? *Clinical Kinesiology, 43,* 96–103.

Wright, J., & Cowden, J. E. (1986). Changes in self-concept and cardiovascular endurance of mentally retarded youths in a Special Olympics swim training program. *Adapted Physical Activity Quarterly, 3,* 177–183.

Wyatt, F. B., Milam, S., Manske, R. C., & Deere. R. (2001). The effects of aquatic and traditional exercise programs on persons with knee osteoarthritis. *The Journal of Strength and Conditioning Research, 15,* 337–340.

Zach, M. S., Purrer, B., & Oberwaldner, B. (1981). Effect of swimming on forced expiration and sputum clearance in cystic fibrosis. *Lancet, 11,* 1201–1203.

Chapter 5
Assistive Technology

Ellen Broach and John Dattilo

Give me a lever long enough and a place to stand
and I will move the earth.

—Archimedes

Introduction

Access to appropriate assistive technology (AT) services and devices can remove barriers, unmask abilities, stretch imaginations, and increase expectations (Deavours, 1997). Regardless of disability severity, when individuals are given appropriate equipment, they are able to make choices important for leisure participation and demonstrating self-determined behavior. Despite the advantages, providers of services underutilize AT (Magee, 2006). Since extensive dependence on others can severely inhibit quantity and quality of leisure participation (Besio, 2004), AT is important to many people with disabilities because it allows them to become more independent and self-determined.

Through play and leisure participation children discover effects of their actions, develop social and cooperative skills, experience fun and enjoyment, and learn social roles (Besio, 2004). Accordingly, if children do not play and experience leisure, their development will be impaired. Therefore, it is important for children with disabilities to be provided with opportunities to play.

While access to leisure is considered important, it is also perceived as less available to individuals with disabilities, caregivers, and providers (Wilcox, Gulmond, Campbell & Moore, 2006). This access is often hampered when individuals lack necessary skills to make choices and participate in traditional leisure activities. Assistive technology creates opportunities for individuals to express choice in enjoyable activities.

Dattilo, Light, St. Peter, and Sheldon (1995) reported that 91% of 55 children using augmentative or alternative communication (AAC) systems desired assistance in learning to access leisure activities. This desire of individuals to participate in leisure and their associated limited leisure repertoire is relevant to TR service delivery because, as the range of leisure activity decreases, opportunities for enjoyment and development decline (Besio, 2004).

Crows and Deavours (1993) explained that technology should be considered a medium for leisure experiences for all people. Technology in leisure programming facilitates opportunities for: successful and independent participation; competition and cooperation; expression and creativity in activities such as spin art, air brush, music, stereos or tape players, and creative writing; choice between numerous toys, games, and hobbies; multi-sensory stimulation through auditory, visual, and motor feedback with lights, pictures, sounds, and movement responses and/or participation; and, lastly, inclusion and equal participation with peers.

A variety of outcomes are associated with use of technology in leisure activities. Physical outcomes include increased hand-eye coordination, fine motor control, respiration control using sip and puff devices, responses to auditory or visual stimuli, and bilateral coordination. Cognitive and linguistic outcomes include the ability to track visual stimuli, sequence movements, respond to directions, control impulses, remember information, solve problems, focus on a task (attention) for a period of time (concentration), and discriminate left and right. By learning through play and leisure experiences, individuals improve their movements, thoughts, ability to plan, social skills, and acquire a personal play style (Besio, 2004).

Although technology available to people with disabilities has greatly expanded in recent years, benefits of these innovations cannot be realized unless TR specialists can operate the technology and integrate it into their interventions. Unfortunately, some practitioners are not always able or willing to modify their strategies to accommodate access to technology by individuals with disabilities (Magee, 2006).

> For example, in a qualitative study of 28 teachers and 28 students (ages 6–17, 16 males) with severe disabilities, Carey and Sale (1994a) identified barriers to full inclusion: (a) limited access to technology; (b) lack of consistent power sources; (c) lack of mobility of equipment; (d) cost of equipment; (e) maintenance of technology systems; and (f) lack of curricular outcomes that consistently included use of technology. These barriers could be addressed with consistent use of interventions, knowledge of adaptive technology, and creative professionals (Wilcox et al., 2006).

Providers are aware of the importance of AT in facilitating children's participation in activities and in promoting family interactions (Wilcox et al., 2006). These providers viewed parental attitudes as important factors in making decisions about AT. Therefore, a family-centered approach is recommended practice in AT decision making for clients. Involving families requires assessing information on family strengths, needs, priorities and culture, the individual's community environments, and activities where devices and services will be used. Dattilo (2002) suggested that when assessing needs for technology and providing services, professionals can encourage independence and facilitate inclusion.

Because it is helpful for practitioners to be aware of issues related to technology, this chapter provides information on using technology to increase function and leisure participation. Definitions associated with technology are provided followed by a discussion of assistive technology devices, the history of assistive technology, efficacy of assistive technology, case examples of assistive technology services, and resources.

Definitions

The Individuals with Disabilities Education Improvement Act (IDE/A) of 2004 defines AT as "any item, piece of equipment, or product system, whether acquired commercially, modified, or customized, that is used to increase, maintain, or improve functional capabilities of individuals with disabilities" (20 U.S.C. § 1401(251)). There is a multitude of devices and services associated with assistive technology; however, when considering the most important terms associated with this topic three phrases merit discussions:

- Assistive Technology (AT)
- AT Device
- AT Service

Assistive Technology (AT)

The Individuals with Disabilities Education Improvement Act (IDE/A) of 2004 defines AT as "any item, piece of equipment, or product system, whether acquired commercially, modified, or customized, that is used to increase, maintain, or improve functional capabilities of individuals with disabilities" (20 U.S.C. § 1401(251)).

AT Device

An AT *device* can be a simple or complex device such as Velcro, adaptive toys, seating systems, computer hardware and software, wheelchairs, augmentative and alternative communication systems, and other commercially available or adaptive, modified, or customized items that are used to increase, maintain, or improve function of individuals with disabilities.

AT Service

AT *service* is defined as service that directly assists an individual with a disability in selection, acquisition, or use of an assistive technology device (PL, 100–407). Public law identifies a broad spectrum of services including evaluating needs and skills for assistive technology, acquiring assistive technologies, selecting, designing, and repairing systems, and training individuals with disabilities and those working with them to use technologies effectively.

Descriptions

The area of assistive technology includes a great deal of information that can be used to enhance the life of people with disabilities. To provide information about technology, the following three topics will elaborate on this topic:

- General Considerations
- Assistive Technology Devices
- Examples of Assistive Technology Services

General Considerations

Based on Bedini's (1993) identification of ethical issues related to technology and leisure services and Dattilo's (2002) discussion of inclusive leisure services, the following suggestions associated with assistive technology are provided:

- Focus on the person
- Focus on abilities
- Provide technology
- Encourage independence
- Obtain competence in assistive technology

Focus on the person. To increase the chance that practitioners will establish appropriate priorities when using assistive technology, it is helpful if the focus is on the individual rather than the technology. AT is deemed appropriate when the device is related to precise and clear goals that are meaningful to the person and family (Long, Huang, Woodbridge, Woolverton, & Minkel, 2003). These sentiments are similar to Deavours (1997), who argued that the lack of individual focus results in inappropriate and expensive technological purchases when more appropriate and less expensive solutions would have been best.

It is essential to consider the individual's entire life when designing and choosing technology since behavior in one context can rarely be understood fully in isolation from other contexts.

> For example, Brady and Cunningham (1985) examined the life of a woman with cerebral palsy by conducting observations across school and home settings and interviewing the woman, her family, and friends. When viewed separately, each program or service seemed appropriate and beneficial. However, when viewed in the context of her entire life, many discrepancies were identified. As an example, her adapted headrest served to restrict her field of vision at school, thus limiting her ability to be involved in socialization opportunities. This example supports the benefit of looking at the person's entire life when using assistive technology.

Focus on abilities. When using technology, it is useful to focus on an individual's abilities rather than limitations. Focusing on a person's abilities is important because, too often, decisions are made based on what participants cannot do which stifles problem solving and limits options. When abilities become the focus, practitioners are more likely to make adaptations that capitalize on participants' skills, thus, creating more options.

For example, when using an augmentative communication device to play a guessing game, a child's cognitive abilities, motivations, and physical skills are important when determining usability of a certain device (Besio, 2004).

Provide technology. It is vital to recognize that technology cannot provide enablement, access, or opportunities unless support is in place. Parette, Van-Biervliet, and Hourcade (2000) emphasized that AT is only appropriate when it is compatible with practical considerations such as funding sources. Including individuals with disabilities in leisure settings has and will continue to spur requests for inexpensive and versatile technologies (Carey & Sale, 1994a) as well as increase use among people with disabilities.

Community recreation agencies can acquire and maintain selected adaptive equipment to encourage continued usage by people with disabilities after rehabilitation because cost of AT is a major barrier that prevents use of technology (Besio, 2004). Provision of appropriate AT can increase benefits of treatment and satisfaction of leisure participation. While provision of AT is important, support is often needed, such as teaching individuals and families how to use devices and systems, disseminating information and resources, and assessing and reassessing needs.

Encourage independence. AT is only useful when it results in outcomes that meet goals to maximize skills. When working with children, TR specialists consider family issues and preferences and collaborate with families to determine technology intervention strategies (Long et al., 2003). A participant's level of self-determination is considered by TR specialists to determine which AT services would be appropriate (Parette & Brotherson, 2004).

Encouraging self-determination means supporting people's engagement in problem solving, development of autonomy, and ability to make an impact on their environment (Erwin & Brown, 2003). Dependence may occur when technology does too much for individuals with disabilities; thus, they are discouraged from achieving their potential. Practitioners are encouraged to use technology when it is needed, but must continue to facilitate skill acquisition so that participants can be as independent as possible.

Develop competence in assistive technology. One barrier to people using AT is their lack of knowledge of what is available and how to select appropriate devices (Long et al., 2003). However, there is a shortage of professionals trained to provide AT services. TR specialists who are informed about AT can be helpful to people with disabilities that might benefit from technology.

For example, AT may be used for computer access, speech access, and accessing recreation equipment, such as electric fishing reels, rifles, cameras, toys, bicycles, billiards, scuba, or beep balls. TR specialists who are knowledgeable about the potential of AT in facilitating these activities can be helpful to participants and be a valuable resource for an interdisciplinary team in rehabilitation and in the community.

As access to technology becomes increasingly important for individuals with disabilities, there is a need for TR specialists to become competent in evaluation, operation, and adaptation of assistive technology. Long and colleagues (2003) emphasized that providers need skills and knowledge to address AT needs and services, strategies for funding and measuring outcomes, and contextual factors such as family, community, and finances that impede or facilitate attitudes and use of AT.

To address the issue of practitioner competencies in AT, TR professional organizations have established AT committees and networks. While Stoner, Parette, Watts, and Wojcik (2008) focused on AT in an educational setting, suggestions for discussing AT with teachers including prior knowledge and concerns could be applied in the TR setting. Additional competencies can be obtained from interdisciplinary groups and agencies, such as Closing the Gap, United Cerebral Palsy Association, the Easter Seals Society, and other organizations listed in the resource list of this chapter.

Assistive Technology Devices

Assistive technology devices augment existing abilities or compensate for limits of impairments. Areas of support for development of self-determined action include positioning, communication, recreation and play, learning, self-fulfillment, mobility, and self-care (Lane & Mistrett, 1996). Within each of the noted areas a wide range of high- and low-tech devices exists for support. Devices discussed in this chapter are those commonly noted in the literature that result in independent leisure functioning. These devices include:

- Switches
- Computers
- Virtual reality
- Video games
- Augmentative and alternative communication systems
- Electronic aids to daily living
- Aids for manipulation

Switches. The introduction of switch technology to people with disabilities has increased their ability to manipulate objects and gain a sense of control over their environment (Dugan, Campbell, & Wilcox, 2006). Activating a toy or audio-visual entertainment can provide enjoyment as well as a learning experience (see Figure 5.1).

> For instance, individuals who have cognitive impairments
> can be taught cause and effect tasks by pressing a switch that
> activates a toy. Individuals with speech difficulties can activate
> a communication device to lead a game. In addition, those with
> physical disabilities can use a switch to play while improving
> motor control.

Crows and Deavours (1993) described types of switches that are commonly used in recreation settings (see Table 5.1 on p. 118). Participants can turn on any battery-powered or low-wattage device by activating a single switch. Although

Figure 5.1

single switches can be used to turn on the device, pressure must be maintained to operate a momentary switch, while a latch switch is activated with one touch and then disconnected with another. The switch consists of an input area for touching, a cord with a 1/8th-inch mini-plug on the end that goes into the receptor of the adapted device. Although some commercially available switches are expensive, the cost of any switch can be minimized with simple soldering.

It is important for switches to be paired with the most reliable motor movement (mount set-up should be minimal). It can be helpful to consider the degree of tension required to activate the switch, and how the switch will be used for activating objects such as a toy, computer, communication, mobility, or video game.

> For example, if a person has control of one finger it may be best to use a small, sensitive switch. In contrast, a foot switch should be able to withstand impact from shoes.

The aesthetic preferences of the consumer are an important consideration. Also, it is very important to complete a safety check of all equipment. Finally, evaluating the effectiveness of a microswitch for accomplishing the objective is another key consideration.

Computers. Today, computers can be operated by anyone, in any place, and are sometimes no bigger than a hand-held calculator or credit card. Computers typically consist of hardware such as a keyboard, visual screen, printer, and software which are the instructions that tell a computer what to do.

Many individuals with disabilities can access computers with instructions and/ or adaptations. Ryan and Heaven (1986) described the impact of computers on older adults to facilitate communication, access information and entertainment, and increase independence. They reported that older adults can best be induced to view computers as useful and enjoyable through hands-on experience with user-friendly

Table 5.1

Switch	Description	Typical Mounts (not limited)	Sensitivity and Auditory Feedback
Plate	3"–6" in diameter; pushing switch for response	Hand, head, elbow, knee, foot	Sensitivity varies; some provide auditory click
Sensor	Attaches to skin; detects small, controlled muscle movements (i.e., eyebrow) or touch w/o pressure	Face, fingers	Very sensitive; no auditory feedback
Proximal	Activates when movement occurs in proximity of a switch	Hand	Very sensitive; no auditory feedback
Lever	4"–6" in length	Usually head/cheek	Has limited travel; may have auditory feedback
Leaf/tape	4"–6"; toggle or bend to activate	Head, cheek, arm	No auditory feedback; very sensitive
Grasp	Switch inserted in pillow, pad, or small cushioned grip; squeeze to activate	Usually hand	May have auditory feedback; sensitivity varies
Sip/puff	Sip or puff straw to activate	Mouth	Sensitive; requires lip closure/breath control
Pull/string	String can attach; pull to activate	Usually hand, wrist or finger	Sensitive; can have auditory feedback
Mercury switch	Mercury switch capsule enclosed in protective material; activates when tilted	Head, hand	Very sensitive; no auditory feedback

computer applications. Campbell, Milbourne, Dugan, and Wilcox (2006) found that various computer interventions resulted in improved social interactions, problem-solving abilities, and vocabulary for children with disabilities. Specific to computerized leisure education, studies show improved knowledge of social skills (e.g., Cory, Dattilo, & Williams, 2006) and self-determination (Dattilo, Williams, Guerin, & Cory, 2001).

The two major methods of computer access are *input* and *output*. *Input* involves the means by which instructions are given to the computer. The two primary forms of computer input devices are the keyboard and mouse. Alternative input devices provide access solutions for those who cannot use one or both of these. Alternative keyboards may be expanded or reduced and can have customized overlays. Keyboard layouts can be altered for users with limited hand or finger movement or even users who are new to typing (Ross, 2007). Keyboards might be on the monitor and be accessed with a pointing device, with a switch that scans the keyboard, or with one or two switches that emulate Morse code to directly select letters.

The mouse movements may be emulated with an alternative keyboard or by other devices such as a head mouse that tracks head movements to move the cursor, a pneumatic switch that is also known as a sip and puff switch to produce mouse clicks, trackball, track-pad, touch screen that allows pointing with a finger or stylus to move the cursor, and a joystick or directional switches. Voice input can control both the mouse and keyboard input when combined with speech recognition software.

Other computer-assistive technology includes input tools such as word prediction, screen readers, or magnifying software. Word prediction improves productivity by increasing rate of input for users who are only able to access standard or alternative keyboards one letter at a time. Word prediction identifies the word or series of words most likely to follow an initial letter based on surrounding words. Screen reader and magnifying software solutions make computers with typical input devices more accessible to people who are blind or have low vision by reading text and menu items, or magnifying the entire screen up to 16 times.

Output is the product that is delivered by the computer to the screen, or on a printed page, or as audio. Because typical outputs do not accommodate individuals with sensory impairments, adaptations for output are required. The output may include large print, text to speech identified as screen readers, refreshable Braille that displays output by dots that protrude and recess to convey information, and Braille print. Software programs may facilitate writing journals, poetry and song lyrics, composing and playing music, drawing and painting, and simulation of dance. Buckley (1993) suggested development a software analysis inventory prior to implementing any computer-assisted treatment services using a matrix that indicates software name, access modality, problem or skill areas addressed, and level of difficulty.

There are also features inherent to system software designed to accommodate input and output needs of individuals with disabilities. See Table 5.2 on p. 120 for descriptions of access features built into computer operating systems.

An increasingly important input and output concern for individuals with disabilities is internet access. As the Internet becomes increasingly replete with multimedia representations, animation, and audible sources of information, challenges for people with disabilities increase (Cook & Hussey, 2002). Websites for assistance are available including the Universal Usability Resource Center (http://universalusability. com/resources.html), the World Wide Web consortium Web Accessibility Initiative (http://www.w3.org/WAI/), and the Trace Center (http://www.trace.wisc.edu/world/web/index.html).

Virtual Reality. Virtual reality (VR) describes a computer-generated scenario of objects in a 3-dimensional virtual world with which a person can interact (Yang & Poff, 2001). For example, VR can give an individual with a disability the sense of swimming in the ocean and coming face-to-face with various fish. Aukstakalnis and Blatner (1992) stated that virtual reality exists in three distinct systems including: *passive*, *exploratory*, and *interactive*.

In *passive* VR systems, the user can see, feel, and hear what is happening in the environment, but he or she cannot control it. *Exploratory* VR systems allow the user to move around the environment by such actions as walking, flying, or crawling through and around objects. The *interactive* VR is the most powerful form of technology, in that the user is not only able to move around within the environment, but

Table 5.2

Feature	Description
Slow Keys	Specifies time key must be pushed before registered by computer
Sticky Keys	User can press modifier key, then press second key without pushing both simultaneously
Bounce Keys	Prevents typing double characters when key accidentally hit
Mouse Keys	Substitutes arrow keys for mouse movements
Toggle Keys	Provides tones representing status of Caps Lock, Scroll Lock, and Number Lock keys
Serial Keys	Permits communication aids as computer input devices
Show Sounds	Displays captions for speech and sounds
Sound Sentry	Generates a visual warning when the system generates sound
Repeat Keys	Permits adjusting time a key is held before repeating repeat rate and key
Mouse Speed	Adjusts tracking, double-click speed, size of cursor, adds mouse tails, making cursor easier to track
Filter Keys	The combination of Slow Keys, Bounce Keys, and Repeat Keys

can interact with it and change it as well. The two primary characteristics of virtual reality systems currently being developed are: *immersion* and *dynamic simulations*.

Immersion involves actual presentation and display of information that causes people to feel that they are "actually inside and surrounded by the environment" (Aukstakalnis & Blatner, 1992, p. 26), resulting in a sense of self in the virtual world. Immersion into a new reality is possible through interfaces that provide a connection between the user and the virtual environment in the computer and require the following hardware: head-mounted displays, headphones, body suit, flying mouse, floating joysticks, and data gloves that recognize gesture (Yang & Poff, 2001). The sensory experience depends on the person's movements in the environment that are relayed back to the computer from a control device that may include a joystick, data glove, or body suit.

Dynamic simulation involves the ability to simulate and create accurate representations of reality environment, anything from a busy mall or playground to an undersea floor. Dynamic simulations are created by interactive computer graphics that update images several times per second so that lag time between actions of the user and their representation by the computer is short enough to give the impression that the experience is really happening.

Thiers (1993a) described VR as a technology that allows individuals to experience the sensation of a real-life experience such as climbing a mountain, running, dancing, active games, sports, or recreation experiences without the real-life risks or physical capabilities of doing the actions. A VR user interacts with simulated environments through fiber optic sensors that monitor hand-eye motions and provide feedback and the illusion of movement. VR simulates interactive experiences for all senses and body parts, making it an ideal tool for improving function.

> For example, an individual could manipulate a virtual object before that person has the strength to pick up actual objects, which can facilitate improved coordination and fine motor skills.

Kuhlen and Dohle (1995) described how individuals with motor difficulties, paralysis, or speech impairments can benefit from VR. In VR, people can move parts of their virtual body such as legs or arms by blinking their eyes or making facial movements.

> For example, the Biomuse system is used to detect and act on bioelectric signals from the human body and to grab objects by looking at them (Thiers, 1993a). Thiers described a young child with extensive paralysis who was taught to move a smiley face around on a computer screen simply by moving her eyes. This technology could eventually allow people with no controlled movement but their eyes to operate environmental controls.

VR play can influence motivation levels (Harris, 2005). Using the Pediatric Volitional Questionnaire to measure motivation in a variety of VR environments, Harris found that the features of VR environments that produce high levels of motivation included challenge, variability, and competition. VR development is slowly changing the nature of rehabilitation. VR has been used to improve body image (Riva, 1998), enhance self-perception (Reid & Campbell, 2006), treat phobias (Olsen, 2000), improve cognitive abilities (Grealy, Johnson, & Rushton, 1999), and has been used as a distraction for cancer treatment (Schneider & Workman, 2000). VR can also assist people in controlling their environment.

> For example, using a VR technique called bio-cybernetics, a computer acts on changes in brain waves, which people can learn to control through biofeedback. A person can remain immobile but control tones on a synthesizer through slowing alpha brain waves. Eventually, a person may be able to use brain waves to trigger a light switch (Thiers, 1993a).

VR input devices, such as a data glove, can be used to assist people in functioning in the "actual" world by assisting them in areas such as social skill development. An example of social skill development through VR involves assisting individuals in overcoming phobias.

> Specifically, researchers are testing use of simulated height and depth experiences to desensitize individuals with acrophobia (fear of heights) and other fears (Olsen, 2000). VR social skill experiences for individuals with behavior disorders in a leisure education program were described by Muscot and Gifford (1994),

who offered examples of virtual reality outcomes: active problem solving, cooperative learning, interactive role-playing, resulting in consequences, and training through behavioral modeling.

Muscot and Gifford explained that social skills instruction should be a fundamental aspect of programs for children and youth with behavioral disorders. While VR could provide an excellent medium for social skill instruction, various challenges exist including cost, availability, computer power, and the need for staff training.

Based on current trends in VR, one goal of TR could be to encourage use of virtual environments where people can use virtual community-based simulations and leisure skills. The environments could allow individuals to experiment with solving problems, making choices, experiencing consequences, and improving abilities in the real world.

> For example, Germann, Broida, Broida, and Thompson (2001) have developed software that TR specialists can use with patients to preview community sites that they may want to later visit. The purpose of the software is to increase client confidence and greater independence in the community after treatment.

Video games. Although many games have evolved into VR games, uses of video games that do not involve simulated immersion are abundant. Chaffin, Maxwell, and Thompson (1982) identified variables associated with motivational aspects of video games and applied these results to learning situations requiring high levels of motivation. They noted that video games inherently provide motivational properties that may be of particular relevance to learning and enjoyment of individuals with disabilities because they often include immediate feedback, equal challenge skill ratio, no ceiling on performance, and opportunities for improvement.

In addition to motivational and enjoyment value, benefits of video games extend to individuals who have had cerebral vascular accidents and acquired physical disabilities (Goode, 1982). Goode emphasized the games' ability to facilitate improvement in tracking, eye-hand coordination, concentration, reaction time, scanning, and problem solving. Sedlack, Doyle, and Schloss (1982), who successfully taught video games to three individuals with severe cognitive impairments, noted that skills learned while playing video games generalized to other situations and facilitated more inclusion in community settings.

> An example of adaptations to video games was described by Buckley and Smith (1991) who emphasized use of arcade games as an avenue for active participation. Specifically, they described Arcade Access, an adapted pinball machine, that not only includes a surface that is adjustable to varying heights, but is operable through numerous modalities including pressure sensitive pads, a sip and puff device, a joystick, or a tongue or toe control. Adaptive arcade machines such as Arcade Access and video games can provide a means to facilitate improved leisure, physical, social, and cognitive function.

Augmentative or alternative communication (AAC) systems. Augmentative communication systems supplement a person's existing method of communication, such as writing when speech is not clear, while alternative communication systems allow for speech to occur through another medium such as a computerized system of speech. Devices for communication range from a non-electronic communication symbol board to electronic devices such as computers with voice output and extensive memory programmed to meet the needs of each individual.

AAC devices can also be *dedicated* to function solely as a communication device or multi-purpose otherwise known as *non-dedicated* to provide additional functions such as word processing. Separation between dedicated and non-dedicated devices has decreased as microprocessors increase in power and decrease in size. Because computerized AAC systems are decreasing in cost, and laptop computers are becoming more available and versatile, computerized systems can be used for promoting independence in communication and choice making.

According to Dattilo and colleagues (1995), communication using AAC devices is important because many individuals who have speech difficulties often do not function actively and equally in interactions. If people are to express leisure choices, they must have some control over conversations. The skill to engage in conversations increases the person's opportunity to experience leisure and play. AAC systems are an integral component in aiding the involvement of children with significant disabilities in leisure pursuits and community involvement (Bingham, Spooner, & Browder, 2007).

Visual displays for electronic AAC devices may be static or dynamic. *Static displays* do not change in appearance as they are used. Multiple meaning icons, such as pictures that stay in the same place on the keyboard, represent concepts included on static displays. *Dynamic displays* change in response to commands by the user.

> For example, if someone wants *go out to eat*, the user may activate a restaurant icon that, when touched, will access a sub-menu of actual restaurants to choose from.

Dattilo and Light (1993) demonstrated that individuals who use AAC devices might learn to exert and maintain conversational control. In addition to the importance of instructing people with AAC systems to take control in conversations, there is a need to teach ways to decrease interaction dominance by parents, peers, and other practitioners. One recommendation is to provide individuals with adequate time, at least 10 seconds, to formulate a communication turn (Dattilo & Camarata, 1991). Then, as individuals improve their ability to communicate and are encouraged to make choices, their ability to experience satisfaction in leisure activities should increase (Dattilo & Barnett, 1985).

The importance of use of AAC systems for conversational control was noted in a survey of 87 mothers and 47 fathers of adolescents who used AAC systems (Angelo, Kokoska, & Jones, 1996). Mothers ranked social opportunities with others, integrating AAC into the community, and planning for future needs as highest priorities for AAC use. Fathers ranked planning for the future, repair knowledge, and integration of AAC into educational settings as priority.

Electronic Aids to Daily Living (EADL). EADLs provide a means to control electronic devices such as televisions, DVD players, lights, locks, and telephones that are ordinarily used in the home. EADL was changed from the term *environmental control unit* (ECU) to more accurately describe the purpose of the technology to improve functions of recreation and leisure, independence, communication, and safety (Angelo & Buning, 2002). These aids can be simple switches or more complex systems with sophisticated control for individuals who have significant physical impairments.

Aids for manipulation. Manipulation refers to activities that are normally accomplished using upper extremities. Some of these assistive devices include switches and other computer input devices and EADLs discussed in the previous sections; therefore, they will be excluded from this discussion. Aids not yet identified include low-technological, non-electronic aids for grasping, eating, and manipulation of physical objects. General purpose aids include mouth-sticks, head pointers, and reachers. Mouth-sticks can be used for activities such as turning pages of a book, writing, sketching, typing, turning off lights, and dialing a telephone. A mouth-stick can have attachments that allow pinching an object or a suction cup end to grip items. Reachers are used to extend a person's range to grasp an item when participating in activities such as gardening and cooking.

Special purpose aids are designed for one or two tasks only. Most special purpose aids involve lengthening a handle, modifying a handle such as enlarging it, bending it, or cuffing it to make it easier to grasp, converting two-handed tasks to one-handed tasks, and amplifying the force of a movement (Cook & Hussey, 2002).

> Examples for recreation participation include extending the shutter release on a camera; modifying the handle on garden tools, golf clubs, pool cues, or fishing reel; eating utensils and drinking cups; using grasping cuffs for holding fishing rods, racquets or paddles, or even string for flying a kite. Adaptations that enable one-handed activities might include a gooseneck arm that is clamped to a table with the other end holding an embroidery frame. This adaptation allows the use of one hand for sewing or crocheting activities. Another one-handed adaptation could include the use of a rod holder that is attached on a wheelchair or an individual's chest for one-handed fishing. For one-handed cooking suction cups or mats under bowls and cutting boards that stabilize food can be used. Other one-handed adaptations include card-holders and shufflers, book holders, and knitting needle holders. Examples of special purpose aids for reaching include a mobile bridge for holding the end of a pool cue off the table and ramps for bowling. Contact information of suppliers for many of these aids is included at the end of this chapter.

Devices for individuals with visual impairments that allow them to manipulate objects include enlarged versions of games such as dominos, cards, or board games. In addition, tactually labeled playing cards and board games are common. Sport adaptations, as identified in the chapter on sports, might include balls and bases with beeps or jingles so players can locate objects via sounds.

Examples of Assistive Technology Services

According to Public Law No. 100-107 (Technology-Related Assistance for Individuals With Disabilities Act of 1988), assistive technology service is defined as "any service that directly assists an individual with a disability in the selection, acquisition, or use of an assistive technology device." The following are examples of assistive technology services:

- Camps
- Computer programs
- The Internet

Camps. Assistive technology camps are increasing in popularity for individuals with disabilities. Numerous descriptions of camps can be found through Internet search engines.

> For example, Deavours (1997) described a computer camp that facilitates inclusion of children with disabilities through play opportunities. The camp encourages children with disabilities to bring a sibling or friend and involves children playing cooperatively, using alternative input devices when necessary. Groups of three children rotate through two play stations each day for 1 week including games, graphics, music, and story time. Each station has two computers and alternative input devices such as Intellikeys, keyguards, trackballs, switches, and touch windows to promote inclusive participation. Based on the demand for the program it seems that technology can offer a viable venue in recreation programming that enhances inclusive opportunities.

Camps, such as the one described above, can be designed for all individuals regardless of disability.

> For example, Thiers (1993b) described a computer camp for individuals with multiple sclerosis and their families and friends. The camp included a brief lecture and demonstration about computer technology, followed by practical usage. Computer adaptations such as key guards and enlarged keyboards are used.

Computer programs. Carey and Sale (1994b) described using portable computers to provide affordable inclusion for children with learning disabilities in a 3-year project with seven students with severe and multiple disabilities titled "Project FIT" (Full Inclusion through Technology).

> Apple Powerbook computers were chosen for their color capability, small space requirement, built-in speaker for voice and sound, portability, accommodation of numerous input devices, and the use of icons or audio for students with severe communicative and/or reading problems. Participants used single switch devices, trackballs, touch windows, joysticks, button switches, sensor switches, and sip and puff switches to access the technology.

Internet. The Internet provides a medium for interactions and participation in enjoyable activities. McGarry (1994) described the Internet as the largest electronic network in the world and as the World Wide Web. In addition to e-mail as a common resource, individuals subscribe to electronic mailing lists. Many lists store messages that allow users to search for information using a keyword, such as *cerebral palsy,* and retrieve information in seconds.

Online services can empower people to expand their world and decrease isolation by opening new avenues of social interaction and communication, provide a community where people are more interested in what is said than who is doing the saying, and allow people to present themselves equally regardless of looks, age, or voice (Green, 1994). Common items used for entering an online service include personal computer, modem, and a subscription to an Internet service provider.

Freeman (1997) emphasized advantages of older adults going online and explained that while the typical lifespan has increased and the aging process has not changed, many adults are living longer with physical problems associated with aging. As people age, they can become isolated from their community and family resulting in limited social interactions. The Internet is one way for people to deal with the decline in traditional communities.

> Examples of online usages could include researching interest areas, conversing with family and online friends, playing chess or the stock market, or using an online service such as the SeniorNet. SeniorNet is an organization designed to help people develop computer skills through its many training centers and to cultivate online communities for older adults where people can meet in designated places around interest areas.

To further illustrate online usage, Smith (1994) reported on the 300 e-mail responses from parents of individuals with various disabilities who shared their experiences with online support and information. According to Smith, responses were expressive of emotions and themes of close friends, family, and community when describing others that they met online. For many respondents, telecommunications provided their first contact with other similar families. Some expressed benefits of going online and communicating with individuals with similar disabilities, or with parents of children who are somewhat older yet similar in function to discuss the future of their children.

As the number of individuals with disabilities who use the Internet is increasing, more attention is paid to accessibility of web pages. The Rehabilitation Act Amendments of 1998 include Section 508, which requires that federal websites be accessible to individuals with disabilities. Many individual states have included similar laws that extend to state-funded facilities (Cunningham, Shelar, & Perry, 2007).

History

Prior to 1976, technology consisted of limited materials, tools, systems, and techniques associated with "microcomputers." In more recent years, there has been a decrease in cost and an increase in scale and scope of technology that provides individuals with disabilities with greater choice in relation to leisure, education, and employment (Vincent, 1989). Much progress in AT is due to the work of people with disabilities who have impacted legislation (Fine & Asch, 1988). The following legislative acts accelerated efforts to adapt technology so that all have equal opportunities in education, work, and recreation:

- IDEA: Individuals with Disabilities Education Act Amendments of 1997 (PL 101-476) and the Education for all Handicapped Children Act (PL 94-142)
- Rehab Act: Section 504 and 508 of the Rehabilitation Act of 1973 (PL 93-112) and its Amendments of 1986 (PL 99-506)
- Tech Act: Technology-Related Assistance for Individuals with Disabilities Act of 1988 (PL 100-407)

IDEA

The Education for all Handicapped Children Act (EAHCA) created accessible education and recreation for students with disabilities. The law has been revised many times over the years. One provision requires a mandated Individualized Education Plan for each child, to include consideration of AT devices and services, and to enable students to speak, write, and read in schools. The IDEA also mandates services and devices for infants and toddlers.

Rehab Act

Section 504 and 508 (amended in 1998) of the Rehabilitation Act of 1973 (reauthorized in 1992) mandates nondiscrimination in access to computers in colleges and equal access in any federally funded program. Section 504 resulted in more technology that included speech devices to enable independent access to federally funded programs. Section 508 of the Rehabilitation Act, requires that all electronic office equipment purchased by the federal government be usable by people with disabilities. According to the American Council on Education (1994), the computer industry has responded positively to Section 508 by producing and marketing more accessible computers for people with disabilities.

Tech Act

The most notable legislation that has led to advances in assistive technology is the Tech Act. This legislation is the first legislation act that has focused exclusively on making AT; it supports making such technology more readily available to people with disabilities (Fein, 1996). Administered by the National Institute on Disability and Rehabilitation Research, the Tech Act provides funding for states to implement consumer-responsive, comprehensive programs of technology-related assistance and access for people with disabilities of all ages.

> For example, low-interest to no-interest loans funded under the Tech Act are used to purchase technology that enables people with disabilities to leave home and drive to school or work. Also, information and referral programs are funded under the Tech Act.

Theoretical Foundations

Although the literature related to assistive technology does not consistently connect certain theories to practice or research, two theories seem relevant. Two theories that can provide insight into the usefulness of assistive technology include:

- Self-Efficacy
- Self-Determination

Self-Efficacy

Self-efficacy, one of the cognitive processes influencing behavior, pertains to peoples' belief in their ability to perform behaviors to achieve desired outcomes. Shary and Iso-Ahola (1989) stated that self-efficacy is affected by how people evaluate competence in their ability to successfully execute behaviors. Most research on change in cognitive structures involves self-efficacy. Shifts in a person's accessibility to information may lead to more enduring changes in that person's sense of self (Howard, 1995).

Research based on Bandura's (1986) theory of self-efficacy has found it to be an important cognition in health-related behaviors. Self-efficacy serves as a mediating or buffering role between stress and depression (Coleman & Iso-Ahola, 1993). Mannell and Kleiber (1997) stated that this expectation of individual control underlies motivation of many leisure behaviors and the degree of effort that people expend to achieve outcomes. Shary and Iso-Ahola (1989) suggested that TR can improve perceptions of self-efficacy, choice, and control. AT can enhance these perceptions by providing choice and control.

Self-Determination

Self-determination involves flexibility and ability to choose options (Deci & Ryan, 1985). Self-determination is affected by cognition, affect, and motivation and reflects an interaction between freedom and constraint (Mannell & Kleiber, 1997). When self-determination occurs, an increase in learning, perceived competence, and enjoyment results (Deci & Ryan). Assistive technology is one modality that can increase a person's perceptions of control and self-determination in live activity participation.

Assistive technology has the potential to increase a person's sense of self-determination (Dattilo et al., 2001). Testing efficacy of AT that could enhance self-determination will provide information necessary for developing strategies for enhancing concentration, effort, control, and competence, thereby fostering enjoyment (Broach, Dattilo, & McKenney, 2007).

> For example, grounded in the theory of self-determination Dattilo and Light (1993) examined effects of teaching significant others to promote communication with people with severe motor and speech impairments by using augmentative and alternative communications. The enhanced ability to engage in reciprocal communication increased communication and choices, and, therefore, the potential for leisure experiences.

Effectiveness

This section includes efficacy research that has examined:

- General Technology
- Switches
- Computers
- Virtual Reality
- Augmentative and Alternative Communication Systems
- Computerized/Video Games

General Technology

Hutinger, Johanson, and Stoneburner (1996) conducted a 2-year qualitative analysis of 14 children with multiple disabilities who had 2–10 years of use with AT. Technological usage, effects of usage, and barriers to usage were examined. Using direct observation and videotapes of participants, interviews and questionnaires with teachers and parents, and school records, the researchers found that by using assistive technology, the children accomplished cognitive and physical tasks previously not possible. The greatest improvement was in areas of social and emotional development.

> For example, one participant who acquired a speech device and computer participated in activities by telling jokes and communicating spontaneously with other children and adults. His family and teachers cited numerous benefits for him, including increased interaction, confidence, happiness, and ability to demonstrate abstract thinking.

While type of technology varied, teachers and parents reported that benefits from AT outweighed challenges associated with obtaining and maintaining equipment. Barriers included lack of staff competencies, ongoing reassessment, availability of software and maintenance, and lack of available equipment across settings.

Using open-ended, in-depth interviews and field observations, **Bell and Hinojosa (1995)** examined perceived impact of AT on three males with spinal cord injuries. Recurrent themes were identified that included the fact that mobility to participate in social and community leisure activities was important to their independence and freedom. Another theme was that active participation and use of simple devices influenced continued use of technology. Another valuable aspect of technology was that it increased free time and when technology was available they were less bored. A theme that emerged was that respondents wanted to engage in meaningful activities with support of technology. A final theme addressed was that technology influenced daily activities such as traveling, socializing, using a computer, playing the stock market, and using the telephone. Primary issues included importance of freedom, choice, independence, usefulness, and control. Assistive devices perceived as advantageous were simple, while complex devices were abandoned or modified. Therefore, complex and expensive equipment might not be better, it is important that the user be included in the entire process, and technology should be prescribed with community use in mind.

Summary. There was limited research found examining effects of general technology. Although research supports use of general technology as an effective intervention, since this research lacked adequate rigor, general technology has not yet been identified as an empirically supported facilitation technique. Nevertheless, these two studies indicate social and emotional gains important to daily work, school, and leisure activities of individuals with disabilities. For individuals in the studies, use of simple devices for adaptive technology was important to enhance their personal choice and control and, thus, increase their enjoyment.

Switches

Lancioni and colleagues (2006) used three students with profound multiple disabilities and provided microswitch programs as a TR intervention. Efficacy was determined by active engagement of manipulating the switch and mood. Mood was observed by instances of smiling and positive vocalizations or frowning and negative vocalizations such as crying. The study identified improvements in mood and an increase in switch manipulations.

Lancioni, Singh, O'Reilly, and Oliva (2005) searched for microswitch studies conducted between 1986 and 2005 to identify responses researchers used to determine switch activation. Switch activation included responses such as vocalizations, pushing with one or both hands, tapping with one or both hands, turning head, repeated eye blinks, etc. They were able to identify 48 research studies with 190 participants out of which 151 identified a positive outcome.

Stewart, Ormond, and Seeger (1991) examined effects of three techniques in training single-switch-activation on attention to task and task completion of nine preschool children (ages 4–7). Training techniques included: the Toy Control program that combines use of a computer with battery-powered toys, a battery-powered toy only program, and a computer program that provides only computer screen reinforcement. The Toy Control program is designed to teach single-switch scanning with a visual screen and activation of a battery-powered toy to reinforce performance. "Scanning" is used when a person is unable to point to an item to make a selection. While not significant, participants paid more attention to tasks in all conditions with the Toy Control program resulting in the greatest attention to task. There was a significant difference in attention to the reinforcer for each condition with the toys-only condition receiving most attention. No significant difference was found for task completion between three conditions. Findings supported use of a program such as the Toy Control program that integrates instruction via a computer with reinforcement potential of a toy, and use of toys with children with perceptual and cognitive difficulties to increase attention.

Williams and Matesi (1989) presented a case study of a boy (age 6) with athethoid-type cerebral palsy who lacked trunk stability and was unable to use his arms for purposeful activities. The boy used a radio-controlled toy truck adapted to encourage development of head and neck control, purposeful movement of the upper extremities, and performance of reaction time tasks. Although he had limited physical skills and had difficulty with speech, he had cognitive and receptive language skills at or above his age level. The truck was adapted so that he could control the toy's switch and speed. The toy was important in motivating him to work towards accomplishing therapeutic goals that included: improving stability, using accurate hand placement, making decisions using augmentative devices, and involving his family in instruction through home participation. He continued to use the device at home 10 months after the intervention ended, indicating adherence to engage in the enjoyable activity.

To assess choice within a specific leisure activity, **Dattilo (1988)** used a single-subject, multiple-baseline design across six conditions to examine application of a switch technology assessment procedure to determine music preferences of three children diagnosed with severe mental retardation who were nonverbal. After teaching participants to activate switches, six conditions were provided to give them a choice of two of four types of music (rock, classical, Christmas, and pop). The first phase consisted of computerized music, and the second phase used identical music from cassettes to determine whether the computer music provided a generalizable sample of the different types of music. As in the Gutierrez-Griep (1984) study, while individual preferences were different, there were specific preference patterns for each participant, demonstrating that switch technology can be used to establish preference patterns for individuals who have severe disabilities. This assessment procedure extended previous findings that used this technology to establish a preference hierarchy of visual, auditory, and tactile stimulation to include a preference profile related to music. This study supports use of switch technology to facilitate choice making to subsequently improve an individual's self-determined behavior and enjoyment through participation in a preferred activity.

Realon, Favell, and Davault (1988) used a single-subject withdrawal design across participants to evaluate effects of instruction on continued use of switch-operated leisure materials by 10 non-ambulatory and nonverbal individuals diagnosed with profound mental retardation. The leisure materials that included battery-operated toys, tape player, vibrating doll, and a racecar set were selected based on recommendations from staff, observed participant preferences, participants' habilitation plans, and, availability of items. Seven participants independently used switch-activated items after prompts and reinforcement were withdrawn. Five participants required demonstration of switch technique, and two of the remaining five participants required verbal prompts, positive verbal reinforcement, and physical guidance. Adapting leisure materials with switches is a cost-effective way of increasing independent leisure activity of individuals who are profoundly, multiply disabled. Using AT may permit more accurate assessment of abilities and preferences.

Wacker, Wiggins, Fowler, and Berg (1988) described three projects evaluating use of switches as a means for participants with profound and multiple disabilities to demonstrate preferences between toys and to make requests for specific activities. In the first project, five participants (ages 13–20 years), used switches to activate battery-powered toys. Two items were chosen for each participant from a selection of a tape player, a radio, and battery-powered devices that moved and made sounds. When participants exhibited target behaviors, a device remained activated and duration of the behavior was recorded. During treatment condition, when switches activated toys, all participants increased their duration of responding. Preference analysis may be considered a part of an active leisure skills program, since at the completion of this study, participants were independently and actively engaged in leisure activities. For most participants, this intervention was the first time they performed an activity independently and had reinforcers systematically identified for them. Thus, this project replicated previous studies that demonstrated switches can be used to identify reinforcers and that individuals can activate these independently as preferred leisure activities.

In the second project, **Wacker and colleagues (1988)** used switches to activate messages that signaled the instructor to attend to nine participants (ages 12–20) who were non-ambulatory and nonverbal and dependent on staff for care in order to evaluate their preferences for social attention. A condition where the audio tape with the teacher's name was played when participants emitted the target behavior was compared to a name-plus-attention condition where the teacher responded to participants with attention. By completion of treatment, social attention appeared to be reinforcing for eight of nine participants, and for seven participants it was more reinforcing than the name-only condition. Results suggested that participants are responsive to social environments, find social contact reinforcing, and can request attention.

In the third project by **Wacker and colleagues (1988),** participants used switches and messages to make requests. This study, conducted over 2 years, evaluated participants' requesting of specific activities rather than simply signaling for attention. Participants demonstrated activity preferences by using a switch and a tape recorder. Participants continued to use their switches in a shopping mall showing preferences for a restaurant, shopping, or ordering preferred drinks with a taped message. Participants requested reinforcers, specific attention, and activities. Application of switches were helpful in increasing self-determined behavior of individuals with profound and multiple disabilities.

Dattilo and Mirenda (1987) demonstrated application of an assessment procedure using the computer for determining leisure preferences of people with severe disabilities. A single-subject, multiple-baseline design across three participants and five leisure activity conditions (listening to music, watching videos, using a blender and drinking a milkshake, watching slides, and feeling vibrations from a pad) was used. Participants activated a computer program via a switch to choose between two of five leisure activities in five conditions. The information resulted in individualized leisure preference profiles for participants that were prioritized. The research demonstrated that leisure preferences can be assessed systematically for individuals who are nonverbal, who have severe multiple disabilities, and who use switches to select activities independently. This study applied a protocol that estimated leisure preferences more efficiently than Dattilo (1986) to produce a hierarchical ranking.

To further examine usages of switch technology, **Dattilo (1986)** investigated use of switch technology to determine preferences using a single-subject, multiple-baseline design across three participants with severe disabilities and three conditions: videos, songs, or vibrating pad. These conditions were initiated by pressing a switch to select between conditions. Each participant demonstrated specific but different preferences, indicating that preferences of individuals with severe disabilities can be systematically assessed and analyzed, thereby providing individuals with greater control in leisure activity selection.

Dattilo and Rusch (1985) used switches to determine effects of choice on leisure participation of four individuals with severe disabilities. A single-subject, multiple-baseline design across participants was used in three conditions that included: (a) contingent participation with choice, (b) non-contingent participation in the same activity without choice, and (c) a second contingent participation with choice. Mean scores for manipulating and attending to behaviors were higher in the third choice phase than during the no choice phase; these findings support the contention that once participants were given a choice, they participated more in the activity than when they did not have control. Implications include making previously determined reinforcers, such as watching television, contingent on manipulation responses of choice to facilitate active participation, attending, and control.

Wacker, Berg, Wiggins, Mulson, and Cav (1985) reported similar findings with five adolescents with profound and severe multiple disabilities. Each participant was provided with at least two sensory devices such as taped music and battery-operated games activated by mercury switches. The devices were presented one at a time and participants activated the devices by producing a designated motor response such as raising an arm or their head. Presentations of devices were counterbalanced across days and evaluation of preferences was conducted by recording frequency and duration of participants' responses. All participants displayed substantial increases in response duration when behavior resulted in activation of a sensory device. Participants performed differently across devices, suggesting they had preferences.

To examine choices related to leisure, Gutierrez-Griep (1984) used switch technology to identify sensory preferences of three boys with severe and multiple disabilities with a mean age of 6 years. The Electrical Leisure Activities program (McIntosh, 1982) was used to distinguish between passive sensory information and active controlling of reinforcers by turning them on or off. The intervention consisted of 20 reinforcement trials (4 x wk, 30-min sessions) when a timer automatically turned off reinforcement in 30-second intervals. Participants demonstrated individual sensory reinforcement preferences. The greatest change in behavior was associated with participants looking around less, self-stimulating less, and laughing more when the vibration began. Since sensory items can be rewarding and durable over time, it is helpful to base item provision on individual preferences. Switch technology that enables individuals to make choices might provide participants with satisfaction.

Fehr, Wacker, Trezise, Lennon, and Meyerson (1979) found that children with profound/multiple disabilities could be taught to use switches. Four children with profound and multiple disabilities were taught to activate three types of sensory stimuli (light, vibration, and sound) by touching microswitches. Motor responses of all four children increased substantially when switch-pressing resulted in specific stimulation. This study was one of the first indicating that sensory stimuli could reinforce behavior of people with profound disabilities, but also because it suggests that given the opportunity and appropriate adaptation, these individuals may independently select reinforcers resulting in greater control in activities.

Summary. There was an extensive amount of research found examining effects of switches that strongly indicates that switches are an empirically supported facilitation technique. Switches influence attention to task and task completion, purposeful movement, reaction times, opportunities for an expression of preferences of activities, request for social attention, hierarchy of preferences, adherence to activities, and duration in activity participation. While most studies were conducted with individuals who have developmental disabilities, these outcomes may have implications for all individuals with disabilities who have difficulty communicating preferences or performing tasks without use of switches. Adaptive switches can provide individuals with a chance to participate in challenging and stimulating activities.

Computers

In a case study, **Fisher (1996)** described a project that used computers for cognitive stimulation of older adults with dementia in adult day care. The purpose of this project was to provide practitioners with recommendations for computer usage in adult day care. Fisher found that to facilitate initiation and continued participation, it was important to: provide interesting, motivating, and cognitively demanding software; put the computer on a portable cart that routinely exposed the computer to participants, facilitating participants' curiosity and subsequent desire to use it; and create a group to introduce the computer to participants.

Howard, Greyrose, Kehr, Espinosa, and Beckwith (1996) examined ways computer activities can be used with children with disabilities to elicit behaviors that may occur during other play activities. Social play behaviors, social pretend-play behaviors, communication, and affect exhibited by young children participating in computer activities as compared with behaviors exhibited while they engaged in other types of play (3 x wk for toddlers, 15-min sessions and 5 x wk for 3–5-year-olds, 20-min sessions) were evaluated. Participants had speech and language delays, physical impairments, and/or cognitive impairments. The experimental group (22) attended two schools that routinely implemented computer activities, while the comparison group (15) enrolled in another school did not use computers. The comparison group engaged in supervised play with uniform sets of toys that matched topics addressed by the software programs. Using a modified version of the Peer

Play Scale (Howes, 1980), positive significant differences were found in social play, communication, and affect when comparing groups; however, there was no difference in amount of communication when not using the computer. When comparing non-computer activities of the group who had experience using the computer with similar activities for the comparison group who had not used the computer in activities, the comparison group was significantly less occupied and engaged in simple social play, less cooperative in social pretend-play, and less positive in affect than the experimental group during non-computer activities. This study has positive implications for use of AT to facilitate social pretend play with children who have multiple disabilities.

Buning and Hanzlick (1992) used a single-subject research design using multiple baselines across behaviors to compare traditional adaptations, such as the use of readers, to adapted computer technologies for typical reading activities performed by an adult with severe visual impairment. A computer using a speech synthesizer was paired with a page scanner to convert printed text into computer documents applied to three reading behaviors: proofreading of word-processed documents, reading of printed research articles, and reading common printed articles such as letters and instruction sheets. Use of AT, rather than traditional methods, increased participant's reading efficiency and frequency.

Summary. There was limited research found examining effects of computers. The research modestly indicates that computers are an empirically supported facilitation technique. Computers can be used to elicit social and pretend behaviors, communication, and positive affect in play activities of children with developmental disabilities, and to facilitate functional independence of individuals with visual impairment. Although more research is needed, use of computers may have positive implications for older adults with dementia for activity initiation and adherence.

Virtual Reality

Virtual reality (VR) is an emerging technology used for physical and psychosocial rehabilitation. A number of studies have been conducted using VR to examine improved life function of individuals with disabilities. This section will highlight a few of the studies that pertain to functional and leisure-related outcomes for varied populations.

Bryanton and colleagues (2006) asked 10 children (ages 7–17) with cerebral palsy and 6 without a disability to complete conventional ankle motor control exercises using a VR system that imbedded the child's image into an exercise scenario in a game format. Following each exercise, the child and parent indicated how interesting and fun the exercise was using a visual analog scale. Analysis provided physical outcomes for ankle position, time to complete each repetition, hold time, and number of repetitions. Although participants completed more repetitions during conventional exercises, range of motion, hold times, and enjoyment were greater during VR exercises. Using VR to guide exercises tended to improve compliance and enhance exercise effectiveness.

To test efficacy of VR for pediatric pain distraction, **Gold, Kim, Kant, Joseph, and Rizzo (2006)** used a VR program, *Street Luge* by Fifth Dimension Technologies, on a head mount display or standard topical anesthetic with 20 children (12 boys, ages 8–12) who required IV placement for a magnetic resonance imaging/computed tomography. Prior to participating, the children, their caretakers, and nurses completed standardized and non-standardized questionnaires related to anxiety, pain, sickness, and engagement. Responses from the Faces Pain Scale-Revised (Hicks, bon Baeyer, & Spafford, 2001) indicated a significant increase in affective pain for control conditions while no differences were detected in the VR condition. There were significant relationships between anticipatory anxiety, affective pain, IV pain intensity, and perceived pain. *Street Luge* was effective during IV placement as indicated by no VR simulator sickness and significantly greater child, nurse, and caregiver satisfaction as compared to the control condition. While this study demonstrated usability and effectiveness of VR pain distraction, further examination with larger samples are recommended.

You and colleagues (2005) examined effects of VR games on motor function of 10 people who had a stroke. Participants were assigned to a 4-week control or a VR group (5 x wk, 60-min sessions). The VR group provided practice environments where the skill parameters were individualized to enable appropriate challenge for motor relearning. Walking function was determined by the Standardized Functional Ambulation Category (FAC) and the walking item from the Modified Motor Assessment Scale (MMAS). The FAC examines assistance required during a walk without an assistive device and the MMAS is a 7-point performance-based scale that assesses walking ability. The VR system was IREX VR (Hedenberg & Ajemian, 2003). Stepping and snowboard games were used to facilitate range of motion, balance, mobility, stepping, and ambulation. There was a significant difference in the FAC and MMAS scores between groups. The VR may have contributed to positive changes in functional ambulation and associated motor functioning.

To address stroke survivors' difficulties resuming enjoyable leisure activities, **Farrow and Reid (2004)** conducted in-depth interviews with 16 participants (ages 49–86) after they engaged in a recreation VR program. Participants chose from VR applications, including sports such as volleyball and soccer and creative activities such as painting, dancing, and playing drums and general games. A constant comparative method of data analysis was used to identify four themes: doing and engaging, enabling competence, this has got me moving, and recommendations. The experience was described as a chance to participate in activities they missed or were unable to do in the usual manner. Participants described a sense of accomplishment, control, and ability to use cognitive skills. They felt the activity got them to move around because they typically participated in sedentary activities and viewed VR as a chance to participate in enjoyable activities. VR was felt to motivate and encourage participants to be challenged. Theoretical constructs considered important based on findings included experience flow and self-efficacy.

Weiss, Bialik, and Kizony (2003) examined effects of VR on five young adults with severe intellectual disabilities who were non-speaking, used wheelchairs for mobility, and had cerebral palsy during three games using the Gesture Xtreme VR system. While playing games the users see themselves on screen in the virtual environment and their movements direct completion of the task. Scenarios used included touching birds and balls, playing soccer, and snowboarding. The researchers hypothesized that increasing opportunities to engage in independent leisure activities would decrease learned helplessness. Participant responses to questionnaires showed a high level of focused attention in all VR scenarios and high enthusiasm during VR experiences. Participants indicated preferences for games and some goal-directed movements associated with games. With minimal instruction and practice, participants understood how to use the system.

Germann and colleagues (2001) examined effects of a software program that allows people to virtually visit a community facility, navigate through various scenes, and view short movies of the process. Thirty-four participants (21 males, ages 23–84) with varied physical disabilities were randomly assigned to a control group, VR group, and a leisure education-VR group. The VR group viewed the community center virtually prior to the on-site tour with staff providing instruction on how to use the computer program. The leisure education-VR group experienced the virtual tour facilitated by a TR specialist who guided them through a specific program process. Results indicated that participants who completed the virtual tour prior to visiting a new location demonstrated reduced anxiety. Participants in the leisure education-VR group showed greatest anxiety reduction.

Strickland, Marcus, Mesibov, and Hogan (1996) conducted a case study of two children (ages 7 and 9 years old) with mild to moderate autism to determine if they would accept VR equipment and respond to VR. The researchers assumed that (a) multiple sensory input problems can be addressed by designing less complex stimuli controlled by participants, (b) difficulty generalizing behaviors is addressed through realism of VR, (c) because individuals with autism are primarily visual VR may be useful for learning, and (d) VR can be individualized based on needs and skills. Using a ProVision 100 VR system, a program was used for crossing a street. One participant had 21 3–5-minute sessions over 7 days, while the other had sessions of shorter duration over 4 days. The two children tolerated use of helmets, became immersed in VR scenes enough to label objects and colors, moved their bodies in the VR scenes, and attempted to use hand controls. While results are not generalizable, this study supports use of VR to help understand perceptual processes of children with autism.

Summary. Research indicates the potential of VR to assist in improving physical, cognitive, and leisure experiences. Several studies that were predominately small group studies have been conducted using VR to effect change with individuals who have disabilities. However, it is recommended that TR specialists cautiously explore possibilities of VR to assist in treatment and leisure experiences of individuals with disabilities.

Augmentative and Alternative Communication (AAC) Systems

Using a multiple case study approach, **Salminen, Petrie, and Ryan (2004)** examined effects of an AAC system using a computer on daily activities and communication of six children with speech impairments. Interviews were conducted with children, their primary adult discussion partners, and their therapists. Videotapes showed that motivation to use devices declined over 3–6 months. Participants and discussion partners blamed poor device usability such as being too slow or too complicated to set up; however, the AAC was important and was used mostly for schoolwork and recreation such as drawing, playing games, teasing others, and writing messages, thoughts, and stories. For two participants, the devices facilitated play with siblings. While study design limits generalization, it was useful to discover participant and discussion partner perceptions of ACC.

Dattilo and colleagues (1995) conducted a survey to examine leisure patterns of children with disabilities such as cerebral palsy, mental retardation, and acquired brain injury that resulted in speech and language impairments and use of AAC systems. The Leisure, Communication, and Social Participation survey was administered to parents of 55 children with disabilities and their 35 siblings. While siblings had significantly greater diversity in leisure participation and social interactions, children with disabilities required significantly more assistance with leisure participation and choice in recreation activities. No differences were found in levels of enjoyment. While both groups desired leisure education, children with disabilities had significantly increasing diversity of recreation activities, choice-making, and independence in leisure and other life activities for individuals using AAC systems.

Using a single-subject multiple baseline design across participants, **Dattilo and O'Keefe (1992)** demonstrated effects of instruction in conversational control and social interaction with three participants diagnosed with moderate mental retardation who used AAC systems. Participants were instructed to take control of conversations by responding to initiations of others and then initiating conversation. During baseline, participants demonstrated little or no control. Immediate positive changes were observed for each participant's control over conversations during the intervention and were maintained in follow-up sessions. Social validation measures indicated that parents and caregivers perceived an increase in conversational control by participants. Although there is a need to extend this study, findings indicate promise for increased self-determination and leisure experiences through communication training.

To extend work of Dattilo and O'Keefe (1992), **Dattilo and Light (1993)** used a single-subject, multiple-baseline design across three dyads to examine effects of instructing adults to promote reciprocal communication with participants using AAC systems. Participants' significant others were instructed in four 1-hour sessions to decrease their conversational control and provide more opportunities for participants to communicate with devices. Frequency of initiations, responses, and communicative turns indicated increased reciprocity in interactions across dyads. Engaging in reciprocal communication increased participants' ability to communicate preferences and make choices. Findings identified the value of environments that are responsive to participants' communication attempts.

Summary. There was limited research examining effects of AAC systems on leisure participation. Research moderately indicates that AAC systems are an empirically supported facilitation techniques. AAC systems are beneficial for allowing individuals to increase diversity of recreation activities, choice making, independence in activities, conversational control, social interaction, reciprocal communication, and enjoyment. For individuals with speech and language disabilities, AAC seems to be a viable way to enhance opportunities for cognitive and leisure experiences.

Computerized/Video Games

McKenney, Dattilo, Cory, and Williams (2005) examined effects of a computerized leisure education program on four boys (ages 11–12 years old) with emotional or behavior disorders using a single-subject multiple probe design across participants to assess changes in social skills. The computerized intervention involved a woman who encountered environments that involved social interactions during recreation activities. When the woman encountered social situations, participants attempted to choose the correct social response for the woman. The game addressed skills such as paying attention, speaking at an appropriate volume, speaking at an appropriate speed, letting people know your thoughts, listening, assertiveness, and keeping appropriate distance with others. Improvement was assessed with social interaction scores improved across three participants upon initiation of the intervention and improved for the fourth later in the program. Five week follow-up scores were maintained for three participants. Findings indicated that participants learned about social skills and maintained this knowledge after instruction ended.

In another study of computerized leisure education, **Dattilo, Williams, and Cory (2003)** examined knowledge of social skills that included communication, verbal behaviors, initiating conversations, assertive behavior, and friendship, using a multiple baseline single-subject design across three participants (ages 6–15 years old) with moderate intellectual impairments. All participants improved their scores upon intervention initiation. Follow-up probes taken 9 weeks after the intervention ended showed participants' social skill knowledge was maintained. Findings support development, implementation, and research of computerized leisure education for youth with disabilities.

Dattilo and colleagues (2001) examined effects of a computerized leisure education program (Williams & Dattilo, 2000) on self-determination across four youth with disabilities ages 10–14 years old. The program involved a man confronted with 20 different situations that required self-determined behavior. Participants had to choose correct behavior that allowed the man to continue his journey. While immediate level changes on measures of knowledge of self-determination were not observed upon program initiation, accelerating trends and higher scores were observed for three participants during the intervention compared to baseline scores. After some intervention modification, the fourth participant showed improved scores. Follow-up scores 8 weeks after the intervention were maintained from intervention level. Results were consistent with research identifying the value of using computerized instruction to improve self-determination associated with leisure experiences.

To replicate and extend a previous study that found improved self-efficacy of participants (Maughan & Ellis, 1991), **Ellis, Maughan-Pritchett, and Ruddell (1993)** examined effects of: internal/stable verbal persuasion, external/unstable verbal persuasion, no persuasion, imagery of a successful experience, imagery of a failed experience, and no imagery experience on the self-efficacy of judgments, persistence at task, and score of a video game for adolescents with clinical depression. A social-cognitive theory was tested stipulating that persuasion attributions can have their greatest effects on an individual who can attribute success to self-ability and that vicarious experience such as mental imagery of success should enhance performance in a task. Ninety adolescent volunteers, ages 13–18 years old, were randomly assigned to a control group, a verbal persuasion group, or an imagery group. Internal persuasion resulted in significantly higher scores on self-efficacy, persistence to task, and game score than the other groups. Success imagery resulted in significantly greater self-efficacy than other groups. Attribution-based verbal persuasion might be a potent force in efficacy judgments. This study was important because it showed that a TR intervention using a social-cognition construct could positively effect self-efficacy and skill development.

Riddick, Spector, and Drogin (1986) examined effects of video game play on emotions and affiliating behavior of 10 nursing home residents (mean age 76) and 11 residents in a control group (mean age 78) using the Emotional States Scale and the Approach Avoidance Behavior Scale. Results revealed that opportunity to play a selected video game (3 x wk; 6 wks, up to 3-hr sessions) significantly increased arousal states and social interaction compared to the control group. Video games can improve at least one aspect of emotional well-being and social integration.

Schueren (1986) conducted a survey to examine perceptions of video games used by older adults in nursing homes. Areas examined included acceptance and reaction to the program, how many and how often residents used equipment, and analysis of residents most interested in and capable of participating. The activity managers submitted a weekly game evaluation (2 x wk, 40-min sessions). After reviewing reports by four nursing homes for 6 months, averages were calculated finding that approximately 15 residents with minimal cognitive impairments with varied levels of upper extremity ability participated. Although staff's initial attitude was negative, their reactions improved as participants successfully operated games and showed enjoyment. The staff stated that games could improve function as well as create a context for enjoyment. They stated that the games enhanced socialization, group interaction, friendly competition, and provided observer entertainment as well as improved eye-hand coordination, sensory stimulation, concentration, vestibular normalization, and kinesthetic and proprioceptive awareness. Equipment was adapted to address difficulties with vision, attention, and manipulation of controls, such as use of a large screen television, larger graphics, a well-lit room, giving simple and concise verbal instructions, and using a lapboard with Velcro surface to prevent joystick controls from slipping during one-handed play.

Summary. There was a moderate amount of research found examining effects of computerized games. Research modestly indicates that computerized games are empirically supported facilitation techniques. Research has been conducted with a variety of populations including older adults, individuals with physical and intellectual disabilities, and youth with emotional and behavior disorders. Numerous outcomes have been suggested from the use of computerized games in TR programs including eye-hand coordination, sensory stimulation, concentration, vestibular normalization, and kinesthetic and proprioceptive awareness. Computer games may have positive effects on self-determination and social skills.

Conclusion

There is extensive research examining effects of AT, especially switches. Existing research strongly indicated that use of AT is an empirically supported facilitation technique. There is evidence to indicate that AT has numerous physical and psychological benefits. Furthermore, AT can help to improve function, as well as maintain activity participation in daily life functioning. AT can result in increased function while participating in an enjoyable leisure activity in an inclusive environment. Because AT increases opportunities for self-determined behavior, challenges, self-efficacy, and enjoyment, TR specialists are encouraged to seek ways to enhance the lives of certain individuals with disabilities through this medium.

Case Studies

Deavours (1997) presented case studies to demonstrate how AT enhances leisure participation. In this section of the chapter three cases are presented which include Kathryn, an individual with cerebral palsy, Daniel, who has been diagnosed with amyotrophic lateral sclerosis, and Bryant, who has an acquired brain injury.

Kathryn

Kathryn is a 9-year-old girl who has spastic quadriplegia from cerebral palsy and an associated visual impairment. Kathryn uses a power wheelchair for mobility, which she operates with her right hand. She is assessed on a continuous basis for AT needs to enhance her leisure participation since 2 years of age. When Kathryn was ready to begin school, the TR specialist worked with the Individual Education Program team regarding her educational needs. Kathryn uses her power wheelchair, trackball, key-guard, word prediction, and a voice amplification device to participate in leisure activities such as playing computer games with family and friends, communicating with her teachers, playing wheelchair team handball, doing homework, and participating in class activities.

The TR specialist also uses VR based on Gesture Xtreme technology. Kathryn attended individual recreation therapy for 4 weeks (2 x wk, 90-min sessions). The virtual play environment provides Kathryn with an opportunity to increase play engagement and control over actions that resulted in improved self-efficacy. Kathryn's mother stated that AT increases Kathryn's proficiency, confidence, enjoyment, and length of time in activities.

Daniel

Daniel is a 36-year-old man diagnosed with amyotrophic lateral sclerosis for 10 years. He has been working with a TR specialist to increase his leisure participation. Daniel's disease has progressed and he is currently paralyzed. He uses a sip-and-puff device to control his wheelchair and also uses a single switch placed under his left index finger for computer access and speech.

Daniel states that AT enables him to rediscover activities from the past, such as hunting, where he uses a sip-and-puff system to activate a crossbow and rifle while using his communication device to call "gobblers." Daniel reported that one of his favorite activities is reading to and playing with his children. He described how he downloaded the story "Twas the Night before Christmas" from the Internet and read it to his children on Christmas Eve. He also cites activities such as playing cards and entertaining his son's friends with games such as "hangman" by using his computer.

Bryant

Bryant has an acquired brain injury from a motor vehicle accident 10 years ago, which resulted in spastic quadriplegia and cognitive processing difficulties. Bryant has been using AT for 2 years. Prior to using AT, Bryant used a communication board for his limited ability to communicate and was not independent in leisure activities. The TR specialist assessed his technology needs, recommended appropriate equipment, and trained him to use AT devices.

Since this assessment, the TR specialist works with him at home and on community outings to teach Bryant practical usage of his AT. Currently, Bryant uses Intellikeys, word prediction, and a track ball to access his computer. Prior to using AT, he had difficulties with communication. Bryant now speaks during all of his leisure activities including outings to the museum, zoo, movies, and dining out. He also utilizes the computer to play games and use the Internet to read the news, to access information, and to use e-mail. Bryant states that he uses his computer for all of his activities that he considers enjoyable.

Summary

These actual case studies describe three of many individuals who have benefited from AT used to enhance life functions. Kathryn benefited in school, sports, general communication, and through the ability to enjoy leisure activities with family and friends. Daniel used AT to continue participation in pre-disability activities. Bryant used AT to learn new activities since acquiring his disability as well as relearn communication skills necessary for pre-injury activities of interest. These examples illustrate a few of the many benefits of using AT in TR.

Intervention Implementation Exercises

A computer lab is recommended for these exercises. The exercises will encompass three areas of computer access needs of people with disabilities:

- Choose Accessible Software
- Explore System Access Features
- Access Alternative Input Devices

Choose Accessible Software

It is important to determine access needs of people with disabilities so their experience will be positive and successful. Software is carefully chosen to encourage exploration of new forms of computer input without requiring the user to be extremely accurate.

For example, when instructing an individual with quadriplegia to use a Head Mouse, beginning with word processing would not be useful, because click locations are extremely small and frequently require the user to drag or hold the button down and an on-screen keyboard. This experience would result in the user having to learn multiple new tasks, which the person may soon find overwhelming.

As another example, if participants with cognitive disabilities were being introduced to the computer, they may need exploration opportunities to learn how to track a mouse cursor and coordinate the skills of point and click.

It is recommended, regardless of the level of the user, that the first experience include software such as music or art. Generally, these offer open-ended exploration that do not test "right or wrong." In addition, art and music are appropriate for people of all ages. Many software programs have multiple levels of difficulty that enable the therapist to control how many choices are presented or change certain features.

Painting. Open a paint program and explore the tool and color palettes. Create the letter *M* with five dots. Now have your partner connect the dots with a mouse or alternative pointing device. Try "locking" the mouse button. How does this affect the skills required of the user? Experiment with colors, contrasts, line sizes, and tools.

Be a musician. Open a music program. Notice that moving the pointer enables anyone to be a musician. Experiment with instruments. Does the mouse button need to be locked or held down?

Explore System Access Features

Often solutions for access can be found within the operating system. Participants can learn how to access and use these features in treatment or instruction.

Use mouse keys. When this feature is activated, the cursor can be moved with the numeric pad of a mouth stick (pencil) to play a game such as solitaire.

Try slow keys or key delays. You have a client who types letters accidentally because he "bumps" keys in error when moving to press a target key. What access feature would help eliminate this problem? Answer: slow keys or key delay. This feature sets a delay on the acceptance time of the keystroke and ignores brief hits.

Use sticky keys. You are a one-fingered typist. This makes typing key combinations with modifier keys that require holding down more than one key simultaneously difficult. What access feature enables you to press these keys in sequence? Answer: sticky keys, because sticky keys allow the individual to go to a word processor and type.

Access Alternative Input Devices

These exercises are designed to demonstrate accessing the keyboard and mouse through alternative sources. The access devices can be acquired though local organizations that specialize in AT.

Try expanded keyboard. Using the expanded keyboard Intellikeys, use only one finger for access and experiment with the various overlays. What happens if you press a letter? Now put in the set-up overlay. What feature can fix this problem?

Try adapted trackball. You have two users of differing ability level. One can use only a switch and the other has no significant motor impairment. Use the adapted trackball and a switch to set up a cooperative activity.

Summary

The intervention implementation exercises can be used to increase understanding about use of computers as AT. Techniques of computer access are starting points for understanding possibilities of AT. Intervention techniques, such as those described in previous sections of this chapter, require modifications to meet needs of participants so that they access AT.

Conclusion

AT can enable individuals with disabilities to have more choice and enhanced opportunities for a variety of experiences. However, AT cannot, in isolation, provide solutions unless effective support is in place. It is essential that the needs and abilities of the individual are matched to the technology. Since many individuals who use AT desire leisure education services by a TR specialist, it is important that opportunities are provided to enhance leisure experiences of people using AT.

Discussion Questions

1. What is assistive technology (AT)?
2. Describe four AT devices.
3. Provide an example of an AT device used by a TR specialist.
4. According to research, what are six benefits of AT?
5. What legislation influenced development of AT services and devices?
6. What is the social-cognitive theory?
7. How may AT affect a person's self-determination?
8. Describe considerations for choosing a proper switch for an individual.
9. What are types of keyboard and monitor adaptations?
10. What is virtual reality and its relevance to AT and TR?

11. What are AAC systems?
12. How have video games been used to facilitate treatment outcomes?
13. Describe potential benefits of using switches, computers, and AAC systems.
14. What are some potential benefits of computer online services?

Resources

Websites for Assistive Technology Information

ABLEDATA: http://www.abledata.com

Adaptive Switch Laboratories, Inc: http://www.asl-inc.com

Administration on Aging: http://www.aoa.dhhs.gov

Age of Reason: http://www.ageofreason.com

Alzheimer Research Forum: http://www.alzforum.org

American Therapeutic Recreation Association: http://www.atra-tr.org

Apple Computer: Special Needs Curriculum: http://www.apple.com/education/solutions/accp/special_needs/

Center for Applied Special Technology (Universal Design): http://www.cast.org

Closing the Gap: http://www.closingthegap.com (Promotes the use of microcomputer technology for people with disabilities.)

Disability Access Symbols: http://www.gag.org/resources/das.php

Disability Information and Resources: http://www.makoa.org/index.htm (Please note: this is an individual's website, and as such, may move.)

Don Johnston Incorporated: http://www.donjohnston.com/

Disability Graphics: http://www.lareau.org/disgraph.html

Inclusion Press International: http://www.inclusion.com

International Association for Gerontechnology: http://www.gerontechnology.org

Lekotek of Georgia: http://www.lekotekga.org

Mental Health Infosource: http://www.cmellc.com/

Microsoft Enable: http://www.microsoft.com/enable

Our Kids (Internet resource information): http://www.our-kids.org/

SeniorCom: http://www.senior.com

SeniorNet: http://www.seniornet.org

Simplified Technology: Making Switches and simple assistive technology: http://www.lburkhart.com/

Stitchtime Accessable games and software: http://www.switchintime.com/

Therapeutic Recreation and Technology: http://www.recreationtherapy.com/trnet/trntech.htm

Trace Research and Development Center: http://www.trace.wisc.edu/world/web/index.html

Universal Usability Resource Center: http://universalusability.com/resources.html

World Wide Web Consortium Web Accessibility Initiative: http://www.w3.org/WAI/

Yahoo-Special Education Links: http://www.yahoo.com/education/special_education

References

American Council on Education. (1994). *Computers, technology, and disability.* Washington, DC: Department of Education.

Angelo, D. H., Kokoska, S. M., & Jones, S. D. (1996). Family perspective on augmentative and alternative communication: Families of adolescents and young adults. *Augmentative and Alternative Communication, 12,* 13–22.

Angelo, J., & Buning, M. E. (2002). High-technology adaptations to compensate for disability. In C. A. Trombly & M. V. Radomski (Eds.), *Occupational therapy for physical dysfunction,* 5th ed. (pp. 389–420). Philadelphia: Lippincott Williams & Wilkins.

Aukstakalnis, S., & Blatner, D. (1992). *Silicon mirage: The art and science of virtual reality.* Berkeley, CA: Peachpit Press.

Bandura, A. (1986). *Social foundations of thought and action: A social cognitive theory.* Englewood Cliffs, NJ: Prentice Hall.

Bell, P., & Hinojosa, J. (1995). Perception of the impact of assistive devices on daily life of three individuals with quadriplegia. *Assistive Technology, 7,* 87–94.

Bedini, L. A. (1993). Technology and people with disabilities: Ethical considerations. *Palaestra, 9*(4), 25–30.

Besio, S. (2004). Using assistive technologies to facilitate play by children with motor impairments: A methodological proposal. *Technology and Disability, 16,* 119–130.

Bingham, M. A., Spooner, F., & Browder, D. (2007). Training paraeducators to promote the use of augmentative and alternative communication by students with significant disabilities. *Education and Training in Developmental Disabilities, 42*(3), 339–352.

Brady, M., & Cunningham, J. (1985). Living and learning in segregated environments: An ethnography of normalization outcomes. *Education and Training in Mental Retardation, 20,* 241–252.

Broach, E., Dattilo, J., & McKenney, A. (2007). Effects of aquatic therapy on perceived fun or enjoyment experiences of participants with multiple dystrophy. *Therapeutic Recreation Journal, 41,* 179–200.

Bryanton, C., Bosse, J., Brien, M., McLean, J., McCormick, A., & Sveistrup, H. (2006). Feasibility, motivation, and selective motor control: Virtual reality compared to conventional home exercise in children with cerebral palsy. *CyberPsychology and Behavior, 9,* 123–128.

Buckley, T. J. (1993). Computer-assisted treatment in therapeutic recreation. *Palaestra, 9,* 31–39.

Buckley, T. J., & Smith, R. W. (1991). Arcade access: Pinball providing active recreation opportunities to persons with upper extremity impairment. *Palaestra, 2,* 40–45.

Buning, M. E., & Hanzlick, J. R. (1992). Adaptive computer use for a person with visual impairment. *The American Journal of Occupational Therapy, 47,* 998–1008.

Campbell, P. H., Milbourne, S., Dugan, L. M., & Wilcox, M. J. (2006). A review of evidence on practices for teaching young children to use assistive technology devices. *Topics in Early Childhood Special Education, 26,* 3–13.

Carey, D. M., & Sale, P. (1994a). Practical considerations in the use of technology to facilitate the inclusion of students with severe disabilities. *Technology and Disability, 3,* 80–86.

Carey, D. M., & Sale, P. (1994b). Notebook computers increase communication. *Teaching Exceptional Children, 3,* 62–70.

Chaffin, J. D., Maxwell, B., & Thompson, B. (1982). The application of video game formats to educational software. *Exceptional Children, 19,* 1973–1978.

Cook, A. M., & Hussey, S. M., (2002). *Assistive Technologies: Principles and Practice.* St. Louis: Mosby.

Coleman, D., & Iso-Ahola, S. E. (1993). Leisure and health: The role of social support and self-determination. *Journal of Leisure Research, 3,* 111–128.

Cory, L., Dattilo, J., & Williams, R. (2006). Effects of a leisure education program on social knowledge and skills of youth with cognitive disabilities. *Therapeutic Recreation Journal, 40,* 144–121.

Crows, J., & Deavours, M. (1993). Switch technology in therapeutic recreation programming: An idea whose time has come. *Palaestra, 9*(4), 41–44.

Cunningham, P., Shelar, D., & Perry, T. (2007, June). Tangled in the web: Creating an accessible web page can prove to be a winning opportunity for park and recreation departments. *Parks and Recreation, 42*(6), 45-48.

Dattilo, J. (1986). Computerized assessment of preference for severely handicapped individuals. *Journal of Applied Behavior Analysis, 19,* 445–448.

Dattilo, J. (1988). Assessing music preferences of persons with severe disabilities. *Therapeutic Recreation Journal, 2,* 12–23.

Dattilo, J. (2002). *Inclusive leisure services: Responding to the rights of people with disabilities, 2nd ed.* State College, PA: Venture Publishing, Inc.

Dattilo, J., & Barnett, L. A. (1985). Therapeutic recreation for individuals with severe handicaps: An analysis of the relationship between choice and pleasure. *Therapeutic Recreation Journal, 19,* 79–91.

Dattilo, J., & Camarata, S. (1991). Facilitating conversation through self-initiated augmentative communication treatment. *Journal of Applied Behavior Analysis, 24*(2), 369–378.

Dattilo, J., & Light, J. (1993). Setting the stage for leisure: Encouraging reciprocal communication for people using augmentative and alternative communication systems through facilitator instruction. *Therapeutic Recreation Journal, 27,* 156–169.

Dattilo, J., Light, J., St. Peter, S., & Sheldon, K. (1995). Parents' perspectives on leisure patterns of youth using augmentative and alternative communication systems. *Therapeutic Recreation Journal, 29,* 8–17.

Dattilo, J., & Mirenda, P. (1987). An application of a leisure preference assessment protocol for persons with severe handicaps. *Journal of the Association for Persons with Severe Handicaps, 14,* 306–311.

Dattilo, J., & O'Keefe, B. M. (1992). Setting the stage for leisure: Encouraging adults with mental retardation using augmentative and alternative communication systems to share conversations. *Therapeutic Recreation Journal, 26,* 38–47.

Dattilo, J., & Rusch, F. (1985). Effects of choice on leisure participation for persons with severe handicaps. *Journal of the Association for Persons with Severe Handicaps, 19,* 194–199.

Dattilo, J., Williams, R., & Cory, L. (2003). Effects of computerized leisure education on knowledge of social skills of youth with intellectual disabilities. *Therapeutic Recreation Journal, 37,* 142–155.

Dattilo, J., Williams, R., Guerin, N., & Cory, L. (2001). Effects of computerized leisure education on self-determination of youth with disabilities. *Journal of Special Education Technology, 16,* 5–17.

Deavours, M. N. (1997). A summer computer camp for children with disabilities and their friends. *Therapeutic recreation: Innovative programs in community recreation.* Arlington, VA: National Therapeutic Recreation Society, National Recreation and Park Society.

Deci, E., & Ryan, W. (1985). *Intrinsic motivation and self-determination in human behavior.* New York: Plenum Press.

Dugan, L. M., Campbell, P. H., & Wilcox, M. J. (2006). Making decisions about assistive technology with infants and toddlers. *Topics in Early Childhood and Special Education, 26,* 25–32.

Education for All Handicapped Children Act of 1975, Pub. L. No. 94-142, 89 Stat. 773 (1977).

Ellis, G. D., Maughan-Pritchett, M., & Ruddell, E. (1993). Effects of attribution-based verbal persuasion and imagery on self-efficacy of adolescents diagnosed with major depression. *Therapeutic Recreation Journal, 27,* 83–97.

Erwin, E. J., & Brown, F. (2003). From theory to practice: A contextual framework for understanding self-determination in early childhood environments. *Infants and Young Children, 16,* 77–87.

Farrow, S., & Reid, D. (2004). Stroke survivors' perceptions of a leisure-based virtual reality program. *Technology and Disability, 16,* 69–81.

Fehr, M., Wacker, D., Trezise, J., Lennon, R., & Meyerson, L. (1979). Visual, auditory, and vibratory stimulation as reinforcers for profoundly retarded children. *Rehabilitation Psychology, 26,* 201–209.

Fein, J. (1996). A history of legislative support for assistive technology. *Journal of Special Education, 13,* 1–3.

Fine, M., & Asch, A. (1988). Disability beyond stigma: Social interaction, discrimination, and activism. *Journal of Social Issues, 44,* 3–21.

Fisher, S. (1996). Increasing participation with a computer in an adult day care setting. *Activities, Adaptation and Aging, 8,* 31–44.

Freeman, B. (1997). Seniors on the internet: Implications for practice. *OT Practice,* May, 43–48.

Germann, C., Broida, J. K., Broida, J. M., & Thompson, K. (2001). Improving access using simulations of community resources. *Rehabilitation Services Administration* (Ed.), Washington, DC.

Goode, E. (1982). When video games can help out. *San Francisco Chronicle, 2,* (15), 16.

Gold, J., Kim, S. H., Kant, A. J., Joseph, M. H., & Rizzo, S. (2006). Effectiveness of virtual reality for pediatric pain distraction during IV placement. *CyberPsychology and Behavior, 2,* 207–212.

Grealy, M. A., Johnson, D. A., & Rushton, S. K. (1999). Improving cognitive function after brain injury: The use of exercise and virtual reality. *Archives of Physical Medicine Rehabilitation, 80,* 661–667.

Green, P. (1994). Getting started with telecommunications. *Exceptional Parent, 6,* 30–38.

Gutierrez-Griep, R. (1984). Student preference of sensory reinforcers. *Education and Training of the Mentally Retarded, 4,* 44–47.

Harris, K. (2005). The influence of virtual reality play on children's motivation. *Canadian Journal of Occupational Therapy, 72,* 21–29.

Hedenberg, R., & Ajemian, S. (2005). *IREX 1.3 Clinical Manual.* New York: Jestertek, Inc.

Hicks, C. L., bon Baeyer, C., & Spafford, P. (2001). The faces pain scale-revised: Toward a common metric in pediatric pain measurement. *Pain, 93,* 173–183.

Howard, J. A. (1995). Social cognition. In K. Cook, G. Fine, & J. House (Eds.), *Sociological perspectives on social psychology* (pp. 90–115). Needham Heights, MA: Allyn and Bacon.

Howard, J., Greyrose, E., Kehr, K., Espinosa, M., & Beckwith, L. (1996). Teacher-facilitated microcomputer activities: Enhancing social play and affect in young children with disabilities. *Journal of Special Education Technology, 1,* 36–47.

Howes, C. (1980). Peer play scale as an index of complexity of peer interaction. *Developmental Psychology, 16,* 371–372.

Hutinger, P., Johanson, J., & Stoneburner, R. (1996). Assistive technology applications in educational programs of children with multiple disabilities: A case study report on the state of the practice. *Journal of Special Education Technology, 13,* 16–35.

Individuals with Disabilities Education Improvement Act of 2004, 20 U.S.C. § 1400 et seq. (2004).

Kuhlen, T., & Dohle, C. (1995). Virtual reality of physically disabled people. *Computers in Biology and Medicine, 25,* 205–211.

Lancioni, G. W., Singh, N. N., O'Reilly, M. F., La Martire, M. L., Stasolla, F., Smaldone, A., & Oliva, D. (2006). Microswitch-based programs as therapeutic recreation interventions for students with profound multiple disabilities. *American Journal of Recreation Therapy, 5*(2), 15–20.

Lancioni, G. E., Singh, N. N., O'Reilly, M. F., & Oliva, D. (2005). Microswitch programs for persons with multiple disabilities: An overview of the responses adopted for microswitch activation. *Cognitive Process, 6,* 177–188.

Lane, S. J., & Mistrett, S., G. (1996). Play and assistive technology issues for infants and young children with disabilities: A preliminary examination. *Focus on Autism and Other Developmental Disabilities, 11,* 96–119.

Long, T., Huang, L., Woodbridge, J., Woolverton, M., & Minkel, J. (2003). Integrating assistive technology into an outcome-driven model of service delivery. *Infants and Young Children, 16,* 272–283.

Magee, W. L. (2006). Electronic technologies in clinical music therapy: A survey of practice and attitudes. *Technology and Disability, 18,* 139–146.

Mannell, R. C., & Kleiber, D. A. (1997). *A social psychology of leisure.* State College, PA: Venture Publishing, Inc.

Maughan, M., & Ellis, G. D. (1991). Effect of efficacy information during recreation participation on efficacy judgments of depressed adolescents. *Therapeutic Recreation Journal, 25,* 50–59.

McGarry, B. (1994). Cruising the internet. *Exceptional Parent, 6,* 39–44.

McIntosh, D. (1982). *Electrical leisure activities program, a training guide for teachers of the severely multiply handicapped.* San Diego: San Diego Unified School District Programs for the Handicapped.

McKenney, A., Dattilo, J., Cory, L., & Williams, R. (2005). Effects of a computerized therapeutic recreation program on knowledge of social skills of children and youth with emotional and behavioral disorders. *Annual in Therapeutic Recreation, 13,* 12–23.

Muscot, H. S., & Gifford, T. (1994). Virtual reality and social skills training for students with behavioral disorders: Applications, challenges, and promising practices. *Education and Treatment of Children, 17,* 417–434.

Olsen, F. (2000). Scholars in medicine and psychology explore uses of virtual reality. *Chronicle of Higher Education, 47,* A46.

Parette, P., & Brotherson, M. J. (2004). Family-centered and culturally responsive assistive technology decision making. *Infants and Young Children, 17,* 355–367.

Parette, P., Van-Biervliet, A., & Hourcade, J. J. (2000). Family-centered decision-making in assistive technology. *Journal of Special Education Technology, 15,* 1–35.

Realon, R. E., Favell, J. E., & Davault, K. A. (1988). Evaluating the use of adapted leisure materials on the engagement of persons who are profoundly, multiply handicapped. *Education and Training in Mental Retardation, 9,* 237–241.

Reid, D., & Campbell, K. (2006). The use of virtual reality with children with cerebral palsy: A pilot randomized trial. *Therapeutic Recreation Journal, 40,* 255–268.

Rehabilitation Act of 1973, Pub. L. No. 93-112, 87 Stat. 355 (1974).

Rehabilitation Act Amendments of 1986, Pub. L. No. 99-506, 100 Stat. 1807 (1989).

Riddick, C., Spector, S. B., & Drogin, E. B. (1986). The effects of video game play on the emotional states and affiliative behavior of nursing home residents. In F. McGurie (Ed.), *Computer Technology and the Aged* (pp. 95–107). New York: Hawthorne Press.

Riva, G. (1998). Modifications of body image induced by virtual reality. *Perceptual and Motor Skills, 86,* 163-170.

Ross, J. (2007). Computer accessibility part II: hardware. *American Therapeutic Recreation Association Newsletter, 23*(2), 5–8.

Ryan, E. B., & Heaven, R. K. B. (1986). Promoting vitality among older adults with computers. *Activities, Adaptation and Aging, 8,* 15–29.

Salminen, A., Petrie, H., & Ryan, S. (2004). Impact of computer augmented communication on the daily lives of speech-impaired children. Part I: Daily communication and activities. *Technology and Disability, 16,* 157–167.

Schneider, S. M., & Workman, M. L. (2000). Virtual reality as a distraction intervention for older children receiving chemotherapy. *Pediatric Nursing, 26,* 593–599.

Schueren, B. (1986). Video games: An exploration of their potential as recreation activity programs in nursing homes. *Activities, Adaptation and Aging, 8,* 49–58.

Sedlack, R. A., Doyle, M., & Schloss, P. (1982). Video games: A training and generalization demonstration with severely retarded adolescents. *Education and Training of the Mentally Retarded, 17,* 332–336.

Shary. J. M., & Iso-Ahola, S. E. (1989). Effects of a control-relevant intervention on nursing home resident's perceived competence and self-esteem. *Therapeutic Recreation Journal, 23,* 7–16.

Stewart, H. A., Ormond, C., & Seeger, B. R. (1991). Toy control program evaluation. *The American Journal of Occupational Therapy, 45,* 707–710.

Stoner, J. B., Parette, H. P., Watts, E. H., & Wojcik, B. W. (2008). Preschool teacher perceptions of assistive technology and professional development responses. *Education and Training in Developmental Disabilities, 43*(1), 77–91.

Smith, K., (1994). Parents online. *Exceptional Parent, 6,* 27–29.

Strickland, D., Marcus, L. M., Mesibov, G. B., & Hogan, K. (1996). Brief report: Two case studies using virtual reality as a learning tool for autistic children. *Journal of Autism and Developmental Disorders, 26,* 651–657.

Technology-Related Assistance for Individuals with Disabilities Act of 1988, Pub. L. No. 100-407, 102 Stat. 1044 (1990).

Thiers, N. (1993a). Virtual reality: High tech help for rehab. *OT Week,* August, 14–16.

Thiers, N. (1993b). Computer camp exposes people with MS to technology. *OT Week,* June 19–22.

Vincent, T. (1989). *New technology, disability, and special education needs. Working together?* Paris, France: Organization of Economic Cooperation and Development.

Wacker, D., Berg, W., Wiggins, B., Mulson, M., & Cav, J. (1985). Evaluation of reinforcer preferences for students with profound multiple handicaps. *Journal of Applied Behavior Analysis, 18,* 173–178.

Wacker, D., Wiggins, B., Fowler, M., & Berg, W. (1988). Training students with profound multiple handicaps to make requests via microswitches. *Journal of Applied Behavior Analysis, 21,* 331–343.

Weiss, P., Bialik, B. A., & Kizony, R. (2003). Virtual reality provides leisure time opportunities for young adults with physical and intellectual disabilities. *Cyberpsychology and Behavior, 6,* 335–342.

Wilcox, J. M., Gulmond, A., Campbell, P. H., & Moore, H. (2006). Provider perspectives on the use of assistive technology for infants and toddlers with disabilities. *Topics in Early Childhood Special Education, 26,* 33–49.

Williams, R., & Dattilo, J. (2000). Og [Computer software]. Athens: University of Georgia.

Williams, S. E., & Matesi, D. V. (1989). Therapeutic intervention with an adapted toy. *American Journal of Occupational Therapy, 45,* 673–677.

Yang, H., & Poff, R. (2001). Virtual reality therapy: Expanding the boundaries of therapeutic recreation. *Parks and Recreation Magazine,* May, 53–57.

You, S. H., Jang, S. H., Kim, Y., Hallet, M., Ahn, S. H., Kwon, Y., Kim, J. H., & Lee, M. Y. (2005). Virtual Reality - Induced cortical reorganization and associated locomotor recovery in chronic stroke. *Stroke, 36,* 1166.

Chapter 6
Expressive Arts as Therapeutic Media

Mary Ann Devine

Art is the only way to run away without leaving home.
—Twyla Tharp

Introduction

"Expressive Arts uses five art disciplines to assist individuals to make contact with his/her authentic self" (Arts in Therapy Network, n.d., 2007). These mediums can be used as therapeutic interventions by TR specialists to promote nonverbal communication of feelings as well as improve physical, social, cognitive, and emotional functioning (Magee & Andrews, 2007). The goal of using expressive arts as therapeutic media is to improve participants' functioning, self-expression, and quality of life (Kellman, 2005).

This chapter introduces the reader to the use of expressive arts in TR. Included in this chapter is a definition, description, and history of use of expressive arts as therapeutic media. Primary theories from which to base the use of expressive arts as therapeutic media and a review of relevant literature provide further information on cognitive, behavioral, and emotional concerns addressed through the use of visual art interventions. A case study is presented as an example of how one form of expressive art may be planned and implemented in a TR setting. Finally, exercises and discussion questions are offered to further the reader's understanding of use of expressive arts as therapeutic media.

Definitions

There are a variety of terms associated with expressive arts as a therapeutic media. The following terms are described in this section:

- Expressive art activity
- Expressive art therapies
- Expressive art as a therapeutic media

Expressive Art Activity

Expressive art activity includes use of several different techniques with the intent to produce and achieve a final product (Silver, 1989). According to Silver, the purpose of an expressive art activity is to master the craft of the art. Involvement in expressive arts, whether through playing music, acting out a favorite scene, or sketching a landscape, can be enjoyable, relaxing, and challenging. Expressive arts can also provide a sense of accomplishment, a path for self-expression, or fulfillment of personal satisfaction. People may find expressive art activities private, contemplative, exhilarating, and liberating (Anderson, 1994).

While most expressive art activities have some therapeutic qualities, the primary purpose of art activity is to learn a craft or produce and achieve a final product (Drummond, 1990). The distinguishing characteristics of expressive arts as activity are the aesthetic uses of art to promote independent functioning instead of the more therapeutic process of using art to treat disorders. Use of expressive arts as therapeutic media have been used primarily to improve cognitive, physical, social, and emotional functioning as well as to promote various forms of art as a means for self-expression and leisure experiences for people with disabilities (Ludins-Katz & Katz, 1990).

Expressive Art Therapies

According to Essex (2006), expressive art therapies are defined as a process by which visual arts, music, dance, poetry, or drama are used to treat mental, social, emotional, and physical illnesses. Sausser and Waller (2006) noted the abilities of expressive art therapies as useful in promoting verbal and nonverbal communication of feelings.

The aim of each art therapy is to use methods that promote a therapeutic relationship where participants can be involved in their healing through use of various art forms (Essex, 2006). According to Troeger (1992), the various expressive art therapies have their roots in psychology and have been used to treat psychological disorders, sexual abuse, and neurological dysfunction.

Expressive Art as Therapeutic Media

Use of expressive art as therapeutic media merges the process of creating art and needs of the person with the final product (Sausser & Waller, 2006). According to Broudy (1984), expressive arts are used as therapeutic media when the purpose of using arts is to promote change in individuals. Individual changes may include improvements in cognitive, physical, emotional, or social functioning (Uhler, 1979). The process is therapeutic in that it is multi-sensory, involving sensory, motor, and cognitive skills (Arts in Therapy Network, n.d., 2007).

Primary considerations for involving people with disabilities in expressive arts are needs of the individual. Needs of the individual are assessed and addressed through clear treatment goals. Expressive arts are applied through a process of creating art to meet treatment goals and the needs of the person (Essex, 2006). Expressive arts as therapeutic media involve use of visual arts, music, dance, drama, and poetry to improve an individual's cognitive, physical, social, and emotional functioning (Dalley, 1984).

Descriptions

Depending on needs of the individual, expressive arts can be used as media to promote self-expression, develop muscular and motor movements, advance learning of language skills, facilitate learning of problem-solving skills, practice choice-making skills, or provide a context for empowerment (Corbett, 1999). In using expressive arts, individuals are first instructed and guided in development of visual art, musical, dance, and dramatic skills, and then offered the opportunity to practice these skills.

Descriptions of each type of expressive art skills that can be used as interventions are too many to discuss in this chapter. The reader is referred to the resource section at the end of this chapter for information that may offer techniques on developing various expressive art skills. Descriptions of expressive arts as therapeutic interventions in this chapter are limited to general descriptions of how the following expressive arts categories may be used as interventions:

- Visual Arts
- Music
- Dance
- Drama
- Poetry

Visual Arts

Visual arts are defined as the formation of visual art products using various art materials and artistic technical knowledge (Waller & Gilroy, 1992). According to Waller and Gilroy, examples of visual art products are paintings, drawings, sculptures, ceramics, crafts, pottery, and glassware. Artistic materials can include paint, chalk, canvases, marble, clay, and glass (Atack, 1980). Examples of artistic technical knowledge include application of paint to a canvas, molding of clay, carving of marble, or blowing of glass.

Visual arts as therapeutic media can be defined as the use of creating visual art products to bring about improvements in physical, social, cognitive, or mental functioning, self-expression, and leisure experiences of people with disabilities (Anderson, 1994). In contrast to art as therapeutic media, the American Art Therapy Association defines *art therapy* as use of visual methods of communicating conscious and unconscious thoughts and feelings to diagnose and treat illness and conditions (Jennings & Minde, 1993).

Use of visual arts as therapeutic media is based on the premise that by adapting, teaching, and using visual art skills, an individual's physical, cognitive, emotional and mental functioning, self-expression, and meaningful leisure experiences may improve (Anderson, 1994). Visual arts can be used as a means to help participants recognize, identify sources of, and come to terms with their feelings (Arts in Therapy Network, n.d., 2007). These forms of art can be used in a psychotherapeutic environment with the purpose of self-disclosure. Visual arts are used by adapting, teaching, and offering the opportunity to use painting (see Figure 6.1 on p. 156), drawing, and sculpting skills (Silver, 1989).

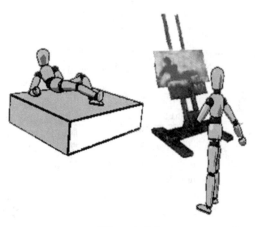

Figure 6.1

Atack (1980) suggested that painting may be used as a therapeutic medium by adapting and teaching various ways an individual may apply paint to paper, canvas, or objects.

> For example, paint may be applied by using brushes or sponges of various sizes or textures. In addition to various tools that may be used to apply paint, painting techniques may also be adapted. Specific adaptation techniques can include enlarging the grip on a paintbrush, placing paper or canvas on a slanted surface such as a drafting table, using larger pieces of paper or canvas, or using a variety of materials for a painting surface such as stone, fabric, or wood. Techniques may also be adapted such as the use of up and down or right-to-left strokes, dabbing or blotting motions, and swirling or figure-eight motions.

Silver (1989) recommended that by using various sculpting substances, sculpting could be used as a therapeutic medium.

> For example, lightweight substances such as paper, foam board, or fabric may be used with individuals who have arthritis and may have difficulty using heavy materials. In addition, tools used to create visual arts can be adapted by enlarging the handles with fabric, using Velcro to secure tools to an individual's hand, or using a helmet to secure a brush to the front of an individual's head (Anderson, 1994).

Photography can also be considered a visual art (Koretsky, 2001). Traditional film photographs can be used as a therapeutic medium, by focusing on certain subjects for self-disclosure purposes or using adaptive equipment such as tripods with shutter extension devices. Digital photography is a versatile use of photography as it can be downloaded and saved on a computer or printed for framing.

Music

Music is the ordering of sounds and tones in succession and combining sounds and tones with a tempo to produce a musical composition (Allen & Allen, 1988). Sounds can be vocal, instrumental, or mechanical, and should be produced with rhythm, melody, and harmony (Sherrill, 1979).

According to Arts in Therapy (Arts in Therapy Network, n.d., 2007), use of *music as therapeutic media* includes techniques such as singing, playing, or listening to music, as well as composing music. The purpose of music as therapeutic media is to address individualized objectives such as increasing language skills, promoting pro-social behavior, expressing emotions, gaining self-control, and improving gross and fine motor functioning.

According to Allen and Allen (1988), to use music as therapeutic media, adaptations may be made to equipment, instruments, techniques, or procedures so an individual can listen to music, play an instrument, sing, or participate in a band. Adaptations are based on the purpose and intended outcome in relation to the needs of the individual (Sherrill, 1979).

The American Music Therapy Association defines *music therapy* as the systematic study and use of music to address physical, cognitive, emotional, and social needs of individuals with disabilities of all ages. Music therapy can promote communication, emotional health, wellness, stress management, pain reduction, emotional expression, and memory retention (Magee & Andrews, 2007).

Listening to music has been used as a means to reduce stress, relieve depression, and increase relaxation with people before and after operative time periods (Allen & Allen, 1988). Sherrill (1979) reported that singing songs could be used with children with mental retardation to improve recall and memory. Allen and Allen discussed the use of music to assist someone in regaining a sense of self, following an accident.

> Tony, a 51-year-old man who had a stroke which resulted in hemiplegia, played the piano prior to his stroke. When he thought he could no longer play the piano because of the loss of the use of his right hand, Tony felt that he lost a sense of himself. After learning to play musical pieces designed for people who have the use of only one hand, Tony felt that he had a way to express his creativity.

Dance

In TR dance can be used as an expressive art or as therapeutic media. *Dance as an expressive art* is defined as rhythmic and patterned bodily movements performed with or without music (Lewis, 1984). For dance to occur, bodily movements must not only be rhythmic and patterned, but carried out in specific sequences and within specified time frames (Allen & Allen, 1988).

Dance as therapeutic media is use of movement to bring about improvements in physical, social, cognitive, or mental functioning, self-expression, and leisure experiences of people with disabilities (Arts in Therapy Network, n.d., 2007).

In contrast to dance as therapeutic media, *dance therapy* is defined by the American Association of Dance Therapy (n.d., 2009) as "use of movement experiences which guide a client to work, to feel, to find the source of his or her inner problems, to uncover his or her unconscious attitudes and feelings and find new life action" (p. 12). According to Hopkins (2007), dance therapy is the observation and analysis of kinesthetic movement and body language. Following an observation, a dance therapist conducts a debriefing with the person to verbally process the psychodynamics of the movements.

Allen and Allen (1988) suggested that a wide variety of dances, such as folk, jazz, ballet, or modern dance, can be used as therapeutic media. Use of dance in this way requires adapting and teaching bodily movements in a specific sequence and then timed to music (Hopkins, 2007).

> Adaptations may include reducing or expanding the size of the dance area, simplifying dance steps, marking the dance floor with tape to indicate a specific sequence, or modifying dance steps for a wheelchair user (Lewis, 1984).

Bojner Horwitz, Kowalski, Theorell, and Anderberg (2006) suggested that dance as therapeutic media is used to improve physical functioning, self-expression, social skills, or cognitive functioning.

> For example, by using repetitive movements or movements familiar to individuals with cognitive disabilities, dance may be used to improve recall and sequencing skills.

Dance assists people with disabilities in understanding themselves and the world in which they live by serving as an outlet to express fears, dreams, desires, and joys through rhythmic body movements (Ludins-Katz & Katz, 1990).

> As an example, Allen and Allen (1988) discussed how "Ed," a 17-year-old man with spina bifida, break dances to show his joy outwardly by using his crutches to spin around, do handstands, and swing back and forth.

Drama

Drama is defined as a process of enactment that tells a story or portrays a character (Landy, 2006). According to Lewis and Johnson (2000), drama involves a creative process that expresses a tale or story. The distinguishing characteristic of drama is that it contains an element of being *unreal* that requires people to behave or act as someone other than themselves or treat the present time frame as if it was not the present (Landy, 2006). Examples of drama include play or character acting, storytelling, mime, improvisations, or puppetry (Allen & Allen, 1988).

Drama as therapeutic media can be defined as the use of acting, storytelling, mime, improvisations, or puppetry to assist in the social, cognitive, imaginative, and physical improvements of people with various disabilities (Landy, 2006). *Drama therapy* is defined by the National Association of Drama Therapy (National Association for Dance Therapy, n.d., 2007) as the systematic and intentional use of drama or theater processes and/or products to achieve therapeutic goals. Theatrical techniques can be used to facilitate personal growth and promote health. It can involve role-play, theater games, mime, puppetry, and improvisational techniques.

Drama as therapeutic media can include play or character acting, storytelling, mime, improvisations, or puppetry (Jennings, 1997). Drama involves thinking, feeling, and behaving in a way that communicates a certain message, image, time frame, place, character, mood, or atmosphere that allows the person to act in "theatrical reality" rather than what the person experiences in everyday reality (Landy, 2006). According to Landy, *theatrical reality* refers to thinking, feeling, and behaving in ways that reflect characters, time frames, or themes not currently a part of the person's reality.

Play and character acting, storytelling, mime, improvisations, or puppetry can be used as therapeutic media by adapting dramatic techniques, modifying dramatic sequences, using repetition to teach dramatic techniques, reducing or enlarging props such as puppets, or reducing the size of a group. The following section contains a description of:

- Play and character acting
- Storytelling
- Mime
- Improvisation
- Puppetry

Play and character acting. Play and character acting is a form of portraying an image of others. Individuals who participate in play and character acting assume roles of others in a way that is non-threatening (Jennings, 1997).

> For example, an individual may play the role of Captain Hook, but the evil nature of the character is done in a non-threatening way.

Landy (2006) recommended using character acting and identifying specific emotions so as to act out anger and decrease aggressive behaviors of children with emotional disabilities. People with cognitive impairments may improve recall, social, and language skills through use of play acting that involves a simple script and repetition of script lines (Jennings & Minde, 1993).

Storytelling. Storytelling involves communicating scenarios to others in an orderly, systematic, and logical manner (Lewis & Johnson, 2000). Storytelling allows participants to increase communication skills through language development, often using verbal communication, gestures, movements, and visual aids to express and add to the effect of the story (Hoffman, 1992). It can also improve listening skills, comprehension, and attention to detail.

> Examples of storytelling include the telling of personal stories, folk or fairy tales, moral or religious stories, and historical stories (see Figure 6.2 on p. 160).

Figure 6.2

Mime. Mime (or pantomime) is a way to speak without words, using body move-ments to transmit ideas (Hoffman, 1992). Individuals who participate in mime express thoughts and feelings by using bodily movements that can range from large, explosive movements to small, subtle ones. Mime is similar to play or character acting, in that the participant assumes a role; however, a necessary element of the mime role is nonverbal communication and use of body language to tell the complete story (Lewis & Johnson, 2000).

Improvisation. Improvisation allows individuals to solve a problem by beginning with no preconception as to how it will be done (Fuller, 1979). Improvisation can be used when a therapist attempts to interpret the verbal or nonverbal messages conveyed by an individual during improvisation. According to Jennings (1997), this requires a therapist who is specially trained to analyze improvisations, a method that is different from using improvisation as therapeutic media. Use of improvisation as therapeutic media can apply simple actions such as playing a card game or ice-skating to inspire self-expression.

Puppetry. Puppetry is a form of drama that involves incorporating use of puppets and can be performed for audiences that include both adults and children (Landy, 2006). Puppetry allows individuals to disguise themselves and often provides people who are shy with a means of non-threatening self-expression (Bailey, 1993). Puppets can also be used to enhance social and language skills and hold the attention of children (Gerber & Gerber, 2003). In addition, the puppeteer can become both the character and the audience while creating and observing the puppet character.

> Different types of puppets include finger puppets, hand puppets, rod puppets (puppets on a stick or rod), combination hand-and-rod puppets, and marionettes.

Shadow puppetry is another technique that can incorporate puppets to make shadows for the audience to view instead of the puppets themselves. Individuals can design and make puppets that allows for self-expression, use of fine motor and eye-hand coordination skills (Lewis & Johnson, 2000).

Another example of the use of puppetry as therapeutic media is to use lightweight puppets with children with muscular dystrophy to improve strength and range of motion.

Poetry

Poetry is a new and burgeoning area of expressive arts that can be used in TR interventions. Mazza (1999) defined *poetry therapy* as use of language arts in therapeutic capacities. It can be described as language that relies on image, rhythm, evocative language, and often metaphor within the framework of patterned structures (Furman, Collins, Langer, & Bruce, 2006). Poetry is often used by writers to express the relationship between their internal and external worlds (Hennessy, 2004).

Poetry has a history in mental health as a tool for expression of emotions including anger and frustration (Corbett, 1999). Poetry as a therapeutic medium can include bibliotherapy, narrative, and metaphoric use of language. These media can be used with individuals who experience difficulty with verbal communication as a way to assist them with self-expression.

> For example, writing poetry can be a way for someone who has had a traumatic brain injury and can no longer speak to express his or her feelings.

Davis (1997) recommended using poetry to create a sense of belonging. Davis reports that poetry provides a forum for a dialogue between community members with and without disabilities through which people get to know each other better.

> For example, Cisco, an adolescent with a cognitive impairment, was able to express the hurt he felt when his peers excluded him in their physical education class through writing poetry. He was able to bridge the gap between himself and his peers that resulted in inclusion.

Health care providers may be able to improve their knowledge, extend their empathy, and possibly develop better treatment interventions by reading poetry written by people they are treating.

> Specifically, professionals working in the field of mental health found they were better able to understand mental illness by reading poetry written by their patients with mental health disorders (Furman et al., 2006).

According to Furman and colleagues, practitioners need to understand the lived experiences of their clients to design appropriate interventions that account for complexities of their lives. Insights gained from non-traditional sources, such as reading their clients' poetry, may be valuable ways to learn about their lives.

Summary

Art activity involves use of specific materials and techniques to produce visual, musical, dance, or dramatic products (Sausser & Waller, 2006). The purpose of participation in a particular expressive art is the primary distinguishing factor between art activity and expressive arts as therapeutic media. According to Landy (2006), addressing specific therapeutic needs of a person is the primary purpose of using expressive arts as therapeutic media, whereas the product or outcome is the primary purpose of art activity. Expressive arts as therapeutic media differ from art therapy because they do not involve diagnosis of an illness.

While expressive arts as therapeutic media and art therapy use various forms of art as interventions, art therapy is primarily concerned with diagnostic or psychoanalytical aspects of interventions (Lewis & Johnson, 2000). Expressive arts as therapeutic media employ use of visual arts, music, dance, and drama with the intent of improving cognitive, physical, social, and emotional functioning (Essex, 2006). In addition to improving functioning, expressive arts as therapeutic media may be used to facilitate expression of thoughts and feelings of people with disabilities.

Individuals with disabilities may benefit from improved verbal skills, enhanced self-expression, or an expanded leisure repertoire. By applying expressive arts in a systematic manner, consistent with goals and objectives designed to meet needs of the individual, expressive arts can be used as therapeutic media (Magee & Andrews, 2007). Using expressive arts as therapeutic media can serve as a way to meet individuals' functional, expressive, and leisure needs.

History

Expressive arts as therapeutic media evolved as a result of viewing art as a way to facilitate positive changes in the physical, social, and emotional functioning of a person with a disability (Anderson, 1994). Use of expressive arts as therapeutic media is thought to have evolved from art therapy (Waller & Gilroy, 1992). Initially, art therapy was used in institutional settings as a diverting activity to assist people in passing time (Reynolds, 1993). Jennings and Minde (1993) noted that art therapy began before World War II, when a group of artists and psychiatrists initiated an interest in more diagnostic uses of art.

According to Reynolds (1993), in the 1930s, institutional personnel became increasingly aware of benefits of recreation, including art, for people with disabilities. For example, a 1930 White House conference on child health protection generated interest in the use of recreation, and art in particular, for people with mental retardation to improve functional skills necessary for community living (Anderson, 1994).

During the 1940s and early 1950s, World War II spurred use of art as therapeutic media in military hospitals (Reynolds, 1993). Jennings and Minde (1993) noted that a pioneer in use of art as therapeutic media was Adrian Hill, an artist from Great Britain. During World War II, Hill first used painting to relieve boredom of military personnel who were convalescing and then used it as a way to facilitate expression of fears and feelings of living with a disability (Jennings & Minde). Reynolds (1993) stated that during World War II military hospital personnel recognized that art activities, as well as other leisure activities, learned by people who were convalescing, could be used to develop skills useful after discharge. It was then that the focus broadened from offering diverting activities to facilitate positive changes in the physical, social, and emotional functioning of a person with a disability (Anderson, 1994).

The 1960s and 1970s were periods that markedly influenced the provision of leisure services, including art, for people with disabilities (Reynolds, 1993). The passage of the Rehabilitation Act of 1973 (29 U.S.C. 701-796) and the Education for All Handicapped Children Act of 1975 (PL 94-142) by federal legislators were among the most influential factors of this era (Anderson, 1994). The Rehabilitation Act of 1973 prohibited discrimination of otherwise qualified people with disabilities, on the basis of their disability, from participation in or benefits of programs and activities receiving federal funding. The Education for All Handicapped Children Act of 1975 required that education and supportive services be conducted in the least restrictive environment and be appropriate to the needs of children with disabilities.

These laws primarily influenced extension of expressive arts as therapeutic media to include people with disabilities. Inclusion in expressive arts related to leisure and educational services facilitates and promotes self-expression as well as the expression of a leisure lifestyle by individuals with disabilities (Sherrill, 1979).

In 1990, the Americans with Disabilities Act (ADA) (PL 101-336) was signed into law, prohibiting discrimination of people with disabilities in school, community settings, and the workplace. The ADA extended the provisions outlined in the Rehabilitation Act of 1973 by prohibiting discrimination of people with disabilities by public and private organizations.

The Education for All Handicapped Children's Act (PL 94-142) was reauthorized in 2004 as the Individuals with Disabilities Education Act (IDEA) (PL 101-476). Under the provisions of IDEA, children with disabilities are entitled to a free and appropriate education in the least restrictive environment.

Together these laws enforce a nondiscrimination policy toward people with disabilities in school, community, and employment settings. Implications of these two laws further extended the use of expressive arts as therapeutic media to include participation in school and community settings by ensuring that individuals: learn and use art skills in community and school-based art programs, receive modifications to art-related equipment to increase their inclusion, and participate in art activities alongside peers without disabilities. Expressive arts can be used in a variety of rehabilitation, school, and community settings to facilitate achievement of functional objectives and promote healing and health.

Summary

Expressive arts as therapeutic media began as a way to facilitate positive changes in the physical, social, and emotional functioning of a person with a disability. Evolving from art therapy, expressive arts were used in institutional settings as a diversional activity to assist people in passing time (Waller & Gilroy, 1992). During World War II and through the 1950s, healthcare professionals recognized that art activities, as well as other recreation activities, learned by people who were convalescing could be used to develop skills useful after discharge. The advent of civil rights-related laws from the 1960s–1990s introduced and furthered the inclusion of people with

disabilities in school- and community-based art programs by mandating nondiscrimination of people with disabilities. Through inclusion of people with disabilities
in art-related classes and programs, use of expressive arts as therapeutic media
extended opportunities to use art-related skills learned in institutional settings.

Theoretical Foundations

Much of the literature on use of expressive arts as therapeutic media does not
explicitly indicate theories on which interventions were based. According to Shank,
Kinney, and Coyle (1993), interventions, services, and research that result in
outcomes or benefits for participants are developed based on theoretical perspectives. Application of theory to use of expressive art as therapeutic media would
contribute to the base of knowledge for TR practice and research (Sylvester, Voelkl,
& Ellis, 2001).

Theory allows for the suggestion of relationships so that outcomes can be
controlled, understood, or explained (Henderson, 1994). When practice and research
using expressive arts as therapeutic media are not theoretical, a gap is created
between building outcomes-focused services and research (Shank, Coyle, Boyd &
Kinney, 1996). Based on studies examining use of expressive arts as therapeutic
media, the following two theories are reviewed:

- Contact
- Self-Determination

Contact Theory

Contact theory asserts that if contact and interactions between people with differences is positive, then their attitudes toward one another will be positive (Tripp &
Sherrill, 1991). Contact, intended to change one group's attitudes toward individuals
of another group, is described as a situation in which expectations and assumptions
about group members are altered or confirmed (Roper, 1990). According to contact
theory, changes in attitudes depend primarily on conditions under which contact
occurs (Allport, 1954).

> For example, favorable conditions tend to improve attitudes,
> whereas unfavorable conditions tend to foster harmful attitudes.

Conditions of contact determine success or failure of the contact (Roper, 1990).
According to Allport (1954) and Tripp, French, and Sherrill (1995), unfavorable
attitudes tend to occur when: contact produces competition between groups; the
environment is unpleasant, involuntary, or has an air of tension; group members
are in a state of frustration; and groups have standards that are objectionable to
each other.

Conversely, these authors noted that favorable conditions that tend to foster
positive attitude changes between differing groups involve contacts that:

- Produce equal status and create rewards
- Are personal and persist over time
- Establish common goals

Produce equal status and create rewards. Contact theory can increase understanding of how expressive arts as therapeutic media could be used to promote self-expression and leisure experiences. The environment in which expressive arts are conducted can be designed to produce equal status and create a mutually rewarding experience between people with and without disabilities. By creating an environment for expressive arts where social status is equal, contact between people may be positive and mutual. If contact between people is positive and mutually rewarding, people may be more likely to feel comfortable expressing themselves through art.

> For example, if individuals with disabilities have equal access to and use of art equipment, equal social status between people with and without disabilities is increased. Adapting art equipment, such as increasing the grip size on ceramic art tools so that the use of the equipment is greater for people who have difficulty grasping, is one way to adapt a visual art activity so that the experience is mutually rewarding for individuals with and without disabilities.

Are personal and persist over time. Expressive arts can be conducted in an environment conducive to fostering positive contacts when contact is personal rather than casual and persists over time. If an expressive art environment is designed so that people with and without disabilities can interact together, contact is more likely to be personal rather than casual. In addition, if contact persists over several weeks rather than a one-time contact, then expressive arts may be an environment that fosters positive contact.

> For example, storytelling may be used to foster personal contact by giving each person in the group an interacting role to play in telling the story. Conducting the storytelling exercise over several weeks is also a way to foster positive contact between people with and without disabilities.

Establish common goals. Contact theory suggests that contact may be positive if common goals are established. Expressive arts environments can be conducive to focusing on the establishment of common goals.

> For example, through use of a group visual art project, such as creating a group sculpture, all individuals could work toward the common goal of creating a sculpture. Participants with and without disabilities can individually contribute to creation of the sculpture, with the final product being the common goal towards which all are working.

This theory supports the idea that structured expressive arts experiences are more likely to result in positive changes in attitudes toward people with disabilities and may increase inclusion opportunities (Allport, 1954). In particular, peer interactions are important to consider when designing inclusive expressive arts services for people with and without disabilities.

> For example, Schleien, Rynders, and Mustonen (1988) considered creating an environment in an art class that promoted contact and was mutually rewarding for children with and without disabilities. While the researchers did not identify a theory as the basis of their study, they addressed the quality of contact and interaction between children with and without disabilities participating in a visual arts program. When negative attitudes toward people with disabilities were addressed, children with and without disabilities increased their social interactions as they participated together in visual arts classes.

Self-Determination

Self-determination includes the perception of freedom to make choices and the ability to initiate chosen activities. According to Deci (1980), self-determination asserts that if people acquire attitudes and abilities to make choices or adjust to situations when few choices are available, then they will make choices or respond with flexibility to a lack of choices.

At the core of self-determination is personal freedom to choose and have those choices become determinants of one's actions. When individuals are self-determined they act out of choice rather than obligation. When self-determination is achieved, learning increases, and perceptions of competence are enhanced.

Traditionally, people with disabilities have experienced a lack of self-determination (Bambara, Koger, Katzer, & Davenport, 1995). According to Wehmeyer and Metzler (1995), many people with disabilities have not had the opportunity to assume responsibility for choices and decisions that impact their lives. A lack of self-determination has resulted in people with disabilities being dependent on people without disabilities to make choices for them, not engaging in preferred activities, and lacking the ability to take responsibility for choices made (Wehmeyer & Metzler).

Self-determination theory assists in our understanding of expressive arts as therapeutic media in that expressive arts can be used as a method to teach and reinforce choice making. Perceived control over an expressive art activity (rather than being controlled or being limited in an expressive art activity) is important to functional improvements, self-expression, and the leisure experience (Shamir, 1988).

> For example, Bambara and colleagues (1995) found that by including choice making in the daily routine of adults with mental retardation, participation in activities increased and disruptive behaviors decreased. Structuring expressive arts so as to embed choice making in the experience may provide people with

disabilities the opportunity to improve choice-making skills. For instance, a painting program may be structured so participants can choose various canvases or paper, paints, size of brushes, and subjects to paint.

Another way that self-determination theory enhances our understanding of expressive arts as therapeutic media is by using expressive arts to teach choice making. Dattilo (1988) recommended systematic planning to teach individuals with disabilities to make choices and express preferences. Systematic planning should include instruction related to assisting people in learning to make choices or acquire skills to adjust to situations in which there may be only one choice.

> For example, when using improvisations as therapeutic media people can be taught to choose characters or places to act out, or can be taught to adjust to situations when the improvisation is selected for them.

Expressive arts can be used as therapeutic media to improve and promote self-expression (Perks, 1979). In the process of expressing oneself, individuals have the opportunity to identify preferences that are symbolic of themselves. Basing expressive arts interventions on self-determination theory can assist in creating a link between choice making and preferences, which may improve one's self-expression.

> For example, when playing musical instruments, TR specialists could use a wide variety of instruments so participants may identify preferences for a particular instrument.

Summary

Expressive arts as therapeutic media have the potential to improve functioning, self-expression, and leisure experiences (Sherrill, 1979). Based on contact theory, if expressive arts environments are structured so that contact and interactions between people with differences is positive then their attitudes toward one another will be positive (Allport, 1954). Self-determination asserts that through expressive arts, if people acquire attitudes and abilities to make choices or adjust to situations when a lack of choices are available, then they will be able to make choices or respond with flexibility to a lack of choices.

Effectiveness

Many studies have been conducted using expressive arts as therapeutic media to improve cognitive, emotional, or physical functioning. While some of these studies support effectiveness of art as therapeutic media, some lack scientific controls necessary to link effects of an intervention with the person's functional change or improvement in leisure lifestyle. Studies examining effects of the following forms of expressive arts are reviewed:

- Visual Arts
- Music
- Dance
- Drama
- Poetry

Visual Arts

Recent studies have produced much documentation on effects of visual arts as therapeutic media. Researchers have investigated the impact of a visual art and video intervention on reducing post-traumatic stress disorder (PTSD), examined effects of the instruction of a visual arts activity to promote personal expressiveness with individuals with a dual diagnosis, and used personal photographs of older adults to encourage communication and dialog in a non-threatening way.

Gantt and Tinnin (2007) examined use of a 2-week art therapy and video program (7 x wk) on 72 adults with post-traumatic stress disorder to determine if use of visual arts or video reduced effects of the disorder. The intervention consisted of first drawing a graphic narrative of the trauma they experienced. The drawing had to include at least one drawing of the startle, thwarted intention (fight or flee), state of consciousness, body sensations, submission, and self-repair. Drawings were posted on a display board for analysis and discussion. Next, video recording was used to promote a discussion to address auditory hallucinations and dissociation relative to the trauma. In the video recording, participants looked at the video camera and first talked to it as if they were addressing the person they were before the trauma. Then, the person would reverse roles and speak to the camera from the perspective of the person before the trauma addressing their post-traumatic self. From both positions, the individual was encouraged to ask questions (e.g., Why didn't you run? Why didn't you scream for help?). During the video sessions, minimal intervention was provided by the therapist, but following, extensive discussions occurred. Following the interventions, participants completed several self-report instruments 1-week, 3-months, and 6-months post-intervention. Thirty-three participants (45%) experienced recovery from PTSD, 32 (44%) reported that their PTSD was improved, and 11% of the participants either experienced no change or their symptoms increased. Findings indicated that through intensive intervention, and one that used media that they could manipulate, especially drawings, people diagnosed with PTSD address effects of a trauma and reduced or eliminated the effects.

In two different studies using the same five participants (ages 17–21), **Malley, Dattilo, and Gast (2002)** examined effects of instruction of visual arts activity skills designed to promote personal expressiveness with individuals who had a dual cognitive impairment and mental health diagnosis. In the first study, effects of instruction designed to teach visual arts activity skills on art skill development, maintenance, and generalization were examined. Art media used were mixed media drawing, water color painting, and acrylic painting. Data were collected using a single subject multiple probe design over 43 sessions with each session including set up, use of materials, and clean up. Participants were taught each session task, were prompted to complete the tasks using a 5-second time delay and then probed for maintenance and generalization. Effects could not be controlled because selected art tasks were not totally independent of each task; however, each person learned three art activity skills as well as maintained and generalized these skills. The purpose of the second study was to promote personal expressiveness by using art materials in appropriate ways, based on skills learned in the first study. The difference between the two studies was that in the second study the instructor encouraged self-expression instead of teaching arts. The instructor used seven different techniques to facilitate self-expression, such as verbal suggestions about kinesthetic experiences, use of feelings, representation of things, or content-based subject matter. Data were collected through observations of videotaped sessions and 1:1 interviews. There was an increase in expressiveness, self-references in art products, and self-selection behaviors (e.g., an interest in bringing own art supplies to class). This study was inconclusive relative to decreasing inappropriate behaviors, or the quality or richness of the art products.

Koretsky (2001) used personal photographs of older adults to encourage communication and dialog in a non-threatening way about a variety of mental health issues. Individuals showed photographs of themselves or family members and the dialog began that made it easier to understand their family system. Photographs helped people to discuss issues such as loneliness, depression, memories, and feelings. Using photographs as therapeutic media can also be used to address end of life issues. For instance, having older adults put together a collage to give to family members is an empowering experience. Expressing feelings that are provoked by a photograph may be helpful. For example, the researcher discussed how one woman talked to her brother in the photograph who died shortly after the picture was taken. Photographs can help with memory problems that people with dementia may be experiencing. They could be used to help recognize family members who may be unfamiliar to them given their memory limitations. They could also be used to identify past leisure interests and patterns. Using photographs as therapeutic media can be an effective way to help with life's transitions in a non-threatening way with older adults.

Summary. Research examining effects of visual arts as therapeutic media is beginning to point to the effectiveness of such interventions. The three studies reviewed in this section lacked experimental control but were rich in what they had to offer regarding use of different types of visual arts. Although designs of the studies were limited, there was some support for the positive effects of visual arts for people with disabilities.

Music

The nature of music appears to inherently lend itself to having therapeutic effects. The following studies support what is anecdotally known about music and its use as therapeutic media, such as positive effects of music programs on older adults undergoing cardiovascular surgery, as well as those with Alzheimer's disease. Also, music can assist with inclusion of children with and without disabilities, and music can be used to treat children's behaviors associated with autism spectrum disorder.

Twiss, Seaver, and McCaffrey (2006) used a randomized control design to determine if listening to music reduced post-operative anxiety in 60 older adults (age > 65) who underwent cardiovascular surgery. The authors based their study on previous inquiries that found that listening to music when recovering from a surgery can reduce anxiety in the recovery process since anxiety before, during, and after surgery increases cardiovascular workload, thereby prolonging recovery time. The experimental group listened to music during and after surgery in addition to receiving standard post-operative care, while the control group received only standard post-operative care. The Spielberger State Trait Anxiety Inventory (Spielberger, Hammper, & Schur, 1984) was administered to both groups before surgery and 3 days post-operatively. Those participants who listened to music had significantly lower anxiety scores compared to those who did not. The researchers concluded that music had a positive effect on reducing anxiety associated with surgery and recovery and speculated that findings could be generalized to others who may experience significant medical procedures.

Children who have autism spectrum disorder (ASD) often have significant limitations with traditional forms of verbal and nonverbal communication. **Wigram and Gold (2006)** used two randomized controlled trials to examine short-term effects of a structured music intervention on a variety of social interaction and communication behaviors on four children with ASD. Structure and predictability found in music appeared to assist in developing reciprocal social interactions and resulted in increases in verbal and nonverbal communication and language development. The researchers recommended that future research should focus on effects of music on attention span, behavioral control, and relationship building with children with ASD.

Pollack and Namazi (1992) examined effects of a 2-week music program (3 x wk, 20-min sessions) on social behavior of five women and three men (ages 67–85) diagnosed with Alzheimer's disease. Specific music activities were singing; vocalizing; whistling to familiar songs; dancing to folk music; playing hand percussion instruments, drums, or the piano; as well as reminiscing about past experiences associated with music. Frequency of social behavior was measured 15 minutes before and after each session by direct observation. There was a significant increase in social behavior for the group during and after the music sessions. Specifically, participants responded positively to the music treatment by increasing their smiling behavior, eye contact, and positive verbal feedback during and after activities. The researchers concluded that 1:1 music activity may be used to encourage social interaction during and after activity sessions. However, results are limited by the lack of procedural analysis, small sample size, and no control group.

Humpal (1991) examined effects of an integrated early childhood music program on social interaction between children with and without disabilities. Fifteen children without disabilities (age 4) from one preschool and 12 children with moderate mental retardation (ages 3–5) from a developmental center participated in a 15-week integrated music program (1 x wk) designed to facilitate interaction between participants. Interaction increased among the children during and after the music intervention. Questionnaires distributed to the program staff supported the researcher's contention that the program fostered peer interaction and acceptance of differences among individuals. The researcher concluded that an early childhood music program could be effective in context for social interaction between children with and without disabilities.

Summary. While this review is far from complete, there appears to be research indicating therapeutic benefits of music. The studies reviewed suggest that music can be beneficial when used in programs with people recovering from an invasive surgical procedure, in an inclusive process, with children with autism spectrum disorder, and people with Alzheimer's disease. Music may be an appropriate element to include in some TR programs.

Dance

It is common for dance and movement therapy (DMT) interventions to be an integral part of TR programs. DMT programs have been found to be beneficial for older adults with geriatric depression and Parkinson's disease, adults with fibromyalgia, individuals with developmental disabilities, people with visual impairments, and children in an inpatient psychiatric setting. Dancing can also be adapted for wheelchair users.

Hackney, Kantorovich, Levin, and Gammon (2007) randomly assigned adults with Parkinson's disease to a 13-week exercise group that was conducted primarily in a seated position or a tango group (20 1-hr sessions) to examine effects on their functional mobility. Pre- and post-test measures were collected via the Unified Parkinson's Disease Rating Scale (UPDRS), Motor Subscale 3, the Berg Balance Scale, 5-meter gait velocity, Timed Up and Go mobility test (TUG), and a Freezing of Gait Questionnaire. Both the tango and exercise groups improved significantly on the Motor Subscale 3 and the UPDRS; however, only the tango group significantly improved on the Berg Balance Scale and showed a trend toward improvement in the TUG test. Overall, both groups showed improvements in motor abilities; however, the tango group demonstrated greater improvements in mobility, especially in the area of balance.

Haboush, Floyd, Caron, LaSota, and Alvarez (2006) investigated use of an 8-week ballroom dancing program (1 x wk, 45-min sessions) to decrease depression of 20 older adults (mean age of 69), diagnosed with depression and living independently in the community who participated in the intervention and 20 individuals on a waiting list and used as a control group. Ballroom dancing was selected as the treatment intervention because it is a popular form of recreational dance for individuals in this life phase and could help to facilitate social interaction. Scores on the Geriatric Depression Scale (GDS) for those in the treatment were compared to control group scores. No significant differences were found between scores of the two groups; however, when post-treatment scores were compared to pre-treatment scores, a significant difference was found for the treatment group. The significant difference between pre- and post-intervention scores indicated that depression decreased for those who received the ballroom dance intervention while there was no change in depression scores for those on the waiting list. The researchers recommended the use of dance with individuals experiencing depression to increase levels of activity, community involvement, and social interaction with others.

DMT was examined to determine its effectiveness in reducing pain with 36 women who had a diagnosis of fibromyalgia. **Bojner Horwitz and colleagues (2006)** conducted a 6-month dance intervention with 20 participants, while the other 16 served as a control group. The intervention was conducted once a week for 1 hour and focused on free-form movement associated with themes such as personal space, feelings, and weather. Effects were analyzed through drawings by participants that reflected their self-image and a global assessment of well-being and pain questionnaire. Positive results were found in the areas of increased mobility, decreased pain, and energy for those in the treatment group compared to those in the control group.

Erfer and Ziv (2006) used a DMT intervention (3 x wk, 45-min sessions) with seven children (ages 5–8) residing in a psychiatric unit of a hospital to create group cohesion and decrease maladaptive behaviors. The children had diagnoses of depression, attention deficit/hyperactivity disorder, anxiety, psychosis, and post-traumatic stress disorder. Some exhibited behaviors of social isolation while others were verbally and physically aggressive, oppositional, and defiant. The DMT included self-expressive and free-form movements using props such as balls and scarves, mirroring experiences, and turn-taking dancing to instruments such as drums. The DMT was effective in increasing positive body image, self-awareness, awareness of others, and group cohesion.

Boswell (1993) investigated effects of a 12-week creative dance program (1 x wk, 50-min sessions) on balance of 25 children with mild mental retardation. Twelve participants were randomly assigned to an experimental group that participated in a creative dance program and 13 participants were assigned to a control group that participated in a gross motor program. The post-test group mean of the experimental group was significantly higher than the post-test group mean of the control group.

Bachman and Sluyter (1988) investigated effects of a 16-week aerobic dance program (3 x wk, 45 min) on inappropriate behaviors, such as repetitive movements and off-task behaviors, in adults with severe and profound mental retardation. During baseline, participants were observed twice daily in a classroom. During intervention, behavioral observations of participants occurred in a classroom setting immediately prior to and following aerobic dance. Fewer inappropriate behaviors occurred during intervention than during baseline. The researchers concluded that aerobic dance can be an effective means of controlling inappropriate behaviors.

Chin (1988) investigated effects of a DMT on spatial awareness of children with visual impairments. Participants were randomly assigned to a control group that participated in a physical education class or to an experimental group that participated in both a physical education class and a DMT program. The Hill Test was administered before and after the intervention to determine spatial awareness of participants. There were no apparent differences between groups' scores before the intervention, but there were significant differences between the two groups' scores after the intervention. Improvements in the experimental group's scores were significantly better than improvements in the control group. The researcher concluded that a DMT program could be beneficial in improving spatial awareness of children with visual impairments.

Summary. Based on the research, there is support that DMT interventions can be beneficial for people with disabilities and some elements of DMT could be incorporated into TR programs. From the reviewed research, it appears that DMT programs can benefit older adults with geriatric depression, adults with fibromyalgia individuals with developmental disabilities, people with visual impairments, and children in an inpatient psychiatric setting.

Drama

Investigators have examined use of drama therapy with people with emotional disabilities and conduct disorders, post-traumatic stress disorder (PTSD), older adults, and young adults with moderate depression.

Dramatic reality was used by **Pendzik (2006)** to address PTSD associated with sexual assault. Pendizk used a 10-week drama therapy intervention individually with eight people (1 x wk, 1-hr session). Dramatic reality is a technique that brings together the imaginary and real worlds with the purpose of addressing difficult feelings and re-living difficult memories. In particular, it is intended to create a safe environment for individuals experiencing PTSD to express their feelings and address difficult memories. Using qualitative methods including in-depth interviews and debriefings it was determined that the intervention assisted each person in coming to terms with their trauma and decreasing traumatic stress present in their everyday life.

A 3-month psychodrama therapy program (1 x wk, 3-hr sessions) was used to treat depression as reported by **Hamamci (2006).** The purpose of this randomized control group study was to examine effects of using drama therapy to treat 31 young adults diagnosed with moderate depression. The Beck Depression Inventory (BDI), Automatic Thoughts Questionnaire (ATQ), and Dysfunctional Attitude Scale (DAS) were administered prior to treatment. The drama therapy group participated in warm-up exercises such as role-playing to identify irrational beliefs, dysfunctional attitudes or behaviors, or depressive thoughts. A second phase of drama therapy used a technique called enactment when the therapist selected one of the dysfunctional behaviors identified in the warm-up phase and asked the individual to pinpoint the stage of life this behavior occurred. Using role-play, the individual was then asked to act out this behavior in that stage of development. Eventually, the same technique was used but instead acting out positive beliefs, attitudes or behaviors, and thoughts. The researcher concluded that using drama therapy was effective in reducing depression, negative automatic thoughts, and dysfunctional attitudes.

Johnson (2000) examined effects of lifetime storytelling on social and cognitive skills of older adults with dementia. Using an experimental design, five participants were randomly assigned to the treatment and five participants were assigned to the control group. During the 15-week intervention (3 x wk, 30-min sessions) the activity coordinator verbally began telling a fictional story, and each participant verbally added to the story. The sessions then progressed to participants telling their life stories ending with periods of debriefing and verbal interactions between participants. Social interaction and reminiscence about important life events increased across time with individuals in the storytelling group. The researcher concluded that storytelling may be an appropriate intervention to increase social interaction and reminiscence skills with older adults experiencing dementia.

Landy (1994) examined effects of a 20-week program using dramatization and role-playing (1 x wk, 45-min session) to teach conflict resolution techniques with 26 adolescents with emotional and conduct disorders. Participants were randomly selected and assigned to a control group or an intervention group. Landy provided the adolescents with a conflict they might encounter in daily life, such as losing a table tennis game. The adolescents were required to act out and problem-solve the conflict with two other group members. There was a significant increase in conflict resolution abilities among the adolescents during and after the intervention, as compared to the control group. Landy concluded that adolescents with emotional and conduct disorders can learn to effectively problem solve conflicts through use of dramatizations and role-playing.

Summary. While there is limited evidence of effectiveness studies, there appears to be evidence indicating therapeutic benefits of drama. The studies showed that drama as a therapeutic medium may be effective with people with emotional disorders, anxiety disorders, mental retardation, and physical disabilities, as well as disoriented individuals.

Poetry

Poetry as therapeutic media may be useful with individuals who have a variety of disabilities. Efficacy research has been predominantly conducted with people who have cognitive impairments including, but not limited to, developmental disabilities, dementia, brain injuries, and cerebral vascular accidents as well as those with sensory impairments such as visual impairments.

Furman and colleagues (2006) examined how poetry could provide insight into the lives of individuals with mental illness. Poetry was used as an intervention by the therapist writing the poem about the person experiencing mental illness in an effort to develop effective treatment. Poems were written and analyzed about individuals with schizophrenia, mid-stage Alzheimer's disorder, Tourette's syndrome, or depression. In writing and analyzing poems, people's strengths, resourcefulness, difficulties, and sense of humor became apparent. From these findings, the researchers developed treatments to address issues each individual was experiencing such as difficulty fitting in with others in treatment, social isolation, powerlessness, or adjusting to semi-independent living.

Kahn-Freedman (2001) used qualitative methods to examine effects of a 10-week poetry program designed to provide four adults with cognitive impairments who had limited verbal skills an opportunity for self-expression. Poems written by famous poets, such as Audre Lorde, were rewritten in simplistic style and read to the group. Various qualitative strategies were used to initiate the poetry-writing phase. For instance, sometimes the session began with the instructor soliciting ideas from the group to compose a group poem. In this case, a phrase was used as the beginning of each line of the group poem, such as: *Autumn smells like . . .,* with group members completing a designated line. Participants were guided in poetry writing to express anger, memories, emotions, anxiety, and likes and dislikes. Front-loading and debriefing techniques were used to determine impact of the poem on self-expression. The researcher concluded that poetry is an effective intervention to promote self-expression with individuals who have limited verbal skills.

Summary. Since use of poetry as therapeutic media is a relatively new facilitation technique, there are few studies examining effects of this intervention. However, there is some preliminary support for using poetry effective with individuals with developmental disabilities in promoting self-expression. Also, researchers have written and analyzed poetry identifying that participants better understood their issues and that poetry provided an effective treatment.

Overall Summary

In summarizing literature reviewed in this section, research indicates that the expressive arts as therapeutic media are empirically supported facilitation techniques. Evidence supports use of expressive arts as therapeutic media to improve function, self-expression, and the quality of one's leisure lifestyle; however, additional research is needed to examine strategies effective in teaching individuals with disabilities expressive art skills, how participation in arts programs contributes to increasing self-determined behaviors, and effective techniques to increase and improve inclusive art opportunities.

Case Study

This case study highlights the use of dance as a therapeutic medium with women and children residing in a homeless shelter. Effects of homelessness has been widely documented and includes stress, depression, feelings of loss, feelings of abandonment, lack of sense of accomplishment or sense of belonging, and deprivation of leisure opportunities (Klitzing, 2003; 2004). Dance was used in this case to facilitate and encourage the development of social bonding and connections, encourage self-determination, decrease stress, and provide a safe, structured, and stable context for leisure.

Participants and Setting

Participants were residents of a shelter for people who are homeless. The adult participants were white, African-American, and mixed-race women between the ages of 18–42 years. Eight women participated in the dance program which was conducted twice a week for 1 hour over 8 weeks. The setting was a private nonprofit homeless shelter in a small suburban city in Ohio. The shelter had the capacity to house 70 people for up to 6 months at a time. The dance program was conducted in a large multi-purpose room.

Dance as Therapeutic Media for Participants

To determine the effectiveness of the dance program on creating social bonding and connections, self-expression, decreasing stress, and providing a safe, structured, and stable context for leisure, Marcy, the TR specialist, conducted a verbal assessment with each woman individually and recorded their responses. She chose to complete a verbal assessment rather than a written one due to the varied reading abilities of the residents. It also allowed her to establish a rapport with each woman and set a relaxed tone and atmosphere for the program.

The assessment was developed by Marcy for the purpose of the dance program and consisted of questions such as: "Have you ever taken a dance class before?"; "What type of music do you enjoy?"; "What do you hope to get out of the dance class?"; "Who are your friends here in the shelter?"; "On a scale of 1–10, with 10 being the highest, what would you say your level of stress is?" Additionally, prior to and immediately following each dance session, participants completed a Likert-type scale indicating levels of emotions and feelings including happiness, depression, energy, and stress. Marcy recorded responses from each participant using a Microsoft Excel computer program.

Dance sessions were 50 minutes long beginning with 15 minutes of warm-up exercises, then 30 minutes of dance, and concluding with 10 minutes of a cool down session. The goal of the warm-up exercises was to stretch the muscle groups that would be used in the day's class. Marcy planned the warm-up exercises to consist of gentle stretches such as standing with feet parallel, shoulders width apart and gently rolling down the spine to hang the torso over the legs and stretch the muscles in the back of the legs. Another warm-up exercise she used was having the participants reach their arms overhead and gently bend at the waist to the right and then the left to loosen torso muscles. Marcy also integrated some elements of the dance combination to be taught that day into the warm-ups as an introduction and to make them recognizable later in the class. Some examples she included were box steps, clapping out rhythms of the music, and footwork that was combined in the dance session with upper body movements.

Based on the assessment responses from the participants about preferred type of dance, Marcy used four styles of dance in the 8-week program: hip-hop, country-line dancing, ballet, and creative movement/improvisational movement. One style was selected each day on a rotational basis so all types of dance could be incorporated. Marcy used a moderate pace to teach dance steps, and incorporated repetition, similar movements, and accompanying music. At each session she brought a variety of music for selection and asked for input on music, dance moves, and props (i.e., scarves) from the participants. Marcy also encouraged questions, created a relaxed atmosphere that was conducive to socializing, and instilled an element of fun. In addition to teaching dance steps, sequences, and routines, Marcy incorporated a technique called imagery. Imagery involves the use of imagination, self-expression, and a bit of role-playing all incorporated into a dance. For instance, participants could use a boxing- or arm-punching move to release anger or smooth flowing arm sweeping moves to reflect caring or compassion.

Marcy concluded each class with a cool down session. The cool down included similar stretching exercises as the warm-up session to further stretch muscles. If a good deal of physically active dance was used, Marcy used exercises to reduce heart rates such as marching in place or stepping from side to side. During the cool down, Marcy conducted a debriefing with the participants asking questions such as: "What did we do today that you liked best/least?"; "What suggestions or ideas do you have for the next class?"; "In what ways did this help your stress level?" She recorded the responses immediately after each class for future reference. Lastly, Marcy compared the participant's pre- and post- responses from the Likert scale of emotions and feeling rate how the dance class affected them. This data was compared across each session and charted to determine changes. Marcy found that the participants reported an increase in motivation, joy, happiness, and energy and a decrease in stress and fatigue.

Summary

Participants living in this homeless shelter were experiencing a lack of social bonding and connections, limited sense of self-determination, stress, and a lack of stability especially in the context of leisure. Participation in the dance program provided an opportunity for them to bond with others in a relaxed environment, express their wishes and interests, and decrease their stress. In addition, through this program, participants had the opportunity to develop and strengthen relationships as well as discover mutual leisure interests. By using dance in a therapeutic way, participants had the opportunity to practice the use of the skills so as to improve their ability to generalize the skills in other areas of their lives.

Intervention Implementation Exercises

The following exercises are offered as suggestions to use expressive arts as a way to increase individuals' functioning and skills, and to promote engagement in recreation programs. While these exercises lack empirical testing, they provide a starting point for TR specialists in using expressive arts as therapeutic media. The exercises are categorized in the following way:

- Visual Arts
- Music
- Dance
- Drama
- Poetry

Visual Arts

Photography. Photography can be used for a variety of therapeutic purposes. The following is an example of an exercise that provides participants the opportunity to express their feelings that may be difficult to verbalize through photographs. This exercise may be used with people over the age of 7 years who have a variety of emotional or cognitive disabilities. Groups should include between 3–8 people.

Provide each participant with a camera. While digital cameras allow participants to instantly view their photographs to determine if it captures their feelings, cameras that use film can be used as well.

Begin by having participants make collages of pictures from magazines and various print media to pictorially represent their feelings. One guide that should be established is that pictures should not include people, but instead be of objects, places, animals, plants, or other non-people subject matter. This guide is important when the group ventures into the community; participants should not be taking pictures of people without their permission. After collages are completed have participants write words, a letter, or compose an essay or poem that represents what is depicted in the collage.

Before conducting a photography session at a site, instruct participants on how to use and care for the cameras. Based on the collages, have the group meet to discuss where they can go to take photographs.

> For instance, the group could go to a local park, hike and bike
> trail, shopping mall, public gardens, or historic site. If this exercise
> is conducted with individuals who are unable to leave a facility,
> facility grounds (e.g., gardens, gymnasiums, reading rooms) may
> be used.

Using leisure education methods, participants can be a part of the outing planning process as well. When at the photography site, instruct participants to photograph things, except people, that represent how they feel, emotions they are experiencing, or an issue they have difficulty verbally expressing. Allow approximately 30–45 minutes for photographing. Have participants write about their photographs in between the photo session and the next group session.

> For example, they can add to the writing they did following
> completion of the collage, write one or two word descriptions, title
> their photographs, or compose a poem or a letter.

At the next session, one at a time, place one participant's photograph in the middle of the group and have that participant identify the feeling or issue represented in the photograph. That person should be encouraged to read what he or she wrote if that would increase his or her level of comfort. That participant then listens while the group members comment on what they perceive in the photo.

Positive and constructive comments are encouraged as well as modeled by the TR specialist. The participant then responds to peers as to how the photograph represents the difficult emotion he or she is experiencing. This exercise, like most expressive arts activities, provides the opportunity for participants to express feelings, develop trust, explore common interests with others, and learn how to express feelings in a constructive way. Another way to use photography is through art appreciation in a museum or gallery setting. Corbett (1999) cites a study where children with learning disabilities found gallery and museum visits valuable as evidenced by displaying enthusiasm and excitement during the experience.

Group Acrylic Painting Activity. Group activities are one way to promote bonding, a sense of belonging, and feelings of accomplishment (Erfer & Ziv, 2006). One activity that can be used to accomplish these goals and promote self-expression is through a group painting project. The project can be to paint murals on a wall, canvas, or other material.

For the purposes of this example, a wall-size canvas will be used. Materials needed include acrylic paints; paintbrushes in a variety of bristle sizes (interior painting brushes, sponges, paints rollers, mops, or scrub brushes also can be used to apply paint); small containers of water to rinse brushes between colors; paper towels; and a piece of canvas of at least 8' x 12' (available at most art supply stores).

Provide participants with a wide variety of colors of acrylic paints from which to choose. Demonstrate the use of the paints, application tools, including the various strokes that may be made using the different tools on practice paper as well as brush cleaning techniques.

Begin by discussing and selecting a subject for the mural. Include all participants in the discussion so all have a sense of having their voice heard and a feeling of
ownership in the project. The group can select roles that each member could play in
constructing the mural.

> For instance, some group members could sketch a preliminary
> drawing of the selected subject; others could decide to paint
> specific areas. Participants who use wheelchairs could paint the
> mid and lower sections, or those with visual impairments could
> have their section bordered with tape so they are aware of where
> their portion of painting needs to be completed.

The group facilitator plays an important role in assuring that all participants are
actively involved in the painting project, encouraging each person to provide positive
and constructive feedback to their fellow painters, and celebrating the group's
accomplishment. The facilitator encourages participants to comment on others'
contributions to the painting in a non-judgmental positive way. Debriefing discussions could center on each person describing their role in the project, discussing the
role other members played in completion of the project, and how they feel when the
project is completed.

Music

Playing rhythmic musical instruments can be a way for people to express emotions
(Espenak, 1981). For example, playing musical instruments at slow rhythms may be
used to express sadness or calmness, whereas playing instruments at a fast pace may
be used to express fear or joy (Sherrill, 1979).

> Materials that can be used to express emotions are: (a) instruments
> such as bells, cymbals, drums, musical blocks or triangles, rhythm
> sticks, tambourines, thumb guitars, or xylophones and (b) musical
> tools to strike the instruments such as drum sticks with and without
> padded tips, musical triangle sticks, and wooden spoons.

Begin by asking participants to select and strike a musical instrument. Verbally
and physically demonstrate the slow and fast rhythms that can be played with each
instrument, providing opportunities for participants to practice each rhythm. Choose
an emotion and ask all of participants to demonstrate and explain their expression of
each emotion on the rhythm instrument.

Participants can be instructed and persuaded to experiment with various tempos
and patterns of rhythms to express the emotion. While demonstrations and explanations may sound similar or different, participants should be encouraged to express
their rhythmic interpretation of that emotion. After demonstrations and explanations
have been conducted with a variety of emotions, instruct participants to demonstrate
and explain the emotions they are currently feeling.

Following participation in this exercise, encourage participants to independently use rhythmic instruments to express emotions. Using rhythmic instruments to depict emotions may expand the individual's repertoire of ways to express emotions.

Dance

Many types of dance can be used to achieve therapeutic outcomes including, folk, modern, jazz, formal, and improvisational.

> One type of dance that can be used with individuals with
> mobility impairments is chair dancing, using either wheelchairs
> or a traditional chair without arms. Chair dancing can be used
> to promote self-expression, enjoyment, physical activity, social
> interaction, and a sense of belonging. To conduct chair dancing, a
> variety of music, a means to play music, an open space, and chairs
> without arms are needed.

A discussion on the role of dance in self-expression and health can lead the session. Warm-up or stretching exercises are conducted for approximately 7 minutes. These exercises can include torso stretches, bicep and tricep stretches, deep breathing, and leg muscle stretches if possible.

Prior to beginning the dance portion, various dance moves can be demonstrated and practiced. Some of these moves can include moving arms above your head in a left-to-right swaying motion; moving one arm toward the floor and the other toward the ceiling in an alternating pattern; leaning the torso back and rolling the shoulders back then leaning the torso forward while rolling the shoulders forward. All of these and other movements can be accomplished from a sitting position.

The dance session includes the demonstrated moves, repetition of these moves, and a sequence of moves that can be in rhythm to music. Each dance session is concluded with a cool down of approximately 10 minutes. The cool down can include stretching exercises similar to those done during the warm-up period, moving slowly to bring the heart rate to resting capacity, and deep breathing. Using dance as a therapeutic medium can promote physical activity, self-expression, and social relationships.

Drama

Improvisations allow people to act spontaneously and require imagination (Sherrill, 1979). Use of improvisations as a therapeutic medium may be a way for people to develop and practice self-expression skills. Improvisations may be done individually or in small groups.

To teach improvisation skills to promote self-expression, Tanner (1973) recommended beginning with teaching simple actions that require use of an object, such as taking a photograph, sawing a board, putting on shoes, or ironing a shirt. The simple actions can be taught using objects related to the action. Specifically, participants can be taught to remember movements, sequences, and details of the objects in relation to the action they are learning. Movements, sequences, details of the objects such as weight, size, and texture may be taught through demonstration, repetition, and gradual elimination of objects as actions are learned. Participants may be persuaded to be creative by using facial expressions, various postures, or self-talk vocalizations to further promote self-expression.

Poetry

Poetry can be a way to facilitate communication, express difficult feelings, and connect with others (Furman et al., 2006). Poetry has potential as a therapeutic medium to meet goals as it can be done not only in writing but electronically recorded, and verbalized, using simplistic as well as complex language.

One way to use poetry is to use it as a means of problem solving. This exercise can be used on an individual basis or as a group activity. Begin by discussing what determines a poem. Traditional literary rules of writing poetry do not need to be adhered to. Next, assist the participant with identifying an issue of concern. Ask participant to talk about it in a free-flowing manner while electronically recording the verbalization. Following the recording, have the person listen to the recording and put the words that had the most significance to the problem on paper. If the individual has difficulty with writing skills, the TR specialist can write while the person dictates the words. This process is the beginning of the composition of the poem. Poems can be revised, edited, or added to as part of the problem-solving process.

> A debriefing process can be conducted using questions such as: (a) How did writing this poem help to understand the problem?, (b) What did you learn about your problem that was new to you?, and (c) What things can you do to solve this problem?

Summary

TR specialists can use the implementation exercises found in this chapter to facilitate nonverbal communication skills, coping, and creativity. Interventions described in this chapter are starting points for TR specialists. As with most interventions, modifications are needed for different individuals who participate in expressive arts activities.

Conclusion

Expressive arts, such as visual arts, music, dance, and drama, have the potential to be used as therapeutic media by TR specialists to promote communication of feelings and creative skills. In addition, expressive arts can promote inclusion in recreation participation. Studies indicate that use of expressive arts as therapeutic media may improve individuals' cognitive, physical, social, and emotional functioning (Dalley, 1984).

Discussion Questions

1. What is the difference between "drama" and "drama as a therapeutic medium"?
2. Develop an argument for or against TR specialists conducting art therapy.
3. Identify three music activities that may be used as a therapeutic medium.
4. How can dance be used as a therapeutic media?
5. In what ways can poetry be used as a therapeutic media?
6. How did the use of expressive arts as therapeutic media evolve?
7. What influence did the Rehabilitation Act of 1973 have on expressive arts as therapeutic media?
8. How did IDEA and the ADA influence the use of expressive arts as therapeutic media?
9. How does the theory of self-determination enhance understanding of expressive arts as therapeutic media?
10. Identify three ways in which contact theory may be applied to expressive arts as therapeutic media.
11. What are the goals Marcy has for using dance as a therapeutic media?
12. What are some other ways music can be used as a therapeutic media that are different from those provided in the Implementation Exercise section?

Resources

Agency Resources

Very Special Arts
John F. Kennedy Center for the Performing Arts
Washington, DC 20566

American Art Therapy Association, Inc.
428 E. Baltimore Street
Baltimore, MD 21202

American Dance Therapy Association
2000 Century Plaza
Columbia, MD 21044

National Association of Music Therapy
910 Kentucky Avenue, Suite 206
Lawrence, KS 66044
http://www.artsintherapy.com

Material Resources

Mazza, N. (2007). Poetry Therapy. Retrieved April 11, 2007,
http://www.artsintherapy.com

References

Allen, A., & Allen, G. (1988). *Everyone can win: Opportunities and programs in the arts for the disabled.* McLean, VA: ERM Publications.

Allport, G. W. (1954). *The nature of prejudice.* New York: Addison-Wesley.

American Association of Dance Therapy (n.d.). Retrieved August 30, 2009, from http://www.adta.org/

Anderson, F. E. (1994). *Art-centered education and therapy for children with disabilities.* Springfield, IL: Charles C. Thomas.

Arts in Therapy Network. (n.d.). Retrieved March 23, 2007, from http://www.artsintherapy.com

Atack, S. M. (1980). *Art activities for the handicapped.* London, United Kingdom: Souvenir Press.

Bachman, J. E., & Sluyter, D. (1988). Reducing inappropriate behaviors of developmentally disabled adults using antecedent aerobic dance exercises. *Research in Developmental Disabilities, 9,* 73–83.

Bailey, S. D. (1993). *Wings to fly: Bringing theatre arts to students with special needs.* Rockville, MD: Woodbine House.

Bambara, L. M., Koger, F., Katzer, T., & Davenport, T. A. (1995). Embedding choice in the context of daily routines: An experimental case study. *The Journal of the Association for Persons with Severe Handicaps, 20*(3), 185–195.

Bojner Horwitz, E., Kowalski, J., Theorell, T., & Anderberg, U. M. (2006). Dance/movement therapy in fibromyalgia patients: Changes in self-figure drawings and their relation to verbal self-rating scales. *The Arts in Psychotherapy, 33,* 11–25.

Boswell, B. (1993). Effects of movement sequences and creative dance on balance of children with mental retardation. *Perceptual and Motor Skills, 77,* 1290.

Broudy, H. (1984). *Nature of aesthetic experience.* Unpublished paper presented at G. I. E. V. A. Conference, Los Angeles (October).

Bruininks, J. P., Woodcock, P. B., Weatherman, T. L., & Hill, J. (1984). *Scales of independent behavior.* New York: DLM Teaching Resources.

Carter, M. J., Van Andel, G. E., & Robb, G. M. (2003). *Therapeutic recreation: A practical approach.* Prospect Heights, IL: Waveland Press.

Chin, D. L. (1988). Dance movement instruction: Effects on spatial awareness in visually impaired elementary students. *Journal of Visual Impairment and Blindness, 82*(5), 188–192.

Corbett, J. (1999). Disability arts: Developing survival strategies. *Adults with disabilities: International perspectives in the community,* 171–181.

Dalley, T. (1984). Introduction. In T. Dalley (Ed.), *Art as therapy* (pp. xi–xxviii). New York: Tavistock.

Dattilo, J. (1988). Assessing music preferences of persons with severe disabilities. *Therapeutic Recreation Journal, 22,* 12–23.

Dattilo, J., & Kleiber, D. A. (1993). Psychological perspectives for therapeutic recreation research. In M. J. Malkin & C. Z. Howe (Eds.), *Research in therapeutic recreation: Concepts and methods* (pp. 57–76). State College, PA: Venture Publishing, Inc.

Davis, S. L. (1997). The miracle of poetry. *Impact, 10*(1), 10–11.

Deci, E. L. (1980). *The psychology of self-determination*. Lexington, MA: Lexington Books.

Drummond, A. E. R. (1990). Leisure activity after a stroke. *International Disabilities, 12*, 157–160.

Erfer, T., & Ziv, A. (2006). Moving toward cohesion: Group dance/movement therapy with children in psychiatry. *The Arts in Psychotherapy, 33*, 238–246.

Espenak, L. (1981). *Dance therapy: Theory and application*. Springfield, IL: Charles C. Thomas.

Essex, J. G. (2006). Expressive arts therapy. Retrieved March 2, 2007, from www.artsintherapy.com

Fuller, L. (1979). The dance of childhood: Focus on wellness, not emotional disturbance. In C. Sherrill (Ed.), *Creative arts for the severely handicapped* (2nd ed., pp. 75–82). Springfield, IL: Charles C. Thomas.

Furman, R., Collins, K., Langer, C., & Bruce, E. A. (2006). Inside a provider's perspective: Using practitioner poetry to explore the treatment of persons with mental illness. *The Arts in Psychotherapy, 33*, 331–342.

Gantt, L., & Tinnin, L. (2007). Intensive trauma therapy of PTSD and dissociation: An outcome study. *The Arts in Psychotherapy, 34*, 69–80.

Gerber, B. L., & Gerber, E. (2003, April/May). Use the arts to light up your curriculum. *Council for Exceptional Children, 9*(7), 12.

Haboush, A., Floyd, M., Caron, J., LaSota, M., & Alvarez, K. (2006). Ballroom dance lessons for geriatric depression: An exploratory study. *The Arts in Psychotherapy, 33*, 89–97.

Hackney, M. E., Kantorovich, S., Levin, R., & Gammon, M. (2007). Effects of tango on functional mobility in Parkinson's disease: A preliminary study. *Journal of Neurologic Physical Therapy, 31*(4), 173–179.

Hamamci, Z. (2006). Integrating psychodrama and cognitive behavior therapy to treat moderate depression. *The Arts in Psychotherapy, 33*, 199–207.

Henderson, K. (1994). Theory application and development in recreation, parks, and leisure research. *Journal of Park and Recreation Administration, 12*(1), 51–64.

Hennessy, C. (2004). Timothy Liu: An interview. *The Writers Chronicle, 36*(5), 4–11.

Hoffman, D. H. (1992). *Arts for older adults: An enhancement of life*. Englewood Cliffs, NJ: Prentice Hall, Inc.

Hopkins, C. (2007). Dance/Movement Therapy. Retrieved March 25, 2007, from http://www.artsintherapy.com.

Humpal, M. (1991). The effects of an integrated early childhood music program on social interaction among children with handicaps and their typical peers. *Journal of Music Therapy, 28*, 161–177.

Jennings, S., & Minde, A. (1993). *Art therapy and drama therapy: Masks of the soul*. Philadelphia: Jessica Kingsley.

Jennings, S. (1997). *Introduction to drama therapy: Ariadne's ball of thread*. London: Jessica Kingsley.

Johnson, D. R. (2000). Developmental transformations: Toward the body as presence. In P. Lewis & D. R. Johnson (Eds.), *Current approaches in drama therapy* (pp. 87–110). Springfield, IL: Charles C. Thomas.

Kahn-Freedman, E. (2001). Finding a voice: Poetry and people with developmental disabilities. *Mental Retardation, 39,* 195–200.

Kellman, J. (2005). HIV, art, and a journey toward healing: One man's story. *Journal of Aesthetic Education, 39*(3), 38–41.

Klitzing, S. W. (2003). Coping with chronic stress: Leisure and women who are homeless. *Leisure Sciences, 25,* 163–181.

Klitzing, S. W. (2004). Women who are moneyless: Leisure and affiliation. *Therapeutic Recreation Journal, 38,* 348–365.

Koretsky, P. (2001). Using photography in a therapeutic setting with seniors. *Afterimage, 29*(3), 8.

Landy, R. J. (1994). *Drama therapy: Concepts, theories, and practices* (2nd ed.) Springfield, IL: Charles C. Thomas.

Landy, R. J. (2006). The future of drama therapy. *The Arts in Psychotherapy, 33,* 135–142.

Lewis, P. (1984). *Theoretical approaches in dance movement therapy.* Dubuque, IA: Kendall-Hunt.

Lewis P., & Johnson, D. (Eds.) (2000). *Current approaches in drama therapy.* Springfield, IL: Charles C. Thomas.

Ludins-Katz, F., & Katz, E. (1990). *Art and disabilities: Establishing the creative art center for people with disabilities.* New York: Brookline Books.

Magee, W., & Andrews, K. (2007). Multi-disciplinary perceptions of music therapy in complex neuro-rehabilitation. *International Journal of Therapy and Rehabilitation, 142,* 70–74.

Malley, S. M., Dattilo, J., & Gast, D. (2002). Effects of visual arts instruction on the mental health of adults with mental retardation and mental illness. *Mental Retardation, 40,* 278–296.

Mazza, N. (1999). *Poetry therapy: Interface of the arts and psychology.* Boca Raton, FL: CRC Press.

National Association of Dance Therapy. (n.d.). Retrieved March 23, 2007, from http://www.nadt.org/

Pendzik, S. (2006). On dramatic reality and its therapeutic function in drama therapy. *The Arts in Psychotherapy, 33,* 271–280.

Perks, W. (1979). Self-expression through the arts: A human right. In C. Sherrill (Ed.), *Creative Arts for the Severely Handicapped* (2nd ed.) (pp. 25–28). Springfield, IL: Charles C. Thomas.

Pollack, N. J., & Namazi, K. H. (1992). The effect of music participation on the social behavior of Alzheimer's disease patients. *Journal of Music Therapy, 29,* 54–67.

Reynolds, R. (1993). Recreation and leisure lifestyle changes. In P. Wehman (Ed.), *The ADA mandate for social change* (pp. 217–240). Baltimore: Paul H. Brookes.

Roper, P. (1990). Changing perceptions through contact. *Disability, Handicap, & Society, 5*(2), 15–23.

Sausser, S., & Waller, R. J. (2006). A model for music therapy with students with emotional and behavioral disorders. *Arts in Psychotherapy, 33*(1), 1–10.

Schleien, S. J., Rynders, J. E., & Mustonen, T. (1988). Art and integration: What can we create? *Therapeutic Recreation Journal, 22*(4), 18–29.

Shamir, B. (1988). Commitment and leisure. *Sociological Perspectives, 31*(2), 238–258.

Shank, J. W., Coyle, C. P., Boyd, R., & Kinney, W. B. (1996). A classification scheme for therapeutic recreation research grounded in the rehabilitative sciences. *Therapeutic Recreation Journal, 30,* 179–196.

Shank, J. W., Kinney, W. B., & Coyle, C. P. (1993). Efficacy studies in therapeutic recreation research: The need, the state of the art, and future implications. In M. J. Malkin & C. Z. Howe (Eds.), *Research in therapeutic recreation: Concepts and methods* (pp. 301–328). State College, PA: Venture Publishing, Inc.

Sherrill, C. (1979). *Creative arts for the severely handicapped* (2nd ed.) Springfield, IL: Charles C. Thomas.

Silver, R. A. (1989). *Developing cognitive and creative skills through art.* Mamaroneck, NY: Albin Press.

Spielberger, C. D., Hammper, E., & Schur, S. B. (1984). *The Spielberger state-trait anxiety inventory.* Boston: Functional Resources Enterprise.

Spinack, G., Spotts, J. R., & Haines, P. E. (1985). *The Devereux child behavior rating scale.* Philadelphia: Devereux Foundation Press.

Stephenson, J. (2006). Music therapy and the education of students with severe disabilities. *Education and Training in Developmental Disabilities, 41*(3), 290–299.

Sylvester C., Voelkl, J., & Ellis, G. (2001). *Therapeutic recreation programming: Theory and practice.* State College, PA: Venture.

Tanner, B. (1973). The circle of drama. *English Journal, 62,* 737–741.

Tripp, A., French, R., & Sherrill, C. (1995). Contact theory and attitudes of children in physical education. *Adapted Physical Activity Quarterly, 12,* 323–332.

Tripp, A., & Sherrill, C. (1991). Attitude theories of relevance to adapted physical education. *Adapted Physical Activity Quarterly, 8,* 12–27.

Troeger, B. J. (1992). Application of child art theories to the interpretation of children's art. *Art Therapy, Journal of the American Art Therapy Association, 9*(1), 30–35.

Twiss, E., Seaver, J., & McCaffrey, R. (2006). The effect of music listening on older adults undergoing cardiovascular surgery. *Nursing in Critical Care, 11*(5), 224–231.

Uhler, E. (1979). The arts as learning and socialization experiences for the severely handicapped. In C. Sherrill (Ed.), *Creative arts for the severely handicapped* (pp. 183–190). Springfield, IL: Charles C. Thomas.

Waller, D., & Gilroy, A. (1992). *Art therapy: A handbook.* Philadelphia: Open University Press.

Wehmeyer, M. L., & Metzler, C. A. (1995). How self-determined are people with mental retardation? National consumer survey. *Mental Retardation, 33*(2), 111–119.

Wigram, T., & Gold, C. (2006). Music therapy in the assessment and treatment of autistic spectrum disorder; Clinical application and research evidence. *Child: Care, Health, & Development, 32,* 535–542.

Chapter 7
Leisure Education

John Dattilo and Richard Williams

If you think education is expensive, try ignorance.
—Derek Bok

Introduction

Therapeutic recreation (TR) is a profession committed to helping people with illnesses and disabilities develop and maintain appropriate leisure lifestyles (National Therapeutic Recreation Society, 1993) and to provide recreation resources and opportunities in order to improve health and well-being (American Therapeutic Recreation Association, 1998). People experience leisure by partaking of enjoyable activities that individually and in combination help them to realize their human potential leading them to self-fulfillment and enhanced well-being and quality of life (Cohen-Gewerc & Stebbins, 2007).

Leisure education is particularly suited to the task of helping individuals in that it addresses the challenges to enjoyable leisure experiences that are often faced by people with a variety of disabilities. Researchers recommend that increased emphasis be placed on leisure education to encourage people with disabilities to actively participate in physically and mentally healthy programs, to empower them to make decisions and discover new information and resources about leisure, and help them navigate through stressful transitions throughout their lives (Patterson, 2007). This chapter serves as an introduction to the topic of leisure education; however, readers are encouraged to explore the topic in more depth than can be provided within this chapter.

Definitions

When discussing leisure education, several terms are used that, on first glance, may seem interchangeable. For instance, people may discuss the same activity yet use different words to label the activity as either "play," "free time," "recreation," or "leisure." Additionally, while *leisure education* is a term that is often used by professionals in TR, what is meant by the term can vary widely.

One source of possible confusion has been the use of the term *leisure education* interchangeably with the term *leisure counseling*. Perhaps, initially, there were discernable differences between leisure education and leisure counseling; however, those differences appear now to be largely semantic, and the use of "leisure education" over "leisure counseling" enjoys nearly universal preference. This section will contain definitions of the following:

- Play
- Free Time
- Recreation
- Leisure
- Leisure Education

Play

Play does not seem to be a behavior limited to humans. Most people have played games with pets or watched young animals playfully romp at the zoo or on television programs. For humans, play has been defined as behavior that is engaging, intrinsically motivated, and chosen (Huizinga, 1955), that results in a transformation of reality (Schwartzman, 1978). Usually, play appears to involve making believe that one object is another (Hughes, 1991).

> For example, Sarah and Anna can play for hours with even the crudest of toys, creating a fantasy construction project or battlefield out of sticks, rocks, and piles of dirt.

Social scientists have long speculated about the functions of play, and disagreements remain among researchers and theorists. However, the universality of play behavior suggests that it is an important part of development.

Although play is usually associated with children, it seems that adults play as well. For people with disabilities, particularly people with developmental disabilities and older adults, it is important to engage in play that is age-appropriate. Leisure education may be used to impart age-appropriate leisure skills, knowledge, and attitudes.

Free Time

Another phrase associated with free time is *discretionary time*. Often, free time is conceived as a time when there are few or no obligations to work, school, chores, or other responsibilities. People can use free time however they choose, since, by definition, they are free from obligation.

Frequently, free time is valued because people choose to use free time in ways that are enjoyable. However, free time can sometimes pose a serious challenge to people. Many people with disabilities have an abundance of free time (Hoge & Dattilo, 1995), but lack the leisure skills needed to make the time meaningful (Dattilo, 2008). Therefore, systematic instruction for the meaningful use of free time seems appropriate.

Recreation

Usually, recreation is associated with an organized activity that people do for enjoyment. Often, recreation activities are believed to be beneficial for individuals or society or both. Additionally, such activities are characterized by being rule-bound.

While there are many varieties of recreation activities, some common examples include sports, crafts, and games. Even though people participate in recreation activities for enjoyment, occasionally results of participation can be less than enjoyable.

> For instance, David and Calvin are playing a game of checkers. However, both of the boys become very angry and begin to argue loudly when David accuses Calvin of intentionally not following the rules.

Traditionally, many community recreation programs have discriminated against people with disabilities, thus limiting their recreation participation (Dattilo, 2002). Leisure education may be beneficial in helping people with disabilities gain the recreation skills they need to participate in inclusive recreation.

Leisure

Leisure is perhaps the most difficult of the five terms to define. Essentially, leisure has been defined as a subjective state of mind when individuals experience a sense of freedom and are motivated to participate in an activity primarily for the enjoyment associated with the activity (Neulinger, 1981). Leisure is not coerced and, as such, it is a positive experience that requires people to use their abilities and resources to engage in personally satisfying and fulfilling experiences (Stebbins, 2005).

Clearly, much of the literature describing leisure originates from western-based individualistic attitudes. Dieser (2002) suggested that the core leisure components of self-determination and intrinsic motivation are not universal norms and may not be appropriate for all people. Given this bias, additional attributes of leisure may include relatedness, interdependence, affiliation, and camaraderie.

Since leisure is not tied necessarily to one type of activity, any activity could be a context for a leisure experience. For instance, even though most people think of mowing the lawn as a work activity, some people describe it in terms usually reserved for more typically leisure-related activities.

Leisure is subjectively experienced; therefore, some individuals may experience leisure engaging in an activity, while others may not experience leisure in the same activity. Reading is considered leisure by many people, but not by everyone. Thus, whether an activity is considered leisure depends on a personal evaluation of the activity. While not confined to a list of particular activities, the leisure experience is characterized by choice, freedom, enjoyment, and personal growth.

The ability to experience leisure depends on several fundamental skills such as the ability to choose. For a variety of reasons, many people with disabilities often lack skills necessary for experiencing leisure independently (Dattilo, 2002). Leisure education has evolved to address these leisure skill deficits.

Leisure Education

Although developing activity skills is important, leisure education involves more than simply teaching activity skills. Dattilo and Murphy (1991) identified leisure education as a human right in that it can enable choice, freedom, and self-determination.

Leisure education is important to improving the human condition since it is a way to enrich the lives of people who feel their leisure lifestyle is too uninteresting, unexciting, incomplete, or even nonexistent (Cohen-Gewerc & Stebbins, 2007). If individuals have the right for leisure and leisure contributes to human development, it is imperative that individuals and societies be educated for leisure (Sivan, 2007).

The skills learned in leisure education create options for people, thus allowing for choice and a broad range of activities from which to choose (Dattilo, 2008). Specific elements of leisure education are discussed in later sections of this chapter, but leisure education can be broadly defined as a process of teaching recreation and leisure-related skills, attitudes, and values (Johnson, Bullock, & Ashton-Shaeffer, 1997).

Descriptions

There have been many leisure education interventions developed over the years, far too many to be reviewed here. However, many of the models have common elements.

Similar discussions of frequently used components of leisure education models have appeared in several recent text books. In their texts, Bullock and Mahon (1997) as well as Dattilo (2008) recognized the importance of other writings on leisure education. Cited as particularly influential were the leisure education models proposed by Mundy and Odum (1979); later updated by Peterson and Gunn (1984), Mundy (1998), and Stumbo and Peterson (2009). This section contains descriptions of the components of leisure education discussed in these texts including:

- Leisure Appreciation
- Self-Awareness
- Decision Making
- Self-Determination
- Leisure Activity Skills
- Community Skills
- Social Skills
- Leisure Resource Awareness

Leisure Appreciation

One of the primary tasks of many leisure education programs is to help individuals become more aware of the concept of leisure. Leisure can be a complicated concept.

While there is not universal agreement concerning the nature of leisure, one of the characteristics of leisure widely discussed is that leisure is associated with several benefits such as pleasure, happiness, and satisfaction. Defined broadly, leisure can be associated with biological benefits such as physical fitness through sports, social benefits such as increased social support through friends met during leisure, and psychological and emotional benefits such as stress relief through yoga or meditation.

By becoming aware of leisure and by gaining a deeper understanding of it, people may be in a better position to access the experience. To facilitate leisure appreciation, a TR specialist can help participants understand leisure, the important roles leisure plays in society, and the beneficial outcomes of participating in leisure.

> For instance, some people have negative attitudes about leisure or feel that they do not deserve to experience leisure. By addressing such attitudes, a TR specialist can help participants experience a more enjoyable and meaningful event.

Self-Awareness

Leisure is often identified as a subjective experience. That is, what is leisure to some people will not be leisure to other people. Evidence for the subjective nature of leisure rests in the startlingly wide array of activities in which people participate for leisure. It is remarkable that activities as different as bungee jumping and reading a novel can both facilitate leisure experiences.

Many people with disabilities have limited options for leisure experiences and find dissatisfaction with the options available to them.

To develop a satisfying leisure lifestyle, having an understanding of oneself is important. To understand one's self requires self-examination. This process can involve questions of preferences, past involvement, goals, skills, attitudes, and satisfaction related to leisure. Leisure education can help people with disabilities to explore options for leisure expression.

> For example, to facilitate self-awareness, Brent, a TR specialist, has Ashanti, Caleb, and Careen list all leisure activities that they have done in the past, do currently, and would like to do in the future. Such a catalogue of activities could be used as the source for a discussion of leisure satisfaction, goal setting, benefits, needs, likes, and dislikes.

Having an awareness of self is an important step toward independence in leisure.

One of the most prevalent barriers to recreation participation for people with and without disabilities alike is the lack of time. Between work, school, cooking, shopping, cleaning, and other responsibilities, making time for recreation can be difficult. Considering that it may take more time for many people with disabilities to accomplish tasks than it does for people without disabilities, it may be even more complicated for people with disabilities to squeeze recreation into their daily routines than for people without disabilities. TR specialists can help people find time for recreation in a number of ways. By charting the time devoted to activities in a typical week, people are often startled at how much free time they have.

Another frequent source of surprise is the number of hours that people spend watching television. By gaining a better understanding of the ways they use their time, people might be able to address barriers due to time.

Decision Making

Many leisure service professionals have identified the ability to make decisions as a fundamental skill needed for independent leisure experience. It is widely held that decision-making skills can be taught (Bullock & Mahon, 1997).

Some people with disabilities live in environments that do not foster decision-making skills, which lead them to be dependent on others (Dattilo, 2002). Skills associated with decision making include making appraisals, forming realistic goals, gathering information, and problem solving (Mahon, 1994). Each of these skills can be addressed through leisure education. Goal setting is offered as an example.

A TR specialist could help participants learn to make appropriate leisure goals. However, simply asking a person to set a leisure-related goal may not be sufficient. A specialist could teach a number of techniques for the formation of effective goals.

> For example, Judi, the TR specialist could explain to Lionel and Julie that goals are personal expressions of desires, so their goals should be their own. Judi encourages the two participants to record goals that are clear and precise. Judi then works to facilitate successful goal-attainment after realistic goal setting, by encouraging Julie and Lionel to begin with short-term and easily attainable goals that have measurable results.

Once participants learn effective goal setting, they are more capable of making decisions about leisure. As discussed in the next section, decision making is an important element of self-determination.

Self-Determination

The state of self-determination has been described as being in control of the course a life takes (Wehmeyer, 1996). While there are external and uncontrollable influences in everyone's life, people who are self-determined perceive that they are free and make decisions as they negotiate their lives.

Being self-determined is important to being able to experience leisure fully (Dattilo & Kleiber, 1993). Although illnesses and disabilities can negatively affect self-determination, leisure education can help individuals to address these adverse conditions (Dattilo, Kleiber, & Williams, 1998).

Being self-determined in leisure involves taking responsibility for leisure expression. To help participants take this responsibility, a TR specialist could facilitate exploration of preferences. Once preferences are identified, participants can be taught ways to become more assertive in the expression of preferences.

Participants can be taught assertive methods of speaking and assertive body language. Often, it is important to distinguish between aggressive and assertive behaviors. To be assertive, people need a degree of self-confidence. To facilitate confidence, TR specialists can conduct role-playing exercises that allow participants time to practice assertive behaviors. Even in the process of leisure education, TR specialists can facilitate self-determination in participants.

The environment in which leisure education is taught can contribute to or impair self-determination of participants. Settings and programs that are structured too tightly tend to control the actions of participants and are likely to inhibit self-determination.

Well-designed programs facilitate self-determination in participants by allowing room for autonomy and meaningful decisions. By incorporating opportunities for choice into their programs, TR specialists can structure leisure education so that self-determination is facilitated in participants.

> For instance, during a leisure education drawing activity, Clarisse, Tahtah, Samuel and Sonya are encouraged to make a variety of choices such as between types of paper, colors of pencils, and subjects for drawing (see Figure 7.1).

Even these relatively small choices can encourage self-determination.

Figure 7.1

Leisure Activity Skills

To make decisions and to become self-determined, it is necessary for people to have options. Even the most fundamental leisure-related activities require skills, and each activity has a unique set of skills required for full participation. Without a variety of leisure activity skills, people will not have many options, and thus little opportunity for self-determination.

Leisure education programs might best serve participants by teaching skills associated with activities likely to lead to leisure and enjoyment. It is important for participants to choose the activities they would like to learn.

To help facilitate independent leisure involvement of participants, a TR specialist might begin by determining which activities are most attractive to participants. By focusing at least some of the available time and resources on skills associated with activities chosen by participants, TR specialists not only encourage self-determination, but increase the likelihood that participants will employ the skills once they have acquired them.

> For example, Homa, a TR specialist working with a group of
> adolescents, might conduct brief interviews with participants to
> determine which recreation activities they are most interested in
> learning. Finding that most participants are interested in sports,
> Homa plans several sessions when participants learn fundamental
> skills associated with sports of interest. In addition, Homa
> recognizes the value of having a variety of recreation skills, so she
> includes additional sessions that introduce participants to other
> types of activities such as art and cooking.

Community Skills

According to Bullock and Mahon (1997), community skills enable people to participate in community-based programs. Although there are certainly others, two of the most common community skills addressed by leisure education are use of public transportation and money management.

Lack of transportation is one of the barriers to leisure participation that is frequently identified by people with disabilities. Without the ability to drive or use public transportation, it is difficult to travel to places where people often go for recreation, such as shopping malls, movie theaters, libraries, and athletic facilities. TR specialists can facilitate acquisition of transportation-related skills in several ways.

> For example, Chinwei informs participants about public
> transportation resources that can help them overcome some
> transportation barriers. He explains that often, communities
> have services that meet the unique transportation needs of some
> people with disabilities. Additionally, Chinwei teaches and
> has participants practice both in a classroom setting and in the
> community specific skills such as map reading and appropriate
> behaviors for public spaces.

Many private and public recreation activities and events cost money. People who are generally not accustomed to handling money can experience barriers to independent leisure participation due to the lack of money-handling skills. TR specialists can help participants address this barrier in a number of ways including teaching them how to make change, count money, and appropriately and safely handle money in public. Role-playing in a nonthreatening classroom setting may help participants gain confidence when handling money in public.

The use of public transportation and money are two of the primary community skills that are needed for independent leisure expression. TR specialists can design leisure education programs to help participants address barriers associated with these and other community skills.

Social Skills

Because socializing can be an integral part of many leisure activities, social skills are a valuable component of leisure education. Additionally, deficits in social skills may be particularly noticeable in leisure settings; therefore, social skills are among the most important skills needed for people with disabilities to be accepted in inclusive community settings. Some people with disabilities may have few or no social skills deficits, while others may have significant deficits.

Social skills can include sharing, cooperating, communicating verbally and nonverbally, and determining appropriate rules for different situations. TR specialists can help people learn social skills in a number of ways.

> Most fundamentally, Lynne, a TR specialist, models appropriate social skills when interacting with participants (see Figure 7.2). She also uses role-plays of various social situations to help participants learn appropriate social interactions. In addition, Lynne uses cooperative games that require teamwork to teach lessons about sharing and the importance of communication.

Because so many leisure activities are done with others and because friendship is so important to people, social skill development is often included in leisure education.

Figure 7.2

Leisure Resource Awareness

Dattilo and Bemisderfer (1996) identified "the 3 Ps" of community resources: people, places, and printed materials. People can be community resources by acting as sources of information related to recreation opportunities. Places might include resources such as community centers, shopping malls, movie theaters, and athletic facilities. Printed materials like phone books and newspapers can be a source of information pertaining to recreation opportunities.

An important additional leisure resource is the Internet. There are a variety of websites that assist people in determining valuable information about various recreation activities. By making people aware of both personal and community leisure resources, leisure educators can help people with disabilities become more independent in leisure.

TR specialists can help people learn about community leisure resources both in a classroom setting and by taking a more "hands-on" approach.

> For example, Lanora, a TR specialist, brings resources such as brochures, phone books, newspapers, and schedules into a classroom and encourages participants to examine the materials. Additionally, Lanora has participants practice making specific plans for recreation participation by using the materials.

With appropriate support, TR specialists can work with participants in their communities to help them explore leisure resources.

Summary

While many leisure education programs have been developed and evaluated, there are common components of many of these programs. Drawing heavily on the textbooks by Bullock and Mahon (1997) and Dattilo (2008), this section reviewed many common elements of leisure education.

Leisure appreciation includes helping people become more aware of leisure and its benefits. Self-awareness involves helping people become more aware of their own attitudes toward leisure. Decision-making skills contribute to both self-determination and the leisure experience. Actions associated with self-determination help individuals take control of their lives. Such control is important to the ability to experience leisure. By acquiring a range of leisure activity skills, people have a greater chance of becoming self-determined and experiencing leisure. Community skills such as the use of public transportation and handling of money help people participate independently in leisure activities. Social skills can facilitate friendships and contribute to leisure experiences. Finally, the ability to identify leisure resources can help people independently experience leisure.

When conducting leisure education programs associated with the content listed above it is often useful for the instructor to process the experience with participants. *Processing* is the umbrella term for many facilitation techniques designed to assist people in describing, reflecting on, analyzing, and communicating about experiences directed toward helping people transfer or generalize what they have learned to other life situations by not only attending to the immediacies of the experience but also relating important aspects of the experience to future issues (Dattilo, 2008).

Dieser (2002) identified a legitimate concern of many leisure education programs that they are predominately individualistic in their emphasis on self-awareness, skill development, and mastery. Programs are typically developed by privileged segments of society. Leisure educators are encouraged to become culturally competent so that they can move beyond their individual perspectives and expand service delivery to include individuals who have differing perspectives and characteristics. If leisure educators fail to recognize the complex nature of cross-cultural service delivery, they may act with best intentions but unknowingly perpetuate oppressive and harmful behaviors by following unexamined common practices (Ryan & Fox, 2002).

History

The first part of this review of the history of leisure education relies heavily on a chapter of the same subject in Mundy and Odum (1979). Formalized leisure education has its origins in progressive education reform early in the twentieth century. Schools became widely recognized as having responsibility for a variety of societal roles, including education for the responsible use of leisure. National education policy statements identified leisure as an important topic for education. Increased (if undesired) free time for many adults due to widespread unemployment during the Depression era convinced many of the potential merits of leisure education.

For years following the Depression era, leisure education received only sporadic attention. There were a number of education initiatives and scholarly publications in the United States, Canada, and the United Kingdom, but there was no organized effort to institutionalize or formalize leisure education until the 1960s.

Two books in particular mark the beginning of current manifestations of leisure education. Kraus's (1964) *Recreation and the School* identified goals for leisure education similar to many of the leisure education programs in use today. Soon thereafter, Brightbill's (1966) *Educating for Leisure-Centered Living* documented philosophical justifications for leisure education. The pace of scholarship concerning leisure education has increased steadily since the introduction of these two works (World Leisure & Recreation Association, 1993).

The introduction of Mundy and Odum's (1979) text on leisure education was an important milestone for recreation therapists and it continues to influence both practice and research. The National Therapeutic Recreation Society's (NTRS) Philosophical Position Statement (1982) included leisure education as one of the three components of the therapeutic recreation process, further establishing the role of leisure education in the field. Currently, there are many different permutations of leisure education, and there has been a comparably large amount of research into the effectiveness of leisure education. The text books by Bullock and Mahon (1997) and Dattilo (2000; 2008) further delineate the boundaries and codify the practice of leisure education.

International influences contribute to development of leisure education as a variety of programs are administered in different regions of the world. An issue of *World Leisure and Recreation* (2nd quarter, 1997) contained discussions of leisure education in Egypt, Canada, Brazil, Belgium, Israel, and Hong Kong. Later, the World Leisure Organization (2005) produced documents delineating the main aim of leisure education to be to help the individual, family, community, and society achieve a suitable quality of life and good health. Also, Cohen-Gewerc and Stebbins (2007) edited a book with contributions from international scholars designed to integrate on a world scale the main elements of a manifesto on leisure education. While it is difficult to anticipate future developments, it seems likely that leisure education will continue to be an integral part of therapeutic recreation.

Theoretical Foundations

At first glance, topics included in leisure education are quite varied. As a result, one might expect a wide range of theories underpinning the various elements of leisure education. However, it appears that social psychological theories of motivation are at the foundation of the most familiar ingredients of leisure education. One common topic of study in social psychology is motivation. Social psychologists such as Deci (1975), Seligman (1975), and Bandura (1986) have long grappled with the question, "Why do people do what they do?"

Motivation is also an issue of particular interest for leisure educators. Leisure researchers and practitioners alike have asked questions such as "Why do people participate in one leisure activity and not another?" and "How do I motivate people to participate in leisure activities?" By understanding what motivates people to engage in leisure-related activities, TR specialists are in a better position to help people gain the skills needed for independent leisure expression. Two approaches that have been taken to explain motivation in leisure include:

- Intrinsic Motivation
- Goal Orientation

Intrinsic Motivation

Neulinger (1974) posited that there are three types of motivation relevant to discussions of leisure: (a) intrinsic motivation, (b) extrinsic motivation, and (c) extrinsic/intrinsic motivation. People are thought to be *intrinsically motivated* when they participate in activities simply for the fun and excitement they experience while participating in those activities. Most often, people are intrinsically motivated while participating in recreation activities. Extrinsic motivation is often associated with work. People are *extrinsically motivated* when they engage in an activity for some external reward such as money, praise, or food. Sometimes people are motivated intrinsically and extrinsically at the same time.

> For example, some professional athletes continue playing their sports long after they have a financial need to earn a living. In his waning years as a professional football player, Herschel Walker was reportedly among the richest athletes in the National Football League, yet he continued to play for a small fraction of what he earned during his most financially successful years.

Extrinsic motivation is rarely associated with leisure experiences. Neulinger (1974) described *pure leisure* as a state of mind that comes about when people feel strong intrinsic motivation and perceive that they are free. The content of leisure education programs is often devoted to two tasks that reflect Neulinger's model of pure leisure: (a) the exploration, identification, and development of those activities and experiences that are intrinsically motivating; and (b) addressing barriers to the perception of freedom. As such, Neulinger's model serves as a theoretical guide to the provision of leisure education services. Others in leisure studies have proposed different models to explain motivation in leisure.

Goal Orientation

Mannell and Kleiber (1997) described a model of motivation in leisure that included four components: (a) needs or motives, (b) behavior or activity, (c) goals or satisfactions, and (d) feedback. The model holds that when *needs arise* in people, they will try to reduce or eliminate the need by *performing behaviors and activities* to *satisfy these goals*. By reaching their goals, people receive *feedback* as to whether they are satisfied or whether they still have a need. Recognizing that the need has not been fulfilled would start the process again. In the context of leisure, the following example may be helpful.

> Most people feel the need to be near other people and to have friends and intimate relationships. To satisfy social needs, some people join organizations such as clubs and churches in hopes of meeting other people and making friends. If, by joining a local synagogue, Amelia feels that her goals have been satisfied, then the feedback was positive, and the need disappeared or become weaker. If however her goals had not been satisfied, then the feedback was negative, and the process began again.

By understanding that people are motivated to be involved in recreation activities and respond to feedback provided by these activities, TR specialists can understand how people become involved in activities. Leisure education can be a forum for helping people identify and develop activities that satisfy leisure needs and provide positive feedback.

Summary

While the two theoretical models of motivation reviewed in this section are quite different, they are not necessarily incompatible. Each presents a different way of understanding motivations people have for their actions. Of particular interest to the leisure educator are the ways in which people are motivated to participate in leisure.

Effectiveness

This section contains a review of some of the research examining effects of leisure education. While not a comprehensive review, these studies represent predominant trends in leisure education research. This material should aid in development of rationales for including leisure education in TR services. The limited scope is not to suggest that leisure education is appropriate only for people discussed in the following sections. Rather, this section focuses on groups who have received leisure education services and effects of these services have been researched. This summary is organized in the following categories:

- Programs for Older Adults
- Programs for People with Chemical Dependence or At Risk for Substance Abuse
- Programs for People with Cognitive Impairments
- Programs for People Receiving Mental Health or Behavioral Services

Programs for Older Adults

Generally as people age, there are changes in their lifestyles. For instance, when people age, often there is a decline in physical health, and after retirement, people often have more discretionary time than they have had prior to retirement. Leisure education can help people negotiate these often dramatic lifestyle changes.

Janssen (2004a) measured effects of a 6-week leisure education program using 60–90 minute sessions twice a week on quality of life of 47 residents from 3 Midwest retirement centers (37 women) who were 62–99 years of age. These residents were alert and oriented to time, place, and themselves. Participants were randomly assigned to a control or experimental group. Sessions involved awareness of self and leisure, leisure appreciation, self-determination and leisure, making decisions involving leisure participation, and awareness and use of leisure resources. There was a significantly higher post-test score for the experimental group but not for the control group in their *Quality of Life Profile: Senior Version, Leisure sub-domain* (Renwick et al., 1996). The experimental group scores were significantly higher for the leisure sub-domain with the largest increase in *getting out with others.* It appears that the leisure education program improved participants' leisure skills and offered an opportunity for participants to successfully age via development of new leisure skills.

Janssen (2004b) examined effects of a 6-week leisure education program using 90-minute sessions twice a week on quality of life. The participants were 18 older adults (13 women) who were 61–93 years old in an assisted living facility. Participants were randomly assigned to experimental and control groups and given the *Quality of Life: Senior Version (QOL: SV)* as a pre- and post-test to measure three domains: being, belonging, and becoming. The intervention included addressing the role of leisure in an individual's life and included definitions of leisure, developing leisure attitudes, leisure resources, self-determination, and quality of life. The leisure education group showed significant improvements in the *belonging* and *becoming* domains and an enhanced perception of quality of life. The findings identify the different aspects of participants' lives that could be enhanced by such a program and highlight the importance of quality leisure education programs for older adults who are entering assisted living facilities.

Nour, Deroseirs, Gauthier, and Carbonneau (2002) examined effects of a 10-week in-home leisure education program (1 x wk, 60–75-min sessions) on 13 older adults (10 men) who were 55 years and older recovering from a stroke.

Six participants were randomly assigned to an experimental group and seven to a control group. Pre- and post-test measures of psychological quality of life using the *Beck Depression Inventory* (Beck et al., 1974) and physical quality of life using the *Sickness Impact Profile* (Van Staten et al., 1997) were collected. While the leisure education program was associated with a significant increase in participants' physical quality of life, psychological quality of life did not increase significantly.

Dunn and Wilhite (1997) used a single-subject design to examine effects of a leisure education program on leisure behavior and emotional well-being of older adults who were home-centered. The leisure education program consisted of units addressing leisure awareness, skills, and knowledge. The leisure education program led to an increase in the frequency and duration of leisure participation as indicated by participant self-reports. Despite the apparent increases in leisure participation, there appeared to be few changes in participant emotional well-being.

Lovell, Dattilo, and Jekubovich (1996) conducted a study to determine effects of leisure education on older women with disabilities. Half the participants received a 3-week leisure education program (5 x wk, 1-hr sessions) while the other half did not. The leisure education program consisted of the content areas outlined by Dattilo and Murphy (1991) including leisure awareness, awareness of self, social skills, decision making, self-determination, leisure activity skills, and leisure resources. Data were collected through participant interviews and the *Leisure Diagnostic Battery* (LDB) (Witt & Ellis, 1987). Results of the LDB were inconclusive except with the finding that the women who received leisure education were more aware of barriers to leisure involvement. However, the interviews revealed that participants in both groups had common concerns related to leisure involvement. Themes that emerged from the interviews included reduced leisure repertoires, requirements to make decisions, desires for control, and importance of personal goals.

Searle, Mahon, Iso-Ahola, Sdrolias, and van Dyck (1995) investigated effects of an 18-week leisure education program (1 x wk, 1-hr sessions) on independence and psychological well-being of older adults. Thirteen participants were assigned to an experimental group that participated in a leisure education program, and 15 participants were assigned to a control group that received no intervention. To determine psychological well-being, both groups were pre- and post-tested on the Perceived Leisure Control Scale and the Perceived Leisure Competence Scale (Witt & Ellis, 1987), the Life Satisfaction Index A (Neugarten, Havighurst, & Tobin, 1969), the Locus of Control Scale (Levenson, 1974), and the Leisure Boredom Scale (Iso-Ahola & Weissinger, 1990). The leisure education group improved leisure control and satisfaction and reduced leisure boredom, therefore improving perceived locus of control and competence.

Searle and Mahon (1991) investigated effects of an 8-week leisure education program (1 x wk, 1-hr sessions) on older adults. Twenty-six participants (mean age of 77) were assigned to an experimental group that received leisure education and 27 participants were assigned to a control group. Instruments to measure social psychological variables included the Perceived Leisure Control Scale and the Perceived Leisure Competence Scale (Witt & Ellis, 1987) and Rosenberg's (1965) Self-Esteem Scale. The experimental group showed significantly improved scores on locus of control, perceived competence, and self-esteem as compared to the control group.

The leisure education intervention was successful and the intervention contributed to participants' ability to live independently.

Backman and Mannell (1986) compared effects of a program designed to teach recreation activity skills to the effects of a leisure education program on attitudes toward new activities of 40 residents of a facility for older adults. The leisure education intervention focused on topics of leisure attitudes and leisure awareness. Results indicated that the leisure education intervention positively affected participants' attitudes toward the new activities, while the activity skills program did not. Backman and Mannell concluded that more positive attitudes toward new activities could lead to higher levels of satisfaction from participation in the activities.

Summary. From the available research, it appears that there are several benefits of leisure education for older adults. For instance, leisure education appears to positively influence locus of control, perceived leisure competence, leisure participation, attitudes toward new leisure activities, and awareness of barriers to leisure.

Programs for People with Chemical Dependence or At Risk for Substance Abuse

Chemical dependence or being at risk for substance abuse inhibits people from interacting in healthy ways with others. While results are preliminary in nature, it appears that leisure education may carry benefits for those with chemical dependence or at risk for substance abuse.

Caldwell, Baldwin, Walls, and Smith (2004) examined effects of a 3-year leisure education program on 634 rural middle school adolescents (315 females). Youth in four schools were the experimental group and youth in five other schools were the controls. Data were collected via self-administered *Free Time Motivation Scale for Adolescents* (Baldwin & Caldwell, 2003) and the *Leisure Experience Battery for Adolescence* (Caldwell, Smith, & Weissinger, 1992) 3–6 weeks after the program ended each year. During the first year, six 50-minute sessions were administered to the experimental schools. These sessions were designed to promote personal development through healthy leisure engagement and prevent substance abuse and other unhealthy behavior. The experimental group reported higher levels of interest and well-being in leisure activities and scored higher in their ability to plan and make decisions during free time. Respondents identified participating in new and interesting activities more frequently than students in the control group.

Carruthers and Hood (2002) developed a 7-session leisure education program for individuals with alcoholism and addictions. The *Coping Skills Program* based on the *Stress Program Process Model* (Shiffman & Wills, 1985) was implemented with adults receiving inpatient outpatient services in three hospitals across the United States. The authors recognized that individuals recovering from addictions often lack motivation and skills necessary to cultivate new supportive relationship and satisfying activities. Therefore, they developed, implemented, and evaluated an intervention designed to motivate participants to pursue self-reinforcing activities and to teach them skills needed to engage is social and leisure activities that support their recovery. All sessions had an instructional phase, a homework application phase, and a debriefing phase. Due to differing lengths of treatment among participants, the program was evaluated after each session using social validation and behavioral measures and therapist feedback. Data supported the conclusion that participants felt the intervention was socially valid and that it improved their behaviors. The study provided support for implementing similar programs; however, lack of time and use of cognitively complex material were barriers to the usefulness of certain sessions.

Jekubovich (1994) used multiple research methods including field observations and interviews to investigate effects of a 12-week leisure education intervention (3 x wk, 1-hr sessions) on adults with addictions to alcohol and other drugs. The program included defining leisure, personal barriers to leisure, strategies to overcome barriers, personal leisure interests, benefits of leisure, community resources, and meeting personal needs through leisure. Although statistical analyses indicated no effects of the program, field notes and responses to open-ended questions suggested that the program was successful in helping participants learn to meet personal needs through leisure and to be confident in leisure participation decisions.

Rancourt (1991) used a qualitative design to examine effects of a leisure education program on 40 women who were residents of a substance abuse treatment facility. The program focused on concerns identified by participants, including playfulness, self-esteem, spirituality, mothering, decision making, and the benefits of leisure participation. Results indicated benefits of leisure education, including increased leisure awareness particularly related to family leisure, and increased abilities to find leisure resources appropriate to their needs. Based on participant statements leisure education appeared to be a valuable ingredient in recovery.

Summary. It appears that leisure education can address some of the issues faced by people with chemical dependence or those at risk for substance abuse. People who have abused substances might benefit from participation in a leisure education program during their recovery. Leisure education seems to be an appropriate response to social constraints that inhibit the appropriate expression of leisure.

Programs for People with Cognitive Impairments

There are characteristics of cognitive disabilities that can be constraining to leisure participation. These can include leisure skills, lack of professional and family support, and attitudinal and transportation barriers. A significant amount of leisure education research has been conducted with people with cognitive impairments.

Based on the Social Information Processing Model (Crick & Dodge, 1994), **Dattilo, Williams, and Cory (2003)** examined effects of the computerized leisure education program (4 x wk, 30-min sessions) on knowledge of social skills of 3 boys (ages 6–15) with intellectual, emotional, or learning disabilities. The main character had to determine the best way to handle a number of social situations. A baseline game was used where participants moved the character through the game without feedback about response accuracy. The *Social Interaction in Leisure Assessment* was used before every session to assess participant knowledge of social skills in leisure. Once the scores stabilized, the leisure education intervention was initiated to help show participants their correct and incorrect responses. Increased social knowledge was associated with the intervention and maintained for at least 2 months.

Dattilo, Williams, Guerin, and Cory (2001) assessed the achievement of objectives associated with a computerized leisure education program designed to provide information about becoming self-determined in leisure of four youth with disabilities (ages 10–14). To assess program validity, participants were interviewed and family and staff completed surveys. The intervention was socially valid and resulted in increases in knowledge of self-determination in leisure. These positive results were replicated across participants and maintained during probes up to 2 months post-intervention.

O'Reilly, Lancioni, and Kiernans (2000) examined effects of a social skills problem-solving intervention (3 x wk, 1-hr sessions) on four adults with moderate mental retardation. Participants were taught to decode social situations, make decisions, perform the behavior, and evaluate their performance. Role-plays were provided in a variety of contexts. The intervention produced immediate positive changes in social skills that were generalized to other settings and maintained for up to 3 years.

Dattilo and Hoge (1999) examined effects of the Transition through Recreation and Integration for Life (TRAIL) leisure education program on affect of 19 young adults with mental retardation who were members of three special education classes in three public high schools. TRAIL is composed of four main components: (a) a leisure education curriculum based on Dattilo and Murphy (1991) including units on leisure appreciation, social interaction and friendship, leisure resources, self-determination, and decision making; (b) leisure coaching; (c) family and friend support; and (d) follow-up services. A single-subject, multiple-baseline across participants design was used. Data were collected across various settings, including classrooms and a recreation setting. Since positive affect was higher during the intervention than during baseline and this effect was replicated across all classes, the leisure education program was determined to be effective at enhancing the leisure expressions of young adults with mental retardation.

Hoge and colleagues (1999) examined effects of a 20-week leisure education program (3 x wk, 1-hr sessions) on perceived freedom of 40 high-school male and female students (ages 15–20) with mild to moderate mental retardation. Participants were separated into two groups, 21 in the control group and 19 in the experimental group. The control group was taught, just as before, in self-contained classrooms and received no intervention. Individuals in the experimental group received 54 leisure education lessons and were assigned a trained leisure coach to help identify leisure skills and opportunities. All participants were pre- and post-tested using the *Leisure Diagnostic Battery* (LDB) (Ellis & Witt, 1986). The authors concluded that the leisure education program, along with leisure coaches and family involvement was associated with participants' improved perceived freedom. These higher scores on the LDB by the experimental group indicate higher perceived confidence and control that are important when making the transition to adulthood.

Williams and Dattilo (1997) used a single-subject, multiple-baseline across participants design to examine effects of a 8-week leisure education program (3 x wk, 1-hr sessions) on decision making, social interaction, and positive affect of two female and two male young adults (mean age of 24) with mental retardation. The program included instruction on decision-making, social interaction, and leisure awareness. The leisure education program had little effect on decision making and social interaction, but participants exhibited positive affect during discretionary time more frequently after participating in the leisure education program.

Mahon (1994) used a multiple-baseline design to study effects of a leisure education program on four adolescent males with mental retardation. The leisure education program was designed to facilitate self-determination and contained elements of leisure awareness, decision making, planning, and self-monitoring. Participants become more self-determined in leisure than they had been prior to the intervention. Mahon concluded that leisure education might facilitate self-determination in leisure for young adults with mental retardation.

Bedini, Bullock, and Driscoll (1993) investigated effects of the Wake Leisure Education Program on high-school students in special education classes. Program participation resulted in increases in competence, perceived control, self-esteem, leisure satisfaction, life satisfaction, assertiveness, and choice making, and decreases in communication barriers and social barriers. Curiously, some participants, despite improvements in many leisure-related areas, expressed discontent with leisure following their involvement in leisure education. A similar phenomenon was reported by Caldwell, Adolph, and Gilbert (1989), who speculated that awareness of leisure may become a constraint if expectations are raised but level of involvement in leisure remains constant. The researchers concluded that leisure education was valuable for participants, but may be more effective if offered to people younger than those in high school.

Mahon and Bullock (1992) used a single-subject alternating treatment design to investigate effects of a leisure education program on decision making and leisure awareness of adolescents with mental retardation. For decision making, a system of self-instruction techniques was taught to four adolescents with mental retardation. Behavioral observations were used to determine percentage of times the participants used the techniques successfully and leisure awareness was measured by percentage of correct answers given by participants to a number of questions. Encouragement and verbal praise were used as reinforcement during one phase of the leisure education program. Participants increased their frequency of use of self-instruction techniques to make decisions and displayed enhanced leisure awareness. Although participants largely continued to rely on the therapist for prompts to use the self-instruction techniques, Mahon and Bullock concluded that people with mental retardation can learn to make decisions, thus creating more satisfying leisure lifestyles.

Lanagan and Dattilo (1989) compared effects of a leisure education program for adults with mental retardation and a recreation participation program on frequency of involvement in recreation activities. The 39 participants in the leisure education program increased frequency of participation significantly more than participants in the recreation participation program. The leisure education group appeared to retain information from the program. The researchers concluded that leisure education might be an effective element of comprehensive leisure services.

Anderson and Allen (1985) investigated effects of a leisure education program on 40 people with mental retardation. Results indicated that participation in the leisure education program increased frequency of activity involvement but not duration of activity involvement or frequency or duration of social interaction. The researchers concluded that leisure education is a valuable intervention and that social skills training should be emphasized in leisure education programs developed in the future.

Summary. Perhaps more research has examined effects of leisure education on people with cognitive impairments than any other group of people. Results of this research are encouraging. For instance, it appears that leisure education can increase frequency of participation, self-determination, perceived control and competence, leisure awareness, and positive affect. Therefore, leisure education would seem to be a valuable tool for TR specialists working with people with cognitive impairments.

Programs for People Receiving Mental Health or Behavioral Services

Parsons (2006) used videotaped role-plays of 12 youth (ages 12–21), with autism or Asperger's syndrome that allowed participants to observe themselves, make helpful suggestions to their peers, and rehearse social skills within the context of play. Perceptions of parents, peers, and participants were assessed via structured surveys. Parents and youth reported observing positive changes in social skills used in leisure contexts, in their homes, and at school. The findings provide support for examining effects of videotaped role-plays on enhancing leisure and social skills.

　　McKenney, Dattilo, Cory, and Williams (2004) examined effects of a social skills intervention. The intervention was conducted five times per week for 30 minutes. Participants were 4 boys (ages 11–12) with IQ scores 59–75 who had behavioral or emotional disabilities. The *Social Interactions in Leisure Assessment* (SILA) (Dattilo et al., 2001) was used to determine participants' social knowledge in leisure. Baseline sessions involved the 5-minute SILA test along with playing a computer game for 25 minutes. Once SILA scores were stable the intervention was initiated. The intervention sessions were the same as baseline except the computer game gave participants feedback on how to act. After the session was complete the SILA was again administered. Once students achieved 3 consecutive sessions of 85% or more accuracy the follow-up phase began. This involved administering SILA four times over 5 weeks to test for knowledge retention. During follow-up sessions, participants' scores were similar to their improved scores at the end of the intervention. Three participants scored 100s, which was equal or higher than their last few sessions of the intervention. The social skills computer program shows promise in helping children with behavioral and emotional disabilities not only learn, but also maintain proper social skills.

　　Pegg (2003) examined the relationship between leisure participation and health incorporating different leadership styles in a 24-week leisure intervention. The program met once a week for 3-hour sessions. There were 46 participants (35 men) who were 18–58 years old with mental health disorders. Fifteen participants were randomly assigned to the comparison group, 15 to the first intervention group (traditional leadership style) and 16 to the second intervention group (interactive leadership style). Participants' perceived control in leisure was tested with the LDB short form (version B) (Ellis & Witt, 1986) before, during, and 6 months after the intervention. Perceived control was significantly higher for those who participated in an intervention than those who did not. There was a larger increase in perceived control for those who had an interactive leader than those who had a traditional leader. The study supports the contention that leisure education can increase perceptions that individuals with disabilities have control over their leisure. In addition, the study illustrates the importance of having an effective interactive program leader to achieve the best possible results.

Yang, Huang, Schaller, Wang, and Tsai (2003) examined effects of a social-emotional skills curriculum on the ability of six children (4 boys) 7–9 years-old with autism to generalize or transfer socio-emotional skills. The program was conducted once a week for 80 minutes over a 13-week period. Homeroom teachers recorded behaviors using the *Behavior Record Form* (BRF) (Alberto & Troutman, 2002) while students were in the regular classroom. The BRF was developed to monitor student's everyday activities. Four children were randomly assigned to the experimental group, and two to the control group. The four children who participated in the experimental group showed marked social growth over time; however, the two children in the control group did not show these trends.

Dieser and Ruddell (2002) examined effects of attribution training on sixteen adolescents (ages 14–17 years) diagnosed with depression. Attribution relates to how people assign cause to their performance; that is, how they identified reasons for their failures and successes. Attributions were measured by the *Causal Dimension Scale* (McAuley, Duncan & Russell, 1992) and the *Attribution Style Questionnaire* (Peterson et al., 1982; Tennen & Herzberger, 1985). Participants were interviewed after activities twice per week so that they could discuss recreation experiences and reasons that those experiences were positive or negative. While the intervention that used verbal persuasion may have been helpful, significant changes were not found. Further studies with larger samples may provide insight into effects of the intervention. It appears that an important aspect of leisure education is teaching individuals how to view or *attribute* their successes and failures in healthy ways.

Mahon and colleagues (1996) developed a leisure education program for adults with severe and persistent mental illness titled *Reintegration through Recreation*. Three surveys were administered to determine: social significance of goals for the leisure education program, social appropriateness of the leisure education program, social appropriateness of the leisure education intervention strategies, and social importance of the effects of the leisure education program. The authors reported that, in general, participants, family members, and service providers considered the goals, interventions, and outcomes of a leisure education program to be socially valid. Results underscored the importance of including participants, their families, and their friends in the process of refining leisure education interventions.

Summary. Individuals with mental health or behavioral disabilities have symptoms that are frequently treated by medication. While medication may be necessary for certain individuals and circumstances, leisure education programs are another effective treatment for diminishing symptoms associated with mental health and behavioral disabilities. While results in the literature are primarily positive, researchers recommend involving participants, their families, and friends in refining programs, teaching individuals how to attribute success and failures in healthy ways, and educating instructors to be highly interactive.

Overall Summary

This section contained a review of research examining effects of leisure education. Leisure education has been used with a variety of people and effects of leisure education appear to be quite varied. While results are mixed, there is ample evidence to support use of leisure education for many people with disabilities to facilitate independent and appropriate leisure expression.

After examining the literature on leisure education, Patterson (2007) reported that people with disabilities benefit from leisure education that emphasizes instruction related to social skill, decision making, accessing leisure information and resources, and motor skills. Through leisure education, people with disabilities develop competencies necessary for leisure participation, confidence to use community-based resources, and friendships that are the foundation of social inclusion (Patterson, 2007).

In summarizing the literature reviewed in this section, there was limited research found examining effects of leisure education. Existing research moderately indicated that leisure education is an empirically supported facilitation technique.

Case Study

Jaime

Jaime is an 11-year-old boy with mild mental retardation. He resides in a rural community with his parents and two younger sisters. Jaime attends a public middle school and spends most of his day in special education classes, but he is involved in an inclusive after-school recreation program.

While Jaime reported enjoying his participation in the after-school program, teachers observed that he rarely interacted with other youth or participated in the activities during the after-school program. Instead, he sat on a bench and watched others play. A TR specialist designed a leisure education program to help facilitate inclusion of students with disabilities into the program.

Leisure Education Intervention

In designing the leisure education program, the TR specialist realized that to facilitate inclusive and independent leisure participation during the after-school program, she had to address needs and concerns of not only students with disabilities, but also students without disabilities. She conducted assessments of the children with disabilities, focusing first on their strengths and abilities, then on their barriers. Results of the assessment suggested that the leisure education program should focus on leisure activity and social skills deficits and a general lack of self-determination. To address the concerns, fears, and attitudes of students without disabilities about disabilities, the TR specialist incorporated disability awareness and sensitivity into the leisure education program.

Working with the special education teachers to schedule sessions for leisure education, the TR specialist designed a leisure education class that was taught 3 days per week during a homeroom period. She used the books by Dattilo (2000; 2008) as a resource to help her design sessions related to development of social skills and self-determination. By identifying the games most often played by participants in the after-school program, she determined activity skills she would teach.

During each session, the TR specialist reviewed material from the previous session and then introduced the main topic of that day's session. Rather than merely talking about various leisure skills, the TR specialist incorporated games, projects, activities, and role-playing into each session. Following each activity, the TR specialist conducted a debriefing by asking questions to assess participant level of understanding and to answer any questions. Jaime and the other participants were encouraged to practice skills they were learning during the after-school program.

To address the children without disabilities, the TR specialist enlisted the support of the school's administrators and homeroom teachers. Visiting a different homeroom class each day for 2 weeks, the TR specialist presented information about people with disabilities through the use of professionally prepared videotape and led a discussion. She hoped that these presentations and discussions would diminish some of the apprehension that many of the children in the after-school program had demonstrated toward Jaime and other children with disabilities.

Although progress was slow at first, Jaime's skills and confidence increased with time. During leisure education, Jaime learned how to throw a football and a Frisbee and how to play several games that were popular among his classmates, including kickball and tetherball. While Jaime had generally strong social skills, the TR specialist helped Jaime become more assertive by practicing social skills such as eye contact and introducing himself to others. Jaime learned about his leisure preferences and about some positive outcomes of participating in recreation activities.

Previously, Jaime seemed too shy to participate, but with his newfound skills, he began to participate in games more often during the after-school program. By the end of the formalized leisure education instruction, the TR specialist observed Jaime's behavior during the after-school program and made discreet suggestions and reminders to him. Jaime continued participating in the program throughout the school year.

Summary

By identifying leisure-related abilities and skills deficits, the TR specialist was able to design a leisure education intervention to help Jaime and his classmates more fully participate in the after-school recreation program. Learning activity and social skills and other leisure-related skills enabled Jaime to play with and befriend other children with and without disabilities.

Intervention Implementation Exercises

This section includes several exercises that can be used in leisure education programs. Exercises are presented for each of the components of leisure education discussed in the section titled "Description of Leisure Education Interventions." The sections include:

- Leisure Appreciation
- Self-Awareness
- Decision Making
- Self-Determination
- Leisure Activity Skills
- Community Skills
- Social Skills
- Leisure Resource Awareness

Leisure Appreciation

Leisure Bingo. This activity works best with a large group of people. Prior to the session, the instructor makes Leisure Bingo cards by drawing a large square on a piece of paper, then drawing two horizontal and two vertical lines so that the square is divided into nine equally sized boxes. The instructor writes a leisure-related activity in each of the squares using both common and slightly obscure recreation activities. Everyone in the group should be provided with a copy.

The activity is introduced while the bingo cards and pencils are being distributed to each participant. Participants can be instructed that when prompted, their task is to find people who have participated in various activities on their cards and to ask what benefits they receive from participating in an activity on the card. Benefits should be written in the square with the activity to which it corresponds. Each person can supply a benefit for only one square on his or her activity card, so that when a card is complete, each participant will have spoken to nine different people. Additionally, each person can initial only one square per bingo card. The activity will continue until the first person to complete a card announces, "Bingo!"

The activity can be debriefed by asking participants if they had learned about any new or interesting recreation activities. Participants can be encouraged to participate with other group members who identified an interest in similar activities.

Self-Awareness

This section contains several activities designed to promote self-awareness that include:

- Inner-view
- Leisure Continuum
- Time Table

Inner-view. This activity helps participants explore their preferences for leisure. Pencils and paper are the only materials needed for this activity. Participants are divided into pairs. Each participant is directed to write five different questions concerning the leisure of their partner. The questions can focus on preferences, dislikes, frequency, or any number of topics related to leisure. Encourage participants to write probing but not overly personal questions.

Once participants complete writing their questions, they can be instructed to trade lists with their partner so that each participant will be asked questions they had designed for someone else. The instructor can have participants begin to interview each other, taking notes on the responses. After interviews are completed, the instructor debriefs the exercise by asking participants to share several of their responses with other participants. The instructor can ask participants if they learned anything new about themselves or others in the group.

Leisure Continuum. Prior to the activity, a list can be prepared of approximately 10 contrasting pairs of leisure-related activities. This list might include items such as a hike in the mountains or a nap in a hammock, a monster movie or a romantic movie, a good book or a good sale, and eating out or dining in. The list can be tailored to the backgrounds of participants.

For this activity, a clear open space is needed, such as a large room with furniture pushed to the sides of the room. Participants can be asked to stand as a group in the center of the room, and they can be instructed that they are to move to one side of the room or the other when an item is read aloud. For instance, the facilitator will say aloud, "If you prefer a hike in the mountains, move to my left. If you prefer a nap in a hammock, move to my right." Time should be allowed for participants to decide their preferences and to move to the appropriate area of the room before reading the next item aloud. The activity continues until all of the prepared items have been read aloud.

To debrief, participants can sit on the floor in a circle. Participants can be asked if they recognized any patterns in their leisure preferences and whether they were surprised by any of their preferences. Time should be allowed for participants to ask questions or to make statements about their observations of the activity.

Time Table. This activity was adapted from the TRAIL Leisure Education Curriculum (Dattilo & Bemisderfer, 1996). While some people have an abundance of free time that they have difficulty occupying with rewarding activity, the opposite is true for many other people. One of the most common constraints to leisure that people mention is the lack of free time. This activity is designed to help people realize the amount of free time they have and to help people organize their time.

To begin, a pencil and a piece of paper can be distributed to each participant. Next, participants are to draw seven equally sized boxes on the paper. Each box represents one day of a hypothetical week in the participant's life. Participants can be instructed to label each box in order with a different day of the week and to write the hours of the day down the left side of each box. Finally, participants can record typical responsibilities for each day, including maintenance activities (such as cleaning or sleeping), work, school, family responsibilities, and anything else they feel is a daily necessity.

Once participants have completed their Time Tables, they can be asked to share their results with others in the group. Often, people are surprised by the amount of blank space left in their Time Tables, even people who felt like they had very little free time. The facilitator can debrief the activity by identifying blocks of free time that might be used for leisure-related activities and by offering suggestions on ways to reorganize commitments.

Decision Making

How to Decide? This activity will help illustrate the process involved in decision-making. Prior to the session in which this activity will be used, four small paper bags (such as lunch bags) can be numbered (1–4). A banana can be placed in bag #1, a resealable soda bottle filled with water can be placed in bag #2, an orange in bag #3, and a dollar bill in bag #4. The tops of the bags may be folded over so the contents are not visible.

During the activity, the four bags are to be positioned side by side on a table in front of the group. Volunteers from the group can each stand behind a different bag. Each volunteer can be asked why he or she selected the bag he or she stood behind. Next, volunteers are instructed to lift the bags without looking into them. Participants can be asked if they would like to trade their bags with someone else now that they have some information. If two or more people want to trade, they may do so. Next, participants are to feel the object in their bag without looking. Again, any trades may occur if two or more want to make a trade based on the information they just gained. Participants can be reminded that they are making a decision based on only what they believe is in their bag since they do not know what might be in the other bags. Once all trades have been completed (if there are any), participants can take the object out of the bag in their possession and show their objects to the class. If any of the volunteers choose to trade their objects once they have seen them, they may do so. Volunteers may then return to their seats.

The activity can be debriefed by discussing the importance of having information before making decisions. Participants can be asked if they ever make decisions before gathering the information necessary, or if they have ever made a decision that they regretted because they had not gathered sufficient information first.

Self-Determination

Spaced Out. To be self-determined, it is necessary for people to take responsibility for their leisure. This activity is designed to help participants understand what it is like to take sole responsibility for their leisure.

Participants are given a sheet of paper and markers and told that they are to plan for an imaginary extended voyage to another planet aboard a spaceship. The leader can explain that the trip will take exactly 1 year, and with the exception of essentials like food, water, and air, they must remember to take everything that they will need for a year. However, because of limitations of weight and space, participants only take seven items.

Participants can draw a rough outline of a spaceship on their pieces of paper. Once participants have finished drawing their spaceships, they can be instructed to draw and label the seven objects they will take with them on their voyage. The leader can explain that the quality and accuracy of the drawings is not important.

Once everyone has finished their drawings, participants can share the list of items they chose to take with them. Participants can be asked why they chose specific items and whether they could take sole responsibility for their own leisure for a year with only the items they took with them.

Leisure Activity Skills

There are many activity skills that can be taught during leisure education. This section will offer several guidelines in choosing activity skills to teach. Simply asking participants which activities they would like to learn more about is an effective way to determine activity skills to be included in a leisure education program. In addition, it is helpful to:

- Consider the Setting
- Contextualize Activities

Consider the Setting. Considering the variety of settings in which leisure education can occur, it may be helpful to choose activities that suit the setting of leisure education.

> For instance, a classroom setting might lend itself naturally to such activities as board games and arts and crafts projects. An outdoor setting might lend itself to activity skill instructions related to active games and sports such as soccer or throwing a ball, or camping skills such as setting up a tent.

Contextualize Activities. Regardless of activity skill or setting, it is important to contextualize activities so that they have meaning to participants. To make it more likely that participants find activities meaningful, TR specialists can place activities in wider historical and social contexts than the leisure education setting.

> For example, learning to play volleyball while in treatment may have no meaning for participants if the experience is isolated from their lives outside of leisure education. If, however, there is a community volleyball league in which participants want to participate, then the activity would have more meaning.

Without such contextualization, TR specialists are at risk of teaching activity skills that will be of little use to participants.

Community Skills

Mo' Money, No Money. This activity is designed to help participants learn to plan recreation activities with both large and small budgets. Participants are divided into two groups. Both groups are instructed to plan a recreation activity such as an event involving a sport or a trip. One group receives a large imaginary budget while the other is given a small imaginary budget. Participants use their knowledge of local resources to plan a recreation activity including any relevant elements such as transportation, scheduling, and accommodations. It may be helpful to make available to participants such resources as brochures, phone books, and local guidebooks.

Once both groups finish planning, a representative from each group presents the activity that the group planned. If time allows, participants plan a second activity with the larger-budget group planning a smaller-budget activity and the smaller-budget group planning a larger-budget activity.

Social Skills

Friendship Tree. This activity involves participants drawing a "Friendship Tree." The leader distributes paper and markers to the participants. Participants are instructed to draw a tree including roots, a trunk, branches, leaves, and circles scattered among the leaves that represent fruit. The drawing covers nearly the entire page.

Once participants finish drawing their trees, they are told to label the roots of their trees with things that are needed to nourish friendships. If participants find this task too challenging, the facilitator can suggest words and phrases such as *trust, respect, common interests,* and *fun experiences.* Once participants complete labeling the roots of their trees, they may label fruits of the trees with benefits of friendship. Once again, if participants find this difficult, the facilitator can suggest words such as *happiness, companionship,* and *intimacy.*

This activity is debriefed by asking participants to share and discuss ingredients and benefits of successful friendships. It may be helpful to ask participants to share stories about their friends and what their friendships have meant to them.

Leisure Resource Awareness

Resourcerer. This activity is designed to facilitate discussions of local resources. The leader distributes pencils and paper to participants. Prior to the session, a list of varied activities is prepared. Activities that are very different from each other such as basketball, sewing, socializing, and making crafts can be included on the list.

Participants write the alphabet on the left side of a piece of paper so there is one letter of the alphabet on each line of the paper. The leader explains that a leisure activity will be named from a list, and when cued, participants will have 1 minute to write as many local resources related to that activity as they can imagine. However, participants are instructed to write only one resource for each letter. Resources can include a place where the activity occurs, a person who has information about the activity, printed material that contains information about the activity, and a website that contains information about the activity. Using a timepiece, the leader indicates that participants are allowed 1 minute to complete the activity.

After 1 minute, participants stop writing. Next, participants read aloud their complete list of resources. Participants score 1 point for each response deemed to be a resource by the facilitator. The same resource may be named by different participants without penalty. The activity may be continued for several rounds, until a participant reaches a predetermined number of points.

Throughout the game participants can ask questions about the resources. The facilitator asks questions of participants who name particularly interesting resources. To focus participants' attention on cooperation, each distinct answer given by participants can count toward a predetermined group goal. Following the game, participants are asked what they learned about any local resources that interested them.

Summary

Intervention implementation exercises presented in this chapter can be used to increase understanding about relevance of leisure education. Gaining skills related to leisure appreciation, self-awareness, decision making, self-determination, activities, community, socialization, in addition to an increased repertoire of leisure resources expands the number of leisure opportunities available to people with and without disabilities. These exercises may require modifications to meet unique needs of individuals so that they acquire skills contributing to fulfilling leisure experiences.

Conclusion

Leisure education is a valuable facilitation technique designed to assist individuals in establishing an enjoyable leisure lifestyle. The components of leisure education described in this chapter encourage individuals to acquire skills that can enhance their overall quality of life.

Leisure education interventions have been used with a variety of people and are empirically supported as effective facilitation techniques. Overall, improving people's leisure lifestyle through leisure education can lead to benefits that influence all aspects of their lives.

Discussion Questions

1. What are some benefits of leisure education that research has suggested?
2. Which different types of disabilities have been included in the study of leisure education?
3. What are some ways in which leisure education might benefit older adults?
4. What are some of the most common components of a leisure education program?
5. What is the importance of self-determination to leisure?
6. How is motivation related to leisure education?
7. How might a TR specialist facilitate self-determination during leisure education?
8. Other than in a classroom, where might leisure education occur?
9. What criteria would you use to determine content presented in a leisure education program?
10. What is the ultimate goal of leisure education?

Resources

Material Resources

Dattilo, J. (2000). *Leisure education specific programs*. State College, PA: Venture Publishing, Inc.

Dattilo, J. (2002). *Inclusive leisure services: The rights of people with disabilities* (2nd ed.). State College, PA: Venture Publishing, Inc.

Dattilo, J. (2008). *Leisure education program planning: A systematic approach* (3rd ed.). State College, PA: Venture Publishing, Inc.

Mundy, J. (1998). *Leisure education: Theory and practice* (2nd ed.). Champaign, IL: Sagamore.

Stumbo, N. J. (2002a). *Leisure education I: A manual of activities and resources* (2nd ed.). State College, PA: Venture Publishing, Inc.

Stumbo, N. J. (2002b). *Leisure education II: More activities and resources* (2nd ed.). State College, PA: Venture Publishing, Inc.

Stumbo, N. J. (1998). *Leisure education IV: Activities for individuals with substance addiction*. State College, PA: Venture Publishing, Inc.

Stumbo, N. J. (1997). *Leisure education III: More goal-oriented activities*. State College, PA: Venture Publishing, Inc.

Stumbo, N. J., & Thompson, S. R. (1986). *Leisure education: A manual of activities and resources*. State College, PA: Venture Publishing, Inc.

References

American Therapeutic Recreation Association. (1998). *ATRA mission statement* [Online]. Available: http://www.atra-tr.org.educat.html

Alberto, P. A., & Troutman, A. C. (2002). *Applied behavior analysis for teachers*. (6th ed.). Upper Saddle River, NJ: Merrill.

Anderson, S. C., & Allen, L. R. (1985). Effects of a leisure education program on activity involvement and social interaction of mentally retarded persons. *Adapted Physical Activity Quarterly, 2*, 107–116.

Backman, S. J., & Mannell, R. C. (1986). Removing attitudinal barriers to leisure behavior and satisfaction: A field experiment among the institutionalized elderly. *Therapeutic Recreation Journal, 20*(3), 46–53.

Baldwin, C. K., & Caldwell, L. L. (2003). Development of the free time motivation scale for adolescents. *Journal of Leisure Research, 35*, 129–151.

Bandura, A. (1986). *Social foundations of thought and action: A social cognitive theory*. Englewood Cliffs, NJ: Prentice-Hall.

Beck, A. T., Rial, W. Y., & Rickels, K. (1974). Short form of depression inventory: Cross validation. *Psychological Reports, 34*, 1184–1186.

Bedini, L., Bullock, C., & Driscoll, L. (1993). The effects of leisure education on factors contributing to the successful transition of students with mental retardation from school to life. *Therapeutic Recreation Journal, 27*(2), 70–82.

Brightbill, C. K. (1966). *Educating for leisure-centered living*. Harrisburg, PA: Stackpole.

Bullock, C. C., & Mahon, M. J. (1997). *Introduction to recreation services for people with disabilities: A person-centered approach*. Champaign, IL: Sagamore.

Caldwell, L. L., Adolph, S., & Gilbert, A. (1989). Caution! Leisure counselors at work: Long-term effects of leisure counseling. *Therapeutic Recreation Journal, 23*(3), 4–7.

Caldwell, L., Baldwin, C., Walls, T., & Smith, E. (2004). Preliminary effects of a leisure education program to promote healthy use of free time among middle school adolescents. *Journal of Leisure Research, 36*(3), 310–335.

Caldwell, L. L., Smith, E. A., & Weissinger, E. (1992). The relationship of leisure activities and perceived health of college students. *Loisir et société/Society and leisure, 15*(2), 545–556.

Carruthers, C. P., & Hood, C. D. (2002). Coping skills programs for individuals with alcoholism. *Therapeutic Recreation Journal, 36*, 154–172.

Cohen-Gewerc, E., & Stebbins, R. A. (Eds.) (2007). *The pivotal role of leisure education: Finding personal fulfillment in this century*. State College, PA: Venture Publishing, Inc.

Crick, N. R., & Dodge, K. A. (1994). A review and reformulation of social information-processing mechanisms in children's social adjustment. *Psychological Bulletin, 115*, 74–101.

Dattilo, J. (2000). *Leisure education specific programs*. State College, PA: Venture Publishing, Inc.

Dattilo, J. (2002). *Inclusive leisure services: The rights of people with disabilities* (2nd ed.). State College, PA: Venture Publishing, Inc.

Dattilo, J. (2008). *Leisure education program planning: A systematic approach* (3rd ed.). State College, PA: Venture Publishing, Inc.

Dattilo, J., & Bemisderfer, K. (1996). *Project TRAIL leisure education curriculum*. Athens, GA: University of Georgia.

Dattilo, J., & Hoge, G. (1999). Effects of leisure education on youth with mental retardation. *Education and Training in Mental Retardation, 34*(1), 20–34.

Dattilo, J., & Kleiber, D. (1993). Psychological perspectives for therapeutic recreation research: The psychology of enjoyment. In M. J. Malkin & C. Z. Howe (Eds.), *Research in therapeutic recreation: Concepts and methods* (pp. 57–76). State College, PA: Venture Publishing, Inc.

Dattilo, J., Kleiber, D., & Williams, R. (1998). Self-determination and enjoyment enhancement: A psychologically based service model for therapeutic recreation. *Therapeutic Recreation Journal, 32*, 258–271.

Dattilo, J., & Murphy, W. D. (1991). *Leisure education program planning: A systematic approach*. State College, PA: Venture Publishing, Inc.

Dattilo, J., Williams, R., & Cory, L. (2003). Effects of computerized leisure education on knowledge of social skills of youth with intellectual disabilities. *Therapeutic Recreation Journal, 37*(2), 142–155.

Dattilo, J., Williams, R., Guerin, N., & Cory, L. (2001). Effects of computerized leisure education on the self-determination of youth with disabilities. *Journal of Special Education Technology, 16*(1), 5–17.

Deci, E. L. (1975). *Intrinsic motivation*. New York: Plenum Press.

Dieser, R. B. (2002). A personal narrative of a cross-cultural experience in therapeutic recreation: Unmasking the masked. *Therapeutic Recreation Journal, 36*(1), 84–96.

Dieser, R., & Ruddell, E. (2002). Effects of attribution retraining during therapeutic recreation on attribution and explanatory styles of adolescents with depression. *Therapeutic Recreation Journal, 36,* 35–47.

Dunn, N. J., & Wilhite, B. (1997). The effects of a leisure education program on leisure participation and psychosocial well-being of two older women who are home-centered. *Therapeutic Recreation Journal, 31*(1), 53–71.

Ellis, G. D., & Wit, P. A. (1986). The Leisure Diagnostic Battery: Past, present, and future. *Therapeutic Recreation Journal, 29*(4), 31–47.

Hoge, G., & Dattilo, J. (1995). Recreation participation patterns of adults with and without mental retardation. *Education and Training in Mental Retardation and Developmental Disabilities, 30*(4), 283–98.

Hoge, G., Dattilo, J., & Williams, R. (1999). Effects of leisure education on perceived freedom in leisure of adolescents with mental retardation. *Therapeutic Recreation Journal, 33,* 320–332.

Hughes, F. P. (1991). *Children, play, and development.* Boston: Allyn and Bacon.

Huizinga, J. (1955). *Homo ludens: A study of the play element in culture.* Boston: Beacon Press.

Iso-Ahola, S. E., & Weissinger, E. (1990). Perceptions of boredom in leisure: Conceptualization, reliability and validity of the leisure boredom scale. *Journal of Leisure Research, 22,* 1–17.

Janssen, M. (2004a). The effects of leisure education on quality of life in older adults. *Therapeutic Recreation Journal, 38,* 275–289.

Janssen, M. (2004b). The use of leisure education in assisted living facilities. *American Journal of Recreation Therapy, 3*(4), 25–30.

Jekubovich, N. (1994). The effects of a leisure education program on adults with chemical dependencies. Unpublished master's thesis. University of Georgia.

Johnson, D. E., Bullock, C. C., & Ashton-Shaeffer, C. (1997). Families and leisure: A context for learning. *Teaching Exceptional Children,* Nov./Dec., 30–34.

Kraus, R. G. (1964). *Recreation and the schools.* New York: MacMillan.

Lanagan, D., & Dattilo, J. (1989). The effects of a leisure education program on individuals with mental retardation. *Therapeutic Recreation Journal, 23*(4), 62–72.

Levenson, H. (1974). Activism and powerful others: Distinctions within the concept of internal-external control. *Journal of Personality Assessment, 38,* 377–383.

Lovell, T. A., Dattilo, J., & Jekubovich, N. J. (1996). Effects of leisure education on women aging with disabilities. *Activities, Adaptations, & Aging, 21*(2), 37–58.

McAuley, E., Duncan, T. E., & Russell, D. (1992). Measuring causal attributions: The Revised Causal Dimension Scale (CDSII). *Personality and Social Psychology Bulletin, 18,* 566–573.

McKenney, A., Dattilo, J., Cory, L., & Williams, R. (2004). Effects of a computerized therapeutic recreation program on knowledge of social skills of male youth with emotional and behavioral disorders. *Annual in Therapeutic Recreation, 13,* 12–23.

Mahon, M. J. (1994). The use of self-control techniques to facilitate self-determination skills during leisure in adolescents and young adults with mild and moderate mental retardation. *Therapeutic Recreation Journal, 28*(2), 58–72.

Mahon, M. J., & Bullock, C. C. (1992). Teaching adolescents with mild mental retardation to make decisions in leisure through the use of self-control techniques. *Therapeutic Recreation Journal, 26*(3), 9–26.

Mahon, M., Bullock, C., Luken, K., & Martens, C. (1996). Leisure education for persons with severe and persistent mental illness: Is it a socially valid process? *Therapeutic Recreation Journal, 30,* 197–212.

Mannell, R. C., & Kleiber, D. A. (1997). *A social psychology of leisure*. State College, PA: Venture Publishing, Inc.

Mundy, J. (1998). *Leisure education: Theory and practice* (2nd ed.). Champaign, IL: Sagamore.

Mundy, J., & Odum, L. (1979). *Leisure education: Theory and practice*. New York: John Wiley and Sons.

National Therapeutic Recreation Society. (1982). Philosophical position statement of the National Therapeutic Recreation Society.

National Therapeutic Recreation Society. (1993). Philosophical position statement of the National Therapeutic Recreation Society.

Neugarten, B. L., Havighurst, R. J., & Tobin, S. S. (1969). The measurement of life satisfaction. *Journal of Gerontology, 16,* 134–143.

Neulinger, J. (1974). *Psychology of leisure: Research approaches to the study of leisure*. Springfield, IL: Charles C. Thomas.

Neulinger, J. (1981). *The psychology of leisure* (2nd ed.). Springfield, IL: Charles C. Thomas.

Nour, K., Deroseirs, J., Gauthier, P., & Carbonneau, H. (2002) Impact of home leisure educational program for older adults who have had a stroke. *Therapeutic Recreation Journal, 36,* 48–64.

O'Reilly, M. F., Lancioni, G. E., & Kiernans, I. (2000). Teaching leisure social skills to adults with moderate mental retardation: An analysis of acquisition, generalization, and maintenance. *Education and Training in Mental Retardation and Developmental Disabilities, 35*(3), 250–258.

Parsons, L. D. (2006). Using video to teach social skills to secondary students with autism. *Teaching Exceptional Children, 39*(2), 32–38.

Patterson, I. (2007). Leisure education for special groups. In E. Cohen-Gewerc & R. A. Stebbins (Eds.). *The pivotal role of leisure education: Finding personal fulfillment in this century* (pp. 111–130). State College, PA: Venture Publishing, Inc.

Pegg, S. (2003). Improving recreation therapy outcomes for community-based consumers of a regional mental health service. *American Journal of Recreation Therapy, 2*(2), 35–45.

Peterson, C. A., & Gunn, S. L. (1984). *Therapeutic recreation program design: Principles and procedures*. Champaign, IL: Sagamore.

Peterson, C., Semmel, A., von Baeyer, C., Abramson, L. Y., Metalsky, G. I., & Scligman, M. E. P. (1982). The Attributional Style Questionnaire. *Cognitive Therapy and Research, 6,* 287–299.

Rancourt, A. (1991). Older adults with developmental disabilities/mental retardation: A research agenda for an emerging sub-population. *Annual in Therapeutic Recreation, 1,* 48–55.

Renwick, R., Brown, I., & Nagler, M. (Eds.). (1996). Quality of life in health promotion and rehabilitation. Thousand Oaks, CA: Sage.

Rosenberg, M. (1965). *Society and the adolescent self-image*. Princeton, NJ: Princeton University Press.

Ryan, S., & Fox, K. (2002). Working to honour difference. *Leisure/Loisir, 26*(1–2), 61–84.

Schwartzman, H. (1978). *Transformations: The anthropology of children's play.* New York: Plenum Press.

Searle, M., & Mahon, M. (1991). Leisure education in a day hospital: The effects on selected social-psychological variables among older adults. *Canadian Journal of Community Mental Health, 10*(2), 95–109.

Searle, M., Mahon, M., Iso-Ahola, S., Sdrolias, H., & van Dyck, J. (1995). Enhancing a sense of independence and psychological well-being among the elderly: A field experiment. *Journal of Leisure Research, 27*(2), 107–124.

Seligman, M. E. P. (1975). *Helplessness: On depression, development, and death.* San Francisco, CA: Freeman.

Shiffman, S., & Wills, T. (Eds.) (1985). Coping and substance abuse. Orlando, FL: Academic Press.

Sivan, A. (2007). Educating for leisure. In E. Cohen-Gewerc & R. A. Stebbins (Eds.). *The pivotal role of leisure education: Finding personal fulfillment in this century* (pp. 51–65). State College, PA: Venture Publishing Inc.

Stebbins, R. A. (2005). Choice and experimental definition of leisure. *Leisure Sciences, 27,* 349–352.

Stumbo, N. J., & Peterson, C. A. (2009). *Therapeutic recreation program design: Principles and procedures* (5th ed.). San Francisco: Benjamin Cummings.

Tennen, H., & Herzberger, S. (1985). Attribution style questionnaire. In D. J. Keyser & R. C. Sweetland (Eds.), *Test critiques* (Vol. 4, pp. 20–32). Kansas City: Test Corporation of America.

Van Straten, A., de Haan, R. J., Limburg, M., Schuling, J., Bossuyt, P. M., van den Bos, G.A.M. (1997). A stroke-adapted 30-item version of the Sickness Impact Profile to assess quality of life (SA-SIP30). *Stroke, 28,* 2155–2161.

Wehmeyer, M. L. (1996). Self-determination as an educational-outcome: Why is it important to children, youth and adults with disabilities? In D. J. Sands & M. L. Wehmeyer (Eds.), *Self-determination across the life span: Independence and choice for people with disabilities* (pp. 15–34). Baltimore, MD: Paul H. Brookes.

Williams, R., & Dattilo, J. (1997). Effects of leisure education on choice making, social interaction, and positive affect of young adults with mental retardation. *Therapeutic Recreation Journal, 31*(4), 244–258.

WRLA International Charter for Leisure Education. (1993). In A. Sivan, Recent developments in leisure education research and implementation. *World Leisure and Recreation, 39*(2), 43.

Witt, P., & Ellis, G. (1987). *The leisure diagnostic battery: Users' manual.* State College, PA: Venture Publishing, Inc.

Yang, N., Huang, T., Schaller, J., Wang, M., & Tsai, S. (2003). Enhancing appropriate social behaviors for children with autism in general education classrooms: An analysis of six cases. *Education in Training Developmental Disabilities, 38*(4), 404–416.

Chapter 8
Moral Development Discussions

Alexis McKenney and John Dattilo

*To educate a person in mind and not in morals is
to educate a menace to society.*
—Theodore Roosevelt

Introduction

In 1991, Thomas Lickona argued that America is faced with an escalating moral decline "ranging from greed and dishonesty to violent crime to self-destructive behaviors such as drug abuse and suicide" (p. 3).

> For example, in 2007, the Culture and Media Institute, a division of the Media Research Center found that 74% of Americans believe the United States has experienced a moral decline over the past 20 years. Kirschenbaum (1995) reported that the number of youth who have engaged in illegal sexual behavior such as date rape and gang rape and engaged in hate-related violence has increased. In 2002, one in twelve murders committed in the United States involved a juvenile offender (Office of Justice Programs, 2006).

Therapeutic recreation (TR) specialists are in a position to take a role in confronting violence and juvenile crime. Ipson and Cruse (1991) encouraged leisure professionals to join in moral development of today's youth and advocated reinforcement of social responsibility in leisure programs. By not acknowledging moral development within a leisure context, leisure professionals risk losing sight of the humanity and dignity of freedom associated with leisure (Fain, 1991). One approach TR professionals can take to address issues of moral development is through use of moral development discussions.

This chapter introduces the reader to moral development discussions as a TR intervention. After definitions associated with moral development are offered, an example of a description of a moral development discussion is presented. Next, the theoretical foundations of the cognitive-developmental approach to moral development are provided, followed by examples of studies that have demonstrated effectiveness when moral development discussions have been used. A case study is offered as an example of the potential effectiveness of a moral development discussion. Finally, a list of professional resources is provided.

Definitions

How people learn to think and behave morally depends on the stage of moral development in which they are functioning. To better understand how people develop morally, it is helpful to understand concepts of morality and developmental stages separately, as well as how these concepts are combined for implementation of moral development discussions. This section of the chapter is designed to help the reader develop an understanding of moral development by examining the following definitions:

- Morality
- Developmental and Moral Stages
- Moral Development
- Moral Development Discussions

Morality

"Morality in its broadest sense can be defined as interpersonal behavior that involves the rights, duties, or welfare of either party" (Leming, 1991, p. 268). Each one of us has a moral sense that helps us understand a universal set of rules; however, an understanding of particular exceptions is determined by each culture (Hauser, 2006). According to Leming, morality is a necessary element of any society and directs behavior in a way that promotes the rights and well-being of members of society. Societies require rules of moral behavior such as avoiding violence and respecting the rights of others that help to regulate relations among people (Leming, 1991). An individual's sense of morality develops through interaction with, and is challenged by, other members of the society.

Developmental and Moral Stages

Development is defined as the sequence of changes over an organism's life span (Reber, 1985). According to Reber, developmental stages are those periods of growth when certain characteristics surface within a human. Examples of human development include social, intellectual, emotional, and moral development. The advancement toward moral reasoning maturity is typically characterized in terms of a sequence of moral stages (Shields & Bredemeier, 2005). According to D'Alessandro and Power (2005), a moral stage is an organized pattern of thinking that gives particular moral concepts meaning. Stage development applies to moral development in that a general trend for moral behavior is associated with an individual's developmental and moral stage (Nucci, 2004).

Moral Development

The idea of moral development emerged from the study of morality as it is related to human development. Moral development, therefore, is development of the ability to distinguish right from wrong, to develop a system of ethical values, and to learn to act morally (Rich & DeVitis, 1994). Leming (1991) argued that moral development is a process by which a person develops from an egocentric state to one in which the person recognizes society's norms as just, and therefore, chooses to adhere to them.

Moral Development Discussions

Moral development discussions are based on Kohlberg's (1958) model of moral development. Moral development discussions use ethical dilemmas written to challenge participants to examine their thinking about moral issues such as social norms, conscience, life, and truth. Dilemmas generally focus on participants' lives, involve a central individual (or group of individuals) about which participants can make moral judgments, and involve a conflict for participants (Galbraith & Jones, 1976). Discussions require interacting with other people with the intention of changing the way participants orient themselves toward the social world. According to Nucci (2004), when such changes occur, the direction is typically toward the moral. For progression to occur, participants typically experience some distress when their moral judgment is challenged (D'Allesandro & Power, 2005). This experience is referred to as *cognitive disequilibrium*.

Summary

Morality functions to direct societal behavior in a way that promotes citizens' rights. Development involves changes over the course of a person's life. Just as people develop intellectually, socially, or emotionally, they develop morally. A person's sense of morality develops as that person's thoughts and beliefs are challenged by other members of a society. Moral development is comprised of a sequence of developmental and moral stages through which an individual moves from being selfish to choosing to follow societal norms perceived to be fair and just. An individual's stage of moral development can be influenced by moral development discussions comprised of dilemmas that challenge participants' thinking on moral issues.

Descriptions

One particular moral development discussion is designed to encourage participants to examine their thinking about moral issues and is based on Kohlberg's (1958) model of moral development. The discussion is comprised of moral dilemmas and associated probe questions. Probe questions are designed to stimulate discussion among participants about moral aspects of the dilemma stories (Galbraith & Jones, 1976). Galbraith and Jones suggested that moral development discussions be based on the following premises set forth by Kohlberg. First, if facilitators understand the developmental process of moral reasoning, they will be more prepared to implement a discussion that helps participants move toward moral maturity. Second, the discussion is designed to encourage self-reflection and a consideration of others when confronted with a dilemma. The discussion goes beyond the idea of telling participants to be fair by challenging their responses to moral problems. Third, compared to discussions designed to encourage value-neutrality, moral development discussions are designed to encourage participants to confront and work through moral dilemmas.

This section includes descriptions of the two major techniques used in moral development discussions:

- Moral Dilemmas
- Probe Questions

Moral Dilemmas

Moral dilemmas include issues such as social norms, property, conscience, civil liberties, life, authority, punishment, and truth. Recreation activity experiences offer authentic moral dilemmas and a means for participants to discuss their thoughts and ideas. Based on the essential ingredients provided by Galbraith and Jones (1976), each dilemma involves: (a) focusing on participants' lives or contemporary society; (b) a central individual (or group of individuals) that participants can make moral judgments concerning what individuals should do; (c) a genuine conflict for the involved individuals; (d) a central focus related to a moral issue such as property, life, or truth; and (e) a "should" question, such as "What should the involved individuals do in this situation?" Moral dilemmas can be presented associated with the following three categories:

- General
- Recreation-related
- Spontaneous

General dilemmas. General dilemmas involve situations that may be experienced by participants. Part of the dilemma involves individuals other than the population being served as the central character(s) and a portion of the dilemma includes the population being served at the time.

Recreation-related dilemmas. Recreation-related dilemmas involve situations that may occur during a person's free time or may involve decisions an individual may experience while engaged in a recreation activity.

Spontaneous dilemmas. Spontaneous dilemmas include dilemmas presented by participants before or during discussion. These dilemmas are unprepared and originate from participants' experiences or thoughts.

Probe Questions

Probe questions assist the facilitator in encouraging participants to remain focused on moral issues of the dilemma story and to interact with one another during discussions (Galbraith & Jones, 1976). According to Galbraith and Jones, the facilitator can combine four different kinds of probe questions to accomplish this task:

- Clarification
- Issue-related
- Alternative dilemma
- Interaction

The following is an example of a recreation-related dilemma and associated probe questions:

> Rosa and her best friend, Karen, are shopping in a department store. Karen finds a shirt she wants but cannot afford. She takes it into a fitting room and puts it underneath her jacket. She shows it to Rosa and, despite Rosa's protests, leaves the store. Rosa is stopped by a security guard. The manager searches Rosa's bag, but finds nothing and concludes that Karen stole the shirt. The manager asks Rosa for Karen's name, threatening to call both Rosa's parents and the police if she does not tell.

This dilemma provides an example of the essential ingredients of a dilemma story as described by Galbraith and Jones (1976). First, the dilemma focuses primarily on the life of Rosa; however, Karen's life would be affected by Rosa's decision. Second, the central individual who is faced with a moral decision is Rosa. Third, Rosa is faced with the conflict of deciding whether she should provide the manager with information about Karen. Fourth, the central focus related to a moral issue is that of truth and property. Finally, the primary *should* question would be, "What should Rosa do?"

Clarification probes. Clarification probes should be the same for each dilemma. The following questions are examples of clarification probes:

1. Who is/are the main character(s) of the story?
2. What is the problem faced by the main character(s)?

Issue-related probes. Issue-related probe questions are designed to provoke discussion among participants about the dilemmas. "Why" or "why not" questions follow most of the probes. The following questions are examples of issue-related probes:

1. What should Rosa do?
2. Should Rosa give the manager Karen's phone number?
3. Was it correct for Karen to steal the shirt from the store?
4. Is it ever correct for Karen to steal clothing from a store?
5. Should Rosa tell her parents what happened?
6. Should Karen be angry with Rosa if Rosa gives the manager Karen's phone number?

Alternative dilemma probes. Alternative dilemma probes are designed to provoke disagreement when the participants are all in agreement about how to solve a dilemma. The following statements are examples of alternative dilemmas probes:

If the group agrees that Rosa *should* give the manager Karen's phone number, the following alternative dilemma can be used to provoke disagreement:

Karen has been caught shoplifting before, and was grounded by her parents for 3 weeks as a result. If Karen is grounded, this time she will miss the prom, which is scheduled for the next week.

If the group agrees that Rosa *should not* give the manager Karen's phone number, the following alternative dilemma can be used to provoke disagreement:

Rosa has a police record because she has been arrested once before for shoplifting. The judge warned her that if she was arrested again, she would be taken to a juvenile detention center.

Interaction probes. Interaction probes are designed to promote discussion among the participants and are developed by the facilitator once the discussion has begun. The following questions are examples of interaction probes:

1. Angelina, do you agree with what Ben's just said about the dilemma story?
2. Sayeed, you disagreed earlier with Jack's position concerning Jin. Could you restate his position and respond to him from your point of view?

Summary

According to Galbraith and Jones (1976), moral development discussions are designed to encourage participants to examine their thinking about moral issues. The discussions are designed to help participants move toward moral maturity. Primary goals of moral development discussions are to encourage self-reflection and consideration of others. To achieve these goals, moral development discussions consist of general and recreation-related dilemmas as well as probe questions. Probe questions are used to encourage discussion and help participants focus on the dilemma. Examples of probe questions include those used for clarification, ones that are issue related, or alternative dilemmas and questions used to promote participant interactions.

History

The history of cognitive developmental moral development discussions can be traced to the work of Piaget (1932/1965). Piaget tested his theory of moral development by examining boys (ages 5–13) on how they played a game of marbles and how they responded to stories of moral events. Piaget proposed a two-stage model of moral development involving heteronomous morality and autonomous morality. When an individual operates within the *heteronomous morality* stage of development, that person's moral judgment is based on respect for authority figures. As individuals move to middle childhood or early adolescence, they begin to develop a morality of cooperation and autonomy, which Piaget referred to as *autonomous morality*. In the stage of autonomous morality, "social experience, principally peer interaction, becomes the main way to increasing cooperative and ethical growth" (Rich & DeVitis, 1994, p. 46).

Based on writings of Piaget, Kohlberg (1958) researched and formulated a model of moral development. According to Gibbs (2003), Kohlberg almost single-handedly changed the field of cognitive moral development. Kohlberg researched moral development by interviewing 75 adolescents using nine moral dilemmas (Lande & Slade, 1979). Kohlberg asked participants to solve dilemmas in an attempt to learn how they solved them and to discover their reasoning behind their solutions (Lande & Slade, 1979). From his study, Kohlberg proposed a theory of moral development in which all people move through a series of successive stages at varying rates when developing morally. Long-term results from his original study eventually led to refinement of the description and scoring of the stages (Gibbs).

Based on Kohlberg's work, moral development discussions have been used with students in regular classroom settings (e.g., Binfet, 2004), students considered to be behavior disordered (e.g., Niles, 1986), and youth identified as being delinquent (e.g., Gibbs, Arnold, Ahlborn, & Cheesman, 1984). Moral dilemma discussions are typically used as the primary discussion.

Theoretical Foundations

Kohlberg's model of moral development is based on a cognitive-developmental theory of moral judgment. As individuals develop their capacity for moral judgment, they are considered to be maturing morally (Nucci, 2004). According to Kohlberg, the cognitive-developmental theory maintains that the cognitive processing that occurs when a person experiences a conflict varies depending on the stage of moral development within which an individual is operating. Moral stages are primarily the products of an individual's social interactions (Kohlberg, 1987).

According to Kohlberg, the fundamental factor that influences structuring of moral order is social participation and role taking. Moral role taking involves an emotional component and an ability to define situations in terms of rights and duties, and the perspectives of other people. Based on his research, Kohlberg argued that all people advance through the stages in a successive order, and neither skip stages nor revert to prior stage reasoning. Kohlberg proposed that stages of moral development clustered into three levels:

- Preconventional
- Conventional
- Postconventional

Preconventional

At the preconventional level of moral development, the individual is responsive to labels of good and bad, right or wrong. People interpret these labels in terms of the consequences of action. This level is divided into the first two stages of moral development and may be labeled:

- Punishment and obedience
- Instrumental relativism

Punishment and obedience. Individual reasoning at the first stage of Kohlberg's moral development model, punishment and obedience, is egocentric in behavior and thinking. Physical consequences of actions determine whether the action is seen as good or bad by the individual. Avoiding punishment is important, but not because of a respect for *moral order*. People are valued according to the amount or quality of possessions, and justice is defined in terms of power and possessions.

Instrumental relativism. In the second stage of Kohlberg's model, instrumental relativism, the self is considered first, yet the idea of sharing is present. Correct action consists of actions that satisfy one's own needs and occasionally the needs of others. Individuals operate with the belief that how they treat others will determine how they will be treated. Fairness is a matter of equal exchange.

Conventional

One who operates at the conventional level of moral development is concerned with conformity to social order. Despite potential consequences, maintaining expectations of one's family or nation is imperative. Kohlberg divided this level into the next two stages of moral development:

- Good boy/nice girl
- Law and order

Good boy/nice girl. In the third stage of moral development, good boy/nice girl, good behavior requires approval by others. Being *nice* earns approval, while avoiding disapproval is motivation for conformity. Individuals who function at level three strive to follow role models such as being a good parent, a good employee, or a good student. Comparison of behavior is to others such as coworkers or peers occurs at this stage.

Law and order. Maintaining fixed order; that is, an orientation to authority and law, is the premise of stage four, law and order. Law and order are perceived as the most superior societal values. Laws uphold tradition, and are therefore necessary. Moral behavior means showing respect for authority and doing one's duty to maintain social order.

Postconventional

Apart from identifying with authority associated with groups, individuals make noticeable efforts to define moral values in the post-conventional level of moral development. Kohlberg's postconventional level includes the last two stages of moral development and may be labeled:

- Social contract
- Universal ethical principle

Social contract. At the fifth stage of moral development, social contract, correct action is defined in terms of general individual rights and standards critically examined and agreed upon by society. Unlike stage four, where the law is maintained at all cost, at this stage of moral development, an individual might question the fairness of a law. Conflicts between the group and individual beliefs surface in stage five. The individual may hold beliefs not generally held by a particular group.

Universal ethical principle. The sixth stage of moral development, universal ethical principle, is based on the idea that every person has the same rights. In particular, every human being has the right to freedom and human dignity. The universal ethical principles are justice, reciprocity, and equality of human rights. Also important is respect for dignity of human beings. Nucci (2004) argued that progression toward Stage 6 culminates in thinking that produces morally binding decisions.

Support for cognitive developmental theory. Colby and Kohlberg (1981) conducted a 20-year longitudinal study to demonstrate that people develop morally in the stages presented by Kohlberg. Fifty-three boys (ages 10–16) were presented with nine hypothetical moral dilemmas in an interview format at 3–4 year intervals. The authors predicted that participants would not move downward or omit stages. Results were consistent with Kohlberg's stage model of development. All participants reached a stage by advancing through a preceding stage. Changes were generally less than a full stage at each interval. Participants were typically in transition between two stages showing developmental change that involved primarily an increase in the next higher stage. Participants neither skipped stages nor reverted to prior stage reasoning. Nucci (2004) suggested that no schema can be skipped because each one is needed to move onto the next one.

Moral judgment and behavior. Although Kohlberg argued that knowledge of good will translates into good behavior, Blasi (1980; 1983) found that research that supported this argument were weak. Through his research on moral identity, Blasi discovered a link between moral judgment and moral behavior and suggested that moral identity serves as a linking variable between the two. Nisan (2004) explained that people's perception of morality as a part of their identity serves as a basis for motivating individuals to connect their moral judgment with their behavior.

Summary

Kohlberg's model of moral development is based on the cognitive developmental theory, which holds that cognitive processing occurring when one is faced with a conflict, varies depending on the individual's present stage of moral development. Kohlberg argued that all people advance through the six stages in successive order. The stages of moral development cluster into one of three levels including *preconventional*, *conventional*, and *postconventional*.

Effectiveness

Based on Kohlberg's model of moral development, researchers have incorporated the use of moral dilemma discussions into the practice of moral education (Gardner, 1983). Kohlberg's model of moral education uses group discussions of controversial dilemmas to create dissatisfaction with the participants' understandings of what is good. In particular, researchers have sought to examine how moral development can be advanced through the use of moral-dilemma discussions in adolescents considered to be behavior disordered, delinquent, or without behavior problems in a classroom and physical education setting.

Binfet (2004) examined effects of two moral reasoning interventions on 97 sixth and seventh graders (49 girls and 48 boys; ages 10–13) from four different classes. The two moral reasoning interventions included one during which students discussed moral dilemmas and one during which students reflected on moral dilemmas independently. Participants completed a questionnaire on demographic information and Gibb's Sociomoral Reflection Measure Short-Form (SRM-SF; Gibbs, Basinger, & Fuller 1992) to assess their moral reasoning levels. Next, participants were randomly assigned either to a moral dilemma discussion group, a non-moral discussion group, a moral reflective abstraction group, and a non-moral reflective abstraction group. All groups were presented with either moral or non-moral vignettes, respectively. After reviewing the vignettes, the discussion group was asked a series of probe questions designed to encourage discussion about the story. The reflective groups were asked to answer the probe questions in a written format. Following the experiment, the SMR-SF was used to measure participants' moral reasoning. No statistically significant differences between the post-test and the pre-test scores of the moral discussion group and moral reflection group were found; however, when compared to placebo groups, the two experimental groups (moral reasoning discussion and moral reflection groups) experienced statistically significant increases in moral reasoning.

For 16–20 weeks, **Arbuthnot and Gordon (1986)** conducted sessions involving moral-dilemma discussions, role-plays, and spontaneous situations (45 min, 1 x wk) with 35 male and 13 female adolescents (ages 13–17) reported by teachers as demonstrating aggressive, impulsive, and disruptive behavior. Participants were interviewed before and after the discussion using the Kohlberg Moral Judgment Interview (Kohlberg, 1958). Compared to 24 participants in the non-treatment control group who did not advance in moral reasoning scores after the discussion, the scores for the 24 participants in the experimental group increased significantly by advancing nearly one half of a stage.

Niles (1986) conducted an experimental moral development study with male adolescents (ages 13–15), 27 of whom were enrolled in an institutional school program, and 32 of whom attended a day school special education program. Participants were interviewed before and after the discussion to assess their stages of moral reasoning. Nineteen participants were then assigned to a treatment group, 19 to a placebo (values clarification) group, and 21 to a control group. The 16-week treatment group engaged in problem-solving activities aimed at consensus based on presented dilemmas (2 x wk). Although the same dilemmas were presented to the placebo group, the facilitator sought interaction and consensus using values clarification. Compared to the placebo and control groups, the moral-dilemma discussion group significantly affected the participants' moral development scores. Six out of seven participants in the treatment group moved from the first stage to the second stage of moral development, and the remaining participants in the treatment group who were tested at stage two before the discussion remained at stage two after the discussion. Participants in the placebo and control groups did not demonstrate movement to stage two.

Romance, Weiss, and Bockoven (1986) examined effects of an 8-week moral development physical education program on 32 elementary school children. The nine males and seven females in the experimental group received regular physical education instruction and special moral development teaching strategies. The eight males and eight females participated in physical education classes without moral development teaching strategies. Five strategies were used: (a) built-in dilemma/dialogue (a game with a built-in dilemma); (b) built-in dilemma/problem solve (participants encouraged to change the game as they wished); (c) self-created inclusive and fun games; (d) two cultures (one game with a built-in dilemma, one without); and (e) the listening bench (when faced with a conflict, participants would sit on a bench and discuss a dilemma). The experimental group demonstrated significantly more moral growth than the control group.

Gibbs and colleagues (1984) used a small-group 8-week moral-dilemma discussion (40 min, 1 x wk) with 30 male and 30 female incarcerated juvenile delinquents (ages 14–18). Participants were administered the Sociomoral Reflection Measure (Gibbs, Widaman, & Colby, 1980) and the Dilemma Decisions Survey before and after the discussion. Participants were assigned to one of three groups: discussions aimed at consensus, discussions that did not seek consensus, and no discussions (comparison group). Of participants who were assessed at stage two before the discussion, 88% advanced to stage three after the discussion, compared to only 14% of the comparison group. Participants who were assessed at stage three before the discussion remained at stage three after the discussion. Nonconsensus dilemma discussions were as effective in stimulating moral stage growth as were consensus dilemma discussions.

Rosenkoetter, Landman, and Mazak (1980) examined effects of a 7-week moral dilemma discussion (90 min, 1 x wk) with 13 male and 6 female adolescents (ages 13–16) found to be reasoning morally at stage two. Participants were administered the Kohlberg Measure of Stage assessment before and after the discussion, and were randomly assigned to either a treatment or comparison condition. Following the discussion, significant gains were found in the treatment group with 82% increasing one-fifth of a stage. Similar gains were not found with the comparison group.

In a study conducted with 132 sixth and tenth grade students, **Blatt and Kohlberg (1975)** examined effects of a 9-week direct discussion of moral-dilemma program stimulated moral development compared to simple exposure to dilemmas (45 min, 2 x wk). Using two treatment groups and a control group, one group engaged in discussions in which the instructor used a one-plus matching approach such as providing dilemmas designed to elicit responses one stage above the stage the participants indicated via testing prior to the discussion. The second group discussed the dilemmas without systematic leadership or the use of the one-plus matching. The group that received one-plus matching approach demonstrated significant increases in moral reasoning scores and maintained the effects after 1 year.

Summary

In summarizing literature reviewed in this section, existing research moderately indicates that the use of moral-dilemma discussions is an empirically supported facilitation technique. Although sample sizes overall have been low, moral-dilemma discussions have shown positive results when researchers have sought to promote moral stage growth in adolescents with behavior disorders (Arbuthnot & Gordon, 1986; Niles, 1986), youth categorized as juvenile delinquents (Gibbs & colleagues, 1984; Rosenkoetter & Landman, 1980), and youth receiving classroom training (Binfet, 2004; Blatt & Kohlberg, 1975) or a physical education class setting (Romance, Weiss, & Bockoven, 1986). Consequently, each study has helped to substantiate Kohlberg's (1958) argument that individuals develop morally in successive stages.

Case Study

Sam

Sam was a 16-year-old adolescent in the tenth grade residing in a long-term psychiatric treatment facility for adolescents. Sam was 1 year behind in school because of being incarcerated in a juvenile detention center for 6 months. Prior to his incarceration, Sam was admitted on three different occasions into short-term psychiatric facilities. Sam was originally diagnosed with oppositional defiant disorder; however, upon this admission he was diagnosed with conduct disorder. Sam's last admission to short-term psychiatric care followed a suspension from school for disruptive behavior demonstrated in the classroom. Sam's teacher reported that Sam was repeatedly verbally abusive toward him and his peers. Sam was taken to the juvenile detention center after being arrested for breaking and entering and possession of narcotics. After remaining incarcerated for 6 months, Sam was transferred to the long-term psychiatric facility.

Two weeks after his admission to the facility, Sam continued to demonstrate impulsive and violent behavior when frustrated. Sam told staff that when he was angry nothing mattered but "revenge" against whoever made him angry. As a result, Sam verbally or physically attacked his targets before taking time to think about what was making him angry or how his anger affected others or his treatment progress. Sam told staff that since he wanted to learn to think before he acted, he would therefore agree to cooperate with the treatment program. Sam was then assigned to the life management program, as well as the education, therapeutic recreation, and group therapy programs he already attended. Included in the life management program was a moral development discussion facilitated by the TR specialist.

Moral Development Discussion for Sam

The moral development discussion in which Sam participated involved the discussion of moral dilemmas with the TR specialist and 11 other adolescent participants. The moral development discussion was conducted three times per week for 1 explain what the discussion would involve and what was expected of him. Furthermore, Sam was administered the Sociomoral Reflection Measure-Short Form (SRM-SF) developed by Gibbs, Basinger, and Fuller (1992). The SRM-SF results revealed that Sam was reasoning at Kohlberg's stage two (instrumental relativism). Sam agreed to participate cooperatively in the program.

During the first two sessions, Sam sat quietly and listened to his peers. When interaction probe questions were used to encourage Sam to participate, Sam would answer with short answers without elaboration. Concerned that Sam was not motivated to participate, the TR specialist met with Sam after the group and asked him why he had not joined in the discussions. Sam explained that he was nervous and felt that he did not know the "right answers." The TR specialist explained to Sam that it was not a matter of "right answers"; rather, what was important was that Sam contributed so that he would benefit from hearing what others thought of his opinions as well as learning from other opinions. Sam stated that he would try to offer his thoughts during the next session.

During the next five sessions, Sam contributed his thoughts and opinions about most of the dilemmas discussed. On two occasions, Sam took a leadership role by asking probe questions himself. Sam, however, became angry with another participant during the sixth session, who challenged Sam's opinion in a dilemma about whether or not to use drugs. Sam left the group angry, and did not return until the seventh session. Sam explained to the TR specialist after the group that he became angry because "doing drugs" was one of the reasons he had been arrested and he felt that by using drugs he wasn't harming anyone, including himself. The TR specialist asked Sam if he would be willing to listen to how others felt after having a couple of days to calm down. Sam agreed and returned to the group.

Sam initially appeared angry after another participant pointed out to Sam that by his doing drugs he risked not only hurting or killing himself, but hurting his family. Sam sat quietly and listened while clenching his fists. To give Sam a moment to calm down, the discussion was directed toward another peer who also had used drugs in the past. After 10 minutes of discussion, Sam yelled, "Damn it! I know I'm making a bad decision when I use drugs. I just don't think about it when it's there in front of me." A few of the other participants said they understood because they too had the same problem. The TR specialist used this moment to ask several probe questions related to the dilemma. After the discussion ended and the group talked about how the activity went, Sam commented that this was the first time he ever felt that he might be able to stop and think when faced with problems. The TR specialist agreed that Sam demonstrated that he was capable of thinking before acting, but it would take practice.

Sam participated in the remainder of the moral development discussion groups. Sam maintained a leadership role by asking questions, participating actively in the discussions, and offering dilemmas that he has faced. Sam's teachers and therapist reported that he continued to demonstrate some impulsive behaviors; however, overall he had shown improvement. Sam's therapist stated that Sam was tempted to run away with two peers who had planned to leave for 2 days to "smoke cigarettes and drink beer." Instead, he was successful in convincing them that their plan would prolong their treatment. Upon completion of the discussion, Sam was, again, given the SRM-SF. Whereas Sam scored at Kohlberg's stage two (instrumental relativism) before the discussion, Sam scored at stage three (good boy/nice girl) after the discussion. At 1-month follow-up, Sam continued to demonstrate improved behavior in recreation therapy, group therapy, and school, and remained at Kohlberg's stage three of moral development.

Summary

Sam's diagnosis of conduct disorder stemmed from his oppositional behavior in school and his difficulties with the law. An evaluation of the moral development discussion group indicated that the discussion had a positive effect on Sam. Specifically, the discussion helped Sam to learn to consider what he should do and why he should do what is right when confronted with a conflict. Through his experiences during the discussion, Sam learned to accept feedback, the opinions of others, and to challenge others. As the discussions progressed, Sam demonstrated less impulsive behavior in school and in recreation therapy. Sam, furthermore, demonstrated moral stage growth.

Intervention Implementation Exercises

The following moral development discussion exercises have been developed for use in TR programs. Approximately three moral dilemmas can be presented during each activity period. If one dilemma is not presented due to time restrictions, it may be addressed during the next session. Some examples of dilemmas are adapted from Galbraith and Jones (1976) and Lande and Slade (1979); however, dilemmas can be created by the TR specialist based on personal experiences and examples depicted in the media. The following two guidelines are recommended if the TR specialist chooses to develop dilemmas. First, participants can identify the actual dilemma; therefore, the dilemmas do not exceed the ability levels of the participants. Second, the TR specialist includes the major elements of dilemma story which are: (a) a central individual or group of people that participants can make moral judgments concerning what the person(s) should do; (b) a genuine conflict for the involved individual(s); (c) a central focus related to a moral issue; and (d) a *should* question. The following six examples specific to recreation are presented:

- The Surprise
- The Open Window
- The Championship
- New Friends
- The New Club
- The Boyfriend

Dilemma One: The Surprise

Alex and Ike went to the video game store on Saturday morning to buy some video games. The store was very crowded and several other kids were lined up at the counter paying for video games. Ike picked up two games and Alex picked out one. Alex and Ike went to the counter to buy the games and had to stand in a crowd of other people also trying to buy things. There were several clerks working to help the many people in the store. One clerk was taking money and another clerk was putting the materials in bags for the customers. Alex and Ike paid the clerk, picked up their bags, and started home. When they got to their house and looked in the bags, they were surprised. In Ike's bag, he found two extra video games. In Alex's bag, she found extra batteries.

1. What should Alex and Ike do about the extra merchandise they found in their bags?
2. Should Alex and Ike keep the surprises?
3. Should Ike take the two games back to the video game store?
4. Is it okay for Alex to open the package of batteries?
5. Should Alex and Ike tell anyone else about their surprise? If so, who should they tell?
6. Should Alex and Ike try out the video games even if they plan to take them back to the store?
7. If Alex and Ike disagree about whether to return the surprises, how should they solve their disagreement?
8. If Alex and Ike do not return the surprises and their parents find out, should they be punished in any way?
9. What should Alex and Ike think about, before they use the surprises they found in their bags?

Dilemma Two: The Open Window

Each Friday evening after the recreation center had closed, the big playground next to the recreation center was always filled with teenagers. Teenagers from the neighborhood were always hanging out, talking to one another, playing games, or listening to music until after dark. On this particular evening, Cindy, Jason, and Paul, along with a lot of other teenagers had been listening to music and talking. It was almost 11:00 p.m. and the group was about to break up when one of the girls shouted, "Hey, look what I found!" Eight or nine of the teenagers ran over to the side of the building to find out why the girl was shouting. One of the windows in the recreation center was open. Jason had an idea: "Hey, let's boost each other up and go inside the center.

That will be fun! No one will be in the building except us and we can have fun." The kids all agreed and one by one were boosted up through the window and into the building. Cindy was one of the last ones to go in through the window and the other kids had started running through the halls of the empty building. A few kids took balls out and threw them around, some smoked cigarettes and others wrote graffiti on the walls with markers. Cindy was afraid. She wasn't sure she wanted to be part of this. She knew it was against the law to be inside the center after it was closed. She thought for a minute and decided that she better go home. It was almost curfew, anyway. She crawled back out of the window and ran home.

When Cindy arrived at the center the next Monday after school, she noticed that there was a lot of confusion. The recreation leaders were talking out in the hall, and a lot of teenagers were talking and laughing in the gymnasium. Cindy soon found out what all the confusion was about. The recreation director had visited each group and told the teenagers what had happened the night before: "Somebody had broken into the center and had caused quite a bit of damage that is still being repaired." The director explained that this was more than just a prank. The teenagers were not supposed to be in the center after it was closed. The recreation leader explained, "We are all proud of our recreation center and we all have to take responsibility for protecting the building and grounds. If anyone in the program knows about what happened in the building this weekend or who was involved, she or he should go to the director some time during the day and tell her what she or he knows."

1. Have you ever looked in the window of a building after it was closed?
2. Have you ever been playing with a group of your friends when someone said, "Let's go do something," and you were not sure whether you really wanted to do it or not, but you wanted to go along with your friends?
3. Should Cindy talk to the director and explain what happened on Friday?
4. Should she talk to her parents about what happened at the recreation center?
5. If she tells the director or the leader about what happened on Friday, should she mention that she was inside the center for a few minutes?
6. Is it right to go into a building if you find a window open?
7. Should her friends be angry with Cindy if she tells the director what happened?
8. Should Cindy say anything to any of the other teenagers about who was involved in the incident?
9. What was the worst thing that the teenagers did in the center? Place graffiti on the walls? Throw the balls out on the floor? Smoke cigarettes?
10. If Cindy's friends are discovered and taken to the director's office, should they be punished in any way for what they did?

If the group agrees that Cindy *should* tell the director about what happened on Friday, the following alternative dilemma can be used to provoke disagreement:

> Some of the teenagers who entered the center were caught entering the center last year, and were told that if they were caught again, legal charges would be brought up against them.

If the group agrees that Cindy *should not* tell the director about what happened on Friday, the following alternative dilemma can be used to provoke disagreement:

> The director announced to the teenagers that if no one took responsibility for the incident, then the recreation center grounds would have to be closed to everyone after hours.

Dilemma Three: The Championship

Prior to the track season, Coach Roberts of the Recreation Department received a complaint concerning the bias against girls in the program. According to the complaint, girls were not being given the same opportunities as boys to participate in the track program. Coach Roberts and the recreation director agreed that this complaint needed to be addressed promptly.

After meeting with the community's recreation board, Coach Roberts agreed to open the tryouts to girls. During the tryouts, Patty Connors did extremely well in the 440-yard dash. Patty worked very hard and her time for the event was excellent, but several of the boys could run the 440 faster. Patty was about equal to Tom, but not as good as Rico, Jamaal, and Harold.

Coach Roberts told Patty that she had made the team, and would run in the mile relay. Usually, Tom, Rico, Jamaal, and Harold ran the important relay race, but the team agreed that Patty and Tom would alternate for each track meet. Tom would run in every other meet for the season. During the season, the team of Tom, Rico, Jamaal, and Harold went undefeated, winning five relay races. When Patty ran, the team won two and lost two.

May 15 was the big day. Seven teams would compete for the city championship. The Recreation Department had a chance to win the city championship for the third straight year. As the meet progressed, it appeared that the mile relay could determine the championship. Patty knew that it was her turn to run on the relay team, and she was doing some warm-up exercises in preparation for the race.

The day before the city championship, Rico, Jamaal, and Harold talked about the possibility that the championship might hinge on the last relay. They knew that they could win the mile relay if the all-boy team ran. They decided that if the last relay were crucial to the outcome of the meet, they would ask Patty to withdraw voluntarily. With only two events to go, the boys looked at the scoreboard. Their team was one point out of first place and followed by a team one point behind them.

Rico, Jamaal, and Harold decided to go ahead with their plan. They approached Patty as she was doing her warm-up exercises. Harold asked Patty to fake a pulled muscle and tell the coach that she could not run in the relay. The boys explained to Patty that their team could win another championship if Tom could run with the team. Patty had to agree that the chances for a win would be better with Tom in the relay. She didn't know what to do.

1. Is winning the championship more important than giving Patty an opportunity to run in the race?
2. What is Patty's obligation to the team and winning the championship?

3. Should the fact that the coach and the team agree to let Patty run in alternative races be more important than the immediate situation of the championship?
4. From the point of view of Coach Roberts, what should Patty do?
5. What is the purpose of athletic programs in recreation settings?
6. Should women be allowed to participate in sports on an equal basis with men?
7. Should Patty go along with the request of the other team members?
8. Is it ever right to fake an injury?

If the group agrees that Patty *should* withdraw from the race, one of the following alternative dilemmas can be used to provoke disagreement:

1. A college sports scout is in the stands to watch Patty run. She is considering her for a track scholarship to college. Should that make a difference in the decision Patty makes?
2. A newspaper reporter is at the track meet to do a special feature on Patty. Should that make a difference in Patty's decision?

If the group agrees that Patty *should not* withdraw from the race, one of the following alternative dilemmas can be used to provoke disagreement:

1. Coach Roberts also asks Patty to voluntarily withdraw for the benefit of the team and the championship. Should that make a difference in the decision Patty makes?
2. The boys decide to boycott the relay race if Patty will not withdraw. Should that make a difference in the decision Patty makes?

The following are examples of additional recreation-related dilemmas that can be used and for which probe questions can be developed.

Dilemma Four: New Friends

Sid is 14 years old and recently completed the first half of his freshman year of high school. Sid spends a lot of time alone and has always had difficulty making friends. He has always enjoyed solitary recreation activities such as making models or drawing and painting. Sid does not like sports but wishes that he fit in with a group.

During the winter break from school, Sid started riding his bike each day down to the local convenience store where many of the other kids from his school were hanging out. One day, one of the boys in the group, Rocky, yelled out to Sid, "Hey kid, whatcha doing?" Sid, appearing shocked, asked, "Who? Me?" "Yeah, you!" responded Rocky. Sid went over and said, "Hi." The boy who yelled told Sid that he had seen him around school and wondered who he was. The boys talked for a while when Rocky suggested that they go to the park and get high. Rocky asked Sid if he would like to join them. Sid was not sure what to do. This was the first time a group of his peers had shown any interest in him as a friend.

1. Should Sid go with Rocky and the other boys to the park?
2. If Sid decides to go to the park, should he "get high" with the other boys?
3. Have you ever wanted to be part of a group?
4. Should Sid go along with the boys so that he could feel like part of a group?
5. If Sid felt uncomfortable with the idea of using drugs, what could he do?
6. Is it all right to use illegal drugs?
7. What are the consequences of using illegal drugs?

If the group agrees that Sid *should* join Rocky and his friends, the following alternative dilemma can be used to provoke disagreement:

> Although Sid chooses to visit the local convenience store each
> day, the local recreation department offers group programs for
> youth. Sid has not gone because he is afraid to go alone. What
> should Sid do?

If the group agrees that Sid *should not* join Rocky and his friends, the following alternative dilemma can be used to provoke disagreement:

> This is the first time Sid has ever been invited by another teenager
> to participate in a group activity. Sid feels that if he doesn't join
> them, he will never have another opportunity.

Dilemma Five: The New Club

Sid has just finished his freshman year of high school and has continued to hang around Rocky and his friends at the convenience store. Sid is now frequently smoking cigarettes and marijuana with his friends and has lost interest in activities he had been doing alone, such as model building and drawing. Some of the kids who were hanging out at the store are now going on summer vacation, but two new kids have started hanging around the store. One of the kids, Rob, has become the leader of the group and Sid feels intimidated by him.

The two new kids are involved in a *skinhead* group. Rob explained to Sid that the skinheads are a neo-Nazi group that works to maintain rights of white people. Rob went on to explain how they feel that Jews and blacks are receiving too many rights, and it is time to take a stand. Sid agreed to attend a meeting. At first, Sid felt uncomfortable because everyone at the meeting was drinking alcohol or using drugs other than marijuana, and many of members carried guns.

At the end of the first meeting, Sid had a chance to walk around and meet many of the members. Everyone was very friendly to Sid. One of the members even asked Sid if he would like to join. Sid had never felt more accepted by a social group.

1. Should Sid join the neo-Nazi group?
2. What should Sid think about when considering whether to join the group?
3. If Sid joins the group, should he consider using drugs?
4. Is it right to discriminate against people based on their religion or race?
5. Is it right to ever carry a gun?

6. If Sid chooses not to join the group, what should he do?
7. Should Sid talk to an adult about his experience with the group?

If the group agrees that Sid *should* join the neo-Nazi group, the following alternative dilemma can be used to provoke disagreement:

> Sid has made one friend who is African American in school since he began hanging around at the convenience store. Should Sid consider him when making the decision? Should Sid risk losing this friendship?

If the group agrees that Sid *should not* join the neo-Nazi group, the following alternative dilemma can be used to provoke disagreement:

> Rob has a lot of influence over the group that hangs around the convenience store. Sid feels that if he does not do what Rob asks him, he will no longer be part of the group. Sid also fears that he may be physically hurt if he does not do what Rob asks of him. What should Sid do?

Dilemma Six: The Boyfriend

Pasha is a junior in high school, and has been dating the same boy since she was a freshman. Pasha has recently discovered that her boyfriend, Justin, has been secretly dating a girl from another school. Pasha confronted Justin on the affair and he agreed to stop seeing the other girl. Two weeks later, Justin tells Pasha that he has to spend the weekend with his family, so he won't be able to do anything with her.

That Saturday night, Pasha and her friends saw Justin at the beach with the other girl. Pasha's friend, Leona exclaimed, "That jerk! I'm going to let the air out of his tires." Pasha starts to giggle and says to Leona, "You're the best. You wouldn't really do that, would you?" "Oh, yes I would," Leona responds. "But what if he catches you?" Pasha asks. Leona responds, "So what if he catches me? He deserves it—the creep. Besides, he's not even paying attention." Pasha then said, "But if you give him four flat tires, he'll probably not get home on time and get in trouble with his family. He's already in trouble with his family and that won't help."

Ignoring what Pasha said, Leona hopped out of her car, removed a screwdriver from the trunk and started working on Justin's tires. Pasha sat in the car feeling a bit uncomfortable. Although she was not certain if Justin would get in trouble, Pasha did not really want to risk getting Justin in trouble with his family. Pasha also could not help but enjoy the fact that somebody was doing something other than sympathize with her. A bit nervous, Pasha kept glancing at the beach walkway while Leona walked toward Justin's car.

1. Should Pasha allow Leona to let the air out of Justin's tires?
2. Does Pasha have a good reason to take revenge on Justin?
3. Is it ever right to destroy another person's property?

4. Is it ever right to physically hurt another person?
5. Is it right if someone else is taking the revenge for you?
6. What else could Pasha do about the situation?
7. Was it right for Leona to get involved?
8. Is it right to lie to another person?
9. What could Justin have done differently?

If the group agrees that Pasha *should* allow Leona to let the air out of Justin's tires, the following dilemmas can be used to provoke disagreement:

1. Pasha knows that Justin's parents have warned him that if he returns home late one more time, he will be grounded for a month.
2. Pasha and Leona can tell Justin is with somebody, but they cannot tell if it is the other girl Justin has been seeing, or if it is a male friend.

If the group agrees that Pasha *should not* allow Leona to let the air out of Justin's tires, the following dilemma can be used to provoke disagreement:

> Justin's car is parked only one block from his home and he has an emergency car service that he can call if he has an emergency.

Summary

The intervention implementation exercises presented in this chapter can be used to increase understanding on how to facilitate moral development discussions. In addition to using the presented examples, moral development discussions may be promoted based upon personal experiences or situations depicted in movies, television, or media. The moral dilemmas presented are starting points and can be modified to accommodate different groups of participants based on their needs and skills.

Conclusion

America is faced with a moral decline among youth (Lickona, 1991). This decline is consistent with the numbers of youth who have engaged in illegal behaviors such as rape, violence, and cheating (Kirschenbaum, 1995). Leisure professionals are in a position to confront this moral decline by addressing the issue of moral development. One moral development discussion that TR specialists can employ to address this issue is the cognitive-developmentally based moral development discussion. This chapter presented a description of moral development as it relates to TR that included related definitions, a description of the strategies, theoretical foundations, effectiveness studies, a case study, and professional resources and references.

Discussion Questions

1. What is the definition of moral development?
2. What are the two stages of moral development as defined by Piaget?
3. What are the six stages of moral development as defined by Kohlberg?
4. What three premises identified by Galbraith and Jones are followed when designing moral development discussions?
5. What do Galbraith and Jones suggest be included in moral dilemmas?
6. What are four types of probe questions used in moral-dilemma discussions?
7. What is the cognitive developmental theory of moral development?
8. What did Colby and Kohlberg find in their longitudinal study of moral development?
9. How have moral development discussions been effective with adolescents with behavior disorders?
10. What was the outcome of the moral development discussion used with "Sam?"

Resources

Agency Resources

Association for Moral Education
National-Louis University
Psychology Department
122 South Michigan Ave.
Chicago, IL 60603
http://www.amenetwork.org/

Character Education Partnership
1025 Connecticut Avenue, N.W.
Suite 1011
Washington, D.C. 20036
Phone: (800) 988-8081
http://www.character.org

CharacterCounts!/ Josephson Institute of Ethics
9841 Airport Blvd.
Suite 300
Los Angeles, CA 90045
Phone: (800) 711-2670 & (310) 846-4800
http://www.charactercounts.org

School for Ethical Education
440 Wheelers Farms Rd.
Milford, CT 06460
Phone: (203) 783-4439
http://www.ethicsed.org

Association for Moral Education
http://www.amenetwork.org

Center for the Advancement of Ethics and Character
Boston University
621 Commonwealth Ave.
Boston, MA 02215
Phone: (617) 353-3262
http://www.bu.edu/education/caec

References

Arbuthnot, J., & Gordon, D. A. (1986). Behavioral and cognitive effects of a moral reasoning development intervention for high-risk behavior-disordered adolescents. *Journal of Consulting and Clinical Psychology, 54,* 208–216.

Binfet, T. (2004). It's all in their heads: Reflective abstraction as an alternative to the moral discussion group. *Merrill-Palmer Quarterly, 50,* 181–201.

Blasi, A. (1980). Bridging moral cognition and moral action: A critical review of literature. *Psychological Bulletin, 88,* 1–45.

Blasi, A. (1993). The development of identity: Some implications for moral functioning. In G. G. Noam & T. E. Wren (Eds.), *The moral self* (pp. 99–122). Cambridge, MA: MIT Press.

Blatt, M. M., & Kohlberg, L. (1975). The effects of classroom moral discussion upon children's level of moral judgment. *Journal of Moral Education, 4,* 129–161.

Colby, A., & Kohlberg, L. (1981). *Invariant sequence and internal consistency in moral judgment stages.* (ERIC Document Reproduction Service No. ED 223514). Cambridge, MA: Graduate School of Education, Harvard University.

Culture and Media Insitute (2007). *Madonna's dilemma: Survey shows America in cultural, spiritual confusion.* Retrieved October 10, 2008, from the Culture and Media Insitute, from http://www.cultureandmediainstitute.org/articles/2007/20070307144654.aspx.

D'Alessandro, A. H, & Power, F. C. (2005). Character, responsibility, and the moral self. In D. K. Lapsley & F. C. Power (Eds.), *Character Psychology and Character Education* (pp. 101–120). Notre Dame, IN: University of Notre Dame Press.

Fain, G. S. (1991). Moral development and leisure experience. In G. S. Fain (Ed.), *Leisure and ethics: Reflections on the philosophy of leisure* (pp. 21–23). Reston, VA: American Alliance for Health, Physical Education, Recreation, and Dance.

Galbraith, R. E., & Jones, T. M. (1976). *Moral reasoning: A teaching handbook for adapting Kohlberg to the classroom.* Anoka, MN: Greenhaven Press.

Gardner, E. M. (1983). *Moral education for the emotionally disturbed early adolescent: An application of Kohlbergian techniques and spiritual principles.* Lexington, MA: Lexington Books.

Gibbs, J. C. (2003). *Moral development and reality: Beyond the theories of Kohlberg and Hoffman.* Thousand Oaks, CA: Sage Publications.

Gibbs, J. C., Arnold, K., Ahlborn, H., & Cheesman, F. (1984). Facilitation of socio-moral reasoning in delinquents. *Journal of Consulting and Clinical Psychology, 52*, 37–45.

Gibbs, J. C., Basinger, K. S., & Fuller, D. (1992). *Moral maturity: Measuring the development of sociomoral reflection*. Hillsdale, NJ: Lawrence Erlbaum Associates.

Gibbs, J. C., Widaman, K. F., & Colby, A. (1980). The sociomoral reflection measure. In L. Kuhmerker, M. Mentkowski, & V. L. Erickson (Eds.), *Evaluating moral development and evaluating educational programs that have a value dimension* (pp. 101–111). Schenectady, NY: Character Research Press.

Hauser, M. (2006). *Moral minds: How nature designed our universal sense of right and wrong*. New York: Harper Collins.

Ipson, N. M., & Cruse, D. L. (1991). Character education: Something's missing—Whose responsibility? In G.S. Fain (Ed.), *Leisure and ethics: Reflections on the philosophy of leisure* (pp. 260–263). Reston, VA: American Alliance for Health, Physical Education, Recreation, and Dance.

Kirschenbaum, H. (1995). *100 ways to enhance values and morality in schools and youth settings*. Boston: Allyn & Bacon.

Kohlberg, L. (1958). The development of modes of moral thinking and choice in the years ten to sixteen. Unpublished doctoral dissertation, University of Chicago, Chicago, IL.

Kohlberg, L. (1987). The development of moral judgment and moral action. In L. Kohlberg (Ed.), *Child psychology and childhood education: A cognitive developmental view* (pp. 259–328). White Plains, NY: Longman.

Lande, N., & Slade, A. (1979). *Stages*. San Francisco, CA: Harper & Row.

Leming, J. S. (1991). The contribution of leisure to moral development. In G. S. Fain (Ed.), *Leisure and ethics: Reflections in the philosophy of leisure* (pp. 267–285). Reston, VA: American Alliance for Health, Physical Education, Recreation and Dance.

Lickona, T. (1991). *Education for character. How our schools can teach respect and responsibility*. New York: Bantam Books.

Nisan, M. (2004). Judgment and choice in moral functioning. In D. K. Lapsley & D. Narvaez (Eds.), *Moral development, self, and identity* (pp. 133–160). Notre Dame, IN: University of Notre Dame Press.

Niles, W. J. (1986). Effects of a moral development discussion group on delinquent and predelinquent boys. *Journal of Counseling Psychology, 33*, 45–51.

Nucci, L. (2004). Reflections on the moral self construct. In D. K. Lapsley & D. Narvaez (Eds.), *Moral development, self, and identity* (pp. 133–160). Notre Dame, IN: University of Notre Dame Press.

Office of Justice Programs/U.S. Department of Justice (2006). *Juvenile Offenders and Victims: 2006 National Report*. Retrieved October 10, 2008 from http://www.ojjdp.ncjrs.gov/ojstatbb/nr2006/index.html.

Piaget, J. (1965). *The moral judgment of the child*. New York: Free Press. (Original work published 1932.)

Reber, A. S. (1985). *Dictionary of psychology*. New York: Penguin Books.

Rich, J. M., & DeVitis, J. L. (1994). *Theories of moral development*. Springfield, IL: Charles C. Thomas.

Romance, T. J., Weiss, M. R., & Bockoven, J. (1986). A program to promote moral development through elementary school physical education. *Journal of Teaching in Physical Education, 5,* 126–136.

Rosenkoetter, L. I., Landman, S., & Mazak, S. G. (1980). Use of moral discussion as an intervention with delinquents. *Psychological Reports, 46,* 1, 91–94.

Shields, D. L., & Bredemeier, B. L. (2005). Can sports build character? In D. K. Lapsley & F. C. Power (Eds.), *Character psychology and character education* (pp. 121–139). Notre Dame, IN: University of Notre Dame Press.

Chapter 9
Stress Management

Travis Meckley, John Dattilo, and Sharon Malley

Things are neither good nor bad, but thinking makes them so.

— William Shakespeare

Introduction

Stress is believed to be the leading cause of illnesses in modern society (Goliszek, 1987). Although primarily associated with work, stressful situations can occur during any aspect of individuals' lives and can impact their capacity to experience leisure.

Although the effects of stress can be extensive, there are specific ways to prevent, counteract, and alleviate them. The number and variety of popular self-help books devoted to the management of stress indicates that stress is recognized as a problem across many segments of society. However, individuals experiencing problems associated with disabilities may not possess the resources to understand and address effects of stress; therefore, stress management programs provided by TR specialists may be helpful.

This chapter examines the topic of stress and ways to manage negative stress. After definitions associated with stress are provided, there are descriptions of two stress-management techniques. Following a discussion of the history and theoretical foundations of stress management, current research is reviewed. Additionally, two case studies, intervention implementation exercises, discussion questions, and stress management resources are provided.

Definitions

To help promote an understanding of stress management, four definitions related to stress and two definitions related to stress management techniques are presented. The definitions in this chapter include:

- Stress
- Distress
- Eustress
- Yoga
- Hatha
- Progressive Relaxation

Stress

Stress is defined as an external force that produces strain on a structure. The external force is the stressor and the strain it produces is stress (Goliszek, 1987). Another definition focuses on the subjective experience of stress, in that stress is the "perception that events or circumstances have challenged, or exceeded, a person's ability to cope" (Time-Life Books, 1987, p. 8). Taken together, the definitions and explanations provided in this section indicate that the perception of a stressor leads to the physical changes that result in the emotional feelings of stress.

Distress

Derived from the Latin word, *dis*, which means bad, distress is defined as an "unpleasant or disease producing stress" (Selye, 1976, p. 465). Examples of the damaging effects of stress include high blood pressure, emotional disturbance, gastric ulcers, and various types of sexual, allergic, and vascular conditions.

Eustress

Eustress, derived from the Latin word, *eu*, which means good, is positive stress that represents challenge for personal growth (Selye, 1976). Certain recreational activities, such as mountain climbing, skiing, competitive sports, and games are chosen for their ability to induce eustress (Leitner, Leitner, & Associates, 1996). This type of stress promotes optimal arousal in the individual, resulting in positive experiences such as enjoyment, improved self-esteem, and competence.

Yoga

The practice of yoga today involves a system of physical controls. In Western culture, the purpose is to bring about physical and mental well-being (Hewitt, 1977). Hatha yoga, one of the many classifications of yoga, uses physical postures and proper breathing to relieve stress and provide physical rejuvenation. It is the most widely practiced and understood form of yoga in Western culture (Hewitt, 1977) and here-after will be referred to as simply "yoga." In yoga, to realize the self beyond the ego is to find the union between the individual being and the "Cosmic Being." That union is called "yoga" (Smith, 1986).

Hatha

The word *hatha* is derived from two root words in Sanskrit. *Ha* means *sun,* and *tha* means *moon.* The regulation of breath is central to hatha yoga, with the flow of breath in the right nostril representing "sun breath" and the flow of breath in the left nostril representing "moon breath" (Hewitt, 1977).

Progressive Relaxation

Progressive relaxation, also known as relaxation therapy, relaxation training, progressive muscle relaxation, and progressive relaxation training, is a method for treating individuals experiencing psychological stress and physical symptoms associated with stress (Lehrer, Batey, Woolfolk, Remde, & Garlick, 1988). *Progressive relaxation* is defined as the systematic application of techniques that enable people to relax or reduce physical tension (Lucic, Steffen, Harrigan, & Stuebing, 1991).

Descriptions

The routines, habits, and attitudes associated with daily life determine how well individuals will respond to stress. The underlying theme of stress management is control. Individuals who feel that they are in control of situations and events are less likely to experience stress. Although it is difficult to control every stress-inducing event, individuals can control how they react to such events.

Increases in stress affect leisure participation; more specifically, when individuals are confronted with stressors, they decrease their leisure involvement in most areas except for relaxing activities (Patterson & Coleman, 1996). Activities particularly designed to manage stress that are often used as interventions by human service personnel include yoga, meditation, progressive relaxation, and biofeedback. To manage stress in individuals with disabilities, it is often helpful for TR specialists to possess the knowledge of specific interventions. Many stress management techniques have been used by TR specialists. The following two techniques are presented in this chapter:

- Yoga
- Progressive Relaxation

Yoga

Yoga is the oldest and most complete system of personal development that focuses on the mind, body, and spirit. It is a living science that has evolved over thousands of years from the beliefs of Indian Hinduism (Smith, 1986). Yoga was developed to reveal humans' essential nature by increasing understanding of the relationship between the body and the mind.

Although yoga is directly linked to a spiritual foundation, researchers have begun to study effects of yoga. Anticipated benefits of yoga are based on the belief that reduction in stress and anxiety results from the practice of yoga (Angus, 1989). Yoga has also been linked with increased strength and flexibility.

Yoga is based on several assumptions including the beliefs that:

- Proper exercise stimulates body systems and develops muscles.
- Breathing full, regular breaths increases energy.
- Relaxation releases deep tension in the body and mind.
- Diet in harmony with nature aids in development of a steady mind.
- Positive thinking and meditation increases happiness.

The physical exercise associated with yoga is achieved through a series of *asanas,* or body postures, which are designed to increase flexibility and static muscle strength

(Berger & Owen, 1992). Participants relax into the postures to stretch and strengthen their muscles as much as possible. The combination of regulated breathing and body postures enables participants to focus inward on internal physical and mental states. This inward focusing frees participants from distractions and mental stresses and provides a respite from life's responsibilities.

Programs that offer yoga vary widely, but a group yoga session led by a qualified teacher typically lasts about 90 minutes (Hannon, 1994). Typically, sessions begin with about 10 or 15 minutes of breathing exercises, continue with 30 minutes of seated postures, and then 30 minutes of standing postures. The session often culminates with about 15 minutes of relaxation postures or guided relaxation.

There are more than 1,000 postures practiced in yoga (Hannon, 1994). The postures can be combined and adapted to address individuals' body types and needs. Because agility and advanced lung capacity are not prerequisites for yoga, many people who either lead sedentary lifestyles and/or have a disability can practice yoga.

Many postures associated with yoga are named for the visual image that the position of the body projects.

> For example, a participant in the "cobra" posture (see Figure 9.1) begins by lying face down on the floor and then slowly pushing up on the hands to extend the head, neck, shoulders, and upper torso up in an arch. The posture resembles a cobra rearing back its head to strike.

Although the general intention of yoga is to quiet the mind, according to Hewitt (1977) each of the postures is designed to address specific bodily functions.

> For example, the cobra posture is intended to exercise the spine, vertebra by vertebra, and nourish the spinal nerves with blood. Inverted postures, such as "shoulder stand" (see Figure 9.2), are intended to address circulatory problems.

The postures in hatha yoga are often paired to provide opposite stretches or strengthening.

> A posture that stretches the spine in a backward arch, such as the cobra, would be followed by a posture that stretches the spine in a forward curve, such as "back stretching" (see Figure 9.3). The back-stretching posture involves sitting on the floor with legs outstretched straight in front and bending the upper torso from the waist to stretch over the legs. Postures that require asymmetrical movements of the body are repeated on the other side of the body. For example, "tree" posture, which involves balancing on one leg (see Figure 9.4), is always repeated by balancing on the other leg (see Figure 9.5).

Progressive Relaxation

A stress management technique used extensively over the last two decades is progressive relaxation (Lehrer et al., 1988). According to Bernstein and Borkovec (1973), it is essential that the facilitator of progressive relaxation be familiar with the procedures, the complexity of the technique, its limits, and the problems that may arise in its use.

Bernstein and Borkovec's manual was designed specifically for professionals in human services, providing a detailed description of a modified version of Edmund Jacobson's technique, procedures, case examples, and possible problems associated with the training. Because the work of Bernstein and Borkovec simplified Jacobson's technique, it is often referred to as "abbreviated progressive relaxation training" (Carlson & Hoyle, 1993). Bernstein and Borkovec provided specific suggestions for developing an effective environment. For instance, they suggested using a quiet room with a chair that is completely supportive, ideally a well-padded recliner chair. They also suggested focusing on helping participants feel comfortable. One way to

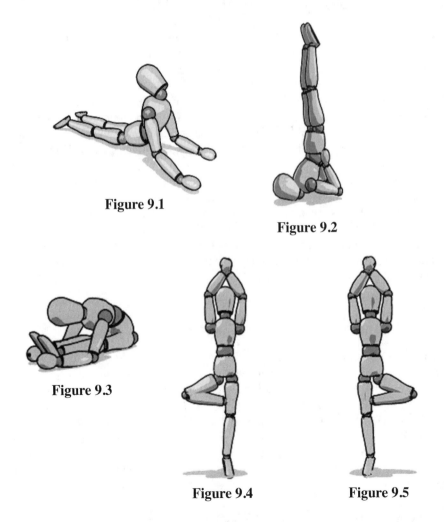

Figure 9.1

Figure 9.2

Figure 9.3

Figure 9.4

Figure 9.5

do this is to encourage participants to wear loose-fitting clothing and to remove their glasses, watch, jewelry, and shoes.

In addition, Bernstein and Borkovec explained that the first session is devoted to instilling confidence in and appreciation of the procedure. The role of tension in relation to the participant's life is explained, with further discussion of how management of the tension can result in certain improvements. A description of the technique is given, with an explanation of how it works. The participant is then guided through a full relaxation session while seated comfortably in the recliner chair.

The basic procedures outlined by Bernstein and Borkovec to be followed by the participant during each relaxation session include:

- Focus attention on muscle group named by facilitator.
- Tense muscle group at a predetermined signal from facilitator.
- Maintain tension for a period of 5 to 7 seconds.
- Release muscle group tension at predetermined signal from facilitator.
- Maintain attention on the muscle group as it relaxes.

The order of tension and release of the 16 muscle groups is dominant hand and forearm, dominant biceps, non-dominant hand and forearm, non-dominant biceps, forehead, upper cheeks and nose, lower cheeks and jaws, neck and throat, chest, shoulders, upper back, abdominal or stomach region, dominant thigh, dominant calf, dominant foot, non-dominant thigh, non-dominant calf, and non-dominant foot. Bernstein and Borkovec concluded that when guiding participants through the succession of tension and release, the facilitator should maintain a calm comforting tone of voice. Please refer to the exercises at the end of this chapter to obtain a narrative of the process.

The major difference between the techniques developed by Jacobson and by Bernstein and Borkovec is in the use of muscle contractions (Lucic et al., 1991). Although Jacobson's initial procedures required participants to contract muscles individually and sequentially to acknowledge the sensations, he emphasized that contractions were not to be used as an aid in relaxation. Bernstein and Borkovec indicated that the contractions used during the relaxation sessions aid participants in attaining greater relaxation.

History

The stress response, also known as the "fight or flight" response was vital to the survival of our ancestors (Rowshan, 1993). Although life-threatening situations are uncommon in modern society, individuals continue to respond to more commonplace events as if they were life threatening (Goliszek, 1987). According to Eliot (1994), many individuals experience the physiological changes necessary to adapt to life-threatening situations on a daily basis. In many people, these physiological changes lead to further problems, both physically and emotionally.

A variety of techniques have been used over the years to manage stress. A brief history of the following two techniques is provided in this section:

- Yoga
- Progressive Relaxation

Yoga

Hewitt (1977) indicated that to understand yoga's history is to understand Hindu and Indian culture. Yoga is intertwined with India's religion, literature, and folklore, serving as a basis for its culture. Unlike other major world religions, which center on the activities of a founder, Hinduism evolved gradually over a period of 5,000 years (Smith, 1986). One possible origin is from the Aryans, who migrated to the valleys of the Indus and Ganges about 2,000 B.C. (Hewitt, 1977).

The earliest indications of yoga practice are found in 5,000-year-old ceramics, which were decorated with yogic meditative postures. The first Upinshads, which are sacred literature describing the purest yogic philosophy, were written between 800 and 500 B.C. Hinduism has become a national Indian religion that is centered on the belief that there are four paths to spiritual truth (Smith, 1986). It is a way of conduct, rather than a system of doctrines, with the practice of various yogas providing the paths to spiritual truth.

Progressive Relaxation

Progressive relaxation training was developed by Edmund Jacobson after he conducted studies at Harvard University in 1908 and continued the studies at Cornell University and at University of Chicago (Birch, 1987). He first published a description of his technique in the *American Journal of Psychology* in 1925 and he reported on the culmination of his studies in his book *Progressive Relaxation*, published in 1938. Since Jacobson's developments, there have been numerous modifications, adaptations, and applications of the technique, most notably, that of Wolpe's (1958) "systematic desensitization" technique used often with individuals who express anxiety surrounding a particular setting or event.

Theoretical Foundations

Theoretical foundations related to the value of stress management interventions are based on current knowledge of the body's response to stress. The negative effects of stress on the body and mind vary for every individual and are described below. Two theories found in the literature include:

- Physiological Disruption Due to Stress
- Analytical Introspection

Physiological Disruption Due to Stress

According to Eliot (1994), there are two major ways in which the body responds to stress. The two bodily responses include:

- Acute alarm
- Chronic vigilance

Acute alarm. The acute alarm reaction is the short-term "fight or flight" response that begins in the hypothalamic region of the brain. A message is sent along the sympathetic nervous system to the adrenal glands located near the kidneys. The adrenal glands release catacholamines into the bloodstream, which, along with other physiological reactions, cause the following to occur:

- increase in heart rate for additional power and blood volume
- elevation in blood sugar levels for increased muscle energy
- shift of blood volume from digestive organs to skeletal muscles for added power
- faster blood clotting in the event of a wound
- widening of pupils for greater awareness and visual acuity
- increase in rate of breathing for greater oxygen supply to vital organs

While the adrenal glands release catacholamines, the brain releases endorphins (Goliszek, 1987). Endorphins decrease the body's sensitivity to pain (Eliot, 1994). A chronic state of acute alarm causes neglect of other bodily functions which can weaken the immune system or leave the body vulnerable in previously injured areas.

Chronic vigilance. The chronic vigilance response to stress enables the body to respond to long-term persistent danger. This response is triggered by the pituitary gland at the base of the brain which stimulates the adrenal gland to release cortisol into the bloodstream (Goliszek, 1987). Accoring to Eliot (1994), cortisol causes the following physical changes to occur:

- irritability and hyper-alertness
- fat storage for insulation and energy reserves
- salt retention
- elevated blood pressure
- loss of potassium, magnesium, and other essential minerals
- erratic heart rhythms
- increased fats and cholesterol in the bloodstream
- suppression of sex hormones
- increased gastric acid

When someone experiences physiological changes associated with stress more than is necessary for the situation or event, certain negative symptoms are likely to occur. Rowshan (1993) proposed that symptoms of stress may be categorized into five types:

- spiritual
- social
- emotional
- mental
- physical

Spiritual symptoms include feelings of emptiness and hopelessness, loss of direction, and hostility toward others. Social symptoms include self-centeredness, loneliness, withdrawal, and intolerance. Emotional symptoms include anxiety, anger, depression, apathy, and nervous laughter. Mental symptoms include frequent lapses of memory, racing thoughts, poor concentration, and poor judgment. Physical symptoms include sudden weight changes, headaches, muscle tension, high blood pressure, frequent colds, stuttering, and chronic fatigue.

Analytical Introspection

The theory upon which Jacobson based progressive relaxation training was derived from his interest in analytical introspection. Analytical introspection is the process by which individuals gain the ability to control their thoughts and emotions with thoughtful reflection. Interested in developing a method that would "bring quiet to the nervous system" (Jacobson, 1925/1987, p. 523), Jacobson hypothesized that if individuals practice specific relaxation techniques they can gain introspective control over the psychological processes that lead to tension. Jacobson proposed that it might be possible to identify and reduce the physiological accompaniments to emotions, resulting in a reduction in psychological tension. In other words, Jacobson theorized that if physical tension could be removed, then a reduction in emotional tension would follow.

Effectiveness

Many studies have been conducted examining effects of stress management techniques. Some studies associated with the following two stress management techniques are reported in this section of the chapter:

- Yoga
- Progressive relaxation

Yoga

Yoga programs are used or recommended by TR specialists and other human service professionals because studies indicate that they can positively impact health. Yoga has been beneficial in reducing anxiety and depression, treating chemical dependency, improving body awareness and motor performance, improving learning, the treatment of hypertension, and mood alteration. These are but a sample of the many studies of the effects of yoga, addressing problems that TR specialists might encounter. The studies selected for review in this chapter are presented in the following sections:

- Yoga decreases anxiety and depression
- Yoga decreases hypertension and pulmonary tuberculosis
- Yoga decreases pain
- Yoga increases alcohol abstinence
- Yoga increases physical performance
- Yoga increases learning
- Yoga enhances mood

Yoga decreases anxiety and depression. Krishnamurthy and Telles (2007) examined effects of a yoga program on depression of older adults. Sixty-nine adults over the age of 60 participated in a 24-week yoga program designed to decrease their depression levels. Participants were randomly divided into three groups; a control group, an ayurveda group which received an herbal supplement twice daily, and the yoga group (6 x wk, 75-min sessions). The intervention involved different yoga poses such as backbends, standing poses, and inversions. Spielberg's Trait Anxiety Inventory (Spielberger et al., 1970) and the Profile of Mood States (POMS) (McNair et al., 1971) were used to measure changes in participant depression. Participants in the yoga group showed significantly lower depression ratings than participants receiving herbal treatment and those in the control group. Therefore, the yoga program showed promise in treating depression.

Another study done on individuals with hypertension, along with a number of other varying illnesses was conducted by **Gupta, Khera, Vempati, Sharma, and Bijlani (2006).** There were 175 participants involved in a 10-day study which included eight 3–4 hour sessions. A 2-day break occurred in the middle of the study. The intervention involved physical posturing, breathing exercises, breakfast with classical music, and instructional videos on diet, stress management, and yoga exercises. Anxiety levels were measured using the state trait anxiety disorder test (Spielberger et al., 1970). Significant decreases in anxiety of individuals suffering from illnesses such as hypertension, coronary heart disease, and obesity were observed.

Michalsen and colleagues (2005) examined effects of yoga on depression and anxiety of 24 women volunteers who reported experiencing emotional distress at least every other day for the past 3 months, were not currently diagnosed with any psychological condition, and were not currently participating in yoga. Sixteen women were randomly selected for the first yoga group, while the other 8 did not receive treatment immediately and were used as a control group. The women participated in a 12-week intervention that met twice a week for 90-minute sessions. Spielberger State-Trait Anxiety Inventory (Spielberger, Gorsuch, & Lushene, 1970), the Cohen Perceived Stress Scale (Cohen et al., 1983), the Profile of Mood States (McNair et al., 1971), the ADL-S which measures depression (Farmer, Locke, & Moscicki, 1988), the Zerssen well-being scales (Von Zerssen & Koeller, 1976), and the 70-item Freiburg Complaint List (Fahrenberg, 1994), were used during the yoga intervention. The stress, anxiety, and depression levels of the participants in the intervention group decreased significantly, and the overall well-being of the women increased significantly compared to the control group

Another study that examined depression and anxiety as well as physical effects of yoga, was completed by **Oken and colleagues (2004),** who examined the effects of a 26-week yoga program (1 x wk, 90-min sessions) on 69 individuals with

Multiple Sclerosis. Participants were randomly assigned to one of three groups; an exercise group, a control group, or the iyengar yoga group. The intervention consisted of 19 postures all using some sort of support (i.e., a chair) and different types of relaxed breathing. Positions were modified to meet participant needs. Multiple tests were used to determine possible improvements throughout the intervention: (a) The Stroop Color and Word Test assessed ability to focus attention (Gronwall, 1977), (b) the Paced Auditory Serial Addition Test assessed alertness and attention (Perret, 1974), (c) the Stanford Sleepiness Scale (Hoddes et al., 1973) assessed alertness, (d) the Profile of Mood States (McNair et al., 1971) assessed changes in mood and state of mind, (e) the State Trait Anxiety Inventory (Spielberger et al., 1970) assessed anxiety, and (f) physical tests such as the sit and reach, and the 25-foot timed walk (Hui & Yuen, 2000) assessed physical changes. Physical skills of participants in the yoga group were higher than that of those in the control group and there was a significant decrease in depression and anxiety between the two groups.

Waelde, Thompson, and Gallagher-Thompson (2004) examined effects of a yoga program on participants' anxiety and depression. Fourteen women who were caregivers for older adults with dementia participated in 5 yoga sessions per week for 6 weeks. The first 4 sessions each week were 90 minutes; the 5th session was 180 minutes. The intervention consisted of meditation, hatha yoga, breathing techniques, guided imagery, mantra repetition, and discussion on how and when these techniques can be best applied. Participants kept journals indicating when they used these techniques at home and how effective they were. Pre- and post-test measures were taken using the Center for Epidemiological Studies Depression Scale (CES-D) (Radloff, 1977), the Self-Efficacy for Controlling Upsetting Thoughts about Caregiving subscale of the Revised Scale for Caregiving Self-Efficacy (SEC) (Steffen et al., 2002), and the State-Trait Anxiety Inventory (STAI) (Spielberger et al., 1970). Researchers found that the intervention significantly lowered participant anxiety and depression, while increasing self-efficacy.

Carlson, Speca, Patel, and Goodey (2001) selected 42 participants who had recently survived breast cancer or prostate cancer to participate in an 8-week yoga intervention (1 x wk, 90-min session) with an additional 2-hour session between weeks 6 and 7. During yoga sessions participants were taught theoretical material, practiced meditation and yoga, and examined practical applications for these ideas. Participants were given an audiotape with instructions on how to meditate and do yoga at home and asked to practice every day and keep a journal. Stress levels, depression, and anxiety of participants decreased significantly throughout the intervention. These findings indicate that yoga could be useful for individuals with depression, anxiety, or stress problems.

Yoga decreases hypertension and pulmonary tuberculosis. Visweswaraiah and Telles (2004) examined effects of yoga on individuals with pulmonary tuberculosis. Seventy-nine people participated in an 8-week program (6 x wk, 60-min sessions). The sessions consisted of 30 minutes of simple breathing exercises, 20 minutes of regulated yogic breathing, and 10 minutes of relaxation in the supine position. Measurements were taken using body weight, tracking of symptoms, FEV (American Thoracic Society, 1990) which measures lung capacity, and a Sputum Culture

(National Tuberculosis Institute, 1993). Participants increased their body weight, reduced symptom scores, and increased lung capacity.

Brownstein and Dembert (1989) reported the case of a U.S. Air Force aviator who benefited from yoga to treat his hypertension. The aviator wanted to lower his hypertension without using antihypertensive medications so that he could resume an active flight career. He was instructed in yoga postures, breathing, and relaxation so that he could practice at home. After 6 weeks of daily yoga practice, his blood pressure was reduced to normal limits. His medical waiver for flight duty was discontinued and he resumed his career. He continued to practice yoga and was reevaluated 6 months later, with blood pressure measurements remaining in the normal range.

Yoga decreases pain. Williams and colleagues (2005) examined effects of a 16-week yoga program (6 x wk) on pain and improving physical functioning of individuals experiencing lower back pain. Sixty participants took part in a 16-week intervention where they participated in one 90-min in-class session and five 30-min at-home sessions per week. Participants were taught numerous yoga poses throughout the in-class session and were taught how to do them at home. Pain levels and movement ability were assessed using the Pain Disability Index (Tait et al., 1990), the McGill Pain Questionnaire (Melzack, 1987), the Survey of Pain Attitudes (Jensen et al., 1994), the Coping Strategies Questionnaire Revised (Robinson et al., 1997), and the Back Pain Self-Efficacy Scale (Anderson et al., 1995). Range of motion was tested using a Saunders Digital Inclinometer. Participants increased their movement and decreased lower back pain and disability.

Bonadies (2004) studied effects of an 8-week yoga program (2 x wk, 60-min sessions) on four participants (2 female) diagnosed with AIDS. Sessions consisted of 10 minutes of meditation, 10 minutes of light stretching, and 40 minutes of yoga positions modified for individuals needs. The Numeric Pain Rating Scale (McCaffrey & Pasero, 1999) measured pain and anxiety (pre- and post-intervention). Participants experienced an increase in balance and ambulation witnessed by staff after the intervention. Participants decreased their pain levels, indicated by a 35% decrease in pain medication and a reduction in anxiety.

Yoga increases alcohol abstinence. Calajoe (1986) reported two case histories of use of 6-month yoga program (4 x wk, 45-min sessions) and meditation techniques in treating chemical dependency. Each individual attended a day treatment program for alcohol and substance abuse with yoga sessions as an aspect of the treatment plan. Both individuals had been addicted to alcohol, experienced stress and anxiety when they were sober, and reported using alcohol as a coping mechanism in social situations and as a means of relaxation. One individual experienced panic attacks in public places. In addition to attending yoga sessions, each individual was provided with a packet of information and cassettes for practicing yoga postures and meditation at home. Both individuals reported greater confidence and relaxation, increased comfort in social situations and continued abstinence from alcohol. Two years after leaving treatment one continued to abstain from alcohol, attended college full time, and continued to practice yoga daily. One and a half years after leaving treatment the other worked full-time in his computer business, practiced yoga biweekly at home, and abstained from alcohol.

Yoga increases physical performance. Culos-Reed and colleagues (2004)
examined effects of yoga (1 x wk, 75-min sessions) on physical and mental health
of 38 cancer survivors. Participants were randomly assigned to a wait list group or
the yoga group before the intervention. The intervention included: gentle breathing
exercises, stretching and strengthening exercises, and shavasana or corpse pose (the
individual lays flat on their back with arms and legs relaxed at their sides, palms facing up), for relaxation. The following were used to measure effects of the program:
(a) The Profile of Mood States (McNair, Loir, & Droppleman, 1971), (b) European
Organization for Research and Treatment of Cancer Quality of Life Questionnaire
(Aaronson et al., 1993), (c) the Symptoms of Stress Inventory (Leckie & Thompson,
1979), and (d) the Leisure Score Index, part of the Leisure Time Activity Index
(Godin & Shephard, 1985). The post-test demonstrated that the yoga group had
significantly increased their walking distance compared to the control group, and
significantly decreased resting heart rate, heart rate after exercise, tension, depression, anger, and confusion compared to the control group. The 3-month follow-up
showed a continued decrease in stress and mood disturbance among participants;
however, there was a slight decline in the other measures.

Another study which addressed motor performance and physical functioning
was completed by **Greendale, McDivit, Carpenter, Seeger, and Huang (2002)**.
They examined effects a 12-week yoga program (2 x wk, 60-min sessions) on
flexibility, stature, and functional skills of 21 older adults with hyperkyphosis.
Sessions included modified classical forms of yoga specifically adapted to meet
participant needs. Every 3 weeks, more difficult positions would be included in
the intervention as participants' abilities increased. Functional measurements were
taken related to height, forward body curvature, balance, reach, fine motor skills,
strength, and ambulation pre- and post-intervention. Tests indicated increased
height, decreased curvature, decreased time taken to pick up a penny (fine motor
performance) and significantly longer functional reach on average compared to
baseline. It appears that yoga can be used to help increase physical functioning
and motor skills.

To study effects of yoga on body awareness, **Rani and Rao (1994)** used a
body awareness questionnaire developed by Shields and Mallory (1989) with two
independent groups of participants. A yoga training group of 17 participants (ages
20–36) received 3 months of yoga training (5 x wk, 60-min sessions) at the Institute
for Yoga and Consciousness, Andhra University, Vishakhapatnam, India. The control
group of 19 participants consisted of individuals (ages 17–36) who sought admission to the institute but had not begun training. Both groups were administered the
questionnaire. The difference between mean scores of the two groups was significant,
indicating that the yoga group had greater body awareness than the control group.
The authors stated that the tests were administered at different times, and a pre-test
of the yoga-training group would have revealed more information about the actual
increases in body awareness.

A study of school children's static motor performance after yoga training was
conducted by **Telles and colleagues (1993).** The authors used two groups of 45
children each (ages 9–13), with one group receiving 10 days of yoga and the other
group not receiving training. Yoga sessions included breathing techniques and games
designed to improve attention and memory. Each group received a pre- and post-test

requiring them to insert a metal rod into increasingly smaller holes of a metal plate without touching sides of the holes. Performance was approximately the same for both groups during pre-test, but the yoga training group displayed significant improvement in the post-test and the control group did not. Certain asanas could have improved voluntary control and eye-hand coordination and overall calming of the mind and relaxing the body might have contributed to improved performance.

Yoga increases learning. Peck, Kehle, Bray, and Theodore (2005) also examined effects of yoga on children's learning capabilities. Ten children (grades 1–3) were selected by their school psychologist to participate in a 3-week yoga fitness for kids intervention (2 x wk, 30-min sessions) using videotapes to improve their attention deficits. The intervention consisted of deep breathing, physical postures, and relaxation exercises. Baseline measures were taken comparing participants to other students of the same sex in the classroom using the Behavior Observation Form (Rhode, Jenson, & Reavis, 1993). During the intervention students showed marked improvement in their attention deficits; however, this improvement decreased after the intervention was completed. Although effects did not continue to occur at the same level as when the intervention occurred, attention to task was significantly higher than baseline measures.

Effects of 10-months of yoga on children with mental retardation were studied by **Uma, Nagendra, Nagaranthna, Vaidehi, and Seethalakshmi (1989)**. Forty-five children with mental retardation (ages 6–16) were compared to a control group of 45 children with mental retardation who were matched for age, sex, IQ, socioeconomic status, and socio-environmental background. The children in the yoga group received 10-months of treatment (5 x wk, 60-min sessions), while the control group received no treatment. Both groups received the same school training, other than yoga. The yoga techniques included breathing exercises, physical postures, and meditation. Pre- and post-test data were taken in the form of standardized tests for IQ and social maturity, the Binet Kamath for General Mental Ability, the Seguin Form Board, and the Vineland Social Maturity Scale. Children in the yoga group made significant improvements in test scores after the yoga program, whereas children in the control group did not. While yoga is known to improve physical, mental, and emotional well-being in individuals without disabilities, children with mental retardation also can improve with regular yoga practice.

Yoga enhances mood. Lavey and colleagues (2005) completed another study examining effects yoga has on mood of 113 individuals residing in a psychiatric center with a variety of illnesses including: mood disorder, psychotic disorder, borderline personality disorder, and adjustment disorder. The 10-day intervention (1 x wk, 45-min sessions) included a yoga class consisting of gentle stretching and strengthening exercises with a strong focus on breathing and sensations experienced while demonstrating different poses. The Profile of Mood States (POMS) (McNair et al., 1971) was used pre- and post-intervention. There was a decrease in negative mood and a decrease in anxiety, depression, and fatigue. Even with the brevity of the intervention, yoga may be a viable option for enhancing mood in its participants.

A study comparing mood benefits of hatha yoga and swimming was conducted by **Berger and Owen (1992)**. In previous studies the authors had found aerobic swimming to alter mood, with reduction in scores on tension, depression, anger, and confusion in addition to increased vigor following swimming. Four groups of college students were examined, two beginning swimming classes having 20 and 17 participants, a yoga class having 22 participants, and a control group in a health science lecture course having 28 participants. Swimming and yoga students exercised 60 minutes per week in the class settings. All participants were administered the Profile of Mood States (McNair et al., 1971) immediately pre- and post-class on three different days evenly spaced throughout the semester. The State-Trait Anxiety Inventory (Spielberger et al., 1970) was administered on the first test day and the last test day. Both swimmers and yoga participants reported significantly greater short-term mood benefits than did participants in the control group. Differences between types of benefits in yoga and swimming were reported by gender. Mood alteration can occur in exercise that does not require aerobic training, and yoga might be a form of exercise for individuals who are unable or unlikely to engage in strenuous exercise.

Allen and Steinkohl (1987) examined effects of a physical activity program for older adults who attended a geriatric clinic. The individuals who attended the clinic often presented a wide range of affective symptoms related to depression and anxiety and expressed somatic complaints. The authors piloted a 6-month yoga project (2 x wk, 90-min sessions) with nine people (ages 65–78). Results were derived from group process recordings after each session and observations. Eight of the nine individuals reported positive results from attending the yoga sessions. The other individual dropped out before the completion of the 6 months. Results included reports of feeling more relaxed, more energetic, and less fearful about dying. The authors concluded that controlled studies of effects of yoga on older adults are needed.

Summary and conclusions of studies on yoga. As Hindu practitioners of yoga have long believed, the benefits of yoga are many. Although each of the studies indicated positive effects, not all studies utilized sound methodologies. Allen and Steinkohl (1987) found their yoga project to be beneficial, but indicated a need for more controlled studies with older adults. Calajoe's (1986) report of the benefits of yoga in treating chemical dependency was based on two case studies, and Brownstein and Dembert (1989) used a case study to report on benefits of yoga in treating hypertension. Although case studies provide compelling results, controlled studies are needed of individuals with chemical dependency and with hypertension.

Early studies reporting benefits of yoga with sound methodologies and favorable results included those by Rani and Rao (1994), Telles and colleagues (1993), Uma and colleagues (1989), and Berger and Owen (1992). The study by Rani and Rao provided evidence for increased body awareness as a result of practicing yoga. The study of school children by Telles and colleagues indicated improved static motor performance as a result of yoga training. Uma and colleagues found that children with mental retardation might benefit from yoga, with the identification of improvements in social adaptation and IQ scores. When comparing benefits of yoga and swimming, Berger and Owen found that both activities positively altered mood, indicating that exercise need not be strenuous to alter mood.

More recently, Krishnamurthy and Telles (2007), Gupta and colleagues (2006), Michalsen and colleagues (2005), Waelde and colleagues (2004), Oken and colleagues (2004) and Carlson and colleagues (2001) found a positive relationship between yoga participation and decreases in anxiety and depression. Also, Visweswaraiah and Telles (2004) extended the work of Brownstein and Dembert by identifying positive effects of yoga on lung capacity with a sample of 79 individuals with pulmonary tuberculosis. Bondais (2004) and Williams and colleagues (2005) identified the association between yoga and decreases in pain of people with AIDS and lower back pain, respectively. A study by Greendale and colleagues (2002) and Curlos-Reed and colleagues (2004) complemented the work of Telles and colleagues, as well as Rani and Rao, by demonstrating increases in physical performance associated with yoga participation. Also, findings by Peck and colleagues (2005) supported previous research by Uma and colleagues by noting that yoga is associated with improved learning. Finally, Lavey and colleagues (2005) extended the work of Allen and Steinkohl, as well as Berger and Owen, supporting that yoga participation is associated with enhanced mood.

Therefore, in summarizing the research, given the support of the use of yoga as an effective facilitation technique, there is a substantial amount of research found examining effects of yoga. Existing research strongly indicates that yoga is an empirically supported facilitation technique.

Progressive Relaxation Training (PRT)

Progressive relaxation techniques are used by TR specialists and other human service professionals because studies have indicated that they elicit physiological changes that influence feelings of well-being (Bernstein & Borkovec, 1973). For example, effects of progressive relaxation have been shown to produce positive changes in electromyographic (EMG) and heart rate measures (Lehrer, Carr, Sargunaraj, & Woolfolk, 1994), thus reducing stress. Other studies indicating decreased stress associated with progressive relaxation include those by Burish, Vasterling, Carey, Matt, and Krozely (1988); Foley, Bedell, LaRocca, Scheinberg, and Reznikoff (1987); and Taylor (1995). Decreased anxiety was associated with progressive relaxation training and its modifications in studies by Rankin, Gilner, Gfeller, and Katz (1993); Rickard, Collier, McCoy, Crist, and Weinberger (1993); Carlson, Ventrella, and Sturgis (1987); Lindsay, Baty, Michie, and Richardson (1989); and Lindsay, Fee, Michie, and Heap (1994). Engle-Friedman, Hazlewood, Bootzin, and Tsao (1992) indicated that progressive relaxation can decrease insomnia. Lucic and colleagues (1991) studied the amount of relaxation experienced when comparing the use of muscle contractions to no muscle contractions during sessions. Other studies examined side effects (Rickard et al., 1993) and the relaxation benefits associated with progressive relaxation training for individuals with psychiatric disorders (Rickard, McCoy, Collier & Weinberger, 1989). Increased self-esteem and internal locus of control were benefits of progressive relaxation in a study by Bensink, Godbey, Marshall, and Yarandi (1992), as were the reduction of symptoms associated with various illnesses in a study by Carlson and Hoyle (1993). The studies selected for review in this chapter are presented in the following sections:

- Progressive relaxation decreases stress
- Progressive relaxation decreases anxiety
- Progressive relaxation decreases insomnia
- Progressive relaxation decreases illness symptoms
- Progressive relaxation increases relaxation
- Progressive relaxation increases self-esteem and locus of control

Progressive relaxation decreases stress. Studies have been conducted on effects of progressive relaxation on stress and other side effects associated with various disorders. Studies reviewed are those that examined effects of progressive relaxation on side effects of chemotherapy (Burish et al., 1988), on coping with the stress of multiple sclerosis (Foley et al., 1987), and on stress and stress-related symptoms in men who were HIV-positive (Taylor, 1995). In addition, effects of progressive relaxation on stress compared to other stress management techniques have been studied (Lehrer et al., 1994).

Stress inducement influences the body's immune response, as observed in lower T-cell counts (Taylor, 1995). Stress can have a devastating effect on individuals who are HIV-positive, because lowered T-cell counts can lead to full-blown AIDS (Taylor, 1995). In a study of 10 men who were HIV positive, Taylor evaluated effects of a 10-week stress management program (2 x wk, 60-min sessions) which included training in progressive relaxation, electromyographic (EMG) biofeedback-assisted relaxation, self-hypnosis, and meditation on anxiety, mood, self-esteem, and T-cell counts. The electromyographic biofeedback involved use of a biofeedback device during 20-min relaxation practice sessions, the self-hypnosis involved visualizing deep relaxation while repeating positive statements about being relaxed and healthy, and the meditation involved visualizing the body becoming a white light of pure love and compassion. Compared to the five people in the control group, the five people in the treatment group changed significantly on the four measures from pre- to post-treatment. Consequently, Taylor argued that stress management techniques can elicit positive outcomes in individuals who are HIV positive.

Recognizing that stress management techniques are becoming widely accepted as treatment components of therapy, **Lehrer and colleagues (1994)** examined studies that compared progressive relaxation to electromyographic biofeedback (12 studies) and to mantra meditation (13 studies). Electromyographic biofeedback measures muscle tension using surface electrodes located on various parts of the body. Mantra meditation involves sitting quietly and silently repeating a word. The techniques were compared to discern whether each technique elicited the same relaxation response or whether there are specific effects for each technique. Biofeedback seemed to be more effective than progressive relaxation in producing changes in the electromyographic measurements. In these studies, live instruction in progressive relaxation was more effective than taped instruction. Although self-reported reductions in symptoms based on techniques were mixed, participants tended to favor electromyographic biofeedback for reducing stress over taped relaxation training. Results of comparing effects of progressive relaxation to mantra meditation were mixed. Progressive relaxation seemed to have a greater effect than mantra meditation in reducing heart rate. For electromyographic effects, the techniques were equally effective. For electroencephalographic effects involving measurement of brain waves, mantra meditation was more effective. Although results found by Lehrer and colleagues (1994) were mixed when comparing progressive relaxation to other forms of stress management, many studies have reported positive effects as a result of progressive relaxation. Most notably, individuals receiving chemotherapy, those with multiple sclerosis, and those who are HIV positive appear to have benefited from progressive relaxation training.

In their survey of 50 individuals with cancer, **Burish and colleagues (1988)** were not only interested in effects of progressive relaxation, but also in whether participants continued to use it after discontinuing chemotherapy. The 34 participants who responded to the questionnaire rated progressive relaxation as being highly effective in reducing the distress of chemotherapy. Approximately 72% of the 34 participants reported using the technique after chemotherapy had ended to cope with stress-related problems.

Foley and colleagues (1987) conducted a study of individuals with multiple sclerosis, applying a stress-inoculation training program as a means of reducing stress associated with the social and psychological consequences of the disease. The term "stress-inoculation training" refers to the introduction of stress management techniques to individuals as a protective or coping mechanism. The training entailed having participants self-monitor daily stressors, responses to those stressors, and participate in a progressive relaxation training program. Compared to the 21 participants in the control group, the 20 participants in the treatment group experienced significantly more decreases in depression and state anxiety, as well as improved coping with daily stressors and problem-focused coping efforts.

Progressive relaxation decreases anxiety. Progressive relaxation training (Bernstein & Borkovec, 1973) has been effective in reducing anxiety in older adults (Rankin et al., 1993; Scogin, Rickard, Keith, Wilson, & McElreath, 1992) and in people with limited physical abilities when adapted (Scogin et al., 1992). Progressive relaxation techniques, furthermore, have positive effects when conducted individually or with additional cues (Lindsay et al., 1989; 1994).

Rankin and colleagues (1993) studied effects of progressive relaxation on anxiety and memory in 30 older adults. Participants who tested high on anxiety before receiving the intervention were randomly assigned to either a progressive relaxation treatment or control group. The authors predicted that progressive relaxation would enhance participant memory skills. Although the single session of progressive relaxation did significantly reduce participant anxiety, memory did not improve significantly. One possible reason for the lack of improvement was that relaxation effects dissipated too quickly to influence memory.

Scogin and colleagues (1992) compared effects of progressive relaxation to imaginal relaxation, which involved asking participants to imagine performing the muscle tension-release cycles. Imaginal relaxation was hypothesized to be an appropriate substitute for progressive relaxation for individuals who might be physically unable to tense and release muscles. Three groups of participants were formed: 19 people in the progressive relaxation group, 19 people in the imaginal relaxation group, and 16 people in a control group. The authors found that both techniques were effective in reducing anxiety. An implication of their study was that people could benefit from imagined muscle tension and release procedures when physical limitations preclude actual tension-release experiences.

An alternative to contracting muscles during progressive relaxation was proposed by **Carlson and colleagues (1987).** They suggested that muscle stretching allowed participants to sense the muscles, as in muscle contracting, but the physiological benefits of stretching enabled stronger contrast effects when coupled with relaxation. Using procedures by Bernstein and Borkovec, a case study was conducted using exercises of the head, neck, and arm muscles, substituting stretching muscles for contracting muscles. Based on self-reported measures, levels of anxiety and muscle tension decreased; however, there was no measure of comparison between the two techniques of stretching muscles versus contracting muscles.

Because several authors have indicated that progressive relaxation training has not been successful in reducing anxiety with adults with moderate to severe mental retardation, a group of researchers suggested the use of behavioral relaxation to achieve such results (Lindsay et al., 1989). *Behavioral relaxation* is a modification of progressive relaxation involving the modeling of relaxed and non-relaxed behaviors in 10 areas of the body. By focusing on observed behaviors modeled by the trainer rather than subjective states of tension and relaxation, participants who do not conceptualize relaxation states are more likely to respond. **Lindsay and colleagues (1989)** studied 50 participants with moderate to severe mental retardation who were randomly assigned to one of five groups: individual behavioral relaxation training, individual progressive relaxation training, group behavioral relaxation training, group progressive relaxation training, and control group. Measurements of rated anxiety were taken using pulse rate and a behavioral assessment that measured observed behavioral anxiety of voice, trunk, head, eyes, lips, throat, shoulders, hands, feet, and general relaxation/tension. Participants who received individual behavioral relaxation training displayed significantly lower levels of rated anxiety than participants assigned to other treatment groups.

After establishing that behavioral relaxation training can be more effective with adults with moderate to severe mental retardation than progressive relaxation training (Lindsay et al., 1989), **Lindsay and colleagues (1994)** suggested that the addition of cues such as "quiet" and "still" to behavioral relaxation training might enable individuals to relax without following the entire relaxation procedure. In a single case design across five participants, initial training was provided in behavioral relaxation coupled with cues. Participants demonstrated a decrease in rated anxiety during a "cue only" condition.

Progressive relaxation training has been effective in reducing anxiety in older adults as indicated by the studies of Rankin and colleagues (1993), and Scogin and colleagues (1992). In addition, Scogin and colleagues demonstrated that a modification for individuals with limited physical abilities might be just as effective as the accepted tension and release program. As the two studies by Lindsay and colleagues (1989; 1994) indicated, progressive relaxation with individuals who have difficulties conceptualizing relaxation states may require modification. Behavioral relaxation training may be an effective substitute for such individuals and can be coupled with a cue to elicit responses of decreased anxiety.

Progressive relaxation decreases insomnia. Progressive relaxation was a treatment component in a study by **Engle-Friedman and colleagues (1992)** to determine effects of behavioral treatments for insomnia in 53 older adults. Participants were assigned to one of four conditions: (a) support and sleep hygiene; (b) support and sleep hygiene plus progressive relaxation; (c) support and sleep hygiene plus stimulus control; and (d) a control group. In all conditions, improvement in sleep patterns occurred, although those in the control group reported feeling least refreshed and had the least total sleep time and longest times prior to sleep onset. Behavioral interventions, including progressive relaxation training, show promise for improving the sleep of older adults with insomnia.

Progressive relaxation decreases illness symptoms. A meta-analysis was conducted by **Carlson and Hoyle (1993)** on effects of progressive relaxation training in 29 experiments including a total of 1,206 participants. Relaxation training was administered to individuals experiencing stress, chronic headaches, hypertension, cancer, and tinnitus, as well as people receiving chemotherapy and adolescents with depression. Because effect size estimate for the combined sample was significant, the authors concluded that progressive relaxation is an effective treatment technique for a range of disorders.

Progressive relaxation increases relaxation. Considerable debate exists surrounding use of the tension-release sequence versus relaxing muscles to increase relaxation. To determine effects of muscle contractions versus no muscle contractions before relaxation, **Lucic and colleagues (1991)** studied effects of muscle contractions versus no muscle contractions before relaxation in three groups of 16 participants. When given a single session of progressive relaxation, those who had received training without muscle contractions were more relaxed than those who self-induced relaxation, or who had been instructed to contract muscles. A limitation to this study was in the application of only one session, which is used as a training session. During an initial session, contracting and relaxing muscles is more difficult to learn than merely relaxing muscles. Development of relaxation skills over several sessions could affect outcomes.

Studies on the effectiveness of progressive relaxation with individuals with psychiatric disorders have been limited because of earlier suggestions that the technique would be problematic with such individuals. After studying side effects of progressive relaxation training (Rickard et al., 1989), **Rickard and colleagues (1993)** conducted a study indicating that progressive relaxation training can be effective in achieving greater relaxation with individuals in a psychiatric hospital.

Rickard and colleagues (1989) examined the extent to which individuals in a psychiatric program of a hospital reported relaxation training side effects. Sixty-four participants were randomly assigned to two groups, one receiving progressive relaxation training and the other receiving passive suggestions of relaxation. After seven training sessions, only one individual experienced side effects resulting in removal from the program. There were no significant differences between groups in reported side effects such as unwanted thoughts, which averaged a total of less than two reported side effects per session for each group.

In a later study, **Rickard and colleagues (1993)** examined effects of three sessions of progressive and imaginal relaxation training on 51 individuals receiving psychiatric care. Imaginal relaxation was used with participants who could not tolerate the structure of the muscle tension and release sequences. Participants experienced significantly greater relaxation after sessions with both types of relaxation, as measured by a relaxation inventory administered pre- and post-intervention. However, significant carryover effects were not found with only three treatment sessions. Unfortunately, a control group was not used for this study.

Studies of individuals needing psychiatric services receiving progressive relaxation training have elicited positive results. Not only have such individuals benefited from the training by experiencing increased relaxation, but reported side effects have been minimal.

Progressive relaxation increases self-esteem and internal locus of control. Effects of progressive relaxation on the perceived locus of control and self-esteem of older adults in long-term care were studied by **Bensink and colleagues (1992)**. Fifteen participants in a progressive relaxation group were compared to 13 participants in an activities group. Both groups experienced increases in self-esteem and internal locus of control. Self-esteem was significantly higher for participants in the relaxation group than for those in the activity group when compared over time. Participants in the relaxation group demonstrated a stronger positive correlation between internal locus of control and self-esteem than those in the activities group.

Summary and conclusions of studies on progressive relaxation. Although efficacy research has indicated that progressive relaxation can elicit positive changes in participants' experiences of stress and stress-related symptoms, many studies have not been methodologically sound, such as the Lucic and colleagues (1991) study, which used only one training session; the Carlson and colleagues (1987) study, which tested a modification to progressive relaxation without comparing it to the unmodified version; the Rickard and colleagues (1989) study, which lacked a control group; and other studies, which used more than one stress management technique in a package without isolating the interventions (Engle-Friedman et al., 1992; Foley et al., 1987; Taylor, 1995). Results of the Lehrer and colleagues (1994) meta-analysis were mixed, with progressive relaxation not always being as effective as other forms of stress management. In summarizing the aforementioned studies, there was a moderate amount of research found examining effects of progressive relaxation. Although extant research supports use of progressive relaxation as an effective intervention, since this research lacks adequate rigor, progressive relaxation cannot yet be identified as an empirically supported facilitation technique.

Studies of use of progressive relaxation with sound methodologies and favorable results included those by Burish and colleagues (1988), Lindsay and colleagues (1989), Lindsay and colleagues (1994), Rankin and colleagues (1993), and Scogin and colleagues (1992). The two studies by Lindsay and others provided evidence that individuals with moderate to severe mental retardation can be taught modified versions of progressive relaxation successfully. Burish and colleagues used self-reports to indicate that progressive relaxation was effective for individuals coping with the stresses of cancer. Studies by Rankin and colleagues and Scogin and colleagues indicated the effectiveness of progressive relaxation in reducing anxiety in older adults. Although these studies provide favorable evidence for the use of progressive relaxation training, more studies of individuals with disabilities and illnesses are desirable to elicit continued support for the use of progressive relaxation training.

Case Studies

Two case studies are presented that exemplify the application of stress management techniques by TR specialists. The first case provides an example of the application of yoga and the second case study illustrates the use of progressive relaxation. The following two cases are described:

- Susan
- Juan

Susan

Susan was diagnosed with anorexia nervosa at the age of 17 and was admitted to an eating disorder unit of a private psychiatric hospital. The 40-bed hospital unit provided a 30-day treatment program for individuals with eating disorders, most of whom were diagnosed with anorexia nervosa.

At the time of admittance, Susan weighed 90 pounds and was having trouble eating. She had begun to diet when she was 16, feeling that her 110 pounds was too fat for her 5-foot 4-inch frame. Along with dieting, she engaged in a rigorous exercise routine, which included jogging four miles daily and attending aerobics twice weekly. As she began to lose weight, she continued to regard herself as fat even though she was quite thin. During the previous month she had found it difficult to eat and often was too weak to jog more than a mile. When she entered the hospital program, she admitted that she still felt fat and as if her body belonged to somebody else. She wanted to have more energy again, but was afraid to eat for fear of getting fat. She expressed great anxiety about getting fat, and indicated that she spent all of her waking hours worrying about it.

Yoga for Susan

The TR specialist developed a program for Susan that included a yoga session three times during the first week and daily during the remaining 3 weeks. During the first week it was important that Susan's medical condition stabilize. The yoga sessions were 30 minutes each during that week, and the focus was on relaxing and centering the body. The postures included corpse posture, spinal rock, plough posture, fish posture, back-stretching posture, and cobra posture. Each posture was executed very slowly to allow Susan time to feel her muscles working in a calm and relaxed manner. Benefits of yoga were explained to Susan, and she was surprised that one could "exercise" without getting out of breath. After the third session, Susan indicated that she liked doing the yoga, but wasn't sure if she would ever substitute it for jogging or aerobics.

During the 3 weeks that Susan attended daily yoga sessions, her need for vigorous exercise gradually changed. The sessions were increased in length to 45 minutes, with the focus being to relax and center the body as well as increase strength and improve balance. In addition, the sessions were designed to enable Susan to feel good about her body, and, at the same time, forget about having an ideal body image. The therapist introduced more postures, including standing postures that develop balance and strength. Each session started with the corpse posture and spinal rock and included other seated postures. A series of standing postures followed and the corpse posture concluded the session. Susan was encouraged to go at her own pace and the therapist monitored her closely to make sure she was not overexerting herself. Some sessions were shortened with the more difficult postures left out when Susan seemed weak or tired.

To enable Susan to feel the full benefits of the postures, and thus feel good about her body and herself, positive verbal guidance was provided for each posture.

> For example, during spinal rock the therapist would say *"Clasp your knees as if you are hugging them and rock yourself. Feel the rhythm of your body as you rock back and forth, much as a baby feels the rhythm of a cradle."*

The verbal imagery gave Susan the opportunity, and perhaps the permission, to take care of herself.

During the last week of her hospital stay, Susan expressed an interest in continuing to practice yoga at home. She indicated that she would prefer to practice yoga rather than aerobics or jogging. She felt that yoga enabled her to exercise and stay calm at the same time. From the information she had learned during her hospital stay, she realized that yoga would help her to take care of herself without risking too much weight loss. Following each yoga session she felt more relaxed and happy about herself. The therapist contacted a community center that offered yoga classes and shared the scheduling information with Susan and her parents. Susan enrolled in the program and continued to practice yoga over the next year.

Juan

Juan was in his mid-twenties and lived in a group home for adults with mental retardation and mental illness. Although he was admired by his housemates because he could read the newspaper and write letters to his friends and family and he was musically and artistically talented, he was feared because he could suddenly accuse others of bothering him or his belongings without provocation. Juan was able to enjoy his free time in the community with a high degree of independence. He traveled using public transportation to shop and go to the library. Because Juan was artistic he had been referred to a creative arts day-treatment facility that included a community work component. He seemed quite satisfied with the new program, and although he experienced few problems at work, he began to have more difficulties at home.

Juan's difficulties included his obsession to relocate to another city and his fears of people bothering him in public. Juan's obsessions were manifested in extremely anxious behavior. He repeatedly asked the staff at the group home, clinicians, and visitors if he could move to a particular city. He asked when he could move, the reasons for him not being able to move, and then spoke repeatedly about how he needed to move. He carried a postcard of the city in his pocket, kissing it, and showing it to anyone who was willing to talk to him about it. Juan's fear of people bothering him while he was at the library and when he rode the bus coincided with his increased perseverations about relocating. Spending afternoons at the library had been one of his favorite activities and now he avoided going there. Then he began to walk home from work rather than take the bus. It was a long walk that often made him tired and more anxious as he arrived home. Overall, Juan's behavior indicated severe anxiety, making it difficult for him to focus on the activities that he had previously enjoyed after work, such as drawing, cooking, shopping, visiting the library, and reading.

Progressive Relaxation for Juan

The TR specialist developed a program of progressive relaxation to aid in reducing anxiety during leisure activities. The program was designed to be implemented daily (20–25-min sessions) by either the TR specialist, or one of two group home staff members trained to provide guidance. The progressive relaxation program was based on the work of Bernstein and Borkovec. Juan and the facilitator sat in a quiet room, with Juan in a comfortable chair. Juan would remove his shoes and jewelry prior to the start of the session. The facilitator would first tell Juan to take a couple of deep breaths, close his eyes, and relax. Then the facilitator would guide him through the tension and release exercises of the 16 muscle groups. At the end of each session, Juan was given time to sit quietly with suggestions provided to remain relaxed. After a quiet period of about 5 minutes, the facilitator offered suggestions to begin to move various parts of his body. After Juan opened his eyes and moved his arms, hands, head, and neck, the facilitator would ask him general questions about how he felt.

Juan followed the program daily after he arrived home from work, sometimes initiating the start of sessions and always willingly participating. Behavioral measurements of his anxiety level were taken pre- and post-session with two observers rating him on a scale of 1–5. After each session Juan was consistently calmer, and after about 10-days of training, effects of the relaxation began to carry over into evening activities. His anxious behavior gradually diminished and, although he continued to talk about moving, he spent time in the evening drawing and cooking.

Although relaxation training is meant to be conducted by individuals alone and in the privacy of their homes after training, Juan responded best to the program when someone was there to guide him. On weekends he practiced the relaxation techniques by himself, but during the week, when more was expected of him, he followed the lead of a staff member or the TR specialist. Because Juan lives in a group home designed to provide active treatment, it was easy to incorporate this program into his schedule. Two years have passed and Juan continues to practice progressive relaxation. It has been a part of his daily program when his anxiety has interfered with enjoyment of activities. During periods of relative stability, he does not practice it daily, but may use it during times when he feels particularly anxious.

Summary

The two case studies presented in this chapter are examples of successful implementation of stress management techniques by TR specialists. Using a progressive relaxation intervention, Juan diminished his anxiety and increased his participation in productive activities associated with daily living. A yoga program enabled Susan to feel more relaxed and happy. Participation in stress management programs allowed both Juan and Susan to overcome physical and mental barriers and benefit from reduction of stress in their lives.

Intervention Implementation Exercises

Regular physical exercise counteracts effects of stress (Time-Life Books, 1987). In fact, Lutz, Lochbaum, Lanning, Stinson, and Brewer (2007) state that exercise and stress have an inverse relationship, where as one goes up the other goes down. Vigorous exercise is associated with lower hypertension and a reduced risk of cardiovascular disease. Exercise helps maintain clear passages in the blood vessels. Not only does exercise counteract the physical effects of stress, but some emotional effects of stress can be counteracted as well. Exercise releases endorphins into the bloodstream which elevates mood and are responsible for such phenomena as *runner's high*.

Other suggestions for reducing stress involve maintaining control over one's life as much as possible. Suggestions for maintaining control include being assertive in bodily and verbal communication, maintaining positive and loving relationships with other people, and creating harmony in one's living environment. Although activities such as meditation and biofeedback are specifically designed to manage stress, this section of the chapter includes exercises that provide a starting point for TR specialists using stress management techniques and are categorized as follows:

- Yoga
- Progressive Relaxation

Yoga

A short program of yoga, such as that suggested by Hewitt (1977), provides an introduction to a range of postures. Participants can be led in each of the nine postures. Participants are instructed to wear comfortable, loose-fitting clothing and remove their shoes and socks. Each participant needs a blanket or mat that can be spread on the floor and used for seated postures. The following are the postures in the order in which they are led and the associated precautions:

- Corpse
- Spinal rock
- Shoulder stand
- Plough
- Modified fish
- Back stretching
- Cobra
- Bow
- Corpse

Corpse. Lie flat on back with legs stretched out and feet slightly apart (see Figure 9.6). Allow each foot to relax and fall limply outward. Allow arms to rest at sides with palms up and relaxed. Focus on breathing quietly, smoothly, and evenly. Starting with feet, allow each body part to relax or "let go." After all parts of the body feel relaxed, focus again on breathing for 1–2 minutes and then again on relaxing body parts.

Spinal rock. Continue to lie flat on back and bring knees up to chest, clasping hands behind knees (see Figure 9.7). Rock slowly and gently back and forth on rounded back, keeping head tucked. Breathe out when rocking back-ward and breathe in when rocking forward. Rock back and forth about 10 times.

Shoulder stand. Lie flat on back with legs stretched out together (see Figure 9.2 on p. 251). Bring knees to chest and then roll legs so that knees are over the head. Stretch legs vertically into the air, using hands as a brace against small of back. Straighten back and legs as much as possible so that they make a right angle with the floor. Feet will remain together. Breathe deeply and balance in this posture for 20–30 seconds. To come out of the posture, gently lower legs over head and roll the back slowly down.

Plough. This posture can be performed after the shoulder stand posture when lowering legs over head (see Figure 9.8). From a resting or corpse posture, bring knees to chest and roll legs so that knees are over head with legs straight and parallel to floor. Use hands as a brace against the small of the back. Continue to stretch legs back, with feet together, until toes are touching the floor behind head. Continue to use hands as a brace against the small of the back. Breathing will be short and through the nostrils in this pose. Keep toes on floor for about 6–10 seconds. If unable to touch floor with toes, let weight of legs keep them balancing over the head while straightening spine as much possible. To come out of the posture, slowly roll down on the spine, one vertebra at a time, keeping knees bent and legs tucked over chest.

Modified fish. This is a modified version for beginners (see Figure 9.9). Lie flat on back and with feet crossed at ankles and pulled up as close to the body as possible. Keep knees spread apart and as close to the floor as possible. Bring arms up behind head and cross them at the wrists, resting head on arms. Breathe deeply and remain in the posture for about 30 seconds. A more advanced version follows: Begin by sitting on the floor and crossing legs in the lotus position. In the lotus position, legs are crossed and each foot is crossed over opposite thigh with the sole turned up. Using elbows as support, lean back, arch back and extend neck. Let head touch the floor, continuing to arch the back and keeping back and shoulders off the floor. Press top of head on to the floor and hold feet with the hands. Breathe deeply and remain in the posture for 15–30 seconds. To come out of the posture, slowly lift head, while grasping feet, and sit up.

Back stretching. Sit on the floor with legs extended together and straight out in front (see Figure 9.3 on p. 251). Breathe in and then slowly exhale and stretch forward, sliding hands down sides of legs. Allow lower back to stretch as much as possible, but do not force the stretch. Let head rest on or as close to knees as possible. Hold posture for 10–20 seconds, breathing deeply. To come out of the posture, slowly raise head and sit up.

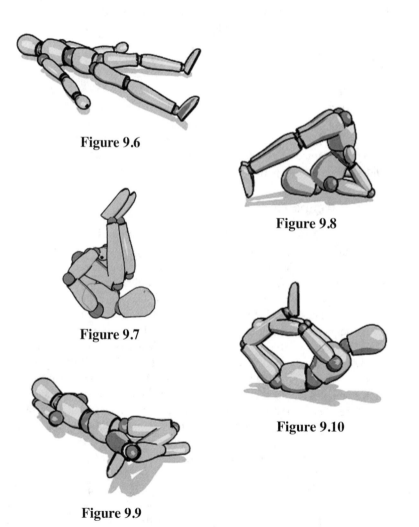

Figure 9.6

Figure 9.8

Figure 9.7

Figure 9.10

Figure 9.9

Cobra. This is a modified version for beginners (see Figure 9.1 on p. 251). Lie flat on abdomen with legs straight and together, with soles facing up. Place hands flat on floor with palms down and elbows bent, about 6 inches in front of shoulders. Inhale and slowly raise head, then neck, then shoulders and upper back, straightening the arms. The body from waist to feet remains pressed against the floor. Keep arms straight, breathe deeply, and remain in the posture for 10–20 seconds. To come out of the posture, slowly bend elbows and lower upper body to a reclining position. In the advanced cobra posture, hands are placed beside shoulders rather than in front of shoulders. The rest of the posture remains the same.

Bow. Lie flat on the abdomen with chin on the floor and legs spread apart (see Figure 9.10 on p. 273). Bend knees, bringing feet back to buttocks. Reach back and grasp ankles while lifting head, neck, and shoulders as high as possible. At the same time, stretch legs up as high as possible, keeping arms straight. Hold posture and breathe freely for about 6 seconds. To come out of the posture, lower legs, head, neck, and shoulders and then release grasp of ankles.

Corpse. Repeat the first posture, allowing for at least 5 minutes of relaxation.

Precautions. Heaner (2003) identified precautions to take when participating in yoga. Prior to starting a yoga exercise, it is important to warm up by stretching. Stretching or using a treadmill for 10 minutes can help prevent strains during activity. To avoid joint pain, Heaner suggests not engaging in movements that bend or twist joints in an uncomfortable manner. Beginners are encouraged to avoid head and shoulder stands until experience is gained to prevent injury.

Progressive Relaxation

Probably the most efficient way to learn how to provide progressive relaxation training to participants is to experience it and then practice guiding others. The instructor can guide participants through an actual progressive relaxation session following the order of 16 muscle groups. There is a standard set of directional statements that the instructor uses to guide tension and release cycle, as outlined in the Bernstein and Borkovec manual. The following are instructions for directing the procedure.

After participants are comfortably seated, the instructor will say, for example, "Let's begin by focusing all of your attention on the muscles of your right hand and lower arm." After waiting about 5 seconds, the instructor will say, "By making a tight fist I'd like you to tense the muscles in the right hand and lower arm, *now*." The tension statement includes an instruction on how to achieve tension and an indication of the muscle group on which participants should be focused. Participants will not actually begin tensing until the instructor says "now," and thus participants should be told that "now" is the tension cue. Participants hold the tension for 5–7 seconds, during which the instructor makes statements to remind participants to hold the tension, such as "Feel the muscles pull, notice the tension in these muscles." A standard cue statement follows to indicate it is time to relax the muscle group. The statement can be simply "Okay, now relax." For the next 30–40 seconds, the muscle group is relaxed and the instructor makes statements designed to focus attention on the relaxation process. Rather than making direct prescriptive statements to relax, the instructor says, "Just let the muscles go, feel the muscle group as it becomes more and more relaxed, feel the tension being released from the muscle group." After 30–40 seconds the tension-release sequence is repeated for the same muscle group, but with 45–60 seconds allotted for the relaxation segment.

Each muscle group is tensed and released twice. At the end of the second tension-release sequence for each muscle group the instructor determines if deep local relaxation has been achieved. A predetermined signal is used by participants to indicate relaxation. For example, the instructor says, "If the muscles in the right hand and right lower arm feel completely relaxed, please signal." The signal can be the raising of the little finger of the right hand, or some other predetermined signal. If a participant fails to signal, the tension-release sequence is repeated for that muscle group.

When all muscle groups have been tensed and released, the instructor allows some minutes for participants to enjoy the state of relaxation. The instructor may continue to make indirect suggestions to direct participants to remain focused on the relaxation state, at 15–20 second intervals. Then, participants are directed to slowly begin to move legs and feet, then arms and hands, then head and neck, then the remaining portions of the body.

After completing the progressive relaxation session, the instructor focuses discussion on techniques that were used to guide the session. Participants are asked to describe what the instructor did that enabled them to relax, using the following questions:

- What was the rationale for the order of the tension and relaxation of the muscle groups?
- What did you notice about the instructor's tone of voice?
- Before tensing a muscle group, what did the instructor tell you to do?
- What was the cue the instructor used for you to tense your muscles?
- Approximately how long did you hold tension in each muscle group?
- What did the instructor say while you were tensing the muscle groups?
- What was the cue the instructor used for you to release tension in the muscle groups?
- What did the instructor say while you were relaxing muscle groups?
- What signal was used to indicate that your muscles were relaxed?
- Why is it important to provide a signal for complete muscle relaxation?
- What was different about the procedures for the chest, shoulders, and upper back muscle group?
- Why do you think this was different?
- How did the instructor end the session?
- Why do you think that you were asked to move slowly at first?

After the progressive relaxation session, participants are asked to form groups of two and practice guiding each other through the tension and release cycle of the first four muscle groups. After practice in guiding each other, the instructor asks if any problems occurred, or if there are any questions about the procedure.

Summary

The stress management exercises outlined in this section are intended for use as preliminary guides to help facilitate stress management. It is helpful for TR specialists to be aware of participants' diagnoses so that exercises can be modified to accommodate all participants.

Conclusion

Support exists for therapeutic use of stress management techniques for individuals with or without disabilities. Stress management techniques such as progressive relaxation and yoga can be utilized in settings such as community centers, nursing homes, psychiatric facilities, and hospitals with participants having various diagnoses. The area in which the session will occur should be spacious enough for comfortable movement of participants, should allow for dimmed lighting, and should maintain a low noise level to induce a sense of calmness and relaxation among participants. TR specialists can facilitate the therapeutic effect of stress management techniques by adapting exercises to meet individuals' needs.

Discussion Questions

1. What is the definition of progressive relaxation?
2. What is the definition of yoga?
3. Who first developed progressive relaxation training?
4. When was yoga first developed?
5. What is the theory that led to the development of progressive relaxation training?
6. What are the five points of yoga as it is practiced today?
7. What manual is most often associated with progressive relaxation training?
8. Briefly describe a progressive relaxation session.
9. Name and describe five yoga postures.
10. Name five effects of progressive relaxation training demonstrated in various studies.
11. Name five effects of yoga as demonstrated in the studies.
12. Describe two different ways that progressive relaxation training has been modified successfully.
13. What was the rationale for each of the modifications?

Resources

Agency Resources

American Psychological Association
750 First Street, NE
Washington, DC 20002
http://www.apa.org
The organization has numerous divisions based on specialty areas that are described at the website. Each division has a president with address and phone number provided. Although there is not a separate branch devoted specifically to progressive relaxation therapy, questions can be addressed within specialty areas, such as rehabilitation psychology, clinical psychology, and so on.

Material Resources: Yoga

Fields, R. (Ed.). (1975–present). *Yoga Journal* [Magazine]. Berkeley, CA: California Yoga Teachers Association.

Living Arts. (1995). *Yoga Journal's Yoga: Six Volume Collection* [Videos]. (Available from Living Arts, Box 2939 Dept. YJ303, Venice, CA 90291.)

The Sivananda Yoga Video. (1988). *Yoga* [Video]. (Available at 163 Amsterdam Ave., Suite 207, New York, NY 10023.)

Material Resources: Progressive Relaxation

Benson, H. (1976). *Relaxation response*. New York: Avon Books.

Benson, H. (1985). *Beyond the relaxation response*. New York: Berkley Publishing.

Davis, M., & McKay, M. (1995). *Relaxation and stress reduction workbook* (4th ed.). Oakland, CA: New Harbinger Publishing.

Gunther, B. (1986). *Sense relaxation*. N. Hollywood, CA: Newcastle Publishing.

Khor, G. (1994). *Tai-chi: For stress control and relaxation*. Torrance, CA: Heian International.

Pepper, E., & Holt, C. (1993). *A self-healing workbook using dynamic relaxation, images, and thoughts*. New York: Plenum Publishing.

References

Aaronson, N. K., Ahmedzai, S., Bergman, B., Bullinger, M., Cull A., Duez, N. J., Filiberti, A., Flechtner, H., Fleishman, S. B., & De Haes, J. C. (1993). The European organization for research and treatment of cancer QLQ-C30: A quality of life instrument for use in international clinical trials in oncology. *Journal of National Cancer Institute, 85,* 365–376.

Allen, K. S., & Steinkohl, R. P. (1987). Yoga in a geriatric mental clinic. *Activities, Adaptation & Aging, 9*(4), 61–68.

American Thoracic Society. (1990). Diagnostic standards and classification of tuberculosis. *American Review of Respiratory Disease, 142,* 725–735.

Anderson, K. O., Dowds, B. N., Pelletz, R. E., Edwards, W. T., & Peeters-Asdourian, C. (1995). Development and initial validation of a scale to measure self-efficacy beliefs in patients with chronic pain. *Pain, 63,* 77–84.

Angus, S. F. (1989). Three approaches to stress management for children. *Elementary School Guidance and Counseling, 23,* 228–233.

Bensink, G. W., Godbey, K. L, Marshall, M. J., & Yarandi, H. N. (1992). Institutionalized elderly: Relaxation, locus of control, self-esteem. *Journal of Gerontological Nursing, 18*(4), 30–36.

Berger, B. G., & Owen, D. R. (1992). Mood alteration with yoga and swimming: Aerobic exercise may not be necessary. *Perceptual and Motor Skills, 75,* 1331–1343.

Bernstein, D. A., & Borkovec, T. D. (1973). *Progressive relaxation training: A manual for the helping professions.* Champaign, IL: Research Press.

Birch, D. (1987). Progressive relaxation. Special issue: 100 years of the American journal of psychology. *American Journal of Psychology, 100,* 522.

Bonadies, V. (2004). A yoga therapy program for AIDS-related pain and anxiety: Implications for Therapeutic Recreation. *Therapeutic Recreation Journal, 38,* 148–166.

Brownstein, A. H., & Dembert, M. L. (1989). Treatment of essential hypertension with yoga relaxation therapy in a USAF aviator: A case report. *Aviation, Space, and Environmental Medicine, 60,* 684–687.

Burish, T. G., Vasterling, J. J., Carey, M. P., Matt, D. A., & Krozely, M. G., (1988). Post-treatment use of relaxation training by cancer patients. *The Hospice Journal, 4*(2), 1–8.

Calajoe, A. (1986). Yoga as a therapeutic component in treating chemical dependency. *Alcoholism Treatment Quarterly, 3*(4), 33–46.

Carlson, C. R., & Hoyle, R. H. (1993). Efficacy of abbreviated progressive muscle relaxation training: A quantitative review of behavioral medicine research. *Journal of Consulting and Clinical Psychology, 61,* 1059–1067.

Carlson, C. R., Ventrella, M. A., & Sturgis, E. T. (1987). Relaxation training through muscle stretching procedures: A pilot case. *Journal of Behavior Therapy and Experimental Psychiatry, 18*(2), 121–161.

Carlson, L., Speca, M., Patel, K., & Goodey, E. (2001). Mindfulness-based stress reduction in relation to quality of life, mood, symptoms of stress, and immune parameters in breast and prostate cancer outpatients. *Psychosomatic Medicine, 6,* 571–581.

Cohen S., Kamarck T., & Mermelstein R. (1983) A global measure of perceived stress. *Journal of Health and Social Behavior, 24,* 385–96.

Culos-Reed, N., Carlson, L., Daroux, L., & Hately-Aldous, S. (2004). Discovering the physical and psychological benefits of yoga for cancer survivors. *International Journal of Yoga Therapy, 14,* 45–52

Eliot, R. S. (1994). *From stress to strength: How to lighten your load and save your life.* New York: Bantam.

Engle-Friedman, M., Hazlewood, L., Bootzin, R., & Tsao, C. (1992). An evaluation of behavioral treatments for insomnia in the older adult. *Journal of Clinical Psychology, 48,* 77–90.

Fahrenberg, J. (1994) *Die Freiburger Beschwerdenliste FBL (The Freiburg complaint list FBL).* Göttingen, Hogrefe.

Farmer, M. E., Locke, B. Z., & Moscicki, E. K. (1988). Physical activity and depressive symptoms: the nhanes I epidemiologic follow-up study. *American Journal of Epidemiology, 128,* 1340–1351.

Foley, F. W., Bedell, J. R., LaRocca, N. G., Scheinberg, L. C., & Reznikoff, M. (1987). Efficacy of stress-inoculation training in coping with multiple sclerosis. *Journal of Consulting and Clinical Psychology, 55,* 919–922.

Godin, G., & Shephard, R. J. (1985). A simple method to assess exercise behavior in the community. *Canadian Journal of Applied Sport Sciences, 10,* 141–146.

Goliszek, A. G. (1987). *The book of stress survival.* New York: Simon & Schuster.

Greendale, G., McDivit, A., Carpenter, A., Seeger, L., & Huang, M. (2002). Yoga for women with hyperkyphosis: Results of a pilot study. *American Journal of Public Health, 92*(10), 1611–1614.

Gronwall, D. A. (1977). Paced auditory serial-addition task: A measure of recovery from concussion. *Perceptual and Motor Skills, 44,* 367–373.

Gupta, N., Khera, S., Vempati, R. T., Sharma, R., & Bijlani, R. L. (2006). Effect of yoga based lifestyle intervention on state and trait anxiety. *Indian Journal of Physiology and Pharmacology, 50*(1), 41–47.

Hannon, K. (1994, May 16). Yoga goes mainstream. *U. S. News and World Report, 116*(19), 79–83.

Heaner, M. K. (2003, May). When om turns to ouch. *Health, 17*(4), 90, 94.

Hewitt, J. (1977). *The complete yoga book.* New York: Schocken Books.

Hoddes E., Zarcone, V., Smythe, H., Phillips R., & Dement, W. C. (1973). Quantification of sleepiness: A new approach. *Psychophysiology, 10,* 431–436.

Hui, S. S., & Yuen, P. K. (2000). Validity of the modified back-saver sit-and-reach test: A comparison with other protocols. *Medical Science in Sports and Exercise, 32,* 1655–1659.

Jacobson, E. (1987). Progressive relaxation. Special issue: 100 years of the American journal of psychology. *American Journal of Psychology, 100,* 523–537. (Original work published 1925.)

Jacobson, E. (1938). *Progressive relaxation.* Chicago, IL: University of Chicago.

Jensen, M. P., Turner, J. A., Romano, J. M., & Lawler, B. K. (1994). Relationship of pain-specific beliefs to chronic pain adjustment. *Pain, 57,* 301–309.

Krishnamurthy, M. N., & Telles, S. (2007). Assessing depression following two ancient Indian interventions: Effects of yoga and ayurveda on older adults in a residential home. *Journal of Gerontological Nursing, 33*(2), 17–23.

Lavey, R., Sherman, T., Mueser K. T., Osborne, D. D., Currier, M., & Wolfe, R. (2005). The effects of yoga on mood in psychiatric inpatients. *Psychiatric Rehabilitation Journal, 28*(4), 399–402.

Leckie, M. S., & Thompson, E. (1979). *Symptoms of stress inventory.* Seattle: University of Washington.

Lehrer, P. M., Batey, D. M., Woolfolk, R. L., Remde, A., & Garlick, T. (1988). The effect of repeated tense-release sequences on EMG and self-report of muscle tension: An evaluation of Jacobsonian and post-Jacobsonian assumptions about progressive relaxation. *Psychophysiology, 25,* 562–569.

Lehrer, P. M., Carr, R., Sargunaraj, D., & Woolfolk, R. L. (1994). Stress management techniques: Are they all equivalent, or do they have specific effects? *Biofeedback and Self-Regulation, 19,* 353–401.

Leitner, M. J., Leitner, S. F., & Assoc. (1996). *Leisure enhancement*. Binghamton, NY: The Haworth Press.

Lindsay, W. R., Baty, F. J., Michie, A. M., & Richardson, I. (1989). A comparison of anxiety treatments with adults who have moderate and severe mental retardation. *Research in Developmental Disabilities, 10,* 129–140.

Lindsay, W. R., Fee, M., Michie, A., & Heap, I. (1994). The effects of cue control relaxation on adults with severe mental retardation. *Research in Developmental Disabilities, 15,* 425–437.

Lopata, C., Nida, R. E., & Marable, M. A. (2006). Progressive muscle relaxation: Preventing aggression in students with EBD. *Teaching Exceptional Children, 38*(4), 20–25.

Lucic, K. S., Steffen, J. J., Harrigan, J. A., & Stuebing, R. C. (1991). Progressive relaxation training: Muscle contraction before relaxation? *Behavior Therapy, 22,* 249–256.

Lutz, R., Lochbaum, R., Lanning, B., Stinson, L., Brewer, R. (2007). Cross-lagged relationships among leisure-time exercise and perceived stress in blue-collar workers. *Journal of Sport & Exercise Psychology, 29,* 687–705.

McCaffrey, M., & Pasero, C. (1999). *Pain: Clinical manual* (2nd ed.). St. Louis: Mosby.

McNair, D. M., Loir, M., & Droppleman, L. F. (1971). *Profile of mood states manual*. San Diego: Educational and Industrial Testing Service.

Melzack, R. (1987) The short-form McGill pain questionnaire. *Pain, 30,* 191–197.

Michalsen, A., Grossman, P., Acil, A., Langhorst, J., Ludtke, R., Esch, T., Stefano, G., & Dobos, F. (2005) Rapid stress reduction and anxiolysis among distressed women as a consequence of a three-month intensive yoga program. *Medical Science Moniter, 11*(12), 555–561.

Oken, B. S., Kishiyama, S., Zajdel, D., Bourdette, D., Carlsen, J., Haas, M., Hugos, C., Kraemer, D. F., Lawrence, J., & Mass, M. (2004). Randomized controlled trial of yoga and exercise in multiple sclerosis. *Neurology, 62,* 2058–2064.

Patterson, I., & Coleman, D. (1996). The impact of stress on different leisure dimensions. *Journal of Applied Recreation Research, 21*(3), 243–262.

Peck, H., Kehle, T., Bray, M., & Theodore, L. (2005). Yoga as an intervention for children with attention problems. *School Psychology Review, 34*(3), 415–424.

Perret, E. (1974). The left frontal lobe of man and the suppression of habitual responses in verbal categorical behavior. *Neuropsychologia, 12,* 323–330.

Radloff, L. S. (1977). The CES-D Scale: A self-report depression scale for research in the general population. *Applied Psychological Measurement, 1,* 385–401.

Rani, H. J., & Rao, P. V. K. (1994). Body awareness and yoga training. *Perceptual and Motor Skills, 79,* 1103–1106.

Rankin, E. J., Gilner, F. H., Gfeller, J. D., & Katz, B. M. (1993). Efficacy of progressive muscle relaxation for reducing state anxiety among elderly adults on memory tasks. *Perceptual and Motor Skills, 77,* 1395–1402.

Rhode, G., Jenson, W. R., & Reavis, H. K. (1993). *The tough kid book*. Longmont, CO: Sopris West.

Rickard, H. C., Collier, J. B., McCoy, A. D., Crist, D. A., & Weinberger, M. B. (1993). Relaxation training for psychiatric inpatients. *Psychological Reports, 72,* 1267–1274.

Rickard, H. C., McCoy, A. D., Collier, J. B., & Weinberger, M. B. (1989). Relaxation training side effects reported by seriously disturbed inpatients. *Journal of Clinical Psychology, 45,* 446–450.

Robinson, M. E., Riley, J. L., Myers, C. D., Sadler, I. J., Kvaal, S. A., Geisser, M. E., & Keefe, F. J. (1997). The coping strategies questionnaire: A large sample, item level factor analysis. *Clinical Journal of Pain, 13*, 43–49.

Rowshan, A. (1993). *Stress, an owner's manual: Positive techniques for taking charge of your life*. Oxford, United Kingdom: Oneworld.

Scogin, F., Rickard, H. C., Keith, S., Wilson, J., & McElreath, L. (1992). Progressive and imaginal relaxation training for elderly persons with subjective anxiety. *Psychology and Aging, 7*, 419–424.

Selye, H. (1976). *The stress of life*. New York: McGraw-Hill.

Shields, S. A., & Mallory, M. E. (1989). The body awareness questionnaire: Reliability and validity. *Journal of Personality Assessment, 53*, 802–815.

The Sivananda Yoga Video. (1988). *Yoga* [Video]. (Available at 163 Amsterdam Ave., Suite 207, New York, NY 10023.)

Smith, H. (1986). *The religions of man*. New York: Harper & Row.

Spielberger, C. D., Gorsuch, R. L., & Lushene, R. (1970). *State-trait anxiety inventory manual*. Palo-Alto, CA: Consulting Psychologists Press.

Steffen, A. M., McKibbin, C., Zeiss, A., Gallagher-Thompson, D., & Bandura, A. (2002). The revised self-efficacy for caregiving interview: Two reliability and validity studies. *Journal of Gerontology: Psychological Sciences, 57B*, 74–76.

Tait, R. C., Chibnall, J. T., & Krause, S. (1990). The Pain Disability Index: Psychometric properties. *Pain, 40*, 171–182.

Taylor, D. G. (1995). Effects of a behavioral stress-management program on anxiety, mood, self-esteem, and T-cell count in HIV-positive men. *Psychological reports, 76*, 451–457.

Telles, S., Hanumanthaiah, B., Nagarathna, R., & Nagendra, H. R. (1993). Improvement in static motor performance following yogic training of school children. *Perceptual and Motor Skills, 76*, 1264–1266.

Time-Life Books. (1987). *Managing stress from morning to night*. Alexandria, VA: Rebus.

Uma, K., Nagendra, H. R., Nagaranthna, R., Vaidehi, S., & Seethalakshmi R. (1989). The integrated approach of yoga: A therapeutic tool for mentally retarded children: A one-year controlled study. *Journal of Mental Deficiency Research, 33*, 415–421.

Visweswaraiah, S., & Telles, S. (2004). Randomized trial of yoga as a complementary therapy for pulmonary tuberculosis. *Respirology, 9*, 96–101.

Von Zerssen, D., & Koeller, D. (1976) *Die Befi ndlichkeits-Skala (The well-being questionnaire)*. Weinheim: Beltz-Test Gesellschaft.

Waelde, L., Thompson, L., & Gallagher-Thompson, D. (2004). A pilot study of a yoga and meditation intervention for dementia caregiver stress. *Journal of Clinical Psychology, 60*(6), 677–687.

Williams, K., Petronis, J., Smith, D., Goodrich, D., Wu, J., Ravi, N., Doyle, E., Juckett, G., Kolari, M., Gross, R., & Steinberg, L. (2005). Effect of Iyengar yoga therapy for chronic low back pain. *Pain, 115*, 107–117.

Wolpe, J. (1958). *Psychotherapy by reciprocal inhibition*. Stanford, CA: Stanford University Press.

Chapter 10
Therapeutic Use of T'ai Chi

John Dattilo and Ijnanyah Wingate

Success isn't measured by money or power or social rank.
Success is measured by discipline and inner peace.
—Mike Ditka

Introduction

Although T'ai Chi is a traditional Chinese martial art that has been thought to have therapeutic effects for more than 600 years, some therapists and physicians are just beginning to investigate effects of T'ai Chi (Honda, 1995). Because T'ai Chi emphasizes body relaxation, mental concentration, and movement coordination, it is considered to be an exercise that has effects on both physical and psychological behaviors for a variety of individuals (Wolfson et al., 1996).

This chapter provides information to individuals who would like to learn more about T'ai Chi and the effective use of it as a therapeutic medium. T'ai Chi can provide a variety of individuals with disabilities the opportunity to be active in an alternative to high-impact forms of exercise that has both mental and physical effects.

Because T'ai Chi is a form of exercise or recreation that is new to some countries in comparison to other forms of exercise, T'ai Chi is defined in this chapter and a discussion is included addressing the theoretical basis of T'ai Chi. A description of the origin and technique is also presented to clarify different styles and evolution of T'ai Chi. The chapter contains a section that explains the theoretical basis of T'ai Chi. A review of the literature is provided that presents research examining effects of T'ai Chi as a therapeutic intervention. This chapter concludes with suggestions for professional resources and potential ideas that a TR specialist can use to promote physical and psychological functioning of individuals with varying abilities utilizing T'ai Chi.

Definition

T'ai Chi Ch'uan, better known as T'ai Chi, is a Chinese martial art that has been documented as being practiced for over 600 years; however, its origin is neither clear nor certain (Honda, 1995). Tai Chi emphasizes relaxation, and is essentially a form of *meditation in motion* (Crompton, 2000, pg. 82). Unlike other martial arts, Tai Chi is characterized by precisely executed soft, slow, flowing movements that emphasize force, rather than intense strength (Lan, Lai, & Chen, 2002).

Many styles of T'ai Chi Ch'uan have evolved, such as Yang, Chen, Wu, and Sun styles. T'ai Chi Ch'uan is comprised of three Chinese characters: *Tai* meaning "entire, all-encompassing," *Chi* meaning "ultimate, extreme point" (Kuo, 1991, p. 6), and *Ch'uan* meaning "an exercise involving fists and boxing," or "force" (Sun & Chen, 1995).

T'ai Chi Ch'uan refers to the martial art, or the actual sequence of movements, whereas *T'ai Chi* refers to the philosophical idea. *T'ai Chi* is usually the phrase used when describing the movement for brevity, and will be used in this chapter for the movements and philosophy, unless otherwise specified. The T'ai Chi philosophy is defined as "all things are continuously moving and restless, yet each is proceeding back to the source," so the movements of T'ai Chi are continuous. The Yin-Yang philosophy, described in detail in the section of this chapter devoted to theoretical foundations, provides the basis for movements that are included in a T'ai Chi form.

Descriptions

Although T'ai Chi is a type of martial art, it is a slow, graceful, learned sequence of movements that, at first glance, resembles swimming in the air in slow motion (Jacobsen, Ho-Cheng, Cashel, & Guerrero, 1997). T'ai Chi can be comprised of 24 sequential movements (simplified T'ai Chi Ch'uan) or can have 85 movements (traditional Yang Long style) or more, and has been described as a dance, exercise, sport, way of life, and method of reaching mental and physical relaxation (Sun & Chen, 1995). What all styles of T'ai Chi have in common are the coordinated, slow, rhythmical movements and relaxed muscles with weight shifting from foot to foot to maintain balance combined with deep breathing techniques of karate (Meditation in Motion, 1994). This section contains:

- Characteristics of T'ai Chi
- Training Essentials of T'ai Chi
- Program Considerations for T'ai Chi

Characteristics of T'ai Chi

According to Yan (1995), T'ai Chi can be an accessible, enjoyable activity that has health and fitness benefits. The positive response by participants to T'ai Chi may be due to T'ai Chi having the following characteristics:

- Noncompetitive
- No equipment is required
- Perfect form is not required
- Different styles and levels to choose

Noncompetitive. T'ai Chi is an exercise that does not require direct competition and is paced by the individual; therefore, individuals at different fitness levels can participate. When involved in T'ai Chi, participants do not compete against other people; rather, they perform at the level at which they feel comfortable. Although there is a style of 2-person T'ai Chi that requires participants to push against one another, this style consists of controlled, slow motions in a noncompetitive manner, called Push Hands. The purpose of the 2-person Push Hands is to allow participants to practice their form movements.

No equipment required. T'ai Chi requires no equipment to practice. As long as the person has enough space to perform the movements, T'ai Chi can be practiced anywhere. In some styles of T'ai Chi, individuals wear uniforms or loose shirts, but no particular clothes are required to perform T'ai Chi. Loose-fitting clothing, and comfortable shoes or no shoes are recommended to allow freedom of movement. Videos, cassettes, books, and the Internet can assist in learning and practicing of T'ai Chi, but they are not required.

Perfect form not required. In the Westernized styles of T'ai Chi, such as Beijing Short Form and Yang Short Form, the movements have been simplified and made shorter in comparison to some other styles of T'ai Chi that are older or no longer practiced. The purpose of T'ai Chi is to combine physical movement with mental thoughts to promote *chi,* or energy flow, from one's inner self (Sun & Chen, 1995). T'ai Chi relies on how participants feel about themselves during and after practice. Perfect form is not required because the intent of T'ai Chi is not to create stiff movements, but rather relaxed, fluid movements. Therefore, T'ai Chi is a potential exercise and form of recreation for children, older adults, or individuals with varying abilities (Sun & Chen, 1995).

Different styles and levels to choose. T'ai Chi has evolved from martial arts in the Chinese culture. Therefore, some styles of T'ai Chi are taught with more rigor than others, and individuals are judged based on the quality of movements performed. However, the more rigorous styles of T'ai Chi are usually the longer forms. Fortunately, the longer forms have been adapted for the Western world and those individuals who would like to have the physical and psychological benefits of T'ai Chi without the rigor or rank competitiveness. The shorter, more simplified styles, such as Beijing Short Form and Yang Short Form, are two styles that are based on the traditional T'ai Chi forms but were created to be less time-consuming and less difficult for the beginner. Therefore, individuals can chose between different styles and levels of T'ai Chi, and therapists can guide participants to the style that the individual might enjoy most.

Summary. Because T'ai Chi does not require direct competition or perfect form, and participants can choose the style and level that they might enjoy, T'ai Chi is a desirable exercise for individuals who are interested in physical and psychological health. Also, because no equipment is required, T'ai Chi can be practiced almost anywhere and with limited resources.

Training Essentials of T'ai Chi

With Tai Chi, emphasis is placed on exercising of the mind and the conscious (Li, Hong, & Chan, 2001). The meditative component, which allows participants to focus on the body as a whole, makes this physical activity unique (Hogan, 2005). During T'ai Chi practice, participants relax all areas of the body, allowing their body to assume a comfortable posture and alignment (Crompton, 2000). According to Li, Hong, and Chan, the circular continuous movements help the body shift weight back and forth while successful completion of the precise movements facilitate muscle control.

When practicing T'ai Chi, participants attempt to keep their mind calm and focused, maintain a relaxed body, engage in deep breathing, and demonstrate movements that are agile, smooth, very slow, and made in a circular motion (Metzger & Zhou, 1996). Although perfect form is not required during T'ai Chi practice, training essentials can be helpful to perform and understand the movements of T'ai Chi. These essentials include:

- Slowness
- Continuity
- Relaxation
- Weight distribution
- Breathing
- Posture
- Internal strength
- Light movement

Slowness. All movements in T'ai Chi are performed as slowly as possible. This aspect makes T'ai Chi different from most martial arts. Each movement is slow and calculated.

Continuity. T'ai Chi is not only practiced very slowly, but the sequence of movements is continuous. Therefore, after a series of movements are learned, they will not be recognized as single movements, but rather a fluid sequence, or form. In addition, participants' upper and lower body are coordinated to create a harmonization of body movements, making T'ai Chi look more like a slow, fluid dance rather than a martial art.

Relaxation. The body and upper limbs are relaxed as much as possible when performing T'ai Chi. Muscles of participants' shoulders and chest remain relaxed during T'ai Chi practice. It is helpful to have relaxing thoughts during T'ai Chi with the mind remaining clear, while maintaining a focus toward bringing all energy to the center of the body, or the *Dantian*.

Weight distribution. Body weight is never distributed equally on both legs during T'ai Chi practice; rather, participants shift back and forth placing different amounts of weight on each leg. Although weight distribution is constantly changing, participants maintain their balance by maintaining a stance with feet shoulder-width apart.

Breathing. Breathing is natural during T'ai Chi practice, with participants taking deep, long, even breaths. Over a period of time and after regular practice, breathing becomes slow and steady during T'ai Chi movements.

Posture. The bodies and spines of T'ai Chi participants are held upright as they control their waists with their arms slightly out to their sides, as if small balls were placed under the armpits. While practicing T'ai Chi, participants keep their heads in an upright position with their eyes focused on their hands, instead of their feet. Participants maintain relaxed shoulders, pushed slightly back and down in order to open up and lift the chest.

Internal strength. During practice of T'ai Chi, it is important for participants to concentrate and focus on using their minds to move their bodies. During T'ai Chi, it is helpful for participants to focus on keeping their body relaxed when it is moving, unlike many other sports.

Light movement. The stepping pattern of T'ai Chi has been referred to being like that of a cat. The movement is light and agile as participants use their hips and bend their knees to keep their body in one plane and shift their center of gravity when needed. Participants keep their upper bodies in an upright position that is relaxed and undisturbed by the movement of the lower body.

Summary. Essentials of T'ai Chi practice are natural to the body and are interrelated. These essentials, which include slowness, continuity, relaxation, weight distribution, breathing, posture, internal strength, and light movements, become integrated into the T'ai Chi performance with practice over time. T'ai Chi participants become more aware of their bodies' movement as they practice their technique.

Program Considerations for T'ai Chi

It is important for TR specialists to be prepared before implementing a T'ai Chi program. To become knowledgeable about T'ai Chi and to prepare the agency and participants it is helpful to do the following in advance:

- Gather resources
- Develop a budget
- Assess participants
- Determine staff capabilities
- Establish program focus
- Evaluate facility size
- Examine environmental conditions

Gather resources. Because T'ai Chi has only recently been adopted in Western society, many people are not familiar with T'ai Chi. Therefore, it is helpful to gather as many resources as possible to learn about the various styles of T'ai Chi and determine which style is appropriate for participants. Resources include books, magazines, videos, Internet sites, and other programs offered by colleagues. A list of resources is included at the end of this chapter to assist the TR specialist in learning more about T'ai Chi.

Develop a budget. In some cases, funds are needed to initiate a T'ai Chi program. Since little or no cost is necessary for equipment and if space is available (such as a gym or spacious room), the only cost may be for an instructor. If available, volunteers can be used in the class instead of paid personnel to assist clients.

Assess participants. Assessment of participants who will attend the T'ai Chi program is important. Each participant may have a different ability level and will need an individualized plan which also takes into account any chronic conditions. Some participants may need extensive assistance during the program, an accessible location, or a style of T'ai Chi that is simple and repetitive. Other participants may be ready to participate in higher, more difficult levels or styles of T'ai Chi.

Determine staff capabilities. There are many resources associated with T'ai Chi such as the National T'ai Chi Ch'uan Association that provide workshops on T'ai Chi to enable individuals to become certified as instructors. In addition, agencies can help locate a certified instructor who can be contracted to conduct a T'ai Chi class. For those who might need extensive assistance during T'ai Chi class, additional staff might be needed if volunteers are not available.

Establish program focus. To achieve desired outcomes when using a T'ai Chi program, it is useful to establish a clear purpose statement for the program. In addition, goals are helpful in clarifying the intent of the program as well as specific objectives and clearly articulated performance measures.

Evaluate facility size. The facility in which the T'ai Chi program is conducted can be a large room, a gymnasium, or the outdoors (weather permitting). The critical aspect of the facility is that participants have sufficient room to move without making contact with one another. Individuals should remain at least an arms' length in any direction from each other.

Examine environmental conditions. The environment of a T'ai Chi class should allow for all participants to see the instructor throughout the class. A comfortable room temperature should be maintained and adequate lighting should be available so participants can easily see the instructor. Because T'ai Chi is slow moving with relaxed muscles, soft music can be played at a low volume to help to create a relaxed atmosphere.

Summary. When planning a T'ai Chi program, gathering resources, developing a budget, assessing participants, determining staff capabilities, establishing goals (objectives and performance measures), evaluating facility size, and examining environmental conditions can help. Following these steps may help TR specialists develop a program that provides participants with an enjoyable and meaningful experience.

History

T'ai Chi has been used for many years in the Chinese culture and has recently been introduced to Western societies (Sutton, 1991). Although use of T'ai Chi has been documented for over 600 years as a therapeutic martial art, its history extends to ancient Chinese times.

Tai Chi was originally taught as a martial art and longevity exercise and was considered to be a secret practice passed down through families and loyal students. When people began to report health benefits of T'ai Chi in the early 20th century (Fei, 2001), the Chinese art form acquired a new role as a preventive medicine or as a wellness exercise (Crompton, 2000). People choose to participate in Tai Chi, not only for its health benefits, but because it is an exercise that may be practiced throughout the lifespan.

Since many current experts on T'ai Chi believe that T'ai Chi originated from martial arts, it is helpful to understand the origin of martial arts. This section reviews the:

- Origin of Martial Arts
- Origin of T'ai Chi
- Origin of T'ai Chi Styles
- T'ai Chi Chih Style

Origin of Martial Arts

According to Kuo (1991), martial arts can be traced to the beginning of human culture in ancient China. According to legend, humans were given the ability to defend themselves against animals and the environment because they could study and learn from animals and the environment. Martial arts developed from observation and imitation of animals and the environment, such as animals stretching, rivers flowing, and clouds floating.

Origin of T'ai Chi

According to Sun and Chen (1995), the creation of T'ai Chi evolved over time and surfaced in the Liang region of South-North dynasty in China between 502 and 577 A.D. A series of basic movements were formulated that evolved during the Tang dynasty (618–907 A.D.) which are believed to be pre-T'ai Chi exercises and the basis of the forms present today. The person usually credited as the first recorded T'ai Chi teacher and practitioner is Zhang San-feng. However, the origin of T'ai Chi is not clear, since many individuals, such as the monks of Shao-Lin Temple in China (772 A.D.), are believed to have contributed to the creation of T'ai Chi.

Origin of T'ai Chi Styles

After the first record of T'ai Chi in the 1500s, a split of T'ai Chi practice occurred that divided China into different T'ai Chi styles. The T'ai Chi styles were split into branches involving northern and southern China. Most T'ai Chi that is practiced today is believed to be from the northern branch, and has evolved into a combination of martial art, relaxation technique, dance, exercise, and philosophy of life (Sun & Chen, 1995). There are many styles of T'ai Chi, all of which have similar movements, with each style named after the instructor who began the style and school. All styles are practiced and taught today; however, many take a considerable length of time to complete and require years of practice to master.

T'ai Chi Chih Style

While T'ai Chi Chih is similar to T'ai Chi Ch'uan, it lacks all aspects of martial arts and instead focuses on circulating, developing, and balancing your Chi, or your individual energy flow, within your body. T'ai Chi Chih was developed and first taught in 1974 by Justin Stone, a T'ai Chi Ch'uan master. T'ai Chi Chih includes 19 soft, gentle movements and one closing posture (T'ai Chi Chih, 2008).

- Chen
- Yang
- Wu
- Hao
- Sun
- Beijing Short Form 24

Chen. The origin of T'ai Chi is not quite clear; however, in China many people believe Chen Wangting (1597–1664) is the founder of T'ai Chi (Metzger & Zhou, 1996). Chen style has 32 forms that consist of smooth flowing forms of T'ai Chi, as well as explosive jumps that are not seen in many other forms practiced today. According to Metzger and Zhou, the Chen Style of T'ai Chi was used for military training and is closely related to fighting types of martial arts.

Yang. The most widely used style in research and practice is the Yang-style (Thornton, Sykes, & Tang, 2004). The founder of this style is Yang Luchan (1795–1842), who was born in the Hopeh province of China. The Yang style is rooted in the Chen style, because Luchan was a student of Chen Wangting and the styles have similar movements. However, Luchan modified the Yang style throughout his lifetime and developed three branches within the style. These branches include (a) Traditional Yang Form (85 postures), (b) Beijing Short Form (24 postures), and (c) Yang Short Form (40 postures). These branches of Yang style are characterized by balanced, fluid movements that are sequential, simple movements (Metzger & Zhou, 1996).

Wu. As Yang Luchan was a student of Chen Wangting, Wu Jianquan, the founder of Wu style T'ai Chi, was a student of Yang Luchan. Wu taught the Yang style for many years; however, he developed a style that is less gentle, with movements that are less relaxed and fluid than the other styles. Although Wu schools are present today, the Wu style is probably the least popular style of T'ai Chi.

Hao. The Hao style, developed by Hao He (1849–1920), is a variation of Yang Luchan style. He expanded the Yang form by adding more variations of the postures and repeating them within the form. The Hao style is similar to the Wu style and is characterized by a quick succession of movements (Metzger & Zhou, 1996).

Sun. Sun Lutang (1861–1932) was first a master of the art of fist fighting in China before he became involved in T'ai Chi. After visiting Beijing, China, he met Hao He, who became very sick. Lutang cared for He until he recovered. In return, He taught Lutang his style of T'ai Chi. Sun integrated what He taught him and created the Sun style with 85 forms in a different sequence than the Hao style. The Sun style is characterized by distinct hand movements and gentle, fluid movements of the legs (Metzger & Zhou, 1996).

Beijing Short Form 24. As the interest in T'ai Chi grew, including not only people from China but people from other countries, the Chinese National Physical Education Administration met in 1970 in Beijing, China at a conference. At this conference, instructors or masters from all different styles of T'ai Chi formulated a simplified form of T'ai Chi that has 24 forms or movements. This style is often referred to as Simplified, or Beijing, Short Form T'ai Chi (Sun & Chen, 1995). Although this style of T'ai Chi is easier to learn because it only has 24 movements as compared to other styles that have up to 108 movements, some problems accompany the shortening of T'ai Chi styles.

> For example, the shortened technique is less focused on breathing, eye movement, and concentration, all of which are believed to be critical aspects of effective T'ai Chi.

Summary. Although all styles of T'ai Chi are similar, some are practiced more than others. The Yang style and Beijing Short Form 24 are the most popular in the United States; however, many variations of these forms exist. These styles may be the most applicable for TR specialists to utilize for treatment and recreation participation because of their simplicity and the ability of participants to complete the forms in a manageable amount of time. The more difficult styles may be more beneficial for individuals who desire to be challenged extensively and for people who possess advanced physical skills.

Theoretical Foundations

Although T'ai Chi has varied styles and forms that have different movements and founders, one theoretical premise is consistent across all forms. Yin-Yang is an important belief which is central in T'ai Chi. In addition, the five element theory is a component of all forms of T'ai Chi. This section contains information on:

- Yin-Yang
- Five Element Theory

Yin-Yang

In Chinese philosophy, T'ai Chi derives its energy from the Yin and the Yang. Chinese philosophers believed in the beginning that the world was "void and boundless" (Kuo, 1991, p. 6). This state, or time, of the world was called *wu chi*. However, it is hypothesized that two forces evolved called the *Yin* and the *Yang*. The union of these two forces is what the Chinese call *T'ai Chi* and is recognized as the Yin-Yang symbol (see Figure 10.1).

Figure 10.1

The Yin and Yang are opposite or alternating forces that complement each other in the universe. Because T'ai Chi is based on the natural world and surroundings that human beings encounter every day, the Yin and the Yang are viewed in Chinese philosophy as the two primal forces (Kuo, 1991). Separate definitions of Yin and Yang and a description of what the phrase *Yin-Yang* means may help clarify the Yin-Yang philosophy and why the circle made up of two parts symbolizes Yin-Yang.

Yin symbolizes *stillness*, *dark*, or *rest* (Crompton, 2000). Therefore, in the circular symbol with the two opposing tear drops, Yin is represented as the darker half of the Yin-Yang design, symbolizing that which is static, or still, in the universe. According to Chinese philosophy, movement must occur when stillness is not present (Sun & Chen, 1995). According to Crompton (2000), Yang symbolizes *movement*, *light*, or *activity*. This definition demonstrates the opposite symbolization of Yang in comparison to Yin. Yang is, therefore, symbolized in the Yin-Yang design as the lighter half, representing activity.

These two alternating forces, Yin and Yang become the basis of the philosophy of T'ai Chi when they are combined. The two sectors of the Yin-Yang combined depict dual forces that are complementary to each other and forever present in our universe. The Yin and Yang are treated as polarities: moon and sun, woman and man, softness and firmness, earth and the heavens, and stillness and movement (Sun & Chen, 1995). According to Chinese philosophy, humans experience all of these polarities, and they all influence the human body.

For example, in T'ai Chi, when the right hand pushes forward in a movement, the left hand draws back. Another example is when the leg kicks, the quadricep muscle (front of upper leg) contracts while the hamstring muscle (back of upper leg) extends in an opposing fashion; furthermore, the muscles complement each other in natural inhalation and exhalation movements.

The opposing forces of Yin and Yang are not necessarily separate entities, but rather, some portion of the one force exists in the other. Therefore, in the practice of T'ai Chi philosophy, or T'ai Chi Ch'uan, the movements are not comprised of starting and stopping, but rather of constant, flowing, and circular movements, with no true beginning or ending. Although the two dots, or small circles, within each of the teardrops of the Yin-Yang symbol represent the beginning and the end, as Yin and Yang contain a portion of each other, so does the beginning and end, according to Chinese philosophy (Metzger & Zhou, 1996).

When learning T'ai Chi, each movement is usually taught separately, and a beginning form and commencement form are taught, as well as a sequence. However, when the movements are learned, participants can complete the sequence of movements as many times as desired. Each time the movements are practiced, it is viewed as a continuation of the previous time, never beginning again and never ending.

Five Element Theory

According to Chinese philosophy, when the Yin and Yang work together to form T'ai Chi, they generate the five directions of the universe, creating five basic elements found in nature (Kuo, 1991). The five elements are symbolized in the T'ai Chi form in the movements, describing what direction the body, hands, and feet move while practicing. The Five Element Theory, also known as the Five Phase Theory, includes the elements of:

- Earth
- Metal
- Wood
- Water
- Fire

The relationship of these five elements is often illustrated by a circle with five points. The element *earth* represents direction and possible movement in T'ai Chi Ch'uan practice. The earth is the center, and in practice the position is being on guard or in the center. The *metal* element represents the west, and movement in a T'ai Chi form that it represents is to advance or move forward. The element *wood* represents the east. A retreat or stepping-back motion in T'ai Chi is represented by wood. *Water* results in the left, and represents the direction north. *Fire* is associated with the south, and movement in T'ai Chi that is associated with fire is shifting the body to the right.

Effectiveness

The value of T'ai Chi as a therapeutic exercise has been described for centuries (Hine, 1992). Only recently has research begun to document effects of T'ai Chi. For example, Taggart (2001) used a single-factor, within-participants design, to determine benefits of a 3-month T'ai Chi (2 x wk, 30-min sessions) as reported by 45 older women (ages 72–96) living within retirement communities. Self-reported health status and perception of changes in health were assessed at baseline, after 3 months of typical activity, and after participating in the T'ai Chi program using a scale developed by the National Center for Health Statistics (1991). During an exit interview, participants completed an open-ended question about perceived benefits of T'ai Chi. Mean score of the self-assessed health measure increased significantly from the initial application of T'ai Chi practice to post-intervention. Eighty-eight percent of participants reported experiencing various benefits from T'ai Chi practice, including a decrease in use of assistive devices for walking, reduction in pain, and increased bladder control. Although data were collected via self-report, participants did identify some potential benefits for T'ai Chi practice.

Effects of T'ai Chi have been studied using a variety of indicators. The next section reviews the research examining effects of T'ai Chi on the following behaviors:

- Balance and Postural Stability
- Metabolic Responses and Cardiorespiratory Function
- Immune Responses and Physical Systems
- Neurological Function
- Psychological Effects

Balance and Postural Stability

Due to the exercise components of flexibility, balance, and muscle strengthening, T'ai Chi has been effective in reducing falls and slowing declines in ambulation and balance for older adults with mild to moderate Parkinson's disease (Weber, 2008). Several studies are reviewed that indicated that participants experienced improved balance and postural function associated with participating in T'ai Chi.

Fong and Ng (2006) examined effects of T'ai Chi on the muscle reflex latency of lower limbs, active knee joint repositioning accuracy, and balance performance of 48 participants (24 men, 24 women, ages 40–70) based on the amount of T'ai Chi experience. Of the 40 participants, 16 had 3 months of experience in T'ai Chi training, 16 had 1–3 years of experience in T'ai Chi training, and 16 had no experience in T'ai Chi training. Reflex was tested using a posteroanterior perturbation test, in which stimulus is applied to a muscle to produce a reaction from that muscle (Ng, 2005) and a system of electrodes attached to the hamstrings and gastrocnemius muscles. Ankle positioning was assessed using a method created by the researchers that involved knee flexion of the dominant leg while the dominant leg is suspended. Balance was assessed using the Dynamic Balance Test (Jacobson et al., 1997). Participants who practiced T'ai Chi for more than a year exhibited significantly faster reaction times in terms of reflex in hamstrings and gastrocnemius muscles and a longer balance time than those who practiced T'ai Chi for 3 months or not at all. Participants who practiced T'ai Chi for more than 3 months had significantly less knee joint angle-repositioning error than those who did not practice T'ai Chi. Although the study supported the benefits of regular practice in T'ai Chi, types or level of activity among participants were not reported, which may have affected participants overall physical functioning levels.

T'ai Chi has been shown to increase balance and reduce factors associated with falls. **Lin, Hwang, Wang, Chang, and Wolf (2006)** used a quasi-experimental design to examine long-term effects of a community-based T'ai Chi program on the gait, balance, and number of injurious falls of 1,200 people (ages > 65) from six rural villages in Taichung, Taiwan. Participants were given educational flyers and could view educational posters in public areas. Two villages (experimental group) were provided the option of participating in a free 1-year T'ai Chi program consisting of learning and practicing 13 movements from Chen-style T'ai Chi available (6 x wk, 60-min sessions). Immediately before and after the intervention, participants completed a personal interview and the Performance-Oriented Assessment of Mobility Problems test. Telephone interviews were conducted and postcards sent to participants every 3 months for 2 years to determine number of falls experienced post-participation and exercise frequency and duration. Despite the fact that both the control group (44%) and experimental group (75%) experienced a decline in number of injurious falls, the decline of the experimental group was 31% higher, although not statistically significant. In terms of balance, the experimental group (-0.2) experienced less of a decline in balance than did the control group (-1.4). Although this study supports T'ai Chi as a means for maintaining and improving gait and balance, caution is advised because implications of participants' physical activity levels were not adequately addressed. In addition, participants who encountered health problems during the follow-up period may not have completed all phone interviews, and this may have influenced results. Future research that measures such factors and health and activity levels when examining effects of T'ai Chi is encouraged.

There is support for the use of T'ai Chi to increase balance and reduce falls over time. For example, using an experimental randomized control trial, **Li et al. (2005)** examined effects of a 6-month T'ai Chi intervention (3 x wk, 60-min sessions) on the number of falls for 256 community dwelling adults (ages 70–92) identified as being physically inactive. The T'ai Chi program included a 5–10-minute warm-up, 40–50-min T'ai Chi practice, and 5–10-min cool-down. Participants were randomly assigned to the T'ai Chi group or to a control group that participated in a stretching program for 6 months. The intervention phase was followed by a 6-month follow-up in which no exercise classes were provided. Participants kept a daily record of number of their falls. In addition, the Berg Balance Scale (Berg, Wood-Dauphinee, Williams, & Maki, 1992), Dynamic Gait Index (Wrisley, Marchetti, Kuharsky, & Whitney, 2004), Up&Go Test (Podsiadlo & Richardson, 1991), and Functional Reach Test (Duncan, Weiner, Chandler, & Studenski, 1990) were used to measure additional outcomes such as functional balance. The T'ai Chi group decreased frequency of falls by 55% and showed improved scores for the Up&Go Test. The control group experienced approximately 3 times as many falls than the T'ai Chi group. Although the 6-month T'ai Chi program effectively decreased falling and improved physical performance for the older adults, these results are a concern since the number of falls and other related data were often self-reported. Also, some researchers who conducted the assessments were aware of the intent of the intervention and, therefore, results may have been influenced.

T'ai Chi has the potential to affect balance of participants with visual impairments as well. **Ray, Horvat, Keen, and Blasch (2005)** used a case study design to examine effects of a 10-week T'ai Chi class (2 x wk, 90-min sessions) on balance of two women (ages 54 and 25) with visual impairments. The intervention included modified, descriptive instructions for T'ai Chi, hands-on positioning of participants, and use of dowel spacers to assist participants in determining appropriate distance between their hands or feet during a movement. The Equitest System, developed by NeuroCom®, was used to assess participants' balance and use of sensory information based on anterior and posterior sway. Participants' balance increased, more so for the 54-year-old participant who improved her overall equilibrium score from 58 (at-risk) to 78 (within normal range based on age). Although the balance for both participants improved following participation in the T'ai Chi program, generalization of effects is limited since a case study design was used.

Research supports T'ai Chi's potential to improve balance and posture. For example, using a cross-sectional design, **Tsang, Wang, Fu, and Hui-Chan (2004)** examined effects of long-term T'ai Chi practice on balance control of healthy older adults over the age of 60. The ability of 20 long-term practitioners of T'ai Chi to control balance while standing under somatosensory, visual, and vestibular conditions were compared to a group of 20 older adults who did not practice T'ai Chi and 20 young adults. Balance control was assessed using the Sensory Organization Test (Nashner, 1993) while placing participants within three conditions: eyes open, eyes closed, and eyes open on a sway-referenced platform. There was no significant difference in balance when participants' eyes were open. For the eyes closed and eyes open on a sway-referenced platform conditions, T'ai Chi practitioners scored significantly lower than the young adults and non-T'ai Chi practitioners group. Also, T'ai Chi practitioners swayed significantly less than the older adults who did not practice T'ai Chi. Although T'ai Chi was associated with enhanced balance control among older adults in this study, future research that includes observations in a natural setting to help to triangulate measurements taken in the controlled environment may provide additional insight into the impact of T'ai Chi.

During T'ai Chi practice, participants repeatedly perform circular, continuous motions that have the potential to develop muscle coordination and joint control (Lan, Lai, & Chen, 2002). Using a nonrandomized cross-sectional controlled trial, Fong and Ng (2006) examined effects of T'ai Chi on the muscle reflex latency of lower limbs, active knee joint repositioning accuracy, and balance performance of 48 participants (24 men, 24 women, ages 40–70) based on the amount of T'ai Chi experience. Of the 40 participants, 16 had 3 months of experience in T'ai Chi training, 16 had 1–3 years of experience in T'ai Chi training, and 16 had no experience in T'ai Chi training. Reflex was tested using a posteroanterior perturbation test, in which stimulus is applied to a muscle to produce a reaction from that muscle (Ng, 2005) and a system of electrodes attached to the hamstrings and gastrocnemius muscles. Ankle positioning was assessed using a method created by the researchers that involved knee flexion of the dominant leg while the dominant leg is suspended. Balance was assessed using the Dynamic Balance Test (Jacobson et al., 1997). Participants who practiced T'ai Chi for more than a year exhibited significantly faster reaction times in terms of reflex in hamstrings and gastrocnemius muscles and a longer balance time than those who practiced T'ai Chi for 3 months or not at all. Participants who practiced T'ai Chi for more than 3 months had significantly less knee joint angle-repositioning error than those who did not practice T'ai Chi. Although the study supported the benefits of regular practice in T'ai Chi, types or level of activity among participants were not reported, which may have affected participants overall physical functioning levels.

To provide a general understanding of effects of T'ai Chi on fall prevention, balance, and cardiorespiratory functions in older adults (age > 50), **Verhagen, Immink, van der Meulen, and Bierma-Zeinstra (2004)** performed a systematic review of the literature using a meta-analysis as developed by Verhagen, de Vet, de Bie, Boers, & van den Brandt (2001). The seven studies included in the review used either a randomized or concurrent controlled trial. The application of T'ai Chi programs ranged from 1-hour weekly sessions for 10 weeks to 1-hour sessions every morning for 1 year. Most studies reviewed supported the conclusion that T'ai Chi significantly improved physical functioning. Although efficacy of T'ai Chi was supported, caution is advised because some of the studies did not assign participants randomly into groups, but rather placed participants into groups based on preferences, which, in turn, may influence outcomes. As well, some of these studies did not focus on fall prevention, balance, or cardiorespiratory functioning as primary outcome measures.

Shih (1997) investigated changes in velocity of postural sway for a group of four women and seven men (ages 20–34) who volunteered from a T'ai Chi club to participate in this quasi-experimental pre- and post-test study. During the 16-week program (3 x wk, 55-min sessions) participants learned the Beijing, or Simplified form of T'ai Chi, and practiced 15 minutes on their own each day. The average velocity of sway was collected by first recording the static state of participants (standing with arms at sides on a force platform) and at a dynamic state (rocking toe to heel while keeping balance on a force platform). The T'ai Chi program did not produce a change in the static sway; however, there was a significant difference from the pre-test to the post-test between static state and dynamic state, as well as during the dynamic state of the velocity of sway. This suggests that participants in the T'ai Chi program reduced their risk of falling. A limitation of the study was the absence of a control group. Future research could provide insight on why T'ai Chi could be an intervention for targeting increases in dynamic sway for older adults.

Schaller (1996) conducted a quasi-experimental pre- and post-test study of 46 sedentary older adults living in the community to determine effects of a 10-week T'ai Chi Chih (a Westernized form of T'ai Chi Ch'uan consisting of 20 simple movements) program (1 x wk, 1-hr sessions) on balance and flexibility, mood, health, and blood pressure. Twenty-two individuals were randomly assigned to a control group and remained sedentary for 10 weeks, and 24 individuals were randomly assigned to an experimental group and participated in the T'ai Chi Chih program. Although the T'ai Chi Chih group increased their balance by 50%, whereas the control group decreased by 2% (a significant difference), measures of flexibility, mood, health, and blood pressure were not significantly different. The T'ai Chi Chih program may not have been vigorous enough to influence flexibility, mood, health, and blood pressure, but it did improve balance for older adults with difficulty or limited balance.

Some studies examining effects of T'ai Chi have focused on physical determinants of balance, such as postural sway, control, or velocity. **Wolf and colleagues (1996)** examined effects of a 15-week T'ai Chi program (2 x wk, 1-hr sessions), computerized balance training (1 x wk, 1-hr sessions), and an educational group (control group) (1 x wk, 1-hr sessions) on 72 older adults (mean age = 80) who were healthy and independently living within their community. A quasi-experimental pre- and post-test design was used with a four-month follow-up. The 72 adults were randomly placed in one of three groups. Few significant differences between groups for the 40 variables of demographic data were found. Participants were evaluated for postural sway on the Chattecx Balance System for 20 seconds on each of the four parts of the system (quiet standing with eyes open, quiet standing with eyes closed, toes up with eyes open, and toes up with eyes closed), on three consecutive times for an average. Although the computerized balance training and education group had a significant increase of postural stability, they had an increase in fear of falling. While there was no statistically significant increase in postural stability for the T'ai Chi group as compared to the computerized balance training group, the T'ai Chi group demonstrated significantly more confidence in postural stability than the other two groups, without reducing sway. Also, 40% of the individuals in the T'ai Chi group were still participating after 4 months, and 30% after 2 years as compared to the other groups. Findings support the use of T'ai Chi as a consistent, long-term method to promote confidence for postural sway in older adults.

Wolfson and colleagues (1996) explored effects of a three-month intense balance and strength training program and effects of 6 months of T'ai Chi as a maintenance intervention to sustain changes from initial training. One hundred ten older, independent adults (mean age = 80) who were healthy and residing in the community volunteered for this random control, quasi-experimental study and participated in one of four interventions (3 x wk): balance (equilibrium control) training (45 min), strength (weights) training (45 min), balance plus strength (combination) training (90 min), or an educational control group (5 x total). Losses of balance during Sensory Organization Testing (LOB), single stance time (SST), usual gait velocity (GVU), voluntary limits of stability (FBOS), and summed isokinetic torque of eight lower extremity movements (ISOK) were measured. The balance training group improved on LOB, FBOS, and SST, and the strength training group increased in ISOK and SST (lower extremity and stance stability), while the balance plus strength group showed similar results to the balance training group, combined with results of the strength training group. Although positive effects were found, recorded complaints of muscle pain from participants were common (10 of 55) in the strength group and in the balance plus strength group. During the T'ai Chi maintenance phase, participants in all four groups participated (72% attendance). Improvements in both balance and strength were maintained after the T'ai Chi phase, although the control group was not mentioned. These results present T'ai Chi as a possible low-intensity therapeutic method that can maintain improvements in balance and strength.

Tse and Bailey (1992) examined effects of T'ai Chi practice on postural control in an ex post facto study on two groups of six older men and three older women, Chinese adults, who were healthy, living independently, and ambulatory. Five balance tests and a questionnaire were administered to one group consisting of nine T'ai Chi practitioners with 1 to 20 years of experience (ages 64–84), and the other group of nine sedentary older adults (ages 66–86). The T'ai Chi practitioners did significantly better on all five tests for postural control in comparison to their sedentary counterparts. Although further research is needed to determine the cause of these results, the authors concluded that T'ai Chi could have positive effects on the postural control of older adults. These results may have some hereditary basis that was not controlled in the study; therefore, possibly a matched participant study could be used in future studies.

Summary. The slow movements and precision associated with T'ai Chi may serve as a means to help enhance a person's ability to control body movement and posture. The increase in control may prevent people from losing their balance and decrease the tendency to fall and possibly injure oneself. Therefore, T'ai Chi could be considered as a possible intervention for older adults to improve balance and stability.

Metabolic Responses and Cardiorespiratory Function

The impact of T'ai Chi on metabolic responses (heart rate and blood pressure) for various individuals has been studied. Slow deep breathing and integration of body movements are emphasized during T'ai Chi. The breathing practice may increase respiratory functioning and therefore assist with cardiorespiratory challenges. For example, using a randomized control design, Wolf and colleagues (2006) examined effects of a 48-week T'ai Chi program (2 x wk) on physical performance and cardiovascular functioning of 311 older adults (ages 70–97) who were becoming frail and had fallen at least once within the previous year. The program included six T'ai Chi movements completed with assistive devices as needed and increased from 60-minute sessions to 90-minute sessions at an unspecified point during the 48-week period. Participants were asked to perform home-based exercises 4–5 times a week in addition to their T'ai Chi training. The control group participated in lectures on fall prevention, exercise and balance, diet and nutrition, age-related changes in body function, and mental health issues. Over the course of the intervention, physical status was measured by performance-based tests including the Functional Reach Test (Duncan, Weiner, Chandler, & Studenski, 1990) and gait speed. Although systolic and diastolic blood pressure decreased for both the T'ai Chi group and the control group, the T'ai Chi group experienced a statistically significant improvement, approximately twice as much improvement as the control group. As well, the control group and the T'ai Chi group experienced similar percent gains in functional reach and gait speed. Although the T'ai Chi group's blood pressure decreased significantly more than the control group, the overall increase in physical functioning was comparable to that of the control group.

Some forms of T'ai Chi encompass strenuous movements and, depending on the form, may require intense practice. The intensity of the exercise may affect the effectiveness of the heart to circulate blood. **Thornton, Sykes, and Tang (2004)** used an experimental design to examine effects of a 12-week T'ai Chi program (3 x wk, 60-min sessions) on balance and blood pressure of 17 relatively inactive women (ages 33–35). The T'ai Chi program, using the Yang style, included a 20-min warm-up, 30-min of T'ai Chi activity, and 10-min cooldown. Five minutes post-cooldown, a certified health care assistant recorded the average of two blood pressure measurements using a sphygmomanometer, according to American Heart Association guidelines (American Heart Association, 1989). The Functional Reach Test (Duncan, Weiner, Chandler, & Studenski, 1990) was used to assess balance within 1-week pre- and post-intervention. The pre- and post-test results of the T'ai Chi group were compared to a control group comprised of 17 women matched to participants based on similar housing, activity level, age, and body size. The T'ai Chi group experienced a significant increase in balance and a significant decrease in systolic and diastolic blood pressure. Among the control group, there was no significant change in either blood pressure or balance. Given that the study supports the effectiveness of T'ai Chi in reducing blood pressure and increasing balance for women, replication of this study with men would provide additional insights into effects of T'ai Chi.

With a similar purpose, **Jones, Dean, and Scudds (2005)** used an experimental design to examine effects and feasibility of a 12-week community-based T'ai Chi program (3 x wk, 90-min sessions) on residents (ages 39–71) of Hong Kong. Fifty-one participants in this novice T'ai Chi program were compared to a 49 individuals who had practiced T'ai Chi for at least 6 months. Lung function and physical activity were evaluated at baseline and post-intervention using a spirometer. At baseline, 6 weeks, and 12 weeks, resting heart rate, blood pressure, oxygen saturation, and flexibility were assessed using a portable blood pressure device, pulse oximeter, and the Sit-and-Reach Test, respectively. Although the novice group experienced an increase in flexibility and oxygen expiration, the experienced group showed a statistically significant, greater flexibility and lower resting heart rate. Subsequent research examining how various intensities associated with each form of T'ai Chi may influence flexibility and heart rate is warranted.

Using an experimental pre- and post-test design (2 x wk for 4 wks, followed by 1 x wk for 5 wks, 1-hr sessions), **Channer, Barrow, Barrow, Osborne, and Ives (1996)** examined differences between 126 people (including 90 males) who had experienced acute myocardial infarction (mean age = 56) randomly assigned to one of three groups (a) T'ai Chi (Wu Chian Ch'uan style), (b) aerobic exercise, or a (c) non-exercise support on their heart rate and blood pressure (systolic and diastolic). Although a lowering of systolic blood pressure after intervention was present in both aerobic and T'ai Chi groups, a decrease in resting heart rate and diastolic blood pressure was found only in the T'ai Chi group. According to Channer and colleagues, although aerobic exercise has cardiovascular benefits, not all people recovering from a myocardial infarction could, or should, do heavy or even moderate exercise. The T'ai Chi group had positive effects in both blood pressure and heart rate in small increments that could provide improvement for exercise tolerance during recovery. This suggests that T'ai Chi could be used as an alternative to aerobic exercise, especially for people not able to engage in more aerobic types of exercise. Attendance at the T'ai Chi class was high (82%), slightly more than the aerobics (73%), and much higher than the support group (8%).

Lai, Lan, Wong, and Teng (1995) initiated a cross-sectional study with a 2-year trend follow-up to examine effects of T'ai Chi on cardiorespiratory functioning of 84 healthy, community-dwelling older adults assigned to two groups, one group of 23 men and 22 women who had practiced an average of 6.7 years of T'ai Chi, and a sedentary group consisting of 21 men and 18 women, who were matched for body size and age with the first group. The intervention consisted of a 2-year T'ai Chi group (5 x wk, 55-min sessions). After 2 years, rate of change of cardiorespiratory functioning in both groups were assessed using heart rate, VO2max, VEmax, and maximum oxygen release (WRmax) that were taken at baseline. The only measure that indicated significant differences between the T'ai Chi and control groups after 2 years was VO2max. The VO2max of males in the T'ai Chi group decreased significantly less than the control group, who had a decline in VO2max and pulse, although not statistically significant. The female sedentary group showed a greater decline in aerobic functioning (VO2max, VEmax, WRmax), a 7.4% decrease per year in comparison to a 2.9% decrease per year for the T'ai Chi practicing women. Although not statistically significant, women in the T'ai Chi group increased their heart rate to 122 bpm (positive increase) and the men in the group increased to 128 bpm (positive increase) while the control group had no change in heart rate. Therefore, T'ai Chi practiced regularly may have long-term effects on delaying deterioration of cardio-respiratory function of older adults. Since this was a cross-sectional study, possible influences of heredity were not controlled and longitudinal studies are needed to examine effects of T'ai Chi on cardiorespiratory functioning.

Using a quasi-experimental pre- and post-test design, **Schneider and Leung (1991)** examined both T'ai Chi and Wing Chun by recording measurements during a session of practice and effects on cardiorespiratory and metabolic responses with 10 males proficient in T'ai Chi (mean age = 35.5) and 10 males proficient in Wing Chun (mean age = 30.0). Wing Chun, another style of martial arts, uses force in comparison to the relaxed T'ai Chi style of exercise; however, both styles use controlled (almost static) and determined movements in practice. Both groups were pre-tested for VO2max differences on a treadmill exercise, but did not show significant differences. Average heart rate and ECG (electrocardiogram, another heart rate test) was recorded. The session of practice, that included the Wing Chun participants performing the same, repetitive movements (2 x 6-min sessions) and the T'ai Chi practitioners performing movements from their style (2 x 7-min sessions), occurred no more than 10 days after the treadmill test. Previously reported percentages of both heart rate and VO2max from aerobic exercise were used to compare to the same measures of Wing Chun and T'ai Chi. Both martial arts had post-test mean values of heart rate and VO2max significantly higher than pre-test scores. The T'ai Chi group only had an increased heart rate percentage relative to metabolic rate, which did not produce cardiorespiratory changes adequate for aerobic effects. The T'ai Chi exercise was low intensity with many static movements that caused recorded heart rate percentage to positively increase slightly. In contrast, Wing Chun had higher cardiorespiratory effects, such as an increase in breathing and heart rate, but only slightly more than T'ai Chi. The heart rate findings were not negative because either type of these martial arts could be considered as a possible exercise for individuals who require low intensity workouts, such as individuals with cardiovascular disease

Effects of T'ai Chi on metabolic measures (heart rate and blood pressure) and cardio-respiratory changes were examined by **Zhou, Shephard, Plyley, and Davis (1984)**. Eleven healthy males (ages 24–35) with 3–8 years of experience in T'ai Chi were pre-tested for grip force using a Stoelting handgrip dynamometer, maximum oxygen intake and maximum oxygen output, heart rate, and blood pressure (systolic and diastolic), and then performed 108 routine movements for a range of 17.5–25 minutes (this time was according to time it took individuals to complete the movements). Systolic and diastolic blood pressures were significantly higher than at rest during the intervention. Heart rate increased significantly over rates from pre-test an average of 45 beats per minute (bpm) during exercise with peak heart rate reaching an average of 134 bpm. Results indicated that T'ai Chi can be a moderate, safe exercise for individuals experiencing problems associated with tension, range of motion, and cardiac function, but not for healthy, younger adults due to lack of large effects on heart rate and blood pressure. Since no control group was used and all participants were young and had extensive experience with T'ai Chi, this study is limited due to the population studied; yet, it provides information about possible effects of T'ai Chi and potential benefits to particular groups with illnesses or disabilities.

Summary. Although studies have examined a variety of measures, such as heart rate, blood pressure, VO2max, and VEmax, collectively they suggested some benefits of T'ai Chi as a therapeutic intervention for individuals experiencing cardiac problems. Also, it appears that T'ai Chi may help to delay the onset of age-related declines in cardiorespiratory function and has the potential to maintain oxygen expiration and reduce resting heart rates among T'ai Chi practitioners. T'ai Chi may be a safe alternative to traditional exercise, which often requires intense movement to produce results (Hogan, 2005).

Immune Responses and Physical Systems

The aging process can result in deficits in many structural and functional systems of the body (Hogan, 2005). Research suggests that remaining physically active during older adulthood may limit effects of conditions associated with aging (Conroy, Cook, Manson, Buring, & Lee, 2005). For example, Qin and colleagues (2005) used a cross-sectional design to evaluate effects of T'ai Chi practice on bone mineral density and neuromuscular functioning of 99 postmenopausal women (ages 50–65). Participants had been affected by menopause within the last 10 years. Forty-eight participants had been practicing T'ai Chi for more than 3 hours a week for more than 3 years. Bone mineral density was measured in the femur of the participants' non-dominant leg using a dual-energy x-ray absorptiometry. Neuromuscular functioning was determined by measuring strength in the quadriceps muscle using an isometric dynameter, body flexibility using a trunk bend-and-reach test, and balance using a timed single, stance test for the non-dominant leg. Participants who regularly practiced T'ai Chi showed significantly higher bone density, a greater magnitude of trunk bend-and-reach, and statistically significant greater quadriceps strength and longer stance time than did participants who did not practice T'ai Chi.

Using the same population, Chan and colleagues (2004) examined effects of a 12-month T'ai Chi program (5 x wk, 45-min sessions) on the weight-bearing bones of 132 postmenopausal women (mean age of 54) who experienced an onset of menopause within the last 10 years. Using an age-matched and randomized prospective intervention design, participants were placed into the T'ai Chi (n=67) or sedentary control group (n=65). For both groups, bone mineral density (BMD) was measured in the lumbar spine and proximal femur by using dual-energy x-ray absorptiometry and in the distal tibia by using multi-slice peripheral quantitative computed tomography (pQCT) at baseline and 12 months. Fracture rate was also documented. Both groups experienced general bone loss, but with a reportedly slower rate in the T'ai Chi group. A significant 2.6- to 3.6-fold retardation of bone loss was found in the distal tibia for the T'ai Chi group as compared with the control group. Three subjects within the control group and only one subject in the T'ai Chi group experienced a fracture post-follow-up. It may be helpful for subsequent research to examine how the intensity associated with a particular style of T'ai Chi may affect bone mineral density as well as neuromuscular functioning.

Another concern among therapists working with older adults is their ability to maintain a functional immune system. A functional immune system is needed to protect against illnesses that may occur later in life (Hogan, 2005). T'ai Chi has the potential to boost the functioning level of the immune system. Using a randomized experimental design, Irwin, Pike, Cole, and Oxman (2004) compared effects of a 15-week T'ai Chi program (3 x wk, 45-min sessions) as a behavioral intervention on the health status and risk of acquiring shingles as compared to a control group. Thirty-six men and women (ages > 60) who had a history of varicella (chickenpox) were randomly assigned to each group. The intervention consisted of a 10-min warm-up period, 30-min of T'ai Chi practice, and a 5-min cooldown period. Those assigned to the control were asked not to begin any new forms of physical activity such as meditation or yoga. Health functioning was assessed using the Medical Outcomes Study Short Form (Ware, 1993) at baseline, at 5-week intervals during the intervention and 1-week post-intervention. Varicella zoster virus specific mediated cell-mediated immunity (VZF-CMI), a critical component in protecting against reinfection of chickenpox, referred to as shingles in later life, was assessed by measuring the responder cell frequency within the blood samples of participants at baseline and 1 week post-intervention. As compared to control group, the T'ai Chi group received significantly higher scores on the Medical Outcomes Study Short Form as well as in development of VZF-CMI. Although T'ai Chi improved immunity for shingles and health status, it is not clear if these results are sustained over time.

Older adults often experience a decline in organ functioning and an increase in illness (Lai et al., 1995; Xusheng, Yugi, & Ronggang, 1990). Therefore, ways to improve health or maintain it through exercise for older adults are needed. One way the body can promote immunity to illness is having a higher percentage of ZC rosette-forming cells circulating in the body (Xusheng et al., 1990). Xusheng and colleagues explored the possibility that T'ai Chi could create this circulation.

A cross-sectional pre- and post-test study conducted by **Xusheng and colleagues (1990)** examined effects of T'ai Chi on 48 healthy retired staff from Shanghai (ages 59–80) divided into two groups, T'ai Chi practitioners and a matched sedentary group (12 men, 12 women in each group). Measures of the percentage of ZC rosette-forming cells (ZC-RFC %), white blood cells, and the percentage of lymphocytes (LC %) were taken before and after 20 minutes of T'ai Chi exercise by extracting participants' blood. A significant difference was observed between the control and T'ai Chi groups for the ZC-RFC % after exercise intervention, with the T'ai Chi group being significantly higher (8.9%). The number of lymphocytes was related to ZC-RFC % before and after T'ai Chi. Having a higher percentage of ZC rosette-forming cells in the body could represent immunity capacity (humoral), implicating that a larger number of antibodies were dispersed in the body, as detected by these ZC-RFC indicators. Xusheng and colleagues suggested that T'ai Chi may create responses that signal the sympathetic system to discharge cells (antibodies) to areas of the body that provide immunological responses such as lymph nodes, spleen, and blood. Although further research is needed, this study supports the belief that T'ai Chi could be beneficial for older adults to enhance or delay deterioration of humeral immunity.

Summary. A few studies have explored the impact of T'ai Chi on the immune system and skeletal systems. Results of the studies reviewed indicate that T'ai Chi may help moderate the functioning of the immune system and may retard bone density loss. Long-term and follow-up studies are warranted that examine people's ability to continue T'ai Chi and to prevent problems through regular T'ai Chi practice over an extended period of time.

Neurological Function

Often exercise has been recommended as a non-pharmacological way to reduce effects associated with various disorders. T'ai Chi is one form of exercise that has received attention. For example, using a randomized control design, Li et al. (2004) examined effects of a 24-week T'ai Chi program (3 x wk, 60-min sessions) on self-rated sleep quality and daytime sleepiness in 180 older adults (ages 60–90) who reported experiencing sleep problems. Adults participated in either a T'ai Chi practice group consisting of an 8-form version of Yang style T'ai Chi, or a low impact exercise group consisting of seated exercise, stretching, relaxation, or controlled breathing. Sleep quality and daytime sleepiness were measured using the Pittsburgh Sleep Quality Index (Bussye, Reynolds, Monk, Berman, & Kupfer, 1989) and Epworth Sleepiness Scale (Johns, 1991). In comparison to the low-impact exercise group, T'ai Chi participants reported major improvements in sleep quality, sleep onset, sleep duration, sleep efficiency, and sleep disturbance. Although T'ai Chi effectively enhanced sleep for participants, caution is advised since the study involved self-reported measures. Participants may have reported increases in positive sleep outcomes based on expectations of participating in the study.

T'ai Chi has been used to treat individuals experiencing neurological conditions such as traumatic brain injury. For example, using a case study, Shapira, Chelouche, Yanai, Kaner, and Szold (2001) examined effects of T'ai Chi (60-min sessions) on three men who experienced severe head injuries that affected their walking and daily functioning. T'ai Chi was first practiced while in a sitting position once per week. After several weeks, the number of sessions was increased to twice a week and participants began to complete T'ai Chi forms from a standing position. After at least 2 years of therapy, all participants walked without assistance, rarely falling. They also increased their balance and muscle tone control, which they reported led to increased physical (and mental) freedom and performance of daily activities. A controlled experimental method was not used; therefore, conclusions based on this research are limited.

Another common concern of therapeutic recreation specialist who work with older adults is reducing problem behaviors associated with neurological conditions. The mental focus required by T'ai Chi practice may positively influence behavior.

Using a repeated measures design, Hernandez-Reif, Field, and Thimas (2001) examined effects of a 5-week T'ai Chi program (2 x wk, 30-min sessions) on 13 adolescents with Attention Deficit Hyperactivity Disorder (ages 13–16). Each T'ai Chi session consisted of 5-min of warm-up and breathing exercise and 25-min of T'ai Chi practice. Teachers rated the children's behavior using the Conners Teacher Rating Scale-Revised (Goyette, Conners, & Ulrich, 1978) during baseline, after the 5-week T'ai Chi intervention, and 2 weeks post-intervention. After students participated in the 5-week T'ai Chi program, teachers reported that students exhibited less anxiety, improved conduct, less daydreaming behaviors, less inappropriate emotions, and less hyperactivity, which persisted over the 2-week follow up. Although participants exhibited positive changes in behaviors, teachers' prior expectations about T'ai Chi may have prompted them to report more positive behaviors post-intervention.

Summary. T'ai Chi involves every part of the body and benefits all bodily parts and functions, not just the musculoskeletal system. T'ai Chi emphasizes concentration and control through meditation. With a relaxed focus, the nervous system attempts to allow participants to focus on other mental activities that may be important to maintain neurological functioning.

Psychological Effects

Studies have examined effects of T'ai Chi on physical functioning as shown in the previous section. This section reviews research examining potential psychological effects of T'ai Chi. Though the following studies include measures of physical functioning such as heart rate and noradrenaline these measures were used to examine psychological effects. According to Jin (1989), increase in heart rate is one sign of increased stress or anxiety. Therefore, these studies explore psychological effects of T'ai Chi using both psychological measures (questionnaires) and physical measures.

Research supports the ability of T'ai Chi to decrease a variety of psychological problems including depression, stress, tension, and anxiety, as well as increase functions such as confidence (Lan, Lai, & Chen, 2002). For example, using a quasi-experimental design, Taylor-Piliae, Haskell, Waters, and Froelicher (2006) examined effects of a 12-week T'ai Chi program (60-min sessions) on psychosocial status of 39 Chinese adults (ages 58–74) living in the United States at risk for cardiovascular disease. Using the Yang-style 24 posture short form (Fei, 2001), the intervention included a 20-min warm-up, 30-min T'ai Chi exercise, and a 10-min cooldown. Chinese versions of the Perceived Stress Scale (Cohen & Williamson, 1988), Profile of Mood States (McNair, Lorr, & Droppelman, 1992), Multidimensional Scale of Perceived Social Support (Blumenthal et al., 1987), and T'ai Chi Self-Efficacy performance (Taylor-Pillae & Foelicher, 2004) were used to assess elements of psychosocial status including mood and stress reduction. Participants' mood state and self-efficacy increased while perceived stress decreased significantly. Although the study only examined Chinese immigrants, results indicated that the T'ai Chi program improved the psychosocial status of participants. In addition, participants may have had previous expectations about T'ai Chi, which, in turn, may have influenced their self-reports.

Yeh and colleagues (2004) conducted a similar study that examined psychological effects of a 12-week T'ai Chi program (2 x wk, 60-min sessions) on quality of life and exercise capacity of 30 participants (ages 51–77) with heart failure. Each session consisted of meditative warm up exercises and practice of 5 simplified T'ai Chi forms. Pre- and post-test measures of quality of life and exercise capacity were respectively evaluated using the Minnesota Living with Heart Failure Questionnaire (Rector & Cohn, 1992) and determined by the distance participants were able to walk at a comfortable speed within 6 minutes. Participants were randomly assigned to either T'ai Chi or to a control group that did not receive an exercise program. The T'ai Chi group showed statistically significant improvements in quality of life scores and an increase in distance walked as compared to the control group. Although participants' prior expectations may have influenced their responses on self-report items, results support the conclusion that T'ai Chi helped to improve participants' perceived quality of life and exercise capacity.

Since the psychological challenges of stress and tension are extremely prevalent, Abbott, Hui, Hays, Li, and Pan (2006) used an experimental design to examine effects of a 15-week T'ai Chi program (2 x wk, 60-min sessions) on the health-related quality of life and headaches of 30 adults (ages 23–64 years) who experience tension headaches. Participants were randomly assigned to a "wait-list" control group or the Yang-style T'ai Chi group. Health-related quality of life was measured using the SF-36 (Ware, Kosinski, & Dewey, 2000) while a short form of the DYNHA Headache Impact Test (HIT-6) (Kosinski et al., 2003) was used to assess effects of headaches. In comparison to the control group, the T'ai Chi group significantly improved the HIT-6 score and SF-36 score in terms of pain, energy/fatigue, social functioning, emotional well-being, and mental health. Although this study suggests that T'ai Chi is effective in reducing tension headaches and in increasing health-related quality of life, replication of this study would increase confidence in the findings.

Using a randomized experimental design, Mustian and colleagues (2004) compared effects of a 12-week T'ai Chi program to a Psychosocial Support Program (3 x wk, 60-min sessions) on 21 women (ages 31–78) diagnosed with breast cancer who had completed treatment within the last 30 months, on their self-esteem and health-related quality of life. The T'ai Chi group performed 10-min of warm-up stretching and stationary T'ai Chi fundamentals, 40-min of practice using a 15-move short form Yang style T'ai Chi, and 10-min of regulatory breathing, imagery, and meditation as an exercise cool-down. The Psychosocial Support Group attended lectures and discussions guided by Spiegel's Supportive-Expressive Group Therapy model (Spiegel, 1995) that emphasized teaching behavioral coping strategies, peer support, and group cohesion. The T'ai Chi group significantly improved their quality of life, while the Psychosocial Support group reported declines in quality of life. Additionally, the T'ai Chi group exhibited improvements, although not statistically significant, in self-esteem, while the Psychosocial Support group reported declines in self-esteem. Although the study supports the ability of T'ai Chi to improve health-related quality of life and self-esteem, further research using a larger sample is warranted.

T'ai Chi has the potential to reduce effects of symptoms associated with chronic disabling conditions while increasing quality of life. As a pilot study, Taggart, Arsianian, Bae, and Singh (2003) examined effects of a 6-week T'ai Chi exercise program (2 x wk, 60-min sessions) on fibromyalgia symptoms and health-related quality of life of 39 adults (ages 26–80). The self-administered

Fibromyalgia Impact Questionnaire (FIQ) (Burkhardt, Clark, & Bennett, 1991) was used to measure the impact of symptoms of fibromyalgia on ten domains of physical functioning, mental health, and well-being; the SF-36 (Ware & Shelbourne, 1992) was used to assess the health-related quality of life pre- and post-intervention. Participants showed statistically significant improvements in all but 4 of the 10 domains of the FIQ, and 5 of 7 of the domains addressed by the SF-36. In terms of the remaining domains for each measure, participants demonstrated improvements, although not statistically significant. Future research resulting from this study may look at aspects of mental health with respect to quality of life.

Measured effects of T'ai Chi on knowledge, attitude, and behavior, and secondary measures of heart rate, blood pressure, and stress level, were investigated by **Sun, Dosch, Gilmore, Pemberton, and Scarseth (1996)** with a group of 20 Hmong American older adults (ages > 59). Participants were divided randomly for a quasi-experimental pre- and post-test study into two groups, a control group of three men and seven women (ages 60–79) that remained sedentary, and an experimental group of four men and six women (ages 60–74) who participated in a T'ai Chi program for 12 weeks. The T'ai Chi Ch'uan Program Inventory, with a test-retest reliability of .82, was used as pre- and post-test to acquire information on level of understanding of T'ai Chi, perceived stress and measurements of heart rate, blood pressure, and skin temperature (to assess stress level). The experimental group participated in a 12-week T'ai Chi program (1 x wk, 2-hr sessions) that included a mini-lecture on health and stress. Compared to the control group, the T'ai Chi group had significant increases in knowledge, attitude, and behavior on the therapeutic values of T'ai Chi exercise. Decreases in both systolic and diastolic resting blood pressure, decreases in self-perceived scores of stress and stress level according to body temperature, and increases in flexibility were reported. Consequently, this study provides support for use of T'ai Chi as an exercise to promote both mental and physical health, especially for older adults.

Jin (1992) compared effects of T'ai Chi to reading, brisk walking, and meditation in a quasi-experimental pre- and post-test study that randomly assigned 48 healthy men (mean age = 34.6) and 48 healthy women (mean age = 37.8) with various ethnic backgrounds to one of four groups. At the beginning of the study, difficult arithmetic tests and a 1-hour stressful movie were used to produce stressful and anxiety-like emotions. The individuals then participated in T'ai Chi or one of three other programs (reading, brisk walking, or meditation). Using previously documented measures (Jin, 1989) of heart rate, blood pressure, urine, saliva, and mood (POMS and STAI Y-1), T'ai Chi was significantly better at reducing anxiety and improving vigor than the other programs. Although reduction in anxiety, as measured by the STAI Y-1, and improvement with vigor, as indicated by the POMS measure, could have occurred as a result of the T'ai Chi group expecting to have psychological benefits, increases in positive mood and motivation are noteworthy. Relative to heart rate, blood pressure, and urine hormonal results, T'ai Chi appeared to yield similar effects as walking (6 km/hr). However, no significant differences were found between T'ai Chi and the other three groups for salivary cortisol, suggesting that this intervention provided limited physical exercise, but may provide psychological benefits.

Jin (1989) explored physiological and psychological effects following T'ai Chi participation for 66 healthy T'ai Chi practitioners (ages 16–75) divided into two groups, 10 men and 13 women practitioners with at least 1 year of T'ai Chi experience, and 16 men and 17 women beginners with less than 8 months of T'ai Chi experience. Participants' scores were compared across groups for time (morning, afternoon, or night) and phase (before, during, or after T'ai Chi) and were pre-tested by measures of heart rate, noradrenaline, saliva, and urine, as well as two questionnaires containing profile of mood states (POMS) and state anxiety (STAI Y-1). Participants were assigned randomly to a T'ai Chi session (morning, afternoon, or night) and performed T'ai Chi for a 1-hour practice session. After the practice, urine and saliva samples were taken, and participants completed the POMS and STAI Y-1 forms. After one more hour, the POMS and STAI Y-1 forms were completed a third time, the VITALOG (heart rate monitor) was then removed, and saliva and urine samples were taken a third time. During the T'ai Chi practice period (60 minutes), participant heart rates were higher, especially for experienced practitioners; however, these rates did not have a significant cardiovascular or isometric effect. Although tests showed no change in urinary dopamine (affecting mood), there was an increase in noradrenaline and a decrease in salivary cortisol. The noradrenaline effect is consistent with increased heart rate, and the salivary cortisol is related to T'ai Chi being a low-workload exercise (requires < 50% VO2max). The time of day was found to have an effect on both hormonal and cardiovascular measures; participants in the afternoon program showed the highest noradrenaline and those in the evening class showed the lowest amounts of salivary cortisol. Mood states improved significantly during T'ai Chi and remained positive even 1 hour afterwards, suggesting that individuals may benefit psychologically from practicing T'ai Chi. Participants reported "less tension, depression, anger, fatigue, confusion and state anxiety, felt more vigorous" (p. 204). Results of the POMS administered during and after T'ai Chi provides support that T'ai Chi can have positive short-term effects.

Summary. T'ai Chi philosophy suggests that mental attitude can promote physiological change, and, in turn, movement. The mental control associated with T'ai Chi practice may help teach participants how to focus and maintain a high sense of psychological well-being. As well, T'ai Chi may serve as an outlet for aggression, which may reduce stress and changes in mood. Overall, attending T'ai Chi programs with other people provides social benefits and may help to teach self-control.

These studies suggest the possible psychological benefits of T'ai Chi. Some measures of physical functions were observed and recorded; however, the consistent finding shown by these studies was that in comparison to a control group, a T'ai Chi group appeared to have lower stress and anxiety and higher mood levels. Positive psychological results were evident in some of the diastolic blood pressure measures, revealing lower blood pressure in the T'ai Chi groups.

Overall Summary

In summarizing literature reviewed in this section, there was limited research examining effects of T'ai Chi. Existing research moderately indicates that T'ai Chi is an empirically supported facilitation technique. Improvements in balance and postural stability, metabolic responses, and cardiorespiratory function, immune responses, and psychological responses have been reported as a result of practicing T'ai Chi.

Case Study

Leila

Leila was a 43-year-old woman living independently in a two-story home, who was diagnosed with relapsing-remitting multiple sclerosis (MS) after experiencing loss of 20% of vision in her right eye and repeated falls resulting in a sprained ankle and a broken hip. In conjunction with MS, Leila admitted to being in denial and had not told her three children that she had MS. Leila's husband confirmed that she had not told anyone in her family and reported that she seemed to be stressed and depressed much of the time. Leila managed a busy consulting business, was an active snow skier, and an international traveler prior to her diagnosis.

Although Leila continued working and was taking medication prescribed by her neurologist for regrowth of the myelin sheath, Leila did not consistently take the medication and often became fatigued during the day. Leila's neurologist suggested an alternative treatment and referred her to an MS day enrichment program. Upon registration to the day program, Leila displayed antisocial behavior and did not participate in an open discussion about MS and related health concerns. When Leila did interact with other participants, she was often abrupt and did not reveal any personal details of her life. After several days of orientation to the program and discussions with the staff and other participants, Leila was given a choice of programs in which to participate at the center. The staff recommended the T'ai Chi program and Leila chose to participate. Leila's treatment goals were related to her diagnosis of relapsing-remitting MS that resulted in difficulties in balance, gross motor performance, fatigue, and enjoyment.

T'ai Chi Intervention for Leila

The 8-week T'ai Chi program met twice a week, with sessions lasting approximately 55 minutes. Prior to beginning the program, measurement of Leila's balance using a functional-reach test and a stair-climbing test to measure gross motor performance were taken. In addition, she completed a 24-hour medical history survey, a 10-question perceived fatigue questionnaire, and an experience questionnaire to measure enjoyment of the program. The Yang Style Short Form was taught during the T'ai Chi class, which included learning 16 different movements of the form, focusing on balance, muscle relaxation, and concentration.

During the assessment, Leila had difficulty balancing and gripped the railing when walking up and down the stairs for the 2-minute period, and often stopped to catch her breath. Leila walked 25 steps during her assessment. She stated that she had not realized how difficult it was for her to walk up and down stairs. Leila commented that maybe the T'ai Chi program might help her physical symptoms.

Leila began the T'ai Chi program with four other participants. After an introduction related to potential benefits of T'ai Chi, the first movement was demonstrated by the instructor and was repeated by each participant. Leila did not have any difficulty with the first movement. However, when practicing the second movement "Walking on Ice," Leila lost her balance and fell into the arms of a volunteer standing close behind her. Although another participant said that he almost lost his balance as well, Leila appeared embarrassed and often relied on balancing herself with a chair during the remainder of the session. The intent of the movement and the two that followed were focused on practicing weight shifts to promote knowledge of body placement. At the end of the session, Leila reported that she did not enjoy the session.

Leila's balance and gross motor performance improved slightly during the next two sessions; however, the greatest change came during the fourth session when participants completed six movements, which made one subset of the form. Prior to this class, Leila was assessed again. At this time, Leila walked up and down 38 steps, and only used the railing for the last two flights of stairs. Also, Leila stated that she was now enjoying classes and said, "I really think this program has made me less tired."

As the class progressed, Leila learned all the movements taught in the class and was practicing the movements at home and demonstrating what she had learned to her children. Leila shared with the instructor that she felt less stressed at work and was more aware of her needs and abilities. Leila showed marked improvements in her perceived fatigue, stair climbing, and balance.

At her 2-month follow-up, Leila had continued in another T'ai Chi class and convinced her husband to join a class with her at the community center close to their home. Leila could walk 50 steps in a 2-minute period, and reported that she had not fallen due to loss of balance since completing the program. Leila commented in a final interview that even though sometimes she still became stressed and fatigued, T'ai Chi gave her energy to get through those times and helped her relax.

Summary

Leila's diagnosis of MS resulted in her becoming fatigued easily and she would often fall due to loss of balance. The T'ai Chi program continually challenged Leila to be aware of her body and helped her detect when she was pushing herself too hard at work and at home. Through her experiences in the T'ai Chi program, Leila found an enjoyable recreation activity that she engaged in with her husband that resulted in her feeling less fatigued.

Intervention Implementation Exercises

This section of implementation exercises contains information of the beginning form of T'ai Chi and details on a specific form associated with T'ai Chi. Therefore this section is divided into:

- Beginning Form of T'ai Chi
- Parting the Wild Horse's Mane, Left

Beginning Form of T'ai Chi

Although the different styles of T'ai Chi have various movements in their forms, many of the movements are variations or
common in each style. Most styles use a beginning posture that
prepares the body and mind to continue the posture (see Figure
10.2). Participants will perform the following tasks: standing
with legs shoulder width apart, with knees slightly bent, almost
as if sitting on the edge of a high stool; relaxing the neck,
shoulders, arms, and back; and clearing the mind of everything
except for what they're doing. Tell them to pretend that a
ball about the size of a tennis ball is underneath each armpit,
leaving the arms rounded and loose. Have them practice this
posture until it is a relaxed movement. This posture contains
movements that are found in most other postures of T'ai Chi.
Following the starting position the Beginning Form of T'ai Chi
has four distinct upper body movements (see Figure 10.3):

Figure 10.2

- Peng
- Lu
- Ji
- An

Peng. While breathing is normal, raise both arms straight out in front to shoulder level
with palms down and fingers, in a natural position, dangling towards the floor. Without
tightening muscles, visualize raising arms slowly straight out in front of the body.

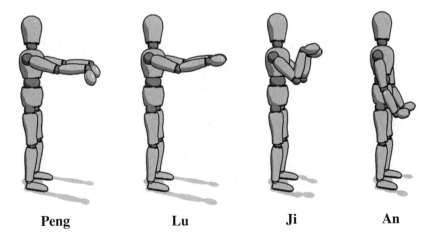

| Peng | Lu | Ji | An |

Figure 10.3

Lu. When arms reach shoulder level, slowly bend wrists up, so palm of hands are facing forward and slightly curved as if holding a small, light, beach ball in front.

Ji. While hands and wrist remain in the same position, bend elbows to bring hands toward chest.

An. With hands still rounded, push hands with bent elbows straight down to navel level and then slightly away from body, acting as if the beach ball is still in hands, but now resting lightly on water at hip level.

Parting the Wild Horse's Mane, Left

One posture or movement of T'ai Chi that is simple to learn is Parting the Wild Horse's Mane, Left, which is movement 17 in Simplified T'ai Chi. Practice this movement until it is natural and smooth; however, it does not have to be perfect. To understand the movement clearly, it has been divided into the first part of the movement and the second part identified as:

- Part 1
- Part 2

Part 1. Maintain an arm's length of space away from other people (see Figure 10.4). Stand relaxed with right leg back and right foot facing straight forward, and with knees slightly bent. Relax shoulders and arms, and then shift weight to left leg and turn torso slightly to left. Shift weight back to right leg (60% weight on right leg). Bring right hand, open palm facing floor, up to shoulder level with elbow bent at 90 degrees. Place left hand directly below right hand. Open palm facing upward at navel level and pretend to be holding a large, round beach ball lightly between two hands.

Figure 10.4

Figure 10.5

Part 2. Step forward with the right leg (see Figure 10.5), leaning slightly to left (60% of weight on left). Turn torso slightly more to left, and bend left knee slightly. Remember to shift weight slowly and relax shoulders and the neck. Meanwhile, push right hand palm down to navel level while simultaneously moving left hand palm in a diagonal motion up (right to left) until hand is eye level.

The intervention implementation exercises found in this chapter can be used to facilitate the learning of T'ai Chi postures and movements. Interventions described in this chapter are starting points for TR specialists and modifications may be required for some individuals who participate in T'ai Chi programs.

Conclusion

TR specialists can use T'ai Chi as a therapeutic intervention when working with people who have physical and psychological limitations. T'ai Chi practiced by older adults and individuals with cardiovascular difficulties has been documented to influence physical functioning and psychological well-being. When using T'ai Chi as a therapeutic intervention, TR specialists are encouraged to learn about T'ai Chi, consider resources to provide such a program, and assess needs of participants. Therefore, with thorough preparation, T'ai Chi can be an enjoyable experience providing both physical and psychological benefits for participants.

Discussion Questions

1.   What is the difference between T'ai Chi and T'ai Chi Ch'uan?
2.   What is the meaning of T'ai Chi?
3.   Describe four training essentials of T'ai Chi?
4.   What is the meaning of Yin-Yang?
5.   What are the two theoretical foundations behind T'ai Chi?

6.   Describe steps that a TR specialist would take to begin a T'ai Chi program.
7.   What individuals have participated in most of the research on T'ai Chi?
8.   Describe one physical and one psychological benefit of T'ai Chi.
9.   What are the different styles of T'ai Chi?
10.   What are the more popular styles of T'ai Chi?
11.   Why are some styles of T'ai Chi more popular than others?

Resources

Material Resources

Jou, T. H. (1988). *The Tao of T'ai-Chi Ch'uan—Way to rejuvenation*. Warwick, NY: T'ai Chi Foundation.
Lowenthal, W. (1991). *There are no secrets—Professor Cheng Man-Ch'ing & his T'ai Chi Chu'an*. Berkeley, CA: North Atlantic Books.
Man-Ch'ing, C. (1981). *T'ai Chi Ch'uan—Simplified method for health and self defense*. Berkeley, CA: North Atlantic Books.
Wile, D. (1983). *T'ai-chi touchstones: Yang family secret transmissions*. Brooklyn, NY: Sweet Ch'i Press.

T'ai Chi Videos

Dunn, T. (1989). *T'ai Chi for health: The Yang long form*. Interarts Productions.
Dunn, T. (1989). *T'ai Chi for health: The Yang short form*. Interarts Productions.

T'ai Chi Websites

T'ai Chi Ch'uan with Ron Perfetti [Online]. Available: http://www.maui.net/~taichi4u/specifics.html#arthritis
Stillness in Motion, Inc.: School of T'ai Chi Ch'uan and Chi Kung. (1997). [Online]. Available: http://www.stillnessinmotion.net
Wu Style Tai Ji Quan Form Site: English list of moves [Online]. Available: http://www.wfdesign.com/tc/tc.htm
Wu Style Tai Ji Quan Instructors [Online]. Available: http://www.wfdesign.com/tc/t.htm
Stress Free with Tai-Chi [Online]. Available: http://www.tai-chi.com/info.html# select
List of Video Clips [Online]. Available: http://www.eastactonvideo.com.au/listvid.htm

References

Abbott, R. B., Hui, K., Hays, R. D., Li , M., & Pan, T. (2006). A randomized controlled trial of T'ai Chi for tension headaches. *Evidence-based Complimentary and Alternative Medicine, 4*, 107–113.
American Heart Association. (1989). *Standards for blood pressure measurement*. Minneapolis: American Heart Association.

Berg, K., Wood-Dauphinee, S., Williams, J. I., Maki, B. (1992). Measuring balance in the elderly: Validation of an instrument. *Canadian Journal of Public Health, 2*, S7–S11.

Blumenthal, J. A., Burg, M. M., Barefoot, J., Williams, R. B., Haney, T., & Zimet, G. (1987). Social support, type A behavior, and coronary artery disease. *Psychosomatic Medicine, 49*, 331–340.

Burckhardt, C. S., Clark, S. R., & Bennett, R. M. (1991). The fibromyalgia impact questionnaire (FIQ): Development and validation. *Journal of Rheumatology, 18*, 728–733.

Bussye, D. J., Reynolds, III, C. F., Monk, T. H., Berman, S. B., & Kupfer, D. J. (1989). The Pittsburgh Sleep Quality Index: A New Instrument for Psychiatric Practice and Research. *Psychiatry Research, 28*, 193–213.

Chan, K., Qin, L., Lau, M., Woo, J., Au, S., Choy, W., Lee, K., & Lee, S. (2004). A randomized, prospective study of the effects of T'ai Chi Chun exercise on bone mineral density in postmenopausal women. *Archives of Physical Medicine & Rehabilitation, 85*, 717–722.

Channer, K. S., Barrow, D., Barrow, R., Osborne, M., & Ives, G. (1996). Changes in hemodynamic parameters following Tai-Chi-Chuan and aerobic exercise in patients recovering from acute myocardial-infarction. *Postgraduate Medical Journal, 72*, 349–351.

Cohen, S., & Williamson, G. M. (1988). Perceived stress in a probability sample of the United States. In S. Spcapan & S. Oskamp (Eds.), *Social psychology of health* (pp. 31–67). Newbury Park, CA: Sage.

Conroy, M. B., Cook, N. R., Manson, J. E., Buring, J. E., & Lee, I. (2005). Past physical activity, current physical activity, and the risk of coronary heart disease. *Medicine and Science in Sports and Exercise, 37*(8), 1251–1256.

Crompton, P. (2000). *T'ai Chi: An introductory guide to the Chinese art of movement*. Shaftesbury, Dorset: Element Books, Ltd.

Duncan, P. W., Weiner, D. K., Chandler, J., & Studenski, S. (1990). Functional reach: A new clinical measure of balance. *Journal of Gerontology: Medical Sciences, 45*(6), M192–M197.

Fei, P. L. (2001). *The principle of Chinese acupuncture*. Concord, CA: Mainstream Publishing.

Fong, S. M., & Ng, G. Y. (2006). The effects on sensorimotor performance and balance with T'ai Chi training. *Archives of Physical Medicine & Rehabilitation, 87*, 82–87.

Goyette, C. H., Conners, C. K., & Ulrich, R. F. (1978). Normative data on revised conners parent and teachers rating scales. *Journal of Abnormal Child Psychology, 6*, 221–236.

Hernandez-Reif, M., Field, T., & Thimas, E. (2001). Attention deficit hyperactivity disorder: Benefits from T'ai Chi. *Journal of Bodywork and Movement Therapies, 5*, 120–123.

Hine, J. (1992). *Yang T'ai Chi Chuan*. London: A & C Black.

Hogan, M. (2005). Physical and cognitive activity and exercise for older adults: A review. *International Journal of Aging and Human Development, 60*, 95–126.

Honda, C. M. (1995). Cultural diversity: T'ai Chi Ch'uan and laban movement analysis. *Journal of Physical Education, Recreation & Dance, 66*(2), 38–40.

Irwin, M. R., Pike, J. L., & Oxman, N. M. (2004). Shingles immunity and health functioning in the elderly: T'ai Chi Chih as a behavioral treatment. *Evidence-Based Complementary and Alternative Medicine, 1*, 223–232.

Jacobson, B. H., Chen, H. C., Cashel, C., & Guerrero, L. (1997). The effect of T'ai Chi Ch'uan training on balance, kinesthetic sense, and strength. *Perceptual Motor Skills, 84*(1), 27–33.

Jin, P. (1989). Changes in heart rate, noradrenaline, cortisol, and mood during T'ai Chi. *Journal of Psychosomatic Research, 33*(2), 197–206.

Jin, P. (1992). Efficacy of T'ai Chi, brisk walking, meditation, and reading in reducing mental and emotional stress. *Journal of Psychosomatic Research, 36*(4), 361–370.

Johns, M. W. (1991). A new method for measuring daytime sleepiness: The Epworth Sleep Scale. *Sleep, 14*, 540–545.

Jones, A. Y., Dean, E., & Scudds, R. J. (2005). Effectiveness of a community-based T'ai Chi program and implications for public health initiatives. *Archives of Physical Medicine and Rehabilitation, 86*, 619–625.

Kosinski, M., Bayliss, M. S., Bjorner, J. B., Ware, J. E., Jr., Garber, W. H., Batenhorst, A., et al. (2003). Six-item shortform survey for measuring headache impact: the HIT-6. *Quality of Life Research, 12*, 963–974.

Kuo, S. (1991). *Long life good health through T'ai Chi Ch'uan*. Berkeley, CA: North Atlantic Books.

Lai, J., Lan, C., Wong, M., & Teng, S. (1995). *Journal of the American Geriatrics Society, 43*(11), 1222–1227.

Lan, C., Lai, J. S., & Chen, S. Y. (2002). T'ai Chi Chuan: An ancient wisdom on exercise and health promotion. *Sports Medicine, 32*, 217–224.

Li, F., Fisher, K. J., Harmer, P., Fisher, J., McAuley, E., Chaumeton, N. R., Eckstrom, E., & Wilson, N. (2005). T'ai Chi and fall reduction in older adults: A randomized controlled trial. *The Journals of Gerontology: Medical Sciences, 60A*(2), 187–194.

Li, F., Fisher, K. J., Harmer, P., Irbe, D., Tearse, R. G., Weimer, C. (2004). T'ai Chi and self-related quality of sleep and daytime sleepiness in older adults: A randomized controlled trial. *Journal of American Geriatric Society, 52*, 892–900.

Li, J. X., Hong, Y., & Chan, K. M. (2001). T'ai Chi: Physiological characteristics and beneficial effects on health. *British Journal of Sports Medicine, 35*, 148–156.

McNair, D. M., Lorr, M., & Droppelman, L. F., (1992). *EdITS Manual for the Profile of Mood States*. San Diego: Educational Testing Service.

Meditation in motion: T'ai Chi and beyond. (1994, September). *The University of California, Berkeley Wellness Letter, 10*(5), 7.

Metzger, W., & Zhou, P. (1996). *T'ai Chi Ch'uan and Qigong: Techniques and training*. New York: Sterling Publishing.

Mustian, K. M., Katula, J. A., Gill, D. L., Roscoe, J. A., Lang, D., & Murphy, K. (2004). T'ai Chi Chuan, health-related quality of life and self-esteem: A randomized trial with breast cancer survivors. *Supportive Care in Cancer, 12*, 871–876.

Nashner, L. M. (1993). Computerized dynamic posturagraphy. In Jacobson, G., Newman, C., & Kurtush, J. (Eds.), *Handbook of balance function and testing* (pp. 280–307). St. Louis: Mosby Yearbook.

National Center for Health Statistics. (1991). *The National Health Interview Survey.* Hyattsville, MD: Author.

Ng, G. Y. (2005). Patellar taping does not affect the onset of activities of vastus medialis obliquus and vastus lateralis before and after muscle fatigue. *American Journal of Physical Medicine & Rehabilitation, 84,* 106–11.

Qin, L., Choy, W., Leung, K., Leung, P. C., Au, S., Hung, W., Dambacher, M. A., & Chan, K. (2005). Beneficial effects of regular T'ai Chi exercise on musculoskeletal system. *Journal of Bone Mineral and Metabolism, 23,* 186–190.

Ray, C., Horvat, M., Keen, K., & Blasch, B. B. (2005). Using T'ai Chi as an exercise intervention for improving balance in adults with visual impairments: Two case studies. *RE:view, 37*(1), 17–24.

Rector, T. S., & Cohn, J. N. (1992). Assessment of patient outcome with the Minnesota Living with Heart Failure questionnaire: Reliability and validity during a randomized, double-blind, placebo-controlled trial of pimobendan. *American Heart Journal, 124,* 1017–1025.

Schaller, K. J. (1996). T'ai Chi Chih: An exercise option for older adults. *Journal of Gerontological Nursing, 22*(10), 12–17.

Schneider, D., & Leung, R. (1991). Metabolic and cardiorespiratory responses to the performance of Wing Chun and T'ai Chi Ch'uan exercise. *International Journal of Sports Medicine, 12*(3), 319–323.

Shapira, M. Y., Chelouche, M., Yanai, R., Kaner, C., & Szold, A. (2001). T'ai Chi Chuan practice as a tool for rehabilitation of severe head trauma: 3 case reports. *Archives of Physical Medicine and Rehabilitation, 82,* 1283–1285

Spiegel, D. (1995). Essentials of psychotherapeutic intervention for cancer patients. *Supportive Care in Cancer, 3,* 252–256.

Sun, W. Y., & Chen, W. (1995). *T'ai Chi Ch'uan: The gentle workout for mind & body.* New York: Sterling Publishing.

Sun, W. Y., Dosch, M., Gilmore, G. D., Pemberton, W., & Scarseth, T. (1996). Effects of a T'ai Chi Ch'uan program on Hmong American older adults. *Educational Gerontology, 22,* 161–167.

Sutton, N. (1991). *Applied T'ai Chi Ch'uan.* London, UK: A & C Black.

T'ai Chi Chih. (2008). *T'ai Chi Chih: Overview.* Retrieved September 20, 2008, from http:// http://www.taichichih.org/overview.php

Taggart, H. M. (2001). Self-reported benefits of T'ai Chi practice by older women. *Journal of Holistic Medicine, 19,* 223–232.

Taggart H. M., Arslanian, C. L., Bae, S., & Singh, K. (2003). Effects of T'ai Chi exercise on fibromyalgia symptoms and health-related quality of life. *Orthopedic Nursing, 22*(5), 353–360.

Taylor-Piliae, R. E., & Froelicher, E. S. (2004). Measurement properties of T'ai Chi exercise on self-efficacy among ethnic Chinese with coronary heart risk factors: A pilot study. *European Journal of Cardiovascular Nursing, 3,* 287–294.

Taylor-Piliae, R. E., Haskell, W. L., Waters, C. M., & Froelicher, E. S. (2006). Change in perceived psychosocial status following a 12-week T'ai Chi exercise programme. *Journal of Advanced Nursing, 54,* 313–329.

Thornton, E. W., Sykes, K. S., & Tang, W. K. (2004). Health benefits of T'ai Chi exercise: improved balance and blood pressure in middle-aged women. *Health Promotion International, 19,* 33.

Tsang, W. W., Wang, V. S., Fu, S. N., & Hui-Chan, C. W. (2004). T'ai Chi improves standing balance control under reduced or conflicting sensory conditions. *Archives of Physical Medicine and Rehabilitation, 85,* 129–137.

Tse, S. K., & Bailey, D. M. (1992). T'ai Chi postural control in the well elderly. *American Journal of Occupational Therapy, 46,* 295–300.

Verhagen, A. P., Immink, M., van der Meulen, A., & Bierma-Zeinstra, S. (2004). The efficacy of T'ai Chi Chuan in older adults: A systematic review. *Family Practice, 21*(1), 107–113.

Verhagen, A. P., de Vet, H. C. W., de Bie, R. A., Boers, M., & van den Brandt, P. A. (2001). The art of quality assessment of RCTs included in systematic reviews. *Journal of Clinical Epidemiology, 54,* 651–654.

Ware, J. E. (1993). *SF-36 Health Survey Manual and interpretation guide.* Boston: Nimrod.

Weber, L. (2008, October). T'ai Chi fits exercise guideline criteria, benefits PD patients. *Biomechanics: The Magazine of Body Movement and Medicine,* 13.

Wolf, S. L., Barnhart, H. X., Kutner, N. G., McNeely, E., Coogler, C., & Xu, T. (1996). Reducing frailty and falls in older persons: An investigation of T'ai Chi and computerized balance training. *Journal of the American Geriatrics Society, 44,* 489–497.

Wolf, S. L., O'Grady, M., Easley, K. A., Guo, Y., Kressig, R. W., & Kutner, M. (2006). The influence of intense T'ai Chi training on physical performance and hemodynamic outcomes in transitionally frail, older adults. *Journals of Gerontology: Series A: Biological Sciences and Medical Sciences, 61A*(2), 184–189.

Wolfson, L., Whipple, R., Derby, C., Judge, J., King, M., Amerman, P., Schmidt, J., & Smyers, D. (1996). Balance and strength training in older adults: Intervention gains and T'ai Chi maintenance. *Journal of the American Geriatrics Society, 44*(5), 498–506.

Wrisley, D. M., Marchetti, G. F., Kuharsky, D. K., & Whitney, S. L. (2004). Reliability, internal consistency, and validity of data obtained with the Functional Gait Assessment. *Physical Therapy, 84,* 906–918.

Xusheng, S., Yugi, X., & Ronggang, Z. (1990). Detection of ZC rosette-forming lymphocytes in the healthy aged with Taichiquan (88 style) exercise. *Journal of Sports Medicine and Physical Fitness, 30*(4), 401–405.

Yan, J. H. (1995). The health and fitness benefits of T'ai Chi. *Journal of Physical Education, Recreation & Dance, 66*(9), 61–63.

Yeh, G. Y., Wood, M. J., Lorell, B. H., Stevenson, L. W., Eisenberg, D., Wayne, P., et al. (2004). Effects of T'ai Chi Mind-Body Movement Therapy on functional status and exercise capacity in patients with chronic heart failure: A randomized controlled trial. *American Journal of Medicine, 117,* 541–548.

Zhou, D., Shephard, R. J., Plyley, M. J., & Davis, G. M. (1984). Cardiorespiratory and metabolic responses during T'ai Chi Ch'uan exercise. *Canadian Journal of Applied Sport Science, 91*(1), 7–10.

Chapter 11
Therapeutic Horseback Riding

Sara Tosado, John Dattilo, and Christine Sausser

Riding a horse was something that gave me an immense freedom.

—Lauren McDevitt

Introduction

An ancient Greek sage once stated "the outside of a horse is the best thing for the inside of man" (Bliss, 2006). For centuries, scholars have been aware of the therapeutic elements that horseback riding has to offer. For people with disabilities, the opportunity to use horseback riding as a treatment method provides people with the chance to experience a sense of freedom and independence (Nichols, 2007). According to Brock (1989), riding a horse can be an opportunity to "control one's destiny and allow mobility far beyond previous capability" (p. 1).

Therapeutic horseback riding has been classified into four main approaches to serve people with different types of disabilities by addressing psychological, physical, social, and behavioral goals. The approaches identified include therapy, education, sport, and recreation and leisure. These different approaches are used depending on the goals identified for the participant.

> For example, participants whose goals consist of increasing trunk control are likely to receive therapy services with the horse rather than using the horse for sport. TR specialists may choose to utilize therapeutic horseback riding as facilitation technique designed to accomplish goals relevant to TR services.

This chapter has been written to assist those who wish to expand their knowledge of therapeutic horseback riding in TR. After definitions relevant to therapeutic horseback riding are presented, specific intervention strategies are described. In the next section of the chapter, a summary of the theoretical foundations of therapeutic horseback riding follows a brief history. A review of the literature as well a case study is included in this chapter so the reader can become familiar with the value of therapeutic horseback riding. This chapter concludes with activity ideas and professional resources that a TR specialist can use with participants.

Definitions

Therapeutic horseback riding utilizes traditional riding disciplines or adapted riding activities to achieve therapeutic goals. The North American Riding for the Handicapped Association (NARHA) uses the title of *therapeutic riding* to describe the range of activities a certified NARHA instructor employs while implementing therapeutic horseback riding interventions (NARHA, 2007). For the purpose of this chapter, therapeutic horseback riding will be the phrase used to refer to all types of therapeutic uses of horses. It may be helpful to consider that overlap exists across approaches to therapeutic horseback riding related to service provision, types of disabilities addressed, and benefits of services. The approaches to therapeutic horseback riding classified by NARHA include:

- Therapy
- Education
- Sport
- Recreation and Leisure

Therapy

Horseback riding activities are considered *therapy* when the participant derives benefits from the activity, shows improved skills, or feels better after engaging in the activity (NARHA, 2007). Therapy may be offered in an individual or group format. Background knowledge is encouraged for those providing therapy services, including training in the following areas:

- Hippotherapy
- Developmental riding therapy
- Equine facilitated psychotherapy

Hippotherapy. Hippotherapy utilizes the movements of the horse as a tool to address impairments, functional limitations, and disabilities (Benjamin, 2000). Hippotherapy does not refer to riding lessons, but instead a prescribed treatment that is implemented by a credentialed therapist (Apel, 2007). During hippotherapy, the participant may be positioned on the horse facing forwards or backwards, sitting sideways or laying prone or supine. While in these various positions, the participant responds to the horse's movement. Benjamin (2000) suggested that hippotherapy can be beneficial in improving the participant's motor coordination, muscle tone, postural alignment, flexibility, and strength. In addition, improvements are often seen in respiratory, cognitive, sensory processing, balance, affective, arousal, and speech/language production functions. To determine long- and short-term goals for participation in a hippotherapy program, a treatment plan is developed by professionals providing services.

Developmental riding therapy. Developmental riding therapy is a multi-disciplinary approach to providing treatment services to hippotherapy participants who have met their long-term goals and are ready to transition to a more challenging program, yet may not have skills required for therapeutic riding (Heine, 1997). According to Heine, the fundamental elements of developmental riding include: individual sessions with a therapist; therapist-controlled sensory stimuli; client-centered focus; use of positions on the horse that correlate with horse's natural movement; and development of relationships between participants, therapists, and horse-selected components of riding skills. Developmental riding therapy is set apart from hippotherapy by its more diverse client population, broader professional participation, and focus on equine skills and training.

Equine facilitated psychotherapy. As a specialized therapy approach, equine facilitated psychotherapy is used to assist participants with psychosocial issues or mental health needs (EFMHA, 2007). Equine facilitated psychotherapy employs a range of activities, such as handling, grooming, riding, driving, and vaulting to address the needs of participants with a variety of psychosocial and mental health needs (NARHA, 2007). Examples of the disability groups that benefit from equine facilitated psychotherapy are participants with social, emotional, behavioral, communication, or cognitive disorders or issues (EFMHA).

Education

The purpose of using educationally oriented activities in therapeutic horseback riding is to have the horse act as a motivator for people with psychological, physical, behavioral, and cognitive impairments while helping the participants learn the following skills:

- Riding
- Driving
- Interactive vaulting

Riding. Riding skills may include: posting, positioning, pacing, and establishing gait. *Posting* is an exercise done by the rider while the horse is trotting. As the horse trots, and the horse's front foot closest to the rail of the ring moves forward, the rider simultaneously lifts his or her seat out of the saddle by standing in the stirrup (see Figure 11.1a). The rider sits as the horse's opposite leg moves forward (see Figure 11.1b). A posting rider appears to be rhythmically alternately standing and sitting as

Figure 11.1a   **Figure 11.1b**

the horse trots forward. *Positioning* requires the rider to sit using correct form. To achieve the correct form, the rider's ankles and shoulders must be aligned while he or she is seated in an upright position. *Pacing* involves communicating with the horse to quicken or slow its pace, adjusting the speed of the horse by using the reins, leaning forward or back, or by using verbal commands. *Establishing gait* requires the rider to have the horse assume a different gait. The various gaits of a horse are associated with different speeds at which the horse moves. Gaits of a horse in ascending order of speed are walk, trot, canter, gallop, and run.

Driving. The same concepts described for riding apply to driving and vaulting except that different types of skills are learned. Driving is the use of a horse to pull a cart or carriage. Skills learned for driving may include directing the horse to move in a specified direction, instructing the horse to change its gait, or balancing when the horse turns or changes its gait. Diving may also improve a participant's upper body strength (Nichols, 2007).

Interactive vaulting. Vaulting is the performance of gymnastic exercises on horseback, such as kneeling or standing on the horse's back independently, or with other people. Skills learned in vaulting might include holding different gymnastic positions on the horse and performing different exercises. The environment created by interactive vaulting offers educational, social, creative, and movement opportunities for the participant (NARHA, 2007).

Sport

Rather than focusing on learning new skills, use of horseback riding as sport is reported to assist individuals in development of balance, skill coordination, and strength through application of learned skills (Brock, 1988) while participating in an enjoyable experience. Although the intention of riding as sport is not necessarily a therapeutic one, therapeutic benefits are often realized (DePauw, 1986). People with various impairments can participate in sport activities using skills, such as riding, vaulting, and driving, learned through the education approach (NARHA, 1996). Therapeutic horseback riding as sport is distinguished from education by its focus on application of these skills rather than attainment of knowledge. Using a sport approach, activities are designed to focus on accomplishment of horsemanship goals.

Recreation and Leisure

Therapeutic riding is a form of therapeutic horseback riding that focuses on attainment of riding skills specifically for the purpose of riding. Although therapeutic value is inherent in the activity, therapeutic riding is recognized as a recreational activity for people with disabilities who may need adaptations or specialized instruction. TR specialists and therapeutic riding instructors are important contributors to therapeutic riding program development (NARHA, 1996). Under the classification of recreation and leisure, people with varying types of disabilities may use therapeutic riding as an experience when therapeutic goals are met in a relaxing, enjoyable setting. Benefits may be obtained in areas of socialization, posture, mobility, and an improved quality of life. Adaptations may be provided for activities, allowing riders to actively participate in an environment with structure, support, and socialization for the purpose of being intrinsically motivated and finding enjoyment through riding.

Summary

Therapeutic horseback riding has been acknowledged as a form of horseback riding that may be offered to people of varying abilities in many different contexts. Therapeutic horseback riding can be provided as a form of therapy, education, sport, and recreation to accomplish physical, cognitive, behavioral, psychological, and social goals. In this sense, its approach to service provision is quite similar to TR. Stumbo and Peterson's (2004) service delivery model described TR as providing treatment, leisure education, and recreation participation through selected leisure activities related to the improvement of functional and behavioral areas and the development of knowledge, attitudes, and skills necessary for leisure participation. Therapeutic horseback riding may be a beneficial facilitation technique used by TR specialists in a variety of contexts because of how it can be adapted based on individual participant needs.

Descriptions

Horses have been used with many people who have a variety of disabling conditions to assist in achieving therapeutic goals (NARHA, 1996). Riders may benefit therapeutically by meeting physical, psychological, and social goals through their interaction with the horse (Britton, 1991). This section provides a description of different approaches to riding and specific interventions used with those approaches. In addition, a description of how these approaches may be beneficial to riders of varying skill levels will be included. This section is divided into the following topics:

- Therapeutic Horseback Riding
- Hippotherapy
- Developmental Riding Therapy
- Equine Facilitated Psychotherapy
- Caring for Horses
- Programming Considerations

Therapeutic Horseback Riding

NARHA, established in 1969, has over 700 accredited operating centers in the United States that serve over 36,000 individuals with disabilities each year (Scott, 2005). NARHA provides standards, guidelines, and certifications for its operating centers and members. The type of interaction the participant has with the horse depends on the participant's goals and desired benefits. Because therapeutic horseback riding serves many different types of people with disabilities, various types of interventions are used to meet the diverse needs of clients.

Interventions for people pursuing therapeutic riding generally include a lesson plan based on an assessment of participant's needs that are incorporated into a lesson during which the participant learns the skills necessary to ride a horse. Lessons may occur in a group or on an individual basis. Individuals who may benefit from therapeutic horseback riding include those with orthopedic disorders, neurological disorders, mental health issues, and developmental delays (Bliss, 2006).

> For example, an intervention used for a person fitting the above description may include lessons provided twice a week for 1 hour. An entire lesson may focus on mounting the horse or becoming familiar with the horse. A more advanced lesson may include exercises that the participant must perform while sitting on the horse.

These exercises help participants to improve their postural and motor responses as well as improve their motor coordination, muscle tone, postural alignment, stiffness/flexibility, and strength. In addition to these positive outcomes, changes in the participant's respiratory function, cognitive ability, sensory processing, balance, affect, arousal, and speech/language functions are often experienced (Benjamin, 2000). Specific exercises that may be used in therapeutic horseback riding include:

- Mounting
- Stretching
- Balancing
- Strengthening
- Using a line
- Jumping
- Vaulting
- Driving
- Incorporating games

Mounting. Therapeutic riding lessons usually begin with an important aspect of horseback riding, mounting the horse. *Mounting* is the process of climbing into riding position from the ground or a platform onto the horse's back. Mounting can be a difficult task during which assistance may be needed. To make mounting easier for the rider, the instructor should be knowledgeable about the possibilities for mounting and have practiced them before attempting to help a rider for the first time.

The ramp should be at a level such that the rider can easily step into the stirrups. Different horses may require different ramp heights for mounting. The ramp generally reaches a height equal to the midpoint of the horse's midsection. The rider should be on the mounting platform before the horse is led into the area. This will keep the horse from being spooked by a sudden movement or loud noise made on the platform (Scott, 2005). The necessary equipment that includes a mounting ramp or mounting block can be in place in an area that is free from distractions.

In addition, it is helpful if riders are informed of the procedure involved in mounting so that they can communicate to the instructor the degree of assistance they feel is needed. Britton (1991) described eight different procedures that may be used for mounting: (a) total lift, (b) assisted lift from wheelchair, (c) partial assisted wheelchair transfer, (d) wheelchair transfer with minimum assistance, (e) crutch/walker mount from ramp, (f) standard mount with partial assistance, (g) standard mount with minimum assistance, and (h) standard mount.

The *total lift* involves trained personnel lifting the rider onto the horse. A hoist may be used for heavier riders. If mounting is done from a mounting ramp, the instructor ensures that the horse is in position and that the stirrups are clear of the ramp before riders insert their feet.

In an *assisted lift from a wheelchair,* the lift is accomplished from a mounting ramp, with the instructor facing the rider and the rider's wheelchair facing the horse. An assisted lift from a wheelchair to a horse is similar to an assisted lift to any other seating area. The position of the rider's wheelchair facing the horse's shoulder is at about a 45–80° angle. Mounting occurs from the left side of the horse. The instructor begins the assist by facing the rider, with the back toward the front of the horse, positioned in front of the horse's midsection. Wheelchair transfers typically occur with riders whose goal is independence, or are too large to be lifted. The instructor places arms around the rider's back with the instructor's knees touching the rider's knees, then lifts the rider forward, and swivels the rider around to lower the rider onto the saddle.

A *partial assisted wheelchair transfer* is accomplished by allowing the rider to have more independence in the mounting procedure. The wheelchair is placed in the same position as in the assisted lift and the rider maneuvers until he or she is sitting on the saddle with both legs on one side. The instructor supports the rider's back until the rider has swung one leg over and is sitting in an astride position.

The *wheelchair transfer with minimum assistance* is accomplished in the same manner as a partial assisted wheelchair transfer, except that the instructor stands by and does not assist unless necessary. A *crutch/walker mount from a ramp*, however, is accomplished with the help of the instructor assisting the rider up a ramp. The instructor then puts the left arm around the rider's chest, enabling the instructor to take the crutch or walker from the rider with the right hand and give it to an assistant. The instructor then encourages the rider to mount normally with the reins in the rider's left hand and the rider's left foot in the left stirrup.

A *standard mount with partial assistance* is done in the same manner as the crutch/walker mount, except that there is no crutch or walker to be removed. The instructor and assistant(s) help riders put their left foot in the stirrup and support riders in lifting themselves and becoming comfortable in the saddle.

The *standard mount with minimum assistance* and the *standard mount* both encourage independence of the rider. The mount with minimum assistance allows riders to mount themselves with help from the instructor only if difficulty is encountered. The *standard mount* is done with no assistance from the instructor. To perform a standard mount, the rider mounts from the left side of the horse by putting the left foot in the stirrup, pulling up, throwing the right leg over the horse's back gently, and then placing the right foot into the right-side stirrup.

Stretching. Many different types of stretching exercises can be accomplished on the horse in a therapeutic riding program (Davies, 1988). Rider stretching is an important part of a lesson and is primarily done before the riding session. Sometimes stretching exercises are accomplished while the horse is walking. Before a ride, the rider may hold a baton in various positions to stretch different areas. A rider may be instructed to reach out and take large rings from the therapist when held in different positions (Scott, 2005). Therapeutic horseback riding can be used to help stretch hands, arms, shoulders, body, neck, and legs.

To stretch the *arms* and *body,* riders may be asked to touch their toes while sitting astride the horse. Stretching can be accomplished by having riders touch their toes with their same-side hand, or by having riders touch their toes with their opposite-side hand. Another stretch for arms and body is forward bending that is accomplished by riders placing their hands on their hips, bending at the waist without losing balance or coming up out of the saddle, and trying to touch their chin to the horse's neck. To stretch the arms in this exercise, riders try to touch the horse's ears (see Figure 11.2). The rider's head should be held in a position so the rider can look forward through the horse's ears.

Figure 11.2

Trunk twisting, used for *body stretching,* is accomplished by riders holding their arms out to their sides at 90 degree angles and twisting from the waist, trunk facing forward, first to the left, and then to the right. The movement is conducted slowly and smoothly. Lying back on the horse's hindquarters is a stretch that is especially beneficial to individuals with spasticity because it straightens the body. The stretch is conducted by assisting riders in leaning back gradually until they are lying directly on the horse's hindquarters with their head resting just above the horse's tail (see Figure 11.3). Before this exercise is completed, riders are asked to remove their feet from the stirrups and cross their arms over their chests.

Neck stretches include turning the head slowly to the left and right, and then "head circling," which is completed by moving the head around in a circling motion (this technique should not be done more than three times in one lesson). *Leg stretches* are done by riders stretching their legs downward, holding the stretch, and then relaxing and stretching them sideways and repeating the procedure. In addition, riders can turn their ankles in a circling motion in both directions in another stretch for the legs.

Arms, hands, and shoulders may be stretched by moving wrists in a circling motions, swinging the arms backwards and forwards, moving arms in a circling motion (large and small circles), and hand clapping (in front of and behind the trunk).

Figure 11.3

Balancing. To help riders improve their balance, an exercise called *Around the World* may be used (Davies, 1988). For most riders, this is a useful exercise because it can be fun while being physically demanding. The exercise is accomplished by asking riders to revolve in a complete circle while seated on the horse. Riders may begin the exercise by raising either leg over the horse's neck and sitting on the saddle with both legs on one side. Then riders lift the leg closest to the horse's tail over the horse's hindquarters so riders are sitting astride the horse facing its rear. This movement is continued until riders are facing their original position. A variation of this exercise is to ask riders to click their heels together over the horse's neck while seated in the forward position and asking riders to click their heels again over the horse's hindquarters while facing the rear of the horse.

Strengthening. All exercises including mounting, stretches, and balancing exercises are designed to improve riders' strength. According to Davies (1988), one exercise used for this purpose is "standing in the stirrups" (see Figure 11.4). This exercise also helps riders improve their balance; however, it should not be used with riders with

Figure 11.4

spasticity. To begin this exercise, the instructor asks riders to stand in the stirrup. This is done properly when the ball of the foot is pushed down into the stirrup with the heel held in a lower position than the toes. The leg straightens but does not lock, the knee presses inward toward the saddle, and the rider's seat lifts up from the saddle by tensing the buttocks while bracing the back and stomach muscles. The lower leg should remain positioned under the rider without the leg swinging forward or back. The rider remains in this position until the signal is given from the instructor.

Using a line. Therapeutic horseback riding can occur with the use of the following types of lines: (a) lead, (b) lunge, and (c) long.

Lessons on a *lead line* are most common for riders with disabilities beginning a riding program (Britton, 1991). A lead line is a rope approximately 6–8 feet long that is attached to the horse's halter or bridle. The *bridle* is the equipment placed onto the horse's head used to direct the horse to move in a specific direction. The leader walks alongside the horse between its head and shoulder (see Figure 11.5). Side walkers are people who walk beside the horse to assist the rider; they may be a part of the lesson to increase safety and to assist riders who need help maintaining their balance. The lead line is held in the right hand of the leader about 6–12 inches from the horse's head. The rider uses reins to direct the horse as the leader walks alongside.

Figure 11.5

When riders become more advanced, lessons may be given on a *lunge line* (Britton, 1991). A lunge line is a rope approximately 20–30 feet long that is longer than a lead line, and gives the rider increased independence and freedom in the control of the horse while receiving assistance from the instructor. The instructor, at a distance, holds the lunge line approximately 15–20 feet from the rider, who rides the horse in circles around the instructor.

Similar to a lunge line is a *long line*. A long line is what appears to be a pair of lunge lines, one attached to each side of the horse's halter or bridle, used by the instructor who walks behind the horse to guide its movement. Lead line and lunge lessons are generally given on an individual basis, which may benefit the rider by having the instructor's full attention. Another benefit of lead line and lunge lessons is that the rider may be more comfortable performing exercises without having to worry about controlling the horse. Lead line or lunge lessons are particularly helpful for novice riders (Britton, 1991). Using a lunge or lead line, riders may more easily focus on their positioning and balance when going over the obstacles while the instructor or leader controls the horse as needed.

Jumping. Providing opportunities for participants to be on a horse when it jumps can be rewarding for the riders. When engaged in therapeutic horseback riding the following items can be used for jumping: (a) poles, (b) caveletti, and (c) jumps.

Poles are simply long poles approximately 4–6 inches in diameter and approximately 12 feet long that are placed on the ground about 4–5 feet apart that the rider directs the horse to walk or trot over. The instructor may ask the rider to move into a specific position, such as raising the seat out of the saddle, while the horse goes over the poles.

Caveletti are poles that may be placed 6–8 inches above the ground. The horse is directed to go over the caveletti at a walk or trot as the rider practices balancing. For this exercise, riders lift their seats out of the saddle.

When riders become more experienced, they may go over *jumps*. Jumps are basically caveletti that are raised to a greater height. This is always accomplished with riders raising their seat out of the saddle.

Vaulting. Vaulting is an exercise in therapeutic riding during which riders perform gymnastics on horseback (Britton, 1991). The benefit of vaulting is that it offers participants an opportunity to progress at their own speed while participating in a group (Rhodes, 2002). Riders who are physically able may mount the horse by walking or jogging alongside the moving animal and leaping onto the horse from the ground with assistance when needed. Those who have more difficulty mounting can mount before the lesson begins and complete exercises on the horse during the lesson. Exercises in vaulting may include taking and holding certain positions while on the horse's back, such as kneeling on hands and knees, kneeling on knees only, or standing on the horse's back. These exercises are generally accomplished while the horse is walking but may be done at a standstill for practice or at a trot for more advanced riders. Britton (1991) suggested that riders participating in vaulting might benefit by experiencing decreased anxieties, hyperactivity, and aggressive tendencies, as well as increased trust, self-awareness, self-esteem, sensory motor abilities, interpersonal skills, and positive social behavior.

Driving. Driving is a form of therapeutic riding that involves activities related to carriage driving (NARHA, 2007). This type of exercise is used with individuals who may be unable to ride a horse. Benefits of driving may include improved upper body strength, balance, hand-eye coordination attention span, and spatial awareness (Scott, 2005). As with all other forms of riding, safety precautions should be taken. A horse trained specifically for driving is used along with a cart that is suited for the driver and may be adapted to accommodate a wheelchair (Britton, 1991). To be safe, a "whip" (experienced driver) accompanies the inexperienced driver (Britton, 1991). Two sets of reins may be used, one set for the driver and one set for the whip in case of emergency. While driving, individuals may participate in different activities, such as maneuvering through obstacle courses, *dressage* that involves horsemanship using slight movements to control horse's direction and pace, and pleasure driving (Britton, 1991).

Incorporating games. Games provide riders with opportunities to work on skills while having a good time. They may be played in teams or individually as long as the riders are enjoying themselves. Games may focus on therapeutic goals or can be offered as respite from lessons. Before choosing a game for riders, the safety of the game is considered. Examples of games that may be played in a therapeutic riding session include: (a) Egg and Spoon Race, (b) Treasure Hunt, (c) Dressing Up Race, and (d) Postal Workers.

The *Egg and Spoon Race* is played by giving riders a serving spoon and then asking them to position their horse at the end of the ring (Britton, 1991). When the instructor signals, riders direct their horse to the opposite end of the ring where they each collect an egg from the instructor or assistants, place it on their spoons, and attempt to return to the starting point without dropping the egg. When riders return to the starting point, the egg is placed into a bucket. The first one to place an egg in the bucket wins.

In *Treasure Hunt,* each rider has a "grandparent" (an instructor or assistant) who has two cards (Britton, 1991). Each card has a drawing of an object on one side and the name of the object on the other side. The grandparent gives one card to the rider and the rider tries to find the object on the card. When the object is found, the rider returns the card and the object to the grandparent and receives the second card. The process of finding the object is repeated. Prior to the beginning of the game, the instructor places the objects that are on the cards in locations where riders, astride their horses, can reach the objects while remaining astride.

Dressing Up Race is similar to relay racing (Britton, 1991). To prepare for this game, the instructor places different types of loose-fitting clothing (usually a jacket or sweatshirt) on a pole positioned perpendicular to the ground at a height that is easily reached by riders on their horses. The first rider rides to the pole, puts the clothing on, and returns to the starting line where the clothing is removed and given to the second rider. The second rider returns the clothing to the pole and returns to the starting line. The third rider rides to the pole, puts the clothes on, and returns. This is repeated until all riders have had a turn.

In the game *Postal Workers,* riders are asked to post cards or letters into a large box with a slit that is within their reach while sitting astride their horses (Britton, 1991). Riders can write actual letters to other group members or use stickers to personalize their letters.

Hippotherapy

Hippotherapy literally means "treatment with the help of a horse" (Heine, 1997, p. 11). The movement of the horse's pelvis and hips at a walk provides a challenge for riders who, without the use of the horse as a tool, may not otherwise be able to experience this movement. Hippotherapy is divided into two classifications:

- Classic hippotherapy
- Hippotherapy

Classic hippotherapy. In *classic hippotherapy,* the rider's response to the horse's movement is evaluated. The therapist may adjust the rider's positioning or the horse's pace to accommodate the rider's abilities and address areas that need improvement. Classic hippotherapy is often used in conjunction with a treatment plan that may be developed by an interdisciplinary team of therapists.

Hippotherapy. *Hippotherapy* is distinguished from classic hippotherapy in that a treatment approach is taken relating to specific goals of healthcare professionals offering the services. Hippotherapy does not focus on the acquisition of riding skills. The purpose of hippotherapy is to "provide a controlled environment and graded sensory input designed to elicit appropriate responses from the client" (Heine, 1997, p. 11).

A rider participating in hippotherapy may be positioned on the horse by the therapist in a manner that may promote and improve posture, mobility, balance, and function. Not all riders can use a saddle. Saddles can be used by riders who can maintain balance, have some knowledge of horses' gaits, and who are learning riding skills. Saddles are rarely used with hippotherapy. Back riding, which includes an experienced rider who sits on the horse behind the inexperienced rider to provide support, may be utilized for riders who do have limited postural control. Riders may be asked to complete stretches, play games, or sit in different positions on the horse to accomplish therapeutic goals. The warmth of the horse's body, its movement, and the tactile sensations that might be experienced through touching the horse can all contribute to improvements in trunk control and strength, pelvic control, gross motor skills, motor planning, and ability to process sensory information (Heine, 1997).

Developmental Riding Therapy

Developmental riding therapy, like hippotherapy, uses a treatment approach to achieve cognitive, affective, perceptual motor, and movement needs (Britton, 1991). Developmental riding therapy is distinguished from hippotherapy by a focus on acquisition of equine skills and training. In addition, it is offered to people with a wider range of disabilities (Heine, 1997). This approach to riding is utilized for people with conditions such as autism, learning disabilities, language delays, sensory integration disorders, emotional disturbances, mild cerebral palsy, mental retardation, and post-traumatic brain disorder (Britton). Because of the focus on acquisition of riding skills, developmental riding therapy is suggested for riders who have reached their long-term hippotherapy goals and are ready to initiate a more challenging form of therapy. As riders progress, they may continue to undertake more challenging situations, eventually participating in therapeutic riding, which is for more advanced riders, as described in the earlier section.

Equine Facilitated Psychotherapy

Equine facilitated psychotherapy may be used in hippotherapy, developmental riding therapy, or therapeutic horseback riding depending on physical abilities of the rider; however, it is generally associated with therapeutic riding. The distinction of this approach to therapeutic horseback riding is related to the type of goals that are addressed. According to the Equine Facilitated Mental Health Association (EFMHA, 2007), equine facilitated psychotherapy can be used with participants who have psychosocial issues or mental health needs that result in altered cognition abilities, moods, judgment, anxiety levels, social skills, communication, and behaviors. Examples of people who report benefits from equine facilitated psychotherapy include: individuals with anxiety disorders, behavior disorders, autism, attention deficit hyperactivity disorder, depression, post-traumatic stress disorder, and expressive language disorders.

> For example, The Inside Look at NARHA (1996) reported on a therapeutic riding center in Longview, Texas, where adolescents who have histories of burglary, theft, assault, drug abuse, and gang relations participate in a horsemanship program. To participate in the program, adolescents must meet specified criteria while in a local detention center. The program includes group therapy discussions, riding lessons, lessons on care of horses, debriefings after lessons, and trail rides related to applying horsemanship skills and knowledge to real-life situations. Ninety percent of teens who participate in the program have successfully reintegrated into their communities.

Caring for Horses

In addition to riding, positive outcomes can be facilitated through care of a horse. Medical, educational, and recreational goals can be accomplished through the process of preparing a horse for a lesson.

> For example, for participants who may have limitations related to gross motor skills, brushing the horse may provide an opportunity to improve abilities. In addition, a sense of responsibility and confidence may be instilled through completion of a job well done.

Programming Considerations

Many considerations are made when conducting therapeutic horseback riding programs. Because risk is involved in using large animals, the selection of the horse is essential in providing a safe environment. Other environmental considerations include the area where the session occurs, instructor qualifications and knowledge, and different types of equipment that may limit risks and provide comfort to the rider. This section will present an overview of the following considerations when providing therapeutic horseback riding services:

- Horse selection and training
- Equipment
- Safety maintenance
- Facilitator and volunteer training
- Environmental management
- Orientation and support
- Caring for the animal

Horse selection and training. Before a horse can be accepted as part of a therapeutic riding program, it must be evaluated to ensure that it embodies the characteristics of a therapeutic riding horse (Nichols, 2007). According to Britton (1991), the following must exist: (a) a therapeutic horse that has a kind and calm disposition and accepts being led, (b) side walkers who walk beside the horse to provide assistance to the rider, (c) a mounting block where riders mount the horse, (d) a wheelchair on the ground, on a ramp, and while transferring participant, and (e) crutches and canes, balls, rings, and games. Ideally, the horse obeys voice commands, lunges by moving in circles on a long lead rope in both directions at different gaits, performs smooth transitions between gaits, and accepts adaptive equipment.

The therapy horse is typically at least 5 years of age. Younger horses may be unpredictable, lack patience, and have short attention spans. Horses used for therapy should be 12–15.2 hands high (a hand is 4 inches) and have good conformation (build or physique).

When selecting a horse, participant characteristics are considered such as age and type of disability, services offered, available space, and budget.

> For example, if participants are children, it may be beneficial to choose ponies and small horses, rather than horses that might be too large for some children. The number of horses owned by an agency is often limited by the amount of pasture and boarding space available.

Although it would be ideal if all horses selected for the therapeutic horseback riding program fit qualifications listed above, some horses can be selected for their ability in specific areas such as pulling a cart. Some horses with disabilities may be used if the program is able to budget for the horse's medical needs such as corrective shoes and a veterinarian has determined the horse to be medically sound. Agencies with limited funds may consider leasing or borrowing horses. In addition, it is not uncommon for therapy horses to be donated (Nolt, 1995).

When selecting a horse for a riding lesson, considerations are made related to rider abilities and goals, condition of the horse such as mood, physical abilities, availability, and conformation. Using stocky, wide-backed horses may be helpful for riders who have limitations associated with coordination and balance (Britton, 1991).

Once a horse has been selected to be part of a program, it must be trained. Training a therapeutic riding horse may take several days or several months, depending on the program and the horse. Facilitators and trainers begin training the horse in a ring where it is led around and taught how to stop, step backwards, and walk in a circle. The horse also learns how to go around and over poles. While in training, the horse becomes familiar with equipment used by participants, such as ramps and mounting blocks (Nichols, 2007).

Equipment. Many types of adaptive equipment are used in therapeutic horseback riding; however, if it is possible for riders to use standard equipment, they are encouraged to do so. Davies (1988) suggested the following guidelines for using adaptive riding equipment: (a) use only when necessary; (b) use only to meet rider's need; (c) do not attach equipment to the horse and rider at the same time (first the rider then the horse); (d) equipment should not cause the rider to be embarrassed; (e) equipment should not interfere with the rider's balance, control, or movement; and (f) equipment should not restrict, cause discomfort, or injure the horse.

Choosing equipment for the rider is generally accomplished after initial assessments (Davies, 1988). Equipment may be changed throughout the therapeutic process to adapt to the progress of the rider. Davies (1988) suggested the following considerations be made when choosing equipment for the rider: (a) physique, age, and health; (b) type and degree of impairment (whether the disability is progressive, stable, or improving); (c) expectations, knowledge, experience, and attitude towards riding; (d) temperament, ambition, and character; (e) length, frequency, and form of lessons; (f) number, breeds, and sizes of horses available; and (g) resources available, such as cost and setting.

Ensuring that a facility has appropriate adaptive equipment needed for some people with disabilities is another consideration for programming in therapeutic riding. Information about the following equipment is provided: (a) safety belt or body harness, (b) saddle pad, (c) stirrups, (d) reins, (e) bridle, (f) hand holds, (g) anti-cast surcingle, (h) surcingle, (i) saddles, (j) riding crops, (k) bandages, and (l) bell.

Equipment used in a therapeutic horseback riding program is meant to assist the rider in obtaining correct posture and positioning on the horse and to help the rider become more comfortable (Davies, 1988). The *safety belt or body harness* is the most commonly used adaptive equipment in therapeutic riding (Davies, 1988). It helps riders with poor posture or balance to maintain correct positioning on the horse. The harness crisscrosses over the rider's chest and back with a belt around the waist and hand holds on the belt. The side helper who walks beside the rider can grab onto the handholds and correct positioning of the rider if the rider begins to lose balance.

Another piece of equipment commonly used in therapeutic riding is a *saddle pad*. Saddle pads are placed directly on the horse's back and are typically used with riders who have spinal cord injuries or people who have a loss of sensation in their legs and seat area. The saddle pads prevent the horse from developing sores and provide a natural padding for the rider. The saddle pad also allows participants to feel warmth of the horse's body (Nichols, 2007).

Specially made *stirrups* can be used to make riding easier. Two different types that may be used are the peacock safety stirrups and the Devonshire boot (Davies, 1988). The peacock safety stirrups have a snap-off rubber band located on the side of the stirrup facing outward and are useful with riders who have weakness in their lower limbs. The peacock safety stirrups help hold the foot in the correct position. The Devonshire boot is a stiff leather boot that attaches to the stirrup and provides protection to the rider as well as encouraging correct positioning of the foot.

Riders who have difficulty grasping may use special *reins* such as the looped rein, the ladder rein, the *Humes* rein, overhead check reins, or side reins to direct the horse (Davies, 1988). The looped rein is designed with three large leather loops attached along different points of the rein so that the entire hand of the rider can be placed through the loop. The ladder rein is similar to a ladder in that *rungs* of leather, at intervals of 6 inches apart, allow the rider to shorten or lengthen the reins by moving up or down a rung. Humes reins are essentially nonslip reins built with webbing, leather stops, or rubber covering. Check reins and side reins run from the horse's mouth area of the bridle through rings in the saddle, and to the rider. Check reins assist in preventing the rider from losing balance if the horse tries to bend its neck to eat grass.

The *bridle* is a leather headpiece worn by the horse, to which the reins are attached, that allows the rider to steer the horse in the desired direction. The bridle may function with use of a bit that is a metal or rubber piece placed in the horse's mouth to which the reins attach, or with a bitless attachment where the reins attach to the noseband of the bridle.

Hand holds are generally used in the beginning stages of therapeutic riding or hippotherapy, especially with riders who have poor balance and control (Davies, 1988). Hand holds allow riders to support themselves by having something in front of them to grasp while riding.

The hand hold is attached to the pommel that is the front mid-portion of the saddle or to the top portion of an *anti-cast surcingle,* which looks like a large belt worn by the horse, used in conjunction with a saddle pad to hold it in place. Hand holds are positioned so that the rider can maintain a natural balance. In addition, they are to be strong and secure. When hand holds are not present on the anti-cast surcingle, the belt device is called a *surcingle*. The surcingle and saddle blanket together may be used for people who do not ride in a saddle.

Saddles are another type of equipment that is required for therapeutic riding (Davies, 1988). When choosing from the many types of saddles, considerations are that they are deep-seated, well made, and made for general purpose. The saddle should not provide total upper body support because riders are encouraged to balance themselves.

Other items that may be used are riding crops, knee bandages, and bells (Davies, 1988). *Riding crops* may reinforce riding aids for people who have weakness in their limbs once they have reached an acceptable level of advancement. *Bandages* can decrease friction of rubbing between the rider and horse and thereby reduce participant's soreness. A *bell* is useful for riders with visual impairments. It is attached to the back of the saddle on the lead horse in a group ride so that the riders can follow the sound of the bell.

Safety maintenance. To achieve a safe therapeutic riding environment Britton (1991) suggested conducting safety checks to detect hazards in the facility, understanding rider disabilities, using equipment for comfort, assistance, and safety, placing riders in groups, and developing rider awareness of safety procedures. All riders, regardless of ability, are required to wear helmets. If a participant has limited head control, a helmet that is lightweight is recommended (NARHA, 2007).

Facilitator training. To become a therapeutic riding instructor, an individual must complete all training course requirements, pass the NARHA exam, and be granted NARHA Registered Instructor Status (Scott, 2005). Instructor certification is available for therapeutic horseback riding through the NARHA (NARHA, 2007). Certification is not required for all individuals who are part of the therapeutic riding team; however, instructors must be certified at accredited therapeutic riding institutions.

Therapists who administer a hippotherapy program must be licensed or registered to practice in their field, have received hippotherapy training, maintain professional liability insurance, and be a NARHA-certified instructor (Heine, 1997). The therapist receives training in classic principles of hippotherapy, equine movement, and equine psychology (Scott, 2005).

Environmental management. According to Bauer (1972), unique considerations related to the therapeutic horseback riding facility include: (a) areas for riding, (b) mounting ramps, (c) pasture and stable areas, and (d) the barn.

An indoor *riding* ring approximately 60' by 120' would be ideal for all weather riding; however, if an indoor ring is not available or feasible, an outdoor ring is acceptable. Sand is often used as a ground cover within the ring because it helps horses maintain their footing. In addition to the main riding ring, a circular ring of about 60' in diameter is helpful for training horses and instructors.

Solidly constructed wooden *mounting ramps* are carpeted to prevent slipping and be accessible so people using wheelchairs may access the mounting area. The mounting ramp platform is at least 6' wide, 4' deep, and 4' high. The ramp is suitable for riders of all sizes and disabilities.

Pasture and stable areas are considered in relation to care of horses. Pastures next to riding rings may cause distractions for the horse and rider; therefore, this type of arrangement should be avoided.

The barn may be an area where horses are stalled or groomed and an area where equipment is stored. The barn may be frequently used by riders and staff and is a safe environment for everyone. Considerations are made related to size of different areas of the barn.

> For example, in the grooming area it is helpful to know whether there is enough room for more than one horse to be groomed at one time and if there is enough walking area for the necessary number of people in this area. The stalls should be large enough so that the horse may move around freely. The tack room, typically located in the barn, should be large enough to store all the equipment owned by the facility as well as any additional equipment that riders choose to store.

Policies that may apply to the entire facility include requiring that all areas, including the tack room and rest room, are accessible to everyone participating in the therapeutic riding program and are maintained so the facility remains clean and safe.

Orientation. Anyone involved in a therapeutic horseback riding program should be oriented to the setting, requirements of involvement, population served, safety precautions, equipment, horse care, handling procedures, and general behavior of horses. The proper location for grooming and lessons is critical to a successful therapeutic horseback riding program. These activities occur in restricted areas away from high traffic roads, unfenced pastures, or in a stall or paddock where another horse may be unsecured.

If volunteers are used, it is helpful for them to have knowledge of expectations of their involvement, and be trained in their duties such as grooming a horse, leading, or side-walking. It is important for professionals associated with the therapeutic horseback riding program to understand unique characteristics of participants so that effective planning occurs. If a facility is used that is open to riders other than people with disabilities, it may be helpful to orient the coordinator of those activities to different disabilities addressed in therapeutic horseback riding lessons. Although volunteers only help riders when necessary, they must be present at all times and be knowledgeable about what to do to help when working with people with various disabilities (Britton, 1991).

All volunteers, therapists, and instructors are trained to implement safety procedures. This is helpful for maintaining a safe environment, and prepares individuals to respond appropriately to emergency situations when necessary.

Orienting people to the different types of equipment used in equine facilitated therapy may be overwhelming, especially if they do not have prior experience with horses.

> For example, giving volunteers an illustrated handout describing the different types of equipment and their uses may be helpful.

In addition, therapists and instructors determine which equipment may best meet needs of individuals receiving the lesson. It is helpful for those who work with the horse to have knowledge related to the handling, care, and behavior of horses. Being able to determine if a horse is anxious or frustrated may prevent accidents from occurring. Knowledge of proper grooming techniques can be beneficial.

> For example, if a stone stuck in the hoof is removed with a hoof pick prior to a lesson, this will prevent pain to the horse during a lesson, thus possibly preventing a rider's fall as well.

Caring for the animal. Time and money involved in housing, grooming, medical care, and food costs for horses can be substantial. Grooming can, and usually is, done by the agency providing the services. However, in addition to daily grooming such as brushing the horse, combing its mane, and removing the dirt from its hooves, horses need their hooves trimmed regularly. If horses are ridden on a rough surface often, such as a road or on concrete, they will also need shoes. General medical care including regular veterinarian checks, vaccinations, dental care, and de-worming is included in the care of a horse. Food can become expensive with a horse possibly consuming 50 pounds of feed a week.

History

Ancient Greeks used horses as a main mode of transportation. Using a horse as transportation was considered a right not denied to anyone, including individuals with disabilities (Britton, 1991). It was common for the early Greeks to use horses not only for transportation, but to alleviate suffering. In addition, horseback rides were given to people considered to be untreatable or incurable to improve their spirits (DePauw, 1986).

According to DePauw (1986), medical literature over the eighteenth and nineteenth centuries contains references to benefits of horseback riding. The value of horseback riding was first documented in Paris in 1875 when Chassigne wrote that riding was beneficial in treatment of hemiplegia, paraplegia, and other neurological disorders. He hypothesized that abilities such as posture, balance, joint movement, and muscle control improved by active and passive movement provided by the horse (DePauw).

At the turn of the century, during World War I, a member of the Chartered Society of Physiotherapy, Olive Sands, brought her horses to the Oxford Hospital to allow men who had been injured in the war to benefit from riding (Britton, 1991). Through Ms. Sands' efforts and with the help of Dame Agnes Hunt, founder of the first Orthopedic Hospital in Owestry in 1901, horseback riding became recognized as being therapeutic; however, therapeutic riding programs were not established until the 1950s.

Liz Hartel is generally considered the founder of modern therapeutic riding. Hartel experienced severe muscle deterioration after contracting Polio in 1943. Despite her disability, Hartel continued to ride and eventually entered the Helsinki Olympics in 1952, where she won the silver medal for the equestrian event, Grand Pris Dressage, competing with riders without disabilities. Hartel's triumph captured the attention of equestrian enthusiasts around the world (Scott, 2005). England quickly moved forward in this new field, followed closely by other European countries (Heipertz, 1981). Since the 1950s, programs have spread throughout Europe and beyond. Therapeutic riding programs in the United States and Canada have developed since the mid-1960s to early 1970s, and are found throughout these countries to this day.

Theoretical Foundations

In 1970, development was undertaken for a theoretical construct for what was recognized as therapeutic riding (Britton, 1991). German theorists designed a three-circle diagram that illustrated the approaches taken and the theory behind service provision in this field. The three circles represented education, medical benefits, and sport. These three circles overlapped to represent the holistic approach taken by therapeutic horseback riding and its ability to address several different types of disabilities through comprehensive and integrative services. Since then, therapeutic horseback riding has become more widely used and additional approaches have been developed to provide specialized services.

NARHA developed a new classification system similar to the previous theoretical diagram, which was discussed in the definition section of this document (NARHA, 1996). The new classification system is a circle diagram as well, but contains four circles that overlap, instead of three. The new circles represent therapy, education, sport, and recreation and leisure. The point at which all circles overlap represents an integration of all four approaches, although the approaches may be utilized individually. The theoretical model reflects beliefs of early theorists and has been adapted to accommodate growth of therapeutic horseback riding. As NARHA continues to evolve, the classification system is constantly changing. Currently, NARHA is progressing towards more equine-assisted activities and therapies approach to therapeutic horseback riding (NARHA, 2007).

Effectiveness

There are many testimonials to support positive effects of therapeutic horseback riding; however, to date, empirical research examining effects of therapeutic horseback riding is limited. Although studies have been conducted to determine effects of therapeutic horseback riding on self-concept (Cawley, Cawley, & Retter, 1994) and language abilities (Macauley & Gutierrez, 2004), most studies have focused on studying effects on physical skills such as balance (Biery & Kauffman, 1989), coordination (Brock, 1988), gross motor movements (Chern, Liao, Leung, & Hwang, 2004), and gait (Kulkarni-Lambore, McGuigan, Narula, & Sepelak, 2001). Therefore, this portion of the chapter contains the following sections:

- Physical Skills
- Self-Concept
- Language Development

Physical Skills

Cherng and colleagues (2004) studied effects of a 16-week therapeutic horseback riding program on gross motor and muscle tone of hip adductors in 14 children (ages 3–11) with spastic cerebral palsy. Gross motor function was assessed prior to and following the intervention with the use of the Gross Motor Function Measure. In the first phase, nine participants received therapeutic horseback riding along with their regular treatment; the remaining participants only received their regular treatment during this period. In the second phase, the groups were reversed. After the program, some participant scores increased in gross motor function in running, walking, and jumping, as well as total scores. These improvements lasted for at least 16 weeks. The researchers concluded that therapeutic horseback riding was beneficial for some children who have spastic cerebral palsy.

Ionatamishvili, Tsverava, Loriya, Sheshaberidze, and Rukhadze (2002) studied effects of therapeutic horseback riding on motor functioning of 100 children (ages 3–4) with cerebral palsy. Participants were divided into two groups, one group received therapeutic horseback riding and the other group did not.

Riding therapy consisted of 40–45 procedures that were divided into two periods: the adaptation period was designed motivate participants to ride, and the main period focused on acquisition of new skills. Participants' motor functioning was examined using a variety of original tests. The researchers developed a protocol for therapeutic riding as well as scales (rating the participant's degree of hyperkineses and spasticity) to assess the effectiveness of therapeutic riding for individuals who have cerebral palsy. With the use of the therapeutic riding protocol and the assessment scales, the researchers found that therapeutic horseback riding is an appropriate treatment for participants with cerebral palsy because it promotes motor skill development and reduces spasticity and hyperkineses. Caution in interpreting these findings is suggested since reliability and validity of measurements used in this study were not reported.

Kulkarni-Lambore and colleagues (2001) studied effects of hippotherapy on walking patterns of a 15-year-old male with cerebral palsy who had right hemipariises. The participant was referred to hippotherapy as part of his physical therapy regimen. A computerized gait analysis tool was used to assess his gait before and after 8 sessions of hippotherapy (2 x wk, 30-min sessions). A comparison was made between initial gait analysis and final gait analysis. The final gait analysis revealed that there were significant changes in joint angles of the right hip in the saggital and coronal plane, as well as the right knee and ankle joints on the saggital plane. The researchers reported that 8 sessions of hippotherapy improved the gait of a participant with right hemipariises as measured by a computerized gait analysis tool.

MacKinnon and colleagues (1995) studied effects of horseback riding (1 x wk, 60-min sessions) on 19 children with cerebral palsy. After being separated into two groups by degree of disability (mild or moderate), 10 children (ages 6–11) were randomly assigned to a 6-month riding group and 9 children (ages 4–8) were randomly assigned to a non-riding group. The Gross Motor Function Measure (GMFM) was used to assess the participant's gross and fine motor control, posture, daily living activities, and psychosocial changes, prior to and at the conclusion of the intervention. Quantitative measures did not reveal statistically significant results; however, qualitative data supplied by the instructor, therapists, parents, and videotaped evaluations revealed perceived improvements in motor control, posture, daily living, and psychosocial behaviors. MacKinnon and colleagues suggested that quantitative assessment of therapeutic horseback riding is difficult due to limitations of available assessment instruments. When interpreting results caution is advised due to measurement challenges and small sample size.

Biery and Kauffman (1989) studied effects of therapeutic riding on balance of five men and three women (mean age 16.5) with mental retardation who followed verbal instructions and had not participated in such a program during the previous 3 years. Participants who served as their own control were involved in a 6-month riding program (1 x wk, 20-min sessions) designed to provide vestibular stimulation with the horse's movement as the base. Each session contained 5 minutes spent following the horse's motion (hippotherapy), 10 minutes of intensive activities (stretching, specific positions, games, goal-directed activity), and 5 minutes of cooling down with positioning emphasizing proper body alignment. Participants were time-tested on 10 balance tasks during an initial evaluation, interim period and second evaluation, and intervention and third evaluation. Participants significantly surpassed their initial testing scores after the riding therapy intervention as determined by the above balance tests. Results support the belief that therapeutic riding has a positive effect on balance involving trunk stability and postural adjustments of individuals with mental retardation. Caution is advised in generalizing these results due to use of such a small sample size and participants' continued involvement in other physical programs, such as swimming and physical education throughout the study.

Brock (1989) studied effects of horseback riding on adults with physical disabilities (ages 19–41), including people with head traumas, visual impairments, arthritis, cerebral palsy, and epilepsy. Participants were randomly assigned to either the riding group (2 x wk, 90-min sessions), having 15 adults assessed before and after the intervention, or the non-riding group, having 24 adults assessed after the intervention. Participants in the riding group demonstrated significant improvement in coordination but no significant improvement in self-concept and strength. Brock concluded that the use of therapeutic riding may assist individuals with disabilities in developing their coordination.

Self-Concept

Elliott, Funderburk, and Holland (2008) collected in-depth descriptive information on 10 individuals, five participants, and a parent of each participant, to determine the perceived impact of a therapeutic riding program on children with physical and cognitive disabilities. The participants reported a common theme of enjoyment in participation, and enjoyment and fun was supported by parents' comments. Other issues brought up by the children and their parents include the child/animal connection, social relationships with volunteers, perceived physical benefits, and the social and mental benefits of the program.

Cawley and colleagues (1994) studied effects of participation in a riding program on self-concept of 13 male and 10 female adolescent "first-time" riders and six "previous experience" riders (mean age 13) who had severe emotional disabilities, mental retardation, or learning disabilities. Participants attended 8-sessions (1 x wk, 120-min sessions) that included care and maintenance of horses and basic riding. Self-concept was measured using the Pier Harris Children's Self-Concept Scale before and after the intervention. Changes were not statistically significant except for the behavioral subset, which reflects extent to which the person admits or denies problematic behavior. Participants under 13 years of age showed greater improvement in measures of self-concept than those 14 and older. Limitations such as use of only one measure of self-concept, a small convenience rather than random sample, and lack of participant background information influence interpretation of results.

Language Development

Macauley and Gutierrez (2004) studied effects of 6 weeks of hippotherapy (2 x wk, 60-min session) on three boys (ages 9–11) with language-learning abilities. Participants and their parents each completed a satisfaction questionnaire at the end of their traditional speech and language therapy and then again at the end of the hippotherapy. While the participant rode the horse, a speech language pathologist led several activities with the participant, such as telling and re-telling stories to one another and determining different sounds in words. Questionnaires were compared and researchers reported that responses were noticeably higher following hippotherapy interventions and their appeared to be improvements with attention and motivation. Caution is advised when interpreting these results given the absence of objective performance measures and that measurement strategies only assessed perceptions of improvement as opposed to actual measurement of these behaviors.

Summary

Research has provided some limited support for the conclusion that physical benefits such as increased coordination and gait (Brock, 1989; Kulkarni-Lambore et al., 2001), motor control and balance (Biery & Kauffman, 1989; Chern et al., 2004), and decreased spasticity and hyperkensis (Ionatamishvili et al., 2002) might be achieved through therapeutic horseback riding. In addition to the physical benefits, participants might experience psychosocial benefits, such as improved problem-solving skills and a feeling that they have learned to cope with their disabilities (Ionatamishvili et al., 2002). Finally, improvements in self-concept (Cawley et al., 1994) and language-learning skills (Macauley & Gutierrez, 2004) were found.

In summarizing literature reviewed in this section, there was limited research found examining effects of therapeutic horseback riding. Although some research supports use of therapeutic horseback riding, since this research lacked adequate rigor, therapeutic horseback riding cannot yet be identified as an empirically supported facilitation technique. More research is needed that investigates immediate and long-term effects of horseback riding on development and improvement of physical skills such as coordination. In addition, research examining effects of horseback riding on psychological measures such as self-concept is needed.

Case Study

Sera

Sera was born with cerebral palsy. By 4 years of age, her speech was slightly impaired and she had spastic diplegia. Before beginning a therapeutic riding program, she sat and remained upright on her own; however, her trunk was rounded and asymmetrical. Her posture was stiff due to the spasticity of her muscle tone. It was difficult for her to relax her muscles in her lower extremities and she had poor support when standing. Her speech impediments were that she tended to stutter and speak unclearly.

Sera's physician suggested that her parents contact a local accredited therapeutic riding center and schedule an assessment. Sera was excited about being near horses and seemed eager and motivated. The therapeutic riding instructor determined that Sera would most likely benefit from exercises that stressed achievement of reduced spasticity and reduction of postural stiffness with a focus on normal movement such as trunk control, rotation through the body axis, weight shift, and dissociation at shoulders and pelvis. The horse would be used as a therapeutic tool.

Therapeutic Horseback Riding for Sera

Sera met Belle at her first lesson. Belle was a 12-year-old grey pony who stood 13 hands tall; an ideal size for Sera. Sera needed a pony with a narrow back due to the spasticity in her lower extremities. Belle's build allowed Sera to sit astride her comfortably. Initially, Sera rode on a sheepskin saddle pad that allowed her to sit in various positions required for exercises completed on the horse including prone, side-lying, or sitting position. When she became more accomplished at her exercises, a saddle with a suede cover was used. The suede cover helped her legs stick to the saddle. No adaptations were made to the reins.

Although Sera was excited about riding Belle, she was slightly apprehensive when participating in exercises the first time. This apprehension quickly faded, and by Sera's third lesson, her self-confidence had improved, with less fear of position change and movement. Sera became an active participant in her therapy.

Sera's lessons with Belle continued for 10 weeks. She rode in a group with two other children, twice weekly, for 1-hour sessions. Belle was lead at a walking pace with side-walkers with one on each side of the horse who helped Sera position herself when she started to lose her balance. A typical lesson would begin with Sera being in a prone position. The therapist would mobilize Sera's pelvis or shoulder and scapula to induce relaxation through horse movement. As muscle tone became more manageable, Sera moved into a side-lying position and a series of prone positions encouraging stretching and relaxation. Belle's pace was quickened or slowed to help facilitate normalized muscle tone in Sera. Some stretching exercises that Sera accomplished were reaching for the horse's ears, her own toes, and around toward Belle's tail while sitting in a forward-facing position on the horse. To help Sera strengthen her lower extremities and practice weight shifting, she sat in a squatting position with her feet in the stirrups supporting her weight while the therapist led Belle in different directions or up and down gradients. Balancing exercises were accomplished through extending her arms in different positions while sitting in a forward-facing position on Belle. Throughout the lessons, Sera was encouraged to give vocal commands to Belle such as walk, halt, and whoa (slow).

Summary

At the end of the 10-week program, Sera showed improvement in both her level of spasticity and her balance. She sat alone with her trunk extended and symmetrical with her upper extremities extended at her sides. Her lower extremities became more relaxed and she stood with fair control. Sera's speech did not improve significantly, but she became more vocal and attempted speech more frequently than when she first began her sessions. She was especially vocal when communicating with Belle. Sera is now 6 years of age and continues to ride Belle at the center. She rides at a trot without the help of side-walkers. Her goal is to eventually show Belle at local horse shows.

Intervention Implementation Exercises

The following exercises can be used as an enjoyable way to learn about horses. For participants who have little experience with horses, learning about horses can be challenging. It is helpful to have some knowledge of horses before handling them and using equipment commonly used during therapeutic horseback riding. The following exercises may be adapted to suit needs of different participants:

- Learning About Horses
- Pin the Tail on the Horse
- Equipment Trivia
- Musical Moves
- Horse Story

Learning About Horses

Often when group lessons are offered with horses, participants may have to share horses; therefore, while one person is with the horse, other participants wait their turn. Since riding lessons may be canceled due to rain, this is an excellent time to increase participants' knowledge of horses through games such as word searches, crossword puzzles, and matching games (Britton, 1991).

> For example, a matching exercise may be done where the rider matches certain equipment to where it fits on the horse's body and is then asked to name the equipment and possibly its different parts. The rider might instead be asked to match the body parts of the horse to the names of those parts. Giving riders different pictures of horses and asking them to talk about them, such as how they look or the breed of horse, may help participants learn to describe the horse while using correct horse terminology. Participants may also be asked to draw a picture or write about what riding means to them and how they feel they have progressed in the lessons.

Pin the Tail on the Horse

In this game, a chalkboard, easel, or other surface on which objects may be taped is needed. A large picture of a horse is cut into pieces according to the names of each body part, such as hoof, mane, withers, and hock. Each participant is given a piece of the horse with tape on the back or tape can be provided by the facilitator when it is each participant's turn. One-by-one participants approach the board, state the name of the body part, and tape the body part to the board where they believe it is found on the horse. The board will be blank so it may be helpful if someone with a head part goes first to provide a reference for the remaining body parts. If participants do not name the body part correctly, they may not put their body part on the horse. They must wait until it is their turn again to guess. If there are body parts at the end that have not been named, allow group members to provide assistance to each other.

Equipment Trivia

Participants identify different types of equipment such as saddle, reins, bridle, and stirrups and the proper usage of them during riding. If the game is played at the riding facility, equipment located in the tack room is suitable for identification and usage description. If equipment is unavailable, a large diagram of a horse can be displayed on a board or easel, and participants can either draw equipment on or attach equipment cutouts to the horse diagram. Participants can describe proper equipment usage while either drawing or attaching equipment cutouts.

Musical Moves

The facilitator may provide various types of music such as marches, waltzes, popular, and commonly known tunes such as *Yankee Doodle*, *Row, Row, Row Your Boat*, or *Mary Had a Little Lamb* for participants to imagine different gaits encountered during horseback riding. Participants can sit in upright positions maintaining postures similar to those required while riding. They can "match" the rhythm of various tunes to different gaits, such as walk, trot, or canter. For example, marching music may be paired with a trot, or waltz music may be paired with a canter. As the music is played, participants can simulate proper upper body movement generally used with walking, trotting, or cantering. Participants may be encouraged to "feel" the music. During riding, music can be played to encourage participants to become relaxed, maintain concentration, and become more animated or expressive (Kluwer, 1987).

Horse Story

The facilitator can ask participants to write a story about themselves and their experiences with horses that are real or imagined. Participants can write a story about the specific goal toward which they are working.

> For example, Adrienne's goal is to accomplish the vaulting task of standing on a horse's back while the horse circles the ring on a long line. Adrienne is currently at the sitting-only phase of her skill development. Adrienne can write about her feelings regarding the pursuit of her goal, her anticipated feelings during various phases of skill acquisition and development, and how she thinks she will feel once she has attained her goal.

Summary

The intervention implementation exercises presented in this chapter can be used to promote learning about horses and equipment related to horseback riding. Activities can be planned by focusing on proper mounting and riding techniques in addition to adaptive equipment required for mounting and riding. Participants' skills and knowledge regarding horses can be increased by utilizing activities described in this section and exercises can be individually designed to best meet the needs of participants.

Conclusion

Some support exists for use of therapeutic horseback riding for people with disabilities. Therapeutic horseback riding can improve the quality of life for individuals with physical, cognitive, emotional, and social disabilities (Scott, 2005). TR specialists can facilitate the therapeutic effect of horseback riding by planning specific goals and outcomes. It is helpful for therapists to prepare participants for riding sessions by gaining information about participants' experiences with and expectations of horseback riding. TR specialists can prepare for the riding session by knowing what types and sizes of horses will be ridden and what exercises will occur. In addition, establishing protocols and procedures that are within agency guidelines is suggested prior to implementing a therapeutic horseback riding program. It is helpful for the TR specialist to ensure accreditation of the riding facility and credentialing of the facilitator prior to the initial session. Overall, although the use of therapeutic horseback riding shows promise, additional efficacy research is needed.

Discussion Questions

1. What is the definition of therapeutic horseback riding?
2. What are the four classifications of therapeutic horseback riding?
3. What are some documented benefits of therapeutic horseback riding?
4. What are the different types of exercises that can be done in therapeutic horseback riding?
5. What are some considerations when choosing a horse to use for therapeutic horseback riding?
6. What are some different types of equipment that may be used during a therapeutic riding lesson?
7. What is the difference between hippotherapy, developmental riding therapy, and equine facilitated psychotherapy?
8. Why would a TR specialist choose therapeutic horseback riding over other interventions?
9. What type of knowledge is important for a volunteer to have?
10. What is the history of therapeutic horseback riding?

Resources

Agency Resources

American Hippotherapy Association, Inc.
136 Bush Road
Damascus, PA 18415
(888) 851-4592, FAX (570) 224-4462
http://www.americanhippotherapyassociation.org

Equine-Facilitated Mental Health Association
http://www.narha.org

Kiwanis Horses & Handicapped, Inc.
http://www.ege.com/kiwanis/

North American Riding for Handicapped Association (NARHA).
P.O. Box 33150
Denver, CO 80233
(800) 369-7433
http://www.narha.org

Patchwork Therapeutic Riding Center, Inc.
http://www. norwich.net/~dgrant/patchwk.htm

Special Equestrian Riding Therapy Inc. (SERT)
http://www. inst net.com/~sert/

References

Apel, L. (2007). Hippotherapy and therapeutic riding highlight. *Exceptional Parent, 37*(6), 28–34.

Bauer, J. J. (1972). *Riding for rehabilitation: A guide for handicapped riders and their instructors*. Toronto, Ontario: Canadian Stage and Arts Publications Limited.

Benjamin, J. (2000). An introduction to hippotherapy. Retrieved October 10. 2007 from http://www.narha.org/PDFfiles/Vaulting.pdf

Biery, M. J., & Kauffman, N. (1989). The effects of therapeutic horseback riding on balance. *Adapted Physical Activity Quarterly, 6,* 221–229.

Bliss, B. (2006). Alternatives: complementary therapies. Therapeutic horseback riding. *RN, 60*(10), 69–70, 83.

Britton, V. (1991). *Riding for the disabled*. London, UK: B. T. Batsford Ltd.

Brock, B. J. (1988). Effect of therapeutic horseback riding on physically disabled adults. *Therapeutic Recreation Journal, 22*(3), 32–43.

Brock, B. J. (1989). *Therapy on horseback: Psychomotor and psychological change in physically disabled adults*. Paper presented at the National Conference of the American Camping Association, Seattle, WA. (ERIC Document Reproduction Service No. ED 313 183).

Cawley, R., Cawley, D., & Retter, K. (1994). Therapeutic horseback riding and self-concept in adolescents with special needs. *Anthrozoos, 7,* 129–134.

Chern, R. J., Liao, H. F., Leung, H. W. C., & Hwang, A. W. (2004). The effectiveness of therapeutic horseback riding in children with spastic cerebral palsy. *Adapted Physical Activity Quarterly, 21*(2), 103–121.

Davies, J. A. (1988). *The reins of life: An instructional and informative manual on riding for the disabled*. London, UK: J. A. Allen & Co. Ltd.

DePauw, K. P. (1986). Horseback riding for individuals with disabilities: Programs, philosophy and research. *Adapted Physical Activity Quarterly, 3,* 217–226.

Elliott, S., Funderburk, J. A., & Holland, J. M. (2008). The impact of the "Stirrup Some Fun" therapeutic riding program: A qualitative investigation. *American Journal of Recreation Therapy, 7*(2), 19–28.

Equine Facilitated Mental Health Association (2007). *Equine Facilitated Psychotherapy Fact Sheet.* Retrieved October 10, 2007 from http://www.narha. org/SecEFMHA/FactSheet.asp

Heine, B. (1997). An introduction to hippotherapy. *Strides, 3*(2), 10–13.

Heipertz, W. (1981). *Therapeutic riding: Medicine, education, sports.* Ottawa, Ontario: National Printers.

Inside look at NARHA: Psychotherapy program. (1996). *Strides, 2*(4), 14.

Ionatamishvili, N. I., Tsverava, D. M., Loriya, M. S., Sheshaberidze, E. G., & Rukhadze, M. M. (2002). Riding therapy as a method of rehabilitation of children with cerebral palsy. *Human Physiology, 30*(5), 561–565.

Kluwer, C. (1987). *Social and therapeutic effects of riding therapy/hippotherapy.* Paper presented at the meeting of the Seminar on Health Benefits of Pets, Bethesda, MD.

Kulkarni-Lambore, S., McGuigan, S. A., Narula, N., & Sepelak, K. (2001). Kinematic gait analysis of an individual with cerebral palsy before and after hippotherapy. *Physical Therapy, 81*(5), A40. Retrieved April 13, 2007 from Expanded Academic ASAP database.

Macauley, B. L., & Gutierrez, K. M. (2004). The effectiveness of hippotherapy for children with language-learning disabilities. *Communication Disorders Quarterly, 25*(4), 205–218.

MacKinnon, J. R., Noh, S., Lariviere, J., MacPhail, A., Allan, D. E., & Laliberte, D. (1995). A study of therapeutic effects of horseback riding for children with cerebral palsy. *Physical & Occupational Therapy in Pediatrics, 15,* 17–31.

NARHA recognized new classification for therapeutic riding. (1996). *Strides, 2*(4), 6.

National American Riding for Handicapped Association Guide Book (NARHA). (1996). [Binder]. Denver, CO: Author.

National American Riding for Handicapped Association Standards and Accreditation Manual for NARHA Centers (NARHA). (2007). [Binder]. Denver, CO: Author.

Nichols, C. (2007) *Therapy horses.* New York: Bearport.

Nolt, B. H. (1995). *Equine facilitated therapy guidelines.* Pennsylvania State University: Department of Agriculture and Extension Education, College of Agricultural Sciences [Online]. Available: http://www.microserve.net/~eclogue/big.txt

Rhodes, G. (2002). *Vaulting: A Dynamic Approach To Therapeutic Riding.* Retrieved October 10, 2007 from http://www.narha.org/PDFfiles/Vaulting.pdf

Scott, N. (2005). *Special needs, special horses: A guide to the benefits of therapeutic riding.* Denton: University of North Texas Press.

Stumbo, N. J., & Peterson, C. A. (2004). *Therapeutic recreation program design: principles and procedures* (4th ed.). San Francisco: Benjamin Cummings.

Chapter 12
Therapeutic Massage

Sarah Brownlee and John Dattilo

Many people still depend on massage for relaxation;
however, the trend is to use massage therapy for medical purposes
such as injury recovery, pain reduction, headache control,
and for their overall health and wellness.

—Rebecca Birr and Kathy Zebrisky

Introduction

Touch is an important element of human behavior, and when used in a positive manner, it can have a positive impact on people's lives. Human service providers can use touch with clients in an attempt to communicate trust and instill a sense of comfort, security, and familiarity established through human connection. The *intentional* use of touch as a therapeutic modality, otherwise known as "therapeutic massage," is designed to use touch to achieve targeted therapeutic outcomes (Quinn, 1996).

One of the most common outcomes targeted through massage is the reduction of stress. Whether emotional, mental, or physical, stress affects the autonomic nervous system (Selye, 1946). The response, commonly called "fight or flight," physically prepares the body for action. Part of this readying process includes muscle tension. Prolonged stress and associated tension can create anxiety and physical pain and discomfort. This happens when mental tension and daily stress manifest in muscle tension through the release of hormones from the adrenal glands (Yates, 1990). Edwards and Bruce (2001) observed that the calming and soothing physical effects produced by massage can reduce anxiety and cause muscles to relax.

The connection between stress and health is an important consideration for therapeutic recreation (TR) specialists. Good health serves as an important foundation to experience leisure, and several models of practice in TR recognize the importance of addressing functional ability in preparing people to participate in recreation activities and experience leisure. By positively affecting management of pain and reducing anxiety, massage can positively affect physical and cognitive functioning. TR specialists can employ massage techniques to assist people in readying for leisure participation.

In addition, families and supporters may be incorporated in this readying process by providing basic massage techniques to their loved ones. Since people's lives are influenced by several "structures" of intimates, acquaintances, and associations, engaging people who are an integral part of someone's life in the therapeutic process can improve the efficacy of interventions (Bronfenbrenner,

1979). Assisting family members, friends, and caregivers to learn massage techniques can strengthen important bonds between the client and their social supports and can positively affect the mood and attitudes of both people receiving and providing massage (Hernandez-Reif, Field, Krasnegor, Martinez, Schwartzman, & Mavunda, 1999).

The purpose of this chapter is to present therapeutic massage as a possible TR facilitation technique. To begin, a series of definitions will be explained to clarify information regarding common terms used in association with therapeutic massage. Descriptions of massage techniques are then provided, and implications for incorporating massage into the practice of TR are also addressed. A brief history of massage will provide a context for the use of massage for therapeutic purposes, and theoretical foundations that support the use of therapeutic massage offer possible explanations of the therapeutic efficacy of massage. A review of the literature presents research that examines the use of massage as a way to reduce anxiety and pain and related effects associated with stress and tension. Case studies provide applied contexts in which massage is shown to be effective. Finally, sample massage routines are offered as suggested intervention implementation exercises.

Definitions

According to the American Massage Therapy Association (1999), massage therapy is the systematic and scientific manipulation of the body's soft tissue for therapeutic purposes. There are many different forms of massage therapy used in various settings by a diversity of professionals. The following is a sampling of some common techniques found in the United States, including:

- Swedish Massage
- Shiatsu
- Sport and Clinical Massage
- Reflexology
- Thai Massage
- Craniosacral Massage

Swedish Massage

Swedish massage uses gliding and kneading strokes on the more superficial layers of muscles for the purpose of increasing circulation and enhancing relaxation. In addition, active and passive joint movements are used to improve range of motion. Passive joint movements require another person to move one's body part through full range of motion around a joint. Active joint movements are performed independently and without assistance.

Shiatsu

Shiatsu, which originated in Japan, is a technique that is used to manipulate pressure points along the entire body with the intent of increasing the body's energy flow. It is based on the belief that the body is composed of meridians (channels of energy); blockages in meridians cause physical discomfort. Therefore, shiatsu is intended to release blockages by applying direct pressure to points along the meridians and restore natural energy flow.

Sport and Clinical Massage

Sport/clinical massage is intended to encourage optimal performance by assisting in recovery from vigorous activity and aiding in the management of injury. Deep pressure applied with the palms and fingers and strokes applied perpendicular to muscle fibers attempt to enhance contractile ability. Sport/clinical massage is frequently used in rehabilitation settings and with athletes.

Reflexology

Reflexology, tracing origins in India, China, and Egypt, uses finger pressure on points of referral found in the hands and feet to effect change in other parts of the body and is intended to impact the entire body. For instance, points at the tips of the toes correspond to the head and sinuses.

Thai Massage

Thai massage incorporates partnered full-body stretches in which one person positions another's body so as to create a stretch for various muscle groups that elongate or stretch tissue. The stretching of tissue is intended to facilitate circulation and range of motion.

Craniosacral Massage

Craniosacral massage is designed to enhance the flow of cerebrospinal fluid to prevent imbalances or blockages that may cause sensory or motor problems. Very light digital pressure applied at the base of the skull, along the spine, and at the sacrum is intended to release areas of restriction and compression.

Descriptions

Since Swedish massage is the most common form of massage practiced in the United States, more description of Swedish techniques will be presented. The following is a discussion of different types of massage strokes and the associated effects on bodily systems. This discussion is intended to provide foundational information to increase awareness of massage techniques to encourage effective communication with colleagues who are professional massage therapists. The following descriptions based on the writing of Claire (1995) are provided:

- Effleurage
- Petrissage
- Tapotement
- Vibration
- Friction
- Range of Motion Stretches

Effleurage

Long, slow, gliding strokes, most of which are referred to as *effleurage*, maintain contact with the body and are typically used to increase muscle relaxation and circulation. Effleurage is mostly performed using the broad palm surface of the hands. Thumbs, fingers, and knuckles may also be used. The term "effleurage" is derived from a French word referring to strokes that glide over the surface of the skin.

Petrissage

Petrissage involves kneading, squeezing, and rolling the muscle tissue and skin using one or two hands. Petrissage often follows effleurage and stimulates circulation at a deeper level.

Tapotement

Short, fast, percussive strokes are called *tapotement*. Applied using fingertips, sides of hands, and loosely closed hands, this technique breaks contact with the body and results in stimulation of the peripheral nervous system, or nerves found in the arms, legs, hands, feet, and superficial layers of the skin.

Vibration

Vibration is another technique that affects the nervous system that is particularly useful in working with people who are sensitive to touch. This technique involves lightly jostling an entire body part, usually an extremity, or muscle tissue. Jostling refers to the practice of lifting and lightly shaking a body part or rapidly shaking the hands while moving them over particular muscles.

Friction

A deeper technique, called *friction*, is often used in physical rehabilitation settings to address scar tissue. This technique involves deep finger or digital pressure and small movements across or along muscle or tendon fibers.

Range of Motion Stretches

Range of motion stretches gently guide body parts through the natural path of movement around a joint. Range of motion stretches are designed to increase and maintain healthy functioning and movement of joints.

Basic Therapeutic Massage Application

While collaborating with a professional massage therapist may be advisable in some situations, basic massage techniques may be learned by TR specialists and/or taught to family members and supporters. Parents of children with chronic health conditions have positively affected and mitigated complicating health factors by administering therapeutic massage, and parents and children have benefited from the interaction and supportive relationship (e.g., Hernandez-Reif et al., 1999). Family education and training sessions conducted by professional massage therapists may provide additional knowledge needed by TR specialists, families, and supporters in assisting people improve health conditions.

Advanced Therapeutic Massage Practice

Continuing education classes and workshops addressing massage technique may be useful for TR specialists interested in learning more about massage. The American Massage Therapy Association (AMTA) (2002), the non-profit professional organization for massage therapists, provides assistance in locating massage professionals and/or continuing education classes.

At times, it may be helpful for TR specialists to seek the advice of professional massage therapists. Building networks in the allied health community tends to promote better services for people who access TR programs.

The professional practice of therapeutic massage involving careful assessment, skilled palpation, and treatment planning to facilitate healing and recovery requires advanced training. The AMTA recommends that those interested in becoming professional massage therapists complete an accredited training program offering a minimum of 500 hours of in-class instruction including anatomy, physiology, kinesiology, massage theory, supervised hands-on practice, ethics, and business practices. In addition, 25 states and the District of Columbia regulate massage therapists, and most of these states legally require a minimum of 500 hours of instruction from state-recognized training programs. Currently, there are 70 U.S. programs accredited by the Commission on Massage Training Accreditation, and more than 37,000 massage therapists have successfully completed the examination to acquire certification through the National Certification Board for Therapeutic Massage (American Massage Therapy Association, 2001).

History

According to Field (1998), early estimates of the first uses of massage date back to at least 1800 B.C. Early forms of massage originated in China, Japan, and India and were usually part of a holistic approach to health, including exercise, diet, and the use of medicinal herbs. Many forms of massage used today, including shiatsu and Thai massage, are very similar to forms of massage used thousands of years ago.

Per Henrick Ling, who was not trained in medicine, applied his ideas and techniques to the treatment of disease and developed Swedish massage, the basis of many modern forms of massage therapy (Moyer, Rounds, & Hannum, 2004). Moyer and colleagues reported that although Swedish massage was resisted by the Swedish medical community, Ling persevered with assistance from some of his influential clients to gain acceptance from the medical community. Fritz (2000) reported that soon after the success of Ling, the Dutch physician, Johann Mezger, successfully reintroduced massage to the medical community using terms that are still used today.

Massage as a medical intervention was used widely until the 1940s, when pharmaceuticals became the predominant treatment. Currently, with the growth of the "alternative medicine movement," health care professionals are again considering therapeutic massage and other modalities to address health concerns (Field, 1998). However, Moyer and colleagues (2004) noted that massage therapy is currently one of the fastest growing sectors of complementary and alternative medical therapy, with visits to the massage therapists increasing 36% between 1990 and 1997 (Eisenberg et al., 1998).

While additional training in therapeutic massage is advisable for treating serious health conditions, massage as a facilitation technique may be provided TR specialists. However, many health care providers do not offer massage services and many insurance companies do not reimburse for therapeutic massage (Opinion Research Corporation International, 2001). Often, massage is used as an adjunct to medical treatment directed by a physician.

Theoretical Foundations

There are several theories and principles that have contributed to the development of massage techniques. The following theories are described:

- Gate Theory of Pain Relief
- Hormonal Influence on Pain Perception
- Muscle Relaxation
- Stress Reduction
- Interruption of Negative Chronic Posture

Gate Theory of Pain Relief

According to a consumer poll commissioned by the AMTA (Opinion Research Corporation International, 2001), one of the most popular reasons for providing therapeutic massage is for pain relief. The Gate Theory proposed by Melzack and Wall (1965) explains how massage influences pain perception. According to this theory, the brain receives signals of pressure before it receives pain stimuli. Nerve cells carrying pain stimuli are shorter than those carrying signals of pressure, thus the signal travels slower. When the central nervous system receives a certain amount, or *threshold*, of stimuli, it ceases to process subsequent signals. When the threshold is reached through pressure signals, the "gate" is closed, and pain is not experienced. It is theorized that the pressure of massage inhibits pain stimuli from being processed due to the phenomena described by the Gate Theory (Field, 1998).

Hormonal Influence on Pain Perception

Hormone levels, especially endorphins, also influence perception of pain (Eliot, 1994). Neurotransmitters, chemical messengers in the central nervous system, control production and release of pain relieving hormones, such as endorphins. Serotonin is an example of a neurotransmitter that triggers release of endorphins and therefore assists in pain management. Ironson and colleagues (1996) found evidence that massage increases serotonin thus decreasing pain perception and creating a sense of well-being.

Muscle Relaxation

While the Gate Theory and hormonal influences on pain perception may account for immediate and short-term pain alleviation, muscle relaxation can produce longer-lasting pain relieving effects. Overusing or overloading a muscle can result in taut muscular bands that may be painful and tender to the touch. These taut bands, referred to as *trigger points*, can also compress surrounding nerves and exacerbate feelings of pain. Managing the reasons for trigger point onset and application of massage techniques has been shown to be an effective approach to reducing pain through muscle relaxation (Simons, Travell, & Simons, 1999).

Stress Reduction

Whether emotional, mental, or physical, stress affects the autonomic nervous system, which controls all involuntary activities of the body (e.g., digestion, heart rate, hormone levels). Two aspects of the autonomic nervous system are the *sympathetic* nervous system that prepares the body for action and the *parasympathetic* nervous system that prepares the body for inaction. The response to stress, commonly called the "fight or flight" response, activates the sympathetic nervous system and physically prepares the body for action. Part of this readying process includes muscle tension triggered through the release of hormones from the adrenal glands (Yates, 1990). Unlike stress, massage activates the parasympathetic nervous system and triggers relaxation (Ireland & Olson, 2000).

Interruption of Negative Chronic Posture

Expanding on the idea that stress induces muscle tension, Reich (1961) claimed that every individual develops physical and mental/emotional "defenses" in response to stress. These defenses, if created through chronic stress, condition muscles to remain tense even after the stressor is no longer present. After time, these defenses become rigid patterns that the body grows accustomed to, and according to Reich, an "armor-like shield" is created. This chronic muscle tension restricts circulation and inhibits full range of motion (Simons et al., 1999). Massage addresses this chronic tension by gently stretching muscle, enhancing circulation, and triggering the parasympathetic nervous response (Ireland & Olson, 2000).

Rolf (1977) offered a similar perspective to Reich by claiming that chronic postural positions adopted in response to psychological stress, such as a stooped posture to avoid abusive blows, come to be integrally connected to the psychological trauma that created these postures. One way to help treat the psychological stress is to treat the problematic musculature and postural positioning through massage.

Effectiveness

Effects of "alternative therapies" in addressing a variety of physical conditions have been increasingly considered in health care (Opinion Research Corporation International, 2001). One alternative therapy, massage, is often used to reduce:

- Pain
- Anxiety
- Related Effects of Disability

Pain

Kunstler and colleagues (2004) conducted a multiple single-subject design with 4 elderly women with histories of chronic pain. The women received individual sessions which included hand massage and aromatherapy. By assessing pain with a pain rating scale, the participants rated significant different pre- and post-intervention. Participants identified satisfaction of results including relaxation, especially improved sleep patterns and pain diversion.

Irnich et al. (2001) compared effects of massage therapy and acupuncture among 177 adults (ages 18–85) with chronic neck pain in Germany using a placebo-controlled trial. Participants received acupuncture, massage, or "sham" laser acupuncture (5 sessions, 3 wks). Measures of pain were assessed using visual analogue scales and range of motion was assessed using 3-dimensional ultrasound motion analyzer. Assessments were performed before, during, 1 week after, and 3 months after treatment. After 1 week of treatment, pain related to motion was significantly reduced for the acupuncture group compared to the massage group. After 3 months, both acupuncture and massage groups showed reductions in pain related to motion; there were no significant differences between the two interventions in this long-term assessment. While immediate effects of massage on pain relief may not be apparent, massage may be effective at reducing chronic or long-term pain.

Preyde (2000) randomly assigned 98 adults with low-back pain (mean age 46) to one of four 6-session 1-month groups containing 22–26 participants: comprehensive massage (30–35-min session), soft-tissue manipulation (30–35-min session), exercise and posture education (15–20-min sessions), placebo "sham" laser therapy (20-min sessions). The Roland Disability Questionnaire (Roland & Morris, 1983), McGill Pain Questionnaire (Melzack, 1975), State-Trait Anxiety Index (STAI) (Spielberger, Gorsuch, & Lushene, 1970), and Modified Schober test for lumbar range of motion were performed before, immediately after, and 1 month after treatment. Compared to members of the exercise and laser groups, the massage group showed significantly improved function and decreased anxiety immediately and 1 month after treatment. The massage group also showed significantly reduced pain compared to other groups. There was no significant difference among groups for range of motion. Results indicate that massage may be effective in pain reduction and increased function among people with low back pain.

Hernandez-Reif, Dieter, and Field (1998) randomly assigned 26 adults (mean age 40; middle SEC; 69% Caucasian, 27% Hispanic, 4% African American) with migraine headaches to a wait-list control group (no intervention) or to a 5-week massage therapy group (2 x wk, 30-min sessions). Assessments taken the first and final days of the study included the Medical and Headache History Questionnaires (Saper, Silberstein, Gordon, & Hamel, 1995); VITAS Pain Scale (visual analogue scale); Symptom Checklist-90-R (Derogatis, 1983) for depression, anxiety, and hostility symptoms; headache log of frequency and intensity; sleep diary of number of hours slept and number of night wakings; and urine levels of serotonin. The massage therapy group showed fewer distress symptoms, reduced anxiety, less pain, more headache-free days, fewer sleep disturbances, and increased serotonin levels. Future research might assess longer-term effects of massage therapy or more intense massage therapy protocols to determine if effects can be maintained over time.

Massage compared to progressive relaxation for pain reduction. Many TR specialists are familiar with the use of progressive muscle relaxation therapy as a facilitation technique (Malley & Dattilo, 2000). A number of studies have compared therapeutic massage and relaxation therapy as experimental treatments and found more consistent positive effects for massage therapy in addressing pain and associated conditions.

Hernandez-Reif, Field, Krasnegor, and Theakston (2001) examined effects of a 5-week massage program (2 x wk, 30-min sessions) and progressive relaxation exercises (2 x wk, 30-min sessions) on 24 adults (13 women; mean age 40, middle SEC; M=2.5 Hollingshead Index; 67% Caucasian, 17% African American, 8% Hispanic, and 8% Asian) with chronic lower back pain. Pre- and post-test health indicators were collected via the Profile of Mood States Depression Scale (POMS-D) (McNair, Lorr, & Droppleman, 1971), STAI, Short-form McGill Pain Questionnaire (Melzack, 1987), and the Visual Analogue Scale. Spine length measures and a trunk flexion measure assessed range of motion. Depression, anxiety, and hostility were assessed using the Symptom Checklist-90 Revised (Derogatis, 1983), and sleep quality was measured using the Sleep Scale (Verran & Snyder-Halperin, 1988). Urine samples were tested for levels of cortisol, catecholamines (norepinephrine, epinephrine, dopamine), and serotonin. Significant improvements in mood and reductions in anxiety were reported for both groups. Both groups showed decreased pain on first day of treatment, but only the massage group showed decreased pain after both first and final days of treatment. Trunk flexion improved for massage group after one day of treatment. The massage group exhibited decreased depression while the relaxation group showed increased depression. The massage therapy group reported less sleep disturbance by the end of the study than did the relaxation group. There was a significant increase in serotonin and dopamine levels for the massage group. While both relaxation therapy and massage positively affected anxiety levels, massage showed better results in decreasing pain and depression and improving sleep quality.

Meyers, Robinson, Guthrie, and Lamp (1999) assessed effects of progressive muscle relaxation therapy and massage therapy on pain associated with sickle cell disease among 16 African-American adults (mean age 33). Participants either received six sessions of massage (30 min) or participated in 6 relaxation therapy sessions (30 min) within an 18-week period. Assessments taken on the first and last days of the study included analog scales of pain intensity and unpleasantness, the McGill Pain Questionnaire (Melzack, 1975), and the Sickness Impact Questionnaire (Bergner, Bobbitt, Carter, & Gibson, 1981). Both relaxation therapy and massage therapy were effective in decreasing short-term affective and sensory dimensions of pain and long-term affective and sensory dimensions of pain. Findings indicate that relaxation therapy and massage may be equally effective in reducing short-term and long-term pain among people with sickle cell disease.

Field et al. (1997b) investigated effects of 30-day massage therapy and relaxation therapy on 20 children (14 girls; mean age 10; middle SEC; 55% Hispanic, 40% Caucasian, 5% African American) with juvenile rheumatoid arthritis. Participants were randomly assigned to a massage group (15 min daily by parent) or a relaxation therapy group (15 min daily with parent). Assessments of anxiety included the STAI and behavioral observation of child anxiety by parents. Salivary cortisol samples were taken to indicate stress levels. Pain was measured using the Varni/Thompson Pediatric Pain Questionnaire—Parent and Child Forms (Varni, Thompson, & Hanson, 1987), and anatomical diagrams of severe pain points. Significant findings for the massage group suggested reduced anxiety for parents and children, lower cortisol levels among children and reduced pain. Reductions in anxiety and stress hormone (cortisol) could have assisted in reduced pain perception. Arthritis pain may be more effectively addressed using massage as opposed to relaxation therapy, and massage provided by family members showed benefits for parents and children.

Summary. Research examining effects of massage on pain (head, neck, and back) has shown increased function and reductions in long-term pain and associated discomforts, such as distress and anxiety. Research examining effects of massage and relaxation therapy on pain relief shows moderate support for use of massage instead of relaxation therapy. Pain management associated with arthritis, sickle cell disease, and back and neck discomfort may benefit from massage.

Anxiety

Nine female medical students (ages 21–25) received a 1-hour full body massage 1 day before an academic examination causing considerable anxiety (**Zeitlin, Keller, Shiflett, Schleifer, & Bartlett, 2000).** Assessments (blood samples testing natural killer cells and t-lymphocytes, self-report psychosocial data, vital signs) were obtained immediately before and after massage. Additional measures included the STAI and a visual analogue scale of perceived stress. Significant decreases in respiratory rate, anxiety, and perceived stress were noted from before and after massages. No significant differences between pre- and post-measures of blood pressure, pulse, or temperature were found. White blood cell count measures increased and percentage of T cells decreased. Although replication of effects with a larger sample and incorporation of a control group are needed, results support use of massage in reducing anxiety.

Field, Quintino, Henteleff, Wells-Keife, and Delvecchio-Feinberg (1997c) assessed effects of five interventions on stress among 100 employees (64 women; ages 22–38; middle SEC – 2.4 Hollingshead Index) of a public hospital. Participants were assigned to one of five groups providing short (10 min), one-time interventions: 2 massage therapy groups, music relaxation, muscle relaxation with visual imagery, and a social support group including discussions held in a supportive, relaxing environment. Results of the STAI and POMS indicated that all groups showed significant decreases in anxiety, depression, fatigue, and confusion as well as significantly increased vigor. Although intervention brevity and Hawthorne effects may have influenced results, there may be implications for workplace stress reduction.

In another study addressing workplace stress, **Shulman and Jones (1996)** used a quasi-experimental pre- and post-test control group design to assess effects of a 6-week massage program (n=18; 15 min, 1 x wk) and work breaks (n=15; 15 min, 1 x wk) among 33 clerical and professional workers (20 women; mean age 40). Participants were selected randomly by gender for one of the two groups. The State-Trait Anxiety Inventory was used to measure anxiety at the beginning and end of the study. The massage therapy group showed significant reductions in state anxiety (but not trait anxiety); however, there were no significant differences for the work break group. While participant homogeneity and small sample size limit generalizations, this study offers further support for massage in anxiety reduction, especially in the workplace.

Ferrell-Tory and Glick (1993) investigated effects of 30 minute massage sessions for 2 consecutive days on anxiety among 9 men (average age 57) diagnosed with cancer (esophageal, prostate, lung, stomach, rectum, leukemia, or lymphoma) and experiencing pain with cancer progression. Anxiety was measured using heart rate, systolic and diastolic blood pressure, respiratory rate, and mean arterial pressure. Visual analog scales were used for self-reported pain and relaxation. Participants experienced reduced pain and anxiety and increased relaxation. Day-one heart rate and diastolic blood pressure showed significant decreases. Respiratory rate and mean arterial pressure also decreased. Results of the STAI showed decreased anxiety. Although the sample was somewhat homogeneous, results provide support for massage as a way to reduce anxiety among people with cancer.

Fraser and Kerr (1993) used a pre- and post-test experimental design to assess effects of massage on muscle tension, relaxation, and anxiety among 21 older adult residents (17 women) of a long-term care facility. Participants were equally assigned to receive a 5-min massage group, a 5-min conversation group, or control group. Systolic and diastolic blood pressure, heart rate, and electromyography apparatus measured muscle activity, relaxation, and muscle tension. EMG activity was significantly lower for the treatment groups compared to the control group. Systolic blood pressure neared significant differences between the massage group and other two groups, and there were no significant findings for diastolic blood pressure and heart rate measures. The massage group showed significantly lower scores on the STAI compared to the control group; no significant differences were found between massage and conversation groups. Although treatment periods were extremely brief, significant differences between experimental and control groups lend support for use of massage to reduce anxiety.

In another study of older adults, **Semington and Laing (1993)** used a double-blind study to test effects of therapeutic touch, which is a massage technique based on transference of energy and intent to heal, on anxiety among 105 older adults living in two rural and two urban long-term care facilities. Participants were randomly assigned to either a therapeutic touch group (n=34) that received a therapeutic touch back rub; a control group (n=37) that received a routine back rub from a nurse trained in therapeutic touch who purposely did not focus on the intent to heal; or a control group (n=34) that received a routine back rub from a nurse unfamiliar with therapeutic touch. Results from the STAI indicated that the therapeutic touch group showed significantly lower anxiety levels than those in the second control group (nurse unfamiliar with therapeutic touch). Findings support the importance of positive intent in creating a healing environment.

Field, Morrow, Valdeon, Larson, Kuhn, and Schanberg (1992) tested effects of massage on anxiety of 72 children and adolescents (40 boys; mean age 13; lower SEC; 40% Caucasian, 40% Hispanic, 20% African American) with adjustment disorder, depression, or dysthymic disorder. Participants were equally assigned to either a massage group (5 x wk, 30-min sessions) or a relaxation video control group (5 x wk, 30-min sessions). Assessments of anxiety included: STAI, POMS, salivary cortisol samples, pulse rate, behavior observation ratings, urine cortisol and catecholamine (norepinephrine, epinephrine, and dopamine) levels, and sleep quality. The massage group showed decreased STAI scores and POMS scores. Improvements in behavior observation ratings were recorded as a result of the massage session but showed few long-term effects. Pulse rates showed immediate decreases for both massage and video groups but returned to baseline for video group by day 5; no long-term effects were recorded. Salivary and urinary cortisol levels decreased for the massage group, but no significant changes were found in urine catecholamine levels. Quality of sleep also improved for the massage group. Objective assessments (STAI and POMS) as well as physical manifestations of anxiety (sleep and cortisol levels) seem to be positively affected by massage among youth with mental health concerns.

McKechnie, Wilson, Watson, and Scott (1983) investigated effects of 10 sessions of connective tissue massage (30–45-min sessions) on relaxation and muscle tension among 5 adults (3 men; ages 26–56). Relaxation and muscle tension were measured using assessments of heart rate, electromyographic (EMG) readings, and skin resistance measures. Results indicated greater relaxation and reduced muscle tension among participants. Four participants experienced a reduction in heart rate, two showed significant increases in skin resistance, and two showed significant decreases in EMG readings. While the small sample size limits generalizations, findings suggest massage may reduce muscle tension often associated with anxiety.

Massage compared to progressive relaxation for anxiety reduction. Reduction of stress and anxiety are the most common goals of massage therapy (Opinion Research Corporation International, 2001) and relaxation therapy (Malley & Dattilo, 2000).

Studies comparing the two techniques have found that massage has more consistent results with anxiety reduction.

Field, Grizzle, Scafidi, and Schanberg (1997a) studied effects of 5 weeks of massage therapy (2 x wk, 30-min sessions) and relaxation therapy (2 x wk, 15-min yoga exercises, 15-min progressive muscle relaxation) on depression and anxiety of 32 adolescent girls of color who had recently given birth at a large urban hospital. All participants had elevated Beck Depression Inventory (Beck, Ward, Mendelson, Mock, & Erbaugh, 1961) scores, a diagnosis of dysthymia on the Diagnostic Inventory Schedule (Costello, Edelbrock, & Costello, 1985), and were free of medication or other treatment for depression. Assessments recorded on the first and last days of the study included: POMS and State Anxiety Inventory for Children (Spielberger, 1973); Behavior Observation Scales; pulse rate; and saliva and urine cortisol levels. State anxiety decreased for the massage group on the first and last day while the relaxation group showed similar decreases only on the first day. POMS depression scores were lower following the massage on the first and last days with significant changes in observed behaviors. Pulse rates decreased after massage therapy on days 1 and 10. Also, salivary cortisol levels were lower after massage, and urine cortisol levels were lower on the last day of massage than the first day. Some participants indicated relaxation therapy as "hard work;" further research incorporating more passive forms of relaxation may decrease negative experiences and create a more comparable control group.

Summary. Positive effects of massage on anxiety have been shown across groups (men and women of various ages) and settings (work, school, residential facilities). Results of these studies indicate flexibility and versatility of massage as an anxiety reduction intervention. Research also supports use of massage, as opposed to relaxation therapy, in reducing anxiety.

Related Effects of Disability

- Cerebral Palsy
- Csytic Fibrosis
- Eating Disorders
- Autism Symptoms

Cerebral palsy. Edwards and Bruce (2001) reported effects of massage therapy with a 24-year-old woman and 15-year-old boy with cerebral palsy. Verbal and written reports by the parent of the woman included reduced tension as well as improved sleep, range of motion, mood, and breathing. The parent of the boy reported reduced tension, improved breathing, and increased relaxation. Although reports consisted of subjective perceptions and observations, data from this study and relaxation effects described in previous studies suggest that massage may help reduce spasticity among people with cerebral palsy.

Cystic fibrosis. Hernandez-Reif and colleagues (1999) used a pre- and post-test experimental design to study 20 children with cystic fibrosis (ages 5–15; lower-middle

SEC; 35% Caucasian, 30% African American, 35% Hispanic) randomly assigned to a massage therapy treatment group (n=10, 20 min daily by parent, 30 days) or to a reading control group (n=10, 20 min daily by parent, 30 days). All parents were called bi-weekly as part of a compliance check. The State Anxiety Inventory for Children and POMS were used to assess anxiety. Peak air flow meters were used to monitor airflow through major airways. Although significant decreases in anxiety, improvements in mood, and improvements in air flow were reported for the massage group, effects for the reading group were not reported. Despite incomplete data reporting, findings indicate that reductions in anxiety and improvements in mood may be correlated with enhanced respiratory function and family members can be included in the provision of massage.

In other respiratory function research, **Beeken, Parks, Cory, and Montopoli (1998)** designed a case study (no control group) to explore effects of 24 weeks of neuromuscular therapy (1 x wk, 60-min session) on chronic obstructive lung disease (n=5; ages 57–74). While type of lung disease was not controlled, all individuals had moderate lung disease as determined by forced expiratory volume and/or forced vital capacity. Peak air flow was measured pre- and post-intervention by the Monaghan Peak Flow Meter, thoracic gas volume (amount of air present in lungs) was measured using the MED-Graphics System 1085 Plethysmograph, and pulmonary function was measured using the Cybermedic Moose Antler PFT System. Oxygen saturation (oxygen-saturated hemoglobin in blood), heart rate, and blood pressure were measured four times using a DINAMAP Vital Signs Monitor with OXYTRAK Pulse Oximeter. Findings showed improvements in peak air flow, decreases in heart rate, and increases in oxygen saturation. Results provide support for use of massage among people with compromised respiratory function.

Eating disorders. Field and colleagues (1998c) investigated effects of 5 weeks of massage therapy (2 x wk, 30-min sessions) and standard treatment (30–40 sessions/ wk of individual, family, small-group, community therapy; meetings with registered dietician; and nonverbal therapy) among 24 adolescent females (ages 16–21; middle-upper SEC; 68% Hispanic, 32% white) diagnosed with bulimia nervosa (DSM-III-R) residing in a treatment center. Assessments included: STAI; POMS Depression Scale; Behavior Observation Scale (Field et al., 1992); salivary cortisol measures indicating stress levels; Eating Disorders Inventory (Garner, Olmsted, & Polivy, 1983); Center for Epidemiological Studies Depression Scale (Radloff, 1977); urine samples to measure levels of cortisol, creatine, serotonin, and catecholamines (dopamine, epinephrine, and norepinephrine). The massage group showed immediate reductions in self-reported and observed anxiety and depression. By the last day of the study, significantly lower cortisol (stress) levels, lower depression scores, higher dopamine levels, and improved Eating Disorders Inventory sub-scales scores were found. No significant findings were identified for the standard treatment group. The treatment incorporated numerous interventions that address various concerns, and results indicate that massage seems to be an effective adjunct to standard treatment for people with bulimia.

Autism symptoms. Field and colleagues (1996) investigated effects of touch therapy on autism on 22 children (12 boys; mean age 5; middle SEC). An equal number of participants were assigned for 4 weeks (2 x wk, 15-min sessions) either a touch therapy group that received massage or a touch control group in which participants sat on the lap of a researcher and engaged in a color recognition activity. Assessments were taken the first and final days of the study. Children were observed for touch aversion, off-task behavior, orienting to irrelevant sounds, and stereotypic behaviors. Other assessments included the Autism Behavior Checklist (Krug, Arick, & Almond, 1979) and Early Social Communication Scales (Seibert, Hogan, & Mundy, 1982). Touch aversion and off-task behavior decreased for both groups. While both groups reduced orienting to irrelevant sounds and exhibiting stereotypic behaviors, the only significant changes were found for the massage group. The massage group also showed significant improvements in scores from the Autistic Behavior Checklist and Early Social Communication Scales. Results indicate that massage may be helpful in increasing attending behaviors among youth with autism.

Massage compared to progressive relaxation in addressing effects related to anxiety. Although some research limitations exist, several studies support massage therapy as a more effective technique than progressive relaxation in reducing anxiety. Anxiety potentially influences a number of body systems and functions in a negative manner (e.g., pulmonary functioning, attention, immune functioning, and hypertension). Therefore, conditions that are exacerbated by anxiety may improve more consistently with massage therapy than with progressive relaxation therapy.

Diego and Field (2001) compared effects of 12 weeks of interventions (2 x wk, 20-min sessions) of 24 HIV-positive adolescent girls (average age 17; 92% African American, 8% Hispanic) equally assigned to massage therapy or progressive relaxation on anxiety, depression, and immune function among participants completed a demographic questionnaire, and on the first and last days of the study, completed the CES-D Scale (Radloff, 1977) and the STAI to assess depression; blood tests determined indicators of immune function. Compared to the progressive relaxation group, the massage group showed improved immune function as indicated by increased levels of t-lymphocytes and natural killer cells. The massage group reported feeling less depressed than the progressive relaxation group. The link between negative mood and depressed immune function may be mitigated through massage therapy more effectively than by relaxation therapy.

Hernandez-Reif et al. (2000) assessed effects of massage and progressive muscle relaxation on hypertension of 30 adults (16 women; average age 52; middle SEC – 2.3 Hollingshead Index; 60% Caucasian, 27% Hispanic, 13% African American). Participants received treatment for 30 min, 2 x wk for 5 weeks and were randomly assigned a massage group or progressive muscle relaxation group. Assessments taken before and after first and final sessions included the STAI; salivary cortisol levels as an indicator of stress; systolic and diastolic blood pressure; the CES-D Scale (Radloff, 1977); Symptom Checklist – 90 Revised, a self-report of depression, anxiety, and hostility symptoms (Derogatis, 1983); and urinary catecholamines and cortisol as indicators of stress. Significant reductions were noted in anxiety for both the massage and relaxation group. Salivary cortisol levels decreased with the massage group. No significant effects were found for systolic blood pressure for either group. However, significant decreases in sitting and reclining diastolic blood pressure were recorded for the massage group. While both groups showed improved scores on the CES-D, only the massage group's scores were significant. Reductions in self-report depression, anxiety, hostility, and decreased urinary cortisol were recorded for the massage group. While objective measures of anxiety were positively affected by both massage and relaxation therapy, only massage had positive effects on subjective reports of anxiety as well as measures of depression and somatic indications of stress (blood pressure and cortisol).

Field et al. (1998a) examined effects of massage therapy and relaxation therapy on 32 children with asthma (62% male; ages 4–14; middle SEC – 3.9 Hollingshead Index, 50% Hispanic, 36% African American, 14% Caucasian) randomly and equally assigned for 30 days for 20 min/day before bed by parent to a massage group or a relaxation therapy group. Assessments taken the first and final days of the study included a salivary cortisol measure of stress; videotapes coded for affect, anxiety, activity, and vocalization; the STAI; and measures of pulmonary function including forced vital capacity, forced expiratory volume, forced expiratory flow, and peak expiratory flow rate. Anxiety levels decreased for the massage group after the first day. Activity, vocalization, and salivary cortisol levels improved for the massage group after the first and final sessions. All pulmonary function measures showed significant improvement for the massage group. No significant changes were recorded for the relaxation group. Results indicate that massage may be effective in reducing anxiety and thus improving respiratory function among youth with asthma.

Field, Quintino, Hernandez-Reif, and Koslovsky (1998b) assessed compared effects of 10 days of 15-min either massage therapy and relaxation therapy on 28 adolescent boys (90% middle SEC; 71% white, 29% Hispanic) with attention deficit hyperactivity disorder (ADHD). Assessments completed on the first and last days of the study included the Happy Face Scale; three-point measure of fidgeting; Center for Epidemiologic Studies Depression Scale (CES-D, Radloff, 1977); Empathy Scale (Bryant, 1982); Conners Rating Scale (Conners, 1985); and teacher reports of time spent on tasks in the classroom. The massage group rated themselves happier and fidgeted less following treatment than the relaxation group. No significant changes were found using the depression and empathy scales. After the interventions were completed, teachers reported that the massage group spent more time on task and exhibited fewer hyperactivity behaviors than the relaxation group. Findings show support for use of massage in increasing attending behaviors among adolescents with ADHD.

Summary. Decreased muscle tension and anxiety associated with massage appear to have positive effects for a number of health conditions. Research examining effects of massage indicate improvements in respiratory function, enhanced recovery from eating disorders, increased attention among people with autism, and decreased spasticity associated with cerebral palsy. Also, research shows support for reducing stress through massage therapy rather than through progressive relaxation therapy to improve immune function, reduce hypertension, improve respiratory function, and increase attention.

Overall Summary

Research on the uses of massage in reducing pain, anxiety, and muscle tension has shown that massage is a versatile facilitation technique that can be used in diverse settings with various populations. Results of studies indicate use of massage has positive effects across the life span and across environments in management of pain and anxiety. In addition, massage has been found to positively influence symptoms associated with compromised respiratory function, eating disorders, cancer, autism, and cerebral palsy. In addition, Moyer et al. (2004) conducted a meta-analysis of 37 studies that used random assignment to examine effects of single-dose and multiple-dose types of massage therapy. They found a statistically significant overall effect of both types for physiological and psychological outcomes.

As research has indicated, massage seems to be an effective facilitation technique in addressing health concerns associated with stress, tension, pain, and anxiety. These effects associated can improve a person's ability to experience leisure. One study of effects of massage on mood and well-being provides further support for use of massage in improving quality of life. Smith and colleagues (1999) used a descriptive, qualitative evaluation of hospital-based massage therapy to assess effects experienced by 70 patients and observed by 18 healthcare providers that included 4 massage therapists; post-treatment questionnaires provided data. Participants reported increased relaxation (98%); sense of well-being (93%); positive mood change (88%); positive changes in mobility, energy, treatment participation, and increased rate of recovery (66%); reduced muscle tension and anxiety (28.6%); pain reduction (25.7%); feelings of psychological support (22.9%); and enhanced ability to sleep (14.3%). Enhanced body awareness and physical functioning were also among reported effects. Approximately one third of participants experienced long-term effects of massage (1–7 days or more), the remaining participants experienced shorter-term effects. Health care providers indicated that relaxation, a sense of well-being, and positive change in mood were most common effects of massage. Use of massage therapy to reduce stress, pain, and anxiety can improve the chance that people will engage in desired leisure pursuits.

Case Studies

Cliff

Cliff was 83 years old and had been living in a nursing home for 3 years. He had broken his right hip 10 years prior, and his activity level had decreased progressively since then. Cliff spent much of the day sitting and playing cards or watching television. He complained of upper back pain. Assessments ruled out nerve impingement, fractured vertebrae, and herniated disk.

The TR specialist at the nursing home suggested to Cliff that massage therapy may help relieve some of his pain. He agreed to participate in 30 minutes of massage twice a week for 4 weeks. The massage sessions were conducted with Cliff seated comfortably in a chair. The massage included light gliding pressure to the back; pressing the muscles that are parallel to the spine; gentle squeezing pressure at the shoulder, neck, and arm muscles; range of motion stretches at the shoulder; and gentle downward pressure on the shoulders.

After completing 4 weeks of massage, Cliff reported reduced pain and more comfort associated with arm and shoulder movement. Since Cliff's activity level had been reduced for several years, an imbalance in muscle strength and flexibility had developed. The TR specialist suggested future sessions with a professional massage therapist to address Cliff's lower body tension, in addition to upper body pain, to facilitate increased activity.

Kashie

Kashie was a 17-year-old senior in high school. She had been dealing with recurring episodes of bulimia for 2 years and had experienced significant anxiety and depression associated with body image and social life. A good friend of Kashie's finally convinced her to visit a community program offering support for those with eating disorders. Everyone participating in the program met with a psychotherapist and dietician and participated in group therapy sessions. In addition, Kashie decided to try basic massage therapy offered by the TR specialist who worked with the program.

Kashie received a 60-minute massage once a week for 8 weeks. Kashie remained fully clothed during the massage sessions, which included 30 minutes in a supine position and 30 minutes in a prone position. The sessions consisted of gentle traction at the neck with the patient in a supine position, light squeezing pressure at the neck and shoulders, depressing the shoulders, traction at each arm, gliding and gentle squeezing strokes over the length of the arm, and hand massage. The same techniques used with the arms and hands were applied to legs and feet. In prone position, the session included gliding and gentle squeezing strokes from the feet to the hips, sacral traction, gliding strokes to the length of the back, friction along the spine and back of the hips, and gentle squeezing pressure at the shoulders and neck.

After participating in half of the massage sessions, Kashie reported feeling more relaxed and experiencing an increased sense of well-being. She commented that her feelings of anxiety had gradually reduced. By completing the final session, Kashie reported that she felt more "in tune" with her body. After further meetings with the dietician and psychotherapist and occasional massage sessions, Kashie felt that she had developed a healthier perspective about her body and health.

Intervention Implementation Exercises

A range of massage therapy techniques and styles exist, and use of certain techniques is dependent on the condition of the individual. However, as evidenced by studies including parents as massage therapists, basic techniques can be learned and taught fairly easily.

The following are sample routines that may be serve as references for performing therapeutic massage. The comfort of the individual is paramount; orthopedic, health, and psychological factors should be considered when deciding on appropriate positioning. Pressure and type of stroke should be modified according to participant feedback. In accommodating participant comfort, it is possible to achieve desired effects when conducting sessions while participants remain fully clothed. However, if clothing is removed, all body parts not being massaged should remain completely covered using a sheet, blanket, or large towel.

Participant in prone position (lying face down) with bolster or pillow under ankles. Unless a massage table with face cradle is available, the prone position may be uncomfortable for long sessions due to a prolonged rotated neck position. If it is not possible to maintain a neutral neck position, the prone position should be used for short sessions lasting no more than 10 minutes.

To begin, warm superficial tissues by using broad flat palm pressure of hands down the back from shoulders to back of hips. This stroke is performed while standing facing the top of participant's head. Repeat these strokes 3–5 times. While keeping a neutral wrist position, use back of fingers and knuckles to apply gliding pressure from shoulders to back of hips. This stroke will stimulate circulation at a deeper level. Gently squeeze shoulder and neck muscles between fingers and palm. Using fingertips, apply short back and forth movements to muscles next to the spine and outward along back of hip bone. Using palms, apply gentle pressure at back of hips in direction of legs to create traction between hips and sacrum and spine. Using broad palm pressure, apply long gliding strokes to back of entire leg. Reduce pressure when passing over the back of knee. Using gentle squeezing pressure between fingers and palm, knead muscles at back of thigh and calves. Press muscles at back of thigh and calves using palm pressure.

Participant in supine position (on back) with a bolster or pillow under knee. While sitting and facing top of participant's head with hands beneath head and fingers at base of skull, gently apply pulling pressure at neck to create traction among cervical vertebrae. With fingers under base of neck and upper shoulder, apply gentle squeezing pressure between fingers and thumb. Place palms on shoulders and gently press shoulders down away from neck.

While standing at the participant's side, hold arm at elbow (their hand should be supported near your elbow), and apply gentle pulling pressure away from shoulder. Using broad palm pressure, apply smooth strokes over length of arm. Using thumbs, apply spreading pressure to participant's palm. This is done by placing both thumbs in center of participant's palm and stroking outward toward sides of hand. Gently squeeze each finger starting near palm and moving to fingertips.

Using broad palm pressure, apply long gliding strokes to entire leg. Reduce pressure when passing over the knee. Using a gentle squeezing pressure between fingers and palm, knead muscles at the thigh. Press muscles at thigh using palm pressure. Use gliding palm pressure on either side of shin. Place fingers at bottom of foot (plantar) near arch and thumbs on top of foot. Gently pull fingers toward side of foot. Repeat stroke to massage entire bottom of foot.

To enhance range of motion, light stretches and easy movements are used. Using one hand to support leg at back of knee gently lift and bend knee to move thigh toward torso (hip and knee range of motion). Cup fingers around heel (participant's toes will rest against forearm) and lift top of foot toward knees to create a calf stretch. With hands holding lower leg, slowly and gently apply pulling pressure to leg away from hips.

Seated Massage. This position may be the most comfortable for participants, particularly if moving or lying is arduous or painful. Seated massage is performed while participant is fully clothed. If a massage chair is available, this is the best option to maximize comfort. However, any chair may be used in seated massage.

Participant should be seated comfortably with enough space to lean forward over lap, a tabletop, desktop, or back of a chair. Participant is encouraged to relax and position self in most comfortable position throughout session (i.e., sitting upright, leaning over lap, forehead resting on arms on top of table or desk).

Using light gliding palm pressure, apply long broad strokes to the back starting at shoulders and moving toward back of hips. While using palms, press muscles parallel to spine and move from shoulders to back of hips. Using gentle squeezing pressure between fingers and palm, knead shoulder and upper arm muscles. Using fingertips, apply short back and forth movements to muscles next to the spine and outward along back of hip bone. Using palms, apply circular strokes at the low back above hips.

Using gentle squeezing pressure between fingers and palm, knead arm from shoulder to lower arm. Using thumbs, apply spreading pressure to participant's palm by placing both thumbs in center of participant's palm and stroking outward toward sides of the hand. Gently squeeze each finger starting near the palm and moving to fingertips. Supporting the lower arm, gently raise participant's arm out to their side and above their head. Gently squeeze shoulder and neck muscles between fingers and palm. Using fingertips, gently apply circular pressure along the base of the skull and along the side of the neck. Using fingertips, apply circular pressure to scalp. Place palms on participant's shoulders, and gently press shoulders down away from neck.

Communication is an important consideration when using massage as a TR facilitation technique. It is helpful to educate participants and colleagues about the process and effects of massage before using this technique.

Conclusion

Therapeutic massage is the manipulation of the body's soft tissue for therapeutic purposes. The physical and psychological effects of massage can reduce pain and anxiety by inhibiting pain perception, encouraging release of neurotransmitters, reducing muscle tension, addressing problematic chronic postural imbalances, and triggering the parasympathetic nervous system. While therapeutic massage used in professional treatment of specific conditions includes careful assessment, skilled palpation, advanced knowledge of anatomy and physiology, and treatment planning, basic therapeutic massage techniques may be learned and applied fairly easily to reduce stress, tension, pain, and anxiety. By providing or coordinating training of basic techniques, TR specialists can help family members and friends assist people in preparing for leisure participation. TR specialists who use basic therapeutic massage techniques and/or rely on referrals to professional massage therapists can help people be able to participate in activities of their choosing.

Discussion Questions

1. What is the most common form of massage practiced in the United States?
2. Name and describe common techniques associated with Swedish massage.
3. What distinguishes applying basic therapeutic massage techniques from advanced professional practice of therapeutic massage?
4. How can using therapeutic massage as a TR facilitation technique engage family members?
5. What is the name of the national organization that represents the massage therapy profession?
6. In which countries and cultures did the earliest forms of massage originate?
7. Name and explain two theories that are important in understanding effects of massage.
8. Although massage has been shown to affect many health conditions, which two conditions has research shown to most consistently benefit from massage?
9. What two benefits did Cliff experience after participating in massage therapy?
10. What effects did therapeutic massage have for Kashie?
11. What is the most important consideration when using therapeutic massage as a therapeutic recreation facilitation technique?

Resources

Agency Resources

American Massage Therapy Association
820 Davis Street, Suite 100
Evanston, Illinois 60201-4444
(847) 864-0123, FAX (847) 864-1178
E-mail: info@amtamassage.org
http://www.amtamassage.org

References

American Massage Therapy Association. (1999). *Massage therapy: Enhancing your health with therapeutic massage*. Retrieved October 2, 2001, from http://www.amtamassage.org

American Massage Therapy Association. (2001). *Massage career brochure: Becoming a professional massage therapist*. Retrieved April 15, 2002, from http://www.amtamassage.org/publications/career_brochure.html

American Massage Therapy Association. (2002). *Starting a career in massage therapy: What you need to know*. Retrieved April 15, 2002, from http://www.amtamassage.org/becometherapist/starting.htm

Beck, A. T., Ward, C. H., Mendelson, M., Mock, J., & Erbaugh, J. (1961). An inventory for measuring depression. *Archives of General Psychiatry, 4,* 561–571.

Beeken, J. E., Parks, D., Cory, J., & Montopoli, G. (1998). The effectiveness of neuromuscular release massage therapy in five individuals with chronic obstructive lung disease. *Clinical Nursing Research, 7*(3), 309–326.

Bergner, M., Bobbitt, R. A., Carter, W. B., & Gibson, B. S. (1981). The Sickness Impact Profile: Development and final revision of a health status measure. *Medical Care, 19,* 787–805.

Bronfenbrenner, U. (1979). *The ecology of human development.* Cambridge, MA: Harvard University Press.

Bryant, B. K. (1982). An index of empathy for children and adolescents. *Child Development, 53,* 413–425.

Claire, T. (1995). *Bodywork: What type of massage to get – and how to make the most of it.* New York: William Morrow and Company, Inc.

Conners, C. K. (1985). *The Conners Rating Scales: Instruments for the assessment of childhood psychopathology.* Unpublished manuscript, Children's Hospital National Medical Center, Washington, DC.

Costello, E. J., Edelbrock, C. S., & Costello, A. J. (1985). Validity of the NIMH Diagnostic Interview Schedule for children: A comparison between psychiatric and pediatric referrals. *Journal of Abnormal Child Psychology, 13,* 579–595.

Derogatis, L. R. (1983). Symptom Checklist 90-Revised. *Administration, scoring and procedures manual II.* Clinical Psychometric Research.

Diego, M. A., & Field, T. (2001). HIV Adolescents show improved immune function following massage therapy. *International Journal of Neuroscience, 106*(1–2), 35.

Edwards, D., & Bruce, G. (2001). For cerebral palsy patients massage makes life better. *Massage Magazine, 92,* 93–110.

Eisenberg, D. M., Davis, R. B., Ettner, S. L., Appel, S., Wilkey, S., Van Rompay, M., et al. (1998). Trends in alternative medicine use in the United States, 1990-1997: Results of a follow-up national survey. *Journal of the American Medical Association, 280,* 1569–1575.

Eliot, R. S. (1994). *From stress to strength: How to lighten your load and save your life.* New York: Bantam Books.

Ferrell-Tory, A. T., & Glick, O. J. (1993). The use of therapeutic massage as a nursing intervention to modify anxiety and the perception of cancer pain. *Cancer Nursing, 16*(2), 93–101.

Field, T. (1998). Touch therapy effects on development. *International Journal of Behavioral Development, 22*(4), 779–797.

Field, T., Grizzle, N., Scafidi, F., & Schanberg, S. (1997a). Massage and relaxation therapies' effects on depressed adolescent mothers. *Adolescence, 31*(124), 903.

Field, T., Henteleff, T., Hernandez-Reif, M., Martinez, E., Mavunda, K., Kuhn, C., & Schanberg, S. (1998a). Children with asthma have improved pulmonary functions after massage therapy. *Journal of Pediatrics, 132*(5), 854–858.

Field, T., Hernandez-Reif, M., Seligman, S., Krasnegor, J., Sunshine, W., Rivas-Chacon, R., & Schanberg, S. (1997b). Juvenile rheumatoid arthritis: Benefits from massage therapy. *Journal of Pediatric Psychology, 22*(5), 607–617.

Field, T., Lasko, D., Mundy, P., Henteleff, T., Talpins, S., & Dowling, M. (1996). Autistic children's attentiveness and responsitivity improved after touch therapy. *Journal of Autism and Developmental Disorders, 27,* 329–334.

Field, T., Morrow, C., Valdeon, C., Larson, S., Kuhn, C., & Schanberg, S. (1992). Massage reduces anxiety in child and adolescent psychiatric patients. *Journal of the American Academy of Child and Adolescent Psychiatry, 31*(1), 125–131.

Field, T., Quintino, O., Henteleff, T., Wells-Keife, L., & Delvecchio-Feinberg, G. (1997c). Job stress reduction therapies. *Alternative Therapies, 3*(4), 54–56.

Field, T., Quintino, O., Hernandez-Reif, M., & Koslovsky, G. (1998b). Adolescents with attention deficit hyperactivity disorder benefit from massage therapy. *Adolescence, 33*(129), 103.

Field, T., Schanberg, S., Kuhn, C., Fierro, K., Henteleff, T., Mueller, C., Yando, R., Shaw, S., & Burman, I. (1998c). Bulimic adolescents benefit from massage therapy. *Adolescence, 33*(131), 555.

Fraser, J., & Kerr, J. R. (1993). Psychophysiological effects of back massage on elderly institutionalized patients. *Journal of Advanced Nursing, 18,* 238–245.

Fritz, S. (2000). *Mosby's fundamentals of therapeutic massage.* St. Louis: Mosby.

Garner, D. M., Olmsted, M. P., & Polivy, J. (1983). The Eating Disorders Inventory: A measure of cognitive-behavioral dimensions of anorexia nervosa and bulimia. In P. L. Darby, P. E. Garfinkel, D. M. Garner, & D. V. Coscina (Eds.), *Anorexia nervosa: Recent developments in research* (pp. 173–184). New York: Alan R. Liss.

Hernandez-Reif, M., Dieter, J., Field, T. (1998). Migraine headaches are reduced by massage therapy. *International Journal of Neuroscience, 96*(1–2), 1–12.

Hernandez-Reif, M., Field, T., Krasnegor, J., Martinez, E., Schwartzman, M., & Mavunda, K. (1999). Children with cystic fibrosis benefit from massage therapy. *Journal of Pediatric Psychology, 24*(2), 175–181.

Hernandez-Reif, M., Field, T., Krasnegor, J., & Theakston, H. (2001). Lower back pain is reduced and range of motion increased after massage therapy. *International Journal of Neuroscience, 106*(3/4), 131–146.

Hernandez-Reif, M., Field, T., Krasnegor, J., Theakston, H., Hossain, Z., & Burman, I. (2000). High blood pressure and associated symptoms were reduced by massage therapy. *Journal of Bodywork and Movement Therapies, 4*(1), 31–38.

Ireland, M., & Olson, M. (2000). Massage therapy and therapeutic touch in children: State of the science. *Alternative Therapies in Health and Medicine, 6*(5), 54–63.

Irnich, D., Behrens, N., Molzen, H., Konig, A., Gleditsch, J., Krauss, M., Natalis, M., Senn, E., Beyer, A., & Schops, P. (2001). Randomized trial of acupuncture compared with conventional massage and "sham" laser acupuncture for treatment of chronic neck pain. *British Medical Journal, 322*(7302), 1574–1580.

Ironson, G., Field, T., Scafidi, F., Kumar, M., Patarca, R., Price, A., Goncalves, A., Hashimoto, M., Kumar, A., Burman, I., Tetenman, C., & Fletcher, M. (1996). Massage therapy is associated with enhancement of the immune system's cytotoxic capacity. *International Journal of Neuroscience, 84,* 205–218.

Krug, D., Arick, J., & Almond, P. (1979). Autism screening instrument for educational planning: Background and development. In J. Gilliam (Ed.), *Autism: Diagnosis, instruction, management and research.* Austin, TX: University of Texas Press.

Kunstler, R., Greenblatt, F., & Moreno, M. (2004). Aromatherapy and hand massage: Therapeutic recreation interventions for pain management. *Therapeutic Recreation Journal, 38*(2), 133–147.

Malley, S., & Dattilo, J. (2000). Stress management. In J. Dattilo (Ed.), *Facilitation techniques in therapeutic recreation* (pp. 215–244). State College, PA: Venture Publishing, Inc.

McKechnie, A. A., Wilson, F., Watson, N., & Scott, D. (1983). Anxiety states: A preliminary report on the value of connective tissue massage. *Journal of Psychosomatic Research, 27*(2), 125–129.

McNair, D. M., Lorr, M., & Droppleman, L. F. (1971). *POMS-Profile of Mood States.* San Diego: Educational and Industrial Testing Service.

Melzack, R., & Wall, P. D. (1965). Pain mechanisms: A new theory. *Science, 150,* 971–978.

Melzack, R. (1975). The McGill Pain Questionnaire: Major properties and scoring methods. *Pain, 1,* 277–299.

Melzack, R. (1987) The short-form McGill Pain Questionnaire. *Pain, 30,* 191–197.

Meyers, C. D., Robinson, M. E., Guthrie, T. H., & Lamp, S. P. (1999). Adjunctive approaches for sickle cell chronic pain. *Alternative Health Practitioner, 5*(3), 203–212.

Moyer, C. A., Rounds, J., & Hannum, J. W. (2004). A meta-analysis of massage therapy research. *Psychological Bulletin, 130*(1), 3–18.

Opinion Research Corporation International. (2001). *2001 Massage Therapy Consumer Survey Fact Sheet.* Evanston, IL: American Massage Therapy Association.

Preyde, M. (2000). Effectiveness of massage therapy for subacute low-back pain: A randomized controlled trial. *Canadian Medical Association Journal, 162*(13), 1815–1821.

Quinn, J. F. (1996). Intention to heal: Perspectives of a therapeutic touch practitioner and researcher. *Advances: The Journal of Mind-Body Health, 12*(3), 26–30.

Radloff, L. (1977) The CES-D scale: A self-report depression scale for research in the general population. *Applied Psychological Measurement, 1,* 385–401.

Reich, W. (1961). *Character analysis.* New York: Noonday Press.

Roland, M., & Morris, R. (1983). A study of the natural history of back pain. Part I: Development of a reliable and sensitive measure of disability in low-back pain. *Spine, 8,* 141–144.

Rolf, I. P. (1977). *Rolfing: The integration of human structure.* Santa Monica, CA: Dennis-Landman.

Saper, J., Silberstein, S., Gordon, C., & Hamel, R. L. (1995). *Handbook of headache management: A practical guide to diagnosis and treatment of head, neck and facial pain.* Baltimore: Williams and Wilkins.

Seibert, J. M., Hogan, A. E., & Mundy, P. C. (1982). Assessing interaction competencies: The Early Social-Communication Scales. *Infant Mental Health Journal, 3,* 244–245.

Selye, H. (1946). The general adaptation syndrome and the disease of adaptation. *Journal of Clinical Endocrinology, 6,* 117–127.

Semington, J. A., & Laing, G. P. (1993). Effects of therapeutic touch on anxiety in the institutionalized elderly. *Clinical Nursing Research, 2*(1), 438–451.

Shulman, K. R., & Jones, G. E. (1996). The effectiveness of massage therapy intervention on reducing anxiety in the workplace. *The Journal of Applied Behavioral Science, 32*(2), 160–173.

Simons, D. G., Travell, J. G., & Simons, L. S. (1999). *Travell and Simons' myofascial pain and dysfunction: The trigger point manual* (2nd ed.). Baltimore: Williams and Wilkins.

Smith, M. C., Stallings, M. A., Mariner, S., Burrall, M. (1999). Benefits of massage therapy for hospitalized patients: A descriptive and qualitative evaluation. *Alternative Therapies in Health and Medicine, 5*(4), 64–72.

Spielberger, C. D. (1973). *State Trait Anxiety Inventory for Children*. Palo Alto, CA: Consulting Psychologists Press.

Spielberger, C. D., Gorsuch, R. L., & Lushene, R. E. (1970*). The State-Trait Anxiety Inventory*. Palo Alto, CA: Consulting Psychologists Press

Varni, J. W., Thompson, K. L., & Hanson, V. (1987). The Varni/Thompson Pediatric Pain Questionnaire. I: Chronic musculoskeletal pain in juvenile rheumatoid arthritis. *Pain, 28,* 27–38.

Verran, J., & Snyder-Halperin, R. (1988). Do patients sleep in the hospital? *Applied Nursing Research, 1*(2), 95.

Yates, J. (1990). *A physicians guide to therapeutic massage*. Vancouver, BC: The Massage Therapists' Association of British Columbia.

Zeitlin, D., Keller, S. E., Shiflett, S. C., Schleifer, S. J., & Bartlett, J. A. (2000). Immunological effects of massage therapy during academic stress. *Psychosomatic Medicine, 62,* 83–84.

Chapter 13
Therapeutic Reminiscence

Lourdes Martinez-Cox, John Dattilo, and Kathleen Sheldon

*Deep in December it's nice to remember the fire
of September that made us mellow.*

—T. Jones

Introduction

This chapter introduces readers to reminiscence, a technique frequently used by TR specialists who work with older adults and with individuals of all ages who are in a transitional period or life crisis (Webster & Young, 1988). Although traditionally reminiscence has been used in gerontology, recent research is moving to expand the use of reminiscence as a facilitation technique used across the lifespan (Bryant, Smart, & King, 2005).

This chapter begins with an explanation of the definitions associated with reminiscence and a description of reminiscence interventions, followed by the history and theoretical foundations of reminiscence therapy. The chapter concludes with a case study, implementation exercises, discussion questions, a list of resources for those who would like to try therapeutic reminiscence, and a list of the references used in this chapter.

Definitions

In the past, several terms have been used interchangeably, though inaccurately, to describe the processes of reminiscence. Unfortunately, there is currently no single unanimous definition of reminiscence (Parker, 1995). Lack of a consistent definition has been noted for some time by reviewers who have attempted to synthesize the body of knowledge on reminiscence (e.g., Haight, 1991). To help alleviate this confusion the following terms are defined:

- Memory
- Recollection
- Reminiscence
- Therapeutic Reminiscence

Memory

To understand the process of reminiscing and how it can be used as a therapeutic intervention, it is helpful to first review the meaning of memory, how memories are made, and types of memories. Memory records our feelings and emotions, our knowledge about ourselves and the world, our experiences, and all the performance skills we have acquired (Gose & Levi, 1985).

Coleman (1999) found that among individuals with high levels of depression, memories tended to resurface in old age. According to Coleman, avoiding a particular memory had the effect of increasing that memory's power to disturb. Although researchers have identified and classified types of memory, there is presently no uniform terminology. For the purpose of this chapter, terms by Hooyman and Kiyak (1993) are used:

- Sensory
- Short-term
- Long-term

Sensory. Sensory memories come to people through their senses of smell, touch, taste, hearing, and seeing. Sensory memories imprint so quickly that people may not be aware of them.

Some people will recognize the sensation of smelling particular cologne and thinking of a friend, or of tasting something and thinking of a special event such as Christmas or summer camp.

Bluck and Levine (1998) recommend use of multiple senses to stimulate memory. They posit that this may be one way in which less frequently remembered material may be accessed.

Short-term. Short-term memory can be thought of as working memory because it consists of whatever one is working on at the moment. Short-term memory lasts for only seconds or minutes and is used for such tasks as looking up a telephone number or following directions down the hall to a particular office (Hayslip & Panek, 1989). Typically, people can only retain six or seven items at once in short-term memory without having a reminder of some sort, such as a written list, verbal cues, or visual cues. If short-term memory is to be retained longer, it must be rehearsed and connected to other memories.

Long-term. Long-term memory is the term used to describe information that has been rehearsed and connected. Long-term memories can be recent, such as what one had for lunch yesterday, or more distant such as the name of one's first dog. According to Hayslip and Panek (1989), the process of transferring material from short-term to long-term memory has four parts: registration, encoding, storage, and retrieval. *Registration* indicates that information was actually perceived. A person registers something that is heard, seen, felt, smelled, or tasted. Meaning is then assigned to the perception through a process known as *encoding*. Encoding requires attaching the new memory to information previously stored. Each individual has a unique system for organization and *storage* of information. Storage involves the collection of information an individual retains and is available for retrieval. *Retrieval* is the recall of information that was previously registered, encoded, and stored (Hayslip & Panek, 1989). Therefore, retrieval allows the person to be cognizant of specific information stored in the individual's memory.

Some information enters a person's memory very deliberately, as when that person wants to memorize a list for school, or when we devise memory gimmicks to help remember someone's name. According to Bluck and Levine (1998), individuals are able to rework memories and still feel that their memories are accurate. This reworking of memories occurs as part of the retrieval during reminiscing. Bluck and Levine stated that each time a memory is recalled, it is molded to the individual's current self and context. Many memories are involuntary.

> For example, Naomi may hear a song and remember a special time in the past, or she may feel a tweed jacket and remember a relative. She may also hear a siren and remember an accident she witnessed in the past, or she may see a big dog and remember having been bitten.

Sounds, smells, tastes, touch, and other sensations can all be used by TR specialists to invoke memories of individuals with whom they work.

From an analysis of three case studies, Mills (1997) found that memory appeared to decline more quickly than did emotions and emotional responses of those being interviewed. Mills found that semantic memory, or memory of the world, is lost with progression of dementia, whereas memory of self is more durable. According to Mills, the autobiographical recall is typically characterized by memories of an emotional nature.

From a case study, Mills (1997) found that a participant experienced increased sense of self-confidence, expressed happiness, and enhanced personhood and well-being as a result of the reminiscing. In a second case study, the individual overcame speech deficits related to his illness during highly charged sessions as a result of reminiscence. In a third case study, that involved an individual who had been a prisoner of war, the authors concluded that, as a result of reminiscence, he may have created such durable memories that they withstood effects of dementia. In a residential setting, the once prisoner of war may have felt similar confinement to his past and thus experienced his memories more vividly.

In rehabilitation settings, involuntary memories are often induced as a therapeutic intervention through sensory stimulation used to treat people who have recently acquired a brain injury or who have dementia. Suggestions for this type of intervention are found in the section of this chapter titled *Intervention Implementation Exercises*.

Recollection

Recollection describes a deliberate, concentrated effort to remember (Soukhanov, 1992). However, simply remembering a past event is not reminiscing. Rather, reminiscence is more elaborate than recollection and is marked by a shift in interpretation of the event (Parker, 1995).

Reminiscence

Bluck and Levine (1998) define reminiscence as a volitional or non-volitional act or process of recollecting memories of one's self in the past. Reminiscing is a way of talking about one's life that can occur as an unstructured or structured process occurring alone, with another person, or in a group (Buchanan et al., 2002).

Therapeutic Reminiscence

Individuals can retrieve memories voluntarily. This type of retrieval is used when one searches for a lost wallet or tells someone how to find the post office. At other times, memories are retrieved to provide comfort, pleasure, or to remind one of how a problem was solved in the past (Tarrant, Dattilo, Driver, & Manfredo, 1995). Intentional retrieval of memories includes recollection, reminiscence, and life review. When a TR specialist facilitates the process of retrieving memories for an individual, the process is called therapeutic reminiscence.

Over the past 30 years, researchers have studied frequency of naturally occurring reminiscence and life review among adults as they age such as research conducted by Beechem, Anthony, and Kurtz (1998). The consensus is that reminiscence occurs naturally and spontaneously for many older adults and contributes to successful aging. Assuming this to be true, facilitating reminiscence for those who have difficulty doing so on their own may enhance their quality of life. According to Buchanan and colleagues (2002), as an intervention, reminiscence involves eliciting memories and is led by a professional who can identify the purposes of the intervention and needs of the person who is reminiscing.

One challenge cited by Brody (1990) is that long-term care residents' concept of self as a competent adult is continuously eroded with decreased physical and mental skills required for their emotional survival. Beaton (1991) postulated that reminiscence varies with personality structure; therefore, each individual may need a unique approach.

Descriptions

Information on characteristics of participants who often benefit from reminiscence is presented in this section followed by different types of reminiscence. After the description of types of reminiscence, specific suggestions for conducting reminiscence programs are provided. Finally, information describing life review is presented. The following headings are used in this section:

- Participant Characteristics
- Types of Reminiscence
- Suggestions for Conducting Reminiscence Programs
- Suggestions for Conducting Life Review

Participant Characteristics

While all individuals can learn at some level, not all are able to store and retrieve memories at will (Hayslip & Panek, 1989). A variety of conditions can impede the ability to acquire information and store it in memory. For example, mental retardation is a form of cognitive impairment that occurs during the developmental period. Other cognitive impairments may occur later in life, such as a head injury, cardiovascular accident, tumor, and substance toxicity. In addition, acute conditions such as depression, boredom, fear, grief, illness, and medication can disrupt the processes of learning and remembering to such a degree as to impair one cognitively. Reminiscence has been used as a therapeutic intervention with individuals experiencing depression or who have some form of dementia.

According to Jones (2003), reminiscence is useful for recently institutionalized older adults who benefit from building rapport with others and older adults with dementia who might benefit from the structure to remember and the validation of feelings. Beaton (1991) supported views of Erikson (1982) and Butler (1963), who argued that reminiscence can be used as a form of continued development in old age. The next portion of this chapter is devoted to describing:

- Depression
- Dementia

Depression. Depression that interferes with memory can be experienced by anyone. Symptoms of depression include apathy, dejection, fatigue, helplessness, hopelessness, loneliness, pessimism, poor personal hygiene, sadness, sleep disturbance, and weight loss or gain (Aromando, 1995). Depression typically follows a loss, such as loss of abilities through an illness or accident, loss of a close personal relationship through death, break up, or relocation, or loss of work through job displacement or retirement.

According to Coleman (1999), regrets about the past accounts for the inability to cope with physical conditions in old age, as well as with depressive moods. Jones (2003) concurs that depression is the most common, and most overlooked, emotional disorder in older adults and is found 2–3 times more in women than in men.

Depression is also a recognized side-effect of more than 300 prescription medications (Podolsky & Newman, 1991). According to the DSM-IV (American Psychiatric Association, 1994),

> In elderly individuals with a Major Depressive Episode, memory difficulties may be the chief complaint and may be mistaken for early signs of dementia. When the Major Depressive Episode is successfully treated, the memory problems often fully abate (p. 322).

Cappeliez and O'Rourke (2002) found that more frequent reminiscence was being done by those who value memories over new challenges. Characteristic of these same individuals is boredom and lack of stimulation. TR specialists are advised to become familiar with medication effects and side-effects through reference guides such as the guide developed by Skalko, Mitchell, Kaye, and Dalton (1994).

Cappeliez and O'Rourke cautioned that a high level of reminiscing may be a sign of someone experiencing a negative event and struggling to find life meaning.

Dementia. Dementia is a condition that causes memory loss. Alzheimer's disease, the most frequent type of irreversible dementia in adults, is characterized by progressive intellectual impairment (Mace & Rabins, 1981). However, since the only absolute diagnosis of Alzheimer's disease is upon autopsy, symptoms observed are best referred to as *dementia of the Alzheimer's type* (Heston & White, 1983). In this chapter, the term *dementia* refers to dementia of the Alzheimer's type.

Progression of dementia is characterized by increasing memory loss. At first there is forgetfulness, initially short-term, such as location of the car keys. Next, recent memory fades, such as not remembering yesterday's lunch and finally long-term memory is impaired, such as eventually forgetting the name of spouse, children, and one's own name. According to Powell and Courtice (1986), people with dementia may experience the following three conditions: aphasia, agnosia, and apraxia.

Aphasia is loss of the ability to find the right word, to complete a sentence, or to understand what is said. In addition, people with dementia may experience *agnosia*, which results in losing the ability to recognize things or people. When people with dementia experience loss of the ability to carry out motor functions, this is termed *apraxia* (Powell & Courtice, 1986).

As dementia progresses, the individual loses the memories that make her or him an individual. This loss of memories is referred to as the loss of self (Cohen & Eisdorfer, 1986). However, progress of dementia is erratic and the individual may remember certain events from the past with astonishing clarity (Powell & Courtice, 1986).

Types of Reminiscence

In the decades since Butler (1963) first wrote about reminiscence and life review, researchers have expressed concern that not all types of reminiscence are the same; yet no system had been developed to classify various types. Beaton (1991) discussed criteria for three styles of reminiscence: affirming, negating, and despairing. These criteria relate to how individuals perceive their life experiences through reminiscing.

A person with an *affirming* style recognizes past conflicts and is able to view them as having resolution. Ownership of one's life experiences, regardless of outcome is characteristic of the affirming style.

A *negating* style tends to result in minimizing personal life experiences highlighting instead, historical events occurring around the same period. The individual may intentionally exclude specific life events perceived to be negative.

The third style, *despairing*, is characterized by a despairing style of reminiscence. This individual displays a preoccupation related to life experiences perceived as negative. In an attempt to deny what has occurred in their life, the individual may even have feelings of regret.

These categories and those of other researchers were refined and revised by Wong and Watt (1991) who identified the following six distinct types, their defining characteristics, and whether or not they were associated with successful aging:

- Integrative
- Instrumental
- Transmissive
- Narrative
- Escapist
- Obsessive

Integrative. Integrative reminiscence is associated with successful aging. It is used to achieve a sense of self-worth, coherence, and reconciliation with regard to one's past.

Instrumental. Similar to integrative reminiscence, instrumental reminiscence is associated with successful aging. Instrumental reminiscence contributes to subjective perceptions of competence and continuity through recollection of past plans, attainment of goals, and successful problem solving.

Transmissive. Transmissive reminiscence involves passing on one's cultural heritage and personal legacy to others. Transmissive reminiscence includes storytelling and moral instruction. Support for this type of reminiscence is inconclusive at this time.

Narrative. Narrative reminiscence is characterized by statements of autobiographical facts. These statements are used in narrative reminiscence without interpretation or evaluation.

Escapist. Escapist reminiscence involves a tendency to glorify the past and belittle the present. Escapist reminiscence may be detrimental to successful aging.

Obsessive. Obsessive reminiscence originates from guilt over one's past and is evidenced by statements of guilt, bitterness, and despair regarding one's past. Similar to escapist reminiscence, obsessive reminiscence can inhibit successful aging.

More recent work by Coleman (1999) supports four types of reminiscence: integrative, transmissive, obsessive, and escapist in his studies of life review.

Suggestions for Conducting Reminiscence Programs

Reminiscence as an intervention can be conducted with a single individual or with a group, with one's peers, or with individuals from different age groups. In the simplest form, one needs merely to listen to another.

Often people will describe their life story to anyone who will listen (Butler & Lewis, 1973). Bluck and Levine (1998) identified the goal of reminiscence to be to encourage personality reorganization or self-change. Suggestions provided in this section are divided into two categories:

- Structure of sessions
- Size of sessions

Structure of sessions. The way in which TR specialists structure therapeutic reminiscence sessions impacts effects of the intervention. Suggestions are provided related to: choosing topics, selecting the setting, getting started, listening, speaking, and establishing session length.

Choosing topics for reminiscence sessions may come spontaneously from the individual ("Did I ever tell you about the time . . ."), and may be initiated by the TR specialists based on a previous conversation ("Mr. Lee, today you promised to tell about how you met Martha."), or may follow an established protocol ("Since Christmas is next week, let's talk about the best Christmas present you ever received.").

If the reminiscence topic is predetermined, it may be helpful to give the individual a written reminder ahead of time to allow time to organize his or her thoughts. The individual may also want to bring along a photograph, a memento, or some other object to serve as a cuing prop (Holzapfel, 1989).

> Some possible topics include airplanes, Arbor Day, poetry, Christmas, circus days, county fairs, Easter, elections, fall, farming, fathers, Fourth of July, gardens, Halloween, heroes, mothers, pets, post cards, quilts, school, spring, streetcars, summer vacations, table manners, toys, Thanksgiving, Valentine's Day, weddings, winter, and zoos.

When *selecting the setting*, it may be useful to consider that therapeutic reminiscence can be conducted at the bedside (see Figure 13.1) or in a more formal office or dayroom setting. The key to establishing an appropriate setting is to make the speaker as comfortable as possible. An environment with few distractions is recommended.

When *getting started* in a reminiscence session, it may be helpful to call the individual by their preferred name, sit or stand on a face-to-face level, and make initial eye contact. The TR specialist can let the person know that the therapist is ready to listen. It is critical to be honest from the outset about how much time is available for the session. It may take some time to convince the person that the TR specialist is genuinely interested and genuinely wants to hear the person's stories.

When *listening*, Wade-Farber (1996) encouraged professionals to be aware of cultural differences as the listening process occurs. For instance, people from some cultures require more personal space than others; some prefer to tell a whole story uninterrupted, others may want the reminiscence to more closely resemble a give-and-take conversation.

When *speaking*, TR specialists may find success when they speak in a normal tone of voice and allow the individual to see their face. Although it is encouraged to avoid finishing the person's sentences to hurry the conversation along, being prepared to supply a missing word if the individual requests help may be useful.

> For example, Participant: "We didn't have clocks like that with no hands—what do you call them?" TR specialist: "Digital clocks?" Participant: "Yes, we didn't have digital clocks back then."

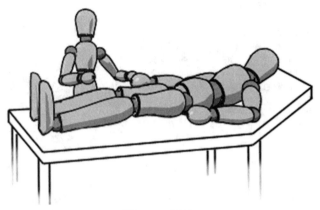

Figure 13.1

TR specialists are encouraged to use corrections judiciously and only if they are critical to the story. Refraining from baby talk, slang, and condescending names like "Honey, Dear, Sweetie, Pal" are characteristics of effective speakers. It is often helpful to speak slightly slower, especially if conducting therapeutic reminiscence with an individual who has a hearing impairment, is not a native English speaker, or has been ill. Although giving feedback to demonstrate listening is helpful, it is important to avoid questions that could be misinterpreted.

> For example, the sentence "It sounds like you were angry about that," sounds less imposing than "Why did you do that?"

Establishing session length appears to be a critical element to the success of one-to-one reminiscence. Haight (1991) discovered five negative outcome studies in which individual reminiscence had been employed. In each of these negative outcome studies the intervention was 1 hour or less in length. Therefore, it appears important to schedule a long or flexible block of time before beginning a reminiscence session. It is helpful to be aware of the time and give adequate warning before the session ends. The TR specialist is encouraged to watch for signs of fatigue and be prepared to conclude the session if the individual agrees.

Size of sessions. Therapeutic reminiscence can occur with different numbers of participants. Suggestions are provided relative to one-on-one sessions and group sessions.

During *one-on-one reminiscence sessions*, the speaker may reveal more intimate details and be more open than in a group session (Haight, 1991). According to Haight, the speaker may also work through more painful details of the past that the person may not wish to reveal to a group.

Zgola (1987) described one-to-one reminiscence as an appropriate activity for individuals who have Alzheimer's disease and related disorders. She suggested using magazines or books of pictures to cue the individual.

Several commercial enterprises produce cuing materials described in the resource list at the end of this chapter. Additional information on commercial materials to facilitate reminiscence is included throughout this chapter and is listed in the resources section.

Figure 13.2

The advantage of **group reminiscence sessions** is the opportunity to receive support from peers (see Figure 13.2). This can be especially helpful when an individual is new to a facility or program and needs to form new relationships. As members of the group share memories and ideas, people may learn how much they have in common with each other. Individuals may learn that they once owned a similar make of car or that they were raised in a similar area. Learning what people have in common can assist them in developing friendships.

According to Jones (2003), positive effects are found when conducting group reminiscence with 6–10 participants, for 30–45 minutes and a frequency of 6–12 sessions (2003). Jones recommended separating groups by gender and age, as well as mental and physical capabilities. According to Austin (1991), group size should be determined by participant characteristics, such as physical frailty, comfort level in groups, and nature of topic for the day.

Huber and Miller (1984) provided a detailed description of how to implement group experiences that involve reminiscence. They suggested calling the time when they met to be a *meeting*, rather than a *group* or *session* in the belief that the word meeting is a more familiar concept for older adults.

Suggestions for Conducting Life Review

Beechem and colleagues (1998) support life review as a therapeutic tool that can be used to problem solve past life experiences and bring resolution or increased sense of well-being. Further, they support life review as a method of facilitating control over one's biography. The authors recognized that the term *life review* continues to have a working definition. Life review is a subset of reminiscing and involves a structured approach to reviewing and looking for meaning in one's life and is conducted at set times involving a guide through different sequential aspects of a person's life (Buchanan et al., 2002).

Studies examined by Beechem and colleagues (1998) were organized by those promoting a sense of well-being, assisting the interviewee through the grieving process, enhancing self-esteem, encouraging the acceptance of one's life accomplishments, and those focusing on cultural and social benefits by passing on wisdom and customs. This is imperative for individuals living in an institutional setting who can easily feel loss of control over time that may lead to depression.

Coleman (1999) outlined four aspects to creating a successful life story: coherence, assimilation of events, a convincing structure, and its truth value. Coherence relates to a connection of goals and life objectives regardless of the many turning points a life may have. Assimilation of events speaks to the ability to interpret events and their meaning to the individual's life. A convincing structure, the third of these aspects, deals with a clear view of the beginning, middle, and end of one's life story. The final aspect is truth value, referring to the true account of a person's life story.

Beaton (1991) found that women with affirming personality styles had a higher level of ego development than women with either negative or despairing styles. Those with affirming styles tended to tell stories characterized by resilience. Beaton concluded that these women were the best candidates for life review sessions that were guided by inexperienced persons due to the nature of the interviewee.

Although reminiscence has been characterized as a generally passive process, life review is said to be more dynamic (Webster & Young, 1988). Three phases occur during life review:

- Recollection of an event
- Evaluation of that event
- Synthesis of that event with other memories

Recollection. Recollection can be conscious and can be identified in statements such as, "Today we planned to talk about how members of our family expressed emotions as we were growing up." In addition, recollection can surface unexpectedly during another discussion such as, "Memories of Christmas."

> As an example, *I remember one Christmas during the Great Depression when all I wanted was a store-bought doll. Mama kept saying money was too dear but I was stubborn. On Christmas morning I got the doll. A week later, I left it in the barn by accident and one of the dogs chewed on it. Mama cried when she saw it and I couldn't understand why—after all, it was my doll.*

Evaluation. Evaluation is developmental; that is, memories are constantly revised as new information becomes available (Webster & Young, 1988). The evaluation of past events changes according to age, stage in life, role, changing values, and changing societal values.

> As an example, *It wasn't until after Mama died that I found a letter she had written to my aunt that Christmas. It seems Mama had given a whole, hand-made quilt for that doll. I know now why she cried but she never said a word.*

Synthesis. During synthesis, memories are reorganized and self-perceptions are revised. Synthesis allows the person to place a memory within a particular context.

> As an example, *That was typical of Mama—she kept everything to herself. She could never say, 'I love you' but she tried to show it by giving me that doll.*

Life review—conducted well—has the potential to result in fewer memory complaints and less depression (Hayslip & Panek, 1989). Recalled memories that support a positive self-image are usually accepted quickly, while memories that are evaluated as negative are often painful. Difficult memories may be rejected, accepted with resignation, or accepted with despair (Webster & Young, 1988). TR specialists can use life review by incorporating activities targeting emotional, social, physical and psychological functioning (Lee, Tabourne, & Yoon, 2008).

Life review can be a painful experience for anyone, but perhaps especially for some older adults. In earlier years, one might have the opportunity to make life changes to alter outcomes or make amends for a wrong done to someone. In later years of life, many of these options no longer exist. It is too late, for example, for one to go back and change one's life career, relationship choices, or lifestyle choices. Hayslip and Panek (1989) reported that some older adults may remember choices that they may regret, such as not finishing high school or marrying young.

Bluck and Levine (1998) stated that life review is common in old age as death becomes an imminent fact. Therefore, it is important for health care professionals to be skilled at conducting reminiscence or life review, especially with people who have encountered traumatic events (Schindler, Spiegel, & Malachi, 1992). Coleman (1999) stated that a refusal to reminisce may be a sign of deep grief, and individuals who want to speak about their experiences typically have positive outcomes associated with life review.

Life review can be achieved through writing. Steward and Croft (1988) conducted workshops for older adults on the joys of writing, whether in the form of personal journals or writing for posterity or publication. The authors stated that as people age, there are many reasons for writing, including to preserve and transmit thoughts and memories and to recall, clarify, and organize thoughts. Writing things gives permanence and makes ideas clearer. Their text contains lists of writing triggers, key words, and story starters that serve to assist writers and help discussion leaders as well.

> Some of these triggers might include getting a haircut, attending class reunions, Christmas morning, when the circus came to town, "the dogs I have owned (and those who have owned me)," and "if I had my life to live over again."

As forms of therapy, reminiscence and life review have the potential to rouse strong emotional memories, both negative and positive. When intentionally focusing on such memories, the TR specialist is encouraged to be present to guide the individual through resolution. According to Teague, McGhee, and Hawkins (1996), there are many who believe that this type of therapy must be dealt with carefully and with professionals trained in the field of mental health. Therefore, it is helpful for TR specialists to be prepared to refer participants to counselors as needed.

Coleman (1999) reported that since nursing staff often feel ill equipped to approach patients experiencing strong feelings, practitioners must develop skills to encourage patients to express their stories orally and in writing. Beaton (1991) recommended that life stories be incorporated as part of the clinical assessment for long term care as it provides an opportunity to build rapport and obtain valuable information. An additional benefit of obtaining a person's personal narrative is that it is never lost and can be used with the person with dementia even as they progress through the illness. Mills (1997) reported that care plans and approaches are influenced by the care provider's knowledge and understanding of the client, thereby providing effective care.

History

The first scholarly examination of reminiscence is attributed to Robert N. Butler, M.D., an American psychiatrist and gerontologist, who wrote a 1963 article on life review. Butler wrote the article to encourage caretakers of older adults to facilitate life review. The type of life review he described employs a process called *introspection*, which Soukhanov (1992) describes as contemplation and self-examination of one's thoughts and feelings. Butler's suggestion that thinking and talking about the past was not maladaptive created interest among professionals working with older adults (Moody, 1988).

Butler was the first to propose that reminiscing is an activity undertaken by those who are aging successfully. Specifically, Butler (1963) proposed that a methodical examination of past experiences was a characteristic of successful aging. Prior to Butler's analysis, it was assumed that thinking and talking about the past was an indication of negative attitudes toward aging (Havighurst & Glasser, 1972). Erik Erikson (1982) later identified the process of life review as the eighth and final psychosocial stage of development. According to Hooyman and Kiyak (1993), a major task of this last stage is to integrate the experiences of earlier stages and to realize that one's life has had meaning.

Although traditionally reminiscence has been used with older adults, more recently reminiscence as a facilitation technique is being used across the lifespan (Bryan et al., 2005). For example, Parker (1999) emphasized the importance of reminiscence in transitional periods of life or during times of transition through a crisis. Although social reminiscing can stimulate positive emotions, Pasupathi and Cartensen (2003) discovered that the occurrence of positive emotions in response to reminiscing about positive events seems to increase with age.

Theoretical Foundations

According to Hooyman and Kiyak (1993), therapeutic reminiscence fits appropriately with any of the four current social theories of aging:

- Role Theory
- Disengagement Theory
- Activity Theory
- Continuity Theory

Role Theory

Role theorists contend that how well one adjusts to aging depends upon how well the role changes of later life are accepted (Rosow, 1976). According to this theory, most people have multiple roles as they age.

Dorothy, for example, had the following roles: grandmother, sister, aunt, cousin, widow, friend, Catholic, member, neighbor, and retired secretary. Role theorists would argue that the status of "retired secretary" will not depress Dorothy because she has many other roles that help to shape her identity. They would further propose that one or more leisure roles such as quilter, bridge player, painter, dancer, and seamstress will help Dorothy adjust to retirement. Reminiscence and life review would be useful in helping Dorothy to identify her many roles and how they contribute to her overall life satisfaction.

According to Lamme and Baars (1993), reminiscing encourages people to define and understand themselves through their histories; they understand and interpret their past from their present. Interpreting the present in relation to the past and creating a coherent life story is the goal of reminiscence. Lamme and Baars supported the idea that reviewing one's life is useful in adjusting to old age.

Disengagement Theory

Disengagement theorists believe that older adults have a natural tendency to withdraw from society and become more introspective (Cumming & Henry, 1961). The withdrawal is physical and psychological.

> For example, Talmage, who is very ill one winter, may withdraw into his home and not venture out to activities in the cold and snow. However, he might be in daily contact with family, friends, and others by telephone so would *not* be considered to have disengaged. In contrast, Theresa might sell the family home and move to a desert retirement colony. If asked, she expresses a desire to live quietly around adults only. Disengagement theorists would say that Theresa has withdrawn from society at the same time that society has withdrawn from her, thus creating a job for a younger person. Reminiscence and life review might be used with Theresa to help identify strong role models in her family or circle of friends who disengaged.

In addition, socially organized transitions may inspire reminiscence such as retirement or empty nest. System changes such as using the Internet rather than the encyclopedia can also bring about reminiscence.

Activity Theory

Activity theorists assume that people who are active will be more satisfied and better adjusted than those who are less active (Havighurst, 1968). They agree with disengagement theorists in that they believe that withdrawal from society occurs after age 65; however, they do not see the withdrawal as contributing to life satisfaction.

Activity theory has been criticized because it does not consider those people who have never been active but report happiness and high levels of life satisfaction. Reminiscence might be used with individuals to try to identify other activities that they were engaged in once before but have since forgotten.

According to Fry (1991), there was no difference noted in frequency of reminiscence engaged in between nursing home and community dwelling elders. Older adults studied who demonstrated more active lifestyles and higher psychological well-being tended to engage less in reminiscence. Fry stated that this is because they have more goal-directed activity in the present and are less concerned about past life events.

Holland and Rabbitt (1991) on the other hand, state that long-term care residents have less to occupy their time and more people doing things for them. Therefore, reminiscing is seen as necessary both for the entertainment value as well as a means to maintain a sense of personal identity outside of the long-term care environment.

Continuity Theory

Continuity theorists assert that as people age, they become more of what they already were in their youth. People deliberately continue familiar patterns (Atchley, 1993). Continuity theorists will readily admit that theirs is *not* a theory of successful aging since a maladaptive pattern in the early years will continue as a maladaptive pattern in the later years, such as a workaholic or a highly controlling mother. Nonetheless, this internal continuity provides a sense of security and predictability that help the individual feel in charge.

Selective investment is the process used to conserve dwindling energy by deciding where to put that energy. Reminiscence and life review are utilized by a continuity theorist to assess to what degree the life patterns established have been optimal for the individual. Conscious decisions could then be made about whether to break the pattern. Sometimes individuals feel that *bad things* happen to them, when in fact they chose the activity that had the negative result.

Effectiveness

Researchers have begun to study the process and outcome of life review interventions. Parker (1995) concluded that there is a lack of consistency concerning how reminiscence is viewed and used, there are contradictory findings with regard to therapeutic benefits, there is confusion across contexts of reminiscence, and there is an absence of a theoretical base. Regardless of these problems, Parker identified improved coping, reduced interpersonal uncertainty, developed or reestablished friendships, and exploration of one's identity benefits of therapeutic reminiscence.

Haight (1991) reviewed 97 articles meeting the following criteria: published between 1960 and 1990, contained in reference journals of the United States, and identified by key words of reminiscing, remembering, aging, life review, history, and oral history. Three articles appeared in the 1960s, 20 in the 1970s, and 71 in the 1980s. Only 7 of 97 articles reported negative outcomes of life review, while the other 90 articles were either non-evaluative or reported positive outcomes. The following is a sample of recent studies that have investigated effects of reminiscence interventions.

Lee and colleagues (2008) implemented a 4-week life review program (2 x wk) plus 2 weeks for assessment and pre- and post-tests with 17 Korean older adults with Alzheimer's disease. The program significantly reduced depression and had some significant effects on self-esteem but did not increase life satisfaction.

Zauszniewski et al. (2004) evaluated effects of focused reflection, using visual images of specific thematic categories on 34 (4:1 female to male ratio) adults (age > 65) living in retirement communities as a result of experiencing chronic health conditions who were experiencing negative emotions described as depression, anxiety, and agitation. Reminiscence sessions consisted of group sessions (6 x wk, 120-min sessions). The authors posited that their study did not confound the reminiscence experience with multiple variables such as music, literature, or other props, and absence of these variables facilitated evaluation of program effects. There was a reduction in negative symptoms demonstrated by participants. With the increase in number of older adults experiencing loss, isolation, and loneliness, health care workers might consider using this method of reminiscence to increase opportunities for socialization and psychological well-being. Recommendations for continued research include using a larger sample size with more ethnic diversity and equal gender representation.

During a 3-week reminiscence intervention, **Jones (2003)** studied elderly women with depression residing in an assisted living facility. The study used a structured nurse initiated reminiscence approach for the experimental group, while the control group received the customary reminiscence interventions. Use of the Geriatric Depression Scale indicated both groups had similar levels of depression at study onset. The experimental group had lower levels of depression post-study. The study supports following a structured approach to facilitating reminiscence and grounding a program in theory.

Buchanan and colleagues (2002) conducted a critical analysis of the literature on therapeutic reminiscing and concluded that there is a scarcity of research evidence to support the facilitation technique. The major value of the review was that there was clarity of operational definitions for reminiscing and life review. A further conclusion was that any study of reminiscing should include several guidelines. Unfortunately, of the many articles reviewed, only a few were data-based.

Tabourne (1995) used a case study to examine effects of a 5-week 1-to-1 life review program (2 x wk) with an 84-year-old man newly admitted to a nursing home, who was depressed. Each session addressed a stage in life from birth to death and introduced an activity typically offered to other residents of the facility. At the conclusion of the program, his scores indicated a moderate decrease in depression and an increase in perceived competence. He improved in his orientation to person, place, and time, which indicated a reduction in confusion. Initially, he reported having no hobbies and no recreation pursuits. Following the intervention, he was more alert, was asking about upcoming programs, and interacted more with peers and staff.

Atkinson (1994) conducted a study on effects of a 2-year reminiscence program (1 x wk) in older adults with learning disabilities in a residential program in the United Kingdom. The purpose of the study was to examine whether seven men and two women (ages 57–77) could use recall and reminiscence to produce oral accounts of their lives. Atkinson divided the study into four phases: (a) public accounts focused on recalling shared themes that were non-threatening, (b) period details concerned with how to maintain people's interests, (c) private accounts centered on small group work examining experiences in depth, and (d) collective accounts combining written and oral accounts. During each phase, reminiscence tools such as slides, photographs, period pieces, and participants' written accounts, were used in aiding recall. Through direct observation, Atkinson reviewed each phase for commonalities by examining the written and oral accounts of each member's experiences. Results showed that reminiscence could lead to an enhanced sense of self and greater self-esteem; the reminiscence group allowed individuals to feel a sense of individual achievement and collective pride; and the group promoted friendships and supportive relationships.

Gibson (1994) examined effects of reminiscence designed to assist with 164 people with dementia experiencing life changes. Many participants were in the process of leaving their homes to enter residential facilities. Participants were separated into 25 small groups. Each group engaged in a 10-month reminiscence program using a thematic approach and a variety of multisensory trigger materials, including slide packages. Each session (1 x wk, 90-min sessions) was documented either with written or tape-recorded accounts. Records were analyzed in terms of programming, attendance, interactions, emotional climate, and content of the reminiscence. Interviews were conducted with staff to further evaluate effects of the groups. Gibson concluded that reminiscence aided participants in feeling a sense of control of their lives, enhanced their self-esteem, and promoted friendships.

Wong and Watt's (1991) taxonomy reported in the description section of this chapter was criticized by **Webster (1993)** as having been derived from adults older than 65 (mean age of 78), therefore limiting generalization of results. Webster surveyed individuals (ages 18–76) to develop a Reminiscence Functions Scale, a 43-item questionnaire used to assess reminiscence functions over the life course. From 710 usable questionnaires, Webster identified 7 functions of reminiscence: (a) boredom reduction, (b) death preparation, (c) identity/problem solving, (d) conversation, (e) intimacy maintenance, (f) bitterness revival, and (g) teach/inform. While these taxonomies and scales have been helpful, some researchers still have concerns.

While some researchers investigate how individuals reminisced, others call for research to determine what individuals reminisce about and how often they do so. **Fry (1991)** interviewed 70 adults to assess the frequency and "pleasantness" of their reminiscence activity. Results indicated that individuals who have high degrees of psychological well-being and engage in a variety of interesting activities are also those who report that reminiscing is most pleasant. Those who are busy reported that they spend less time reminiscing. Fry suggested that older adults who are searching to find meaning in personal existence are likely to resort more frequently to reminiscence.

Summary. Existing research moderately indicates that therapeutic reminiscence is an empirically supported facilitation technique. The current body of literature reveals the following about reminiscing: experiencing reminiscing as pleasant may correlate with a psychological well-being and interesting activity participation. Reminiscing may enhance an individual's self-esteem, sense of self, and help individuals deal with crises, losses, and life transitions. Reminiscence can increase a person's sense of control and their ability to develop friendships as well as reduce their negative emotions and maintain health. In addition, reminiscence can aid communication during the latter stages of dementia and decrease depression and confusion. Reminiscence can potentially help individuals to decrease boredom, prepare for death, identify and solve problems, engage in conversation, maintain intimacy, resolve bitterness, and teach and inform.

Case Study

Estelle

Estelle cried for 2 days and was exhausted when she arrived at the retirement complex in October. After she fell three times last winter, she knew it was time to move out of her house and into a more protected environment. With the help of her three sons and two daughters, plus all the spouses and grandchildren, Estelle sold and gave away her furniture and other goods and sold the house for a profit. Her few favorite pieces of furniture, paintings, lamps, and keepsakes were now arranged in her new room.

The first few weeks went quickly. Estelle was pleased to discover two other widows from her church living in the next wing of the building. She tried many of the activities and selected several to attend on a regular basis. At 78 years old, Estelle was "middle-aged" in the complex. Several of the residents were well into their 90s and a few were in their early 60s. The complex was clean, well-designed, and near her children. Estelle felt very lucky to have found such a nice place to live.

In November, the days grew shorter, leaves fell from the trees, and it began to rain nearly every day. With more free time on her hands, Estelle began to brood. She always imagined that one of her children would want the house in which they were raised. She missed hearing the trains that used to go by in the night. Her friend, Juanita, had a stroke and left the state to live with her daughter. Estelle was sad that she had not been able to say goodbye to Juanita. Eventually, Estelle caught a cold and stopped getting dressed each day. She no longer went to the dining room, but made tea and toast in her room.

Therapeutic Reminiscence for Estelle

A week later Jeni, the TR specialist, knocked on Estelle's door and asked Estelle if she had time to cut out some turkey decorations for Thanksgiving. Estelle declined, complaining that her arthritis was bothering her, that she just did not have the energy, and that she was dreading the whole holiday season. Jeni glanced around the tidy room until she saw a bookcase filled with cups and saucers. She complimented Estelle on the collection and stepped closer for a better look. "Which one is your favorite?" she asked.

Estelle picked up an inexpensive, chipped pair and held the pieces gently. Slowly, she began to tell Jeni about her late husband Daniel throwing baseballs at the county fair to win the cup and saucer for her. He had spent a dollar before he won the set—an extravagant amount of money in those days. "Marry me," Daniel had said, "and someday you'll have a dozen cups to display." Estelle did, and Daniel kept his word. Estelle pointed to cups from Mexico, Hawaii, New York City, and many other places.

Jeni watched Estelle carefully as she reminisced about the cup. Jeni noticed how the wrinkles on Estelle's face smoothed out. "What a wonderful story," Jeni said, "I hope you have written it down for your family." No, Estelle said it had never occurred to her, besides sometimes it was difficult to write with the arthritis. Jeni then suggested that Estelle record the stories of the cups on tape and offered to bring her some equipment. "Would Friday be a good day to start?" she asked.

Jeni returned twice to Estelle's room to assist with the tape recording. At first, Estelle stated that she hated the way her voice sounded, and was intimidated by the buttons on the tape recorder. Eventually, she was able to talk for 30 minutes about each cup and saucer, with additional stories about Daniel and other family members. Estelle decided to give one cup and saucer to each of her children, plus one to each grandchild and great-grandchild. Each cup would be accompanied by an audiotape of Estelle reminiscing about the cup and other topics.

At the New Year's Eve party, Jeni saw Estelle and Lena chatting by the punch bowl. They waved for her to join them. Estelle was happy to report that the cups and tapes had been a wonderful success. Her children had asked for more stories, she said, and they had sent her home with several packages of blank tapes. Furthermore, Lena, another resident of the retirement complex, had heard about the project and wondered if Jeni had another tape recorder. Lena wanted to tell her new great-granddaughter all about the day she first arrived in America many years ago.

Summary

The TR specialist at Estelle's retirement complex encouraged Estelle and other residents to reminisce about their life experiences. In addition to reminiscence, the residents tape-recorded their memories and shared them with their families. Estelle and the other residents remained engaged in their current daily experiences and maintained social and familial contacts providing meaningful relations with others while they successfully recalled memorable times in their lives. In addition to the therapeutic value of the reminiscence program, each participant left a legacy of stories to be shared with their families.

Intervention Implementation Exercises

TR specialists may have the opportunity to implement types of activities associated with a reminiscence program. Examples of each of the following types are described in this section:

- Sensory
- One-on-One Verbal
- Group Verbal
- Written

Sensory Reminiscence Intervention

As individuals with dementia become more confused, they may talk less. At the same time, their need for personally meaningful activity may remain. With this in mind, Durkee (1997) presented a series of reminiscence activities for individuals based on their personal life histories, three of which follow:

- Table Preparation
- Office Work
- Apron Storage

Table Preparation. A former waiter, waitress, maid, or homemaker might like to polish and sort old silverware into a plastic tray and set a table. Use old mismatched spoons and forks with soft rags. A little cooking oil can be substituted for the polish.

Office Work. Former office workers or clerks may enjoy handling file folders and office items. Gather discarded invoices, canceled checks, sales slips, order blanks. Have a supply of pencils with erasers, lined ledger paper, and an older adding machine or typewriter. Provide paper materials that can be sorted, handled, folded, opened, sealed, read, and carried away in someone's pocket.

Apron Storage. Old fashioned tie-in-the-back aprons with pockets for women and nail aprons from the local hardware store for men provide a personal place to carry safe items such as keys, wallet, handkerchief, note pad, pencil, deck of cards, measuring spoons, and combs.

One-on-One Verbal Reminiscence Intervention

Older adults with confusion are often placed in a hospital, long-term care facility, or psychiatric hospital to be evaluated for possible dementia. In a strange place, surrounded by strange people, sounds, and sights, it is not unusual for the older person to refuse to bathe or shower. The following questions are representative of this type of reminiscence:

- Bathroom
- Bathtub
- Water
- Soap

Bathroom. What kind of bathroom did you have when you were growing up? Was it inside the house or outside? Did you have hot running water in the bathroom when you were growing up? Or did you have to heat the water on the stove?

Bathtub. Where did you take a bath when you were growing up? Did you have a built-in tub or a tub that moved around? Was the tub used only for bathing, or did your mother wash clothes in the same tub? Do you remember the first shower you saw?

Water. Did you ever use the water for more than one child? Who got to have the first bath? Who took the last bath? How many times a week did you take a bath?

Soap. Do you remember the soap you used? Did your mother make it herself? Did you ever use Lifebouy soap? Do you remember the Lifebouy commercial on the radio? Did you ever use Camay soap? Ivory soap? Dial soap? Irish Spring? Did you ever have a soap-on-a-rope?

Group Verbal Reminiscence Intervention

Current events can provide a convenient impetus for group verbal reminiscence. The TR specialist can bring in current news magazines, newspapers, snapshots, or objects to serve as visual cues. *Then and Now* can be a successful format with topics such as the following:

- Trials
- The Olympics
- Floods
- Engagements
- Childhood
- Vacations

Trials. There have been many trials repeatedly reported on television and newspaper. Do you remember the trial for the kidnapper of the Lindbergh baby? Do you remember the trial of Dr. Sam Sheppard? Do you remember the Rodney King trial? Do you remember the O. J. Simpson trial? How were trials different in the past? Do you have a favorite movie about a trial?

The Olympics. Do you remember when Jesse Owens ran in Berlin? Do you remember when Dorothy Hamill won the gold medal for skating? Which Olympics do you remember best? Do you prefer the summer or the winter games?

Floods (also tornadoes, snow storms, and drought). Has your house ever been flooded? What did you lose? Where did you go? Did you help to clean up later? Did you stay in that town or move?

Engagements. Here is a picture of a man who rented a billboard to ask his girlfriend to marry him—how did you (your husband) propose? Did you give (get) a ring? What did your parents say? How long had you known each other? How long were you engaged?

Childhood. It says in the paper that the average child will receive $250 of toys and clothes for Christmas. What kind of gifts did you get as a child? What sort of clothes did you wear? Did your mother make any of the clothes for the family?

Vacations. Here is an article about the disappearing American vacation. It says that fewer and fewer families go away for 2 weeks the way they used to. Where did your family go on vacation? Did you go back there year after year? Did your family ever go camping?

Written Reminiscence Intervention

Writing is a highly individual activity that will require some time commitment on the part of the TR specialist if it is to be successful. The following advice from Steward and Croft (1988) has proven successful in facilitating writing by older adults:

- Identify participants
- Provide materials
- Identify location
- Determine topic
- Establish time

Identify participants. Identify those who would like to write.

Provide materials. Provide a selection of mechanical aids. When considering writing implements, have available freshly sharpened #2 pencils, ballpoint pens in several colors and point widths, a fountain pen, fine point felt-tip pens, an upright manual typewriter, an electric typewriter, a word processor, or a computer. When choosing paper, use yellow legal pads, lined loose-leaf notebook paper, school composition notebooks, spiral notebooks, diary, letter stationery, or computer paper. In addition, the following items may be useful: Pink Pearl and art gum erasers, an ink eraser, correction fluids (such as Wite-Out and Liquid Paper), carbon paper, paperback dictionary, and thesaurus.

Identify location. Help writers find a place to write. To establish the habit of writing, one needs to write every day. Identify a room, a corner, a desk, or a table at which to write.

Determine topic. Help writers find something to write about. Any of the topics listed previously in this chapter would also be appropriate for writing. In addition, many older adults will enjoy writing autobiographies to give their families. Encourage writers to use writing for personal reasons. Writing can be a useful tool for reviewing and evaluating the past and future. An individual might consider writing a letter to a deceased relative or friend or to a child not yet born. Such letters are very personal and can be cathartic. If the individual seems anxious after writing the letter, he or she may want to dispose of it symbolically by burying or burning it. Or he or she may choose to mail it to someone.

Establish time. Schedule a writing appointment with each new writer to trouble-shoot problems.

Summary

Examples of reminiscence interventions that can be facilitated by TR specialists include activities that focus on sensory stimulation, one-on-one verbal interaction, group verbal discussions, and written topics. Each intervention provides opportunities for people to address with emotions using memories from their pasts. TR specialists can design the reminiscence activities that are best suited for each participant by becoming aware of individual's treatment goals and their histories.

Conclusion

Reminiscence is a technique that can be used by TR specialists to facilitate social interaction, reconstruction of memories, and coping mechanisms. The memories that are usually evoked during reminiscence are those that have symbolic meaning for the individual. Several types of reminiscence interventions are known and have been documented with varying degrees of success. Practitioners are encouraged to investigate clients' personal histories prior to beginning the reminiscence activities and interventions. Overall, reminiscence is a technique used by TR specialists to assist participants to come to terms with their past, resolve issues, and relate their memories to the present.

Discussion Questions

1. What is the definition of recollection?
2. What is the definition of reminiscence?
3. How does reminiscence differ from therapeutic reminiscence?
4. What are the three types of memory discussed in the chapter?
5. What are the three conditions a person with dementia may experience?
6. How do the six types of reminiscence differ from each other?
7. What are the four parts of the process we call remembering?
8. What is one advantage of group reminiscence?
9. How does life review differ from reminiscence or recollection?
10. What should the facilitator do if an individual clearly makes an incorrect statement during reminiscence?

Resources

Agency Resources

Age Exchange Reminiscence Centre

http://www.lewisham.gov.uk/LeisureAndCulture/MuseumsAndGalleries/
AgeExchangeReminiscenceCentre.htm

The Age Exchange Reminiscence Centre focuses on improving the quality of life for older adults by emphasizing the value of their memories to old and young. The center uses art, education programs, and community involvement (volunteerism) as intervention techniques. Age Exchange offers a training and accreditation program for those interested in working with older adults. The Centre has a number of practical books for both students and practitioners. A monthly magazine is available.

Alzheimer's Association

919 N. Michigan Ave., Suite 1000
Chicago, IL 60611
(312) 335-8700, (800) 272-3900, (312) 335-8882 TDD

American Association of Retired Persons

601 E Street, NW
Washington, DC 20049
(202) 434-2277

A free brochure entitled *Reminiscence* is available.

Briggs Activity Ideas

7887 University Blvd., P.O. Box 1698
Des Moines, IA 50306-1698
(800) 247-2343

A free catalog of products for older adults, including reality orientation kits and books for reminiscing, is available.

Eldergames

11710 Hunter Lane
Rockville, MD 20852
(800) 637-2604

Products designed for sensory stimulation and to encourage reminiscing and life review are available.

Geriatric Resources, Inc.

931 South Semoran Blvd., Number 200
Winter Park, FL 32792
(800) 359-0390, (407) 678-1616

A free catalog of products including conversation starters, memory joggers, and reminiscence aids is available.

Material Resources

Erickson, L. M., & Leide, K. (1993). *Memory: 1993/1994 Kit catalog*. Madison, WI: BiFolkal Productions.

Knoth, M. (1989). *Looking back: Reminiscent party fun for senior citizens*. Lafayette, IN: Lafayette Press.

Knoth, M. (1989). *Remembering the good old days*. Lafayette, IN: Lafayette Press.

Sheridan, C. (1991). *Reminiscence: Uncovering a lifetime of memories*. San Francisco, CA: Elder Press.

Webster, J. D. & Haight, B. K. (Eds.). (2002). *Critical advances in reminiscence work: From theory to application*. New York: Springer.

Weiss, C. R. (1989). TR and reminiscing: The pursuit of elusive memory and the art of remembering. *Therapeutic Recreation Journal, 23*(3), 7–18.

References

American Psychiatric Association. (1994). *Diagnostic and statistical manual of mental disorders* (4th ed.). Washington, DC: Author.

Aromando, L. (1995). *Mental health and psychiatric nursing*. Springhouse, PA: Springhouse Corporation.

Atchley, R. C. (1993). Continuity theory and the evolution of activity in later adulthood. In J. Kelly (Ed.), *Activity and aging* (pp. 5–16). Newbury Park, CA: Sage.

Atkinson, D. (1994). I got put away: Group based reminiscence with people with learning difficulties. In J. Bornat (Ed.), *Reminiscence reviewed* (pp. 96–104). Buckingham, UK: Open University Press.

Austin, D. R. (1991). *Therapeutic recreation: Processes and techniques* (2nd ed.). Champaign, IL: Sagamore.

Beaton, S. R. (1991). Styles of reminiscence and ego development of older women residing in long term care settings. *Journal of Aging and Human Development, 32*(1), 53–63.

Beechem, M. H., Anthony, C., & Kurtz, J. (1998). A life review interview guide: A structured systems approach to information gathering. *International Journal of Aging and Human Development, 46*(1), 25–44.

Bluck, S., & Levine, L. J. (1998). Reminiscence as autobiographical memory: A catalyst for reminiscence memory development. *Ageing and Society, 18*, 185–208.

Brody, C. M. (1990). Women in a nursing home. *Psychology of Women Quarterly, 14*, 579–592.

Bryant, F. B., Smart, C. M., & King, S. P. (2005). Using the past to enhance the present: Boosting happiness through positive reminiscence. *Journal of Happiness Studies, 6*, 227–260.

Buchanan, D., Moorhouse, A., Cabico, L., Krock, M., Campbell, H., & Spevakow, D. (2002). A critical review and synthesis of literature on reminiscing with older adults. *Canadian Journal of Nursing Research, 34*, 123–139.

Butler, R. N. (1963). The life review: An interpretation of reminiscence in the aged. *Psychiatry, 26*, 65–76.

Butler, R. N., & Lewis, M. I. (1973). *Aging & mental health: Positive psychosocial approaches*. St. Louis, MO: Mosby.

Cappeliez, P., & O'Rourke, N. (2002). Personality traits and existential concerns as predictors of the functions of reminiscence in older adults. *Journal of Gerontology, 57b,* 116–123.

Cohen, D., & Eisdorfer, C. (1986). *The loss of self: A family resource for the care of Alzheimer's disease and related disorders.* New York: New American Library.

Coleman, P. G. (1999). Creating a life story: The task of reconciliation. *The Gerontologist, 39*(2), 133–139.

Cumming, E., & Henry, W. E. (1961). *Growing old.* New York: Basic Books.

Durkee, J. (1997). Activities for Alzheimer's residents. *Creative Forecasting, 9*(2), 16–17.

Erikson, E. (1982). *The life cycle completed.* New York: Norton.

Fry, P. S. (1991). Individual differences in reminiscence among older adults: Predictors of frequency and pleasantness ratings of reminiscence activity. *International Journal of Aging and Human Development, 33*(4), 311–326.

Gibson, F. (1994). "What can reminiscence contribute to people with dementia?" In J. Bornat (Ed.), *Reminiscence reviewed* (pp. 46–60). Buckingham, UK: Open University Press.

Gose, K., & Levi, G. (1985). *Dealing with memory changes as you grow older.* Toronto, ON: Bantam.

Haight, B. K. (1991). Reminiscing: The state of the art as a basis for practice. *International Journal of Aging and Human Development, 33*(1), 1–32.

Havighurst, R. J. (1968). Personality and patterns of aging. *The Gerontologist, 8,* 20–23.

Havighurst, R. J., & Glasser, R. (1972). An exploratory study of reminiscence. *Journal of Gerontology, 27*(2), 245–253.

Hayslip, B., & Panek, P. E. (1989). *Adult development and aging.* New York: Harper & Row.

Heston, L. L., & White, J. A. (1983). *Dementia: A practical guide to Alzheimer's disease and related illnesses.* New York: W. H. Freeman.

Holland, C. A., & Rabbitt, P. M. A. (1991). Ageing memory: Use versus impairment. *Journal of Psychology, 82,* 29–38.

Holzapfel, S. K. (1989). Importance of personal possessions in the lives of institutionalized elderly. In AARP, *Reminiscence: Finding meaning in memories resource materials* (pp. 15–17). Washington, DC: American Association of Retired Persons.

Hooyman, N. R., & Kiyak, H. A. (1993). *Social gerontology: A multidisciplinary perspective* (3rd ed.). Boston: Allyn & Bacon.

Huber, K., & Miller, P. (1984). Reminisce with the elderly—DO IT! *Geriatric Nursing,* 84–87.

Jones, E. D. (2003). Reminiscence therapy for older women with depression: Effects of a nursing intervention classification in assisted living long-term care. *Journal of Gerontological Nursing, 29*(7), 26–33.

Lamme, S., & Baars, J. (1993). Including social factors in the analysis of reminiscence in elderly individuals. *International Journal of Aging and Human Development, 37*(4), 297–311.

Lee, Y., Tabourne, C. E. S., & Yoon, J. (2008). Effects of life review program on emotional well-being of Korean elderly with Alzheimer's disease. *American Journal of Recreation Therapy, 7*(2), 35–45.

Mace, N. L., & Rabins, P. V. (1981). *The 36-hour day: A family guide to caring for persons with Alzheimer's disease, related dementing illnesses, and memory loss in later life*. Baltimore, MD: The Johns Hopkins University Press.

Mills, M. A. (1997). Narrative identity and dementia: A study of emotion and narrative in older people with dementia. *Aging and Society, 17*, 673–698.

Moody, H. R. (1988). Twenty-five years of the life review: Where did we come from? Where are we going? *Journal of Gerontological Social Work, 12*, 7–21.

Parker, R. G. (1995). Reminiscence: A continuity theory framework. *The Gerontologist, 35*, 515–525.

Parker, R. G. (1999). Reminiscence as continuity: Comparison of young and older adults. *Journal of Clinical Geropsychology, 5*, 147–157.

Pasupathi, M., & Carstensen, L. L. (2003). Age and emotional experience during mutual reminiscing. *Psychology and Aging, 18*, 430–442.

Podolsky, D., & Newman, R. J. (1991, October 28). Good drugs, bad effects. *U.S. News & World Report*, 82–85.

Powell, L. S., & Courtice, K. (1986). *Alzheimer's disease: A guide for families*. Reading, MA: Addison-Wesley.

Rosow, I. (1976). Status and role change through the life span. In R. H. Binstock & E. Shanas (Eds.), *Handbook of aging and the social sciences*. New York: Van Nostrand Reinhold.

Schindler, R., Spiegel, C., & Malachi, E. (1992). Silences: Helping elderly Holocaust victims deal with the past. *International Journal of Human Development, 35*(4), 243–252.

Sherman, E. (1994). The structures of well-being in the life narratives of the elderly. *Journal of Aging Studies, 8*, 149–158.

Skalko, T. K., Mitchell, R. S., Kaye, A. G., & Dalton, M. J. (1994). *Basic guide to physical and psychiatric medications for recreational therapy*. Hattiesburg, MS: American Therapeutic Recreation Association.

Soukhanov, A. H. (Ed.) (1992). *The American heritage dictionary of the English language* (3rd ed.). Boston: Houghton Mifflin.

Steward, J. S., & Croft, M. K. (1988). *The leisure pen: A book for elder writers*. Plover, WI: Keepsake.

Tabourne, C. E. S. (1995). The life review program as an intervention for an older adult newly admitted to a nursing facility. *Therapeutic Recreation Journal, 29*, 228–236.

Tarrant, M. A., Dattilo, J., Driver, B. L., & Manfredo, M. J. (1995). Physiological response patterning of verbal and mental recreational reminiscence. *Therapeutic Recreation Journal, 29*, 147–162.

Teague, M. L., McGhee, V. L., & Hawkins, B. A. (1996). Geriatric practice. In D. R. Austin & M. E. Crawford (Eds.), *Therapeutic recreation: An introduction* (2nd ed., pp. 227–244). Boston: Allyn & Bacon.

Wade-Farber, F. (1996, Spring). Is anyone listening? *Eldergames News & Views*, 1–2.

Webster, J. D. (1993). Construction and validation of the Reminiscence Functions Scale. *Journal of Gerontology, 48*(5), 256–262.

Webster, J. D., & Young, R. A. (1988). Process variables of the life review: Counseling implications. *International Journal of Aging and Human Development, 26*(4), 315–323.

Wong, P. T., & Watt, L. M. (1991). What types of reminiscence are associated with successful aging? *Psychology and Aging, 6,* 272–279.

Zauszniewski, J. A., Eggenschwiler, K., Preechawoong, S., Chung, C., Airey, T. F., Wilke, P. A., Morris, D. L., & Roberts, B. L. (2004). Focused reflection reminiscence group for elders: Implementation and evaluation. *The Journal of Applied Gerontology, 23*(4), 429–442.

Zgola, J. M. (1987). *Doing things: A guide to programming activities for persons with Alzheimer's disease and related disorders.* Baltimore, MD: Johns Hopkins University.

Chapter 14
Therapeutic Use of Animals

Lynne Cory, Alexis McKenney, and Stephanie Marsden

Animals make such agreeable friends—
they ask no questions, they pass no criticisms.

—George Eliot

Introduction

Pets and animals have become an integral part of American society (Doyle & Kukowski, 1989). The strength of using animals in therapy resides in the ability of animals to elicit emotional and behavioral responses, provide distraction from distress, and enhance mood (Brickel, 1986). Effects of therapeutic use of animals has been hypothesized to be attributed to a sense of normalcy and consistency animals bring to the lives of individuals they encounter (Beck & Katcher, 1983).

This chapter is designed to introduce the reader to the therapeutic use of animals in TR. To achieve this purpose, definitions and a description of the therapeutic use of animals are given. A history and theoretical foundation of the therapeutic use of animals is described. A review of related literature reveals the effectiveness of these therapeutic techniques and a case study is presented as an example of the potential impact of animals on participants. A list of resources and other references are provided to complement the information provided in this chapter.

Definitions

Therapeutic use of animals involves use of a variety of terms and phrases to refer to guided interactions between animals and humans to achieve therapeutic goals. Terminology used to describe programs that integrate animals into TR programs varies greatly; the phrase that will be used in this chapter is the therapeutic use of animals. This phrase will be used because it does not limit the particular approach or type of animal. ***Therapeutic use of animals*** is the use of animals to improve the lives of people with disabilities through interactions and engagement with animals. TR specialists may use a number of facilitation techniques to achieve specific outcomes (Carter, Van Andel, & Robb, 2003); therapeutic use of animals has become an accepted strategy. The following phrases that describe therapeutic use of animals include:

- Pet Therapy
- Pet-Facilitated Therapy
- Animal-Assisted Therapy
- Companion Animals
- Animals as Helpers

Pet Therapy

Pet therapy is a general term that is usually defined as having pets brought into a facility in hopes that the natural therapeutic bond between humans and animals will enhance psychosocial well-being of participants (Kongable, Buckwalter, & Stolley, 1989). Since some animals that are not typically considered to be pets (e.g., farm animals, dolphins, and monkeys) have been used in therapeutic settings, the term pet may be too limiting.

Pet-Facilitated Therapy

The phrase pet therapy is often expanded and is sometimes used interchangeably with the more recently appearing phrase *pet-facilitated therapy*. Brickel (1986) defined pet-facilitated therapy as integrating animals into client-directed, therapeutic activities (p. 309). Although this particular approach considers the therapist as a key element, it continues to focus on animals that are specifically pets. It is helpful to consider that pet-facilitated and all pet- or animal-related therapies are not standardized, have no strict established guidelines, and are used as an adjunctive therapy modality (Brickel, 1986).

Animal-Assisted Therapy

Animal-assisted therapy is a fairly inclusive phrase often used in recent literature (Lefkowitz, Paharia, Prout, Debiak, & Bleiberg, 2005). Although this phrase is inclusive in the sense that it contains the word animal, it infers that the animal is used in conjunction with a therapist, something that may not be inferred by other terms such as pet therapy.

Companion Animals

The phrase *companion animals* is often referred to in the literature in conjunction with the word therapeutic (Valeri, 2006). Household pets, such as dogs, cats, and birds, are considered companion animals. Although owning a pet or having an animal as a companion is, in many ways, therapeutic in terms of improving health and happiness, companion animals are not typically used to achieve therapeutic outcomes (Kavanagh, 1994). If a companion animal is recommended, typically, this decision would not be exclusively that of a TR specialist.

Animals as Helpers

Use of *animals as helpers* for people with disabilities is also frequently discussed in the literature (Eddy, Hart, & Boltz, 1988). Use of "seeing-eye dogs," "hearing-ear dogs," "assist dogs," "service dogs," "canine helpers," or "guide dogs" have been reported to help increase independence and quality of life of individuals with disabilities (Kavanagh, 1994). These service dogs are trained at a myriad of different schools and vary widely in abilities and function. Use of service dogs is not the focus of this chapter because service dogs are often provided by independent agencies whose focus is the specific training of those animals to help people with disabilities. Providing service animals and training animals as helpers is not commonly within the responsibilities of a TR specialist.

Summary

The therapeutic use of animals encompasses a variety of techniques using animals as a component of therapy. The phrases surrounding this type of therapy have yet to be standardized and many phrases used imply use of animals in therapy; however, the actual processes that occur within the therapeutic use of animals are difficult to determine.

> For example, two separate facilities may have programs titled "animal-assisted therapy." One facility may feature a program that involves animals and their handlers entering a room so that program participants can freely interact with the animals (e.g., talking to the animals and handlers, petting the animals, giving the animals treats). The other facility may feature a program that facilitates animals and handlers going into program participants' rooms with specific program objectives and activities identified for participants, such as increasing range of motion while brushing an animal and increasing mobility by walking a dog down the hallway.

Although these programs may share the same name, the structure of the programs may vary. Therefore, it is helpful to specify procedures to be followed for a program employing the therapeutic use of animals.

Descriptions

Use of animals to assist people in achieving therapeutic goals has occurred in a variety of settings, such as nursing homes (Kawamura, Niyama, & Niyama, 2007) and residential psychiatric treatment facilities (Kovacs, Rozsa, Kis, & Rozsa, 2004) and with a diverse range of populations, such as individuals with depression (Lutwack-Bloom, Wijewickrama, & Smith, 2005), autism (Rederfer & Goodman, 1989), aphasia (Macauley, 2006) social limitations (Colombo, Buono, Smania, & Leo, 2006), post-traumatic stress disorder (Lefkowitz et al., 2005), and dementia (Motomura, Yagi, & Ohyama, 2004). In addition, in recent years, animals have been used to assist with development of empathy and positive social behaviors toward humans through humane education (Melson, 2003).

Animal-assisted therapy services are provided by a variety of organizations, some for profit and others volunteer, but perhaps the best known, and largest volunteer organization, is the ***Delta Society***, a nonprofit international organization. The Delta Society's Pet Partners' Program and Animal-Assisted Therapy Services help people with varying illnesses improve their conditions through contact and interaction with trained therapy animals. People with disabilities can increase their independence with the assistance of dogs trained to be helping companions through the National Dog Service Center. In addition, the Delta Society offers a program for the general public, titled People and Pets Activities, which focuses on educating people on ways companion animals can improve their lives such as maintaining good health, growing and developing in positive ways, and coping positively with loss, stress, loneliness, and illness (Delta Society, 1996).

This section contains information on the way animals are used in therapy. Program considerations are provided, as well as the way in which an animal-assisted program can be organized. Therefore, this portion of the chapter contains the following sections:

- Use of Animals
- Program Considerations
- Organization of Programs

Use of Animals

Interventions commonly used with animals can be divided into three sections, depending on the way the animal is used in therapy. The most frequently reported use of animals in the literature is for petting or making contact (Fick, 1993). Another use of animals is in caring for the animal (Mallon, 1994a). Animals are used therapeutically when they are used in conjunction with psychotherapy (Folse, Minder, Aycock, & Santana, 1994). This section is divided into the following topics:

- Contact with animals
- Caring for animals
- Animals used with psychotherapy

Contact with animals. Interventions involving contact with animals can consist of having animals available to be petted by participants or the animals can be used in a more structured manner.

> For example, Loretta, a woman with dementia who lives in an assisted living facility, tells a story about her childhood pet as she holds Elvis the cat in her lap (see Figure 14.1). The TR specialist can assist Loretta with short-term memory recall by asking Loretta questions about Elvis after giving Loretta information about Elvis. Information for recall can include his name, age, color, or weight. Another recall exercise the TR specialist can employ

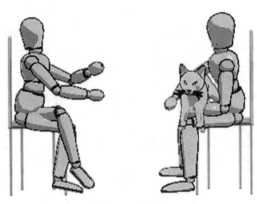

Figure 14.1

is to encourage Loretta to compare her childhood pet to Elvis. In addition, Loretta may be able to maintain mobility, hand-eye coordination, and fine and gross motor skills through the acts of stroking and petting Elvis.

Caring for animals. Some programs that include animals as a component of their treatment approach involve having participants care for the animals. Often, these are farm animals which live at the agency's locale.

> For example, Michael, Ray, and Jim currently reside at an adolescent residential treatment facility for children who have been diagnosed with behavior disorders. The treatment facility is located on a farm in a rural community. The facility has resident animals such as dogs, cats, cows, sheep, horses, and chickens. The three boys, along with other residents, volunteer for the animal care program. As part of this program, the residents alternate responsibilities for grooming, feeding, and cleaning the animals and the animals' living quarters. Program participants might be involved in gathering and selling the products from the animals, such as eggs, milk, or wool. On a regular schedule, the TR specialist meets individually and as a group with Michael, Ray, and Jim for debriefings relative to their feelings toward the animals and their attitudes regarding sole and shared responsibilities for the animals. These programs allow for contact with animals that can foster a sense of nurturance.

Animals used with psychotherapy. Animals can be used in conjunction with psychotherapy to improve the therapist-client relationship by fostering trust and a sense of unconditional acceptance. The animal can be used as a dialogue starter when conducting group discussions and can act to calm participants.

> For example, at a residential treatment facility for people with substance addiction issues, Dooley, a flat-coated retriever, is used by the therapist at the beginning of a discussion group by

introducing her and telling a story about Dooley's life. Beginning the session by first discussing Dooley, rather than an initial focus on participants, might encourage participants to become more relaxed in the group. Another way an animal is used in psychotherapy is to allow participants to pet or stroke the animal while they are talking to the therapist. For example, one therapist regularly takes her small dog, Lucky, to her office on days she has an appointment with Marsha, a child who was physically abused. On initial visits, Marsha was unwilling to talk and sat in the corner and cried. Once Lucky began attending Marsha's appointments, Marsha played with Lucky and spoke to the therapist while holding Lucky in her lap.

Program Considerations

Unless the TR specialist is experienced in the therapeutic use of animals, a reputable external organization can be used to structure the program. There are animal-assisted therapy organizations that charge for services; however, more often, there are well-organized, professionally run volunteer animal-assisted therapy organizations that contract with agencies to provide services on a regularly occurring schedule.

Experienced animal-handler teams can assist TR specialists in building a program that uses the abilities of specific animals for different people. If an external organization is used to facilitate a therapeutic program, a program plan based on the skills and training of the animal-handler teams can be implemented. The animal-handler teams can be matched with participants based on their needs.

It is important to consider many aspects of a program involving the therapeutic use of animals prior to its development and implementation. Considerations relate to the people being served, the available resources, and facilitators of sessions, and include, but are not limited to:

- Selection of animal
- Materials
- Safety and health issues
- Facilitator training
- Environmental management
- Orientation and support
- Care for the animal

Selection of animal. Many considerations surround selection of an animal. The most common animals used in animal-assisted therapy are dogs, cats, and rabbits. The size, age, as well as the temperament and training of the animal are each important considerations.

Sometimes large animals may not be appropriate, especially if the facilitation area is very small. Another consideration relevant to size of the visiting animal pertains to equipment that may be in use by participants, such as poles holding intravenous fluid containers or monitoring equipment. A large dog with a vigorously wagging tail could inadvertently topple or damage some equipment. A large, active dog, albeit gentle, might frighten young children or older adults. Conversely, it may be difficult to continuously use a very small animal such as a gerbil or hamster with a large group. It is most convenient when the participating animal-assisted therapy organizations have different-sized animals which may be used in various settings.

The age of the animal is another important consideration when selecting animals. Animals that are too young may not have had the opportunity to become adequately trained such as being housebroken, obeying commands, and walking on leash properly. In addition, young animals may not be adequately socialized with other people and animals, may be too active, and may be more likely to be distracted. In some therapeutic settings, an older, more mature animal may be a more appropriate choice.

The anticipated behavior of an animal is a crucial consideration in selecting animals or types of animals for a specific setting. It is helpful for the TR specialist to be aware of the type of animal training and evaluation of animal-handler teams employed by the external organizations. Reputable volunteer organizations require stringent testing of animal obedience and temperament prior to admittance of the animal as a member. The handler of the animal is required to accompany the animal throughout testing procedures.

Many organizations require dogs to have successfully completed a basic obedience course prior as well as successfully passing the American Kennel Club's (AKC) "Canine Good Citizenship" (CGC) test and a temperament test. These tests are rigorous and simulate situations animal-handler teams may experience on a visit to various facilities (e.g., clinical settings, settings where participants' voices may be loud and/ or angry, settings where animals may be required to quickly "settle down"). During administration of the CGC, dogs are exposed to equipment commonly present in some settings such as wheelchairs, walkers, and canes. Dogs' reactions to a person's sudden and awkward movements are assessed. In addition, the dogs are exposed to loud noises such as bells clanging, whistles being blown, and people yelling. According to Volhard and Volhard (1993), a well-socialized dog typically will not exhibit behavior indicating stress such as ears flattened onto head, tail down, body lowered, or rapid panting during the testing procedure. Aggressive behavior, such as growling, snarling, or attempting to bite during the testing session, will prevent the dog from successfully passing the CGC and temperament tests. In addition, the overall reactions of the animal being tested and the handler's responses are observed and evaluated.

Evaluations for animals other than dogs differ slightly from the more systematic tests for dogs. Generally, cats, rabbits, ferrets, snakes, and/or birds must tolerate stroking and handling while being held by a stranger and not display reactions associated with stress such as flattening ears onto head, hissing, attempting to escape, biting, scratching, or having episodes of stress-induced urination or defecation when in settings that include unfamiliar animals, equipment, or people. In addition, these animals must tolerate wearing collars and leashes for the duration of the visit. In some facilities, these animals may not be as suitable as dogs as therapeutic companions due to inconsistent reactions and behaviors in varied situations.

Materials. Many types of materials for various methods associated with the therapeutic use of animals can be considered prior to implementing a therapeutic program. Generally, if an external organization is used to assist with the program, the handlers will have materials for their animals. Different types of materials may enhance the therapy experience for participants.

Figure 14.2

For example, people who have difficulty grasping might use a
brush with an enlarged handle to brush animals. Balls of various
weights or textures, such as baseballs or tennis balls may be used
for retrieving (see Figure 14.2). Dogs can jump through hoops held
by people who are targeted to increase fine motor strength or gain
eye-hand coordination. Some dogs can be "dressed" in clothing
with Velcro fasteners.

Safety and health issues. For all types of therapeutic uses of animals, safety and
health issues must be considered. Compliance with all health regulations is of critical
importance and is generally a requirement for facilities implementing animal-
assisted therapy programs. Hospital accreditation organizations regularly review
animal-assisted therapy protocol. These health regulations relate to infection control,
environmental sanitation, and resident rights.

All animals participating in the provision of therapy are to be healthy. Most
organizations devoted to the therapeutic use of animals require veterinary approval
for each animal prior to admission to the organization and require proof of inocula-
tions each year to continue membership. Veterinary approval includes a general
physical exam and parasitological exam for endo- and ectoparasites. Some facilities
administer a tuberculosis test to handlers prior to an initial visit.

Transmission of disease from animals to humans is not common; however,
even inoculated, healthy animals such as cats, birds, monkeys, and domesticated
rodents may carry bacteria that cause infections in people with suppressed or
weakened immune systems (Happy Tails Pet Therapy, Inc., 1994). For that reason,
many facilities will not consider visitation by animals other than dogs. Reputable
organizations involved in the provision of services associated with the therapeutic
use of animals require that animals are clean, well-groomed, and parasite-free prior
to entering a facility for a visit.

To ensure that animals become acquainted with other animal-handler teams
and become oriented to the facility, a visiting animal-handler team usually arrives
at a facility at least 10–15 minutes prior to the session. Animal elimination (i.e.,
urination, defecation) can be addressed during this period reducing the chance of an
"accident" or interruption of the session. Handlers are required to dispose of animal
waste and typically carry plastic bags for this reason.

It is important for facilities using animals in therapeutic ways to develop a written safety plan posted in area where the sessions occur. A first-aid kit should be immediately available to staff facilitating sessions. Emergency numbers, including the closest animal hospital or veterinarian office, should be kept near the phone or carried with the facilitator for on-site visits. It is also helpful for facilitators to have first-aid training.

Facilitator training. If TR specialists choose to facilitate programs involving the therapeutic use of animals rather than contracting with external organizations, it is important that they have a clear understanding of participants' goals and desires so participants can work toward those goals through guided interactions with the animals. To accomplish these goals, it is necessary for the TR specialists to assess participant needs and abilities. Following assessment, TR specialists can utilize specific interventions effectively incorporating specific traits and characteristics of various animals to enhance service delivery and goal attainment.

External organizations involved in therapeutic use of animals typically provide new member training. Their methods include training sessions, observations of actual visits by novice handlers accompanying experienced handlers, and supervised initial visits. Volunteer handlers are required to observe rules of confidentiality with regard to participants' identities and conditions.

Environmental management. Another important factor in the therapeutic use of animals is environmental management. The primary environmental concerns are the facilitation areas (either indoors or outdoors), space available for a resident animal, and procedures to restrain the animal from certain areas (e.g., food preparation areas). An awareness of the type of flooring in the session area can be helpful. For example, although tile may allow for a quick cleanup after sessions, frequently during the session an animal may lose its footing due to tile slickness. How an area is selected can depend on the activities the TR specialist has chosen for the session and the goals of the participants.

If a program involves a resident animal, the animal is given its own space inside the facility and allowed adequate time outside each day (if it is an inside/outside animal).

> For example, Micah, an Australian Shepherd, is a resident animal at a children's psychiatric facility. Often, staff members will take Micah home with them on weeknights and weekends. Micah remains comfortable in a variety of settings due to exposure to various experiences in the community outside the facility. To increase her comfort level with different places and people staff members alternate taking Micah home on weekends.

Orientation and support. Prior to implementing a program utilizing a resident animal in a therapeutic manner, it is helpful to evaluate agency staff to determine if support exists to foster the presence of a resident animal. Evaluation of staff's support for either resident or visiting animal-handler teams is important. Without support of staff, the presence of a resident or visiting animal is unlikely to be successful. It is helpful to identify goals and outcomes desired by using an animal therapeutically and communicate these to all agency personnel. A plan of action can be created that focuses on those goals and desires. Important consideration for a new resident animal is orientation of the animal to the facility, staff, residents, and visitors.

In the case of utilizing visiting animal-handler teams, the handlers are responsible for their animals during the interactions between participants and animals. In addition, handlers must protect their animals from potential dangers. Handlers are not responsible for supervising participants, transporting participants, or providing other services for participants. Therefore, it is important for staff to remain available to assist participants during sessions.

Care for the animal. When initiating a program that involves using a resident animal in a therapeutic manner it is important to consider costs. A budget will depend on the type of animal that is chosen.

> For example, costs for a dog will include food, potential obedience training, equipment such as food and water bowls, bedding, leashes, collars, crates/kennels, fencing, and waste disposal, in addition to grooming, ongoing veterinary and medical costs, insurance, and city/county/state animal licenses.

Other types of animals may require more or less budgetary considerations, depending on what type of animal and specific needs associated with that animal. Housing animals can become costly, especially if an animal sustains injuries or becomes ill. Legal and liability concerns for either resident animals or visiting animals are important considerations. Most organizations involved in the therapeutic use of animals provide liability insurance coverage for their members during therapy visits.

Organization of Programs

It is important for TR specialists to prepare carefully for a session involving therapeutic use of animals. The specialist can communicate with representatives of the external organizations to obtain information about animal-handler teams. Ideally, the TR specialist meets with representatives of the organization prior to program implementation to establish days, times, and rooms most conducive for sessions. In some cases, the specialist can specify which animals might best meet needs of participants and which animals are within the parameters of infectious disease control department of the agency. At the beginning of sessions, it is helpful to inform the animal-handlers of the general session goals.

Often, organizations providing services involving the therapeutic use of animals design groups of specific animal-handler teams that visit facilities on a recurrent basis on scheduled days and times. Groups consist of several animal-handler teams that include animals and the individuals leading the animals (handlers). The number of animal-handler teams can be dependent on the number of participants, goals for the program, size of facility, or other considerations.

Typically, the animal-handler teams are given information prior to the visit about the type of session and activities in which they will be participating. In addition, through recurrent visits, the groups become familiar with the nature of specific sessions at a facility. Nevertheless, it is the responsibility of the TR specialist to manage the session and guide the animal-handler teams to provide an effective therapeutic experience for participants. As the TR specialist becomes familiar with skills and characteristics of various animal-handler teams, sessions can be made increasingly beneficial for participants by matching their needs with animal-handler teams' proficiencies.

A variety of activities can be performed to increase participants' comfort with animals. The following categories are used to organize programs to prepare participants for effective interaction with an animal:

- Preparing for the session
- Visiting with animals
- Implementing intervention techniques

Preparing for the session. The TR specialist can prepare participants for sessions with animals by describing the animal-handler teams who will be attending the session and the organization with which they are associated. Specifically, it is helpful to explain that the animals have received unique training and have been screened relative to their health, disposition, and responsiveness.

An explanation of the nature of the relationship between the animal and the handler can be helpful information for participants. Some handlers own the animals, and the animals are considered family pets. Some handlers borrow animals from animal shelters.

> This therapeutic use of animals generally occurs in collaboration with a local chapter of the Humane Society or other rescue organization and involves the use of untrained puppies and kittens awaiting adoption.

Other handlers participate with animals that are being trained for future service to people with disabilities. Many service animal agencies using dogs require each puppy to live with a family for 1 year prior to formal acceptance into a service program (Volhard & Volhard, 1993).

Participants can be prepared for sessions with animals by being given specific information about the visiting animals. It may be helpful to provide photographs of the animals in addition to short descriptions about them including names, breeds, and activities the animals enjoy. It is also helpful to describe activities planned for a session involving the therapeutic use of animals, such as grooming, petting, walking, and playing with toys.

Although it can be helpful to urge reluctant individuals to participate in the activities associated with the therapeutic use of animals, participants should not feel undue pressure to interact with the animals. When using animals in a therapeutic manner, it is important to respect the rights of all participants. If a participant does not choose to interact with the animals, the participant could watch the interaction between other participants and the animals. Reluctant participants may choose to join the group after they observe interaction between other participants and the animals.

Prior to the session involving animals, a TR specialist can facilitate a warm-up activity or group discussion about animals. The discussion can include asking participants: (a) if they ever owned a pet, and if so the name of the pet, (b) to imagine a friend's pet, (c) to think about some characteristics of their pet or a funny story about it, and (d) why they like their pet. Next, participants can draw a picture of an animal or pet. This activity may stimulate discussion of animals' qualities. If no animals are visiting, the discussion can be used as an exercise for participants to relay information about their past experiences with and feelings toward animals.

Visiting with animals. Before the groups of animal-handler teams arrive, participants can be encouraged to gather in the area where the session will occur. The physical location of the session depends on participants and the agency. Sessions can occur outdoors in an enclosed area or indoors in a room with adequate space to accommodate participants and visiting animal-handler teams.

It is important for the session time to be one that is not an otherwise regularly scheduled time for participants to sleep, have meals, or participate in other activities. Often, sessions are between 30–60 minutes due to limits of participant tolerance of any specific treatment session, mandated length of sessions by agencies, and the potential for some animals to become tired and distracted after more than an hour.

It is helpful to arrange the area where the session will occur that allows for ease of interaction between animals and participants. Chairs can be placed in small groups to enable participants to interact with the animal-handler teams in groups of no more than four participants at a time. Each animal-handler team can move about the room and alternately interact with each group of participants.

If participants use assistive mobility devices such as wheelchairs, walkers, crutches, and canes, and depending on their independence using these mobility devices, the TR specialist or other staff may assist a participant to ensure full participation in the session and unrestricted access to the animals. Participants may also have other portable medical equipment such as intravenous poles, vital sign monitors, and oxygen containers accompanying them during the session. It is necessary to provide opportunities for safe movement by the animal-handler teams among participants and equipment.

In some agency settings, sessions occur in spacious areas having arranged seating. In this setting, sessions are usually less structured and participants and animal-handler teams interact casually. This type of session typically occurs in residential psychiatric settings or assisted-living facilities. The sessions focus on social interaction between participants and animal-handler teams rather than physical rehabilitation. As the animal-handler teams enter the room, certain teams can be directed to specific participants or groups of participants as each animal-handler team offers a different opportunity for a therapeutic experience.

Implementing intervention techniques. Intervention techniques can take many forms and can be used with people who have various disabilities. The following examples of techniques can be used during sessions involving the therapeutic use of animals for people who have physical disabilities. Physical disabilities described below are due to: left cerebrovascular accidents (CVAs), right CVAs, brain injury due to trauma, and disabilities in lower extremities.

A CVA, more commonly known as a stroke, may occur in the left or right side of the brain, or the brainstem. The site in the brain of either the CVA or trauma-induced injury will determine its effects (Bond-Howard, 1993).

People with a *left CVA* experience a stroke on the left side of their brain, which affects the right side of their bodies, and such people often exhibit symptoms that include weakness on the right side of the body and loss of speech or language. Expressive language deficits prevent some people with left CVAs to express desired thoughts. Receptive language deficits can prevent people with left CVAs to understand others. Dysarthria prevents some people from speaking clearly. Other symptoms resulting from a left CVA are memory and attention deficits, difficulty distinguishing left from right, decreased verbal learning, lowered tolerance for frustration, and lengthened response times.

>As an example, to assist in building strength and stamina on his weak right side after a left CVA, the TR specialist assists Jim in using his right hand to groom Bailey, a golden retriever, with a large-handled brush which promotes development of his grasping, fine, and gross motor skills. To promote increases in Jim's coordination, range of motion, and sense of touch, Jim is guided to stroke, pet, or hug Bailey. Throwing Bailey's tennis ball presents an opportunity for Jim to gain hand-eye coordination skills. As Jim follows instructions from the TR specialist on the proper manner in which to command Bailey to retrieve her tennis ball, his receptive language skills can be improved. Jim can hold Bailey's food treats as she eats them from his hand, an activity which enhances his ability to grasp and refine motor skills. In addition, this activity can contribute to an increase in Jim's attention span as he focuses on Bailey and the task at-hand. Depending on Jim's ambulation skills, Jim may be able to walk Bailey around the activity room or down the hall while holding Bailey's leash/harness (see Figure 14.3). Walking Bailey helps Jim develop a sense of balance,

Figure 14.3

additionally increasing expressive and receptive language skills as
he commands Bailey to "Let's go" and "Heel."

Caution is used in determining a participant's ambulation skills following a left
CVA and it is important to review participant records prior to the session to ensure
maximum participant safety.

> In another example of a person with a left CVA and an attempt to
> increase her fine motor skills, coordination, and attention span,
> Alice can "dress" Peaches, a cocker spaniel, with scarves, clothing
> with Velcro fasteners, ribbons, or hair barrettes. The TR specialist
> can assist in development of Alice's expressive and receptive
> language skills by prompting her to give verbal commands to
> Peaches by either repeating commands given by the handler,
> or reading aloud written commands. Another activity aiding in
> language development and increased memory skills is to ask Alice
> to locate and verbally identify parts of Peaches' body. For example,
> Alice may be asked "Where is Peaches' ear?" or "What is this?"
> while pointing to specific areas of Peaches' body and encouraged
> to verbally respond with correct identification of the indicated area.
> It is helpful to give short, concise instructions to Alice throughout
> the session.

People who have experienced a *right CVA* experience a stroke on the right side of
their brain that affects the left side of their body, and exhibit symptoms that include
weakness on the left side of the body and neglect of one side of the body. Neglect of
one side prevents some people from being aware of the presence of a particular side.
Other symptoms exhibited by people who have experienced a right CVA are vision
deficits, memory deficits, dysarthria, decreased reading ability, decreased reasoning
skills, attention deficits, decreased awareness of time (comprehension of past and
future is difficult), decreased ability to recognize familiar faces, increased impulsive-
ness, and poor safety awareness.

> As an example, to help Ted build strength and stamina on a weak
> and neglected left side after a right CVA, the TR specialist can
> have Murray, a Gordon Setter, sit to the left of Ted during a portion
> of the session. Positioning Murray on Ted's left side is intended
> to direct Ted's attention toward his left side so that he can become
> aware of his left side. Murray's handler, Karen, can explain to Ted
> that Murray enjoys chewing on one end of a rawhide toy while a
> person holds the other end. If Ted wants to hold the toy for Murray,
> the TR specialist can assist Ted in grasping one end of the rawhide
> toy while Karen directs the other end of the toy toward Murray's
> mouth. As Murray chews on the rawhide, a gentle tugging on
> the toy results which encourages Ted to increase his grasp on
> the rawhide toy while moving his arm to the rhythm of Murray's

chewing. The movement of Ted's arm can potentially increase his range of motion.

In another example of a person who has experienced a right CVA, Tonia's recall skills can be increased by following 1, 2, 3-step directions. For example, using Brandy, a German shepherd, Tonia can be asked to "Call Brandy's name," "Give a command to Brandy," and "After Brandy obeys the command, give her a food treat." Another activity that promotes development of recall skill is to ask Tonia to recall information about Brandy such as Brandy's name, age, breed, and color then verbally state this information. To promote an increase in reading comprehension skills, the TR specialist can provide written information about Brandy so Tonia can read the information aloud. To promote identification with Tonia's neglected left side, Brandy can be positioned on Tonia's left side during their interaction. It is helpful for the TR specialist to communicate with Tonia in a concise manner throughout the session.

People who have experienced a ***brain injury*** can exhibit symptoms which include decreased attention span, overall weakness or one-sided weakness, inability to follow directions, and poor problem-solving skills. The degree of injury determines the symptoms.

As an example, after Jamal sustained a traumatic brain injury in an automobile accident, the TR specialist attempted to increase Jamal's attention span and increase his ability to follow directions by asking him to complete simple tasks one at a time. For example, using Ranger, a Bernese Mountain Dog, Jamal is asked to "Brush Ranger," or "Pet Ranger with your right hand." In addition, to increase Jamal's ability to focus his attention, he is asked to attend to one animal at a time, completing a simple task before moving to another animal. To promote recall skills, Jamal is asked questions about Ranger such as "What is this dog's name?", "How old is Ranger?" or "What is Ranger's breed?" Jamal can increase his strength and stamina by having Ranger on his weak side during their interaction. Throughout the session, it is helpful to give short, concise instructions to Jamal.

Individuals experiencing a disability as a result of ***hip, knee, or leg injuries/surgeries*** often have weakness in lower extremities and potential limitations with balance. Participants with hip surgeries or replacements are not advised to initially bend hips past 90 degrees. It is helpful for participants to focus on activities which allow them to gain strength in both upper and lower extremities.

As an example, after Allen had hip replacement surgery, he worked with Riley, a Rottweiler, to increase Allen's upper body strength. Allen grasped and held a harness while Riley pulled Allen's wheelchair. To promote tolerance for the standing position, Allen stood while using a walker as an assistive mobility device. He threw a tennis ball for Riley to retrieve. In addition, while using hip precautions such as not bending hips past 90 degrees and grasping his walker for support, Allen leaned to pet Riley. Allen's walking tolerance may be increased as the TR specialist assists him to walk Riley on a loose lead around the room or an outside area. The TR specialist increases Allen's safety by confirming he is securely fastened into his wheelchair or is wearing a gait belt while using his walker prior to activities with Riley.

These are only a few examples of the therapeutic use of animals within a physical rehabilitation setting. The more familiar a TR specialist and the animal handlers involved are with participants' needs and interests, the more likely it is that participants will have a positive experience.

Summary

An important factor that contributes to the success of a program involving the therapeutic use of animals is preparation. It is helpful to prepare participants and the physical area where the session will occur. Intervention techniques using animals in a therapeutic fashion are almost limitless. The type of intervention will vary depending on participant characteristics. It is useful to include the handlers who guide the animals in development and implementation of specific activities in which the animals will interact with participants.

History

The belief that animals positively influence people has a long history. The strength of the animal-human bond has been recognized for thousands of years. Animals have provided humans with a means of transportation, protection, power, and companionship. Throughout history, the popularity of companion animals among human societies has been recorded.

> For example, ancient Egyptians revered dogs, believing nothing exceeded the fidelity of the dog, and worshipped cats, often mourning for months upon their deaths and subsequently mummifying the cats' bodies (Bustad & Hines, 1984).

According to Bustad and Hines (1984), the first documented use of animals in a therapeutic setting was in Gheel, Belgium, in the ninth century. There is evidence of the therapeutic use of animals in the late 1700s in England at the York Retreat, an institution founded by the Society of Friends (Bustad & Hines). Blake (1980) stated that William Tuke encouraged people receiving psychiatric services to care for animals to increase their self-control and involve them with a "being" that would unconditionally provide affection. Stories and medical histories document that people receiving services for psychological disorders were encouraged to spend time with farm animals. An important facet of the treatment involving these farm animals was that the animals became dependent on the people (Blake).

According to McCullough (1983), use of animals in a therapeutic manner occurred in Bethel, Germany at a treatment center for people diagnosed with epilepsy founded in 1867. The facility continues to operate today serving over 5000 individuals on an ongoing basis. The animal-assisted therapy used in Bethel is similar to therapy provided at York Retreat. Bethel's therapeutic use of an animal program includes farm animals and a park housing wild game (Bustad & Hinds, 1984).

The first documented evidence of the therapeutic use of animals in the United States came during World War II in Pauling, New York, at an Army Air Corps Convalescent Hospital (Levinson, 1969). According to McCullough (1983), animal-assisted therapy consisted of working at the hospital's farm with hogs, cattle, horses, and chickens. If patients so desired, they could interact with woodland animals such as snakes, frogs, and turtles (Levinson, 1969).

According to Brickel (1986), Levinson pioneered the pet therapies. Boris Levinson, a child psychiatrist, began to publish his writings in the early 1960s with a clear picture of the potential for animals as part of therapy. In Levinson's first paper (1962), he described the way in which his dog became his co-therapist while he treated children with emotional disturbances. According to Levinson (1972), animals can contribute to psychotherapy by fostering rapport between the therapist and the person during treatment.

> Interestingly, Levinson first observed benefits of animal-assisted therapy with children quite by accident. Levinson's dog, Jingles, was present when a mother and her son entered his office early for the child's appointment. Levinson observed the interaction between the child and Jingles, and felt that Jingles assisted him with the rehabilitation of the son (Bustad & Hines, 1984).

Levinson believed in a connection between humans and animals. He argued that the use of animal companions encouraged mutual support and led to social and emotional adjustment. Through his work, Levinson identified many benefits from using companion and farm animals in training programs (Mallon, 1994a). Levinson outlined procedures for choosing animals used in a therapeutic manner and emphasized the importance of proper selection and training of specific animals for specific populations.

Although animals have had therapeutic effects on the lives of humans for years, it was not until the 1960s and 1970s that the therapeutic use of animals began to be researched. As the popularity of such programs grows, it is hoped that accompanying research will ensue.

Theoretical Foundations

The *human-animal bond* is the basis for people's desire to be with animals. Our natural environment includes animals. Domestic animals influence the physical and mental health of people through the human acts of touching, caring for, and being close (Gammonley & Yates, 1991). It is the bond between that pet and its owner that can be therapeutic. Therefore, to use animals in therapy is a natural extension of that bond.

Most people writing about the therapeutic use of animals show a ***psychoanalytical orientation*** in discussing how pets influence people. Psychoanalysis is based on the premise that unconscious processes or conflicts are at the root of abnormal behavior patterns. Thus, unconsciously, humans may be drawn to animals and interactions with them.

Levinson (1972) extended the premise associated with psychoanalysis by identifying that people have an innate need for affiliating with animals. He introduced the idea that animals are intrinsically therapeutic and affiliation with animals is helpful (Brickel, 1986). According to Brickel (1986), animals have inherent characteristics that might be considered therapeutic, such as unconditional love and protection. Therefore, if people experiencing limitations associated with illness or disability encounter animals in a therapeutic context their lives will be improved and associated limitations reduced.

More recently, a model presented by Lefkowitz and colleagues (2005) emerged as a result of treatment that involved use of animals with individuals who experienced post-traumatic stress disorder (PTSD) following sexual assault. Many treatments for PTSD involve prolonged exposure that call for individuals with PTSD related to a certain event to repeatedly recall that event. Often, prior to prolonged exposure reducing effects of PTSD, it causes fear, increased anxiety, and treatment abandonment due to the stress of recalling the event and/or situation.

The theoretical model developed by Lefkowitz and colleagues (2005) involves including animal-assisted therapy with prolonged exposure to increase individuals' abilities to tolerate prolonged exposure and is based on initial work by Altschuler (1999) and Foa and Rothbaum (1998). The model includes at least 5 sessions with both therapist and dog in sessions. Prior to initial session, the client is assessed to determine this person's willingness to work with a dog during prolonged exposure sessions. The person may have allergies and/or fear of dogs, therefore, if this individual agrees to work with the therapist in conjunction with a dog, then treatment will begin during the session one. During session one, the therapist will introduce the client to the dog so that the client becomes familiar with the dog. In addition, the therapist will provide an overview of treatment and how the dog will be involved in treatment. During session two, the therapist will inquire about the client's reaction to the previous session as well as the client's history of being assaulted.

If the client exhibits anxiety, the client is encouraged to play with the dog as well as practice relaxing breathing techniques, especially as the session progresses and further delves into recalling details of the assault. Sessions advance and include homework assignments that include increased exposure to situations related to similar situations the client may have experienced in addition to in vivo recall; that is, in session the client will verbally recount the experience until her level of anxiety is reduced at recall.

The goal of this model is for the client is to be able to demonstrate distinction between the actual assault and memory of the assault, since PTSD can cause physiological stress states upon memory of a traumatic experience. The researchers argued that by using this model in planning treatment, clients may be more willing to increase their exposure to situations if they have a coach—human or animal—that allows the client to feel safe during exposure.

During sessions, the dog can be used for tactile comfort or as a confidant to whom the client can tell her story. Although the proposed model has not been empirically examined, both prolonged exposure and animal-assisted therapy have been shown to be effective methods of treatment for a variety of psychological diagnoses. Due to the lack of research supporting using this model as a foundation for treatment, caution is advised in applying it for using animals as a facilitation technique.

Effectiveness

In recent years, researchers have begun to find support for what was once only suspected: that contact with animals has specific positive, measurable effects. This section examines research on effects of animals used in therapy. The discussion of effects of therapeutic use of animals is divided into the following sections:

- Contact with Animals
- Caring for Animals
- Animals Used with Psychotherapy
- Human-Animal Bond as a Developmental Tool

Contact with Animals

Although numerous studies examining the effects of AAT increased over the past few years, during the 1980s and 1990s there was limited evidence supporting effects of contact with animals. Early studies include those of Fick, Kongable and colleagues, Hendy, and Sutton.

Fick (1993) studied effects of the presence and absence of a dog on the frequency and types of interactions among 36 men residing in a nursing home. Even though the study included a small sample size of men having verbal communication skills, there was some evidence to support the conclusion that introduction of an animal before an activity might stimulate conversation among group members.

Kongable and colleagues (1989) compared effects of the weekly presence of a dog, the permanent presence of a dog, and no dog (baseline) on social behaviors of 12 Caucasian residents (ages 66–88) who resided in a Veterans' Hospital and who were diagnosed with Alzheimer's disease (AD). There was variability between participants relative to physical skills and medications; however, data suggested that the therapeutic use of pets can have positive effects on the social behaviors of participants with AD.

Hendy (1987) compared effects of different visiting programs (people-alone, people-and-pets, pets-alone, no visit) on behaviors of 25 residents in a nursing home selected from those who regularly used a central lounge area. All three visiting programs showed a higher frequency of smiling and alertness behaviors as compared to the control condition (no visit). Close proximity in the people-alone condition yielded the greatest number of positive resident behaviors. Although extraneous variables existed such as the various personalities of the residents, visitors, staff, and group, there is evidence to support that the presence of pets can increase positive behaviors.

Sutton (1984) examined effects of resident animals (i.e., pets) on the sociable behaviors of 29 residents in a nursing home who were diagnosed as depressed and demonstrated withdrawn behaviors, yet, regularly received weekly visitors. Although limitations were identified, there were indications that introduction of pets resulted in positive changes in social behaviors of residents.

Since the 1990s, additional studies examining effects of AAT provide support for use of contact with animals in a variety of settings and with individuals who have various diagnoses. This section addresses use of AAT contact with animals on older adults and children. The following paragraphs describe these studies that employed contact with animals to achieve therapeutic outcomes. Therefore, the following headings are used:

- Older adults
- Children

Older adults. Using a quasi-experimental design, Martindale (2008) examined the effects of animal-assisted therapy (AAT) on the passivity, engagement, and mood of 20 (ages 53–93; 15 women) residents of a rural nursing home. Ten participants received five 1-hour AAT sessions and 10 participated in a control group that consisted of traditional TR activities. Each session began with the researchers asking participants about their moods and then recording their answers by using the Dementia Mood Picture Scale (Kolanowski, Litaker, & Buettner, 2005). Engagement levels were then recorded during the intervention using the Passivity in Dementia Scale (Colling, 2000). Categories of engagement included: Thinking, Emotions, Interacting with the Environment, Interacting with People, and Activities. Following each session, participants completed a Resident Satisfaction Survey to determine their levels of satisfaction. The researchers found that participants who engaged in AAT demonstrated decreased passive behaviors, increased engagement, improved mood, and high levels of satisfaction. Although the control group demonstrated improvements, none of the improvements were found to be significant.

Using a multi-measure design, **Kawamura and colleagues (2007)** examined long-term effects of a 12-month (2 x mo; 2-hr sessions) AAT program on psychological and behavioral domains of 10 residents in a nursing home (ages 75–95; 9 women). Six had vascular dementia and four had senile dementia including impairment in mental function in daily living. Each participant had deficits in psychological and emotional domains and some had limited physical functioning, including paralysis or aphasia from cerebral infarctions. The intervention included visits by volunteers who brought small dogs. Participants fed, held, and played with the dogs at will; each dog was placed on a separate table and staff and volunteers partnered with participants to assist them in reaching their goals. Data were collected four times using the Gottfries-Bråne-Steen (GBS) (Homma, Niina, Ishii, & Hasegawa, 1991a) dementia scales and the Mental Function Impairment Scale (MENFIS) (Homma, Niina, Ishii, & Hasegawa, 1991b). Total scores for both the GBS and MENFIS decreased in the first 6 months and then increased in the second 6 months indicating an initial improvement then decrease in function; however, the emotional function score on the MENFIS decreased over the 12 months of AAT for all participants, suggesting improvement in emotional function for the duration of AAT. Implications for practice included combining AAT with other therapies to maximize potential for improving functional abilities other than those in the emotional domain, and re-evaluating care plans at 6 months to ensure accommodation related to physical or mental changes, as well as *fresh* stimulation strategies. Limitations included having no control group, small sample size, variability in staff and volunteers, variability in participants' physical, emotional, psychological and general health status, and varying lengths of time each participant spent with the dogs. Further research is needed to determine long-term effects.

Using a quasi-experimental design, **Colombo and colleagues (2006)** examined effects of a 12-week pet therapy program on psychological well-being of 48 older adults residing in a nursing home. The sample of 144 participants tested as cognitively intact (67% female) was randomly divided into three groups. One group (n=48; 30 females) received a canary, one group (n=43; 35 females) received a plant, and the remaining group (n=53; 32 females) received nothing. Instruments used to collect data were the Mini-Mental State Exam (Folstein et al., 1975), the LEIPAD II-SV (De Leo et al., 1995) and the Brief Symptom Inventory (BSI). The LEIPAD II-SV contains 25 items covering physical functioning, self-care, depression and anxiety, cognitive function, social function, and life satisfaction. The 49-item BSI examines such areas as obsessive-compulsivity, interpersonal sensitivity, depression, anxiety, hostility, phobic anxiety, and paranoid ideation. Instruments were administered at baseline and at intervention termination. Psychologists administering the instruments were blind to the study. Animals were examined periodically by two veterinarians. At baseline, there were no significant differences between group members, with the exception of interpersonal sensitivity that was higher for the plant group than the other two groups, and the self-care and social functioning for the animal group as compared to the other two groups. At 12 weeks there were no significant changes in the control group; however, there was a statistically significant improvement in almost all domains for the group that cared for canaries. There was little change in the group that cared for plants with the exception of a statistically significant improvement in self-perception. Limitations included having few males and differences in groups at the beginning of the study in mood and psychological status. For those who cared for a canary, statistically significant findings indicated that improvement in mood might serve as a protective factor against depression and obsessive-compulsive behaviors. Results support previous findings that quality of life is improved through caring for a pet, and that caring for a pet may increase mood and improve psychological status more than caring for a plant or not caring for a living organism or being.

Using a baseline-treatment design with pre-, mid-, and post-testing, **Macauley (2006)** examined effects of a 12-week (1 x wk, 30-min sessions) AAT and traditional therapy on aphasia of three men (ages 59–67) who had left-hemisphere strokes and were enrolled in an outpatient speech-language therapy program. Participants were 4–7 years post-stroke, diagnosed with nonfluent aphasia per the Western Aphasia Battery, and had similar goals including expanding phrases, increasing mean length of utterance, improving articulation, improving word finding, increasing production of noun-verb phrases, and decreasing frustration and effort. Each participant completed a semester of AAT and a semester of traditional speech therapy. The animal used during AAT was an 8-year-old neutered male Newfoundland that was a certified Pet Partner® from the Delta Society. AAT was at least as effective as traditional speech therapy. All participants reached their individual goals in both AAT and traditional speech therapy; however, participants expressed that they preferred the AAT therapy sessions to the traditional therapy sessions, happily anticipated sessions with the dog, and exhibited increased emotion during AAT sessions as they talked about their pets or loss of pets.

Using an experimental design, **Lutwack-Bloom and colleagues (2005)** examined effects of a 6-month AAT program (3 x week, 15–20-min sessions) on depression and general mood of 42 randomly selected participants from two separate nursing homes (mean age 60; 42% female) as compared to depression and mood of 26 members of a control group (mean age 85; 85% female). The intervention entailed structured visits by volunteers that included activities and/or visits with dogs. The AAT group received visits from volunteers and dogs; the control group received visits from volunteers who did not bring dogs. Depression and general mood were assessed with measures taken pre- and post-intervention using the Geriatric Depression Scale (GDS) and the Profile of Mood States (POMS). AAT participants improved their scores dramatically on the POMS and the differences between AAT and control groups were statistically significant. On the GDS, both groups demonstrated a slight score reduction from pre- to post-intervention; however, there were no statistically significant differences. Limitations included not accounting for participants' preferences, meaning-making, and emotion about the variety of dogs (there were 16 dogs ranging in size from teacup Poodle to Great Dane), and potential for *ecological fallacy*, which did not account for differences at the two nursing homes. This study supports previous research, such as Garrity and Stallone's (1998), that suggests pet exposure may not have a significant impact on depression; however, this study does indicate that AAT may be an intervention suitable to improve mood disorders. Caution is advised in that AAT is not a treatment to be used alone but rather in concert with other therapies; participants may fear animals; and use of ATT may compromise the health of participants at risk due to medical fragility.

Motomura, Yagi, and Ohyama (2004) examined effects of a 1-week AAT (1 x day, 4 consecutive days, 60-min sessions) on eight women with dementia (mean age 85) residing in a nursing home. Four participants were diagnosed with dementia of the Alzheimer's type and four were diagnosed with vascular dementia. Mental status evaluation included apathy, irritability, depression, physical self-maintenance, and mental state. The intervention included three different activities and contexts: communicating with dogs by giving dogs commands to *sit* or *wait*, then participants could touch the dogs or call their names; observing dogs do exercises such as jumping through a ring; and freely interacting with dogs. There were no statistically significant differences between pre- and post-test for irritability, depression, activities of daily living, or mental state; however, there was a significant decrease in apathy. Participants stated that they thought AAT was fun and they liked the dogs very much and would participate again. Limitations for this study included the extremely short duration of the intervention and limited number of participants.

In a study examining effects of 16-week (fish aquariums) on 62 adults (24 males; mean age 80, mean length of stay 48 months) with Alzheimer's disease,

Edwards and Beck (2002) found a statistically significant increase in nutritional intake and weight. A time series design was used that incorporated a nonequivalent control group; the researchers chose this design because of its flexibility in collecting data across time and across different groups. Participants were not randomly assigned to groups, but they were observed in their existing groups in their facility. Aquariums were designed for use at facilities where individuals with dementia reside and were self-contained with locks to protect the fish and residents. Eight large, brightly colored fish were placed in each tank and tanks were positioned and lighted to facilitate observation by residents with visual impairments. At two facilities, fish tanks were installed in the activity/dining area. For the control group, an image of the ocean was installed. Weight and nutritional intake were measured prior to study initiation and there were no significant differences across groups at baseline; however, participants in all groups ate less and men consumed more food than women. There was no significant difference between pre- and post-findings for the control group; however, the treatment groups demonstrated statistically increased food intake and weight from pre- to post-test. The researchers suggested that increase in food intake was due to several potential factors, including: individuals who typically wandered and paced during mealtimes sat for longer periods of time following installation of the fish tanks, and the increased sitting time increased intake; and individuals who were typically lethargic demonstrated increased attention to the aquariums, which also increased intake. This study demonstrated that nutritional intake and weight can be increased in individuals with dementia through non-pharmacological means. Limitations included that the study occurred on units that were specifically for individuals diagnosed with dementia and the etiology of the dementia for many of the individuals was not known, there was no indication as to the similarity or differences in the menus for each group, and there was no assessment of participants' feelings about animals (especially fish) or cultural preference for types of food, textures of foods, and/or ability to independently feed themselves.

Children. Kaminski, Pellino, and Wish (2002) examined effects of child-life and pet therapy (1 x wk) on subjective child and parent mood ratings and observation of mood through videotaping. Heart rates, blood pressure levels, and salivary cortisol levels were measured prior to and following therapy. A convenience sample of 70 children was used with 40 children participating in child-life and 30 in pet therapy groups. Participants included individuals who had chronic disorders such as cystic fibrosis, diabetes, transplant, and other medical disorders. Children in the child-life groups spent time in the playroom and participated in play activities of their choosing. Participant mood was assessed using a self-report 7-item scale taken from the Reynolds Child Depression Scale. Participants were asked to rate their mood using a 7-point facial expressions scale. Using a 4-item mood rating scale, mood was reported by parents and or caregivers. Heart rates, blood pressure levels, and salivary cortisol levels were measured prior to completing child-life or pet therapy sessions. Video recordings were examined to determine percentage of time participants displayed different types of affect, time on task, touching, and number of times they initiated activities. Child-life and pet therapy were both viewed as positive experiences for both participants and parents. Although cortisol levels decreased for both groups, the decrease was not significant. Participants in the pet therapy group had higher heart rates than those who attended child-life sessions.

Heimlich (2001) examined effects of an AAT program on 14 children with multiple disabilities residing in a long-term care facility. To evaluate attention span, physical movement, communication, and compliance over time, the Measurement of Pet Intervention (MOPI) was developed. Therapy using one animal and the same handler was delivered in a structured therapy program over eight sessions. The MOPI was completed weekly for 3 weeks prior to beginning the therapy and weekly once therapy began. There was movement of rating on the MOPI in a positive direction with participation in therapy sessions; however, these changes alone cannot accurately measure AAT effects.

Summary. Studies reviewed in this section may indicate that contact with animals contributes to increased social behaviors of older adults and children. Most studies used observations and tally systems to collect data on a variety of conditions. Although there are concerns associated with methods used in the studies reviewed, in general, the conclusion is that contact with animals appears to be beneficial. Additional studies that employ more rigorous research methods and examine effects of the intervention on other groups are needed.

Caring for Animals

Caring for animals and pets is often described as therapeutic in nature. Several facilities recognize the possible benefits and include caring for animals into part of their therapeutic program. Although there are heart-warming anecdotal reports of caring for animals, there remains a lack of research specific to the therapeutic effects of caring for animals, especially at residential facilities.

Rederfer and Goodman (1989) discussed use of pet-facilitated therapy with 12 children (ages 5–10) who attended a center for children with autism. Children participated in a four phase time-lag design study including a baseline, 18 treatment sessions (20 min), post-treatment, and a 1-month follow-up. In the treatment sessions, the therapist and child explored the dog with petting and grooming, and later included games and activities. Each session was coded via a 15-second time sampling procedure to identify isolation and social interaction (87% reliability). Although no trends in social interactions were observed during baseline, a sharp increase in social interaction was noted when the dog was introduced at the beginning of the session. Although results suggest that using an animal as a component of therapy can positively influence social behavior of children with autism, it is not clear if the success of the intervention was a result of the interaction with the dog or interaction with the therapist. Use of a dog to assist therapists may be helpful in teaching children with autism to respond and communicate.

In a follow-up study, Mallon (1994b) examined effects of introducing dogs into the living units (18–20 children per unit) receiving group care for children with significant difficulties (behavioral, emotional, or academic). Once on the unit, dogs were cared for by and available to all residents. An open-ended and Likert-type questionnaire was used to interview 6 staff members and 12 residents about the in-house animal program. Although some problems were noted with the study,

95% of the staff and 100% of the children reported feeling that benefits outweighed difficulties of having a dog reside on the unit.

Summary. Therapeutic use of caring for animals has been researched solely with children with psychiatric disorders and autism. These studies suggest some benefits in using animal care as a facet of a treatment approach. Several themes emerged, including that the children felt better around the animals, and children may find it easier to talk with an animal than an adult counselor. Caring for animals tended to increase social interaction of children with autism (Rederfer & Goodman, 1989), and helped them to notice benefits of having a dog present (Mallon, 1994b). Overall, caring for animals appears to have some therapeutic value for children.

Animals Used with Psychotherapy

Kovacs and colleagues (2004) evaluated effects of a 9-month AAT on seven middle-aged adults with schizophrenia (1 x wk, 50-min sessions). The researchers sought to enhance participants' adaptive functioning and decrease non-adaptive functioning. Outcomes were measured using the Independent Living Skills Survey, which is used to measure living skills of people with chronic psychiatric problems in the eight areas of eating, grooming, health and domestic activities, money management, transportation, leisure, job-seeking or job-related skills. Each session was held in a garden area or in the occupational room. There was a positive effect of AAT in every area assessed by the independent living skills. Significant changes in the areas of domestic and health activities were found.

Using two case studies, **Kogan and colleagues (1999)** examined effects of an 11- and 14-week AAT intervention (1 x wk, 45–60-min sessions) on social skills of a 12-year-old boy with mild mental retardation, attention deficit disorder, oppositional defiant disorder, depression, and explosive tendencies, and an 11-year-old boy with impulse control problems and depression. The 12-year old boy's goals included learning social skills and decreasing time spent fantasizing. The 11-year-old boy's goals included improving social skills, age-appropriate behaviors, and sense of personal control. The intervention included a human-animal team comprised of one adult and one dog from a nonprofit organization, a school professional, and one observer. The intervention included rapport-building and animal training. Rapport-building included activities such as brushing and petting the dog and talking about relevant events during the week previous to the visit. Students chose the commands to teach and were taught how to deliver commands to the dogs. Students used positive reinforcement via treats to train the dogs. Data were collected using the ADD-H Comprehensive Teacher Rating Scale (Ullmann, Sleator, & Sprague, 1991) pre- and post-intervention to assess social skills, in vivo observations, videotaped observations of three AAT sessions, students' IEP plans, and post-intervention interviews with participants, their families, and educators. Both boys made improvements. The 12-year-old did not demonstrate improvement with his self-talk related to his fantasies and scores on the ADD-H Comprehensive Teacher Rating Scale; although other data indicated that he improved relationships with peers. The 11-year-old did not improve his age-appropriate behaviors; he continued behaviors such as tantrums when faced with frustrating circumstances. The AAT intervention reduced most negative behaviors and increased positive behaviors. Triangulation of data collection and analysis increased rigor of study. Although the study was rigorous, it required resources of human effort and time. Caution is advised when attempting to generalize findings since only children were examined, and replication of this study may be difficult because extensive time and resources were used.

Folse and colleagues (1994) investigated effects of AAT on 44 college students (mean age 21) who reported mild to severe depression on the Beck Depression Inventory (BDI). Participants were divided into three groups based on availability. Nine students in the directive group received animal contact in conjunction with psychotherapy, 12 students in the nondirective group received group treatment involving presence of a dog, and remaining participants acted as the control group. Sessions were scheduled for 6 weeks (1 x wk, 45-min sessions). The BDI was re-administered during the seventh session. The nondirective group's scores on the BDI post-test were significantly higher when compared to the control group. Results should be interpreted cautiously because the control group's pretest BDI means were markedly lower than the other two groups, there were only six treatment sessions, and two different dogs and therapists were used. Use of the dog during the directive group may not be considered AAT, even though it may have been therapeutic since the dog was simply present during the psychotherapy session and would wander around the room. The type of AAT may have been very different between the two conditions. The comfort level of participants with dogs was not assessed, and no follow-up test occurred. Although problems with the research methods were evident, findings suggest that college students who receive only AAT demonstrate reduced depression when compared to their peers who do not.

Summary. There is a lack of research in use of animals in conjunction with psychotherapy and when studies are reported the manner in which the animal is used as a therapeutic medium is inconsistent. For example, Folse and colleagues (1994) had the animal just present during group therapy sessions, which is very different from Gammonley and Yates (1991), who defined AAT as an applied science with a goal-oriented approach to use animals to solve human problems.

Approaches to psychotherapy vary from person-centered to situation-centered or individual to group. There appears to be no established standard for animal use in various types of psychotherapy. Although the aforementioned studies resulted in reduced depression levels, social skills, and adaptive functioning, the inconsistent use of the animals is cause for concern.

Human-Animal Bond as a Developmental Tool

There is limited research examining use of the human-animal bond as a developmental tool. Although it has been indicated that some children who are cruel to animals can be diagnosed with some degree and form of psychopathology, research supports the conclusion that empathy toward animals can generalize to empathy toward humans via humane education interventions (Dillman, 1999). Serpell (1999) noted that there has been a lack of research in the child-animal relationship, considering its prominence in our culture.

In a pilot study using a quasi-experimental design, **Valeri (2006)** examined effects of pet ownership and laughter among 95 participants who were divided into four groups: dog owners, cat owners, dog and cat owners, and neither dog or cat owners. Each participant was asked to document in a *laughter log* that included the frequency of their laughter along with sources and presence of others during episodes of laughter over 24-hours. There is a complicated relationship between pet ownership and laughter in that most frequent sources of laughter were spur-of-the-moment laughter following a situation. Individuals who had both cats and dogs logged the most frequent occurrences of spontaneous laughter after an event that involved one or both of their pets. Individuals who owned both cats and dogs as well as those who only owned dogs logged that they laughed more often than individuals who owned only cats. Although findings support that cats and dogs provide social support through laughter and amusing behavior and suggest that dogs can potentially serve as companions or friends that provide humor in their lives, caution is advised with interpreting results considering the short duration of the study as well as the limited detailed information about various aspects of the study.

In a qualitative study using conversational discourse analysis, **Tannen (2004),** examined the role of pets as interactional resources within family conversation. Parents of two families (middle-class, dual-career, and Caucasian) wore or carried audio tape recorders for 1 week to record interactions at home and at work. Analysis of transcripts indicated that pets in these families became voices of the families in various ways; parents spoke to each other, their children, and pets—sometimes *through* their pets—using voices similar to *baby talk*. Humans provided a context for pets to become intermediaries in maintaining positive relationships with family members. Six primary ways in which pets served as intermediaries included instances in which pets helped to soften effects of criticism, reframe position of the speaker as the pet rather than a human so that it was not the human delivering bad news, provide praise, instruct about values, intercede during conflict, and create a family identity. Parents included their pets in their interactions with one another and their children to accomplish conversational tasks listed above. The researcher concluded that families with ongoing conflicts found having an animal mediate the interactions to be helpful. Limitations to this study included that it was only conducted during 1 week with two families, the percentage of interactions including the pet as a mediator was not reported, and typical interaction style of families was not identified.

Melson (2003) posited that the role of companion animals in children's lives contributes to development in social, emotional, perceptual, cognitive, and language areas. Therefore, humane education interventions are designed with the premise that "teaching children to be kind, compassionate, and caring toward animals may foster a heightened respect and sensitivity for all living creatures" (Thompson & Gullone, 2003, p. 3). The following studies represent examples of human-animal interactions related to measures of humane behaviors toward animals as well as the roles of animals in humans' lives and social interaction.

In a repeated measures study designed to investigate psychometric properties of the Children's Treatment of Animals Questionnaire (CTAQ), **Thompson and Gullone (2003)** examined behaviors toward animals of 61 children (ages 8–10, 36 girls) who attended three Catholic schools in Australia. The children were also asked to complete Bryant's Index of Empathy for Children and Adolescents (BIE)

(Bryant, 1982) and the Social Skills Rating System (SSRS) (Gresham & Elliott, 1990). The psychometric properties of the CTAQ were acceptable and the instrument demonstrated satisfactory internal consistency and test-retest reliability. There was statistically significant convergent validity through correlations between the CTAQ and the BIE and SSRS. Findings were consistent with past research demonstrating that boys scored significantly lower than girls on measures of empathy. Seven of the original 19 items in the CTAQ were discarded due to low internal consistency for these items; once these items were discarded, the CTAQ became a measure that primarily assessed humane behavior toward animals. The researchers suggested that humane behavior toward animals and cruelty toward animals were potentially two different, standalone constructs rather than opposite ends of a continuum of behavior.

Using a ranking and interview method, **McNicholas and Collis (2001)** examined 22 participants' (ages 7–8, 13 boys) perceptions of human and non-human social support. Participants included children who attended a middle school in a small town in England, 18 of whom owned pets. Data were collected on 2 consecutive days. On the first day, as a class, participants were asked to make a list of, and explain their relationships to, friends, family, pets, significant others, caregivers who may be important to them. Once participants completed the list, they were asked to choose the top 10 most special relationships and rank them. On the second day, each participant was interviewed individually and were asked to respond to the following themed stories: Who would the children most want to be with them when they: were ill in bed, had to walk down a dark and scary street, were embarrassed during practice for a school play, had a bad day, had a special secret they could only tell one individual, and were being bullied by children they didn't know. Seventeen of 18 children with pets included one or more of their pets in their top 10. Included in the top 10 were nine cats or dogs, four small pets such as rabbits or hamsters, and four had a cat or dog *and* a small pet. The children indicated understanding appropriateness and/or ability of the individual to assist with certain situations. For example, no pets were chosen to assist with bullies. Dogs were chosen over cats for protection in scary situations and for sharing a special secret. Cats were chosen over dogs for comfort when the children were ill. Cats and dogs received higher rankings than some humans not in the children's immediate family such as aunts, uncles, and grandparents. The researchers concluded that pets can play an important social role for children in addition to serving as the provider of certain functions and children discriminate between abilities of pets for support in comparison to human social support.

Summary. Preliminary research findings provide some support that pets may play a role for people in developing social roles, experiencing laughter, and supporting an overall positive family living environment. However, there are substantial limitations associated with existing studies. More research that employs rigorous methods is needed to examine use of the human-animal bond as a developmental tool.

Overall Summary of Literature

There is limited research examining effects of therapeutic use of animals. Although some researchers identified the therapeutic use of animals as an effective intervention, since this research lacked adequate rigor, therapeutic use of animals cannot yet be identified as an empirically supported facilitation technique.

Some benefits have been reported in areas of contact with animals, caring for animals, animals used with psychotherapy, and the human-animal bond as a developmental tool. However, a major problem in understanding studies employing the therapeutic use of animals is the variety of techniques employed. Caution is advised when comparing studies that appear to be similar; the intervention and use of the animals may vary across agencies and programs. Also, since there are many animal therapy programs being provided by independent community groups, there are consequently numerous approaches being evaluated. It is critical that researchers specifically describe the intervention method and role of the animals, therapists, and the participants in the study. Despite the research that has been conducted, more research is needed that examines efficacy of this intervention.

Case Study

Olivia

Olivia lives in a suburban community of a large city. She is 74 years old and was recently widowed when her husband of 43 years died after the onset of a sudden illness. Olivia has two adult children who live in other cities. Olivia and her husband shared a home that she can no longer care for alone. Olivia has arthritis in her hands, knees, and shoulders. After several months of living in her home alone and discussing various residence options with her children, Olivia decided to move into an assisted-living facility. It was a difficult decision and she was sad to leave her home. In addition, Olivia could not take her 10-year-old cat, Mindy, with her. Fortunately, Olivia's daughter provided a home for Mindy. When moving day arrived, Olivia considered that she was alone, she was leaving a home she had shared with her husband, she felt she would lose the independence to which she was accustomed, and she had given up her cat.

Although the move itself was uneventful, Olivia had a difficult time adjusting to the facility. Meal times and activities were scheduled. Olivia had a sense that her new life was extremely scheduled and the only way she could have any semblance of life before the move was to stay in her apartment among her familiar belongings. She missed her husband and spent several hours each week watching home movies and videos in her apartment. Although Olivia was not typically reclusive, she found herself not socializing with the other residents except when necessary, such as for meals and some physical activity sessions such as aqua aerobics. Staff members were familiar with the difficulty of adjustment and encouraged Olivia to join activities, but they did not want her to feel she was forced to participate. Staff members were sensitive to new residents' individual modes of adjustment and closely monitored how each resident coped with relocation from their previous homes into the facility.

Therapeutic Use of Animals for Olivia

One day, while passing the activity board after breakfast, Olivia noticed that a program involving the therapeutic use of animals called Animals and You was scheduled for later in the day. Olivia thought about going to the program, but soon dismissed the idea when she realized it might make her miss her cat even more. As she was going to her room, Olivia passed Tomika, the facility's TR specialist, who reminded Olivia about the program in the afternoon. Tomika and Olivia shared an affinity for cats and had spoken on several occasions about their animals. Olivia thanked Tomika, but said she did not think she would attend the session.

During the Animals and You session, Tomika realized Olivia was not one of the participants. The Animals and You program was one of the most popular activities offered at the facility. Sessions were provided by a volunteer organization that visited once per week for 1-hour visits. Volunteers visited on two teams which alternated weeks. One team had a golden retriever, a long-haired dachshund, a standard poodle, and a Siamese cat. The other team had a chocolate lab, a beagle, a medium-sized shepherd mix, and a rabbit.

Tomika wanted Olivia to have an opportunity to interact with the animals, so she asked the volunteer with the Siamese cat if she would mind making a visit to Olivia's apartment. Tomika called Olivia, said she had a surprise for her, and asked if it was okay for her to visit with a friend. Olivia said that was fine, and provided permission for her to come to the apartment.

When Olivia opened the door and saw Tomika with the volunteer and the cat, she welcomed them in and asked them to sit down. Olivia immediately focused on the cat and talked to the volunteer about the cat, asking her the cat's name and age, while sharing stories about her cat. The volunteer asked Olivia if she wanted to hold the cat and Olivia said, "Yes, very much so." Olivia began to hold the cat, petting and talking to her, telling the cat how much she missed her own Mindy.

Tomika and the volunteer talked with Olivia for several minutes, telling her about the organization and the other animals who were members. Tomika told Olivia about the other team that visited and the volunteer shared stories about each animal on both teams. Olivia continued holding the cat, petting her while they talked. The volunteer indicated the time for the session was almost over and that she should return to the group. She asked Olivia if she wanted to carry the cat to the activity room where the session was being held and meet the other animals. Olivia agreed and accompanied Tomika and the volunteer.

While in the activity room, Olivia met some of the other volunteers and their animals. Seeing the golden retriever reminded Olivia of a childhood pet and she shared a story with the dog's handler about how much her dog had enjoyed swimming with her family during summer vacations at the ocean. Another resident said she too had a retriever and that he enjoyed chasing ducks and swimming in their pond. She and Olivia laughed about their respective dogs' antics. The session ended and the volunteers and animals left. The volunteers told the residents they would see them in a couple of weeks.

It was almost time for supper and Olivia was going to her apartment for a few minutes beforehand. As she was leaving the room, the resident with whom she had shared retriever stories, Mary, asked her what she was doing after supper. The evening activity was an Oktoberfest celebration including specialty German desserts,

German beverages, and a video travelogue through Germany. Mary asked Olivia if she wanted to join her. Olivia agreed, thinking it might be fun. Mary and Olivia attended the Oktoberfest celebration and discovered they were both recently widowed and both were animal lovers. Olivia had traveled with her husband through Europe, and the German evening brought back some pleasant memories.

In the weeks that followed, Olivia and Mary became friends. Mary had lived in the assisted-living facility for several months prior to Olivia's arrival and introduced her to many people. Olivia continued to participate in Animals and You sessions and enjoyed the interaction with the animals and volunteers. At times, Tomika would encourage Olivia to brush the dogs to assist with range of motion in her arms and shoulders. Other days, when the weather was pleasant, she would encourage participants to walk the animals outside, or to play ball in the courtyard. Olivia began to enjoy life at the assisted-living facility. She made new friends and began to participate more in the offered activities. She became team captain of her hall, which entailed various duties such as leading residents' birthday celebrations and keeping the hall bulletin board up-to-date. Tomika observed increases in Olivia's social interaction and decreases in her tendency to be reclusive and depressed. Tomika regularly talked with Olivia, and repeatedly Olivia thanked her for bringing the cat into her room and pets into her life once again.

Summary

Olivia was experiencing social withdrawal after moving into an assisted-living facility. The Animals and You program involving the therapeutic use of animals gave the TR specialist an opportunity to promote Olivia's interest in a social activity. Olivia enjoyed contact with the animals through petting and grooming and reminisced with volunteers and other residents about pets she had owned throughout her life. In addition, Olivia met other residents and, subsequently, became more involved in activities at the assisted-living facility.

Intervention Implementation Exercises

There are many exercises that can be completed to promote an understanding and appreciation for the therapeutic use of animals. Five exercises listed below include:

- Visitation
- Create a Program
- Draw an Animal and Discuss
- List Animal Considerations
- Identify Goals

Visitation

A team of representatives from a visiting pet program can attend class. The organization representative can begin by giving a brief description of the organization, its purpose, and the types of agencies the animal-handler teams visit. Students can simulate characteristics of various disabilities and then interact with the animal-handler teams as such individuals might in an animal-assisted therapy session. Some possible disabilities to simulate might be left-side affected stroke, right-side affected stroke, various vision impairments, and different mobility impairments. Students can prepare and incorporate adaptive equipment as needed.

Create a Program

Create a program involving the therapeutic use of animals for an agency. List the relevant considerations for different types of facilities including nursing homes, psychiatric facilities, and children's hospitals.

Draw an Animal and Discuss

Plan an activity that prepares participants for a visit by an animal-handler team. Start the session by asking participants to draw an animal—an animal from their past, a current pet, or their favorite animal. Then, present a series of questions which will facilitate a discussion about participants' feelings about animals and visits by animals to the facility.

List Animal Considerations

Develop a list of considerations as if an animal had been recently acquired by an agency as a resident animal to be used in a therapeutic manner. Generate a form to assess staff support, analyze budget requirements, consider health department protocols, and other important considerations such as housing, regular exercise, veterinary care, and grooming.

Identify Goals

Identify specific goals and outcomes for participants with various disabilities using resident farm animals.

Summary

The intervention implementation exercises presented in this chapter can be used to increase understanding of the therapeutic use of animals in various settings. Intervention techniques involving the therapeutic use of animals may require modification based on the type of agency, animals available, and the unique needs of individuals participating in the programs.

Conclusion

The therapeutic use of animals can be used with participants having various diagnoses such as depression, right or left CVA, and brain injury. Animals can be used in settings such as nursing homes, psychiatric facilities, and hospitals. Animals may be part of a visiting team or reside at a facility.

TR specialists can facilitate participant benefits by specifying goals and treatment outcomes. It is important to prepare participants for animal visits by gaining information about their experiences with and expectations of animals. It can be useful for TR specialists to prepare for animal visitations by knowing what types of animals will visit and skills of the animal-handler teams. In addition, it can be helpful for the TR specialist to establish protocols and procedures that are within facility guidelines prior to implementation of a program. Staff support of animal visitation or a resident animal allows for increased ease of implementation of a program, whether it is a visiting or resident animal program. The area in which the session occurs should be spacious enough for comfortable movement of participants and animal-handler teams. In summary, therapeutic use of animals shows promise, although, as an intervention technique used by TR specialists, more research is needed to determine effects of such programs.

Discussion Questions

1. What are the various terms or phrases used to refer to the therapeutic use of animals?
2. What is the difference between pet therapy and animal-assisted therapy?
3. What is the general purpose of a service animal?
4. What are some ways that contact with an animal in a structured program may be therapeutic?
5. What are some considerations to make before bringing a visiting animal to a facility?
6. What are some considerations to make before bringing a resident animal to a facility?
7. What are the effects of caring for animals as indicated by the research studies?
8. Why should caution be taken when reading research articles?
9. What are some considerations when choosing an animal to be used for a therapeutic purpose?
10. What are some different types of equipment which may be used with the therapeutic use of animals?

Resources

Agency Resources

The Delta Society
875 124th Ave, NE, Suite 101
Bellevue, WA 98005
(425) 679-5500
http://www.deltasociety.org
The Delta Society is a national society for the interactions of humans and animals whose mission is to promote animals helping people improving their health, independence, and quality of life.

The Latham Foundation
Latham Plaza Building, 1826 Clement Ave.
Alameda, CA 94501
(510) 521-0920
http://www.latham.org
The Latham Foundation is a clearinghouse for information about humane issues and activities, the human companion animal bond (HCAB), animal-assisted therapy, and the connections between child and animal abuse and other forms of violence

Therapet: Animal Assisted Therapy
P.O. Box 305
Troup, TX 75789
http://www.therapet.com
Therapet Foundation's utilizes specially trained and certified animals for the betterment of mankind by promoting health, hope, and healing by establishing and communicating standards of practice for use of specially trained animals in the health care settings, providing education to health care professionals and facility leaders, educating communities on opportunities and benefits of Animal Assisted Therapy, and training, certifying, and assuring competency of human/animal volunteers.

Therapy Dogs International
88 Bartley Road
Flanders, NJ 07836
(973) 252-9800
Email: tdi@gti.net
Therapy Dogs International is a volunteer organization dedicated to regulating, testing and registration of therapy dogs and their volunteer handlers for the purpose of visiting nursing homes, hospitals, other institutions, and wherever else therapy dogs are needed.

Wildlife Conservation Society
http://www.wcs.org/
The Wildlife Conservation Society saves wildlife and wild places worldwide through science, global conservation, education and the management of the world's largest system of urban wildlife parks, led by the flagship Bronx Zoo.

Animal Assisted Therapy and Animal Assisted Activities (AAT/AAA)
http://www.animaltherapy.net/
This website provides links to various resources related to animal assisted therapy.

DogPlay
http://www.dogplay.com/Activities/Therapy/therapy.html.
This website provides information about visiting pets and animal assisted therapy.

Material Resources

Jalongo, M., Astorino, T., & Bomboy, N. (2004). Canine visitors: the influence of therapy dogs on young children's learning and well-being in classrooms and hospitals. *Early Childhood Education Journal, 32*(1), 9–16.

References

Altschuler, E. I. (1999). Pet-facilitated therapy for posttraumatic stress disorder. *Annals of Clinical Psychiatry, 11,* 29–30.

Beck, A., & Katcher, A. (1983). *Between pets and people: The importance of animal companionship.* New York: G. P. Song.

Blake, D. S. (1980). On the introduction of pets for the institutionalized aging: An exploratory descriptive study of an intervention, doctoral dissertation, Columbia University Teachers College, New York, NY.

Bond-Howard, B. (1993). *Introduction to stroke.* Ravensdale, WA: Idyll Arbor, Inc.

Brickel, C. M. (1986). Pet-facilitated therapies: A review of the literature and clinical implementation considerations. *Clinical Gerontologist, 5,* 306–331.

Bryant, B. K. (1982). An index of empathy for children and adolescents. *Child Development, 53,* 413–425.

Bustad, L. K., & Hines, L. M. (1984). The human-animal bond: Historical perspective. In R. K. Anderson, B. L. Hart, & L. A. Hart (Eds.), *The pet connection: Its influence on our health and quality of life* (pp. 15–29). Minneapolis, MN: Center to Study Human-Animal Relationships and Environments.

Carter, M. J., Van Andel, G. E., & Robb, G. M. (2003). *Therapeutic recreation: A practical approach.* St. Louis, MO: Times Mirror/Mosby.

Colling, K. B. (2000). A taxonomy of passive behaviors in people with Alzheimer's disease. *Journal of Nursing Scholarship, 32*(3), 239–244.

Colombo, G., Dello Buono, M., Smania, K., Raviola, R., De Leo, D. (2006). Pet therapy and institutionalized elderly: A study on 144 cognitively unimpaired subjects. *Archives of Gerontology and Geriatrics, 42,* 207–216.

De Leo, D., Carollo, G., & Dello Buono, M. (1995) Lower suicide rates associated with a Tele-Help/Tele-Check Service for the elderly at home. *American Journal of Psychiatry, 152,* 632–634.

Delta Society Pets Partners' Program. (1996). Standards of practice for animal-assisted activities and therapy. Rentaon, WA: The Delta Society.

Dillman, D., (1999). Kids and critters: An intervention to violence. In F. R. Ascione & P. Arkow (Eds.), *Child abuse, domestic violence, and animal abuse: Linking the circles of compassion for prevention and intervention* (pp. 424–432). Indiana: Purdue University Press.

Doyle, K., & Kukowski, T. (1989). Utilization of pets in a hospice program. *Health Education, 20,* 10–11.

Eddy, J., Hart, L. A., & Boltz, R. P. (1988). The effects of service dogs on social acknowledgments of people in wheelchairs. *The Journal of Psychology, 122*(1), 39–45.

Edwards, N. E., & Beck, A. M. (2002). Animal-assisted therapy and nutrition in Alzheimer's Disease. *Journal of Nursing Research, 24,* 697–712

Fick, K. M. (1993). The influence of an animal on social interactions of nursing home residents in a group setting. *The American Journal of Occupational Therapy, 47,* 529–534.

Foa, E. B., & Rothbaum, B. O. (1998). *Treating the trauma of rape: Cognitive-behavioral therapy for PTSD.* New York: Guilford.

Folse, E. B., Minder, C. C., Aycock, M. J., & Santana, R. T. (1994). Animal-assisted therapy and depression in adult college students. *Anthrozoos, 7,* 18–194.

Folstein, M. F., Folstein, S. E., & McHugh, P. R. (1975). "Mini-mental state." A practical method for grading the cognitive state of patients for the clinician. *Journal of Psychiatric Research, 12*(3), 189–98.

Fraser, C. (1989). Sometimes the best therapy has four legs. *RN, 7,* 21–22.

Gammonley, J., & Yates, J. (1991). Pet projects: Animal-assisted therapy in nursing homes. *Journal of Gerontological Nursing, 17*(1), 12–15.

Garrity, T., & Stallones, L. (1998). Effects of pet contact on human wellbeing: Review of recent research. In C. C. Wilson & D. C. Turner (Eds.), *Companion Animals in Human Health* (pp. 3–22). Thousand Oaks: Sage.

Gresham, F. M., & Elliott, S. N. (1990). *Social skills rating system manual.* Circle Pines, MN: American Guidance Services.

Happy Tails Pet Therapy, Inc. (1994). *Volunteer training and information manual.* Roswell, GA: Happy Tails Pet Therapy, Inc.

Heimlich, K. (2001, October/November/December). Animal-assisted therapy and the severely disabled child: A quantitative study. *Journal of Rehabilitation, 67*(4).

Hendy, H. M. (1987). Effects of pet and/or people visits on nursing home residents. *International Journal of Aging and Human Development, 25,* 279–291.

Homma, A., Niina, R., Ishii, T., & Hasegawa, K. (1991a). Behavioral evaluation of Alzheimer disease in clinical trials: Development of the Japanese version of the GBS Scale. *Alzheimer Disease & Associated Disorders, 1*(Supple 1), 40–48.

Homma, A., Niina, R., Ishii, T., & Hasegawa, K. (1991b). Development of a new rating scale for dementia in the elderly: Mental Function Impairment Scale (MENFIS). *Rhonen Seishin Igaku Zasshi, 2,* 1217–1222.

Kaminski, M., Pellino, T., & Wish, J. (2002). Play and pets: The physical and emotional Impact of Child-Life and pet therapy on hospitalized children. *Children's Health Care, 31*(4), 321–335.

Kavanagh, K. (1994). *Pet therapy.* Lansing, MI: PAM Assistance Center. (Eric Document Reproduction Service No. ED 373 462)

Kawamura, N., Niyama, M., & Niyama, H. (2007). Long-term evaluation of animal-assisted therapy for institutionalized elderly people: A preliminary result. *Psychogeriatrics, 7,* 8–13.

Kogan, L., Granger, B., Fitchett, J., Helmer, K., & Young, K. (1999). The human-animal team approach for children with emotional disorders: two case studies. *Child &Youth Care Forum, 28*(2), 105–121.

Kolanowski, A. M., Litaker, M., & Buettner, L. (2005). Efficacy of theory-based activities for behavioral symptoms of dementia. *Nursing Research, 54*(4), 219–228.

Kongable, L. G., Buckwalter, K. C., & Stolley, J. M. (1989). The effects of pet therapy on the social behavior of institutionalized Alzheimer's clients. *Archives of Psychiatric Nursing, 3*(4), 191–198.

Kovacs, Z., Rozsa, S., Kis, R., & Rozsa, L. (2004). Animal-assisted therapy for middle-aged schizophrenic patients living in a social institution. A pilot study. *Clinical Rehabilitation, 18,* 483–486.

Lefkowitz, C., Paharia, I., Prout, M., Debiak, D., & Bleiberg, J. (2005). Animal-assisted prolonged exposure: A treatment for survivors of sexual assault suffering posttraumatic stress disorder. *Society & Animals, 13*(4), 275–295.

Levinson, B. M. (1969). *Pet-oriented child psychotherapy.* Springfield, IL: Charles C. Thomas.

Levinson, B. M. (1972). *Pets and human development.* Springfield, IL: Charles C. Thomas.

Lutwack-Bloom, P., Wijewickrama, R., & Smith, B. (2005). Effects of pets versus people visits with nursing home residents. *Journal of Gerontological Social Work, 44,* 137–159.

Macauley, B. (2006). Animal-assisted therapy for persons with aphasia: A pilot study. *Journal of Rehabilitation Research & Development, 43*(3), 357–366.

Mallon, G. P. (1994a). Some of our best therapists are dogs. *Child and Youth Care Forum, 23,* 89–101.

Mallon, G. P. (1994b). Cow as co-therapist: Utilization of farm animals as therapeutic aides with children in residential treatment. *Child and Adolescent Social Work Journal, 11,* 455–474.

Martindale, B. P. (2008). Effect of animal-assisted therapy on engagement of rural nursing home residents. *American Journal of Recreation Therapy, 7*(4), 45–53.

McCullough, M. J. (1983). Animal-facilitated therapy: Overview and future direction. In A. H. Katcher & A. M. Beck (Eds.), *New perspectives on our lives with companion animals* (pp. 410–426). Philadelphia: University of Pennsylvania Press.

McNicholas, J., & Collis, G. M. (2001). Children's representation of pets in their social networks. *Child: Care, Health and Development, 27,* 279–294.

Melson, G. F. (2003). Child development and the human-companion animal bond. *American Behavioral Scientist, 47,* 31–39.

Motomura, N., Yagi, T., & Ohyama, H. (2004). Animal-assisted therapy for people with dementia. *Psychogeriatrics, 4,* 40–42.

Rederfer, L. A., & Goodman, J. F. (1989). Brief report: Pet-facilitated therapy with autistic children. *Journal of Autism and Developmental Disorders, 19,* 461–467.

Serpell, J. (1999). Animals in children's lives. *Society and Animals, 7,* 87.

Sutton, D. M. (1984). *Use of pets in therapy with elderly nursing home residents.* Paper presented at the Annual Convention of the American Psychological Association, Toronto, Canada. (ERIC Document Reproduction Service No. ED 252 762).

Tannen, D. (2004). Talking the dog: Framing pets as interactional resources in family discourse. *Research on Language and Social Interaction, 37,* 399–420.

Thompson, K. L., & Gullone, E. (2003). The children's treatment of animals questionnaire (CTAQ): A psychometric investigation. *Society & Animals, 11,* 1–15.

Ullmann, R. K., Sleator, E. K., & Sprague, R. L. (1991). *The ADD-H Comprehensive Teacher Rating Scale.* Champaign, IL: MetriTech, Inc.

Valeri, R. M. (2006). Tails of laughter: A pilot study examining the relationship between companion animal guardianship (pet ownership) and laughter. *Society and Animals, 14,* 275–293.

Volhard, J., & Volhard, W. (1993). *The canine good citizen: Every dog can be one.* New York: Howell Book House.

Chapter 15
Therapeutic Use of Exercise

Ellen Broach and Sarah Richardson

*All across the country, there is an expanding interest for people
to include physical fitness activities in daily routines
and this expanded interest includes people with disabilities.*
—P. D. Miller

Introduction

Exercise is inclusive of all human movement including random movement, habitual activity, training done for fitness or health, dance, sports, and recreational activities of all sorts (Brown, 2001). Brown added that exercise is ever-present, appearing everywhere, and is usually practiced in spaces and times set apart from required activities; hence, it is also often considered to be enjoyable.

Exercise can be used by TR specialists to promote muscular strength, endurance, flexibility, optimal body composition, cardiovascular condition (American College of Sports Medicine [ACSM], 2006), mental health (Buckworth & Dishman, 2002), and healthy life activity. Exercise activities are associated with the health and longevity of the individual and general population (Bouchard, Shephard, Stephens, Sutton, & McPherson, 1990) and for individuals with obesity and other disabling conditions (Watts, Jones, Davis, & Green, 2005).

Unfortunately, disability often leads to a sedentary lifestyle, resulting in a reduction in physical function. As physical function is reduced, an even more sedentary lifestyle occurs, which tends to decrease physical capacities. The Institute of Medicine of the National Academies determined that much of modern-day chronic disease is linked to activity level (Suitor & Kraak, 2007). Lieberman (2007) added that inactivity causes early development of heart disease, diabetes, obesity, and hypertension.

The interest in exercise and fitness has resulted, in part, from a trend toward self-help and away from dependence on health care professionals (Sobel, 1995). Exercise can contribute to psychological health as well as physical fitness. Psychological benefits of being actively involved in exercise programs have been reported to include improved mood states as well as decreases in state anxiety, mild to moderate depression, neuroticism, and stress (Hatfield & Brody, 2008). Some authors believe that the positive effect of exercise on depression, mood, and self-esteem has not been demonstrated convincingly (Dishman, 1995).

In this chapter, we introduce the reader to the therapeutic use of exercise and provide a definition, description, and history of exercise. Primary theories from which to base use of exercise and a review of relevant literature provide further information on physiological systems that interact to support aerobic and anaerobic exercise and promote health. Two case studies are presented as examples of how exercise may be planned and implemented in a TR setting. Finally, activities and discussion questions are offered to further the reader's understanding of the use of exercise to promote fitness.

Definitions

Because of the interrelatedness of physical activity, exercise, and fitness, confusion can result as professionals attempt to communicate by using these words and phrases. To alleviate some problems in discussion of these concepts, the following section contains definitions of:

- Physical Activity
- Fitness
- Exercise
- Therapeutic Use of Exercise
- Cardiovascular Endurance
- Muscular Performance
- Muscular Strength
- Muscular Power
- Muscular Endurance
- Body Composition
- Flexibility
- Performance-Related Fitness

Physical Activity

Physical activity is a broad term defined as bodily movement produced by skeletal muscles that result in energy expenditure (Caspersen, Powell & Christenson, 1985). Physical activity covers everything from turning the pages in a book or fidgeting in your seat during a concert to participation in triathlons. Caspersen and colleagues added that physical activity is often measured as caloric expenditure. Hahn, Teutsch, Rothenberg, and Marks (1990) contended that lack of physical activity is believed to cause as many deaths as obesity, high blood cholesterol, and hypertension. Participation in physical activity is said to offer protection from cardiovascular disease (CVD), lung disease, several types of cancer, and diabetes.

Fitness

Fitness is defined as a level of physical condition people achieve that is related to their ability to participate in typical daily tasks and recreation activities (Hornick & Leitner, 1996). Fitness involves participation in aerobic and anaerobic exercises to achieve an optimal level of physical condition.

Overall physical fitness is a state characterized by good muscular strength combined with muscular endurance; however, fitness is viewed in relation to an individual's characteristics such as age, occupation, preferences, disability, needs, goals, and the tasks that must be performed (Lieberman, 2007). Lieberman noted that compared to a less fit individual, a physically fit person demonstrates greater oxygen consumption, cardiac output, stroke volume, total blood volume, oxygen extraction by tissues, cardiac volume, muscular strength, adaptation of circulation, and respiration to effort during exercise and results in lower resting pulse rate, pulse rate, and blood pressure.

Exercise

Exercise is a type of physical activity that involves a deliberate, planned, and repetitive bodily movement done to improve or maintain one or more components of physical fitness (Caspersen et al., 1985). Anaerobic exercise, aerobic exercise, and some sports are generally considered to be *exercise*, while reading and going to the beach are unlikely to be identified as exercise because they are not done to improve physical fitness. *Anaerobic exercises* are activities that can be performed without using inhaled oxygen. According to Hornick and Leitner (1996), *aerobic exercises* are activities that require oxygen for prolonged periods of time and place such demands on the body that requires it to improve its capacity to handle oxygen.

Therapeutic Use of Exercise

While exercise to promote fitness is essentially the same for people with and without disabilities, exercise as a therapeutic medium involves implementation of planned physical activity to improve function as well as remediate impairments to meet treatment goals (Greene & Lim, 2007). TR specialists might use exercise as a therapeutic medium to improve ambulation, joint mobility, circulation, respiratory capacity, coordination, balance, relaxation, strength, endurance, body composition, as well as to decrease rigidity (Lieberman, 2007) and enhance mental health (Buckworth & Dishman, 2002).

Cardiovascular Endurance

Cardiovascular endurance is achieved through aerobic exercises that promote cardiovascular fitness (McCubbin et al., 1997). Hornick and Leitner (1996) defined cardiovascular fitness as the ability of the heart, blood vessels, blood, and respiratory system to supply fuel, particularly oxygen, to the muscles during sustained exercise. One measure of cardiac endurance is VO2 which is an indicator of oxygen transport to the working tissues during exercise participation. VO2 is commonly used in exercise physiology as a measure of exercise intensity. Lower pulse rate and blood pressure during exercise and better adaptation of circulation and respiration to effort are characteristic features of improved endurance (Lieberman, 2007).

Muscular Performance

Kisner and Colby (2007) identified muscle performance as the capacity of a muscle to do work (force x distance). The authors added that performance is a complex component of functional movement and is influenced by all body systems. A TR specialist must consider a participant's ability to anticipate, respond to, and control forces applied to the body. To complete the physical demands of everyday life in a safe and efficient manner, the body's muscles must produce, sustain, and regulate muscle tension to meet these demands. Kisner and Colby stated that key elements of muscle performance are strength, power, and endurance, and if any these elements are impaired, a decrease in function and disability may occur.

Muscular Strength

Muscular strength is the ability of a muscle or muscle group to exert force against resistance during a single effort or repetition without regard to the velocity of the movement (Miller, 1995). Hornick and Leitner (1996) noted that muscular strength decreases the chance of injury, back pain, or poor posture while increasing athletic performance. Lieberman (2007) added that use of resistance training to increase strength has been shown to decrease risk of coronary artery disease, osteoporosis, diabetes, and cancer.

Muscular Power

Muscle power is an aspect of muscle performance that is related to strength and speed of movement and is defined as the work (force x distance) produced by a muscle per unit of time (force x distance/time) (Levangie & Norkin, 2001). In other words, muscle power is the rate of performing work. The rate at which a muscle contracts and produces a force and the relationship of force and velocity are factors that affect muscle power (Brosky & Wright, 2006). Power can be expressed by either a single burst of high-intensity activity, such as lifting a kayak onto an overhead rack or performing a high jump, or by repeated bursts of less intense muscle activity, such as climbing stairs.

Muscular Endurance

Muscular endurance prevents the body from tiring as a result of daily activities (Hornick & Leitner, 1996). Lockette (1995) described muscular endurance as the muscles' ability to repeatedly contract and lengthen between 2–3 minutes. Muscle endurance is an indication of how long the muscles can perform various activities. Muscular endurance is needed to participate in many daily activities, such as wheelchair propulsion, climbing steps, and walking. Anaerobic and aerobic exercises are useful to increase muscular endurance and should be performed at least three times per week (ACSM, 2006). According to Hornick and Leitner, exercises that can increase muscular endurance include weight training, calisthenics, jogging, swimming, and aerobic dancing and should be performed for a minimum of 3–4 minutes.

Body Composition

Body composition is the level of a person's body-fat weight in relation to lean body weight (Hornick & Leitner, 1996). Body-fat weight is the essential and nonessential body tissue as compared to lean body weight which is the muscle, bone, skin, water, and organs of the body. Body composition is influenced by exercise, age, gender, and diet (Faigenbaum, 2008) and is one indicator of a person's level of physical fitness. Specifically, body composition plays a role in how rapidly or slowly a person develops fatigue during aerobic exercise (Figoni, 1995).

> For example, the more body-fat weight that an individual has in relation to lean body weight, the more likely it is that the person will become fatigued.

Flexibility

Flexibility is the ability of a muscle group to elongate, enabling the joint to move through a range of motions. Surburg (1995) described flexibility as the ability to freely move muscles at joints or a group of joints. DiRocco (1995) stated that flexibility permits the body to move freely and improves and maintains range of motion in a joint or group of joints. It is likely that optimal levels of flexibility exist for each activity. Flexibility is important for improving and maintaining posture, reducing muscle soreness, and preventing muscular injury (Miller, 1995). An imbalance in flexibility, hyperflexibility, and inflexibility increases risk of injury (Riewald, 2004). Selected tests for flexibility are included in the implementation exercise section of this chapter.

Performance-Related Fitness

Performance or skill-related fitness involves development of qualities that enhance the performance of physical activities such as sport. Whereas health fitness is concerned with living better, performance-related fitness is concerned with performing sport-related skills better and more efficiently. Different degrees of performance-related fitness are needed, depending on the activity of interest.

> For example, the degree of power, agility, and speed needed to play rugby is different from that required by a wheelchair tennis player, though both individuals need these qualities to perform at an optimal level.

Selected test protocols for performance related fitness are identified by Harman and Garhammer (2008) and others. Wuest and Bucher (2006) identified the following skill-related fitness components:

> Agility - Ability to change direction rapidly with control
> Balance - Ability to maintain equilibrium while stationary or moving
> Coordination - Ability to execute movements smoothly and efficiently
> Power - Ability to produce force at a fast speed
> Reaction - Time elapsed between stimulus and body response to stimulus
> Speed - Ability to move body quickly

Descriptions

Activities that affect fitness involve use of aerobic and anaerobic exercises to produce improvement in an individual's cardiovascular fitness, muscle strength, muscle endurance, flexibility, and body composition (Miller, 1995). According to Bullock and Mahon (1996), fitness activities can be used as a therapeutic medium when the intent is to bring about improvements in an individual. If people wish to increase function or fitness, they can participate in an exercise program following the guidelines set forth by the American College of Sports Medicine (2007) for intensity, duration, frequency, and type.

Because most adults do not pursue vigorous exercise, TR specialists often include opportunities for moderate intensity activity and for vigorous exercise. The goal is to increase the accumulated active time over the course of each day. It is important to do some physical activity on a regular basis, but it is not necessary for it to be strenuous. Moderate activity encourages individuals to be active without mandating participation in vigorous activity.

By applying exercise activities in a systematic manner, consistent with objectives designed to meet the needs of the individual, activities can be used as a therapeutic medium (Bullock & Mahon, 1996). Using exercise as a therapeutic medium can serve as a way to meet functional, expressive, and leisure needs. Facilitating adherence to activities for fitness is one means by which people with disabilities can promote the expression of their leisure lifestyle.

According to the American College of Sports Medicine (2007), recommendations for activities to improve health and fitness include large muscle activities that are rhythmic and repetitive, such as swimming, water and land exercises, weight training, and cycling. These types of activities have the potential for positive physiological outcomes in:

- Cardiovascular Endurance
- Muscular Strength
- Muscular Endurance
- Body Composition
- Flexibility

Cardiovascular Endurance

To help participants achieve improved cardiovascular endurance, a TR specialist uses aerobic exercises to increase and sustain their heart rate for a specified period of time. Aerobic exercises that could be used as interventions include aerobic dancing, running or road racing (see Figure 15.1), step aerobics, walking, bicycling or cycling, machine skiing, rowing, hiking, or jogging (Hornick & Leitner, 1996).

Hornick and Leitner (1996) identified that principles of aerobic exercise for people with disabilities are similar to those for people without disabilities; however, Figoni (1995) recommended that when trying to achieve cardiovascular fitness, a TR specialist considers the person's needs, abilities, and disabilities in relation to the following aspects of activities:

Figure 15.1

- Frequency
- Intensity
- Duration of involvement
- Type of activity
- Adherence

Frequency of activity. Frequency of cardiovascular activity refers to how often people participate in an activity to increase and sustain their heart rate for a specified period of time. Frequency of a cardiovascular activity is important because it contributes to increasing the ability to consume oxygen and increase blood circulation (ACSM, 2007). Maximal oxygen consumption and increased blood circulation contributes to improved fitness.

> For example, people with physical disabilities, particularly those with paralysis, neuromuscular impairments, or degenerative disorders, tend to experience a reduction in active muscle mass which decreases consumption of oxygen and circulation, thus, decreasing cardiovascular fitness.

Frequency of cardiovascular activity for these individuals is important to increase use of large muscle groups to improve oxygen consumption accompanied by increased circulation.

> Specifically, participation in hand cycling by someone with a spinal cord injury for 20 minutes 3–5 times each week could assist in increasing oxygen consumption and contribute to increased circulation.

To improve cardiovascular endurance it is necessary for a person to participate in aerobic exercise at least three times each week if engaging in vigorous exercise and five times a week for moderate exercise (ACSM, 2007). Healthy older adults also need moderate physical activity five times a week or vigorous activity three times a week to maintain health (Nelson et al., 2007). According to the U.S. Department of

Health and Human Services 2008 Physical Activity Guidelines for Americans, adults with disabilities, who are able, should get at least 150-minutes a week of moderate-intensity exercise or 75 minutes a week of vigorous-intensity aerobic activity in episodes of at least 10 minutes and preferably spread throughout the week.

A competitive athlete should be prepared to train as often as six times per week. Everyone should take at least 1 day off to give damaged tissues a chance for repair (Prentice, 1994).

Intensity of activity. The intensity of cardiovascular activity is described as the level of achieved maximal heart rate. Intensity of cardiovascular activity is an important component because it is a measure of degree of exertion during participation in an activity (Figoni, Lockette, & Surburg, 1995). Guidelines for individuals with chronic conditions or for adults over 65 include: (a) moderately intense aerobic exercise 30 minutes a day, 5 days a week or vigorously intense aerobic exercise 20 minutes a day, 3 days a week, and (b) 8–10 strength-training exercises (5–10 repetitions), 2 days a week (ACSM, 2007).

Intensity of physical activity experienced by individuals can vary because it is dependent on personal fitness, target heart zone, and age.

> For example, a moderate intensity walk might be a slow walk for some, particularly older adults, or a brisk walk for others (Nelson et al., 2007).

Figoni and colleagues (1995) offered the following general guidelines to determine intensity: (a) increased heart rate to 70–85% of target heart zone during participation in an aerobic activity is at a *high rate of intensity*, (b) increased heart rate to 50–69% of target heart zone is at a *moderate rate of intensity*, and (c) increased heart rate to 20–49% of target heart zone is functioning at a *low rate of intensity*. It is not recommended to participate in activity above 85% of an individual's target zone.

> Examples of high-intensity aerobic activities are bicycling, jogging, and wheelchair road racing. Moderate-intensity physical activity means working hard enough to raise your heart rate and break a sweat, while still being able to carry on a conversation (ACSM, 2007). Low-intensity aerobic activities include walking and low-impact aerobics.

The unique characteristics of each individual are considered prior to participation so that appropriate intensity of cardiovascular exercise can be suggested.

> For example, certain high-intensity aerobic exercises may be contraindicated for an individual who has had a CVA.

ACSM (2007) noted that to lose weight or maintain weight loss, 60–90 minutes of physical activity may be necessary. The 30-minute recommendation is for the average healthy adult to maintain health and reduce risk of chronic disease.

The 1991 American College of Sports Medicine guidelines made an important distinction regarding intensity of exercise to promote health. While early emphasis was on vigorous activity, moderate physical activities that are performed regularly are now viewed as good to provide protection from disease and early mortality. National objectives for both the ACSM (2007) and Healthy People 2010 (U. S. Department of Health and Human Services, 2000) place emphasis on moderate-intensity activities such as walking, gardening, and moderate cycling as necessary to improve health. *Moderate exercise* involves working hard at about a level six intensity on a scale of 10 and the ability to participate in a conversation during exercise (ACSM).

There are numerous methods of monitoring exercise intensity. The method chosen depends on a participant's fitness level and access to intensity information and experience. Monitoring methods that can be easily used in various settings by the TR specialist include *percentage of maximal heart rate* (220 – age x desired % of intensity x 1.15) and *the Karvonen Formula* which factors in the resting heart rate (220 – age – resting heart rate x desired % of intensity + resting heart rate). While these methods are often used, these formulas only estimate a maximal heart rate that has a variability of + or – 10 to 12 beats per minute (Durstine & Pate, 1988).

Exercise intensity may also be measured by subjective expression of intensity or perceived exertion. Because heart rate is directly related to intensity of exercise and the rate of oxygen consumption, it becomes an easy process to identify a pace that will make heart rate occur at a desired level. Additionally, rates of perceived exertion can be used to monitor heart rate to identify exercise intensity. During exercise, individuals are asked to rate subjectively on a scale from 6–20, or 0–10 exactly how they feel in terms of exercise fatigue relative to their level of exertion (Borg, 1970).

Exercise that requires a high level of energy expenditure and oxygen consumption is related to a higher perceived exertion rate. These scales correlate highly with cardiorespiratory and metabolic factors such as heart rate, breathing rate, oxygen consumption, and fatigue (Forge, 1991). Another subjective means of evaluating exercise intensity is the talk test (Forge, 1991). Participants should be able to talk comfortably and rhythmically throughout exercise to assure safe exercise.

Duration of involvement. According to Miller (1995), duration of cardiovascular fitness is the amount of time one's target heart rate is continuously sustained. Therefore, duration refers to how long individuals raise and maintain their target heart rate. Duration is important to cardiovascular fitness because it contributes to increasing a cardiovascular functioning (Figoni, 1995).

Endurance training is structured to include 5 minutes of warm-up activity, 30 minutes of training, and 5 minutes of cool down (Leiberman, 2007). The American College of Sports Medicine (2006) recommend 20–60 minutes of activity with the heart rate elevated from moderate to intense levels. Prentice (1994) stated that for minimal improvement to occur, the person must participate in at least 20 minutes of continuous activity with the heart rate elevated to a moderate level.

For example, if individuals with multiple sclerosis participate in water aerobics for at least 20 minutes, they may improve or at least maintain their cardiovascular fitness over time.

In the U.S. Department of Health and Human Services 2008 Physical Activity Guidelines for Americans, adults with disabilities, who are able, should engage in aerobic activity in episodes of at least 10 minutes and preferably spread throughout the week. Generally, the greater the workout duration, the greater improvement occurs in cardio-respiratory endurance.

Type of activity. Type of exercise activity is important to consider when people participate in cardiovascular activities. Type of activity refers to which large muscle groups are used during an exercise. Specifically, a TR specialist may want to consider whether an individual needs to use upper body, such as the deltoid muscles, or lower body, such as the quadriceps muscles, during participation in a fitness activity. Kisner and Colby (2007) recommended considering the goals set for the participant and select exercise activities accordingly.

> For example, if a goal set for a participant is to improve distance traveled in by wheelchair, long-distance aerobic wheelchair activities such as road racing could be emphasized.

Adaptive forms of exercises such as walking, running, jogging, dancing, climbing stairs, cycling, swimming, rowing, skating, cross-country skiing are recommended for performance of 60–85% of maximum heart rate or to a heart rate at 50–85% of maximum O2 uptake.

Adherence. Buckworth and Dishman (2002) stated that for exercise to be effective, adherence is necessary. Specifically, after examining many studies examining the effects of exercise, Dishman (1993) concluded that 4 months of exercise may be important for significant long-term changes. While problems with continued participation in programs are emphasized, there is little documentation of effects of techniques designed to promote adherence. Nevertheless, there is some information that suggests determinants and intervention strategies for adherence to physical activity.

Dishman (1993) presented an interrelated list of determinants to habitual fitness activity, which includes demographic variables, biomedical status, access to facilities, past and present behaviors, activity history, and psychological traits and states.

> For example, those people who perceive their health as poor, those who do not expect benefits, and those who do not feel self-determined are unlikely to adhere to an exercise program.

Factors such as socioeconomic status and being overweight may result in selection preferences toward a sedentary lifestyle or may create barriers that can increase resistance to adopting or maintaining a physically active lifestyle. Perceived lack of time, the principal reason given for dropping out of exercise programs, may reflect a lack of interest or commitment to physical activity. Therefore, it is important for TR specialists to incorporate assessments, leisure education, goal setting, and follow-up when using exercise as a therapeutic medium in treatment.

Muscular Strength

The American College of Sport Medicine (1995) described muscular strength as the ability of a muscle to exert maximum force during a single effort or repetition. Muscular strength refers to the amount of force or weight a muscle can exert. According to Brosky and Wright (2006), when using strength training as an intervention, a TR specialist uses anaerobic exercises to exert muscle force during a single effort or repetition over a short period of time (less than 3–4 minutes).

> For example, a TR specialist could use sprinting with a hand-cycle to improve upper body muscle strength (see Figure 15.2). Anaerobic exercises should be completed 3 x a week and include activities such as push-ups, pull-ups, arm circles, and leg lifts using weights (ACSM, 2006).

Strength exercises may produce tissue trauma which temporarily reduces strength output and may cause muscle soreness; therefore, it is desirable to include ample rest between training sessions. When individuals get adequate rest between strength exercises, this time of rest is considered to be the *recovery period* for muscles. During this recovery period, the muscles build slightly higher levels

Figure 15.2

of strength. Since the rebuilding process usually requires about 48 hours, it is recommended that strength workouts be scheduled every other day. Those who prefer to train more frequently should avoid working the same muscle groups on consecutive days.

In the U.S. Department of Health and Human Services 2008 Physical Activity Guidelines for Americans, adults with disabilities, who are able, should do muscle-strengthening activities of moderate or high intensity that involve all major muscle groups on 2 or more days a week. An individual's disability should be considered when using muscular strengthening as an intervention (Kisner & Colby, 2007).

> For example, when using muscular strengthening as an intervention with individuals with arthritis, weight of more than two pounds may be contraindicated.

Miller (1995) noted that the degree of adaptation used with muscular strength exercises is relative to the person's ability to utilize muscle strength effectively.

In relation to adaptations that may be needed, Miller cited several considerations when using muscle-strengthening exercises, which include:

- Muscle contractions
- Amount of weight

Muscle contractions. Muscles are capable of three different types of contractions for strength including: (a) isometric contraction, (b) concentric contractions, and (c) eccentric contraction. An *isometric contraction* occurs when the muscle contracts to produce tension, but there is no change in muscle length.

> Considerable force can be generated against some immovable resistance, even though no movement occurs, such as when pushing against a wall.

Isometric contractions can be effective when joint motion is contraindicated or painful (Lieberman, 2007). In a *concentric contraction*, the muscle shortens in length while tension develops to overcome or move some resistance, such as flexing the arm to begin a bicep curl. An *eccentric contraction* is a contraction that occurs while the muscle is lengthening and still applying force.

> For example, after a bicep curl, if the bicep muscle does not remain contracted when the weight is being lowered, the weight will quickly fall back to the starting position. Thus, to control the weight as it is being lowered, the bicep muscle must continue to contract while at the same time gradually lengthen.

Lieberman added that both concentric and eccentric contractions can be considered *isotonic exercise*, which is when the muscle shortens or lengthens. Isotonic exercise can involve the use of free weights and/or machines.

Amount of weight. The amount of weight that can be moved through tension and lengthening phase of one repetition is an important consideration.

> For example, when a person completes a bicep curl using three pounds of weight, the specific weight has been identified.

It is generally accepted that when weight training for strength, heavier weights with a lower number of repetitions should be used.

Muscular Endurance

According to Hornick and Leitner (1996), muscular endurance prevents the body from tiring as a result of daily activities. As with muscular strengthening, the degree of adaptation used with muscular endurance exercises is determined by the person's ability to tolerate muscle endurance exercises. When using muscular endurance exercises as a therapeutic medium, a TR specialist considers the:

- Amount of weight
- Duration of exercise
- Type of exercise activity
- Repetition of exercise

Amount of weight. Muscular endurance training uses relatively lighter weights with a greater number of repetitions than used for strength training; therefore, when training for muscular endurance, light weights are used. The amount of weight used to increase muscular endurance refers to quantity of weight that a person can lift or tolerate. According to Lockette (1995), as the amount of weight in which a person can tolerate increases, the individual's muscular endurance increases.

An example of a consideration of the amount of weight used to increase muscular endurance is the use of five pounds of weight on the right leg during water exercise activities with someone who has right side hemiplegia.

Duration of exercise. Duration of muscular endurance refers to the amount of time of continuous use of weight (Hornick & Leitner, 1996). Prentice (1994) recommended that endurance training consist of three sets of 10–15 repetitions.

Following the example in the previous section, when the TR specialist considers adequate duration to improve muscular endurance, the use of five pounds of weight (if easily tolerated) on the right leg for 10 minutes of water exercise for a person with right hemiplegia may promote improved duration of exercise.

Type of exercise activity. The type of activity is an important consideration when attempting to improve muscular endurance. Different types of activity target specific muscle groups such as leg lifts, walking, or flutter kicking, and are used to improve muscular endurance for a person's legs.

For example, selection of water exercises utilizing weights on the right leg for 10 minutes could be used to improve muscular endurance of a person who has experienced right hemiplegia.

Repetition of exercise. Repetition refers to the number of times in which the participant can tolerate using a specific amount of weight (Hornick & Leitner, 1996). Repetition of exercise and duration of an exercise is important to consider; however, once a thorough assessment has been conducted, only one of these considerations may be stipulated.

Keeping with the water exercise example, an example of the use of repetition to improve muscular endurance would be to use five pounds of weight on the right leg and to require the person to lift his or her leg in the water for 15 repetitions.

Body Composition

Body composition usually refers to the relative proportions of weight of fat and lean tissue (Harman & Garhammer, 2008). Body fat percentage is the percentage of fat the body contains.

> For example, if a body weighs 160 pounds and 10% fat, it means that the body consists of 16 pounds fat and 144 pounds lean body mass (muscles, blood, bones, ligaments, tendons, and internal organs).

The body needs essential fat because it serves as an important metabolic fuel for energy production and other bodily functions (Kravitz & Heyward, 1992). The authors added that normal body functions may be negatively affected if body fat falls below the minimum level recommended for men (5%) and women (15%). The body fat ranges for optimal health (18%–30% for women and 10%–25% for men) are based on several studies of the general population. For athletes, body fat percentages tend to be lower than optimal health values because excess fat may hinder physical performance and activity.

Body composition is commonly assessed using *skinfold measures*. To measure skinfold, a device called a *skinfold caliper* is used to measure thickness of skin in specific areas of the body including chin, triceps, chest, subscapular, suprailiac, waist, suprapubic, and knees. Skinfold measures are commonly used to predict an individual's percentage of body fat. However, the validity of skinfold measures has been questioned for individuals with disabilities (Lockette & Keyes, 1994). When considering body fat for a participant, Kravitz and Heyward (1992) stressed that the therapist should use a range of values rather than a single value to account for individual differences.

> For example, after age 20, expect at least a 1–3% body fat gain per decade up to the age of 60. After 60, body fat slowly declines. In addition, there is approximately a 2% loss of bone mass per decade in older populations. As a result of these changes, men and women who weigh the same at age 60 as they did at age 20 may have doubled their body fat unless they have been physically active (Wilmore, Buskirk, DiGirolamo, & Lohman, 1986).

Usually body composition information is provided to enable individuals to work toward desirable levels of body fat. When considering body composition, an understanding of the exercise-energy expenditure relationship is essential. The exercise-energy expenditure relationship considers the correlation between amount and type of exercise to the amount of energy expended (Hornick & Leitner, 1996). Exercise for fat loss must be of an intensity, duration, and frequency sufficient of to burn more calories than the number of calories ingested (ACSM, 1991).

> For example, if an individual has a daily consumption of 3,500 calories, this person would then need to expend more than 3,500 calories during exercise to lose weight.

Flexibility

Anaerobic exercises, such as stretching, range of motion, and relaxation exercises can be completed 3 times per week to improve and maintain flexibility (Hornick & Leitner, 1996). According to the American Heart Association, older adults and others should engage in flexibility exercises at a minimum of 10 minutes a day, 2 days a week (Nelson et al., 2007). Older adults and others who have a high risk of injury from falls should also perform exercises that improve balance.

Lieberman (2007) identified the main types of stretching to increase flexibility as being: (a) static, (b) dynamic, and (c) proprioceptive neuromuscular facilitation (PNF). *Static stretching*, the most commonly recommended method to improve flexibility, involves stretching the muscle to a point of mild discomfort and holding for 15–30 seconds. Static stretching has a low risk of injury and requires a small amount of assistance and time. *Dynamic stretching* includes repetitive bouncing movements to produce muscle stretch and may cause soreness and injury. *PNF* is characterized by contraction and relaxation of muscles through a series of motions that may cause soreness and requires a trained facilitator.

> Examples of activities that may promote flexibility through stretching are yoga, tai chi, pilates, and aquatic intervention, such as bad ragaz and watsu.

While the principle of improving and maintaining flexibility is similar for people with and without disabilities (to permit the body to move freely), several factors are considered when flexibility exercises are used as a therapeutic intervention (Kisner & Colby, 2007). These factors include muscle elasticity of surrounding muscle groups, joint structure, joint position, tissue temperature, scar tissue, adhesions, contracture of surrounding muscles, and joint deformities.

> For example, although stretching the lower back muscles is recommended to protect the lower back from injury for people without paralysis of back extensors, it could reduce trunk stability in someone with paralysis of back extensors such as a person with quadriplegia.

History

In ancient societies, it was necessary for people to be physically active for survival; people were required to run from danger, hunt for food, and physically carry everything. Sedentary lifestyles were nonexistent but desired.

Kaplan, Lazarus, Cohen, and Lew (1991) contended that people have put considerable energy into creating a less active lifestyle through inventing step-saving devices. Ironically, people have become so successful at avoiding physical activity that sedentary lifestyles are now a major threat to the health of members of industrialized societies.

According to Lee and Paffenbarger (1996), the concept of physical activity and fitness is not new; early records indicate that organized exercise was used for health promotion in China around 2500 B.C. In addition, Hippocrates and Plato (460–370 B.C.) believed in the importance of a physically active lifestyle for well-being and its usefulness in treating disease and promoting health (Lee & Paffenbarger, 1996).

Despite the known benefits, participation in regular exercise activity has remained relatively low. Dishman (1995) reported that only 12% of adults participated in regular vigorous activity, and while 22% participated in regular moderate activity, the remaining 66% were sedentary. Spangler (1997) reported that 50% of Americans 12–21 years of age did not participate in regular vigorous activity, while only 19% of high-school students were physically active for 20 minutes or more, 5 days a week in physical education courses. She added that 14% of youth report no recent physical activity. Recent studies have also raised alarm regarding the growing percentage of children, youth, and adults who are overweight and obese (Wuest & Bucher, 2006).

Theoretical Foundations

Exercise adherence to an exercise program varies. Some authorities estimate that half of all participants fail to comply with an exercise regimen (Buckworth & Dishman, 2002) often as a result of not having appropriate short-term goals. Garcia and King (1991) stated that the general importance of short-range goals to motivation and behavior change is grounded in social-cognitive theory. Some social-cognitive models discussed in exercise literature related to exercise include the:

- Health Belief Model (Becker, 1974)
- Theory of Reasoned Action (Fishbein & Ajzen, 1975)
- Theory of Planned Behavior (Ajzen, 1991)
- Transtheoretical Model (Prochaska & Velicer, 1997)

Health Belief Model

The Health Belief Model stresses cognitive influences on behavior. The model was originally conceived by Rosenstock (1966; 1990) and further developed by Becker (1974) to explain preventative health behaviors. This theoretical model explains that an individual's beliefs about the susceptibility and severity of illness combine to create an overall perceived threat of illness. The more people feel threatened by illness, the more likely they will participate in actions that promote health. Beliefs about the perceived benefits of a behavior also influence the occurrence of exercise behaviors.

> For example, going on a starvation diet may be perceived as more effective than exercise to lose weight because it achieves weight loss outcomes more quickly.

This leads to an additional point in the health belief theory that perceived actions minus perceived barriers (such as time, money, or effort) influence action. Cost-benefit analyses are suggested to assist a participant in determining if benefits outweigh costs. If benefits of exercise become apparent to a participant to outweigh the costs, then likelihood of participation increases. Self-efficacy, participants' confidence in their capability to perform the desired behavior, is included as an important part of this model. Therefore, TR specialists could educate individuals with disabilities on benefits of exercise prior to their involvement.

As an application of the Health Belief Model, Turner and colleagues (2004) described the Osteoporosis Prevention Program (OPP) for 342 middle-aged women. The purpose of the OPP was to address reasons for non-compliance in osteoporosis prevention by incorporating four major components of the Health Belief Model: perceived barriers, benefits, susceptibility, and severity. Perceived barriers were inconvenient days and time, lack of childcare, cost, and inaccessible location.

To address these barriers, classes were offered at multiple times, with childcare, at no charge, and in a central location. To increase perceived susceptibility, incidences and slides of osteoporosis in women of all ages were presented. Benefits of controlling osteoporosis, such as self-efficacy, skill building, coping skills, and prevention, were presented. Perceived severity was promoted through discussion of death, fractures, reduced quality of life, and physical pain. According to the authors, the OPP increased participation, interaction, and appreciation of the disease.

Theory of Reasoned Action

A major assumption of the theory of reasoned action is that people are usually rational and make predictable use of information. According to Ajzen and Fishbein (1985), intentions are the most immediate influence of behavior. Intentions are influenced by positive or negative attitudes regarding behavior and perceived norms (social influences). It logically follows that if people feel good about a behavior and have positive social influence over time, they will intend to perform a behavior.

Ajzen and Fishbein emphasized that attitudes are influenced by beliefs about the consequence of the action. Subjective norms are affected by the support or pressure of significant others whom participants are motivated to please. TR specialists attempting to involve participants with disabilities in exercise programs might consider effects of social influences on participant intentions. Limiting negative attitudes associated with social influences may increase the likelihood of continued participation.

Theory of Planned Behavior

The theory of planned behavior (TPB) includes the importance of perceived control, attitudes, and social expectations (norms) on intentions to participate in moderate to vigorous physical activity (Ajzen, 1991). Ajzen contended that intentions grow stronger as people perceive control over their action. Therefore, if people think that they can control exercise, they are more likely to continue exercising.

Theodorakis (1994) examined the exercise behavior relationship according to the TPB. He found that role identity is an important predictor of repeated behaviors which are then incorporated into a person's self-image. Martin, Oliver, and McCaughtry (2007) evaluated the ability of TPB to predict children's reported moderate-to-vigorous physical activity. Their analyses provided additional support for the ability of TPB variables to predict activity level. Specifically, participant's attitudes, subjective norm, and perceived control accounted for intention. However, this intention for children may not translate into physical activity unless barriers are addressed.

Keats, Culos-Reed, Courneya, and McBride (2007) used the TPB to examine motivation for physical exercise in 196 adolescent survivors of cancer. A self-administered survey mailed to participants assessed their beliefs, attitudes, perceptions of control, norms, and intentions regarding physical activity. Results revealed that the TPB explained that the most important and significant predictors of physical activity were self-efficacy and intention while affective attitude and instrumental attitude were the significant predictors of intention. Although study limitations were noted, the researchers stated that results can be interpreted to mean that participants view physical activity as a way to regain and maintain their overall health.

In another study describing application of the TPB on people with cancer, Jones and colleagues (2007) examined exercise intention of 100 individuals with primary brain cancer. Results revealed a moderate to large positive correlation of TPB constructs and participants' beliefs toward exercise. Affective attitude and perceived behavior control appeared to be the most important predictors of exercise. An important implication was that promotion of exercise as being enjoyable may improve exercise intentions and adherence. Limitations of the study were use of a self-report survey and a retrospective observation design which limits ability to infer causality.

In conclusion, an understanding of and prediction of behaviors may be improved by models that encourage consideration of a person's preferences, identities, and intentions when developing goals. A TR specialist attempting to involve a participant with disabilities may be more successful at maintaining the participant's involvement if activity is socially supported and the person is given control within the program.

Transtheoretical Model

The transtheoretical model views behavior change as a spiraling continuum, moving from a stage of no intention to change through stages leading to the change being part of an individual's life (Prochaska & Velicer, 1997). Self-efficacy is an important part of the stages in this model. In the context of behavioral change, self-efficacy is a belief that a person can maintain healthy behavior such as exercise, or abstain from unhealthy behavior such as binging or smoking. Seven stages identified by Duffy and Schnirring (2000) are described with suggestions for professional intervention:

- Precontemplation
- Contemplation
- Preparation
- Action
- Maintenance
- Termination
- Relapse

Precontemplation: An individual has no intention to change in the foreseeable future when functioning in the precontemplation stage. The individual may not be fully informed about consequences of behavior or doubt ability to change.

Self-efficacy is low, so the practitioner educates the individual about importance of physical exercise to health.

Contemplation: The second stage involves an individual intending to take action in the next 6 months. In this stage, the person is aware and weighs the pros and cons of changing. This may cause a profound ambivalence and consequential chronic procrastination. The practitioner highlights benefits of change and tries to shift decisional balance to a decision to exercise.

Preparation: With improved self-efficacy, during this stage, an individual may show steps toward changing health behavior, such as developing a plan to decide where and when to exercise. The practitioner helps the individual identify resources and times and teaches safe exercise strategies.

Action: An individual makes lifestyle modifications by engaging in healthy exercise behaviors, such as swimming or walking 3 days a week during the action stage. The practitioner encourages and supports the individual to become active, helps monitor activity level, and discusses program modifications.

Maintenance: An individual sustains the change in healthy behavior for at least 6 months. During this stage, the individual becomes confident in the ability to maintain change. The practitioner discusses ideas for continuing to be active even when schedules change.

Termination: Behavior is fully integrated into an individual's lifestyle. Individuals in this stage have a high degree of self-confidence, meaning that even though they may sometimes relapse, they will continue the positive lifestyle behavior.

Relapse: Discontinuation of the exercise behavior is seen as a return from the action or maintenance stage to an earlier stage during the final stage. While relapse occurs often, Duffy and Schnirring stated that only a small percentage return to the precontemplation stage. The practitioner approaches the individual positively and reminds the person that relapse gives the opportunity to rethink their physical activity attempt. The practitioner then examines what worked and what should be changed with the individual and helps to develop a new plan.

Effectiveness

Many studies have been conducted using exercise as a therapeutic medium to improve physical, emotional, and leisure functioning of individuals with disabilities. The following paragraphs summarize findings associated with effects of fitness on:

- Physical Health
- Mental Health

Physical Health

The impact of physical exercise can be observed in many physical behaviors of participants. This section covers the following physical effects:

- Childhood obesity
- Cardiovascular disease (CVD)
- Cancer
- Bone health
- Diabetes
- Strokes
- Parkinson's disease
- Sleep
- Physical performance
- HIV

Childhood obesity. Obesity in children and adolescents has become an alarming trend throughout the world. Childhood obesity has become problematic because it has increased the amount of juvenile diabetes, high blood pressure, and high cholesterol. Childhood obesity also negatively affects self-esteem, peer relationships, and depression levels. Children who are obese have a higher chance of being obese throughout their entire lifespan leading to cardiovascular disease and coronary heart disease (Kim & Kravitz, 2007). Due to this epidemic, there has been an increase in the amount of exercise related literature that focuses on children and obesity.

Knopfli and colleagues (2008) investigated effects of an 8-week multidisciplinary program including physical activity on 130 obese children and adolescents. The multidisciplinary program consisted of moderate calorie restriction, physical activity, and behavior modification. Body weight, body composition, aerobic fitness, and quality of life were assessed at baseline and at the end of the 8-week intervention. There was a significant decrease in both weight and body fat percentage and a significant increase in quality of life and aerobic fitness.

Chang, Liu, Zhao, Li, and Yu (2007) examined effects of a 1-year exercise program on metabolic risk factors and physical fitness of 49 obese children (ages 12–14). Participants were assigned to a supervised exercise group or a control group, with both groups receiving health education once every 3, 9, and 12 months. Participants in the exercise group showed significant improvement in reducing body mass index, insulin sensitivity, and other metabolic syndrome factors. Physical fitness factors such as body strength, flexibility, and endurance were enhanced. Three months after program termination, health benefits weakened or disappeared.

After reviewing the literature, **Hills, King, and Armstrong (2007)** identified implications and efficacy of physical activity on overweight and obese children. According to the authors, the literature supported the benefits of physical activity in promoting a healthy lifestyle and preventing disease. Moreover, lack of physical activity was associated with disease and chronic health problems. The environment was documented as the most influential factor of physical activity.

Atlantis, Barnes, and Fiatarone Singh (2006) conducted a meta-analysis of efficacy research pertaining to 14 exercise programs (average duration was 16 weeks) and effects on 481 overweight and obese children. All studies consisted of supervised exercise with a treatment and control group. Exercise significantly reduced body fat in obese children, while body weight and obesity outcomes were inconclusive. Caution was advised generalizing results due to brevity of treatments.

Daly, Copelan, Wright, Roalfe, and Wales (2006) examined effects of a 14-week exercise program on 81 adolescents who were obese (63) or morbidly obese (18). Participants were randomly assigned to exercise therapy, equal contact exercise placebo, or usual care groups. The program consisted of one-on-one sessions (3 x wk; 8 wks) before a 6-week home program. Data for physical activity, aerobic fitness, body mass index (BMI), self-esteem, and depression were taken at baseline, and at 8, 14, and 28 weeks. Results revealed statistically significant changes in physical activity, physical self-worth, and self-esteem for participants in the exercise therapy group. There were no statistically significant changes in BMI.

DeStefano, Caprio, Fahey, Tamborlane, and Goldberg (2000) examined effects of a 12-week aerobic and resistance training program on weight and body composition of 15 obese boys (ages 9–12). The exercise program consisted of 30-minute sessions 2 days a week for 12 weeks. There was a significant decrease (10%) in percentage of body fat and a significant increase in peak volume of oxygen uptake, resting energy expenditure, and fat free mass. Participants reported a significant increase in high-intensity activities and a significant decrease in low-intensity activities. Caution is advised generalizing results due to use of a small, male-only sample.

Cardiovascular disease (CVD). In the 1970s, many scientists began to suspect that physical activity played a role in CVD. After reviewing more than 120 articles, including 54 research studies of physical activity and CVD, **Powell and colleagues (1987)** concluded that inactive adults are twice as likely to die from CVD as those who are very active. Thus, the risk of inactivity is about the same as having high blood cholesterol, having high blood pressure, or smoking (Kaplan et al., 1993). Not only does physical activity help prevent CVD, but there is evidence that physical activity aids cardiac rehabilitation and prevents second heart attacks (Haskell et al., 1992).

Haskell and colleagues (1992) argument was substantiated by Wannamethee and Shaper's (2001) review of the literature on effects of physical activity on prevention of CVD. Physical activity appeared to reduce risk of CVD in middle-aged and older adults. A dose response relationship between physical activity and CVD was reported. Furthermore, physical activity reduced risk of stroke by 40–50%. The literature review revealed that physical activity appeared to be both a primary and secondary factor in prevention of CVD.

In a study of 15 men with mental retardation, **McCubbin and colleagues (1997)** investigated three cardiorespiratory fitness tests: (a) maximal exercise test on treadmill (2.5 mph at 0% grade for 2 min and 2.5–4 mph at 2.5% grade for 2 min), (b) submaximal bicycle test (pedal 50 revolutions/min for 6 min), and (c) 1-mile walk (at maximum speed for the individual). The bicycle and 1-mile walk tests were better predictors of aerobic capacity than the treadmill exercise. The researchers recommended promoting cardiovascular fitness for people with mental retardation but cautioned that generalizability of findings was limited due to few participants.

Cancer. Various studies have shown that physical activity has a protective effect against some types of cancer. For example, **Blair and colleagues (1989)** reported a pattern for reductions in cancer deaths associated with fit individuals (age range 40–52). The risk of cancer for males identified as "low fit" was 4.3 times more than that of fit individuals, and 3 times more than that of moderately fit individuals. Low fit women had 16 times greater cancer deaths than the most fit and 2 times the risk of moderately fit. Blair and colleagues contended that the evidence gives at least modest support for the belief that regular exercise provides protection against colon cancer in men and breast cancer in women. Generalizations are cautioned because participants were primarily well-educated, upper- to middle-class Caucasian adults.

To examine effects of exercise, **Rooney and Wald (2007)** reviewed the literature on interventions for weight and body composition in women with breast cancer. A breast cancer diagnosis often leads to weight gain which is associated with an increased recurrence of breast cancer, decreased survival, and other secondary complications. This review identified benefits of exercise interventions for weight loss and the authors called for additional research on therapeutic interventions and preventions that target weight loss.

In a study of people with cancer undergoing chemotherapy, **Quist and colleagues (2006)** investigated effects of a 9-hour a week exercise program on muscular strength, aerobic capacity, and body composition. Seventy participants were assessed at baseline and at 6 weeks. There was a significant increase in muscular strength (41%) and aerobic fitness (15%). Although their weight increased slightly (1%), there was a significant decrease in skin fold measurements (3%). Limitations were a lack of reliability of skin fold measurements and a potentially unrepresentative sample.

Stevinson and Fox (2006) conducted a qualitative study to examine feasibility and acceptability of a group-based exercise program with nine participants who had cancer. The intervention consisted of a circuit training class 1 day a week and a home activity that was 4 days a week. Participants were given the Physical Activity Readiness Questionnaire and CR-1 scale of perceived exertion prior to the study and were encouraged to monitor their exertion throughout the study. After the 10-week program, 20–30 minute interviews were conducted with participants to gather data on positive and negative aspects of the program. Data were processed using an approach which included a cross-case analysis. Participants identified the variety of exercises, empathy, and inspiration from instructors, and social support as positive characteristics of the intervention. Increased fitness, decreased fatigue, enhanced, mood, and enjoyment were reported as perceived outcomes. Although there was a relatively small sample, the researchers noted that the exercise program was feasible and acceptable to participants.

Young-McCaughan and colleagues (2003) examined effects of a 12-week supervised exercise program on exercise tolerance, sleep patterns, and quality of life in 62 adults diagnosed with cancer. Over half of the participants engaged in exercise before their diagnosis, but less than half participated in exercise after diagnosis. Measurement of exercise tolerance was gathered through a graded exercise test, sleep patterns were measured with a wrist actigraph, and quality of life was assessed with the Cancer Rehabilitation Evaluation System-Short Form. All measurements were taken at baseline and at 12 weeks. Exercise tolerance, sleep patterns, and quality of life significantly improved in participants who completed the study. A major limitation of the study was the lack of a control group for comparison of results.

Bone health. There is an interest in using exercise activity for the prevention of osteoporosis (bone loss). While bone health has not been discussed as a cause of premature death, it has often been implicated in bone fractures.

In a similar study, **Swanenburg, Douwe de Bruin, Stauffacher, Mulder, and Uebelhart (2007)** examined effects of a 12-month exercise and nutrition program on balance and risk of falling in 20 older women with osteoporosis and/or osteopenia. Participants were randomly assigned to the control group that received a calcium and vitamin D supplement or the exercise group that received the calcium and vitamin D supplement. Risk of falling, postural balance, body composition, strength, number of falls, and bone mineral content were assessed prior to the program, at 3, 6, and 9 months, and at the end of the study. Compared to the control group, the experimental group reported statistically significant reductions in risk of falling and increases in muscular strength and activity level. The experimental group reported an 89% reduction in falls. Limitations of the study were a small sample size and lack of generalizability due to a women only sample.

Liu-Ambrose and colleagues (2005) investigated effects of an exercise program on risk of falls in 98 older women with low bone mass in a follow up study 1 year after completion of an exercise program. Participants were randomly assigned to a resistance, agility training, or stretching group. Data were taken for fall risk using the Physiological Profile Assessment and for physical activity and participation using the Physical Activities Scale for the Elderly. One year after cessation of the program, all three exercise groups continued to have a lower fall risk than at baseline. Caution should be advised when generalizing results beyond older women.

Various authors have researched effects of athletics on bone mineral density. For example, **Robinson and colleagues (1995)** reported that bone mineral density at the femoral neck, lumber spine, or total body to be greater in gymnasts or weightlifters when compared to a control group. Others have found that adolescent soccer, basketball, or volleyball players have greater bone mineral density than control groups (Risser, Lee & Leblanc, 1990). These studies indicated the importance of exercise activity to lessen bone loss.

Diabetes. Most studies support the relationship between inactivity and the development of diabetes. For example, in a longitudinal study, **Helmrich, Ragland, Leung, and Paffenbarger (1991)** measured physical activity of 5,990 males who were currently University of Pennsylvania athletes and, again 14 years later. Physical activity was measured by the use of a questionnaire that estimated kilocalories expended per week by walking, stair climbing, and sports participation. After the 14-year follow-up, 202 men reported that they developed diabetes. The incidence rate of diabetes decreased, as the reported total kilocalories of physical activity per week increased, suggesting that at least part of the protective effect of physical activity on diabetes development was due to less weight gain in the more active male.

In a recent study, **Ruzic, Sporis, and Matkovic (2008)** examined effects of a 2-week, high-volume, low-intensity exercise camp on glycemic control in 20 children with diabetes. The exercise camp consisted of three sessions a day of exercise, controlling of caloric intake, and monitoring of blood glucose. Data were taken at 10 days and at 2 months. Results revealed that participants had a lower rate of hypoglycemia and improved glycemic control. Two months after the conclusion of the program, the beneficial outcomes of the camp disappeared.

Castaneda (2000) reviewed the literature examining effects of exercise on people with type 2 diabetes mellitus. Benefits of exercise were reported to include better glycemic control, prevention of cardiovascular disease, functional capacity, and quality of life. The literature revealed that physical activity can help people with the management of diabetes mellitus.

Manson, Rimm, Stampfer, Colditz, and Willett (1991) conducted a longitudinal study of 87,253 women (ages 34–59) who did not have diabetes. Participants were asked about their regular physical activity patterns and again asked 8 years later. Women who reported engaging in vigorous exercise at least once a week were found to have lower incidence of self-reported diabetes.

Strokes. Jeong and Kim (2007) used a small-scale randomized control design with pre- and post-test evaluation to examine effects of an 8-week community-based intervention combining rhythmic music with specialized rehabilitation movement incorporating rhythmic auditory stimulation on physical functioning of 33 adults with strokes. Adults who attended a community health center in a metropolitan area in Seoul, South Korea were randomly assigned to an experimental group (16) or a control group (17) that received referral information about available usual care services.

Pang, Eng, Dawson, McKay, and Harris (2005) used a randomized controlled trial to examine effects of a 19-week community-based fitness and mobility exercise program (FAME) (3 x week, 1-hr sessions) on 63 older adults living at home who had the ability to walk more than 10 meters independently and had a single stroke more than 1 year before the study. Adults were randomly assigned to the FAME program or a control group that participated in a seated upper-extremity program. Measures were taken immediately before and after interventions including: VO2max, 6-minute walk test, isometric knee extension, Berg Balance Scale, Physical Activity Scale for Individuals with Physical Disabilities, and femoral neck bone mineral density. The intervention group showed significantly more improvement in cardiovascular fitness, ability to move, and leg strength than did the control group. The control group experienced a significant decrease in bone mineral density while the experimental group maintained their previous density levels. Participants in the FAME program had greater gains than the control group in cardiorespiratory fitness and in bone mineral density.

Parkinson's disease. Hackney and colleagues (2007) randomly assigned adults with Parkinson's disease to a 13-week exercise group that was conducted primarily in a seated position or a tango group (20 1-hr sessions) to examine effects on their functional mobility. Pre- and post-test measures were collected via the Unified Parkinson's Disease Rating Scale (UPDRS), Motor Subscale 3, the Berg Balance Scale, 5-meter gait velocity, Timed Up and Go mobility test (TUG), and a Freezing of Gait Questionnaire. Both the tango and exercise groups improved significantly on the Motor Subscale 3 and the UPDRS; however, only the tango group significantly improved on the Berg Balance Scale and showed a trend toward improvement in the TUG test. Overall, both groups showed improvements in motor abilities; however, the tango group demonstrated greater improvements in mobility, especially in the area of balance.

Protas and colleagues (2005) randomly assigned 18 men with idiopathic Parkinson's disease to a gait and step training or a control group and assessed their gait speed, cadence, and stride length. Although there was no significant difference in participant characteristics between the two groups, significant differences occurred from pre- to post-test for the trained group in gait speed, cadence, and the step test. Therefore, the researchers concluded that task-specific gait and step training resulted in reduction in falls and improvement in gait speed and dynamic balance individuals with postural instability and gait difficulty.

Sleep. The relationship between sleep and exercise has not been adequately examined. However, many professionals believe that a relationship exists between sleep patterns and exercise participation.

King, Oman, Brassington, Bliwise, and Haskell (1997) investigated effects of a 16-week moderate-intensity exercise program (4 x wk, 30–40-min sessions) on quality of sleep among 43 older adults with moderate sleep complaints. Quality of sleep was reported by participants using the Pittsburgh Quality of Sleep Index (PQSI) before and at the end of the program. When compared to the control group, the exercise group reported significant improvement in the PSQI global sleep score, quality of sleep parameters, sleep onset latency, and sleep duration. A limitation of the study was use of a self-report measurement index.

O'Connor and Youngstedt (1995) reviewed literature on the influence of exercise on sleep, because (a) sleep duration is associated with mortality; (b) sleep disturbances are strongly related to mental illness; (c) excessive daytime sleepiness has been estimated to be a problem for 4–5% of the population; and (d) sleep disordered breathing as evidenced by snoring has been associated with increased risk for hypertension, strokes, and myocardial infarctions. However, the authors stated that, despite problems associated with sleep problems and the potential for exercise to impact these concerns, it has largely been ignored by researchers. The authors found exercise to be helpful in promoting sleep and suggested that regular physical activity may be useful in improving sleep quality and decreasing daytime sleepiness.

Physical performance. The following examples represent some of the studies examining immediate effects of exercise or sport. The impact of exercise or sport was studied in relation to the physical performance of adults and children with disabilities.

Fernhall (2008) reviewed benefits of physical activity for individuals with a spinal cord injury and identified a positive relationship between increased physical activity, cardiovascular fitness, bone composition, metabolism, quality of life, and muscle strength. Physical activity was also associated with reduced infections and pressure sores. There is a need for further research involving larger samples.

Rolland and colleagues (2007) examined effects of a 1-year exercise program on performance of activities of daily living (ADLs) on 134 nursing home residents with Alzheimer's disease. ADL performance often deteriorates with progression of Alzheimer's and can affect quality of life. Participants were randomly assigned to an exercise group of a routine medical care group. The 12-month exercise program (2 x wk, 1-hr sessions) consisted of walking, strength, balance, and flexibility training.

ADLs were assessed using the Katz Index. The exercise group showed a significantly slower decline in mean ADL scores than the medical care group.

Nash (2005) examined effects of exercise on overall health in people with spinal cord injuries. The literature revealed that physical activity reduces musculoskeletal and neurological impairments, fatigue, pain, and weakness. Nash contended that improvements in these areas can enhance quality of life and life satisfaction.

Klijn and colleagues (2004) examined effects of a 12-week anaerobic training program (2 x wk, 30-45 minute sessions) on 20 children with cystic fibrosis. Body composition, pulmonary function, peripheral muscle force, physical activity, aerobic performance, and quality of life were measured at baseline, 1 week post-intervention, and 12 weeks post-intervention. Statistically significant improvement was found in the treatment group in anaerobic performance, aerobic performance, and quality of life after the program concluded. There were no significant changes in the control group or in the other dependent variables in the treatment group. Quality of life and anaerobic performance were the only parameters that were significantly higher in the 12-week follow-up for the treatment group.

Santiago and Cole (2004) examined the relationship between free time physical activity and secondary conditions in 170 women with physical disabilities, including multiple sclerosis, cerebral palsy, polio, arthritis, and traumatic brain injuries. The self-rated survey measured physical activity, secondary complications, and functionability. The National Health and Nutritional Examination Survey was used to rank functionability and recreation activities. Physical activity was performed 2.9 times a week and 39.4% reported no physical activity. When functional status was controlled, secondary conditions such as isolation and deconditioning were inversely related to physical activity. The authors noted that functional status and secondary conditions should be considered when conducting an exercise program.

Finley (2002) reviewed literature examining effects of physical exercise on secondary conditions in people with spinal cord injuries. These individuals are eight times less active then sedentary middle-aged men. Secondary complications associated with spinal cord injuries such as pressure sores, urinary tract infections, and respiratory, musculoskeletal, and cardiovascular conditions can severely affect quality of life. Increased physical activity levels in these individuals reduced secondary complications and conditions. There was limited generalization in many studies.

Merriman, Barnett, and Jarry (1996) examined effects of a 12-week physical fitness program (3 x wk, 40-45-min sessions) on individuals who had a dual diagnosis of mental retardation and psychiatric problems (mean IQ of 52). In addition to attending the training program, the 22 participants (mean age of 38) received rewards after each session. A significant improvement in muscular endurance, cardiorespiratory endurance, and flexibility was identified, but no changes were found in body composition.

Pitetti and Boneh (1995) measured isokinetic leg strength and cardiovascular fitness in 13 adults (mean age of 27) with mental retardation who also had Down syndrome (mean IQ of 55) and 24 adults (mean age of 25) with mental retardation who did not have Down syndrome (mean IQ of 60). There was a significant relationship between cardiovascular fitness and knee flexion and extension strength for participants with Down syndrome, while a positive but insignificant relationship was found for participants without Down syndrome. The authors concluded that activity that enhances lower extremity strength or cardiovascular fitness is valuable for individuals with mental retardation.

Suomi, Surburg, and Lecius (1995) examined effects of resistance strength training on isokinetic strength measures of knee extension and hip abduction of 22 males (mean age of 30) with mild-moderate mental retardation (mean IQ of 58). Participants were randomly assigned to 12 weeks of strength training (3 x wk) using Hydra-Fitness Omnikinetic Exercise Machine or to a control group. The treatment group demonstrated a significant increase in strength on the knee extension and hip abduction tests for both legs, while no changes were noted in the control group.

Levinson and Reid (1993) examined effects of two exercise programs (mild walking program for 15 minutes and vigorous exercise program for 15 minutes of jogging) on stereotypic behaviors of three 11-year-old youth with autism. Frequency of stereotypic behavior (motor, vocal, and other) was measured before exercise, immediately after exercise, and 90 minutes post-exercise. A significant reduction in stereotypic behaviors occurred only for vigorous exercise. However, these reductions that were primarily motor behaviors were not found 90 minutes after exercise. The authors contended that results were consistent with the notions of a self-stimulus hypothesis that stereotypic behaviors could be replaced by activity that produces similar sensory consequences.

Bar-Or (1990) reviewed benefits of fitness training in children with asthma, coronary risk, cystic fibrosis, diabetes, hypertension, cerebral palsy, and obesity. Although this review of fitness-related literature associated with children with chronic disease supported benefits of fitness training, many studies had problems with the methodology that resulted in an inability to generalize conclusions.

HIV. There is a growing body of literature supporting benefits of exercise for individuals with HIV. **Lox, McAuley, and Tucker (1996)** examined effects of aerobic and resistance training on body composition, muscular strength, and cardiovascular fitness among 33 men with HIV-1. Participants were randomly assigned to an aerobic training group (n=11), a resistance training group (n=12), or a stretching control group (n=10) for 12 weeks. Measurements were taken prior to intervention and at program's conclusion. The aerobic and resistance group significantly improved muscular strength, lean muscle tissue amounts, and cardiovascular fitness while the stretching control group showed a decline in these outcomes. Caution is advised when considering generalizing results to women and children due to a small, male-only sample.

Summary. Studies reviewed in this section are only a few of the numerous investigations that have demonstrated improved physical health and performance associated with therapeutic use of exercise. The exercise efficacy literature indicates that an exercise program can be designed for risk reduction of chronic diseases, improved health, and enhanced physical ability. As people begin to exercise and achieve a greater level of health, they will increase their vigor to complete routine activities, be less susceptible to fatigue, and therefore, gain an enhanced feeling of well-being.

Mental Health

There is a growing body of evidence supporting psychological benefits of physical activity. It appears that moderate-intensity exercise has the best mental health benefits. While a number of hypotheses have been advanced, including self-efficacy (Cox, 2002), distraction, and endorphin (Petruzzello, 2001), the mechanism by which exercise promotes mental health benefits is not clear. Research investigating these and other hypotheses yields conflicting results. What is known is that there is a positive relationship between exercise and psychological states (Wuest & Bucher, 2006).

Balkin, Tietjen-Smith, Caldwell, and Shen (2007) used a pre- and post-test control group design to examine effects of exercise on depressive symptoms experienced by 110 young adult women as measured by the Beck's Depression Inventory. Participants were assigned to an anaerobic group (n=21), an aerobic exercise group (n=46), or a no exercise group (n=14). A significant decrease in depressive symptoms occurred for the aerobic exercise group only. Although physical exercise appeared to be beneficial, the lack of random assignment for groups and small control sample size are a concern.

Milne, Gordon, Guilfoyle, Wallman, and Courneya (2007) examined effects of physical activity on quality of life among 558 women breast cancer survivors. The Godlin Leisure Time Exercise Questionnaire assessed physical activity and the Functional Assessment of Cancer Therapy-Breast scale assessed quality of life. Physically active, healthy weight survivors reported a better quality of life than physically inactive, obese survivors. Exercise interventions may help breast cancer patients maintain an improved quality of life throughout treatment and into remission. Caution is advised in interpreting results due to use of self report methods.

Lai and colleagues (2006) investigated effects of a 3-month exercise program on depressive symptoms of 100 stroke survivors who had completed acute rehabilitation. Participants were randomly assigned to either an exercise group or a usual care group. Depressive symptoms, quality of life, stroke severity, functional impairments, and perceived social support were assessed at baseline, 3 months, and 9 months. Depressive symptoms scores were lower and quality of life scores improved in the exercise group who had depressive symptoms at baseline. Improvements in mood and functional abilities were reported in the exercise group. A limitation of the study was potential comorbidities that could have interacted with treatment effects.

Four reviews of the literature examining effects of exercise and physical activity in older adults and adults with depression and various mental disorders supported benefits of exercise and physical activity in reducing depression symptoms (Palmer, 2005; Coyle, Denault, Miller, Pham, & Thomas, 2008), psychiatric symptoms, social complications associated with mental illness, and improved physical health (Meyer & Brooks, 2000; Richardson et al., 2005). Richardson added that secondary complications of mental illnesses such as social withdrawal, anxiety, depression, and low self-esteem improved with exercise. The researchers concluded that exercise is a useful coping technique in dealing with mental illness and depression. Limitations of the studies included small samples, lack of control groups, and poor selection methods for control groups.

Coyle and Santiago (1995) used a nonrandomized control trial pre- and post-test design with participants who had mixed physical disabilities such as spinal cord injury, post-polio, and stroke. Seven participants volunteered for the exercise group and 12 for the control group. The exercises were performed at home or at a community center for 12 weeks at 73% of maximum heart rate. VO2 peak increased by 23% in the exercise group compared to a 19% decrease in the control group. The exercise group reported a 59% decrease in depressive symptoms whereas the control group reported a 6% increase. A significant inverse relationship was found from pre- to post-test between changes in depressive symptoms and aerobic functioning. The exercise group demonstrated significantly improved positive affect whereas the control group's positive affect scores did not change. Recreation programs designed to enhance aerobic function may be an effective and cost-efficient means of addressing secondary disabilities in adults with physical disabilities. However, the groups were not equal in age, sex, or race and the experimental group was comprised of people who had experienced a stroke, whereas the control group was mostly comprised of people with paraplegia resulting in heterogeneous groups. The non-randomization of individuals into the exercise or control group and the unsupervised exercise of home exercise prevented generalizability and confidence in reliability.

To better understand effects of exercise on mental health, an overview of a meta-analysis (Dishman, 1995) is presented in this section. A meta-analysis involves systematic examination and statistical testing of a group of related studies. Next, this section contains studies pertaining to older adults that link mental health outcomes to fitness. Finally, this section concludes with examination of literature found to include the impact of exercise on mental health of individuals with physical disabilities.

Dishman (1995) conducted a meta-analysis to address controversy over efficacy of exercise on mental health, specifically anxiety and depression. While positive effects were identified, most literature on anxiety and depression has serious flaws. Dishman found 8 population-based studies and 100 small sample studies indicating that exercise is associated with a moderate reduction in self-rated depression and 150 studies that demonstrated small to moderate reductions in self-rated anxiety. Research indicated moderate intensities of exercise for 30 minutes may be associated with the largest reduction of self-rated state anxiety. Reductions in trait anxiety and depression seemingly require about 4 months of exercise. Alternatively, heavy exertion leads to increased anxiety and depression that accompanies burnout from overtraining in endurance sports.

Netz and colleagues (1994) examined effects of fitness activity on cognition and depression of 31 residents of a geriatric psychiatric and rehabilitation hospital who were hospitalized due to stroke, fractures, or Parkinson's disease. Participants were all diagnosed with cognitive deterioration and/or depression. Seventeen participants in both the rehab-geriatric (mean age of 78) and the psycho-geriatric group (mean age of 67) were divided into an exercise or social group. The exercise group participated in supervised physical exercise designed to improve strength, coordination, balance, agility, and flexibility, mostly conducted in a sitting position. The social group participated in supervised social intellectual activity, such as discussing the news. Both groups lasted 8 weeks (3 x wk, 45-min sessions). There were no changes in scores on the Geriatric Depression Scale for the rehab-geriatric group. While not alleviating clinical depression, significant improvements were observed in the exercise and social intervention groups, with exercise groups improving significantly more than the social group. Activity, in general, not just physical activity, may be an important factor in positively changing mental abilities or depression. Caution is advised when interpreting results because no control group was used.

Bosscher (1993) examined effects of running and mixed exercise on 9 women and 9 men (mean age of 34) residing in a psychiatric facility, matched for depression scores and randomly assigned to an 8-week running group (3 x wk, 45-min sessions) or to a treatment-as-usual group including physical and relaxation exercise. Treatment consisted of a 10-minute warm-up, a 30-minute run (70–85% max. HR), and a 5-minute cooling down. The mixed exercise treatment included several sport activities (2 x wk, 50-min sessions). Although conditions included different activities, they emphasized relaxed, low-intensity physical activity. While participants were not different on any pretreatment measure, the treatment-as-usual group did not achieve any significant improvements. Participants in the running treatment improved significantly on depression, self-esteem, severity of psychoneurotic symptoms, and somatic complaints for an indication of well-being and body satisfaction. Although this study provided some support that running can be a treatment of depression and feelings of discomfort for people receiving inpatient psychiatric care, conclusions are tentative and further study is indicated.

Using a meta-analysis, **O'Connor, Aenchbacher, and Dishman (1993)** reviewed research relating physical activity of older adults and reduced depression. The cross-sectional data suggested a moderate relationship between self-reported inactivity and symptoms of depression. As in the meta-analysis by Dishman (1995), the experimental research focused on individuals without a clinical diagnosis of depression and was methodologically flawed leading to insufficient evidence to conclude that exercise leads to mental health improvement in older adults with depressive disorders. The eight experimental-based studies lacked information describing the relationship between amount of exercise and response.

Thirlaway and Benton (1992) found physical activity, rather than cardiovascular fitness, to be a factor associated with better mental health and mood for 246 white collar volunteers (155 men; ages 18–63), divided into three groups (no activity, some activity, and more activity) based on results of a physical activity questionnaire. Participants completed the Profile of Mood States and a General Health Questionnaire (GHQ) and took fitness measures to include blood pressure, pulse, bicycle submaximal test, lung capacity, VO2max (maximum oxygen intake), and body fat. Activity scores correlated positively with VO2max and pulse but not with blood pressure, weight, or lung capacity. In analysis of mood, higher levels of physical activity were associated with better GHQ independent of fitness. Increased activity was associated with improved mood scores for the fit group. Those with low fitness did not improve mood with increased activity. Although there was a high correlation between physical activity and fitness, as indicated by VO2max, physical activity was associated with mental health while fitness was not. Similarly, activity was associated with positive mood while fitness only demonstrated an association between mood and activity. Since adherence to exercise is a problem and higher intensity exercise is associated with lower adherence, emphasis should be on moderate activity. Therefore, moderate activity is encouraged to promote adherence as well as achieve psychological and physical improvements.

Berger and Owen (1992) examined swimming classes and yoga to determine if aerobic exercise resulted in improved mood by employing a pre- and post-control group design with 87 college students (ages 18–22) enrolled in two swimming classes (2 x wk, 40-min sessions), a yoga course (1 x wk, 80-min sessions), and a lecture control group course (3 x wk, 50-min sessions). Participants completed the Profile of Mood States inventory immediately before and after class on the second session, midway through the study, and on the last day of instruction. A significant reduction in anger, confusion, tension, and depression was reported for swimming and yoga groups when compared to the control group, indicating that aerobic exercise and exercise below a person's target heart rate may enhance mood.

Stein and Motta (1992) compared effects of anaerobic weight training to aerobic swimming on depression and self-concept of 98 volunteers (ages 18–42) randomly assigned to a 14-week structured swimming for fitness aerobic class (2 x wk, 50-min sessions), a structured progressive resistance weight training (2 x wk, 50-min sessions), or a control group that did not exercise. The Beck Depression Inventory, Depression Adductive Check Lists, Tennessee Self-Concept Scale, and Cooper's 12-minute swim were used to assess impact of interventions. Significant improvement in self-concept and depression occurred in both experimental groups when compared to the control group. Although design flaws prevent generalizations, for individuals with disabilities who are unable to withstand land-based weight training, water exercise might be a valuable option for enhancing self-esteem and decreasing depression.

Weiss and Jamieson (1989) evaluated effects of aquatic exercise (range of 8 weeks to 5 years) on subjective depression on 88 women attending an aquatic exercise program. Participants who reported symptoms of depression when beginning the class reported less depressed feelings with 91% of these individuals attributing the aquatic exercise class to their improved emotional state. The subjectivity, lack of information on interview methods and retrospective nature of this study are problematic; therefore, further study is indicated.

Roth and Holmes (1987) examined effects of aerobic exercise and relaxation training on life stress of 55 participants. Nineteen participants were randomly assigned to an aerobic exercise group that included running and a brisk walk when necessary; 18 were assigned to a relaxation group consisting of progressive muscle relaxation and guided imagery, and 18 were assigned to a control group. Although age (mean of 19), sex, life stress, and fitness did not differ across groups, aerobic capacity significantly improved for the aerobic exercise group when compared to the relaxation and control group. The relaxation group had better subjective impressions and plans to continue than the exercise group after the study. The aerobic group showed a greater decrease than the relaxation group and treatment control group in depression. However, at post-intervention and follow-up, there were no significant differences in scores between any groups including anxiety and somatic measures.

Katz, Adler, Mazzarella, and Ince (1985) investigated effects of a 12-week aerobic exercise program on the mood status of a 27-year-old male with paraplegia from spina bifida. He performed on a rehabilitation wheelchair trainer at a rate of 60 revolutions per minute with a predetermined resistance for 5 minutes for an average of four sets. He significantly increased his workload and duration, and demonstrated an improved heart rate and VO2max. Using the Profile of Mood States, a significant decrease in tension, depression, anger, fatigue, and confusion was found, with a marked increase in vigor. Although results provide tentative support for a hypothesis that aerobic exercise is a useful therapeutic strategy for individuals with disabilities, this case study has limited generalizability and control of external variables.

Summary. Although effects of exercise on mental health have been extensively examined on people without disabilities or older adults, individuals with disabilities have received less attention. While effects of exercise on mental health has focused on participants without a clinical diagnosis of anxiety and depression, small to moderate decreases in self-rated depression were noted. The lack of research exploring maintenance effects of exercise suggests the importance of examining activities that facilitate fitness for people with and without disabilities.

Overall Summary

In summary, the research on the effects of exercise is considerable and wide ranging. For example, exercise activity can result in risk reduction of some types of cancer, diabetes, and cardiovascular disease. In addition, exercise as a facilitation technique has improved physical performance of individuals with disabilities and bone health. There is also a growing body of evidence supporting psychological benefits of exercise that include improvements in the areas of social withdrawal, anxiety, depression, mood, and self-esteem. Overall, research indicates that therapeutic use of exercise is an empirically supported facilitation technique that results in improved health, energy level, mood states, quality of life, and well-being.

Case Studies

This section contains two case studies. The first describes how Kim, who has a spinal cord injury, benefited from getting in shape as a result of her participation in an exercise program. The second case involved 11-year-old Christopher who has cerebral palsy, a cognitive impairment, visual impairment, and was deaf and participated in an exercise program. Therefore, the section is divided into the following sections:

- Kim
- Christopher

Kim

Kim lived in a suburb of a large metropolitan city in the Midwest. She had always had a desire to remain physically active. Kim was active, like many 20-year-olds, as she filled most of her free time with cycling, music, and horseback riding. Kim enjoyed cycling on the weekends with her local cycling club and traveled throughout the Midwest competing in various cycling events.

A horseback riding accident that resulted in paraplegia seriously challenged Kim's cycling. Kim found herself to be a different person after the accident as she gained 30 pounds and remained uncertain about her capabilities. Kim wanted a change in her life and chose to begin an exercise program that might ultimately permit a return to competitive cycling. The following information is presented:

- Exercise
- Summary
- Epilogue

Exercise. Kim joined the fitness center at the local hospital where she completed her rehabilitation. Kim knew there would be individuals who could assist her in meeting her fitness goals. This particular center had a TR specialist who assisted participants with disabilities. Kim met with the TR specialist and explained her situation and expressed her desire to improve her physical fitness.

The TR specialist recognized that Kim needed to address five specific fitness goals in the areas of cardiovascular endurance, flexibility, muscle endurance, muscle strength, and body composition. After completing baseline fitness levels, Kim and the TR specialist set realistic fitness goals and objectives in the five areas.

Once medical clearance was received from her physician, Kim attended the fitness center three times a week. Kim participated in an exercise program consisting of 10 minutes of floor exercises and stretching for flexibility, 20 minutes on the arm ergometer (a machine with pedals similar to those on a bicycle that, when moved by participants, measures work output) for cardiovascular and muscle endurance, 20 minutes of upper extremity weight training for muscle strengthening, and consulted the hospital nutritionist for a caloric-intake program.

The TR specialist worked with Kim to monitor her weight and weekly fitness goals and recommended higher or lower intensity exercises based on her ability to participate at 60–75% of her maximum heart rate. Kim continued her program for 6 months without a break. At the end of the 6 months, Kim lost 26 pounds and felt more confident in her capabilities. Kim noticed a difference in her activities of daily living such as transfers, dressing, and her overall energy level. Kim reported fewer negative medical symptoms such as poor circulation and skin breakdowns which had been common prior to her involvement in a fitness program.

Summary. Kim's involvement in an exercise program had made a considerable difference in her life. She received many physical and psychological benefits of participating in an exercise program. With participation in a specific exercise program, Kim met her personal goals of losing weight and increasing her strength and endurance.

Epilogue. Kim has since rejoined her cycling club and participates regularly in local cycling events in surrounding areas. Kim has become a volunteer at her local rehabilitation hospital and continues to tell her story to individuals who are newly injured.

Christopher

Groff, Lawrence, and Grivna (2006) presented a case study on an 11-year-old boy, Christopher, who has cerebral palsy, a cognitive impairment, visual impairment, and was deaf. He lived at home with his parents and two sisters. Christopher was nonverbal and communicated through American Sign Language. He was ambulatory on flat, level surfaces with the assistance of braces, but needed help on uneven surfaces and curbs.

Christopher participated in many leisure activities such as bowling and swimming, but lacked the fundamental knowledge about how to perform these activities. He expressed interest in bowling, weight lifting, football, soccer, basketball, baseball, yoga, bicycling, Frisbee, and rock climbing.

Before beginning a treatment of the growth hormone, his treatment team suggested increasing his exercise to prevent a decrease in physical abilities due to the treatment. His mother wished that his exercise treatment would help him gain gross motor skills and participate in recreational activities with his family. The following information is presented in this section:

- Physical Assessment
- Exercise
- Outcomes
- Summary

Physical Assessment. Christopher was classified as having C5 cerebral palsy according to the Cerebral Palsy International Support and Recreation Association. Based on his classification, Christopher participated in four physical assessments from the Brockport Physical Fitness Test, which measured aerobic capacity, body composition, strength, flexibility, and range of motion. The Target Aerobic Measurement Test was used to measure aerobic abilities for 15 minutes.

Christopher performed physical activity at a moderate intensity for 15 minutes. Christopher's body mass index was 15.6 identifying him as underweight (below 18.5) for his height. During the grip strength test, Christopher applied 3.5 kilograms of force which suggests that he was below average based on his age and gender (avg.=21 kg) and for individuals with cognitive impairments (avg.=14 kg). On the test for flexibility and range of motion, Christopher received a score of 2 on both arms, which meant he was average for his classification.

Exercise. Based on the physical assessment and Christopher's interests, an individualized treatment plan was developed that included exercise with an aide and TR graduate student (2 x wk, 1-hr sessions) for 6-weeks. Three goals for Christopher's exercise intervention were to increase aerobic activity and endurance, strength, and gross motor skills.

Sessions began with a 1/2-mile warm-up to increase aerobic activity. The Functional Independence Measure (FIM) was used for assessment. Christopher was walking with moderate independence (FIM=6) on smooth surfaces and moderate assistance (FIM=3) on irregular terrain. After warm-up, he participated in sit-ups and push-ups with goal to increase core strength. Before his 1/2-mile cool down, Christopher learned fundamental soccer skills, particularly kicking the ball. Throughout the treatment program, the team also used rock climbing and a digital hand strengthener to improve upper body strength, hand strength, and hand-eye coordination.

Outcomes. Christopher completed or partially completed most objectives outlined in his individualized treatment plan. He partially met his goal to increase aerobic activity and endurance because he completed a 5-minute cool down and warm-up in all sessions. He partially met his goal to improve strength because he completes more push-ups and sit-ups than when he started. Christopher's hand strength improved 186% from 3.5 kilograms in the first assessment to 10 kilograms at the final assessment. Christopher also improved his gross motor skills while practicing soccer. He kicked a goal three out of five times from 10 feet, but not from the 36 feet, which was in the objective. Other goals were not met due circumstances such as Christopher's aide resigning. The treatment team also noted that Christopher appeared to enjoy the sessions because he was laughing and smiling more as the sessions continued.

Summary. Christopher's involvement in an exercise and fitness intervention seemed to improve his life. Christopher received both physical and psychological benefits from participating in this exercise program. Through participation in an individualized exercise program, Christopher increased his aerobic activity and endurance as well as his strength and gross motor skills.

Intervention Implementation Exercises

When designing an exercise program for people with disabilities, a TR specialist can explore the various considerations involved in making adaptations. The following section includes five examples of considerations recommended for exploration:

- Determine Resting Heart Rates
- Calculate Maximal and Target Heart Ranges
- Complete Flexibility Tests
- Complete Isolated Arthritis Stretching Exercises
- Participate in a Chair Aerobics Activity

Determine Resting Heart Rates

Participants locate their pulse by placing their index finger on one of three points in the body: the carotid artery in the neck (on each side of the voice box), the radial artery (at the base of the thumb or wrist), or at the temple in front of the ear. When monitoring heart rate with the "finger method," the following procedure should be used: practice locating your pulse until the heart beat is consistently located, apply pressure with one or two fingers to one of the pulse points in the body, count number of heartbeats within a 15-second period counting the first beat as zero, and multiply total frequency by 4 to calculate the heart rate for 1 minute. After participants complete this exercise, their values can be displayed to show the dispersion of heart rates.

Calculate Maximal and Target Heart Ranges

Participants calculate their maximal and target heart rates by using percentage of heart rate and Karvonen Formula. First, complete the mathematical formula with percentage of maximal heart rate (220 – age x desired % of intensity x 1.15) and the Karvonen Formula that factors in resting heart rate (220 – age – resting heart rate x desired % of intensity + resting heart rate). Once maximal heart rate is calculated, multiply rate by .60 and .80 to establish target heart range. Participants' ranges can be displayed and a discussion of how individuals with disabilities might vary from these results can occur.

Complete Flexibility Tests

There is no single test that can tell you your overall flexibility. Each test is specific to a joint, movement, or muscle. Five types of flexibility tests measuring various joints and muscles are discussed. The TR specialist advises participants not do anything that causes discomfort or is painful. The participant is warned that bouncing or performing jerky movements may cause soreness or injury.

One flexibility test is the sit and reach test that measures flexibility of lower back and hamstrings. This test is performed with a partner. The participant sits on the floor or a mat with legs stretched straight out in front. The participant tries to reach his or her toes with hands stretched out palms down while keeping legs straight. The partner places a hand on participant's knees to keep legs straight and measures the distance between participant's fingers and toes. If participant reaches past his or her toes, then the number is as positive. If participant does not reach toes, then the number is recorded as being negative. Exact reach is to be recorded as zero. The participant does not bounce to avoid soreness or injury.

A second flexibility test is the reach behind test which measures shoulder flexibility. The participant places one hand behind their back with palm facing outward. The other hand is placed behind the head with palm facing their back. The participant tries to clasp fingers of both hands. The distance between fingers is recorded. If fingers do not meet, then the number is recorded as negative. If the fingers slide past each other then the number is recorded as positive. A finger to finger touch is recorded as zero.

A third flexibility test is the gastrocnemius test which measures flexibility of the calf muscle. The participant sits flat on the ground with legs stretched straight ahead and heels against a wall. The participant flexes their feet while distance from the wall to the balls of the participant's feet is measured.

The fourth flexibility test is the thigh adductor test which measures flexibility of hip abductors. The participant sits along a right angle with crotch at vertex and one leg along each side of the right angle. The participant moves one leg away from the right angle marker while distance from the ankle to the right angle marker is measured. If the participant cannot get to the marker, then the distance is recorded as a negative number and if the participant can move their leg from the marker then a positive number is recorded. The test is repeated with the other leg.

The last flexibility test is the trunk rotation test which measures flexibility of trunk and shoulders. First, a vertical line is marked on the wall. The participant stands with back to the wall about arms length away and directly in front of the line. The participant's distance from the wall may need to be adjusted once the test has started. The participant extends arms straight in front and parallel to the floor. The participant twists trunk as far to the right as they can go and touches the wall behind them with their fingertips while keeping arms straight and parallel to the floor. The participant is allowed to move his or her shoulders, hips, and knees as long as feet do not move. The point where participant's fingers touched the wall are marked and distance back to the line is recorded. A point before the line is marked as a negative number, while a point after the line is marked as a positive number. The test is repeated on the left side as well.

Complete Isolated Arthritis Stretching Exercises

To complete simple isolated stretching exercises, stand with feet several inches apart and knees slightly bent. Hold right arm straight in front and lock elbow. Make a fist and bring it down toward the body. With the left hand, reach around and gently grasp knuckles. Gently assist by pulling fist back toward the body. Change arms and repeat exercise. After that arm is completed, perform isolated neck exercises. Participants stand with hands on hips, feet several inches apart, and knees slightly bent. Slowly turn head to left of midline until a slight stretching sensation is felt. Return head to midline and turn head to right of midline. Once completed, slowly place left ear on left shoulder. Stretching exercise is then repeated with right ear and right shoulder.

Participate in a Chair Aerobics Activity

Participants sit in desk or chair and place feet 6–12 inches apart and raise weight of legs to toes with heels off the ground. Once this is completed, the action is repeated in alternating pattern with left and right feet. Next, an object is distributed (e.g., Duraband, tube sock, or 18–24 inch piece of material). Grab both ends of the exercising object and lean toward the right, middle, left, and middle. This pattern is repeated for several counts. Finally, stand behind a desk or chair with hands on back of chair and feet shoulder width apart. Step to right of chair, back behind chair, to left of chair, and back behind chair without lifting hands off back of chair. This sequence is repeated for several counts as the instructor calls "right, middle, left, middle." The session is ended by determining if predetermined resting heart rate has elevated.

Conclusion

Research supports the conclusion that participation in exercise activities by people with disabilities is one way to improve muscle tone, balance, mobility, cardiovascular conditioning, flexibility, and functional range of motion, as well as decrease spasticity, muscular atrophy, development of contractures, renal dysfunctions, and pressure sores (DiRocco, 1995). Exercise can play a role in achieving psychological goals such as improved self-image, feelings of independence, self-esteem, and self-determination, as well as reduced levels of stress, chronic fatigue, and feelings of social isolation with people with disabilities (Wuest & Bucher, 2006).

    Unfortunately, not many people are physically active, and more deaths can be attributed to physical inactivity than to hypertension, high cholesterol, or smoking (Bouchard, Shephard, Stephens, Sutton, & McPherson, 1990). In addition, obesity is now becoming an alarming trend in our society. Therefore, it is beneficial for TR specialists to consider providing exercise activity to promote fitness and decrease risks associated with physical inactivity.

Exercise as a therapeutic medium can occur in a variety of settings including hospitals, outpatient rehabilitation centers, long-term care facilities, and wellness centers. Exercise is a viable option for many people with disabilities. Given trends of reduced hospital stays and increased options for independent living in communities, many individuals do not have the opportunity to participate in hospital-based TR services (Austin, 1996). Thus, the range of options needed in communities to provide exercise opportunities is expanding to include services such as those provided by private fitness centers, private recreation organizations, park and recreation departments, colleges and universities, and health care affiliated wellness organizations (Bullock & Mahon, 1996). Because of this, there has been increased interest in the therapeutic use of exercise as one way to improve physical function while the individual resides at home or participates in exercise programs offered through local hospitals, rehabilitation settings, or community recreation centers.

Discussion Questions

1. What is exercise as a therapeutic medium?
2. What are benefits of using muscular strengthening exercises as a therapeutic use of exercise?
3. Why can exercises targeting flexibility be beneficial?
4. What are two considerations when using cardiovascular fitness as a therapeutic medium?
5. What are the physiological outcomes of activities to improve fitness?
6. What does a TR specialist consider to facilitate improved cardiovascular fitness?
7. What are three different muscle contractions that are considered for strength training?
8. What does a TR specialist consider when using exercises to improve muscular endurance?
9. What is the theory of planned behavior?
10. What are the stages and TR implications of the transtheoretical model?
11. What are some of the physical and mental effects of exercise?
12. What are three considerations specific to individuals with disabilities when participating in exercises?

Resources

Agency Resources

The American Association of adaptedSPORTS Programs, Inc. (AAASP): http://www.adaptedsports.org/

American College of Sports Medicine: http://www.acsm.org/

BlazeSports: http://www.blazesports.com

Disabled Sports USA: http://www.dsusa.org/

Disability fitness equipment: http://www.disabilityfitness.com/

International Sports Organization for the Disabled
SRD Guillermo Cabazas
Garcia de Paredos 74
Madrid 3, Spain.

Wheelchair Sports USA: http://www.wsusa.org/

World T.E.A.M Sports: http://www.worldteamsports.org

Ontario Wheelchair Sport Association
585 Tretheway Dr.,
Toronto, Ontario, Canada M6M, 4B8

President's Council on Fitness, Sports, and Nutrition: http://www.fitness.gov

The Athlete Project: http://www.athleticproject.com

United States Association for Blind Athletes: http://usaba.org/

United States Wheelchair Weightlifting Federation
39 Michael Pl.
Levittown, PA 19057

Material Resources

Able Bodies, AAHPERD, 1900 Association Dr., Reston, VA 22091, 703-476-3400
Adapted Physical Activity Quarterly, Human Kinetics Publications, PO Box 5076,
  Champaign, IL 61825.
Kelly, M., & Darrah, J. (2005). Aquatic exercise for children with cerebral palsy.
  Developmental Medicine & Child Neurology, 47, 338–342.
Mondoa, C. T. (2004). The implications of physical activity in patients with chronic
  heart failure. *British Association of Critical Care Nurses, Nursing in Critical
  Care, 9*(1), 13–20.
Sports 'N Spokes, PVA Publications, 5201 North 19th Ave., Suite 111, Phoenix, AZ
  85015.
Thacker, S. B., Gilchrist, J., Stroup, D. F., & Kimsey, D. D. (2004). The impact of
  stretching on sports injury risk: A systematic review of the literature. *Medical
  Science in Sports and Exercise, 36*(3), 371–378.
Therapeutic Recreation Journal, NRPA, 2775 S. Quincy At. Suite 300, Arlington,
  VA 22206

References

Ajzen, I., & Fishbein, M. (1985). From intentions to actions: A theory of planned behavior. In J. Kuhl & J. Beckman (Eds.), *Action-control: From cognition to behavior* (pp. 11–39). Heidelberg, Germany: Springer.

Ajzen, I. (1991). The theory of planned behavior. *Organizational Behavior and Human Decision Processing, 50,* 179–211.

American College of Sports Medicine. (1991). *Guidelines for exercise testing and prescription* (4th ed.). Philadelphia: Lea & Febiger.

American College of Sports Medicine. (1995). *Guidelines for exercise testing and prescription* (5th ed.). Philadelphia: Lea & Febiger.

American College of Sports Medicine. (2006). *Guidelines for exercise testing and prescription* (7th ed.). Philadelphia: Lippincott Williams & Wilkins.

American College of Sports Medicine (2007). *Physical activity and public health guidelines.* Retrieved September 1, 2007 from http://www.ascm.org/AM/ Template.cfm?SectionHome_Page&Template=/CM/HTM

Atlantis, E., Barnes, E. H., & Fiatarone Singh, M. A. (2006). Efficacy of exercise for treating overweight in children and adolescents: A systematic review. *International Journal of Obesity, 30,* 1027–1040.

Austin, D. R. (1996). *Therapeutic recreation processes and techniques* (3rd ed.). Champaign, IL: Sagamore.

Balkin, R. S., Tietjen-Smith, T., Caldwell, C., & Shen, Y. (2007). The utilization of exercise to decrease depressive symptoms in young adult women. *AdultSpan Journal, 6*(1), 30–35.

Bar-Or, O. (1990). Disease-specific benefits of training in the child with a chronic disease: What is the evidence? *Pediatric Exercise Science, 2,* 384–394.

Becker, M. H. (1974). The health belief model and personal health behavior. *Health Education Monographs, 2,* 324–473.

Berger, B., & Owen, D. (1992). Mood alteration with yoga and swimming: Aerobic exercise may not be necessary. *Perceptual and Motor Skills, 75,* 1331–1343.

Blair, S. N., Kohl, W., Paffenbarger, R. S., Clark, D. G., Cooper, K. H., & Gibbons, L. W. (1989). Changes in physical fitness and all-cause mortality: A prospective study of healthy and unhealthy men and women. *J. A. M. A, 262*(17), 2395–2401.

Borg, B. V. (1970) Perceived exertion as an indicator of somatic stress. *Scandinavian Journal of Rehabilitation Medicine, 2,* 92–98.

Bouchard, C., Shephard, R. J., Stephens, T., Sutton, J. R., & McPherson, B. D. (Eds.). (1990). *Exercise, fitness, and health: A consensus of current knowledge.* Champaign, IL: Human Kinetics.

Bosscher, R. J. (1993). Running and mixed physical exercises with depressed psychiatric patients. *International Journal of Sport Psychology, 24,* 170–184.

Brosky, J. A., & Wright, G. A. (2006). Training for muscular strength, power and endurance and hypertrophy. In J. Nyland (Ed.), *Clinical decisions in therapeutic exercise: Planning and implementation* (pp. 171–230). Upper Saddle River, NJ, Pearson Education.

Brown, S. (2001). *Introduction to exercise science.* Baltimore, MD: Lippincott Williams and Wilkins.

Buckworth, J., & Dishman, R. K. (2002). *Exercise psychology*. Champaign, IL: Human Kinetics.

Bullock, C. C., & Mahon, M. J. (1996). Disability awareness: Considerations for the exercise leader. In P. D. Miller (Ed.), *Fitness programming and physical disability* (pp. 3–10). Champaign, IL: Human Kinetics.

Caspersen, C. J., Powell, K. E., & Christenson, G. M. (1985). Physical activity, exercise, and physical fitness: Definitions and distinctions for health-related research. *Public Health Reports, 100,* 126–131.

Castaneda, C. (2000). Type 2 diabetes mellitus and exercise. *Nutrition in Clinical Care, 3*(6), 349–358.

Chang, C., Liu, W., Zhao, X., Li, S., & Yu, C. (2007). Effect of supervised exercise intervention on metabolic risk factors and physical fitness in Chinese obese children in early puberty. *Obesity Reviews, 9*(1), 135–141.

Cox, R. H., (2002). *Sport psychology: Concepts and applications.* New York: McGraw-Hill.

Coyle, C. P., & Santiago, M. C. (1995). Aerobic exercise training and depressive symptomatology in adults with physical disabilities. *Archives of Physical Medicine and Rehabilitation, 76,* 647–652.

Coyle, C., Denault, V, Miller, R., Pham, T., & Thomas, C. (2008). Understanding systematic reviews and their implications for evidence-based practice by examining aerobic exercise as a recreational therapy intervention for individuals with major depressive disorders. *American Journal of Recreation Therapy, 7*(3), 13–22.

Daly, A. J., Copelan, R. J., Wright, N. P., Roalfe, A., & Wales, J. K. H. (2006). Exercise therapy as a treatment for psychopathologic conditions in obese and morbidly obese adolescents: A randomized, controlled trial. *Pediatrics, 118*(5), 2126–2134.

Department of Health and Human Services (HHS). *2008 Physical Activity Guidelines for Americans.* Retrieved October, 10, 2010 from http://www.health.gov/paguidelines/default.aspx

DeStefano, R. A., Caprio, S., Fahey, J. T., Tamborlane, W. V., & Goldberg, B. (2000). Changes in body composition after a 12-wk aerobic exercise program in obese boys. *Pediatric Diabetes, 1,* 61–65.

DiRocco, P. J. (1995). Physical disabilities: General characteristics and exercise implications. In P. D. Miller (Ed.), *Fitness programming and physical disability* (pp. 11–34). Champaign, IL: Human Kinetics.

Dishman R. K. (1993). Exercise adherence. In R. N. Singer, M. Murphey, & L. K. Tennant (Eds.), *Handbook on research on sport psychology* (pp. 790–797). New York: Macmillan.

Dishman, R. K. (1995). Physical activity and public health: Mental health. *Quest: The Academy of Kinesiology and Physical Education papers, 47,* 1–10.

Duffy, F. E., & Schnirring, L. (2000). How to counsel patients about exercise: an office friendly approach, *The Physician and Sportsmedicine, 28,* 53–54.

Durstine, L. J., & Moore, G. E. (2002). *ACSM's exercise management for persons with chronic diseases and disabilities.* Philadelphia: Lea & Febiger.

Durstine, L., & Pate, R. (1988). Cardiorespiratory responses to acute exercise. In American College of Sports Medicine, *Resource manual for guidelines for exercise testing and prescription* (pp. 48–54). Philadelphia: Lea & Febiger.

Faigenbaum, A. D. (2008). Age and sex related differences and their implications for resistance exercise. In T. B. Baechle & R. W. Earle (Eds.), *Essentials of strength training and conditioning* (pp. 142–158). Champaign, IL: Human Kinetics.

Fernhall, B. (2008). *Health implications of physical activity in individuals with spinal cord injury: A literature review*. Retrieved April 6, 2008 from http://findarticles.com/p/articles/mi_m1YLZ/is_4_30/ai_n25014480

Figoni, S. F. (1995). Physiology of aerobic exercise. In P. D. Miller (Ed.), *Fitness programming and physical disability* (pp. 51–64). Champaign, IL: Human Kinetics.

Figoni, S. F., Lockette, K. F., & Surburg, P. R. (1995). Exercise prescription: Adapting principles of conditioning. In P. D. Miller (Ed.), *Fitness programming and physical disability* (pp. 67–77). Champaign, IL: Human Kinetics.

Finley, M. A. (2002). *Impact of physical exercise on controlling secondary conditions associated with spinal cord injury*. Retrieved April 6, 2008 from http://findarticles.com/p/articles/mi_qa3959/is_200203/ai_n9079407

Fishbein, M., & Ajzen, I. (1975). *Belief, attitude, intention, and behavior: An introduction to theory and research*. Reading, MA: Addison-Wesley.

Forge, R. L. (1991). Cardiorespiratory fitness. In M. Sudy (Ed.), *Personal trainer manual: A resource manual for fitness instructors* (pp.195–233). San Diego: American Council on Exercise.

Garcia, A. W., & King, A. C. (1991). Predicting long-term adherence to aerobic exercise: A comparison to two models. *Journal of Sport and Exercise Psychology, 13*, 394–410.

Greene, B., & Lim, S. S. (2007). *The role of physical therapy in management of patients with osteoarthritis and rheumatoid arthritis*. Retrieved August 29, 2007 from http://www.2.arthritis.org/research/Bulletin/Vol52No4/Printable.htm.

Groff, D., Lawrence, E., & Grivna, S. (2006). Effects of a therapeutic recreation intervention using exercise: A case study with a child with cerebral palsy. *Therapeutic Recreation Journal, 40*(4), 269–283.

Hackney, M. E., Kantorovich, S., Levin, R., Earhart, G. M. (2007). Effects of tango on functional mobility in Parkinson's disease: A preliminary study. *Journal of Neurological Physical Therapy, 31*(4), 173–1799.

Hahn, R. A., Teutsch, S. M., Rothenberg, E., & Marks, R. B. (1990). Excess deaths from nine chronic diseases in the United States, 1986. *Journal of the American Medical Association, 264*, 2645–2659.

Harman, E., & Garhammer, J. (2008). Administration, scoring, and interpretation of selected tests. In T. B. Baechle & R. W. Earle (Eds.), *Essentials of strength training and conditioning* (pp. 250–292). Champaign, IL: Human Kinetics.

Haskell, W. L., Leon, A. S., Caspersen, C. J., Froelicher, V. F., Hagberg, J. M. Harlan, W., Holloszy, J. O., Regensteiner, J. G., Thompson, P. D., Washburn, R. A., & Wilson, P. W. F. (1992). Cardiovascular benefits and assessment of physical activity and fitness in adults. *Medicine and Science in Sports and Exercise, 24*, 201– 220.

Hatfield, B. E., & Brody, E. B. (2008) Psychology of athletic preparation and performance. In T. B. Baechle & R. W. Earle (Eds.), *Essentials of strength training and conditioning* (pp. 159–178). Champaign, IL: Human Kinetics

Helmrich, S. P., Ragland, D. R., Leung, R. W., & Paffenbarger, R. S. (1991). Physical activity and reduced occurrence of non-insulin-dependent diabetes mellitus. *New England Journal of Medicine, 325*, 147–152.

Hornick, A., & Leitner, M. (1996). Fitness and leisure. In M. J. Leitner, S. F. Leitner, & Associates (Eds.), *Leisure enhancement* (pp. 145–181). Binghamton, NY: Haworth.

Hills, A. P., King, N. A., & Armstrong, T. P. (2007). The contribution of physical activity and sedentary behaviors to the growth and development of children and adolescents. *Sports Med, 37*(6), 533–545.

Jeong, S., & Kim, M. T. (2007). Effects of a theory-driven music and movement program for stroke survivors in a community setting. *Applied Nursing Research, 20,* 125–131.

Jones, L. W., Guill, B., Keir, S. T., Carter, K., Friedman, H. S., Bigner, D. D., & Reardon, D. A. (2007). Using the theory of planned behavior to understand the determinants of exercise intention in patients diagnosed with primary brain cancer. *Psycho-Oncology, 16,* 232–240.

Kaplan, G. A., Lazarus, N. B., Cohen, R. D., & Lew, D. J. (1991). Psychosocial factors in the natural history of physical activity. *American Journal of Physical Medicine, 7,* 12–17.

Kaplan, R. M., Sallis, J. F., & Patterson, T. L. (1993). *Health and human behavior.* New York: McGraw-Hill.

Katz, J. F., Alder, J. C., Mazzarella, N, J., & Ince, L. P. (1985). Psychological consequences of an exercise training program for a paraplegic man: A case study. *Rehabilitation Psychology, 30*(1), 53–58.

Keats, M .R., Culos-Reed, S. N., Courneya, K. S., & McBride, M. (2007). Understanding physical activity in adolescent cancer survivors: An application of the theory of planned behavior. *Psycho-Oncology, 16,* 448–457.

Kim, D., & Kravitz, L. (2007). Childhood obesity: Prevalence, treatment and prevention. *IDEA Fitness Journal, 4*(1), 22–24.

King, A. C., Oman, R. F., Brassington, G. S., Bliwise, D. L., & Haskell, W. L. (1997). Moderate-intensity exercise and self rated quality of sleep in older adults: A randomized controlled trial. *The Journal of the American Medical Association, 277*(1), 32–37.

Kisner, C., & Colby, L. A. (2007). *Therapeutic exercise: Foundations and techniques* (5th ed). Philadelphia: F. A. Davis.

Klijn, P. H. C., Oudshoorn, A., van der Ent, C. K., van der Net, J., Kimpen, J. L., & Helders, P. J. M. (2004). Effects of anaerobic training in children with cystic fibrosis. *Chest Journal, 125*(4), 1299–1305.

Knopfli, B. H., Radtke, T., Lehmann, M., Schatzle, B., Eisenblatter, J., Gachnang, A., Wiederkehr, P., Hammer, J., & Brooks-Wildhaber, J. (2008). Effects of a multidisciplinary inpatient intervention on body composition, aerobic fitness, and quality of life in severely obese girls and boys. *Journal of Adolescent Health, 42*(2), 119–127.

Kravitz, L., & Heyward, V. (1992). Getting a grip on body composition. *Idea Today, 10*(4), 34–39.

Lai, S., Studenski, S., Richards, L., Perera, S., Reker, D., Rigler, S., & Duncan, P. W. (2006). Therapeutic exercise and depressive symptoms after stroke. *Journal of the American Geriatrics Society, 54*(2), 240–247.

Lee, I. M., & Paffenbarger, R. S. (1996). *Exercise Sport Science Review, 24,* 135–71.

Levangie, P. K., & Norkin, C. C. (2001). *Joint Structure and Function: A Comprehensive Analysis* (3rd ed). Philadelphia: F. A. Davis.

Levinson, L. J., & Reid, G. (1993). The effects of exercise intensity of the stereotypic behaviors of individuals with autism. *Adapted Physical Activity Quarterly, 10,* 255–268.

Lieberman, J. A. (2007). *Therapeutic exercise.* Retrieved August 29, 2007 from http://www.emedicine.com/pmr/topic199.htm

Liu-Ambrose, T. Y. L., Khan, K. M., Eng, J. J., Gillies, G. L., Lord, S. R., & McKay, H. A. (2005). The beneficial effects of group-based exercises on fall risk profile and physical activity persist 1 year postintervention in older women with low bone mass: Follow-up after withdrawal of exercise. *Journal for the American Geriatrics Society, 53*(10), 1767–1773.

Lockette, K. F. (1995). Resistance training: Program design. In P. D. Miller (Ed.), *Fitness programming and physical disability* (pp. 79–89). Champaign, IL: Human Kinetics.

Lockette, K. F., & Keyes, A. M. (1994). *Conditioning with physical disabilities.* Champaign, IL: Human Kinetics.

Lox, C . L., McAuley, E., & Tucker, R. S. (1996). Aerobic resistance exercise training effects on body composition, muscular strength, and cardiovascular fitness in an HIV-1 population. *International Journal of Behavioral Medicine, 3*(1), 55–69.

Manson, J. E., Rimm, E. B., Stampfer, M. J., Colditz, G. A., & Willett, W. C. (1991). Physical activity and incidence of non-insulin-dependent diabetes mellitus in women. *Lancet, 338,* 774–778.

Martin, J. J., Oliver, K., & McCaughtry, N. (2007). The theory of planned behavior: Predicting physical activity in Mexican American children. *Journal of Sport and Exercise Psychology, 29,* 225–238.

McCubbin, J. A., Rintala, R., & Frey, G. C. (1997). Correlational study of three cardiorespiratory fitness for men with mental retardation. *Adapted Physical Activity Quarterly, 14,* 43–50.

Merriman, W. J., Barnett, B. B., & Jarry, E. S. (1996). Improving fitness of dually diagnosed adults. *Perceptual and Motor Skills, 83,* 999–1004.

Meyer, T., & Brooks, A. (2000). *Therapeutic impact of exercise on psychiatric diseases: A guidance for exercise testing and prescription.* Retrieved April 29, 2007 from http://www.EBSCOhost.com

Miller, P. D. (1995). Skeletal muscle physiology and anaerobic exercise. In P. D. Miller (Ed.), *Fitness programming and physical disability* (pp. 35–50). Champaign, IL: Human Kinetics.

Milne, H. M., Gordon, S., Guilfoyle, A., Wallman, K. E., & Courneya, K. S. (2007). Association between physical activity and quality of life among Western Australian breast cancer survivors. *Psycho-Oncology, 16,* 1059–1068.

Nash, M. S. (2005). Exercise as a health-promoting activity following spinal cord injury. *Journal of Neurological Physical Therapy, 29*(2), 87–103.

Nelson, M. E., Rejeski, W. J., Blair, S. N., Duncan, P. W., Judge, J. O., King, A. C., Macera, C. A., & Castaneda-Sceppa, C. (2007). Physical activity and public health in older adults: Recommendation from the American College of Sports Medicine and the American Heart Association. *Medicine & Science in Sports & Exercise, 39*(8), 1435–1445.

Netz, Y., Yaretzki, A., Salganik, I., Jacob, T., Finkeltov, B., & Argov, E. (1994). The effect of supervised physical activity on cognitive and affective state of geriatric and psychogeriatric in-patients. *Clinical Gerontologist, 15*(1), 47–55.

Nichols, D. L., Sanborn, C. F., Bonnick, S. L. B., Gench, B., & DiMarco, N. (1995). Relationship of regional body composition to bone mineral density in college females. *Medicine and Science in Sports and Exercise, 27,* 178–182.

O'Connor, P. J., Aenchbacher, L. E., & Dishman, R. K. (1993). Physical activity and depression in the elderly. *Journal of Aging and Physical Activity, 1,* 34–58.

O'Connor, P. J., & Youngstedt, S. D. (1995). The influence of exercise on human sleep. *Exercise and Sport Science Reviews, 23,* 105–134.

Palmer, C. (2005). Exercise as a treatment for depression in elders. *Journal of the American Academy of Nurse Practitioners, 17*(2), 60–66.

Pang, M. Y. C., Eng, J. J., Dawson, A. S., McKay, H. A., & Harris, J. E. (2005). A community-based fitness and mobility exercise program for older adults with chronic stroke: A randomized controlled trial. *Journal of the American Geriatric Society, 53,* 1667–1674.

Petruzzello, S. (2001). Exercise and sports psychology. In S. B. Brown, *Introduction to exercise science* (pp. 229–376). Philadelphia: Lippincott Williams & Wilkins.

Pitetti, K., & Boneh, S. (1995). Cardiovascular fitness as related to leg strength in adults with mental retardation. *Medicine and Science in Sports and Exercise, 27,* 423–428.

Powell, K. E., Thompson, P. D., Caspersen, C. J., & Kendrick, J. S. (1987). Physical activity and the incidence of coronary heart disease. *Annual Review of Public Health, 8,* 253–287.

Prentice, W. E. (1994). *Rehabilitation techniques in sports medicine.* St. Louis: Mosby-Year Book.

Prochaska, J. O., & Velicer, W. F. (1997). The transtheoretical model of health behavior change. *American Journal of Health Promotion, 12,* 38–48.

Protas, E., Mitchell, K., Williams, A., Qureshy, H., Caroline, K., & Laib, E. (2005). Gait and step training to reduce falls in Parkinson's disease. *Neurorehabilitation, 20,* 183–190.

Quist, M., Rorth, M., Zacho, M., Anderson, C., Moeller, T., Midtgaard, J., & Adamsen, L. (2006). High-intensity resistance and cardiovascular training improve physical capacity in cancer patients undergoing chemotherapy. *Scandinavian Journal of Medicine & Science in Sports, 16,* 349–357.

Richardson, C. R., Faulkner, G., McDevitt, J., Skrivnar, G. S., Hutchinson, D. S., & Piette, J. D. (2005). Integrating physical activity into mental health services for persons with serious mental illness. *Psychiatric Services, 56*(3), 324–331.

Riewald, S. (2004). Stretching the limits of knowledge on stretching. *Strength Conditioning Journal, 26*(5), 58–59.

Risser, W., Lee, E., & Leblanc, A. (1990). Bone density in eumenorrheic female college athletes. *Medicine Science in Sports and Exercise, 22,* 26–35.

Robinson, T., Snow-Harter, C., Taafe, D., Gillis, D., Shaw, J., & Marcus, R. (1995). Gymnasts exhibit higher bone mass than runners despite similar prevalence of amenorrhea and oligomenorrhea. *Journal of Bone Mineral Research, 19,* 26–35.

Rolland, Y., Pillard, F., Klapouszczak, A., Reynish, E., Thomas, D., Andrieu, S., Riviere, D., & Vellas, B. (2007). Exercise program for nursing home residents with Alzheimer's disease: A 1-year randomized, controlled trial. *Journal of the American Geriatrics Society, 55*(2), *158–165.*

Rooney, M., & Wald, A. (2007). Interventions for the management of weight and body composition changes in women with breast cancer. *Clinical Journal of Oncology Nursing, 11*(1), 41–52.

Rosenstock, I. M. (1966). Why people use health services. *Milband Memorial Fund Quarterly, 44*, 194–227.

Rosenstock, I. M. (1990). The health belief model: Explaining health behavior through expectancies. In K. Glancz, F. M. Lewis, & B. K. Rimer (Eds.), *Health behavior and health education: Theory, research, and practice* (pp. 39–62). San Francisco: Jossey-Bass.

Roth, D. L., & Holmes, D. S. (1987). Influence of aerobic exercise training and relaxation training on physical and psychological health followed by stressful life events. *Psychosomatic Medicine, 49*, 355–365.

Ruzic, L., Sporis, G., & Matkovic, B. R. (2008). High volume-low intensity exercise camp and glycemic control in diabetic children. *Journal of Paediatrics and Child Health, 44*, 122–128.

Santiago, M. C., & Coyle, C. P. (2004). Leisure-time physical activity and secondary conditions in women with physical disabilities. *Disability and Rehabilitation, 26*(8), 485–494.

Sobel, D. S. (1995). Rethinking medicine: Improving health outcomes with cost-effective psychosocial interventions. *Psychosomatic Medicine, 57*, 234–246.

Spangler, K. J. (1997). Doing our part to promote healthy lifestyles. *Parks and Recreation, 32*(10), 54–61.

Stein, P. N., & Motta, R. W. (1992). Effects of aerobic and nonaerobic exercise on depression and self-concept. *Perceptual and Motor Skills, 74*, 79–89.

Stevinson, C., & Fox, K. R. (2006). Feasibility of an exercise rehabilitation programme for cancer patients. *European Journal of Cancer, 15*, 386–396.

Suitor, C. W., & Kraak, V. I. (2007). *Adequacy of evidence for physical activity guidelines development: Workshop summary*. Washington, DC: National Academies Press.

Suomi, R., Surburg, P., & Lecius, P. (1995). Effects of hydraulic resistance strength training on isokinetic measures of leg strength in men with mental retardation. *Adapted Physical Activity Quarterly, 12*, 377–387.

Surburg, P. R. (1995). Static stretching: Modified for disability. In P. D. Miller (Ed.), *Fitness programming and physical disability* (pp. 113–118). Champaign, IL: Human Kinetics.

Swanenburg, J., Douwe de Bruin, E., Stauffacher, M., Mulder, T., & Uebelhart, D. (2007). Effects of exercise and nutrition on postural balance and risk of falling in elderly people with decreased bone mineral density: Randomized controlled trial pilot study. *Clinical Rehabilitation, 21*, 523–534.

Theodorakis, Y., (1994). Planned behavior, attitude strength, role identity, and the prediction of exercise behavior. *The Sport Psychologist, 8*, 149–165.

Thirlaway, K., & Benton, D. (1992). Participation in physical activity and cardiovascular fitness have different effects on mental health and mood. *Journal of Psychosomatic Research, 36*(7), 657–665.

Turner, L. W., Hunt, S. B., DiBrezzo, R., & Jones, C. (2004). Design and implementation of an osteoporosis prevention program using the health belief model. *American Journal of Health Studies, 19*(2), 115–121.

U.S. Department of Health and Human Services. *Healthy People 2010* (2nd ed.). With Understanding and Improving Health and Objectives for Improving Health. 2 vols. Washington, DC: U.S. Government Printing Office, November 2000.

Wannamethee, S. G., & Shaper, A. G. (2001). Physical activity in the prevention of cardiovascular disease: An epidemiological perspective. *Sports Med, 31*(2), 101–114.

Watts, K., Jones, T., Davis, E., & Green, D. (2005). Exercise training in obese children and adolescents. *Sports Medicine, 35,* 375–392.

Weiss, C. R., & Jamieson, N. B. (1989). Women, subjective depression, and water exercise. *Health Care for Women International, 10,* 75–88.

Wilmore, J. H., Buskirk, E. R., DiGirolamo, M., & Lohman, T. G. (1986). Body composition: A round table. *The Physician and Sportsmedicine, 14*(3), 144–162.

Winnick, J. P. (1990). *Adapted physical education and sport.* Champaign, IL: Human Kinetics.

Wuest, D. A., & Bucher, C. A. (2006). *Foundations of physical education, exercise science, and sport* (15th ed.). Boston: McGraw Hill.

Young-McCaughan, S., Mays, M. Z., Arzola, S. M., Yoder, L. H., Dramiga, S. A., Leclerc, K. M., Caton, J. R., Sheffler, R. L., & Nowlin, M. U. (2003). Change in exercise tolerance, activity and sleep patterns, and quality of life in patients with cancer participating in a structured exercise program. *Oncology Nursing Forum, 30*(3), 441–452.

Chapter 16
Therapeutic Use of Humor

Richard Williams and John Dattilo

A joyful heart is good medicine, but a broken spirit dries up the bones.
—Proverbs 17:22

Introduction

Humor is a hard concept to pin down. Things that are funny to some people are not funny to others, and comments that are funny in one context fall flat in another. This fleeting nature of humor has led scholars to propose more than 80 distinct theories to explain why certain things are perceived as being funny (Martin & Lefcourt, 1984). Most people who study humor can agree that humor is subjective.

> For instance, a boy who had his friends rolling on the ground with laughter while making rude noises would likely be met with an entirely different reaction were he to make the same noises at the dinner table.

Despite the difficulty people have had in their attempts to intellectually dissect humor, it cannot be denied that people enjoy humor. At least on the surface, humor feels like it might be healthy psychologically and, perhaps, even physically. Suspecting these benefits, some health care practitioners began to use humor as an intervention decades ago.

This chapter provides information and resources concerning the therapeutic uses and benefits of humor. Humor is defined, and there is a brief description of several different humor interventions. Following a discussion of the history and theoretical foundations of humor, current humor research is reviewed. Additionally, a case study, several intervention implementation exercises, discussion questions, and humor resources are provided.

Definitions

To help promote an understanding of the therapeutic use of humor, two definitions are presented:

- Humor
- Therapeutic Use of Humor

Humor

Humor can be generally understood as a mood or disposition (McGhee, 1979) that is, at its essence, non-serious. Recently, humor researchers have identified what they label as the *multidimensional* nature of humor. That is, humor does not have a single element, but it is a concept that is complex and is constructed of different elements. The most sound of these concepts is that of Martin and colleagues (2003) who proposed that there are four humor styles, including humor that is self-enhancing, affiliative, self-defeating, and aggressive.

Self-enhancing humor and *affiliative humor* are adaptive because people can use these styles of humor to counter negative emotions, cope with stress, and build interpersonal relationships.

> For instance, making light of a difficult situation can help people cope. The commonly used quip, "Other than that, Mrs. Lincoln, how did you enjoy the play?" is an example of a humorous comment used to place things in perspective.

Conversely, *self-defeating humor* and *aggressive humor* are maladaptive because these styles of humor can be used to avoid dealing with negative feelings about self, to undermine self-worth, and to alienate others.

> An example of this type of humor is sarcasm, which is, by definition, meant to wound and is not facilitative of positive interactions between people.

Therapeutic Use of Humor

When TR specialists and others use humor in practice, they plan for it to lead to specific therapeutic outcomes. These outcomes will vary according to the abilities and needs of particular participants and should be based on credible evidence of humor's effects. It is critical for practitioners to be sure that the outcomes that they expect for participants can be facilitated by a particular intervention.

That is, TR specialists are encouraged to use interventions with credible evidence of particular outcomes. The same holds true for humor interventions. Some reasonably well-documented outcomes associated with the therapeutic use of humor include its benefits in helping people cope with stress and to reduce depression. These and other documented benefits of humor are reviewed in this chapter and provide support for reductions in anxiety and depression, and improvements associated with pain thresholds, immune systems, and learning.

Descriptions

Researchers have identified different benefits of humor. Curiously, the interventions used in studies of humor have been remarkably similar. The majority of those examining effects of humor used comedy in the form of movies and audio recordings as interventions. For instance, Dillon, Minchoff, and Baker (1985) used a videotaped stand-up comedy performance by Richard Pryor to investigate effects of humor on the immune system. Lefcourt and colleagues (1990) used the videotape *Bill Cosby Himself* as an intervention, and Mahoney, Burroughs, and Hieatt (2001) used the *Soup Nazi* episode of *Seinfeld*. Others simply recommend integrating humor into treatment without specific suggestions of interventions. Thus, few humor interventions have been described in the literature. These are examples of humor interventions that have been described.

- MIRTH
- The Humor Project
- Humor and Wellness in Clinical Intervention
- The Healing Power of Humor
- How to Develop Your Sense of Humor
- The Comedy Club
- Humor Production Procedure

MIRTH

Scholl and Ragan (2003) described a hospital unit (identified as MIRTH) in the Integris Baptist Memorial Hospital in Oklahoma City designed specifically to encourage a therapeutic humor milieu. As such, humor was integrated into the unit's physical design and even the staff's attire. For instance, each patient's door was decorated with humorous quotations and cartoons. Scholl and Ragan observed that the unit's staff did not overtly attempt to get patients to laugh by completing actions such as telling jokes; rather, they attempted to create positive attitudes in their people they served during their interactions, and humor occurred spontaneously as a result. Specific strategies used by the staff to encourage a positive attitude and humor included encouraging older adults to discuss happy times in their youth, encouraging others to shed the "role of patient" by wearing their personal clothes (when medically appropriate) rather than hospital smocks, and getting to know individuals at a meaningful personal level. The authors concluded that humor emerged in interactions between staff and patients because of the environment created by MIRTH. Scholl's (2007) qualitative study of people in the MIRTH unit confirmed Scholl and Ragan's observations.

The Humor Project

Goodman (1983) founded the Humor Project to help people develop and apply their senses of humor, and his newsletter *The Laughing Matters* was among the first resources for people incorporating humor into treatment settings. The project's website (http://www.humorproject.com/) offers access to many therapeutic humor resources.

Goodman suggested four elements to be considered when developing a sense of humor: (a) appreciation of "everyday humor;" (b) laughing at yourself; (c) negative and positive humor; and (d) practicing humor skills. Everyday humor can be found in mundane occasions such as when reading newspaper headlines or while walking down the street. According to Goodman, people can find humor almost anywhere if they search for it. Goodman suggested that if people learn to laugh at their mistakes and faults, they can take themselves less seriously and learn to "play with situations rather than getting stuck in them" (p. 10). Negative humor might involve laughing at someone else while positive humor might involve laughing with someone else. Some other examples of negative humor included sarcasm, ridicule, and scorn. Goodman recommended that humor skills should be practiced. Ways to practice humor skills include watching stand-up comedians and creating jokes using exaggerations and understatements.

Humor and Wellness in Clinical Intervention

Salameh and Frye's (2001) *Humor and Wellness in Clinical Intervention* is both a scholarly and practical resource for use of humor by health care practitioners. Although the primary focus of the book is on use of humor to promote psychological health, humor's relationship to wellness in general is also covered. Essentially, the book is designed to help therapists develop an understanding of humor to help others tap into the benefits of humor. Humor-related topics, such as incongruity, exaggeration, and non-sequiturs are covered. Additionally, Salameh described the difference between therapeutic and harmful humor, and barriers that block client receptivity to humor.

The Healing Power of Humor

Klein's (1989) *The Healing Power of Humor* is divided into three sections. The first, "Learning to Laugh," contains discussions of benefits of humor, connections between laughing and crying, why people laugh, and minimizing the risks of learning to laugh. The second section, "When You Feel Like Crying: Techniques for Getting Through Trying Times," contains 14 techniques for incorporating humor into difficult situations. Several examples of these techniques can be found in the section of the chapter associated with implementation exercises. The final section, *The Last Laugh,* is concerned with the use of humor in coping with death and includes discussions of finding humor in illness and death, religious and cultural traditions, and celebrating loss. Klein's collection of humor development techniques remains a thorough resource for practitioners interested in humor development. More about Klein can be found on his website (www.allenklein.com)

How to Develop Your Sense of Humor

McGhee (1994), who is considered a leader in the area of the therapeutic use of humor, designed a humor development program based on years of research and teaching. The curriculum contains suggestions and activities related to: (a) experiencing playfulness, (b) telling jokes, (c) developing a humorous perspective, and (d) not taking oneself too seriously. McGhee's program is an example of a curriculum for humor development. The program is organized into eight steps, each complete with a lesson, exercises, and *homeplay* (rather than homework). The first step involves "determining the nature of your sense of humor" and then "surrounding yourself with the humor you enjoy" (p. 43). The second step offers suggestions for becoming more playful to prevent taking oneself too seriously. The third step includes ways to laugh more often and more enthusiastically and suggests telling more jokes and funny stories. The fourth step is devoted to playing with language through the use of puns, nonsense words, and exaggerations. The fifth step involves finding humor in everyday life by looking for things such as coincidences, irony, and rigidity of behavior. Step six includes information about taking oneself lightly and laughing at one's mistakes. The seventh step details ways of finding humor in stressful situations. Finally, the eighth step focuses on using humor to cope by incorporating the previous seven steps.

The Comedy Club

Brausa (1993) described a long-running comedy program ("The Comedy Club") developed for a group of people with chronic psychiatric disorders at the Colmery-O'Neil Veteran's Administration Hospital. The program consisted of an active and passive element. During the active element, each participant was responsible for sharing a joke, a funny line, or an act of physical humor with other participants. During the passive element, participants engaged in activities such as watching videotapes of comedies and comedians, listening to audio recordings of comedians and humorous radio shows, and reading aloud biographies of famous comedians. Brausa believed that the Comedy Club helped participants reduce stress, improve the quality of their social interactions, and increase their self-esteem. The Comedy Club is an example of a program that requires no special equipment or training, and it appears that it may be appropriate to many settings and for many people.

Humor Production Procedure

Prerost (1993) described the Humor Production Procedure, which was designed "to enhance a sense of humor by having older adults experience laughter generated at the *imaginal* level" (p. 19). There were four steps to the procedure. First, participants engaged in relaxation exercises such as progressive relaxation and focused breathing. The next step involved guided imagery. For example, participants were told to imagine walking in a forest or on a beach. During guided imagery, participants are encouraged to imagine not only sights, but to imagine sounds, smells, and textures. The third step involved the facilitator introducing incongruous and exaggerated variables into the scene imagined by participants to make it seem suddenly absurd. The final step of the Humor Production Procedure was a debriefing. Participants shared their reactions to the humorous elements introduced during the guided imagery. Although specifically designed for older adults, there seems little reason to limit use of the procedure to this population.

Summary

The humor development programs presented in this chapter are programs that have been disseminated through various publications such as books and journals. It is likely that other programs exist and are in use in various facilities such as hospitals, rehabilitation centers, and schools. In many hospitals, nurses will use a "humor cart" to improve the spirits of the people who they serve. A humor cart might contain materials as varied as videotapes, comic books, and rubber chickens. As discussed in the next section, research suggests that a strong sense of humor can have benefits for a variety of people. TR specialists may choose to design a humor development program or consider using one of the programs discussed previously.

History

While a specific origin of humor is unknown, humor has been part of the human experience for the span of recorded history and may be a uniquely human trait. Aristotle asserted that humor had its origins in improvisation and the lyrics of songs. Classically, tragedy was distinguished from comedy. Tragedy focused on people who were stronger, more powerful, or wiser than average people, while comedy focused on people who were less powerful or not as wise as an average person such as "fools," jesters, and people who were blind.

Comedy and humor can be found in every era of Western civilization. In ancient Greece, Aristophanes, and others wrote comedic plays. Humor permeates Chaucer's *Canterbury Tales*, and Shakespeare is as well-known for his comedies as for his tragedies. The distinction between tragedy and comedy is so strong that scholars refer to Shakespeare's plays that contain nearly equal elements of both tragedy and comedy as "problem plays." The modern entertainment industry produces substantive amounts of comedic material in the forms of situation comedies, routines of stand-up comedians, motion pictures, and other media.

While it has long been suspected that a humorous disposition is somehow healthful, it was not until Norman Cousins published the account of his use of humor in recovering from a potentially fatal disease that many researchers began to seriously consider benefits of humor. In *Anatomy of an Illness,* Cousins (1979) recounted his use of humor and massive doses of vitamin C to overcome a progressive and typically fatal collagen-related illness. Although compared to many areas of inquiry, there has been little research examining effects of humor, the amount of research in the last two decades has steadily increased. Important milestones in the history of humor research include the 1976 Conference on Humor and Laughter held in Wales and establishment of the *International Journal of Humor Research* in 1988 (McGhee, 1989). Despite humor's long history, only in the latter years of the twentieth century has there been substantial investigation on effects of humor.

Theoretical Foundations

There are numerous theories attempting to explain humor; however, one theory seems to be preeminent. McGhee (1979) identified the incongruity theory as central to the explanation of humor, and he posited that incongruity may be a necessary but not necessarily sufficient element of humor. In other words, incongruity is needed for a situation to be perceived as humorous, but incongruity alone may not be enough to make something funny. A wide variety of other elements may influence whether something incongruous is perceived as humorous or not. Sexuality, aggression, and a sense of superiority are common elements in humorous situations. This section contains a discussion of the following theories:

- Incongruity Theory
- Superiority Theory
- Psychological Release

Incongruity Theory

Incongruity is often discussed as the difference between what is expected and what actually happens (Shultz, 1996). Pollio (1983) believed that for something to be funny, it must have an element of unexpectedness. Even while recognizing the importance of the unexpected, incongruity cannot guarantee humor. Shultz (1996) suggested that for something incongruous to be perceived as humorous, there must also be an explanation for the incongruity. Otherwise, humor becomes nonsense.

Much of comedian Jay Leno's humor depends on incongruity. Often, Leno leads an audience in one direction while his punch line comes from an entirely different (incongruous) direction. Consider the following paraphrased joke told on the *Tonight Show*:

> Scientists have announced the development of genetically altered bananas that have the same pain-killing properties as aspirin. Can you believe this? The medicine is in the banana. Of course, there's always a drawback. You have to take it as a suppository.

The joke works in part due to the incongruity of the last line. Without the last line, the joke would not have been funny, but merely an odd statement about bananas.

Superiority Theory

Some of the earliest theories of humor were identified as superiority theories. Aristotle believed that laughter was an expression of ridicule toward people who perceived themselves as superior to others (McGuire et al., 1992). Modern superiority theories are quite similar to Aristotle's beliefs. Pollio (1983) noted that humor and feelings of superiority coincide with one another. Thus, feelings of elation are associated with feeling more intelligent or stronger than another person. So, according to superiority theories, laughter and *making fun* of others are important parts of humor (Keith-Speigel, 1984).

People who subscribe to the superiority theory believe that when someone tells jokes that person takes a superior stance to the audience by confounding those individuals (Fry, 1963). Others have speculated that expressing superiority through humor is an attempt to compensate for feeling inferior (Simon, 1988). Examples of this type of humor might include ethnic jokes and so-called blonde jokes.

Some types of humor may be more appropriate to use therapeutically than others. For instance, derision and sarcasm are examples of humor that are at least partially explained by the superiority theory and should be avoided by TR specialists. Derision entails *making fun* of others and can be destructive to a person's self-concept. Sarcasm is characterized by taunting and sneering and can affect people negatively. These and similar forms of humor are not helpful in therapeutic relationships because of their potential to harm people.

Psychological Release

Theories describing humor as psychological release have their origins in psychoanalysis. In *Jokes and Their Relation to the Unconscious,* Freud (1960) compared the production of jokes to the processes that produce dreams, and he posited that jokes originated in the subconscious. He explained that dreams and jokes share common elements such as absurdity and indirect representations. Freud viewed humor as a higher intellectual function that people use as a psychological defense against strife.

In discussing Freud's analysis of humor, Baker (1993) stated that humor can be a process that allows people to use psychological energy to produce pleasure that typically would have produced pain. Freud (1960) believed humor was a psychic function that allows the release of sexual and aggressive tension in a socially acceptable way. Therefore, according to this theory, if people experience humor, then they will release tension and be more relaxed.

Sexuality and aggression are often subjects of humor. Supporters of psychological release theories hold that humor allows people to release sexual tensions and express repressed emotions related to sexuality and aggression. The most obvious examples of sexual humor are *dirty* jokes. The terms *ribald* and *bawdy* refer to material that is both humorous and sexual. Aggression can be seen in some forms of physical humor such as slapstick and the laughter that occurs when witnessing another person's clumsy fall.

Summary

Any single instance of humor may not be explainable by only one theory; however, by starting with the theoretical foundations of incongruity and superiority, then adding other elements such as aggression or sexuality, many instances of humor can be explained plausibly. Rather than conceiving of a single theory explaining all of humor, it may be helpful to think of incongruity as central to understanding humor with different theories of humor contributing to understanding different types of humor.

Effectiveness

Since the early 1980s, there has been a growing body of research that suggests both psychological and physical benefits of humor. Among the most commonly demonstrated benefits of humor are reduced anxiety and depression, increased pain tolerance, and improved immune system functioning. Other researchers have found support for various other effects of humor. These include a psychologically healthy self-concept, stress reduction, and improved interpersonal relationships. Additionally, humor has been associated with improved memory, successful aging, and successful recovery from surgery.

Humor, however, is a complex phenomenon, and its effects may not all be positive. According to Aarstad, Aarstad, Meimdal, and Olofsson (2005), sense of humor was found to be inversely related to quality of life in people recovering from cancer. In other words, participants in their study with the strongest senses of humor were likely to have the lowest quality of life in the years following recovery from cancer. The authors offered no theoretical explanations for these results. Kuiper, Grimshaw, Leite, and Kirsh (2004) present a possible explanation for these results. The researchers proposed that humor is a concept with both adaptive and maladaptive components. Adaptive types of humor promote successful coping, help people affiliate with one another, and are self-enhancing. Maladaptive humor is self-defeating, aggressive, and rude. Results of their research indicated that adaptive humor was significantly related to low levels of depression, high self-esteem, increased positive affect, and high self-competence beliefs. Conversely, maladaptive humor that was self-defeating was significantly associated with higher levels of depression, anxiety, and negative affect. In particular, individuals who relied on using rude humor scored poorly in their abilities to deal with social difficulties.

Regardless of the occasional caution, most research literature supports humor as a generally therapeutic expression of human emotion, and support for the use of humor is found in the literature of many different professions. The inclusion of humor has been discussed and recommended by professionals in fields as diverse as psychotherapy (Mosak, 1987; Rutherford, 1994), psychiatry (Saper, 1990), nursing (Simon, 1988), crisis intervention (Pollio, 1995), addictions counseling (Sumners, 1988), gerontology (Johnson, 1990; McGuire et al., 1992; Richman, 1995), and TR (Austin, 2009). With such support and a growing number of researchers focusing on humor, it appears that additional benefits of humor will be documented in the future. Brief summaries of some notable studies into the effects of humor are presented in the following sections:

- Anxiety and Stress
- Depression
- Pain Thresholds
- Immune System
- Learning

Anxiety and Stress

Booth-Butterfield, Booth-Butterfield, and Wanzer (2007) examined the role humor plays in helping college students with jobs cope with job-related stress. Participants were 186 undergraduates who completed four surveys designed to measure their senses of humor, job satisfaction, ability to express emotion, and the effectiveness of their individual coping strategies. Results indicated that students with stronger senses of humor were more effective at coping with stress than students with weaker senses of humor. Booth-Butterfield and colleagues concluded that participants with strong senses of humor were not only more effective at coping but also had higher job satisfaction than other participants.

Roussi, Krikeli, Hatzidimitriou, and Koutri (2007) studied patterns of coping of 72 Greek women prior to and following breast cancer surgery. Psychometric scales were administered to and interviews were conducted with participants before and after cancer treatment. Although no relationships were found between descriptive variables (e.g., age) and coping, repeated measures ANOVA analysis revealed that humor was negatively related to levels of distress prior to surgery, 3 days following surgery, and 3 months following surgery.

Szabo (2003) reported results of a study comparing effects of humor to exercise. Thirty-nine university students participated by watching a humorous video, a neutral video, or exercising three times per week. Psychometric tests were administered before and after each 20-minute session. Results indicated that both the exercise and humor interventions caused reduced distress and increased sense of positive well-being, and humor's effect was stronger than the effect of exercise on reduction of anxiety.

Kuiper and Martin (1993) investigated the relationship between humor, self-concept, and affect. One hundred participants completed humor, self-concept, and affective assessments. Results indicated correlations between humor and both positive and healthy self-concepts. Specifically, having high ratings on the humor scales was correlated with: (a) less discrepancy between actual and ideal self, (b) increased stability in self-concept, (c) higher scores on sociability scales, (d) decreased likelihood of depression, and (e) preferring nonextreme and flexible standards for evaluating self. Also, high scores on the humor scales were correlated with both high self-esteem and low perceived stress. The authors concluded that there is a relationship between sense of humor and positive self-concept and affect.

Martin, Kuiper, Olinger, and Dance (1993) conducted follow-up studies to Kuiper and Martin (1993) by investigating humor's role as a moderating influence during stressful life events. The first study investigated humor and coping of undergraduate students preparing to take an examination. Forty-four participants were administered the Coping Humor Scale, the Perceived Stress Scale (PSS) (Cohen, Kamarck, & Mermelstein, 1983), and the Ways of Coping Scale (Lazarus & Folkman, 1984) 1 week prior, immediately following, and 1 week after the examination. During all three testing periods participants were asked whether they viewed the examination as a positive challenge. Participants who used humor as a coping strategy had: (a) greater perceived control over stress, (b) felt less overwhelmed, less anxious, and less stressed, (c) used confrontation and emotional distancing as coping strategies, and (d) viewed the examination as a positive challenge.

The second study by Martin and colleagues (1993) investigated the relationship between positive affect, positive and negative life events, and sense of humor. Thirty-nine participants completed four humor scales to determine number of recent positive and negative life events, levels of positive and negative affect, and role satisfaction. Positive affect increased in participants with high humor scores when the number of recent positive or negative life events increased. Positive affect stayed constant for participants with low humor scores when the number of recent positive life events increased, but positive affect decreased when the number of recent negative life events increased. Finally, it appeared that high humor scores were correlated with high satisfaction with social roles of participants.

Berk and colleagues (1989) investigated the relationship between laughter and stress hormone levels. Five participants were randomly assigned to an experimental group and five participants were randomly assigned to a control group. Blood samples were collected from participants during a baseline period, every 10 minutes during the hour-long intervention, and every 10 minutes during the half-hour-long recovery period. During intervention, the experimental group watched a humorous videotape while the control group received no intervention. Analysis of the blood samples indicated that levels of neuroendocrine and stress-related hormones in participants in the experimental group decreased significantly while neuroendocrine and stress-related hormone levels in the control group did not change. High levels of these hormones are present during the classic stress reaction or what many people call the "fight or flight" response. It was concluded that laughter can reduce levels of hormones related to stress reactions.

Bizi, Keinan, and Beit-Hallahmi (1988) investigated the role humor plays in coping with stress for 159 soldiers in training. Self-report and peer-ratings were used to determine sense of humor of participants. Training course grades and ratings by commanders and peers were used to determine ability to cope with stress. Results suggested that participants who were rated as humorous by peers were more successful at coping with stress than participants who were not perceived as humorous. Correlations were strongest between generated humor such as telling a joke, rather than just responding to something humorous, and successful coping.

Not all studies of humor's role in coping demonstrate positive effects of humor. For instance, **Gelkopf and Sigal (1995)** investigated whether use of humor as a coping mechanism influenced use of other types of coping mechanisms such as aggression, hostility, and anger. Thirty-four adult participants residing in a long-term residential psychiatric hospital completed the Coping Humor Scale and other instruments to determine coping styles. Results suggested no significant correlations between the use of humor as coping and other coping styles. The authors concluded that humor may be used in conjunction with, but not to the exclusion of, other coping styles.

Celso, Ebener, and Burkhead (2003) used structural equation modeling to examine the relationships between use of humor, life satisfaction, and health of older adults in a long-term care facility. The researchers proposed health was a predictor of the likelihood to use humor in coping and life satisfaction. Additionally, it was proposed that the likelihood to use humor affected life satisfaction and to moderate the relationship between life satisfaction and health status. Two hundred and eleven participants completed psychometric scales. While humor was related to health status, the researchers concluded that humor did not play a significant role moderating the relationship between health and quality of life.

Summary. Humor's relationship to anxiety and stress is probably the most studied aspect of the therapeutic benefits of humor, and it appears that humor may indeed help people cope with anxiety and stressful situations. The production of humor, such as creating jokes, seems particularly effective. Considering that so many illnesses and unhealthy behaviors correlate with anxiety, finding ways to help people cope with anxiety is warranted. Although perhaps not effective in all cases, humor appears to have some ability to help people cope with the anxiety and stressful events in their lives.

Depression

The effects of humor interventions on people with depression have been studied by a variety of researchers, but considering that humor seems nearly the opposite phenomenon of depression, surprisingly few researchers have demonstrated therapeutic effects of humor interventions for people with depression.

Walter and colleagues (2007) compared effects of humor interventions to standard pharmacological treatments in two samples of older adults including 20 diagnosed with depression and 20 with Alzheimer's disease. Half of the participants from each group received the humor intervention and all participants continued to receive medications for their conditions. Pre- and post-intervention analysis of psychometric tests revealed that quality of life scores and mood increased significantly in both groups, and the group that received the humor intervention demonstrated higher quality of life scores at post-test measurement.

Similarly, **Thorson and Powell (1994)** investigated the relationship between humor and depression. Three hundred forty-seven participants completed the Multidimensional Sense of Humor Scale (MSHS) (Thorson & Powell, 1993) and the Center for Epidemiological Studies-Depression Scale (CESDS) (Radloff, 1977). Results indicated a significant negative relationship between scores on the MSHS and the CESDS. The authors concluded that depression may decrease as sense of humor increases, but they cautioned that more research is needed to confirm the findings.

Deaner and McConatha (1993) investigated humor's relationship to depression and personality. One hundred twenty-nine undergraduate students completed five questionnaires: (a) the Situational Humor Response Questionnaire, (b) the Coping Humor Scale, (c) the Sense of Humor Questionnaire (Svebak, 1974), (d) the Inventory to Diagnose Depression (Zimmerman, 1983), and (e) the Eysenck Personality Inventory (Eysenck & Eysenck, 1968). Results indicated that participants scoring low on the Inventory to Diagnose Depression scored higher on the Coping Humor Scale. Participants who were more extroverted tended to use humor as a coping mechanism and were more likely to find humor in various situations. Emotional stability was correlated with high scores on the humor scales. Although no significant relationships were found between depression scores and humor scores, it was noted that the mean scores for participants in this study were significantly below normative data for people with depression, suggesting a floor effect. The authors concluded that the study added limited support to a relationship between depression and humor.

Danzer and colleagues (1990) studied effects of humor on induced depression, which consisted of viewing progressively more depressing slides. Physiological measures, such as heart rate and facial expressions, were recorded during the procedure. Following depression inducement, participants completed the Multiple Affect Adjective Check List (MAACL) (Zuckerman & Lubin, 1965) to measure levels of depression. Next, participants were exposed to either an audio recording of a stand-up comedy routine, an audio recording of a non-humorous geology lecture, or no intervention, and a second MAACL was administered. Although there was a statistically significant reduction in depression in the group that received no intervention, only the depression scores of the humor group returned to baseline levels. The authors concluded that humor may be more effective at relieving depression than simply waiting for depression to subside.

Summary. Many researchers have explored the relationship between humor and depression. Although relatively few, findings suggest that humor may alleviate depression (Danzer et al., 1990), may contribute to quality of life (Walter et al., 2007), and may be negatively correlated with depression (Deaner & McConatha, 1993; Thorson & Powell, 1994). As researchers add to this body of knowledge, firmer conclusions will be reached.

Pain Thresholds

Mahoney and colleagues (2001) investigated the influence of expectation of the benefit of humor and relaxation to increase pain thresholds. Participants (n=134) were undergraduate students who were instructed that pain could be moderated through use of humor and relaxation. Blood pressure cuffs were used to induce discomfort while participants watched either a humorous or a relaxing video. Results indicated that both relaxation and humor helped to increase pain thresholds and expectations of benefits positively influenced outcomes.

Rotton and Shats (1996) studied effects of humor, expectancies, and choice on post-surgical mood and amount of self-medication. Seventy-eight participants who had undergone orthopedic surgery were randomly assigned to either the control group or one of eight experimental groups that had various combinations of the following: type of videotape viewed (humorous or serious), perceived control (choice or no choice), and expectation (positive or no expectation). Results indicated that on the first day following surgery, participants in the experimental groups reported more pain than the control group, but by the second day, levels of pain declined in the experimental groups while they remained constant in the control group. There was no significant difference in the number of self-administered pain medication between those who watched comedies and those who watched serious movies. Participants who viewed comedies that they had chosen used significantly less self-administered pain medication than participants viewing: (a) comedies with no choice, (b) serious movies with choice, and (c) serious movies with no choice. Those participants who self-administered the most medication were those who watched comedies they did not choose. The authors speculated, "Few things are as irritating as being exposed to material that fails in its attempt to be funny" (pp. 1786–7), and it appears that the choice factor interacted with the humor factor.

Nevo and colleagues (1993) investigated effects of humor on pain thresholds. Seventy-two participants were divided into two groups. One group watched a humorous film, and the other watched a serious documentary. A hand submerged in ice water was used to induce pain while participants watched the films. While there was no significant difference between groups in pain tolerance, there was a significant correlation between productive humor, such as telling jokes, and pain tolerance, suggesting a difference between active and passive humor. There was also a correlation between how funny participants rated a film and the amount of pain tolerated.

Zillmann, Rockwell, Schweitzer, and Sundar (1993) investigated effects of humor on pain thresholds. One hundred participants watched one of the following videotaped television programs: (a) stand-up comedy routines, (b) a situation comedy, (c) a drama, (d) instructional material (a cooking show), and (e) a sad film. Pain threshold measurements were taken before and after the intervention.

Results indicated that participants viewing the comedy interventions and the sad film had significantly higher pain thresholds than other participants. Stand-up comedy appeared to be the most successful of the interventions.

McGuire, Backman, and Boyd (1990) studied effects of humor on quality of life, including pain reduction, adaptation, and affect, of residents in long term care facilities. Over a 13-week period, 234 participants were divided into three groups: humor, non-humor, and control. The humor group viewed movies found to be humorous by the focus group, the non-humor group viewed serious movies and the control group viewed no films. Movies were shown 3 days a week for 1 hour and at various times. At the beginning of the study participants' affect and adaptability were evaluated. Additionally, participants' charts were viewed on a weekly basis to identify pain medication usage. Results indicated the humor-viewing group had a significant increase in positive affect but no significant changes in adaptability or pain medication use.

Cogan, Cogan, Waltz, and McCue (1987) conducted two experiments to determine effects of humor on pain thresholds. In the first experiment, 40 participants were randomly assigned to a group exposed to one of the following: (a) no stimulus, (b) a 20-minute recording of humorous material, (c) a 20-minute recording of relaxing material, or (d) a 20-minute recording of dull narrative. Following exposure to these conditions, pain threshold measurements were taken. Results suggest that participants exposed to either humorous or relaxing material had significantly higher pain thresholds than other participants. In the second experiment, 40 participants were matched and assigned to a group exposed to one of the following: (a) no stimulus, (b) a humorous recording, (c) a recording of an interesting narrative, (d) a recording of an informative narrative, and (e) a multiplication task. Pain thresholds were measured before and after treatment. Results indicated that the humor group was the only group to have significantly higher pain thresholds after treatment than before.

Summary. Researchers suggest that exposure to humor increases pain thresholds. In several cases, this effect appears to exceed mere distraction of other forms such as educational material and frightening material. Researchers have been reluctant to speculate about the reasons for humor's apparent analgesic effects. Despite the lack of explanation, TR specialist could take advantage of humor's effects on pain when working with participants experiencing pain as a result of a disease or condition.

Immune System

There have been several investigations examining effects of humor on immune system functioning. Of note, all but one of the studies used immunoglobulin A (IgA) as an indication of immune system functioning. IgA is found in human saliva and is believed to combat air-borne disease-causing agents. IgA is a commonly used indication of immune system functioning. Higher levels of IgA equate to improved immune system functioning.

Bennett, Zeller, Rosenberg, and McCann (2005) conducted an experiment to determine if experiencing humor increased natural killer (NK) immune system cell activity in healthy women (n=33). Participants in the experimental group watched a humorous video while participants in the control group watched a tourism video. Results indicated that NK immune system cell activity increased significantly more in the experimental group than in the control group, supporting the conclusion that humor can support a healthy immune system.

Dowling, Hockenberry, and Gregory (2003) reported results of a study of children receiving treatment for cancer. The researchers concluded that a strong sense of humor moderated the relationship between cancer-related stressors and psychological distress, and a strong sense of humor was related to fewer incidences of infections.

Labott, Ahleman, Wolever, and Martin (1990) investigated whether inhibiting or expressing emotions might have physiological and psychological effects on people. Sixteen participants were assigned to an emotion-expression group, 16 to an emotion-inhibition group, and seven to a control group. Participants in the expression and inhibition groups watched sad and humorous films while members of the control group watched emotionally neutral documentaries. Results demonstrated that crying suppresses IgA levels, while laughter increases IgA levels. Even when laughter was inhibited, IgA levels increased when participants were exposed to humorous material. Also, laughter was associated with more positive moods.

Lefcourt and colleagues (1990) investigated the relationship between humor and immunity. In the first and second study, after participants were exposed to humorous material, those likely to use humor as a coping mechanism were more likely to have higher IgA levels, than participants unlikely to use humor as a coping mechanism. In the second study, procedures were identical to the first study except the intervention was a humorous videotape. In the third study, mood disturbances decreased in the 41 participants exposed to humorous material. Additionally, participants with the best senses of humor, as assessed by the Situational Humor Response Questionnaire (SHRQ) (Martin & Lefcourt, 1984), had significantly greater increases in IgA levels compared to participants with lesser senses of humor.

Martin and Dobbin (1988) investigated effects of humor on immunosuppression due to stress. On two occasions (90 days apart), 40 participants were administered the Daily Hassles Scale (Kanner, Coyne, Schaefer, & Lazarus, 1981), the Situational Humor Response Questionnaire (Martin & Lefcourt, 1984), the Coping Humor Scale (Martin & Lefcourt, 1983), and the Sense of Humor Questionnaire (Svebak, 1974). Saliva samples were collected from participants during each testing session to obtain IgA levels. A significant negative correlation was found between stressors and IgA levels. For participants with high humor scores, there was no relationship between stress IgA levels. For participants with low humor scores, there was a negative correlation between the stress and IgA levels. The authors concluded that humor may play a role in reducing stress and, therefore, may counteract the negative influence stress has on the immune system.

Dillon and colleagues (1985) compared effects of humor on the immune system. Ten participants watched both a comedy film and a horror film. IgA levels were measured before and after each intervention. Results indicated that there were significantly higher IgA in participants after viewing the comedy film than before. There were no significant pre- and post-intervention differences in IgA levels when participants viewed the horror film. Additionally, high scores on the Coping Humor Scale were correlated with high IgA levels.

Summary. Humor seems to positively influence the immune system. Not only does it appear that immune system functioning increases when a person is exposed to humorous material, but humorous people appear to have higher functioning immune systems than non-humorous people. The few studies examining effects humor on the immune system confirms the belief that humor and laughter are somehow healthful.

Learning

The following group of studies can be loosely categorized as effects of humor on factors related to learning. Aspects of learning addressed by these studies include memory, group cohesion, fostering interest in mundane tasks, and encouraging people to choose more challenging tasks.

Dienstbier (1996) investigated four hypotheses concerning humor; whether humor would: (a) lead to increased energy without increased tension, (b) influence preference for the difficulty of materials studied, (c) lead to the perception that mundane tasks had become more challenging without becoming more threatening, and (d) lead to enhanced performance on the tasks mentioned in (c). Eighty-one participants were randomly assigned to either a humorous group that watched a video of a Bill Cosby comedy routine or to a non-humorous group that watched a video of an analysis of the comedy routine. Results confirmed hypotheses (a), (b), and (c), but hypothesis (d) was not confirmed. Participants exposed to humor felt more energized (without an increase in tension), were willing to engage in more difficult tasks, and perceived mundane tasks to be more interesting than participants who were not exposed to humor. However, participants exposed to humor did not outperform their non-humor counterparts. The authors concluded that humor may be especially useful for tasks where it is difficult to maintain alertness.

Schmidt (1994) conducted a series of six investigations examining effects of humor on memory. The studies used lists of corresponding sentences. Each humorous sentence had a non-humorous counterpart. Although similar, each study differed from the others in experimental design or research hypothesis. In summary of the studies, it appears that humor can positively influence the ability to memorize sentences. Factors influencing humor's effect on memory included: (a) the method used to measure memory, (b) the context of the sentences, (c) type of memory employed such as incidental, and (d) type of humor. It appears that some humorous material was memorized at the expense of non-humorous material, perhaps because participants paid more attention to humorous material. Incongruous humor appeared to be the most beneficial memory aid.

Banning and Nelson (1987) investigated effects of humor and group structure on group cohesion and affect. Twenty-eight participants were randomly assigned to one of several groups that varied by type of task (humorous or not) and group structure (parallel or project). Members of parallel groups worked side-by-side, but not on a mutual project whereas project groups worked together. Groups met one time for approximately one hour. Results indicated that participants in humor groups enjoyed their activities more than serious groups, and humor groups with both types of group structures had significantly higher cohesion scores than serious groups. The authors concluded that humor and group structure influenced the environment of groups.

Summary. While the studies in this section are loosely connected, each suggests that humor may have positive influences on peoples' ability to learn. Humorous material appears to enhance memorization. Groups seem to work together better when they are assigned a humor-related task. People tend to attempt more difficult tasks with humorous elements than simpler tasks without humorous elements, and humor appears to make mundane tasks more attractive. Each of these findings suggests that humor can be a helpful tool in education and learning.

Overall Summary

Researchers from a variety of disciplines have investigated effects of humor and have reported wide-ranging benefits. Existing research modestly indicates that humor is an empirically supported facilitation technique. Among the benefits suggested by a review of the literature include use of humor as a mechanism for coping with stress. Additionally, humor seems to increase pain thresholds, and it appears that a humorous disposition is related to a healthy immune system. While broad, the research into humor's effects on various conditions cannot be described as deep. In other words, while isolated studies illustrate benefits, there is not overwhelming research evidence supporting the therapeutic use of humor with a particular illness or disability. As researchers continue their investigations of humor, results may well support its use in a many different clinical settings.

Case Study

Chanta

Chanta was a 12-year-old girl receiving treatment for acute myelogenous leukemia from the pediatric oncology center of a large regional hospital. Chanta responded well to her initial treatments of chemotherapy. Following an aggressive series of chemotherapy treatments, the number of visible leukemia cells in her bone marrow dropped dramatically but not completely. Although her sister qualified as a stem-cell donor for Chanta, her doctors decided to try another round of chemotherapy to further reduce the number of leukemia cells. Chanta was very sick during her initial chemotherapy treatments and had a good deal of anxiety about her next round of treatments and hospitalization.

Humor Intervention

Padma was dually certified as a Certified TR Specialist and as a Certified Child Life Specialist and worked in the pediatric oncology center. Padma's primary roles in the center were to help children learn to cope with the stress and unpleasantness of hospitalization and medical procedures and to contribute to their education. She found humor to be helpful in both roles.

Chanta's physician referred Chanta and her family to Padma prior to her procedure. Padma met with Chanta and her family and discussed Chanta's previous experiences in the hospital and her upcoming procedure. During the meeting, Padma asked questions about Chanta's favorite funny movies, funny television shows, and comedians. She suggested that Chanta bring several of her favorite things from home to make her hospital room more comfortable and familiar. Additionally, Padma supplied informational materials for Chanta to review prior to her hospitalization. For younger children, Padma had coloring books that provided information about cancer treatments and hospital stays, but since Chanta was a little too old for coloring books, Padma gave her several comic books that had been prepared by a national cancer foundation. While not humorous, the comic books presented information in an easily-understood format. Chanta and Padma read the first comic book together, and Chanta promised to read the others on her own before she returned to the hospital.

Following the meeting, Padma noted the date of Chanta's next treatment and began to find several movies and television shows that Chanta liked. When Chanta returned to the hospital a week later, Padma and a nurse visited with her immediately before her first treatment to help answer any lingering questions and to help reduce her anxiety. Chanta told Padma that she had read and reread the comic books, and she seemed pleased to hear that Padma had acquired several of her favorite funny movies. Chanta also showed Padma the things she had brought from home, including photographs of her pet dog and a ragged stuffed bear. Padma joked that the bear needed to be in the hospital worse than Chanta. For the next several days, Padma continued to visit Chanta. When Chanta felt very ill, Padma and she simply visited, but several times, Chanta asked to watch one of the movies. After several more days, Padma knew that Chanta had turned an important corner when she entered Chanta's room and heard her laughing out loud as she watched a funny video.

Summary

As an experienced clinician, Padma understood that while humor can help people in a number of ways, there are times when individuals are too sick or too anxious to appreciate humor. So, she subtly used humor with Chanta in her visits with her, and she was sure to respond appropriately to Chanta's level of anxiety and discomfort. Instead of introducing a formal humor intervention, Padma used what she called *ninja humor*, making light-hearted comments in conversation and asking about Chanta's interests and experiences. The comic books that Padma used to help supplement more formal education materials were designed to deliver information in an age-appropriate and familiar way. Padma understood that a large portion of people's anxiety is fear of the unknown.

Padma also understood that humor is a subjective experience and rather than rely on her own taste in humor, she asked Chanta what type of material she found funny. This insured that Padma would have materials available that Chanta would enjoy. In the end, Chanta's procedure was successful, and her hospital stay was less unpleasant that it would have been without Padma's help.

Intervention Implementation Exercises

Humor implementation exercises focus on developing senses of humor. There is an implicit assumption of these exercises (and others like them) that a sense of humor is a skill that can be learned and developed. Each was designed to be not only productive, but fun and rewarding. The following exercises are presented in this section:

- Joke-Jitsu
- Add Some Nonsense
- Laugh at Yourself
- Exercise in Multiple Meanings
- Ha

Joke-Jitsu

The key to the martial art of jujitsu is to use an opponent's strength against him or her. Humor can work in the same way. This exercise can help participants learn to take a humorous stance against personal attacks and potential disasters. The key to joke-jitsu is finding absurd good news as a counterpart to bad news. On a piece of paper, participants write "The bad news is . . ." then they complete the sentence with something that has been causing them stress. It is then up to each participant to write a corresponding sentence that begins, "But the good news is . . ." An example from Klein (1989) is, "The bad news is that my husband ran off with my best friend. The good news is that I now have two fewer people for whom to buy Christmas presents." Once participants have finished their good news/bad news statements, they can be encouraged to read them aloud for the group. If a participant has difficulty thinking of a "good news" statement, other participants can make suggestions.

Add Some Nonsense

Making fun of problems can help people gain new perspectives and perhaps remove some of the power that problems hold. This exercise is designed to help participants gain new perspectives on problems. Have participants sit in a circle, each with a piece of paper and a pen or pencil. Instruct participants to write five things that regularly cause them stress. Next, participants number each sentence in order from least stressful to most stressful. Finally, participants write a different short laugh sound such as "ha ha," or "tee hee hee" following each sentence. Generally, the sillier the sounds the better it will be. Examples might include, "The food in this place is terrible . . . woo ha ha!" and "Nobody ever listens to me . . . ho ho ho!" Once participants have finished writing their sentences and sounds, they can be encouraged to read what they have written aloud.

Laugh at Yourself

Laughing at your own mistakes is quite different than "putting yourself down" (Klein, 1989, p. 134). Laughing at yourself can be a demonstration of security and self-confidence and may actually lead to increased self-esteem. For this exercise, participants write one physical feature and one feature of their personality that they are not completely pleased about. Next, they write a playful sentence poking fun at each of the two faults they just recorded making sure the sentence is not merely mean-spirited. Rather, it should be clever, witty, and funny. Klein offered the examples of two famous comedians. Phyllis Diller once said that she is so ugly that a Peeping Tom once asked her to pull down her window shade, and Woody Allen claimed that he is such a loser that even in kindergarten, he "flunked milk."

Exercise in Multiple Meanings

McGhee (1994) suggested that people who are good at generating humor particularly during conversations, often have developed the skill of finding alternate meanings of words or phrases. These alternate meanings can be used humorously. This exercise will help develop the skill of recognizing multiple meanings to common words. While this exercise will not produce jokes, it should help lead to the creation of spontaneous humor during conversations. Arrange participants around a table with pencils and paper. Read aloud a list of common words, and instruct participants to write the words as you speak them. Next, participants write as many meanings to the words that they can produce. For example, "pen" can mean something to write with or a place for pigs. After everyone has finished with the list of words, encourage participants to look for opportunities to cleverly use alternate meanings to words in conversations.

Ha

Ha has been used at summer camps, and it can be used as an ice-breaker and as a facilitator of social interaction. Have participants lie on the ground on their backs in a circle. Participants can be arranged in a number of ways. For instance, they can be arranged so that they resemble the spokes of a wheel with either their heads or their feet touching in the center of the circle. However they are arranged, it is important that participants are close to one another. Tell participants that, no matter what, they are not supposed to laugh during the activity. Choose one participant to begin the activity. Instruct participants that the first person will say the word *ha,* then the second person will say, "Ha ha," and then each person will add one additional "ha" as it becomes their turn. So, by the time the seventh person speaks, he or she will say "Ha" seven times. Usually, the combination of the laughter restriction and the absurdity of the activity will create an irresistible urge to laugh. The facilitator can process the activity with a discussion of the value of laughter.

Summary

The previous exercises were designed to promote development of senses of humor and to be both therapeutic and fun. As with all exercises of this sort, a debriefing following the activity or other forms of processing the activity are often beneficial to participants. While this chapter contains only a few examples of intervention exercises, others can be obtained through the resources listed at the end of the chapter.

Conclusion

Humor can be used both formally and informally. TR Specialists report that rather than attempt to implement formal humor interventions, they rely on a light-hearted and humorous demeanor when working with clients. In these less formal interactions, humor becomes a complement to whatever other intervention the TR Specialist might be using.

For TR Specialists using leisure education, an element of humor development would be appropriate and might include humor awareness (Klein, 1989), playfulness (McGhee, 1994), *everyday humor* (McGhee, 1994), humor appreciation and production (Klein, 1989; McGhee, 1994), jokes and stories (McGhee, 2010), and stress and humor (McGhee, 1993; Ruxton & Hester, 1987). If nothing else, infusing humor into leisure education presentations and activities could make leisure education more attractive to and productive for participants.

Considering humor's benefit to the immune system, TR Specialists might consider offering humorous materials to people with compromised immune systems such as people with AIDS, people recovering from extensive burns, people receiving treatment for cancer, and others. Also, during uncomfortable physical treatments, exposing participants to humorous material can increase pain thresholds. Although not all treatments are tedious, some can be. Introducing humor can make mundane and tedious tasks more attractive to participants. Humor can ease the pain associated with the recovery from surgery. Humor can be used to *break the ice* and to alleviate anxiety of people in treatment settings. Finally, humorous material may be beneficial in cognitive rehabilitation to aid in memorization skills.

Most commonly, TR Specialists interested in including an element of humor into their treatment have created humor rooms (complete with material such as videos, books, and other resources), humor carts (similar to humor rooms, but portable), funny movies, and skits produced by participants. While not interventions per se, such resources can be valued by clients in a variety of clinical settings.

Discussion Questions

1. Do you use humor to cope with stress? Can you think of a recent example?
2. What are some ways humor might be beneficial in a TR setting?
3. When is it inappropriate to use humor?
4. Which theory or theories of humor make the most sense to you?
5. What type of humor is most appropriate to TR?
6. What are some ways people can improve their senses of humor?
7. Is there enough evidence to support the use of humor in all TR settings?
8. Is humor a skill that can be taught?
9. What are some ways humor can be implemented into TR programs?
10. How might culture influence a sense of humor?

Resources

Agency Resources

Association for Applied and Therapeutic Humor
65 Enterprise
Aliso Viejo, CA 92656
888-747-2284
http://www.aath.org/

The Humor Project Website
http://humorproject.com
Email: humor@wizvax.net

Journal of Nursing Jocularity
P.O. Box 40416
Mesa, AZ 85274
http://www.jocularity.com

Laughing Matters
A newsletter for practitioners who want to incorporate humor into programs. For subscription information, write to:
The Humor Project
110 Spring St.
Saratoga Springs, NY 12866
Also available online: http://community.icontact.com/p/laughingmatters

References

Aarstad, H. J., Aarstad, A. K. H., Meimdal, J., & Olofsson, J. (2005). Mood, anxiety and sense of humor in head and neck cancer patients in relation to disease stage, prognosis and quality of life. *Acta Oto-Laryngologica, 125,* 557–565.

Austin, D. R. (2009). *Therapeutic recreation: Processes and techniques* (6th ed.). Champaign, IL: Sagamore.

Baker, R. (1993). Some reflections on humour in psychoanalysis. *International Journal of Psychoanalysis, 74,* 951–960.

Banning, M. R., & Nelson, D. L. (1987). The effects of activity-elicited humor and group structure on group cohesion and affective responses. *American Journal of Occupational Therapy, 41*(8), 510–514.

Bennett, M. P., Zeller, J. M., Rosenberg, L., & McCann, J. (2005). The effect of mirthful laughter on stress and natural killer cell activity. *Alternative Therapies in Health & Medicine, 9*(2), 38–45.

Berk, L. S., Tan, S. A., Fry, W. F., Napier, B. J., Lee, J. W., Hubbard, R. W., Lewis, J. E., & Eby, W. C. (1989). Neuroendocrine and stress hormone changes during mirthful laughter. *American Journal of the Medical Sciences, 289*(6), 390–396.

Bizi, S., Keinan, G., & Beit-Hallahmi, B. (1988). Humor and coping with stress: A test under real-life conditions. *Personality and Individual Differences, 9*(6), 961–956.

Booth-Butterfield, M., Booth-Butterfield, S., & Wanzer, M. (2007, August). Funny students cope better: Patterns of humor enactment and coping effectiveness. *Communication Quarterly, 55*(3), 299–315.

Brausa, R. (1993). The comedy club. *Psychosocial Rehabilitation Journal, 17*(2), 189–192.

Celso, B., Ebener, D., & Burkhead, E. (2003, November). Humor coping, health status, and life satisfaction among older adults residing in assisted living facilities. *Aging & Mental Health, 7*(6), 438.

Cogan, R., Cogan, D., Waltz, W., & McCue, M. (1987). Effects of laughter and relaxation on discomfort thresholds. *Journal of Behavioral Medicine, 10*(2), 139–145.

Cohen, S., Kamarck, T., & Mermelstein, R. (1983). Humor and laughter in social interaction and some implications for humor research. In P. E. McGhee & J. H. Goldstein (Eds.), *Handbook of humor research, 1* (pp. 135–157). New York: Springer-Verlag.

Cousins, N. (1979). *Anatomy of an illness.* New York: Norton.

Danzer, A., Dale, J. A., & Klions, H. L. (1990). Effect of exposure to humorous stimuli on induced depression. *Psychological Reports, 66,* 1027–1036.

Deaner, S. L., & McConatha, J. T. (1993). The relation of humor to depression and personality. *Psychological Reports, 72,* 755–763.

Dienstbier, R. A. (1996). The impact of humor on energy, tension, task choices, and attributions: Exploring hypotheses from toughness theory. *Motivation and Emotion, 19*(4), 255–267.

Dillon, K. M., Minchoff, B., & Baker, K. H. (1985). Positive emotional states and enhancement of the immune system. *International Journal of Psychiatry in Medicine, 15*(1), 13–17.

Dowling, J. S., Hockenberry, M., & Gregory, R. L. (2003). Sense of humor, childhood cancer stressors, and outcomes of psychosocial adjustment, immune function, and infection. *Journal of Pediatric Oncology Nursing, 20*(6), 271–292.

Eysenck, H. J., & Eysenck, S. B. G. (1968). *Manual for the Eysenck Personality Inventory.* San Diego: Educational and Industrial Testing Service.

Freud, S. (1928). Humor. *International Journal of Psychoanalysis, 9,* 1–6.

Freud, S. (1960). *Jokes and their relation to the unconscious.* New York: Norton.

Fry, W. F. (1963). *Sweet madness: A study of humor.* Palo Alto, CA: Pacific Books.

Gelkopf, M., & Sigal, M. (1995). It is not enough to have them laugh: Hostility, anger, and humor-coping in schizophrenic patients. *Humor, 8*(3), 273–284.

Gelkopf, M., Sigal, M., & Kramer, R. (1994). Therapeutic use of humor to improve social support in an institutionalized schizophrenic inpatient community. *Journal of Social Psychology, 134*(2), 175–182.

Goodman, J. B. (1983). How to get more smileage out of your life: Making sense of humor, then serving it. In P. McGhee & J. Goldstein (Eds.), *Handbook of humor research* (pp. 1–22). New York: Springer-Verlag.

Johnson, H. A. (1990) Humor as an innovative method for teaching sensitive topics. *Educational Gerontology, 16*(6) 547–559.

Kanner, A. D., Coyne, I. C., Schaefer, C., & Lazarus, R. S. (1981). Comparison of two modes of stress measurement: Daily hassles and uplifts versus major life events. *Journal of Behavioral Medicine, 4*, 1–39.

Keith-Spiegel, P. C. (1984). Eight humor theories. In M. Helitzer (Ed.), *Comedy techniques for writers and performers* (pp. 17–22). Athens, OH: Lawhead Press.

Klein, A. (1989). *The healing power of humor.* Los Angeles, CA: Tarcher.

Kuiper, N. A., Grimshaw, M., Leite, C., & Kirsh, G. (2004). Humor is not always the best medicine: Specific components of sense of humor and psychological well-being. *Humor, 17*, 135–168.

Kuiper, N. A., & Martin, R. A. (1993). Humor and self-concept. *Humor, 6*(3), 251–270.

Labott, S. M., Ahleman, S., Wolever, M. E., & Martin, R. B. (1990). The physiological and psychological effects of the expression and inhibition of emotion. *Behavioral Medicine, 16*(4), 182–189.

Lazarus, R. S., & Folkman, S. (1984). *Stress, appraisal, and coping.* New York: Springer.

Lefcourt, H. M., Davidson, K., & Kueneman, K. (1990). Humor and immune system functioning. *Humor: International Journal of Humor Research, 3*, 303–321.

Mahoney, D. L., Burroughs, W. J., & Hieatt, A. C. (2001). The effects of laughter on discomfort thresholds: Does expectation become reality? *Journal of General Psychology, 128*(2), 217–226.

Martin, R. A., & Dobbin, J. P. (1988). Sense of humor, hassles, and immune globulin A: Evidence for stress-moderating effect of humor. *International Journal of Psychiatry in Medicine, 18*(2), 93–105.

Martin, R. A., Kuiper, N. A., Olinger, L. J., & Dance, K. A. (1993). Humor, coping with stress, self-concept, and psychological well-being. *Humor, 6*(1), 89–104.

Martin, R. A., & Lefcourt, H. M. (1983). Sense of humor as a moderator of the relation between stressors and moods. *Journal of Personality and Social Psychology, 45*, 1313–1324.

Martin, R. A., & Lefcourt, H. M. (1984). The situational humor response questionnaire: A quantitative measure of the sense of humor. *Journal of Personality and Social Psychology, 47*, 145–155.

Martin, R. A., Puhlik-Doris, P., Larsen, G., Gray, J., & Weir, K. (2003). Individual differences in uses of humor and their relation to psychological well-being: Development of the Humor Styles Questionnaire. *Journal of Research in Personality, 37*, 48–75.

McGhee, P. E. (1979). *Humor: Its origins and development.* San Francisco: W. H. Freeman and Co.

McGhee, P. E. (Ed.). (1989). *Humor and children's development.* New York: Haworth Press.

McGhee, P. E. (1994). *How to develop your sense of humor.* Dubuque, IA: Kendall/Hunt.

McGhee, P. E. (2010). *Humor as survival training for a stressed-out world.* Bloomington, IN: Authorhouse.

McGuire, F. A., Boyd, R. K., & James, A. (1992). *Therapeutic humor with the elderly.* New York: Haworth Press.

McGuire, F. A., Backman, K. F., & Boyd, R. (1990). *The efficacy of humor in improving the quality of life for residents of long-term care facilities*. Washington DC: American Assocation for Retired Persons.

Mosak, H. H. (1987). *Ha ha and aha: The role of humor in psychotherapy*. Muncie, IN: Accelerated Development.

Nevo, O., Keinan, G., & Teshimovsky-Arditi, M. (1993). Humor and pain tolerance. *Humor, 6*(1), 71–88.

Pollio, D. E. (1995, June). Use of humor in crisis intervention. *Families in Society: Journal of Contemporary Human Services, 76*(6), 376–384.

Pollio, H. R. (1983). Notes toward a field theory of humor. In P. McGhee & J. Goldstein (Eds.), *Handbook of humor research* (pp. 213-230). New York: Springer Verlag.

Prerost, F. J. (1993). A strategy to enhance humor production among elderly persons: Assisting in the management of stress. *Activities, Adaptation and Aging, 14*(4), 17–24.

Radloff, L. S. (1977) The CES-D scale: A self report depression scale for research in the general population. *Applied Psychological Measurement, 1*, 385–401.

Richman, J. (1995). The lifesaving function of humor with the depressed and suicidal elderly. *The Gerontologist, 35*(2), 271–273.

Rotton, J., & Shats, M. (1996). Effects of state humor, expectancies, and choice on postsurgical mood and self-medication: A field experiment. *Journal of Applied Social Psychology, 26*(20), 1775–1794.

Roussi, P., Krikeli, V., Hatzidimitriou, C., & Koutri, I. (2007, February). Patterns of coping, flexibility in coping and psychological distress in women diagnosed with breast cancer. *Cognitive Therapy & Research, 31*(1), 97–109.

Rutherford, K. (1994). Humor in psychotherapy. *Individual Psychology, 50*(2), 207–222.

Ruxton, J. P., & Hester, M. P. (1987). Humor: Assessment and interventions. *International Journal of Aging & Human Development, 25*(1), 13–21.

Saper, B. (1990). The therapeutic use of humor for psychiatric disturbances of adolescents and adults. *Psychiatric Quarterly, 61*(4), 261–272.

Schmidt, S. R. (1994). Effects of humor on sentence memory. *Journal of Experimental Psychology, 20*(4), 953–967.

Scholl, J. (2007, May). The use of humor to promote patient-centered care. *Journal of Applied Communication Research, 35*(2), 156–176.

Scholl, J., & Ragan, S. L. (2003). The use of humor in promoting positive provider-patient interactions in a hospital rehabilitation unit. *Health Communication, 15*(3), 319–330.

Shultz, T. R. (1996). A cognitive-development analysis of humour. In A. J. Chapman & H. C. Foot (Eds.), *Humor and laughter* (pp. 11–36). New Brunswick, NJ: Transaction Publishers.

Simon, J. M. (1988). Therapeutic humor: Who's fooling who? *Journal of Psychosocial Nursing, 26*(4), 9–12.

Sumners, A. D. (1988). Humor: Coping in recovery from addiction. *Issues in Mental Health Nursing, 9*, 169–179.

Svebak, S. (1974). Revised questionnaire on the sense of humor. *Scandanavian Journal of Psychology, 15*, 328–331.

Szabo, A. (2003). The acute effects of humor and exercise on mood and anxiety. *Journal of Leisure Research, 35*(2), 152–162.

Thorson, J. A., & Powell, F. C. (1993). Development and validation of Multidimensional Sense of Humor Scale. *Journal of Child Psychology, 49,* 13–23.

Thorson, J. A., & Powell, F. C. (1994). Depression and sense of humor. *Psychological Reports, 75,* 1473–1474.

Walter, M., Hanni, B., Haug, M., Amrhein, I., Krebs-Roubicek, E., Muller-Spahn, F., & Savaskan, E. (2007). Humour therapy in patients with late-life depression or Alzheimer's disease: A pilot study. *International Journal of Geriatric Psychiatry, 22*(1), 77–83.

Zillmann, D., Rockwell, S., Schweitzer, K., & Sundar, S. S. (1993). Does humor facilitate coping with physical discomfort? *Motivation and Emotion, 17*(1), 1–21.

Zuckerman, M., & Lubin, B. (1965). *Manual for the multiple affect adjective check list.* San Diego: Educational and Industrial Testing Service.

Chapter 17
Therapeutic Use of Play

John Dattilo, Rachel Gordon, and Elizabeth Weybright

Play is to the child what thinking, planning,
and blueprinting are to the adult, a trial universe in which
conditions are simplified and methods exploratory,
so that past failures can be thought through, expectations tested.

—Erik Erikson

Introduction

Play provides people with a chance to enjoy themselves and learn a variety of skills. Play may be used by TR specialists as a medium to encourage individuals with disabilities to develop important skills.

According to many authors play as a therapeutic medium is associated with improved cognition, social interaction, and physical skills of children with disabilities. Play provides an opportunity for children to create and improve their learning. In addition, play can improve children's ability to cope with feelings such as anxiety and anger and in situations involving separation from parents. Children who have benefited from use of play as a therapeutic medium include those with physical and cognitive impairments, behavior and emotional problems, and children who have experienced abuse or chronic illness.

This chapter introduces use of play as a therapeutic medium. Included in this chapter is a definition of play as a therapeutic medium, description of how play may be used by TR specialists, and history of play as a therapeutic medium. Theories that support use of play as a therapeutic medium and a review of current literature on play provide information about effects of play. A case study is presented as an example of how a play intervention may be planned and implemented in a TR setting. Activities and discussion questions are offered to further understanding of use of play as a therapeutic medium.

Definitions

The following section presents characteristics of play and their definitions. Definitions are included for developmental stages of play, social levels of play, play therapy, and developmental therapeutic play. Examples are provided to clarify definitions of various characteristics, stages, and types of play. The following terms and phrases are defined:

- Play
- Cognitive Play Stages
- Social Levels of Play
- Play as a Therapeutic Medium

Play

Play is a complex activity that has several characteristics. There are many definitions of play and many professionals do not try to define play, but simply identify characteristics present for an action to be considered play. Characteristics of play include:

- Intrinsic Motivation
- Positive Affect
- Free Choice
- Fantasy
- Active Engagement

Intrinsic motivation. Intrinsic motivation is the process of doing an activity for its own sake, of doing an activity for the reward that is inherent in the activity itself (Deci, 1995). According to Johnson, Christie, and Yawkey (1987), motivation for play comes from within the individual and activities are pursued for their own sake. Typically, play is intrinsically motivating because people engage in it simply for inherent rewards found in play. Play is an "*end*" in and of itself rather than a means to an end.

> For example, Tonya, who plays in a sandbox and makes objects in the sand, receives no external reward; rather, she plays because it is fun. Children engage in play for its own sake and not to receive external reward such as prizes or verbal praise.

Positive affect. Positive affect includes behaviors which are marked by signs of pleasure and enjoyment (Johnson et al., 1987). For an action to be considered play, a child must value the experience and receive positive feelings associated with engagement in the activity.

> For example, Marcos, who repeatedly swings on a tire swing, may experience some fear and uncertainty, but he will continue to participate in the activity because of the excitement derived from the experience. A positive affect is often characterized by the presence of a smile or laugh.

Free choice. Free choice may be defined as an action involving selection without existence or perception of coercion and outside pressures. When children are assigned or forced to engage in an activity, they regard it as work rather than play. For an experience to be considered to be play it must be free from external influences.

> For example, Latisha decides to play a computer game without the influence from others and/or outside pressures.

Fantasy. Fantasy involves actions that are separated from reality. Within play, participants are "actors," and thus their actions are associated more with an *internal reality* rather than *external reality* (Johnson et al., 1987). Players merely act out an event. Actions by players are separated from reality in that participants may experiment with novel actions and risk failure without "real" consequences.

> For example, children who play "war" act out their characters as soldiers by carrying guns and hiding behind trees.

Active engagement. Active engagement is defined as a child being involved in play physically and psychologically while resisting being distracted or diverted from the activity (Hughes, 1991). When a child plays, the child is absorbed in the activity to the point where the child loses a sense of time and surroundings.

> For example, when Steven is playing captain of the ship at recess, he can become so absorbed in the activity that he is unaware of other students who are returning to the classroom.

Cognitive Play Stages

According to Piaget (1962), there are four stages of play that occur during different points of a child's cognitive development. The child progresses through stages as the child grows during the first year and continues through age five. The stages are:

- Sensorimotor play
- Construction play
- Symbolic play
- Games with rules

Sensorimotor play. Sensorimotor play involves repetitive actions of already learned sensory or motor activities that result in enjoyment associated with the activity (Hughes, 1991). Usually, sensorimotor play occurs during the child's first year, generally between 1–14 months of age. Typically, this type of play involves manipulation of objects without a particular goal.

> An example of this is baby Anna plays with a rattle.

Construction play. Construction play is the manipulation of objects with the intent of making something (Schaefer, 1993). During construction play, the child takes a clear interest in manipulating and creating something out of objects. Construction play generally occurs between 15–24 months of age.

> An example of this type of play would be Jeremiah is stacking
> blocks.

Symbolic play. Symbolic play is defined as using fantasy to change into different people, objects, or situations as evident by verbal expressions and motor movements (Schaefer, 1993). This stage of play typically begins during the second year of life and continues through age six.

> An example of this stage of play is Sonya who feeds her baby doll
> a bottle or plays dress-up.

Games with rules. Games with rules are defined as the active involvement of two or more in a competitive activity where the rules are agreed upon in advance (Hughes, 1991). By the age of five or six, children often begin to develop logic necessary for games with rules. There are two types of games with rules: competitive and cooperative.

Competitive games may be defined as activities directed consistently toward meeting a standard or achieving a goal in which performance by a person or by group is evaluated relative to that of selected people or groups (Martens, 1978). Competitive games often involve a winner and loser and typically entail elimination of participants who are unable to meet standards or performance. Examples of traditional competitive games include basketball, Simon Says, or Musical Chairs.

Cooperative games may be defined as structured games with rules that promote sharing, collaboration, getting along with others, and emphasizing group rather than individual goals (Glakas, 1991). Generally, this type of game promotes teamwork in which everyone works together to achieve a predetermined goal and competition between people or groups is discouraged.

> An example of a cooperative game is Musical Islands, a game
> similar to the traditional game of Musical Chairs. During Musical
> Islands, participants move from hoop to hoop while the music
> is playing; then, each participant must be standing inside a hoop
> when music stops. More than one person can stand in a hoop
> at one time. One hoop is removed each time before the music
> begins and participants assist one another in being in a hoop
> when the music stops. Eventually, only one hoop is left and all
> participants must work together so that they all fit into the hoop.
> Cooperative Musical Chairs (Orlick, 1978) is similar to Musical
> Islands, but participants can sit on one another's laps instead of
> standing in Hula-Hoops.

Social Levels of Play

Parten (1932) identified several levels of play referred to as *social levels of play*. The social levels of play differ from cognitive stages of play in that they are not dependent on cognitive development. Even though children tend to progress to higher levels of social play, all levels of social play occur throughout a person's life.

For example, once Lazarus has mastered a level of play, it is common for him to attempt higher levels of play. However, at other times he will continue to play at lower levels of play. For instance, Lazarus may exhibit cooperative play while playing *house* for 5 minutes and then, during the next 5 minutes, exhibit parallel play while in the sand box.

The primary social levels of play are:

- Solitary play
- Parallel play
- Associative play
- Cooperative play

Solitary play. Solitary play is defined as appropriate action directed toward an object in the environment which may or may not involve proximity to another individual and does not include other individuals (Schleien, Mustonen, Rynders, & Fox, 1990). During solitary play, a child plays independently with no reference to others.

For example, Clarisse may build a castle alone while she is sitting in a corner away from others.

Parallel play. Parallel play is defined as independent play occurring near others (Schaefer, 1993). During parallel play, children may play with the same materials and/or within close proximity to each other but they are not playing with each other.

For instance, although William and Tanasha are both pretending to cook, they do not speak to one another, nor do they make eye contact.

Associative play. Associative play is defined as active involvement of two or more children for short periods of time (Leme, 1993). Associative play is characterized by a child playing with other children with little organization. Although children may play with each other, the individual child's needs and interest take precedence over the groups' needs and interests. Groups exhibiting associative play are often composed of two to three children who interact with each other. Interactions occurring with associative play typically are sustained for short periods of time.

For example, Hiro and Jessica are both playing in a sandbox when Jessica helps Hiro by placing an object on a sandcastle. After this act, the children quickly return to the separate tasks in the sand.

Cooperative play. Cooperative play is organized play intended to meet a group goal chosen by the players. This level of play consists of group play, specific roles, and active cooperation for sustained intervals of time (Schaefer, 1993).

> Examples of this level of play are cooperative games and socio-dramatic play. Socio-dramatic play is defined as social play that has role-plays, reciprocal interaction, persistence, verbal communication, and make-believe present (Throp, Stahmer, & Schreibman, 1995).

Play as a Therapeutic Medium

Play is a medium that allows people to experience autonomy and provides them with opportunities for success and to be in charge of their actions. McMahon (1992) stated that play is a spontaneous and active process in which thinking, feeling, and doing can flourish since they are separated from fear of failure or terrible consequences. Because of these characteristics, play may become an effective therapeutic medium.

Play becomes therapeutic when its intent is to bring a positive change in children who have disabling or limiting conditions. Landreth (1991) suggested that for children to play out their experiences and feelings is the most natural, dynamic, and self-healing process in which children engage. Play as a therapeutic medium can involve use of:

- Nondirective play therapy
- Directive play therapy

Nondirective play therapy. Nondirective play may be used in many different therapeutic ways by several disciplines including TR. Nondirective therapeutic play is an intervention that begins at the child's current cognitive or social play stage and provides support and experiences needed to move the child to the next stage of play. This form of play may be used to improve social, cognitive, and physical abilities in children with disabilities.

> For example, Claire and Mohinder might be taught to build a house with blocks. While they build the house, they are provided with verbal prompts intended to help them imagine what could be happening in the house. This assistance may help these children move from construction play and it might help them improve verbal skills (McMahon, 1992).

Directive play therapy. Directive play therapy creates a natural setting in which children explore their feelings and practice new skills with their peers (Trounson-Chaiken, 1996). This type of play provides children with a realistic social framework where they can practice social interaction skills and develop friendships without fear of rejection (Bell et al., 1989). Directive play therapy is primarily used by clinical psychologists as a modality to treat children's emotional and psychological disturbances.

Summary

Play contains several defining characteristics that include: intrinsic motivation, positive affect, free choice, fantasy, and active engagement. Play as a therapeutic medium differs from typically occurring play in that play situations are designed to meet participant needs. Several cognitive types and social levels of play may be used to meet needs of individuals. Typically, children progress through various types of play from 6 months to 6 years.

Two ways in which play is used as a therapeutic medium include nondirective and directive play. Generally, nondirective play therapy is conducted by a child psychologist and uses play to improve children's emotional skills and help children meet intrapersonal needs. Directive therapeutic play builds on children's current play level to improve social, cognitive, physical, and play skills. TR specialists may use play as a therapeutic medium to provide children with opportunities to develop and improve a variety of skills.

Descriptions

Depending on individual needs, play may be used to teach and improve verbal communication, friendship development, coordination, problem solving, and coping strategies. There are several ways in which play may be used as therapeutic medium. This section provides general guidelines on how to use play as a therapeutic intervention from setting up the environment to the facilitator's role during the session and is divided into:

- Nondirective Play Therapy
- Directive Play Therapy

Nondirective Play Therapy

According to Axline (1947), nondirective play therapy is based on the belief that play, especially for children, is the most natural medium of expression. In nondirective play therapy, toys are viewed as words and people's interactions with toys are interpreted as language.

A distinctive characteristic of nondirective or humanistic play is the role portrayed by the therapist. According to Rasmussen and Cunningham (1995), a nondirective play therapist maintains the following characteristics.

The therapist develops a warm, friendly relationship with the child; accepts the child exactly as he or she is; facilitates free expression of feelings by establishing a feeling of permissiveness; and encourages development of insight by reflecting the child's feelings. The therapist respects the child's ability to solve his or her own problems, make choices, and institute change; refrains from directing the child's actions or conversation; allows therapy to be a gradual, unhurried process; and establishes only those limitations that are necessary to anchor the therapy to the real world and to encourage the child to be responsible in the therapeutic relationship.

The role of the nondirective play therapist is purposeful in nature; however, the course and responsibility of nondirective play is at the discretion of participants. The intent is to provide participants with an opportunity for expression in an environment in which they are free from external pressures (Cattanbach, 1994).

According to Axline (1947), nondirective play therapy begins where individuals are encourages them to go as far as their abilities allow. Children are given opportunities for exploration and growth, are treated with respect, and are given unconditional acceptance. Participants can develop a sense of security within the play environment. According to Axline, therapy sessions are intended to assist children to become mature individuals capable of coping with stressful situations. Components central to effective nondirective play therapy include:

- Facilitator
- Setting
- Participants
- Materials
- Evaluation

Facilitator. Facilitators set the tone for each play session. To be successful, facilitators display unconditional acceptance and understanding such as listening to children and actively participating in play sessions (Cattanbach, 1994).

> For example, when Ando becomes upset, a facilitator might say, "I see that you are feeling sad. Is there anything I can do to make you feel better?"

Facilitators focus their attention on the play session and are sensitive to the needs of each participant. During play sessions, facilitators encourage children to make choices and become responsible for their actions (Trouson-Chaiken, 1996).

> For instance, Maya may approach a facilitator and the child may request that the facilitator play with her. The facilitator will then take an active role in play after the invitation to play.

Typically, facilitators do not initiate play with the child; rather, the facilitator waits for a child's request and then responds. By placing the child in the role of initiator, the facilitator supports the child in developing a sense of autonomy.

Facilitators set limits for the group by presenting rules that are concise and clear. Also, facilitators decide when to present rules; they may choose to explain rules at the beginning of the group play therapy session or present them as necessary (Troester, 1996). When deciding how to present rules, Landreth (1991) provided a helpful acronym, *ACT: acknowledge* the child's feelings, *communicate* limits, and *target* acceptable behaviors.

> For example, when Isaac screams at Simone, the facilitator might say, *It seems you are feeling angry right now. During play sessions, we treat each other with respect. This means that we treat others*

how we would want to be treated. Next time you become angry,
let's try talking to Maya and explain why she is upsetting you or
why you are angry with her.

Setting. The play room is critical to therapy because the room is the first thing children see (Landreth, 1993). It is important that the play room is free of distractions that occur as a result of open windows and cluttered walls (McMahon, 1992). The room's floors, walls, and furniture should be durable. Vinyl floors, washable, neutral paint on the walls, and plastic chairs are preferable in the playroom (Landreth, 1991). It is critical to have a room that can withstand children's play as well as provide a friendly and welcoming atmosphere. Furthermore, it is helpful if play rooms are structured.

As an example, building blocks can be stored in containers on shelves
and art materials can be placed in containers near the art table.

Participants. The number and type of children who participate in play therapy depends on participants' needs. For instance, it is not recommended to have two children who have experienced physical abuse in the same group with two children who are physically aggressive. It is helpful if children in groups have similar backgrounds and experiences so the children may learn from one another (Troester, 1996).

For example, Micah, Elle, and Noah who experience separation
anxiety may learn from one another in various ways. They may
play together and play out their feelings of separation or they may
see how another child has overcome this anxiety and model the
behavior of their peers. For instance, Micah and Elle may observe
Noah who stops playing when he becomes anxious. The children
then observe Noah who moves to an area where he reduces his
anxiety by listening to soft soothing music.

Landreth (1991) suggested that the number of participants in group play therapy should not exceed six in each play session, but contain at least three participants in each group. The children should be within 2 years of age (Sugar, 1991). Despite a close age range, children's developmental levels may be different and can cause problems.

For instance, 3- and 5-year-old children may communicate very
differently. Many 3-year-old children may just be learning how to
express themselves, whereas 5-year-old children often have larger
vocabularies and can express themselves more effectively.

Materials. Although various toys and materials are important to include in a group play therapy session, these materials vary depending on session objectives (Trounson-Chaiken, 1996). For instance, a group of children working on social skills can benefit from materials that encourage interaction such as puppets (see Figure 17.1 on p. 524), kitchen utensils, or musical instruments.

Figure 17.1

It is helpful if materials encourage children to express various feelings and contain media such as a sand table, puzzles, and dress-up clothes. Age-appropriate materials play a critical role in how children express themselves and the degree to which they explore their environment. Toys are age-appropriate when they are of interest to children of a certain age.

> For example, 10-year-old children should have materials available that may be of interest to them such as puzzles or board games, rather than toys such as rattles or blocks, which are associated with infants and toddlers.

Evaluation. There are several ways to evaluate children's behaviors during play therapy. One technique may include videotaping frequency or duration of a behavior such as play initiations. Facilitators may observe children's behaviors during play sessions and write anecdotal reports. Formal assessments can be administered before and after a play therapy program (Trounson-Chaiken, 1996). In each type of assessment, it is helpful to identify and define target behaviors.

> For example, if a group contained children with anxiety problems, a target behavior may include the ability to verbally express oneself during high-stress situations.

Summary. Nondirective play therapy can promote independence, maturity, and coping skills. Components central to effective nondirective play therapy include facilitator, setting, participants, materials, and evaluation. It is important for therapists to consider each person's needs when implementing a group play therapy program.

Directive Play Therapy

Directive play therapy, also known as developmental therapeutic play, focuses on providing experiences necessary to increase the chance that children master a skill or set of skills (McMahon, 1992). Some skills which directive play can address include communication, motor performance, and cognitive awareness. During play sessions, the facilitator provides assistance when the child needs assistance.

> For example, similar to nondirective therapy, if Gabriel is learning how to request help when needed, the facilitator waits for him to initiate a request for help. However, with directive play, if Gabriel does not initiate within a certain time period, the facilitator may provide a verbal prompt (i.e., verbal reminder) to help him learn to request assistance.

In directive play, specific goals and interventions are established when working with children who have disabilities. Generally, during directive play sessions there is a period of skill instruction followed by free play when children can practice skills (Skellenger & Hill, 1994). Directive play can be conducted individually or in small groups, depending on the needs of the individuals.

Facilitators. When preparing for directive play, it is helpful to consider that a child's age will not necessarily determine what skills need to be developed (Leme, 1993).

> For example, a facilitator working with Milo may decide to use socio-dramatic play; however, if he has not mastered parallel play or cannot imitate, Milo will likely encounter difficulties in socio-dramatic play.

Although a child's age may not determine the skills taught, the child's age is considered when determining appropriateness of activities. That is, activities traditionally engaged in by young children are not typically used with older children. Similar to nondirective play therapy, the activities chosen by the facilitator should be age-appropriate and related to the predetermined play objectives (Leme, 1993).

> For example, Hayden, who is 8-years-old and working on hand grip strength, could use a foam ball or plastic baseball bat during play rather than a squeaky Elmo doll.

Facilitators may use a variety of techniques to teach children skills and to encourage their independence in play. Providing verbal and physical prompts can be effective (Broad & Butterworth, 1991). Prompts are commonly used to promote use of appropriate behavior. Schleien, Ray, and Green (1997) identified four common types of prompts including: gesture prompts such as using your hand to motion someone, verbal prompts such as verbal reminders, model prompts such as physically demonstrating desired behavior, and physical prompts such as physically guiding or assisting a child.

Prompts should only be used to help the child start play movement. Once a prompt hierarchy is developed such as verbal, gesture, model, and physical, practitioners can systematically move from least to most intrusive prompt until the child initiates or completes the task, a technique referred to as *system of least prompts* (Cooper et al., 1987).

It is helpful to stipulate the amount of time that a facilitator waits after delivering a prompt before another prompt is provided, such as 10 seconds for the child to initiate movement. As desired behavior occurs more frequently, the prompt is phased out until the child independently demonstrates the behavior.

It is important to provide reinforcement consistently for the correct behavior as well as for close approximations of the desired behavior. *Reinforcement* is the delivery of a consequence that makes the behavior occur more or less often. The technique chosen will depend on the objectives and needs of each child.

> For example, since Ali is visually impaired, modeling and gestures would not be appropriate; however, often the technique of forward chaining in conjunction with physical guidance when the facilitator guides her through the desired behavior may be more appropriate to use.

Setting. The setting will depend on number of participants and goals.

> For example, if Masi's goal is *learning to initiate play with other peers*, then an appropriate setting would be an inclusive playroom or an isolated area with a small group of children.

The environment should make the children feel secure and comfortable. Materials can be organized and set up before the children enter the room. It is helpful to avoid crowding children because it interferes with their ability to process information and focus their attention on specific toys or activities. The environment is arranged to encourage children to be independent and explore.

Some children with disabilities have difficulties with social situations and peer relations. TR specialists may want to consider structuring the play setting to promote play among children. Structuring the play setting may provide more opportunities for social interactions between children with and without disabilities to occur.

> For example, a TR specialist may restrict the physical space in which children may play with the intention of increasing the chance that social interactions will occur.

Participants. The number of participants engaged in directive therapeutic play will vary with individual needs. It is desirable to have participants with and without disabilities participate in small groups. The groups may include 3–4 participants. Individuals who may benefit from this type of therapeutic play are children with cognitive and motor impairments, social skills deficits, and behavior problems (McMahon, 1992).

TR specialists are encouraged to consider teaching children without disabilities to initiate conversations with children with disabilities. Peer modeling involves selecting good candidates who will comply with requests made by a professional, regularly attend programs, exhibit age-appropriate play skills, have limited social history with children with disabilities, and express a willingness to participate. These children are then taught to initiate conversations with children who have disabilities, and then all children are prompted to play together.

Materials. Materials will also depend on participant goals. When selecting materials the facilitator can ask questions, such as: "Will this toy provide opportunities for interactions?" and "Are the materials chosen age-appropriate?" (Leme, 1993). The materials can provide opportunities to develop independence as well as increase chance of children's involvement in the learning process.

Pellegrini and Jones (1994) offered insights into using toys as part of the instructional environment. The facilitator can choose toys that may elicit children's target behaviors. It is important for the facilitator to be aware of certain toys that a child favors. Children will play for longer periods of time when using highly desirable toys. One way to determine what toys are highly desirable is to observe children with a variety of toys and note the amount of time spent interacting with certain toys.

Selection of play materials and activities may promote play between children with and without disabilities.

For example, Loy and Dattilo (2000) suggested that organized games such as Twister may be more effective in promoting social interactions between children with and without disabilities than free play (see Figure 17.2). Socio-dramatic activities such as playing house or acting out a scene from a story may be more effective in promoting play between children with and without disabilities than free play.

Figure 17.2

Evaluation. There are several ways to evaluate participants' progress. If a goal is to increase frequency of initiations of play with another peer, the number of times participant initiated play with peers can be recorded for a designated period of time.

Many behaviors may be divided into individual steps through a *task analysis*. A facilitator may perform a task analysis of the target behavior and record observations about each step of the task and what level of prompt was administered. A systematic recording procedure provides clear and important information to the facilitator.

For example, a facilitator can record what prompt was administered to Clint on each step of the task of throwing a ball. After reviewing

Clint's progress over several sessions, the facilitator may discover that Clint is not initiating or completing a particular step such as picking up the ball. The facilitator can modify the teaching technique based on the information on the data sheet.

Formal assessments and anecdotal recordings may be used depending on the behavior being measured.

For instance, Angela's goal may include improving balance. A formal assessment may be used to assess improvement or anecdotal recording may be used where the facilitator provides information on what activity in which Angela was engaged, how much assistance was provided, and how long she remained balanced.

Summary. Several guidelines are given in this section. Careful considerations about the setting, materials, and methods of evaluation can help increase success of developmental therapeutic play sessions. The setting used in directive therapeutic play is structured and contains a variety of materials that are age-appropriate and geared toward specific goals of participants. The evaluation used reflects program effects and identifies participants' progress, or lack thereof. Finally, it is important to be aware of the impact the facilitator has on determining the success of a program.

History

Although the history of play and its significance have been identified since ancient times, the therapeutic use of play has been recognized and studied only recently. This section of the chapter contains a brief history of the therapeutic use of play. Several theorists who first introduced and demonstrated how play may be used as a therapeutic medium are identified in this section. A description of the current state of play as a therapeutic medium concludes the chapter.

In the first part of the twentieth century, play was viewed as being necessary for the social adjustment of children (Hughes, 1991). Sigmund Freud was the first to record use of play in therapy. Freud sought to apply adult psychoanalytical principles through the child's natural medium of communication, play.

Melanie Klein also used play extensively in psychotherapy (Yawkey & Pellegrini, 1984). In 1927, she was the first to apply rules for working with children. She developed *play analysis* that allowed her to examine children's play behavior which revealed their unconscious thoughts.

The first 20 years of the twentieth century were characterized and dominated by Freud's psychoanalytical principles. By the 1940s, the Rogerian School of nondirective psychotherapy became a dominant force in play therapy (Yawkey & Pellegrini, 1984). Emphasis of this therapy was on child and therapist interactions. The process involved creating an environment of complete acceptance and respect to facilitate the child's self-awareness and self-direction. Although the early pioneers who used play as a therapeutic medium used play in varying ways, play was recognized to have an important role in development and growth of a child (Schaefer, 1976).

Today, many disciplines use play as a therapeutic medium and there is less emphasis on interpretation and self-awareness. Although play therapy is reemerging within the field of child psychology, structured approaches are being used across disciplines (Malone & Langone, 1994). Structured approaches emphasize individual goals, employ clear methods to achieve goals, are client-centered, and utilize the arts, drama, and free play as forms of treatment (Hughes, 1991).

Summary. The emergence of play as a therapeutic medium appeared during the twentieth century. Society began to view play as a valuable part of the child's life. Psychologists such as Freud and Erikson brought play to the forefront and demonstrated the effectiveness of play in working with children (Erikson, 1950). There are several forms of play therapy and structured play approaches being used today.

Theoretical Foundations

This section provides a description of several theories associated with play and their role in child development. The theories presented provide different perspectives on play as a therapeutic medium. Each theory attempts to explain the role of play and demonstrates its benefits to children. The following are theories presented in this section of the chapter:

- Developmental Theory
- Psychosocial Theory
- Sociocultural Theory

Developmental Theory

Piaget (1962) explained play as an activity that influences cognition and associated development. According to Piaget, there are several cognitive stages through which a child progresses. Play is an integral part of the first three stages, including:

- Sensorimotor (0 to 2 years)
- Preoperational (2 to 7 years)
- Concrete operations (7 to 11 years)

Each stage builds on the earlier stage and incorporates previous stages of development. The *sensorimotor stage* is characterized by motor development, exploration of one's body, development of object permanence, and experimentation with objects in the environment. Next, the *preoperational stage* is characterized by development of language and socialization behaviors. Finally, the *concrete operations stage* is characterized by development of logical operations. During the stage of concrete operations, Piaget believed that the child becomes a social being when the child's language is social and communicative. The ability to make logical decisions and solve concrete problems such as fixing a toy or following directions to a game characterizes the concrete operations stage (Wadsworth, 1979).

There are two important processes defined which help a person advance from one stage to the next (Wortman & Loftus, 1988):

- Assimilation
- Accommodation

Wortman and Loftus (1988) defined ***assimilation*** as a process that involves incorporating new information into old ways of thinking or behaving. ***Accommodation*** is the process where people change their way of thinking to adapt to new information (Wortman & Loftus). These two stages must be in balance for an individual to advance to the next level of play.

> For example, Tawny, who believes the word *circle* refers only to balls attends a circus and observes tigers jumping through hoops. She then recognizes the hoops as circles and assimilates this new information into his already-existing understanding. As she grows older, Tawny attends school and is told that wheels on cars are circles. She must now adapt her way of thinking to include the new information into her already existing understanding. This is an example of a*ccommodation*.

Piaget (1962) defined play as the primacy of assimilation over accommodation. For an act to be considered play, it must be done for enjoyment.

> For example, Leonard plays by raising his hands over his head so that he can watch that movement rather than to perform a functional task such as initiating a request. Play serves as a means for Leonard to enjoy and control his environment.

Three types of play are described by Piaget as acts that help a child master the first three levels of intelligence, including sensorimotor, preoperational, and concrete operational. These types of play are:

- Practice play
- Symbolic play
- Play with rules

Practice play involves the repetition of activities, primarily motor activities, until a child develops a sense of mastery. As the child grows, repetitive motor activities diminish and ***symbolic play*** becomes evident as the child begins to use fantasy and imagination. ***Play with rules*** begins to be exhibited around age four and requires at least two people. According to Piaget (1962), the purpose of rules is to acquaint the child with the norms of a social group; therefore, during this form of play, a child learns how to relate with others. Schleien, Heyne, and Dattilo (1995) added that social skill development in children with developmental disabilities is a direct result of advanced play and game playing skills.

Piaget (1962) described play as an activity that is directly related to intellectual acts. Play is the only time when *assimilation* dominates *accommodation* by allowing the child to take control. Therefore, children learn to master their environment through play by repetition of activities. Play serves as a means for children to develop cognitive skills.

Psychosocial Theory

Erikson hypothesized that personality is shaped by outside factors such as society's expectations and social interactions (Wortman & Loftus, 1988). Erikson identified eight stages of life crises that individuals experience. The stages explain personality traits developed depending on how a person resolves each crisis. If a person resolves a challenge positively, positive personality traits emerge which help in overcoming other challenges.

Erikson explained how play aids a child in resolving various challenges in life, thus resulting in development of positive personality traits. Play is a function of the ego, an attempt to bring into synchronization bodily and social processes (Erikson, 1950). Therefore, Erikson believed that the primary purpose of play is ego mastery. He described play as an activity that allows children to gain control over their experiences and their environment.

> The example Erikson used was of a boy who builds a tower and knocks it down. To Erikson, this act may be seen as the child gaining mastery over a previously passive event of learning to walk where a child stands up and wobbles and falls down. By building the tower and knocking it down, the child's ego has gained control over the experience.

According to Erikson, play is divided into three spheres:

- Autosphere
- Microsphere
- Macrosphere

Autosphere is responsible for *autocosmic play*, which occurs during the first life crisis. During this stage of play, the ego is introduced to the world. Children's play during the autosphere centers on their bodies and exploration as they begin to play with other people and things.

The second sphere is ***microsphere***. Play in this category focuses on the small world of manageable toys. Children return to this *thing-world* when they need to *overhaul* their ego. It is important for a child to be properly guided so that the child gains a sense of mastery and derives pleasure from experiences.

The last sphere is ***macrosphere***. Generally, the macrosphere stage occurs during preschool years and is characterized by *the world shared with others*. Play in this sphere focuses on social play.

Erikson emphasized the importance of moving through each sphere with success. Learning is critical so that children acquire knowledge of the content belonging in the correct sphere since each contains its own reality and mastery. Erikson proposed that play is the infantile form of dealing with experiences by creating model situations and to master reality by experiment and planning. Play provides opportunities for children to experience consistent success which Erikson believes is the only way for their egos to become stronger.

Sociocultural Theory

Vygotsky (1967) focused on the social aspect of play which contributes to cognitive development. To him, a child's *capabilities* are shaped by culture and social relationships in which a child is raised. Nicolopoulou (1993) provided a discussion of Vygotsky's sociocultural theory, which is the basis of the description of the theory and stated that play is a social symbolic activity. Cognitive processes are developed through communication with the environment and social interaction with others. According to Nicolopoulou, a child learns and develops in a social context that includes more knowledgeable and capable peers and adults who convey cultural heritage.

A central concept of Vygotsky's theory is the *zone of proximal development*, defined as the difference between a child's actual developmental level as determined by independent problem solving and the level of potential development as determined through problem solving under adult guidance or in collaboration with more capable peers (Vygotsky, 1978). The zone of proximal development is dependent on the social interactions with others.

According to Vygotsky, two components of play include an imaginary situation and rules implicit in the imaginary situation. Thus, play moves along a continuum in which components are not separate, but rather interrelated. Vygotsky believed that as children grow older, their needs and desires become greater and more complex.

Play provides a situation for children to explore their unrealized needs and desires. To achieve this state, children must voluntarily submit to the rules within the imaginary situation that requires them to practice self-control. By practicing self-control, a child learns how to interact with others in social situations structured by rules.

Vygotsky asserted that during preschool years, play serves as the zone of proximal development. "In play, a child is always above his average age, above his daily behavior; in play, it is as though he were a head taller than himself" (p. 16). Therefore, play may be viewed as an activity that prepares children to advance their cognition through stimulation of their imagination which leads to a more advanced way of thinking (Nicolopoulou, 1993).

Summary

This section presented several different theories of play. Each theory contributes to identifying the complexity of play and each theory offers unique perspectives that guide many programs that promote play. Based on works of Piaget, Erikson, and Vygotsky, conclusions can be drawn that play promotes development of cognition, personality, and understanding of social structures within society.

Effectiveness

Play has been used as an intervention in many disciplines with children with developmental disabilities, physical disabilities, and psychological problems. This section presents literature on play as a therapeutic medium. The following areas are examined in this section of the chapter:

- Nondirective Play Therapy
- Directive Play Therapy

Nondirective Play Therapy

The studies presented in this section are reflective of the humanistic or nondirective philosophy of play. Collectively, these studies are indicative of the effectiveness of nondirective play for a variety of individuals with disabilities.

Using a pre- and post-test comparison group design, **Danger and Landreth (2005)** examined effects of a 7-month child-centered group play therapy intervention on articulation, receptive language, expressive language, and anxiety of children with speech difficulties. Twenty-one children (ages 4–6) with speech difficulties were randomly divided into comparison and experimental groups. The experimental group with 11 children received 25 group play therapy sessions along with their regularly scheduled speech therapy. The comparison group with 10 children received only their regularly scheduled speech therapy sessions. Details about the group play therapy intervention and the speech therapy sessions were not provided; however, participants were evaluated before and after the intervention by a speech pathologist using the Goldman Fristoe Test of Articulation (GFTA) (Goldman & Fristoe, 2000) and the Clinical Evaluation of Language Fundamentals Third Edition (CELF-3) (Wilig, Secord, & Semel, 1992). To evaluate anxiety levels of participants, both parents and teachers completed Burk's Behavior Rating Scale (BBRS) (Burks, 1977) pre- and post-intervention. There was an increase in articulation, receptive language, and expressive language for children receiving play therapy compared to those receiving speech therapy alone. Although these findings are promising, differences were not statistically significant and the sample was small.

Using a longitudinal pre- and post-test design, **Reyes and Asbrand (2005)** examined effects of an individual nondirective play therapy intervention (1 x wk, 50-min session) on children (ages 7–16) who were sexually abused. The study purpose was to determine if the intervention reduced symptoms of the trauma related to sexual abuse. The study began with 43 participants; however, by the end of the 9-month period only 18 (13 females) remained. The Trauma Symptom Checklist for Children (TSCC) (Briere, 1996) was used to assess trauma symptoms pre- and post-intervention. Details about interventions were not provided; however, all sessions were conducted in an office using the same play therapy toys such as sand trays, puppets, clay, dolls, books, and various board games. Various significant findings were found including a relationship between the sexual offender and duration of abuse. Children that were abused by a family member had a significantly longer duration of abuse than children abused by a non-family member. Children participating in the intervention significantly reduced their symptoms of anxiety, depression, and post-traumatic stress. However, the intervention did not have a significant impact on anger, dissociation, fantasies, and sexual concerns. While this study demonstrated several significant findings, it had limitations, such as a small sample and limited description of the nondirective intervention.

Using a case study design, **Josefi and Ryan (2004)** analyzed effects of a nondirective play therapy intervention on a 6-year-old boy with severe autism. The intervention consisted of 16 1-hour videotaped play therapy sessions conducted at school over 5 months. Materials present at each session provided expressive, imaginative, relaxing, and interactive opportunities such as finger paints, Play-Doh, musical instruments, puppets, dolls, and pretend food. The therapist and a trained independent observer collected and analyzed qualitative and quantitative data. The qualitative analysis used recurring themes of attachment, autonomy, symbolic play development, and nurture to determine progress. The quantitative analysis was used to scrutinize categories of the child's behavior. Categories included child-initiated physical contact with therapist, child-initiated play activities, time spent by child on play activities, and time spent by child on ritualistic or obsessive activities. Each behavior was matched to the appropriate quantitative themes and was tested for significance. Results indicated that nondirective play therapy is an effective approach for increasing autonomy, play development and initiative, as well as improving social interactions; however, nondirective play therapy resulted in only minor reductions in ritualistic behaviors.

Using a pre- and post-test design, **Scott, Burlingame, Starling, Porter, and Lilly (2003)** examined effects of 7–13 individual client-centered play therapy sessions on mood, self-concept, and social competence of 26 children (ages 3–9) who had experienced sexual abuse. The Abuse Behavior Checklist (ABC) (Chaffin & Wherry, 1993), the Joseph Preschool and Primary Self-Concept Screening Test (JPPSCS) (Joseph, 1979; Sweetland & Keyser, 1986), and the Behavior Assessment System for Children-Parents Rating Scale (BASC-PRS) (Reynolds & Kamphaus, 1992) were administered to participants and their parents prior to the initial therapy session and again 2 months post-therapy. The Social-Environmental Update (Scott & Porter, 1995), a qualitative questionnaire not included with the pre-test assessments, was completed 2 months post-therapy. No details of the sessions were provided. Overall, varied levels of support for child-centered play therapy were found. Although a third of participants demonstrated improvement in mood, social competence, self-esteem, and self-concept, other results indicated that the intervention made no significant positive changes and participation for some children might be contraindicated. Some limitations of this study are sample size, limited duration of therapy sessions, and limited information about the intervention.

Troester (1996) used a case study to examine effects of a 3-year therapeutic play group (1 x wk, 60-min sessions) on social skills and group cohesion for three elementary-aged children with severe-profound hearing loss in a special education class. The facilitator monitored children's play and only played an active role when requested by the children. During group sessions, the children selected play activities and were presented with rules. During the first year, individual and athletic activities were used and, initially, the children displayed frustration and anger. However, by the end of the first year, the children began to compromise, relax, and engage in activities longer. The second year was characterized by formation of group cohesion and children replacing negative behaviors with positive ones, such as turn taking, helping others, and listening to others. The group activities moved from athletic activities to games such as hide and seek and mutual activities such as playing train, in which the children played together in a cooperative manner. The third year was characterized by improved communication among members, formation of a complete team, and an increase in team activities. Teachers and mothers reported generalization to other settings and people. Follow-up showed that all three children maintained their social skills and continued to improve those skills. The three children were moved from self-contained to regular education classrooms. Although the case study showed promising results, formal measurements were not used to assess reported improvements and a control group was not used to address alternate explanations such as maturation and history. Finally, generalization and follow-up sessions were not conducted systematically.

Trounson-Chaiken (1996) examined effects of an 8-month group play therapy program (1 x wk, 45-min sessions) on five preschoolers (ages 2–5) experiencing separation difficulties, cognitive and language delays, aggression, depression, and delayed social development. A case study described changes in the group and children at different phases of therapy conducted in a large hospital room containing several pieces of furniture and toys. Facilitators were active play participants who promoted interactions. Sessions started and ended with group songs and games. Throughout sessions, children played with toys either individually or in groups. As therapy progressed, fewer toys were presented to promote interaction. Clinical vignettes were used to demonstrate progression of group from first phase (confusion and chaos among children and facilitators) to the second phase (stability and security and a shift from individual to more group activities) and to the third phase (group cohesion). Facilitators reported all children showed improvements in language development, independence, social skills, and mastering their feelings. The case study provides information about progression of the play group and children's improvements; however, since the study lacked reliable and valid measurements, caution is advised when considering findings.

Boulanger and Langevin (1992) used a pre- and post-treatment design to examine effects of a 12-week group play therapy (1 x wk, 60-min sessions) on social skills of five 5-year-old boys diagnosed with either oppositional defiant behavior, attention deficit hyperactivity disorder, over-anxiety disorder, or avoidant behavior. During each 30-minute session, the children chose activities and facilitators were passive. Activities such as storytelling, drawing, and role-playing were allowed children to work through certain feelings such as mood changes, accepting positive and negative feedback, and resolving peer conflicts. Facilitators imitated appropriate behaviors with peers to encourage development of social skills. Pre- and post-tests were conducted during the second and fifteenth sessions with no involvement by facilitators. Using the Direct Observation Form to assess behaviors, increases in offering help, apologizing, negotiating, forgiving, and expressing feelings of guilt and gratitude were noted. Maturation and frequent interaction with other children may have influenced children's improvements. Absence of a control group and having two different facilitators reduce confidence in results. Children's contact with facilitators may have accounted for improvements and not play therapy.

Bell and colleagues (1989) compared two groups (treatment and control) of 142 school-aged children who had some form of deprivation (social, environmental, and/or educational). The 72 children in the treatment group received play group therapy. Treatment was conducted for 10 sessions with 5–6 children in each group. Teachers rated the child's behavior, assessments of verbal and reading ability, and social data during baseline. During treatment, type of play and behavior was monitored. Two therapists supervised each group and did not actively participate in play unless invited to play by a participant. Increases in creative play were observed. Because of there were few sessions, children may not have had a chance to develop a positive rapport with other children and supervisors in the group.

Summary. Studies presented in this section demonstrated effects of nondirective play therapy on several variables. For children with speech difficulties, nondirective play therapy was effective in improving articulation as well as receptive and expressive language. For children that were sexually abused, the nondirective approach to play therapy resulted in improved mood, increased social competence and self-esteem, and a decrease in symptoms of anxiety and depression. Lastly, for children with autism spectrum disorder, nondirective play therapy had positive effects on their autonomy, initiative, social interactions, and play development.

Earlier studies presented in this section provided detailed information about the role of facilitators during nondirective play. In general, facilitators were actively included in play activity, closely monitored children's play, and provided activities and modeling of appropriate behaviors and expressions of feeling. Conversely, the more recent studies on nondirective play did not provide the same detailed descriptions creating limitations to interpreting findings.

Another substantial limitation of the studies summarized on nondirective play therapy is their attrition rate. The use of play as a therapeutic medium is a common treatment modality for children who have been sexually abused. As indicated by multiple studies in this section, children who have been sexually abused often do not participate in long-term therapy programs for a variety of reasons.

Results of a meta-analysis by Bratton, Ray, Rhine, and Jones (2005) supported the conclusion that the humanistic, nondirective approach was more effective than the nonhumanistic, directive approach in facilitating play and development. Fortunately, both treatment approaches are considered to be effective.

Directive Play Therapy

Play skills training has incorporated many techniques (Stahmer, 1995). The training has been used primarily with individuals who have developmental disabilities. There have been several studies examining effects of teaching play skills on the level of play, social interaction, and communication skills.

Using play in a directive manner requires therapists to focus on client goals through premeditated interaction and active guidance throughout play therapy sessions. Axline (1947) described directive play as a form of therapy where the therapist assumes responsibility for guidance and interpretation. Examples of directive play include the use of books, known as *bibliotherapy*, or the use of art, known as *art therapy*, to confront issues and achieve therapeutic goals.

Studies reviewed in this section are indicative of a directive approach to the therapeutic use of play. Collectively, these studies provide a foundation for efficacy of non-humanistic or directive play for individuals with a variety of disabilities.

Using a randomized controlled trial, **Li, Lopez, and Lee (2007)** examined effects of a directive therapeutic play intervention on outcomes of children undergoing day surgery. Over 13 months, a total of 203 children (ages 7–12) admitted for elective day surgery participated in the study. Using a complete randomization method, 97 children and their parents were assigned to the experimental group and 106 children and their parents were assigned to the control group. The experimental group was given the directive therapeutic play intervention and the control group was given the hospital's routine services for surgery preparation. Participants were tested pre- and post-intervention on anxiety, emotional behaviors, and post-operative pain. Their parents were tested for anxiety and satisfaction levels pre- and post-intervention. The play intervention included a tour of the operating and recovery room and use of a doll demonstration to help participants understand anesthesia induction. Parents and children in the experimental group had lower pre- and post-anxiety level scores than participants in the control group. There were fewer incidents of participant negative emotional behaviors and higher levels of parent satisfaction for the experimental group than the control group; however, no significant differences were found in children's post-operative pain scores between the control and experimental groups.

Legoff and Sherman (2006) used a long-term non-randomized outcome design to examine effects of a 3-year directive social skills intervention (1 x wk, 90-min sessions) on social competence and autistic-type social behaviors of children with autism spectrum disorder. The children were divided into a control and intervention group. The control group was comprised of 57 children (47 boys). The comparison group consisted of 60 children (49 boys). All participants received similar amounts of other therapies and medications were not changed during the study. The play therapy intervention group was focused on using LEGO bricks. The intervention began with children learning the LEGO Club rules. Here, they not only learned the rules of the intervention but also learned both individual and collaborative building skills. After the first session, children were introduced to a group of peers (some without social skills deficits) and interacted with them on a weekly basis. Each week, participants were assigned different tasks and responsibilities; however, all interventions were focused on verbal and nonverbal communication, joint attention and task focus, collaborative problem solving, sharing, and turn-taking. The Vinland Adaptive Behavior Socialization Domain (VABS-SD) (cf. Klin, Jones, Schultz, Volkmar, & Cohern, 2002) and the Gilliam Autism Rating Scale (GARS: Gilliam, 1995) were used. The play therapy group significantly improved in a broad range of social skills and decreased autistic-type social behavior. Although the control group exhibited similar results, changes were not as significant as the experimental group. Unfortunately, participants were not randomly assigned to groups, the groups utilized different therapists, and there was limited information on treatment provided to the control group.

Using a single-subject design, **Thomas and Smith (2004)** conducted a 2-week study on effects of a directive play therapy approach (7 x wk, 5-min sessions) on specific play behaviors and social interactions of 3 children (ages 3–4) with autism spectrum disorder. The intervention used specific equipment (a table divided by colored tape into 2 sections, 2 chairs facing one another, 2 identical sets of toys, and a typed script indicating how toys should be placed and what participating adults should say and do). Data collection occurred via videotapes and a key worker questionnaire developed by the authors. A positive change in functional use of toys and social interactions with peers was noted. Caution is advised when interpreting results because of the small sample size and brevity of intervention.

Karcher and Lewis (2002) used a pre- and post-test within and between groups design to examine effects of a 9-week directive pair counseling intervention (2 x wk, 50-min sessions) on interpersonal understanding and internal and external problem behaviors of 20 children (9 boys ages 8–12, and 11 girls ages 9–17) with behavioral and mood disorders. Children were divided into two groups, those with behavioral disorders and those with mood disorders. There were three parts to each play session: (a) reflecting on previous session's successes and failures and together selecting the activity for the session, (b) playing games and talking while counselor facilitated interactions by helping them resolve conflicts and by identifying moments of successful cooperation or compromise, and (c) reflecting on their conflicts and successes, to evaluate impact of their actions on ongoing friendships, and to anticipate how they might handle similar conflicts differently in the future. The Relationship Questionnaire (Rel-Q) (Schultz & Selman, 1998) and Achenbach Child Behavior checklist (CBCL) (Achenback, 1990) were used to collect data. Interpersonal understanding of participants increased and external problem behaviors decreased; however, reduction in external problem behaviors was significantly greater than reduction in internal problem behaviors. The intervention was more effective for children with behavioral disorders than children with mood disorders.

Stahmer (1995) used a multiple-baseline single-subject design across subjects to compare effects of a 6-week symbolic play skill and language training program (3 x wk, 1-hr sessions) on play behaviors and interactions of seven students with autism (ages 6–7). Both the symbolic play skills intervention and language training utilized Pivotal Response Training consisting of: (a) introducing toys of interest, (b) modeling appropriate turn taking during play, and (c) providing reinforcement. Play behaviors and interaction skills were measured through direct observation and interval recording procedures. Symbolic play skills training resulted in increases in symbolic play, play complexity, and interaction skills, whereas language training did not result in increases in interaction skills, nor play skills. Six of the seven participants generalized play and interaction skills to other play partners, settings, and toys.

Throp and colleagues (1995) used a multiple-probe single-subject design across subjects to examine effects of socio-dramatic play training (3 x wk, 1-hr sessions) on role-playing, imagination, social behavior, and verbal communication of three children with autism (ages 5–9). Using Pivotal Response Training, the facilitator (a) presented the participant with desired toys, (b) took turns playing, (c) modeled appropriate play behaviors, and (d) provided reinforcement. The intervention appeared to be successful for teaching socio-dramatic play to children with autism.

Stahmer and Schreibman (1992) used a multiple-baseline design across subjects to assess a 4-month self-management treatment package (2 x wk, 60-min sessions) on amount of appropriate play and self-stimulation of three children with autism (ages 7–13). Baseline was conducted across 3 days in 19-minute segments of play. Treatment consisted of four phases: (a) discrimination training when facilitator modeled appropriate and inappropriate behaviors and children identified appropriate behavior, (b) self-management implementation when children learned to monitor their behavior by using a wrist watch and check sheet, (c) a fading of experimenter's presence, and (d) removal of self-management materials. All children increased appropriate play behaviors and decreased self-stimulatory behaviors. Generalization occurred in another setting and behaviors were maintained at follow-up. The study's external validity was limited because only a few children participated.

Skellenger and Hill (1994) used a multiple-probe single-subject design across subjects to assess effects of a 5-month teacher-child play intervention (5 x wk, 10-min sessions) conducted in a classroom with toys on the play skills and verbalizations of three children with visual impairments (ages 5–7). Baseline consisted of 10 minutes of free play observations in the training setting. During the intervention, the teacher followed the child's lead in play utilizing a system of least-to-most prompts during the intervention. The first 5 minutes of play the teacher prompted the child (if the child was not engaged in gross motor, functional, or pretend play) and modeled appropriate verbalization during pretend play. During the last 5 minutes of the intervention, the child played spontaneously while the teacher observed. An interval recording procedure was used to record frequency of targeted play behaviors. All three children increased spontaneous and pretend play and appropriate pretend talk. Although participants exhibited generalization and maintenance of play behaviors, there was a decrease in pretend play from intervention. The study showed that a simple intervention may teach children with visual impairments appropriate play behaviors and verbalizations. External validity was limited in that there were only three participants.

Goldstein and Cisar (1992) used a multiple-probe single-subject design across subjects to examine effects of a 5-week program (5 x wk, 15-min sessions) that taught scripts during sociodramatic play on social interactions of three children with autism and developmental delays and six without disabilities (ages 3-5). During the intervention, children played in triad groups (two without disabilities and one with a disability). There were three themes in which one modeled each individual script, provided feedback, and modeled expansions on scripts or restatements. A system of most-to-least prompts and a token reinforcement system were used. Social interaction, measured using an interval recording procedure, indicated that all children increased their theme-related behaviors such as playing house, playing store, and social interactions. Children's behavior generalized to other settings. Information on whether the training extended to other themes and if there was generalization to other peers was not reported.

Coe, Matson, Fee, Manikam, and Linarello (1990) used a multiple-baseline single-subject design across behaviors to examine effects of a 5-week social skills training and play training program (4 x wk, 10-min sessions) on play initiation, cooperative play, and compliment delivery of three participants with autism and developmental delays (ages 5–6). Participants were taught how to play ball, initiate play, engage in cooperative play, and deliver compliments to other participants. The facilitator used a least-to-most prompting procedure and reinforced the correct behaviors. Each skill was taught independently. An interval recording procedure was used to record ball contact, play initiation, cooperative play, and delivery of compliments.

Although participants acquired these verbal and nonverbal play skills, information concerning fading of reinforcement as well as maintenance and generalization of effects was not reported. Caution is advised when interpreting results since the skill taught was not how to play generally, but rather how to perform a structured activity, such as rolling a ball to another child.

Kohl and Beckman (1990) used a multiple-baseline single-subject design across subjects to assess effects of a teacher-mediated intervention (5 x wk, 10-min sessions) during free play on initiations and responses of eight children with moderate developmental disabilities and their peers without disabilities (ages 3–5). During the first 5 minutes, the facilitator modeled appropriate reciprocal play by providing prompts, reinforcement for correct behavior and corrections for inappropriate behaviors, and 5 minutes of free play with a confederate and the facilitator absent was provided. Prompts and reinforcement were faded until they were eliminated. A continuous event recording procedure was used to assess frequency and duration of initiations and responses. Although increases in frequency and duration of initiations and responses were observed, there was a decrease in initiations and responses from treatment to the maintenance phase. Furthermore, generalization was limited because only five children participated in the study and generalizations to other settings, people, and toys were not reported.

McEvoy, Shores, Wehby, Johnson, and Fox (1990) used a direct observation system to examine effects of a 4-week teacher-managed curriculum (5 x wk, 20-min sessions) in play settings on social interactions of 48 students (ages 4–14) with moderate developmental disabilities, 139 peers without disabilities, and 17 teachers. Three phases conducted in the classroom involved (a) a 4-hour training workshop for teachers on planning and arranging play environments and providing direct instruction by using modeling, prompting, and reinforcement, (b) teachers pairing the students and arranging the play environment, and (c) the same conditions as phase two, except that students without disabilities attended a 30-min training session on topics related to students with disabilities, and that teachers provided prompts, modeling, and reinforcement when needed during the free play sessions. Using direct observations and permanent products, students were assessed on their interaction and participation in play groups, and teachers were assessed on their planning and direct instruction techniques. Student interaction and participation was higher for teachers who planned and utilized the teaching techniques consistently and regularly than teachers who did not utilize techniques. Although the study provided evidence that teachers influenced effects of the intervention on participants, generalization and maintenance of effects were not examined.

DeKlyen and Odom (1989) used an observational design examining effects of a 2-month play program (5 x wk, 30-min sessions) to determine how activity structure and teacher interaction impacted social interactions of 36 children with and without disabilities (ages 3–6). Four children per group completed 15 minutes of one play activity and 15 minutes of another play activity chosen by the teachers chose. Groups were randomly assigned to each activity at least twice per week. Observations were used to assess child-child and child-teacher interactions. Level of structure influenced amount of interaction between peers. When there was high structure in the activity, there was an increase in interaction between peers. There was no statistical difference on activity structure and teacher interaction. Unfortunately, there were no clear definitions to distinguish between low and high structure play activities and there was no control group.

Haring and Lovinger (1989) used a multiple-baseline single-subject design across behaviors to assess frequency of initiations and responsiveness during play training (5 x wk, 30-min sessions) of three children with developmental delays (ages 4–6). During baseline, children engaged in unsupervised play. The intervention consisted of four phases: (a) educating peers without disabilities about children with disabilities, (b) social initiation training, (c) confederate training with children without disabilities, and (d) play initiation training. During play initiation training, the facilitator utilized a least-to-most prompting system. After the 30-minute play initiation training, children were observed in a free play setting with different peers than the confederates. Play initiation and responsiveness were measured by direct observation. Although the children showed increases in initiations and responsiveness during play, most increases occurred during training. Generalization occurred across settings and people, but there was a slight decrease in behaviors.

Singh and Millichamp (1987) used a multiple-baseline single-subject design across subjects to examine effects of a 25-week play teaching program (5 x wk, 60-min sessions) on level of independent and social play of eight participants with profound developmental disabilities (ages 15–25). During baseline, participants played with toys. During intervention, facilitators stood behind participants and provided verbal instruction and graduated guidance to shape play behaviors. Assistance was gradually faded to verbal instruction only. Participants mastered independent play and showed increases in social play and interaction that were maintained at a 1-year follow-up. A major limitation of the study was the use of materials that were not age-appropriate. The study showed promising results in that adults with profound development disabilities may be taught social play and social interaction skills. Replications would enhance external validity.

Summary. Several studies have examined effects of utilizing directive approaches such as modeling, prompting, and reinforcement techniques to improve social and play skills. The studies demonstrated that directive play therapy resulted in improvements in social skills, anxiety levels, emotional behaviors, and problem behaviors. Socio-dramatic play was successful with individuals with autism, mental retardation, and at-risk children who generalized skills to other settings and people. Although, external validity was limited in these studies, internal validity was high resulting in confidence that play and social skills were taught successfully to people of varying ages with various disabilities.

Overall Summary

Studies have used directive and nondirective approaches to play therapy. In nondirective play therapy, the role of the therapist is relatively passive. The therapist develops a relationship with the participant and works at the person's pace to achieve therapeutic goals. In comparison, directive play therapy gives control and direction of play sessions to the therapist. Directive play therapy is focused on achieving outcomes and is less concerned with establishing a therapeutic relationship.

Studies on nondirective and directive play therapy are indicative of their efficacy with a number of populations. These conclusions were supported by a meta-analysis by Bratton and colleagues (2005) that identified both treatment approaches to be effective; however, the humanistic, nondirective approach was found to be more effective than the non-humanistic, directive approach. In addition, research identified that both therapeutic approaches possess limitations.

A study conducted by Rasmussen and Cunningham (1995) suggested integrating the rapport building component of nondirective play therapy with the focused techniques of directive play therapy. It was their belief that a combination of directive and nondirective play therapy would be the most effective approach for treating children who experienced sexual abuse. The outcomes of the studies reviewed in this chapter support Rasmussen and Cunningham's contentions. Perhaps future research could focus on integration of these modalities as a means of increasing efficacy of play therapy.

Case Study

This section presents one case study demonstrating effects of play on developmental changes in children with disabilities. Because play therapy is primarily conducted by trained clinical psychologists, a therapeutic developmental play case study has been selected as an example of the use of play in TR.

Amber

Amber was a 5-year-old girl diagnosed with Asperger's Syndrome, a form of autism. Children with Asperger's Syndrome are often socially withdrawn, have below-average motor planning skills, and display unusual social interactions with peers. Amber's mother was concerned that Amber had very few friends and often displayed peculiar social skills when in settings with peers such as perseveration (continuously repeating a statement or verbalization), inappropriate name calling, and isolating play habits. Amber enrolled in the summer program at her local recreation department. There, Amber's mother explained the situation to a TR specialist. The TR specialist explained to Amber's mother that the facility was offering an inclusive play group (3 x wk) and stated that Amber's participation in the group would provide opportunities to develop social skills that were needed for her to make new friends.

Play for Amber

Prior to participation in the group, the TR specialist observed Amber during unstructured free play. The specialist noticed Amber frequently played alone without initiating conversation with peers, that Amber's motor skills were markedly below skills of her peers, and Amber's peers did not initiate conversation with Amber during play. Based on conversations with Amber's mother and observations of Amber during free play, the TR specialist recommended that Amber first participate in individual social and motor skill development sessions with the specialist before participating in the inclusive play group.

Amber met with the TR specialist three times a week for 30 minutes a day. Amber and the specialist worked on motor planning and social skill development. The TR specialist wanted Amber to develop the physical and social skills needed for successful participation in the play group with her peers without disabilities. The TR specialist focused on improving Amber's hand-eye coordination by using activities such as catching a ball. Basic locomotor skills were the focus of other activities such as skipping and jumping.

In addition to the motor skill development, the TR specialist used verbal and physical prompts to encourage Amber's appropriate behavior when she demonstrated perseveration or inappropriate verbal outbursts. After a period of 2 weeks of participating in individual sessions with the TR specialist, Amber had reduced her inappropriate social behaviors and increased her motor skills to the point where the specialist felt she was prepared to participate in group play activities with her peers.

Feeling that the group might initially be hesitant to accept Amber based on previous observations, the TR specialist decided to lead cooperative games on the first day. The specialist used cooperative games because they were structured to promote sharing and teamwork among the children and might provide opportunities for Amber to model her peers' social behavior. The children played cooperative games including Cooperative Musical Chairs, Partners, Numbers, Shapes, and Letters Together. The children continued playing cooperative games for several weeks. During each session, another staff member recorded the frequency of Amber's positive and negative social interactions. After examining total frequency of positive and negative social interactions, the TR specialist noted four more positive social interactions and seven fewer negative social interactions when compared to the frequency of positive and negative social interactions occurring before participation in the individual play sessions.

Amber's involvement in the play group made an important difference in her development. She continued participating in the inclusive play group for the remainder of the summer program. Her mother reported that her improved social behavior and motor skills continue to improve at school and home.

Epilogue

Amber has continued her participation in an inclusive play group during after-school programs. As a result, Amber has developed a friendship with one of the girls in the play group. Amber was placed in a typical classroom and continues to develop social relationships. Her teachers and parents continue using management techniques and play to further enhance and promote opportunities for Amber to make new friends.

Intervention Implementation Exercises

To gain a sense of therapeutic use of play, it may be useful to encourage an examination of the therapeutic components of play. Playing cooperative games can help to develop a sense of appreciation for the nuances associated with such activities. Since TR specialists must continuously adapt activities to match the needs and skills of participants, it is valuable to practice making such adaptations. Therefore, the following intervention implementation exercises are suggested:

- Examine Therapeutic Components of Play
- Play Cooperative Games
- Adapt Traditional Games

Examine Therapeutic Components of Play

Provide participants with several toys and games such as Hi Ho Cheerio, Candy Land, UNO, and Silly Putty. Ask them to list therapeutic components of each toy or game such as fine motor skills, color discrimination, or counting. Have them brainstorm specific disability groups most appropriate for each toy's use.

Play Cooperative Games (Orlick, 1978)

Various activities can be developed that require cooperation rather than direct competition between individuals. The following activities are described here:

- Collective Blanketball
- Partner Pull-up
- Frozen Bean Bags

Collective Blanketball. Two teams of 8–10 are spread out around two blankets or similarly sized pieces of durable material. Each team grasps the edge of the blanket and a beach ball is placed in the middle of one blanket. First, each team should practice by tossing a ball into the air and catching it again in the blanket. Teams then pass one ball back and forth by tossing it in unison toward the receiving team. One team can pass its ball straight up and move out of the way to let the other team run under and catch it. Groups can see how many times they can pass the ball without dropping the ball.

Partner Pull-up. Partners sit down facing each other with the soles of their feet on the floor, toes touching. Partners reach forward, bending their knees if they must, and grasp hands. By pulling together, both come up to a stand and then try to return to a sitting position. Once this is completed, participants exchange partners.

Frozen Bean Bags (Help Your Friend). Participants begin moving around the room at their own pace, each balancing a bean bag on their head. The leader can change the action or pace by instructing the group to go faster, skipping, hopping, or go backwards. If the bean bag falls off a participant's head, that person is frozen. Another participant must then pick up the bean bag and place it on the frozen player's head to free the person, without losing his own bean bag. The object of the game is to help as many people as possible by keeping them unfrozen.

Adapt Traditional Games

Many traditional games can be adapted to promote play without eliminating participants. Divide the group into 3–4 groups. Provide each group with a piece of paper containing the name of a traditional game such as Simon Says, Hot Potato, or Twister. Have the class examine and adapt the games so they promote participation rather than elimination.

Summary. The exercises presented in this section serve as possible activities that may help students gain an understanding of how play may be used as a therapeutic medium. These exercises provide practice that may help professionals who plan to use play as a therapeutic medium.

Conclusion

Research has demonstrated that play can be effective in promoting development in children with disabilities. Therapeutic use of play may be implemented by TR specialists to teach and develop cognitive, social/communication, and motor skills. Furthermore, therapeutic use of play facilitates inclusion and provides opportunities for development of friendships. Play can be an effective tool with children and adolescents with disabilities. TR specialists may wish to consider using play as a therapeutic medium and to begin developing play programs aimed at assisting children with disabilities.

Discussion Questions

1. What are characteristics of play?
2. What is the difference between "play" and "the therapeutic use play"?
3. According to Piaget (1962), what are the four cognitive play stages?
4. According to Parten (1932), what are the four social levels of play?
5. What is the difference between group play therapy and developmental therapeutic play?
6. How can sociocultural theory be used to explain the therapeutic value of play?
7. How do Erikson's and Piaget's theories enhance understanding of how play may be used therapeutically?
8. How did the therapeutic use of play evolve?
9. How can the social levels of play be applied when using therapeutic play?
10. Why would the ability to play games with rules signify a higher level of childhood development?

Resources

The Able Child
325 West 11th Street
New York City, NY 10014

Achievement Products, Inc.
P.O. Box 547
Mineola, NY 11501

The Best Toys, Books & Videos for Kids: (800-535-1910)

Childcraft Education Corporation
20 Kilmer Road, Edison, NJ 08818
(800) 631-5657

Chinaberry Book Service: (800) 776-2242

Constructive Playthings
1227 East 119th Street
Grandview, MO 64030
(800) 832-0572

Discovery Toys
400 Ellinwood Way
Pleasant Hill, CA 94523

DLM Teaching Resources
One DLM Park
Allen, TX 75002

Educational Teaching Aids
159 West Kinzie Street
Chicago, IL 60610

Ideal School Supply Company
11000 South Lavergne Avenue
Oak Lawn, IL 60453

Kapable Kids: (800) 356-1564

Leisure Learning Products, Inc.
16 Division Street West, P. O. Box 4869
Greenwich, CT 06830

Lekotech Toy Resource Hotline: (800) 366-PLAY

Music for Little People: (800) 346-4445

Toys to Grow On: (800) 542-8338

Toys for Special Children: (800) 832-8697

References

Achenbach, T. M. (1990). Conceptualization of developmental psychopathology. In
    M. Lewis & S. Miller (Eds.), *The handbook of developmental psychopathology*.
    New York: Plenum.

Axline, V. M. (1947). *Play therapy: The inner dynamics of childhood*. Cambridge,
    MA: The Riverside Press.

Bell, V., Lyne, S., & Kolvin, I. (1989). Playgroup therapy with deprived children:
    Community-based early secondary prevention. *British Journal of Occupational
    Therapy, 52*, 548–462.

Boulanger, M. D., & Langevin, C. (1992). Direct observation of play-group therapy for
    social skill deficits. *Journal of Child and Adolescent Group Therapy, 2*, 227–236.

Bratton, S. C., Ray, D., Rhine, T., & Jones, L. (2005). The efficacy of play therapy
    with children: A meta-analytic review of treatment outcomes. *Professional
    Psychology: Research and Practice, 36*(4), 376–390.

Briere, J. (1996). *Trauma Symptom Checklist for Children (TSCC) professional
    manual*. Odessa, FL: Psychological Assessment Resources.

Broad, L. P., & Butterworth, N. T. (1991). *The playgroup handbook* (2nd ed.). New
    York: St. Martin's Press.

Burks, H. F. (1977). *Burks' behavior rating scale*. Los Angeles: Western
    Psychological Services.

Cattanbach, A. (1994). *Play therapy: Where the sky meets the underworld*. London,
    UK: Jessica Kingsley.

Chaffin, M., & Wherry, J. (1993). *Abuse behavior checklist*. Unpublished manu-
    script. University of Arkansas for Medical Sciences, Department of Pediatrics.

Coe, D., Matson, J., Fee, V., Manikam, R., & Linarello, C. (1990). Training nonver-
    bal and verbal play skills to mentally retarded and autistic children. *Journal of
    Autism and Developmental Disorders, 20*, 177–187.

Cooper, J. O., Heron, T. E., & Heward, W. L. (1987). *Applied behavior analysis*.
    New York: Macmillan Publishing Company.

Danger, S., & Landreth, G. (2005). Child-centered group play therapy with children
    with speech difficulties. *International Journal of Play Therapy, 14*, 81–102.

Deci, E. (1995). *Why we do what we do: The dynamics of personal autonomy*. New
    York: G. P. Putnam's Sons.

DeKlyen, M., & Odom, S. L. (1989). Activity structure and social interactions with
    peers in developmentally integrated play groups. *Journal of Early Intervention,
    13*, 342–352.

Erikson, E. H. (1950). *Childhood and society*. New York: W. W. Norton & Company,
    Inc.

Gilliam, J. E. (1995). *Gilliam Autism Rating Scale (GARS)*. Austin, TX: Pro-Ed.

Glakas, B. A. (1991). Teaching cooperative skills through games. *Journal of Physical Education, Recreation, and Dance, 62*(5), 28–30.

Goldman, R., & Fristoe, M. (2000). *Goldman Fristoe test of articulation*. Circle Pines, MN: American Guidance Services.

Goldstein, H., & Cisar, C. L. (1992). Promoting interaction during sociodramatic play: Teaching scripts to typical preschoolers and classmates with disabilities. *Journal of Applied Behavior Analysis, 25*, 265–280.

Haring, T. G., & Lovinger, L. (1989). Prompting social interactions through teaching generalized play initiation responses to preschool children with autism. *Journal of the Association for Persons with Severe Handicaps, 14*, 58–67.

Hughes, F. P. (1991). *Children, play and development*. Needham Heights, MA: Allyn and Bacon.

Johnson, J. E., Christie, J. F., & Yawkey, T. D. (1987). *Play and early childhood*. Glenview, IL: Scott, Foresman, and Company.

Josefi, O., & Ryan, V. (2004). Non-directive play therapy for young children with autism: a case study. *Clinical Child Psychology and Psychiatry, 9*, 533–551.

Joseph, J. (1979). *Joseph Pre-School and Primary Self-Concept Screening Test*. Wood Dale, IL: Stoelting Co.

Karcher, M. J., & Lewis, S. S. (2002). Pair counseling: the effects of a dyadic developmental play therapy on interpersonal understanding and externalizing behaviors. *International Journal of Play Therapy, 11*, 19–42.

Klin, A., Jones, W., Schultz, R., Volkmar, F., & Cohern, D. (2002). Visual fixation patterns during viewing of naturalistic social situations as predictors of social competence in individuals with autism. *Archives of General Psychiatry, 59*, 809–16.

Kohl, F. L., & Beckman, P. J. (1990). The effects of directed play on the frequency and length of reciprocal interactions with preschoolers having moderate handicaps. *Education and Training in Mental Retardation, 25*, 258–266.

Landreth, G. L. (1991). *Play therapy: The art of the relationship*. Muncie, IN: Accelerated Development.

Landreth, G. L. (1993). Child-centered play therapy. *Elementary School Guidance and Counseling, 28*, 17–29.

Legoff, D. B., & Sherman, M. (2006). Long-term outcome of social skills intervention based on interactive LEGO play. *Autism, 10*, 317–329.

Leme, S. (1993). Facilitating play skills: A developmental approach for children with disabilities. In S. J. Grosse, & D. Thompson (Eds.), *Play and recreation for individuals with disabilities: Practical pointers* (pp. 67–79). Reston, VA: American Alliance for Health.

Li, H. W., Lopez, V., & Lee, T. (2007). Psychoeducational preparation of children for surgery: The importance of parental involvement. *Patient and Education Counseling, 65*, 34–41.

Loy, D. P., & Dattilo, J. (2000). Effects of different play structures on social interactions between a boy with Asperger's syndrome and his peers. *Therapeutic Recreation Journal, 35*(3), 317–325.

Malone, M., & Langone, J. (1994). Object-related play skills of youths with mental retardation: A review of single-subject design research. *Remedial and Special Education, 15*, 177–188.

Martens, R. (1978). *Joy and sadness in children's sports*. Champaign, IL: Human Kinetics.

McEvoy, M. A., Shores, R. E., Wehby, J. H., Johnson, S. M., & Fox, J. J. (1990). Special education teachers' implementation of procedures to promote social interaction among children in integrated settings. *Education and Training in Mental Retardation, 25*, 267–276.

McMahon, L. (1992). *The handbook of play therapy*. New York: Routledge.

Nicolopoulou, A. (1993). Play, cognitive development, and the social world: Piaget, Vygotsky, and beyond. *Human Development, 36*, 1–23.

Orlick, T. (1978). *The cooperative sports & games book: Challenge without competition*. New York: Pantheon.

Parten, M. (1932). Social participation among preschool children. *Journal of Abnormal and Social Psychology, 27*, 243–269.

Pellegrini, A. D., & Jones, I. (1994). Play, toys, and language. In J. H. Goldstein (Ed.), *Toys, play, and child development* (pp. 27–45). New York: Cambridge University Press.

Piaget, J. (1962). *Play, dreams and imitation in childhood*. New York: Norton.

Rasmussen, L. A., & Cunningham, C. (1995). Focused play therapy and non-directive play therapy: can they be integrated? *Journal of Child Sexual Abuse, 4*, 1–20.

Reyes, C. J., & Asbrand, J. P. (2005). A longitudinal study assessing trauma symptoms in sexually abused children engaged in play therapy. *International Journal of Play Therapy, 14*, 25–47.

Reynolds, C. R., & Kamphuas, R. W. (1992). *Behavior assessment system for children*. Circle Pines, MN: American Guidance Services.

Schaefer, C. E. (1976). *The therapeutic use of child's play*. New York: Jason Aronson, Inc.

Schaefer, C. E. (Ed.). (1993). *The therapeutic powers of play*. New York: Jason Aronson, Inc.

Schleien, S. J., Heyne, L. A., & Dattilo, J. (1995). Teaching severely handicapped children: Social skill development through leisure skills programming. In G. Cartledge & J. Milburn (Eds.), *Teaching social skills to children and youth: Innovative approaches* (3rd ed., pp. 262–290). Boston: Allyn and Bacon.

Schleien, S. J., Mustonen, T., Rynders, J. E., & Fox, A. (1990). Effects of social play activities on the play behavior of children with autism. *Journal of Leisure Research, 22*, 317–398.

Schleien, S., Ray, M. T., & Green, F. P. (1997). *Community recreation and persons with disabilities: Strategies for inclusion* (2nd Ed.). Baltimore, MD: Brookes.

Schultz, L., & Selman, R. (1998). *Toward the construction of two developmental social competence measures: The GSID Relationship Questionnaires*. Unpublished manuscript, Harvard Graduate School of Education, Cambridge, MA.

Scott, T. A., Burlingame, G., Starling, M., Porter, C., & Lilly, J. P. (2003). Effects of individual client-centered play therapy on sexually abused children's mood, self-concept, and social competence. *International Journal of Play Therapy, 12*(1), 7–30.

Scott, T. A., & Porter, C. (1995). *Social/environmental update*. Unpublished manuscript, Brigham Young University, Utah.

Singh, N. N., & Millichamp, C. J. (1987). Independent and social play among profoundly mentally retarded adults: Training, maintenance, generalization, and long-term follow-up. *Journal of Applied Behavior Analysis, 20,* 23–34.

Skellenger, A. C., & Hill, E. W. (1994). Effects of a shared teacher-child play intervention on the play skills of three young children who are blind. *Journal of Visual Impairment & Blindness, 88,* 433–445.

Stahmer, A. C. (1995). Teaching symbolic play skills to children with autism using pivotal response training. *Journal of Autism and Developmental Disorders, 25,* 123–141.

Stahmer, A. C., & Schreibman, L. (1992). Teaching children with autism appropriate play in unsupervised environments using a self-management treatment packet. *Journal of Applied Behavior Analysis, 25,* 447–459.

Sugar, M. (1991). Planning group therapy for children. *Journal of Child and Adolescent Group Therapy, 1*(1), 5–14.

Sweetland, R. C., & Keyser, D. J. (1986). *Tests: A comprehensive reference for assessments in psychology, education, and business.* Kansas City, MO: Test Corporation of America.

Thomas, N., & Smith, C. (2004). Developing play skills in children with autistic spectrum disorders. *Educational Psychology in Practice, 20,* 195–206.

Throp, D. M., Stahmer, A. C., & Schreibman, L. (1995). Effects of sociodramatic play training on children with autism. *Journal of Autism and Developmental Disabilities, 25,* 265–282.

Troester, J. D. (1996). A therapeutic play group for children with hearing impairments. *Journal of Child and Adolescent Group Therapy, 6,* 101–109.

Trounson-Chaiken, D. (1996). From chaos to cohesion: Group therapy with preschool-aged children. *Journal of Child and Adolescent Group Therapy, 6,* 3–25.

Vygotsky, L. S. (1967). Play and its role in the mental development of the child. *Soviet Psychology, 12,* 6–18. (A stenographic record of a lecture given in 1933; included in J. S. Bruner, A. Jolly, & K Sylvia, Eds., 1976; partly reproduced in Vygotsky, 1978).

Vygotsky, L. S. (1978). *Mind in society: The development of higher psychological processes* (M. Cole, V. John-Steiner, S. Scribner, & E. Souberman, Eds.). Cambridge, MA: Harvard University Press.

Wadsworth, B. J. (1979). *Piaget's theory of cognitive development.* New York: Longman, Inc.

Wilig, E. H., Secord, W., & Semel, E. (1992). *Clinical evaluation of language fundamentals* (3rd ed.). San Antonio, TX: The Psychological Corporation.

Wortman, C. B., & Loftus, E. F. (1988). *Psychology* (3rd ed.). New York: Knopf, Inc.

Yawkey, T. D., & Pellegrini, A. D. (Eds.) (1984). *Child's play: Developmental and applied.* Hillsdale, NJ: L. Erlbaum Associates.

Chapter 18
Therapeutic Use of Sports

John Dattilo, Alexis McKenney, and David Loy

The difference between the impossible
and the possible lies in a person's determination.
—Tommy Lasorda

Introduction

Originally, the use of sports for people with disabilities was guided by a philosophy of rehabilitation (Pensgaard & Sorensen, 2002); that is, sports served as an end in itself. With time, sports have become more, as they now help people with disabilities to experience a sense of empowerment as well. This chapter presents a definition of sports, a description of sports for people with specific limitations, and a brief history of sports for people with disabilities, including some significant legislation influencing these activities. A review of recent literature follows the presentation of some of the theoretical foundations of the use of sports as TR interventions. In addition, two case studies are presented as examples of how sport may be implemented as a TR intervention. A section on implementation exercises presents a sampling of specific sports for people with disabilities. In addition, a conclusion of the chapter is given followed by a list of professional resources and references.

Definition

Sports are competitive physical activities that are performed for pleasure, require physical effort, and are played according to fixed rules (Oxford University Press, n.d.). According to Pensgaard and Sorensen (2002), sport is a term that includes three levels of physical activity. The first level, *recreational sport*, includes sport engaged in primarily for fun and health. The second level, *competitive sport*, involves performance standards and imposed conditions, and the third level, *elite sport*, is limited to people who participate in the top levels of sporting competitions.

Paciorek (2005) argued that people with disabilities have the same desires and needs to participate in sport as people without disabilities. Sports for people with disabilities are essentially the same as those for people without disabilities (Guttman, 1976). The phrase *sports for people with disabilities* does not indicate that such sports are created for people with disabilities by people without disabilities. In fact, many sports engaged in by people with disabilities were developed by and are organized and managed by people with disabilities.

Descriptions

The following section describing sports for people with disabilities is divided into two sections. The first section is devoted to presenting general information about sports for people with various types of disabilities. In the second section, three specific sports (basketball, tennis, and golf) are presented individually as examples to provide detailed information concerning strategies for each sport. Therefore, the two sections are identified with the following headings:

- Sports for People with Specific Limitations
- Specific Sports for People with Disabilities

Sports for People with Specific Limitations

The following section contains general information about sports for people with various disabilities. Although some sports for people with disabilities require modification of equipment and rules, the sports are generally of equal difficulty and rigor to their counterparts for athletes without disabilities. In most cases, modifications are limited to only those essential to accommodating for specific disabilities. Asken (1991) suggested a goal of many athletes with disabilities is to perform at levels equal to or greater than athletes without disabilities.

The following section describes sports for people with specific disabilities. Brief explanations of game and rule modifications are presented below. The descriptions are grouped in three categories:

- Sports for people with physical limitations
- Sports for people with sensory limitations
- Sports for people with cognitive limitations

Sports for people with physical limitations. Sports for people with physical disabilities include a variety of mainstream sports played by participants who use wheelchairs such as basketball, racquetball, tennis, softball, and archery. People who use wheelchairs also participate in track and road racing events such as marathons and triathlons. Common sports for people with amputations include soccer, swimming, and downhill skiing.

Sports for people with sensory limitations. Sports for people who are deaf are among the oldest organized sports for people with disabilities. For example, in the 1930s, athletes from the United States participated in the International "Silent Games." Athletes who have hearing impairments or are deaf also participate in most mainstream sports. The modifications required are usually few, such as pointing the starting gun in a direction to permit the athlete to observe the flash when it is fired.

> Interesting improvisations for people with hearing impairments
> have become traditions in several sports. The football huddle is
> such an improvisation. The football team at Gallaudet University
> (a university founded for people who are deaf) developed the

football huddle so that the team could exchange plays by signing without allowing the opposing team to see the signs.

Sports for people who have vision impairments or people who are blind include a variety of integrated and modified sports. Many of the sports rely on partnerships with assistants who are not visually impaired.

> For example, in track and field, runners use a short cord or rope held by a running partner who is sighted. For jumping events, a coach will verbally signal the athlete when it is time to jump. In downhill skiing, a guide who is not visually impaired skis behind the skier who is blind and gives verbal directions.

Among sports that require little or no modification are wrestling and weightlifting. An internationally competitive sport for people who are visually impaired is goalball. Goalball is played with a large, playground-size ball that has bells inside. When bowling, many people with visual impairments use a rail on the approach to the alley. Golfers who have some visual impairment often use sound beacons on the flags so they can better direct the ball to the hole.

Sports for people with cognitive limitations. People with cognitive limitations are often best served by including them in sports with their peers without disabilities. Modifications that may be necessary are often unique to the individual. Although inclusive sports participation is often the most desirable context for people with cognitive impairments, other programs are available.

A well-known segregated sports program for people with developmental disabilities is the Special Olympics International (SOI). SOI provides local, state, national, and international competitions in track and field events. The SOI program involves extensive training of participants, often beginning a year or more in advance of the event. Although this program has grown to international levels of competition, it has received considerable criticism. For example, Hourcade (1989) listed the following concerns about SOI: segregation, inefficient use of instructional time, a child-like atmosphere, labeling and stigmatization, patronizing treatment of participants which evokes sympathy and pity and lack of verifiable benefits.

Specific Sports for People with Disabilities

To increase understanding of sports for people with disabilities, three specific sports have been selected. Detailed information for following these sports are presented in this section:

- Basketball
- Golf
- Tennis

Basketball. To adapt basketball to accommodate mobility differences, the wheelchair version is similar with a few rule changes and classification requirements (Shepherd

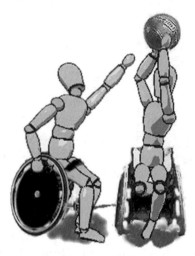

Figure 18.1

Center Therapeutic Recreation Department, 1995). Wheelchair basketball is played in accordance with National Collegiate Athletic Association rules with a few adaptations. The wheelchair is considered a part of the player (see Figure 18.1). General rules of *contact* in regular basketball such as charging or blocking apply in wheelchair basketball. In reference to *time limits,* an offensive player cannot remain more than 4 seconds in the free throw lane while the player's team has possession of the ball.

Players in possession of the ball may not push their own wheelchair more than twice in succession with one or both hands in either direction without *dribbling* or passing the ball. Taking more than two successive pushes constitutes a traveling violation. A player may, however, push the chair and bounce the ball simultaneously just as an able-bodied player runs and bounces the ball simultaneously in regular basketball.

A *loss of ball* (such as when the ball is awarded to the other team) is called by the referee if a player in possession of the ball makes any physical contact with the floor or tilts the chair so far backward that the anti-tip bars touch the floor, or so far forward that the front footplate hits the floor. A player is considered *out of bounds* when any part of the player's body or wheelchair touches the floor on or outside the boundary.

Participants must remain firmly seated in the wheelchair at all times and not use a leg for physical advantage such as in braking or slowing down the chair. Any infraction of this rule (rebound, jump ball, shot) constitutes a *physical advantage foul* and is strictly enforced. Two free throws are awarded and the ball is given to the opposing team. Two such fouls disqualifies a player from the game. If a player *falls* out of the chair during play, the officials immediately suspend play if there is any chance of danger to the fallen player. If not, the officials will withhold their whistles until the particular play in progress has been completed. If a player falls out of the chair to gain possession of the ball or falls to keep opponents from gaining possession of the ball, the ball is awarded to the opposing team.

Teams that compete at a competitive level use a classification system to evaluate the functional abilities of players on a point scale of 1 to 4.5 (Disabled World, n.d.).

When teams include athletes who do not have a physical disability, those teams are classified as a 5. Individuals with the highest degree of disability, such as full paraplegia below the chest, are given the classification of 1. In addition, the following class system is used. *Class 1* includes people with complete motor loss at T-7 or above or comparable disability where there is total loss of muscle functioning at or above T-7. With *Class 2,* individuals who have complete motor loss originating at T-8 and descending through and including L-2 where there may be motor power of hips and thighs are included. Individuals who are amputees with bilateral hip disarticulation fall within this class, as well. *Class 3* includes individuals with all other physical disabilities as related to lower extremity paralysis or paresis originating at or below L-3. Individuals who are lower extremity amputees are included in Class 3 except for those with bilateral hip disarticulation.

Disability specific adaptations to basketball: physical limitations. Many people have physical limitations such as spinal cord injuries, spina bifida, hemiparesis (paralysis of one side of the body), lower extremity amputation, or short stature that impair participation in basketball. (People with short stature were previously referred to as having dwarfism. The word *dwarf* remains in agency/organization titles.) TR specialists provide adaptations that meet the needs of participants desiring participation. Some physical limitations include the following: reduced mobility, smaller hand size, loss of limb, and limited strength or height.

Reduced mobility due to paralysis, amputation, or other neurological dysfunction may require adapting basketball. One adaptation is to modify rules to permit use of a mobility device. For example, some versions of basketball allow the use of mobility aides such as wheelchairs or prosthetic devices for purposes of full participation.

Some disability groups have limited hand strength or *smaller hands* associated with their disability. Programming considerations might include the use of a basketball of smaller diameter to allow better ball control.

Many individuals with disabilities have a *loss of limb(s),* which impairs their ability to participate. TR specialists may encourage players with loss of limbs to consider using adaptive prosthetics to assist with play. For example, a prosthetic device such as the Super Sport can be used for upper extremity amputations. The Super Sport was developed specifically for use in recreational activities and ball sports.

Individuals with *decreased strength* as a result of a disability have an opportunity to participate in basketball. TR specialists may consider adaptations such as using a smaller ball in play. A smaller ball is lighter and allows players with strength limitations to shoot the ball toward the required goal of 10 feet. The Dwarf Athletic Association of America uses a slightly smaller ball in its competitions.

It is helpful to use basketball hoops that can be lowered to allow players with *limited strength or height* to participate more fully. For those with limited endurance, the game can be modified to a half-court version to reduce the amount of running. One final recommendation involves allowing a peer to push the participant who uses a wheelchair around the court.

Disability-specific adaptations to basketball: sensory limitations. Although some people with hearing impairments may participate without rule modifications, individuals with visual impairments may find basketball difficult because modifications of basketball for participants who have visual impairments are limited. Participants with moderate to mild hearing impairments can participate with modifications; however, rule changes are not made.

Considerations for people with *visual impairments* can include having a peer guide the participant around the court during play. Carpet squares or tape to mark the floor can be used for participant orientation. A brightly colored ball or one with a bell can be helpful. Placing a radio under the basket or brightly colored ribbons or streamers placed in the basket can improve shooting percentage. Teammates wearing brightly colored shirts can help a player identify to whom to pass the ball.

Some specific considerations for people with *hearing impairments* include making sure scoreboards are easily visible for all players. Referees or officials can be encouraged to use an abundance of hand signals and manual sign language. Lights can be mounted on top of backboards to alert players with hearing impairments of blown whistles or play being stopped.

Disability specific adaptations to basketball: cognitive limitations. People with cognitive limitations have the opportunity to participate in the game of basketball. For example, Special Olympics International (SOI) offers a variety of basketball events including team competitions, individual skill competitions, and team skill events. Many individuals with cognitive impairments have other limitations associated with their disability such as obesity, lack of fine and gross motor skills, and lack of endurance. Simplifying rules can be helpful. Some rules such as lane violations, back court violations, carrying, shot clock violation, and other rules may be eliminated to simplify the game for participants. Peers can be used to assist participants during the game. The number of offensive plays used by a team can be limited. Participants can be permitted to dribble with two hands. The height of the basket can be varied to increase the opportunity for success. Participants can be allowed to walk while dribbling and encouraged to use the dominant hand until mastery has occurred. Different types of balls such as playground balls, Nerf balls, or punch balls can be used as well.

Nesbitt (1986) provided an example of an adapted version of basketball called *Bankshot Basketball*. Bankshot Basketball is a noncontact, nonrunning, and non-dribbling sport that relies on shooting accuracy, touch, and concentration rather than on athletic ability or experience. The game utilizes a conventional basketball, rims, and scoreboard, but the backboards are not standard, requiring different strategies to score bankshots. The shooting strategies become increasingly more difficult as the player moves from one basket to another. Players are given their own scorecard. At each station, there are three circles marked on the ground. Players shoot twice from each circle. The circles are one, two, and three points respectively. If players score from each circle, they are awarded bonus points and can take a bonus shot from the circle of their choice. It is possible to score a maximum of 10 points from each station. The twelfth station has two baskets, so the perfect score is 130 points. The game includes 12 baskets that are set up on a course approximately 7 feet apart.

Golf. Barriers to golf participation can be the lack of accessibility created by golf course policies and a lack of awareness of course operators (Robb, 1994). Some golf course operators may feel that wheelchairs and other mobility aids will damage the putting greens.

> Public golf courses are included as public entities under the Americans with Disabilities Act of 1990 (ADA). In April 1995, a Portland, Oregon, public golf course agreed to pay $25,000 to settle a suit out of court when they prevented course access to a golfer using a wheelchair (Dade, 1995).

Knowledge of accessibility issues is important. Participation by golfers with disabilities is not always an issue of skill development but of accessibility and advocacy. Knowledge of accessibility issues is essential when providing golf for participants with disabilities. It is helpful to remain current on ADA interpretations and assist golfers with disabilities in advocating and problem solving for course accessibility.

The Association of Disabled American Golfers (ADAG) has taken an active role in advocating accessibility rights for golfers with disabilities (ADAG, 1995; 1996). The creation of the Recreation Access Advisory Committee in 1993 and golf subcommittee provided recommendations for golf course design and alteration issues. These recommendations can be located through the United States Architectural and Transportation Barriers Compliance Board.

The United States Golf Association (USGA) has recently changed *The Rules of Golf* handbook to include modified rules for golfers with disabilities. These changes are meant to aid golfers with disabilities to compete more fairly with all golfers (United States Golf Association, 2001).

Disability-specific adaptations to golf: physical limitations. An interesting feature of golf for people with disabilities is there is not an adapted version of the game. Golf for people with disabilities is the same as golf for people without disabilities (Longo, 1989). Minor adaptations in equipment are typical for golfers with disabilities. A major barrier to golf participation is the physical limitations of some golfers with disabilities. Adaptations are provided which meet the needs of golfers with disabilities desiring participation. Some physical limitations to golf participation include: reduced mobility, limited grip strength, lower extremity impairments, limited balance, decreased strength, and limited flexibility.

A significant limitation to golfers with disabilities is *reduced mobility*. Some strategies to overcome limitations created by reduced mobility may include: attending a golf driving range to involve active participation without the need to ambulate or possess excellent mobility; attending a miniature golf facility to limit amount of mobility required for participation, using mobility devices for access to the entire golf course, and assisting the golfer in contacting the local golf course to assess the facility's policy on use of assistive devices (including wheelchairs) in addition to course access (total or partial). Some mobility assistive devices include single passenger vehicles designed to assist the golfer with a disability (Avery, 1996).

Some people with disabilities have *limited grip strength* due to upper extremity limitations resulting from spinal cord injuries, strokes, amputations, arthritis, birth defects, and other neurological impairments. Lack of grip strength impairs a golfer's ability to securely hold the golf club and produce an effective swing. Adaptations available to overcome grip strength deficits can allow full participation. These devices attach directly to the golf club or the golfer's arm, hand, or prosthesis without altering the club grip. Some devices available for golfers with limited grip that meet USGA requirements include The Amputee Golf Grip and Robin-Aid Golfing Device.

Many golfers with disabilities have *lower extremity impairments*, such as restricted rotation, abnormal gait, and loss of limb, which may impair their ability to play golf. There are many adaptive equipment options available to recommend to the golfer with a disability.

> For example, prosthetics offer a substitute for a loss of limb. Examples of prosthetics include adaptive shoes, artificial hands, and artificial legs. Another adaptation is the use of a wheelchair, stool, or standard chair to assist the golfer who has loss of lower extremity use. Finally, sand shots and putting can be eliminated for those who cannot stand aside from their wheelchair or mobility device.

Many golfers with neuromuscular disorders have *limited balance* and have difficulty participating in golf. Adaptive equipment options include use of a mobility device or seat support that can be portable or affixed directly to the golf cart (see Figure 18.2). Another device that may be used is a camera tripod with a bicycle seat attached on the top. The golfer can sit on the tripod and reduce weight bearing.

Disabling conditions such as arthritis prevent *flexibility* needed to bend at the waist to pick up a golf ball. Consider use of adaptive equipment assisting the golfer with a disability.

> One such example is the Putting Finger, which is a suction cup that fits on the end of the putter and that allows the golfer to retrieve the golf ball without bending at the waist.

A long-handled putter may also aid the golfer with limited flexibility. Rules can be adapted by allowing the player to place the ball on a tee for all shots, excluding putts.

Figure 18.2

Many golfers with physical limitations such as short stature or neuromuscular impairments may have *decreased strength* which can inhibit participation in golf. The golfer with strength limitations can be assisted by providing customized, shortened, or lightweight clubs to assist the golfer in swinging the club effectively. In addition to golf equipment modifications, rules or format of the sport can be adapted.

> One such adaptation includes placing the golfer with decreased strength in a "best ball" format where the best shot of a twosome, threesome, or foursome is selected in play. This allows the golfer with strength limitations to contribute skills to his or her team other than those skills requiring strength. Another strategy to assist the golfer with decreased strength is to allow the player to place the ball on the tee on all shots, excluding putts.

Gary Robb, previous Director of the National Center on Accessibility, provided these guidelines for golfers with disabilities at a 1995 ADAG seminar: (a) call ahead to make a tee time and, if accommodations are required, inform the golf course of the services that might be requested; (b) obtain names of the golf professional and green superintendent; (c) ask specific questions relative to golf course policies including bringing private or modified golf cars, course accessibility for parking and the pro shop, coaches for golfers with visual impairments or personal care attendants, and inform the staff about any assistive devices; (d) become familiar with the golf course and layout; (e) arrive early to ensure adequate time to check in, warm up and, if necessary, answer questions that golf course personnel may have; (f) if you are paired with strangers, introduce yourself early and discuss playing conditions; (g) determine policies for golf carts and/or assistive devices; (h) go to the practice range to warm up and test course conditions; and (i) know your physical limitations and determine the level of course difficulty with which you feel comfortable well in advance of teeing off.

Disability specific adaptations to golf: sensory limitations. Although golfers with *hearing impairments* do not require any adaptations to play golf, golfers with *visual impairments* may require equipment adaptations or alternative programming strategies.

> Some examples of adaptations include using clubs with indented number labeling to allow the golfer with a visual impairment to identify clubs without sight, colored balls, placing a radio in the fairway to give orientation to the golfer with a visual disability, or using devices which emit a beeping sound when placed in the golf hole alerting the golfer as to the location of the hole. One such device is Audio Golf. An example of a program strategy involves pairing a sighted partner with the golfer with a visual impairment. The partner can verbally direct the golfer with a visual impairment in lining up for a swing, identification of the hole, distance, or notification of hazards.

Disability specific adaptations to golf: cognitive limitations. Many people with cognitive limitations play golf. For example, SOI provides local golf clinics to participants with cognitive limitations to increase skills. Techniques that can be used to encourage people with cognitive impairments to play golf include: (a) taking individuals to miniature golf courses for practice in between games and giving simple instructions; (b) using descending ball sizes to increase hand-eye coordination to a level needed to strike a small golf ball such as moving from a beach ball, to a balloon, to a large Wiffle ball, to a tennis ball, to finally, a golf ball; (c) using larger balls or clubs with larger heads; (d) placing balls on tees for all shots except for putting, (e) teeing off from front tee box; and (e) using a peer to provide assistance.

> Frisbee Golf is an example of an adapted version of golf that can be played anywhere where there is a large open area. Holes are simulated with bases or flags. The participant must throw the Frisbee until he or she touches the base or flag. A tally is kept of the number of throws required to touch the base or flag. Nine or eighteen hole competitions can be held.

Tennis. Wheelchair tennis (see Figure 18.3) is played by the same rules used by athletes without disabilities except in wheelchair tennis the ball is allowed to bounce twice before it is returned. According to Paciorek and Jones (1994), experienced wheelchair tennis players rarely use the two-bounce option.

In 1980, the National Foundation of Wheelchair Tennis (NFWT) was established as the organizing body of the sport to: (a) establish a circuit of tournaments and develop these tournaments into quality events; (b) develop a quality junior wheelchair tennis development and sports program; (c) encourage program development through instructional camps and clinics; and (d) provide exhibition events to encourage more people to play the game. The NFWT reported that, since its inception, wheelchair tennis has been the fastest growing wheelchair sport. In 1998, the United States Tennis Association (USTA) assumed responsibility for wheelchair tennis from the NFWT. USTA then became the first National Governing Body of both Olympic and Paralympic tennis events.

Figure 18.3

Disability-specific adaptations to tennis: physical limitations. It is helpful to work with each participant to make adaptations to meet the person's unique needs. Initially, participants may be helped by attaching additional padding and straps to their wheelchair. For those individuals who become more involved in the sport, a specialized tennis chair may be purchased.

> Although there is no single way to set up a wheelchair for sport participation (manual or power), Draney (1997) suggested considering the following: (a) the type of frame; (b) overall weight; (c) width; (d) length; (e) amount of squeeze or pinch; (f) three-wheeler verses four-wheeler; (g) size and type of rear wheels and tubes/tires; (h) amount of camber in rear wheels; (i) size and type of front forks and casters; (j) turning radius; (k) seat height in relation to the ground and to the rear wheels; and (l) seating position with special attention to the elevation of the player's hips in relation to knee elevation.

Modification of equipment is an ongoing process. What works well for one person may not work for another. Constant experimentation with various adjustments allows participants time to adapt to modifications. It may take many alterations to evaluate the benefits of changes to equipment or style of play. Chair setup and equipment modification may be a never-ending process. Three important areas for adaptations to tennis include: stability and balance, rackets, and gripping the racket.

The sport of wheelchair tennis requires frequent, quick motion, and direction change; therefore, *stability and balance* are important considerations. The tennis player in a wheelchair can be assisted with stability and balance by using straps or belts.

> Straps or belts available in various lengths and widths are made from different materials and can be purchased from wheelchair manufacturers, sporting goods stores, or custom-made by upholstery shops. Some tennis players prefer using Velcro to adjust tension and secure straps. Straps with loops at the ends can be used by individuals with limited hand or finger functioning. Straps around the chest or stomach may enhance a player's balance. Straps around a player's waist, knees, and feet may help that player stay in the chair, and thus improve stability. It is important to check skin and joint areas frequently to ensure the chair and straps do not cause injury.

People may make adaptations to their *racket* to accommodate strength and range of motion limitations. For example, lighter rackets with thicker beams require less arm strength to swing. Strings and string tension can be adjusted giving more power and less control; and looser strings adjusted giving less power and more control. It can be helpful to examine what other players with similar skills use.

An individual's ability to *grip a racket* can be determined by observing that person's use of a racket without modifications. When grasping the racket is identified as a problem, there are several options that may be considered. There are specially designed plastic molded hand grips that fasten to the racket with screws or clamps. A person's hand fits inside this plastic grip and is secured with a wrist strap. This device can improve the chance of a consistent grip for the tennis player. Unfortunately, these grips can be very expensive, in excess of several hundred dollars, and make changing rackets difficult (Draney, 1997).

A second option is the use of a soft leather or Naugahyde glove or mitt fastened with a wrist strap. The racket is placed in the gloved hand and fastened with a Velcro strap, ace bandage, or athletic tape. Although use of a glove can be a relatively easy and inexpensive adaptation, it may be too fragile to allow consistency or firmness when gripping the racket handle.

Another simple and inexpensive option is to attach one side of Velcro around the racket handle and the other side of Velcro to a glove (like a baseball batting glove), thus attaching the hand around the racket handle with Velcro in the desired grip (Draney, 1997). Use of an Ace bandage wrapped around the hand while gripping the racket can be reinforced with athletic tape. Although this adaptation is simple and inexpensive, the Ace bandage may stretch and slip under athletic tape, which may lead to inconsistencies with the grip (Draney, 1997). Occasionally, use of athletic tape alone to secure a hand to the racket handle in the desired grip is tried. A glove, such as a baseball batting glove, may be used for cushioning or protection between skin and athletic tape. Taping starts from the back of the hand, pulling each finger around the racket handle, covering each finger (Parks, 1997). The tape then continues around the wrist area, to the back of the hand, and on to the next finger. The tape will then go in the opposite direction to pull the thumb around the racket handle, and then adjustments can be made by adding or removing tape.

The ultimate goal of grip adaptations is for the racket handle to have a firm yet comfortable feeling in the player's hand. A small foam pad placed between the racket handle and a finger or thumb may help with positioning and alleviate pressure and discomfort. Regardless of the gripping technique chosen, it is important that the grip be able to be repeated each time the person holds the racket. It is important to be aware of any numbness, discoloration, or discomfort in the player's hand or fingers. This may be of particular importance if the individual has limited or no sensation hands or fingers. Continuous evaluation and ongoing modification are important.

> Assistance in establishing a wheelchair tennis program is provided
> by the United States Tennis Association (USTA). A guide is
> available that provides tennis instruction guidelines, a directory
> of existing programs, and guidelines for establishing programs
> (Paciorek & Jones, 1994).

Disability-specific adaptations to tennis: cognitive limitations. Tennis among people with cognitive disabilities can be an intervention to promote inclusion. Tennis opportunities within the Special Olympics Unified Sports Program provide tennis training and competition for people with cognitive disabilities. Players with disabilities are paired with players who do not have disabilities at a similar skill level and age. There are a range of tennis games played by people with cognitive disabilities, including unmodified tennis rules to games requiring individual tennis skills such as target stroke, racket bounce, and return shot (Paciorek & Jones, 1994).

Disability-specific adaptations to tennis: hearing impairments. Tennis played by people who are hearing impaired does not differ from the National Federation of Tennis game. Many tennis players with hearing impairments compete with players who have no disabilities. Tennis is a regular event in the World Games for the Deaf.

History

The first sport organization for athletes with disabilities was the International Committee of Silent Sports, formed in 1924 and joined by the United States in 1935. In addition, sports for people who were deaf were popular throughout much of Europe by 1924 (Daquila & Winnick, 1981). After World War II, sports for people with disabilities gained increased recognition (Hedrick & Broadbent, 1996). Wheelchair sports were introduced in England and in the United States in the late 1940s (Asken, 1991). Beginning in the 1950s, people with disabilities formed sport organizations and began competing on local, state, national, and international levels (DePauw & Clark, 1985).

As sports participation for people with disabilities grew, barriers to sports participation such as lack of physical access and discrimination were encountered (Brazile, 1990). Therefore, federal legislative actions began occurring in the late 1960s that provided greater access to facilities and programs for people with disabilities (Kennedy Foundation, 1978). Although each legislative act addresses more issues than sports for people with disabilities, the increased access as a result of legislation has enhanced opportunities. This section of the chapter on history of sports is divided into the following three sections:

- Organizations
- Legislation
- Specific Sports

Organizations

Although there are many sports organizations for people with disabilities, this section highlights two organizations. These two organizations were chosen because of the vast number of people who are served by these programs and the frequency with which TR specialists became involved with the organizations. More detailed descriptions of other organizations are available through resources listed in the back of this chapter. The organizations described are the:

- Special Olympics International (SOI)
- Paralympics

Special Olympics International (SOI). Founded in 1968, SOI is a program of competitive sports events that have been modified to accommodate individuals with mild to profound developmental and/or mental disabilities. This program was created by the Joseph P. Kennedy, Jr. Foundation in 1946, whose missions include research into prevention of mental retardation and improvement of the means by which society treats its citizens with mental retardation (Orelove et al., 1982). The first year the program served 1,000 participants. Within 10 years, the program was serving over 700,000 athletes with mental disabilities from around the world (Canabal, 1988). SOI celebrated its 40th anniversary in July 2008, during which time the organization served almost 3 million athletes from 180 countries (Special Olympics International, n.d.).

Training is provided to athletes for up to a year prior to a Special Olympic event (Orelove et al., 1982), and sponsoring organizations help to offer facilities, accommodations, and volunteers (Canabal, 1988). However, Hourcade (1989) criticized SOI programs as being spectator events that do more to display disabilities of participants than promote sports participation. Poretta, Gillespie, and Jasma (1996) investigated the SOI in terms of issues related to terminology, philosophy, perceptions, and programming by surveying 117 individuals who worked directly or indirectly with the SOI. From their analysis, respondents emphasized that the SOI Committee should create a mission statement that emphasizes inclusion opportunities, have opportunities available to a wider range of individuals with disabilities, and examine their mission statement to stay current on philosophies that drive other organizations.

Paralympics. The Paralympic Games, governed by the International Paralympic Committee, is a competition that involves selected sport events designed for elite athletes with disabilities (International Paralympic Committee, 2009). According to the International Paralympic Committee (n.d.), the word *Paralympic* originates from the Greek prefix *para*, which means beside or alongside, and the word *Olympics*.

The Paralympics Games are held parallel to the Olympic Games, and have shared the same city as the Olympics in 13 locations beginning in Rome, Italy in 1960. The first Paralympics Games consisted of athletes from 23 countries who used wheelchairs. The Beijing Paralympic Games hosted 3,951 athletes, 146 nations, 20 sports, and 12 days of competition. Classes of athletes who participate now include individuals with physical and visual impairments.

Legislation

As the civil rights movement of the 1960s expanded to include the rights of people with disabilities, legislation designed to alleviate some of the existing barriers to participation in society was passed into law. Among these legislative acts were the:

- Mental Retardation Amendments of 1967 (P.L. 90-170)
- Rehabilitation Act of 1973 (P.L. 93-112, Section 504)
- Education for All Handicapped Children Act of 1975 (P.L. 94-142)
- Amateur Sports Act of 1978 (P.L. 95-606)
- Individuals with Disabilities Education Act of 1987 (P.L. 99-457)
- Americans with Disabilities Act of 1990 (P.L. 101-336)

Mental Retardation Amendments of 1967 (P.L. 90-170). This act was designed to provide children with mental retardation access to mainstream classroom education opportunities in public schools (Orelove et al., 1982). Physical education was included among classes mandated to become integrated, thus providing early exposure to sports (Kennedy Foundation, 1978). Researchers have suggested that early exposure to sports participation through physical education instruction may be important in the development of interest in sports by people with disabilities (Wang & DePauw, 1996). According to the Kennedy Foundation (1978), P.L. 90-170 helped to provide for modifications of sports that led to the Special Olympics.

Rehabilitation Act of 1973 (P.L. 93-112, Section 504). With sports participation for people with disabilities increasing in the 1960s, participants found their opportunities limited by barriers to access and segregation (Brickey, 1984). Section 504 of the Rehabilitation Act of 1973 prohibits discrimination on the basis of disability by any program receiving federal funding and further insists that programs be provided in the least restrictive setting possible. Removal of such barriers contributed to increased sports participation by people with disabilities because access to facilities and programs that receive federal funding were now mandated to be made accessible to people with disabilities (Brazile, 1990).

Education for All Handicapped Children Act of 1975 (P.L. 94-142). The Education for All Handicapped Children Act stipulates that physical education classes should be integrated, allowing children with disabilities to experience sports with their peers (Hourcade, 1989). This law helped support programs for children that developed their skills in dance, aquatics, individual and group games, and lifetime sports (Stein, 1978). Connor-Kuntz, Dummer, and Paciorek (1995) suggested that early inclusion and participation of children with disabilities in sports (as mandated in P.L. 94-142) contributed to participation through adulthood.

Amateur Sports Act of 1978 (P.L. 95-606). The Amateur Sports Act required that amateur sports be open to integration of athletes with disabilities and has been a major influence contributing to their participation at national and international levels (Paciorek, Tetreault, & Jones, 1991). Effects of this act extended to the Olympic Committee where athletes with disabilities also became involved (DePauw & Clark, 1985). Opportunities for participation continue to expand.

> For example, in 2008, 3,951 international athletes participated in 12 days of Paralympics competition at the Olympic Games site in Beijing, China during the week immediately following the Olympic Games (International Paralympic Committee, 2009).

Individuals with Disabilities Education Act of 1987 (P.L. 99-457). The Individuals with Disabilities Education Act (IDEA) further supported P.L. 94-142 for earlier inclusion by encouraging provision of integrated school and agency programs. IDEA requires that individuals with physical or developmental disabilities be provided special education and related services including physical education and sports programs (Smith, 1993).

Americans with Disabilities Act of 1990 (P.L. 101-336). The Americans with Disabilities Act (ADA) mandated equitable opportunities for people with disabilities in the areas of employment, transportation, public access, and communication. Within the mandate for public access, participation in sports must be provided for individuals with disabilities in places where sports are available to people without disabilities (McGovern, 1991). The ADA expanded previous mandates such as Section 504 of the Barriers Compliance Act by including facilities which did not receive federal funding, thereby increasing the number of potential opportunities for sports participation for people with disabilities (Kegel & Malchow, 1994).

Summary of Legislation. The trend of inclusion of individuals with disabilities in activities engaged in by their peers without disabilities, including physical education classes, has provided new opportunities for sports experience. In addition, the mandates for barrier removal have increased the possibilities of sports participation and extended hope for even more opportunities.

Specific Sports

Basketball. Many high-schools and colleges include basketball as a component of their athletic program. Basketball originated because of an experiment conducted by James Naismith in 1892. Basketball was developed due to the need for an indoor sport to fill the season between football and baseball.

In its original conception, basketball was played with teams of 9–15 players on a side. Other aspects of basketball that differ from the version played today include use of peach baskets for goals and a football for a ball. During the first 2 years of its existence, basketball was changed as the number of players on the court was reduced from nine to seven. Naismith's version of basketball has since been modified primarily to increase safety for participants.

> As the popularity of basketball grew, the growth of basketball opportunities for individuals with disabilities increased dramatically. Wheelchair basketball began in 1946 in response to the high incidence of World War II veterans who used wheelchairs (Hedrick et al., 1989). The National Wheelchair Basketball Association (NWBA) was established in 1949 after the first National Invitational Wheelchair Basketball Tournament (Savage & Winnick, 1980). Today, there are over 22 conferences (over 200 teams) and seven divisions in the NWBA. In addition to the United States, wheelchair basketball has experienced international popularity evident in the World Championships and Paralympic Tournaments. Wheelchair basketball is one of the few team sports played on an international basis. It ranks as the oldest wheelchair sport in the world.

Golf. The modern game of golf was developed in Scotland. Four centuries ago, it was legally prohibited because its popularity threatened activities that contributed to skill development necessary for military prowess, such as archery. Today, golf is one of the more popular sports in our country. There are over 23,000 golf courses in the United States (World Golf, n.d.). The National Golf Foundation estimates that

12% of the American public participates in the game of golf. Whether recreational or competitive, golf continues to be a sport enjoyed by all genders, ages, and ethnicities.

Despite a decrease in the number of people who play golf from 6.9 million in 2000 to 4.6 million in 2005 (Vitello, 2008), the popularity of golf among Americans led to dramatically more golfers with disabilities who participate in the game. The passage of the Americans with Disabilities Act (ADA) and the formation of the Association of Disabled American Golfers (ADAG) have been instrumental in increasing participation in golf by people with disabilities. Today, there are numerous competitive tournaments held for golfers with amputations, spinal cord injuries, sensory impairments, and persons of short stature. Special Olympics International implements local and district-wide skill workshops to teach golf to individuals with cognitive impairments.

Tennis. Some historians believe that tennis was created by European monks and was played during religious ceremonies (History of Tennis, n.d.). Originally, the ball was hit with the hand, then a leather glove, soon followed by a glove with an adaptive handle attached (History of Tennis, n.d.). The modern game grew from the ancient form and spread throughout the Middle East and Europe. Tennis has been popular in the United States for more than 100 years. Most U.S. public schools, colleges, universities, and parks have tennis courts, as do private clubs and homes.

> The Wheelchair Tennis Tournament Circuit was created in 1981. This circuit consists of championship tournaments among several men's and women's divisions ranging from Open (for the most advanced players) to A and B divisions for beginner or novice players. There are junior divisions (under 18 years), senior (masters) divisions for those over 40, and divisions for people with quadriplegia. Up until 2009, the tennis season culminated each year in Irvine, California, where the U.S. Open Wheelchair Tennis Championships were held. As of 2009, the Championships will be held in Saint Louis, MO. This Championship is an international event that draws over 350 players.

Theoretical Foundations

A range of theories have been used in research of sports for people with disabilities. While not comprehensive, below are introductions to three theories found in the literature. The following three theories include:

- Personal Investment
- Achievement Motivation
- Social Role

Personal Investment

Personal investment has been used to explain motivation of people with disabilities to participate in sports (Brazile, Kleiber, & Harnisch, 1991). The theory of personal investment explains motivation as a two-stage process. In the first stage, factors that give meaning to situations are considered external to an individual. In the second stage, the meaning of a particular situation leads to the degree of personal investment by an individual. The theory frames motivation as a process of choosing how to allocate personal resources such as choosing to use time skiing rather than watching television. According to Maehr and Braskamp (1986), three primary incentives motivate behavior:

- Task
- Ego
- Social

Task incentives are similar to intrinsic rewards in that people set their own criteria for success (Nicholls, 1989). For example, people simply play tennis because tennis is fun.

Ego incentives occur when people compare themselves to each other, such as playing softball because they like to win. An ego incentive might involve a desire to demonstrate superiority compared to others as well (Nicholls, 1989).

Social incentives are things such as friendship and camaraderie, such as enjoying the companionship of teammates (Maehr & Braskamp, 1986).

Achievement Motivation

Atkinson's (1978) theory of achievement motivation has been used in discussions of competitive attitudes in athletes with disabilities (Zoerink & Wilson, 1995). The theory explains competitiveness as an interaction between personality and environment that leads to a desire to succeed. People who are more competitive are theorized to be more interested in sports, set higher goals, and are more persistent in pursuit of excellence in sports. Conversely, those who are less competitive are less likely to pursue sports with the same vigor than their competitive counterparts.

Social Role

Role theory has evolved since Linton's (1936) introduction of the theory. Martin and colleagues (1995) applied social role theory to people with disabilities who partici-pate in sports. For example, people define themselves as athletes when they identify with roles of athletes and expect others to acknowledge them as athletes. An athletic identity is "the degree to which an individual identifies with the role of an athlete" (Horton & Mack, 2000, p. 101) and can have important implications (Martin, Adams-Mushett, & Smith, 1995). For instance, people who identify themselves as athletes are likely to exercise regularly and eat healthfully. An athletic identity is developed through factors such as athletic skill development and social interaction during sport participation (Brewer et al., 1993).

Effectiveness

Researchers have reported a variety of explanations for why individuals with disabilities participate in sports and the various outcomes that result from participation. TR specialists might benefit from gaining an understanding of these effects to better serve participants and to better evaluate progress. In this section, the following categories are presented:

- Participation Incentives
- Physical Effects
- Psychological Effects

Participation Incentives

Goodwin and colleagues (2009) examined the social experience of 11 wheelchair rugby players from the perspective of the players, of which 10 were males with an average age of 33 years. Using semi-structured focus group interviews and artifacts, participants shared their experiences as rugby players. Three themes emerged, including: it's okay to be a quad, don't tell us we can't, and the power of wheelchair rugby. Participants' identified with a shared sense of community and enjoyed the membership, fulfillment of needs, influence, and shared emotional connections. The researchers argued that participants used participation in wheelchair rugby to authentically express themselves through their sport.

In a study that included a sample of 1,307 families and 579 athletes from the United States, **Harada and Siperstein (2009)** examined motivation for sport experiences for athletes with intellectual disabilities who participated in Special Olympics. Athletes primarily participated in sports for fun (54%) and social interaction (21%). Similar to individuals without disabilities, participants discontinued participation because of changes in interest (38%) and lack of program availability (33%).

Fiona, Guy, Faulkner, and Kirsh (2008) investigated perceptions toward physical activity and sport among 13 youth with congenital heart disease. Although participants reported that sports are important in maintaining good health, they did not view them as a valuable pursuit. Participants expressed low-self efficacy and fatigue. Participants low self-efficacy and feelings of fatigue may have decreased the value ascribed to sports participation and physical activity. Results indicated that nontraditional activities, support from other people, and perceptions of mastery each played an important role in enabling participation and helped to facilitate recovery. The findings might help practitioners to design safe and enjoyable physical activities for youth with congenital heart disease.

Farrell, Crocker, McDonough, and Sedgwick (2004) examined perceptions of motivation among 38 Special Olympics athletes from British Columbia, Canada, of which 17 were female with a mean age of 33 years. Upon completion of interviews, the following thematic categories were created: reasons for participating in Special Olympics, dislikes about Special Olympics, social support, and suggestions for program development. Enhanced autonomy, competence and relatedness were linked to motivation for participation. Factors included positive feedback, choice, skill development, demonstrating ability, friendships, social approval, and fun. A primary factor related to participation motivation was social support from family and friends. Motivation was, however, undermined by conflicts with teammates and coaches.

Seeking to investigate "athletic identity" in 678 individuals with spinal cord injuries, of which 84% were males, ranging in age from 20–77 years, with an average age of 45 years, **Tasiemski, Kennedy, Gardner, and Blaikley (2004)** used the Athletic Identity Measure Scale (AIMS) (Brewer et al., 1993) to examine reasons for and barriers to sport participation. Specifically, levels of athletic identity were examined by exploring differences related to gender, number of hours participating in sports per week, and status related to achievement. Participants, including those who competed as athletes, reported lower levels of athletic identity when compared to adolescents with disabilities and adults who did not have a disability. AIMS scores varied according to gender, number of hours participating in sports, and status. Reasons for participating in sports after the injury included: maintaining good physical condition (70.7%), improving upper body strength (57.5%), getting out of the house and meeting people (56.4%), enjoying oneself (55.9%), improving self-esteem (44.8%), improving weight control (41.1%), competing (41.1%), traveling (23.6%), and other reasons (5.7%). Reported barriers to participation included: maintaining good physical condition (70.7%), lacking accessible facilities (38.1%), disliking "traditional" sports for people with disabilities (38.1%), having a high dependency in activities of daily living (30.5%), lacking opportunities to practice favorite sports (25.2%), lacking time (25.1%), lack of money (20.4%), having difficulties with transportation (11.8%), and other reasons (17.6%). No relationship was found when athletic identity and anxiety, depression, and life satisfaction were compared.

Shapiro (2003) examined motives for sport participation among 147 Special Olympics athletes, of which 67 were females, ranging in age from 21–70 years with mean age of 34. Participants completed a 14-item Sport Motivation Questionnaire (SMQ) developed by the researcher. No significant differences were found for gender, age, race, or sport when participation motives were analyzed. Motives included winning medals and ribbons, playing with other people, getting exercise, participating in something they feel good at, and to having fun. Consistent with achievement motivation theory, participants were motivated to participate for task incentives rather than ego incentives.

In a study designed to identify factors that influenced 143 individuals who had a spinal cord injury to participate in sports in the United Kingdom, **Wu and Williams (2001)** examined the relationship between sport participation before and after injuries. Participants were actively engaged in basketball, wheelchair rugby, wheelchair tennis, and wheelchair athletics programs. The researchers developed and administered a disability sport participation questionnaire to collect information regarding personal, impairment, health and fitness, socialization, and participation data on participants. Factors identified included social contexts, social agents, difficulties associated with their disabilities, sources of information, and reasons for participation. Research that involves collecting information specific to the factors identified might provide directions for improving rehabilitation programs and for developing strategies for assisting people with spinal cord injuries to partici pate in sports.

Wang and DePauw (1996) explored incentives among elite athletes with disabilities in China. Forty-three men and sixteen women participants were drawn from the athletes who competed in the second China National Games for the Disabled and were administered the Early Recreational and Sport Experiences of Elite Athletes with Disabilities Survey (Gavron, 1989). Respondents were geographically dispersed throughout seven provinces. Results indicated that participants viewed physical educators and self-motivation as most influential to their participation. Peer influence of other athletes with disabilities was an important component of initial involvement.

To investigate motivation for sport participation, **Kirkby (1995)** surveyed 38 people with disabilities and 19 people without disabilities involved in competitive netball. A 9-item self-administered questionnaire was used to gather demographic and motivational information. Participants reported motivation for participation in the following order: enjoyment, socializing/making friends, fitness, and competition. The authors concluded that there were no differences between motivation of participants with disabilities and those without disabilities.

To examine motivation for participation in triathlon competitions, **Furst and colleagues (1993)** administered a questionnaire to measure participation motives to 25 competitors of the 1990 National Wheelchair Triathlon. Results generated three primary influences for training and competing: other competitors with disabilities, self-motivation, and adapted physical education specialists. The top four reasons for participating were fun, physical development, love of competition, and socialization. Social interaction may be the strongest motivator for sport participation.

Brazile and colleagues (1991) surveyed 158 athletes who used wheelchairs and 116 athletes without disabilities to compare participation incentives. Five factors emerged associated with sport participation including fitness, ego, task, social integration, and social affect. Athletes with disabilities differed from athletes without disabilities in only one factor, that of social integration. In 23 of the 26 reasons for participation in sports, there were no significant differences between people with disabilities and people without disabilities. Being with friends, making new acquaintances, traveling, and pleasing others may be of greater importance to people with disabilities than to those without disabilities. Motivation to participate in sports might be more a factor of individual situation and self-perception than of disability.

Summary. From the research reviewed, social interaction appears to be among the most important incentives for participation in sports by people with disabilities. Other important incentives include maintaining physical fitness, having an opportunity to compete, improving self-esteem, and enjoying sports. TR specialists may want to consider these incentives when planning sport programs for people with disabilities.

Physical Effects

In a study of wheelchair tennis players, **Reina, Moreno, and Sanz (2007)** examined visual behavior and motor responses of five experienced and seven novice players relative to the return in tennis. Both groups engaged in a video-based (two dimensional) series of serves performed to the forehand and the backhand sides, and in a one on court (three dimensional) series of serves. Novice participants initially focused on the expected ball toss area or followed the ball from the toss to the apex and experienced participants focused initially on the head/shoulders and the free-arm. The experienced players obtained helpful information from racket-arm cues during the stroke phase and performed faster motor responses than the novice players.

Goosey-Tolfrey (2005) examined physiological changes in 28 male elite wheelchair basketball players ranging in age from 17–38 years who participated in the 28-month training program that led to the 2000 Paralympics. Twelve participants completed all six sessions. Using a wheelchair ergometer to record data, the focus was on the aerobic and anaerobic assessment of the participants. Physiological changes were measured related to body mass, skin fold assessments, peak oxygen uptake, and peak power obtained during sprinting. Although peak oxygen uptake increased significantly prior to the Paralympics, training had little influence on sprinting. Participants appeared to have high levels of aerobic and anaerobic fitness. Physiological profiles taken during the study demonstrated that participants improved their aerobic capacity while maintaining other fitness levels.

Arnett, Merriman, and Arnett (1998) examined effects of a 9-week (3 x wk; 1 hr) swimming program on the cardiovascular fitness levels and basic water skills of eight individuals who were blind and had severe/profound intellectual disabilities. Cardiovascular fitness was measured before and after the swimming program by having participants complete a Cooper 12-minute walk/run test. Swim skills were assessed with the Special Olympic aquatic level one swimming assessment. The swimming program included a 30-minute changing period before and after sessions, water entry, 12-minute walking in the shallow end of the pool, 16-minute skill practice, and 2-minute cool down. Results indicated that the mean distance walked in the Cooper 12-minute walk/run increased from 569 to 719. The mean percent of completed water skills before and after the program were 18% and 41%, respectively. The authors concluded that individuals who are blind and have severe/profound intellectual disabilities can learn swimming skills and improve cardiovascular fitness levels.

Schaperclaus and colleagues (1997) investigated levels of fitness and risk factors following a myocardial infarction of 67 male and seven female participants in sports groups for people with cardiac problems. Physical fitness was measured with bicycle ergometers designed to establish maximum oxygen intake. Risk factors assessed included hypertension, hyper-cholesterol, obesity, smoking, physical inactivity, and diabetes. Questionnaires and patient files were used to gather personal information. Participants were compared to 52 male and 8 female nonsporting adults with cardiac problems. Compared to the control group, the sport group demonstrated greater maximum oxygen uptake and perceived well-being and a lower risk factor level. The authors concluded that effects of sports programs in cardiac rehabilitation should be further studied.

From a survey of 229 alumni of the University of Illinois with severe locomotor disabilities, **Hedrick and Broadbent (1996)** suggested that levels of participation in physical activities and sports in college and severity of disability could be predictors of current levels of physical activity. Perceived level of physical activity during college was the most significant predictor of current physical activity. The researchers concluded that those alumni who were more active in sports and physical activities while attending the university were less likely to adopt the physically inactive lifestyles so prevalent among people with similar disabilities.

Wells and Hooker (1990) compared specific physical functions between athletes and nonathletes with spinal cord injuries. Results indicated that athletes with disabilities have less body fat, higher lung capacity, and greater aerobic power than their nonathletic counterparts. Participants with spinal cord injuries responded well to strength and muscular endurance training and demonstrated fitness increases at rates equal to those of people without disabilities. The researchers concluded that people with disabilities who participate in sports experience reduce their stress due to wheelchair ambulation and trained athletes with disabilities can attain fitness levels equal to or greater than those of athletes without disabilities.

Pitetti, Jackson, Stubbs, Campbell, and Battar (1989) conducted two studies examining effect of Special Olympic activities on physical fitness of 24 participants ages 9 to 13. In the first study, the authors compared cardiovascular fitness, percent body fat, and blood lipid profiles of participants with mild intellectual disabilities, individuals not disabled, and training adults without disabilities. Special Olympic participants demonstrated lower fitness profiles than training adults without disabilities. Male Special Olympics participants demonstrated fitness profiles similar to individuals without disabilities and female Special Olympics participants demonstrated lower cardiovascular fitness levels than the individuals without disabilities and training adults without disabilities. In the second study, cardiovascular fitness and percent body fat of Special Olympics participants with mild intellectual disabilities were compared before and after 4–18 months of participation. No significant change in body weight, percent body fat, or cardiovascular fitness was found. The researchers concluded that the intensity of activity failed to improve physical fitness.

Summary. According to Healthy People 2010, people with disabilities tend to report more anxiety, pain, sleeplessness, and days of depression and fewer days of vitality than do people without activity limitations (U.S. Department of Health and Human Services, n.d., p. 15). They also experience other challenges such as lower rates of physical activity and higher rates of obesity. Hedrick and Broadbent (1996) suggested that the people with disabilities who remain active in sports experience health benefits. Some physical benefits experienced by people with disabilities who participate in sports include maintaining health, lowering fat levels, increasing lung capacity and aerobic power than nonathletes with disabilities, increased levels of physical fitness, a propensity for adopting an active sports lifestyle, and high levels of aerobic and anaerobic fitness levels.

Psychological Effects

Martin (2008) examined effects of wheelchair basketball on 79 athletes' self-efficacy, including performance, training, resiliency, and thought control, as well as positive and negative affect. There was weak to strong significant relationships among the four types of self-efficacy and among self-efficacy and affect. Participants who were efficacious in their ability to overcome training barriers were confident in their basketball skills and successful in overcoming a focus on distressing thoughts while simultaneously cultivating positive thoughts. Participants with strong resiliency and thought control efficacy reported less negative affect and more positive affect.

Although many researchers have found that sport participation has positive psychological effects, results of a study conducted with 24 adolescents with conduct disorder demonstrated contrary findings. **Maiano, Ninot, Morin, and Bilard (2007)** examined the long-term effects of sport participation on the basketball skills and physical self-concept. Participants were divided equally into three groups: inter-establishment basketball, integrated scholastic basketball, and control-adapted physical activity. A basketball skills test and a physical self-concept measure were administrated 4 times over an 18-month period. Participants' basketball skills in both competitive groups improved. For all three groups a curvilinear trend of physical self-worth was observed. There were no significant changes in physical self-concept for all three groups. The researchers concluded that integrated and segregated competitive programs were not effective in improving physical self-concept of adolescents with conduct disorder.

Castagno (2001) examined changes related to self-esteem, friendship, and sports skills in 58 Special Olympic athletes in grades 6–8 with 24 having intellectual disabilities and only one being female. Data were collected before and after participation in an 8-week (3 x wk, 90-min session) after-school basketball program using the Self-Esteem Inventory (Zigler, 1994), the Adjective Checklist (Siperstein, 1980), the Friendship Activity Scale (Siperstein, 1980), and the Basketball Sports Skills Assessment (Special Olympics, 1992). Scores were significantly higher after participation in the program for both groups. Castagno concluded that the program provided participants with opportunities to interact with a friend, thus providing a vehicle for social interaction. A limitation, however, was that the groups were heterogeneous in relation to age, gender, ethnicity, disability type and severity of disability, and sport.

Similarly, although the literature reveals psychological benefits associated with sports participation, a negative effect, stress, has been examined as well. For example, **Campbell and Jones (2002)** examined causes of stress in an international team of 10 elite, male wheelchair basketball players with a mean age of 32. Structured interviews were conducted to learn about their views; a content analysis was completed to determine stress categories. Ten sources of stress were identified and included: preventive concerns, negative match preparation, on-court concerns, post-match performance concerns, negative aspects major event, lack of appropriate group interaction and communication, negative coaching style/behavior, issues related to relationships, expenses and demands of wheelchair basketball, and lack of awareness about the disability. Identified stress sources experienced were mostly related to the competition process, organization needed for competing at an elite event, and interactions with important people associated with the events. Expenses and demands of wheelchair basketball, and lack of disability awareness among other people, were identified, but not specifically related to competition.

Blinde and McClung (1997) examined effects of participation in horseback riding, swimming, fitness, weightlifting, racquetball, bowling, tennis, fishing, walking, and T'ai chi on perceptions of physical and social selves of 12 males and 11 females with physical disabilities. Based on analyses of tape-recorded interviews conducted after participation, participation impacted four aspects of the physical self: body experienced in new ways, enhanced perceptions of physical attributes, reduced physical capabilities, and increased perceived confidence to pursue new physical activities. Two themes emerged related to respondents' perceptions of the social self: expansion of social interactions and initiation of social activities in other contexts. The researchers concluded that participation in recreation activities enhanced participants' sense of control in both their physical and social lives.

Campbell and Jones (1997) examined competition anxiety and self-confidence in 87 male and 16 female participants ranging in ages from 19 to 46 who engaged in wheelchair sports during three periods (1 x wk, 2 hrs, 30 min) preceding competition. Anxiety and self-confidence were measured at each of the three periods to determine intensity, frequency, and degree to which the experience was facilitated or debilitated. In terms of frequency, anxiety and self-confidence scores consistently rose at each data collection period. Analysis of intensity revealed that anxiety scores consistently rose; however, self-confidence dropped between the 2-hour and 30-minute data collection points. Cognitive and somatic anxiety scores dropped from 1-week to 2-hour data collection points; however, they rose again at the 30-minute data collection point. Competition anxiety and self-confidence responses changed as a function of how close in time participants were to the competitive event.

Riggen and Ulrich (1993) examined differences related to physical ability, social skills, and self-worth, in 75 males who participated in either a segregated Special Olympic program or the integrated Unified Sports Program of Special Olympics. The Perceived Competence Scale for Children (Harter, 1982) was used to assess self-perceptions. A 1-mile run-walk was used to assess cardiovascular fitness, and a standard skills test used for team placement by Special Olympics was used to assess sport skills. An increase in social self-perception was shown among Unified athletes and no significant increases were found in self-perceptions of physical and self-worth for either of the Special Olympics groups. Both groups demonstrated significant increases in sports skills but not in cardiovascular fitness.

Greenwood, Dzewaltowski, and French (1990) conducted a study using the Profiles of Mood States (POMS) and two self-efficacy scales to compare differences between 77 male and 10 female tennis players who used wheelchairs and 32 male and 8 female nontennis players who used wheelchairs in terms of self-efficacy and psychological well-being. The tennis players demonstrated significantly higher levels of self-efficacy and psychological well-being and had better wheelchair mobility skills than those who were not tennis players.

Sherrill and Rainbolt (1988) examined self-actualization profiles of 265 college-age athletes without disabilities and 30 elite male athletes with cerebral palsy, all of whom were international competitors. Profiles were examined in relation to one another and to two normative groups: adults and college students. Both groups demonstrated similar self-actualization profiles. Elite athletes with cerebral palsy were found to be significantly less self-actualized than the normative adults group in areas of time competence, existentiality, self-acceptance, nature of man, and synergy. College-age male athletes without disabilities were generally more self-actualized than the normative college-age group.

Dummer, Ewing, Habeck, and Overton (1987) examined attributions of 147 athletes with cerebral palsy who participated in the 1985 Cerebral Palsy/Les Autres games. Specifically, athletes' reactions to objectively and subjectively (satisfaction with performance) defined success or failure were examined. No significant differences were found related to attributions by gender; however, differences were found when attributions were examined across disability classifications. Compared to participants with cerebral palsy who lost, those who won used both internal and external explanations to a greater degree. Subjective explanations were found to provide a more powerful explanation of achievement behavior than objective explanations. Satisfaction with performance was associated with demonstrating the correct strategy and ability, realistically assessing ability, and enjoying competition.

Mastro, Sherrill, Gench, and French (1987) compared psychological characteristics of tension, depression, anger, vigor, fatigue, and confusion of 33 male and 15 female elite athletes with visual impairments, and contrasted findings with those reported in the literature on athletes without disabilities. Male and female elite athletes with visual impairments were significantly different in levels of confusion, fatigue, and tension. In comparisons between athletes with visually impairments and athletes without disabilities, female athletes with visual impairments demonstrated different psychological profiles from elite athletes with vision, and male athletes with visual impairments demonstrated psychological profiles similar to elite athletes with vision.

Summary. Research modestly suggests that wheelchair tennis players have higher levels of self-efficacy and well-being than those who use wheelchairs but do not play tennis, and improved self-efficacy is associated with participation in wheelchair basketball. Athletes with cerebral palsy have experienced satisfaction when their performance was associated with correct strategy and ability, realistic assessment of ability, and enjoying competition. People with physical disabilities who participate in recreation activities experience enhanced sense of control in both their physical and social lives.

Increases in social self-perception among participants of an integrated Unified Sports Program of Special Olympics have been observed compared to a traditional program. Although positive changes in self-esteem, friendship, and sports skills have been identified for Special Olympics athletes who participate in an after-school basketball program, similar results were not found when examining effects of sports participation on self-esteem and physical self-concept among adolescents with conduct disorders. Although research identified psychological benefits to sport participation, negative effects related to stress have been identified.

Overall Summary

This section provided a summary of studies that examined participation incentives, physical effects, and psychological effects experienced by participants with disabilities in a variety of sports. In summarizing literature reviewed in this section, there was a moderate amount of research found examining effects of sports on people with disabilities. Existing research modestly indicates that sports are an empirically supported facilitation technique.

Case Studies

The following case studies are examples of the implementation of a sports program and the potential impact it has in the life of individuals seeking TR services. As indicated previously, there are many available adaptive sports for implementation in a wide array of settings. The following examples are for:

- Tim with quad rugby
- Danielle with archery

Tim

Tim was raised in a small rural town and was well liked in high school. His plans were to finish college and marry his high school sweetheart. Tim was in his early 20s when injuries sustained in a car accident resulted in quadriplegia at the C-6 level. This level of spinal cord injury left Tim paralyzed from the chest down with moderate impairment in his arms and hands. The accident affected not only Tim's body, but his sense of confidence and self-esteem. According to his family, Tim had always been an individual who was outgoing and confident in his endeavors. The paralysis now left him timid, afraid, and uncertain of his capabilities.

Shortly after Tim entered a rehabilitation hospital, a TR specialist met with Tim to complete an initial evaluation and determine pre- and post-injury interests. The initial evaluation indicated typical interests for a young man in his early 20s: fishing, attending college football games, dining out, board games with friends, participatory and observational sports, and swimming. After Tim and the TR specialist completed the initial evaluation, an individual treatment plan was developed for completion during rehabilitation. Goals were set by Tim and the TR specialist specific to the areas of community mobility, aquatics, billiards, fishing, horticulture, and quad rugby. These goals involved many pre-injury interests such as aquatics, billiards, and fishing, as well as an introduction to new recreation and leisure options such as horticulture and quad rugby.

Quad Rugby for Tim. Although unfamiliar with quad rugby, Tim was willing to learn more about the sport. He verbalized uncertainty with his participation in quad rugby because of his limited muscle function in his arms and hands. The TR specialist assured Tim that the process of adaptive sports involvement worked within his functional abilities and he would not be placed in a situation beyond his skills. The TR specialist wanted Tim to be exposed to quad rugby because of his pre-injury sports interest and quad rugby was one of the few competitive sports outlets for individuals with quadriplegia.

The first step in the process was to teach Tim quad rugby. Tim watched video tapes of quad rugby and learned the rules of the game. Once the basics were understood, Tim was encouraged to attend the practice of the hospital-affiliated team. There, Tim saw quad rugby and interacted with individuals with similar injury levels. Then the TR specialist scheduled an overnight trip to a tournament where Tim met quad rugby players from all over the region.

With Tim's increased knowledge of quad rugby came increased self-esteem and an improved outlook on his future goals. Tim verbalized his desire to progress from a power wheelchair to a manual wheelchair to allow participation in quad rugby. Tim's entire team of therapists used quad rugby as a reinforcement for him to make the transition from a power wheelchair to a manual wheelchair.

The impact of quad rugby on Tim transcended the rehabilitation phase. Tim decided that he would live in the same city in which the hospital was located to allow his participation with the hospital's rugby team. Tim and his family set up an accessible apartment with 12 hours of attendant care to assist him with his daily living activities. With an adequate knowledge of the sport, Tim now practiced the skills necessary for participation. Tim joined the quad rugby team and transferred to the local university, where he resumed his degree coursework in restaurant and hotel management. Tim's functional strength and mobility grew with his continued participation in quad rugby.

The need to travel with the rugby team motivated Tim to increase his independence with his daily living skills. On his first out-of-town trip, he was required to be independent with transfers, dressing, and bowel and bladder programs because of the lack of attendant care resources. Continued participation in out-of-town trips permitted additional practice with daily living skills. Tim's skills progressed to the point where he no longer required attendant care in his apartment. Later in the season, Tim flew on an airplane for the first time. Additionally, some quad rugby players on other teams convinced Tim to try a different technique for feeding rather than using a cumbersome feeding brace. Tim participated on the rugby team for 3 years.

Tim has since returned to his hometown, where he and his wife own and manage their own restaurant. Although Tim has not been involved in quad rugby for the past 2 years, he has not lost interest and is attempting to organize his own team in his hometown. The introduction of quad rugby made an enormous difference in Tim's life.

In this case study, the TR specialist implemented an adaptive sport across a continuum of programming techniques. First, the participant was provided with information about quad rugby. Next, the participant received first-hand experience in practicing the skills to allow full participation. Finally, resources were provided to allow community transition.

Danielle

At the time of this case study, Danielle was 19 years old and had just graduated from the state school for individuals diagnosed as blind and deaf. Danielle was congenitally blind from a condition called retrolental fibroplasia (RLF). Danielle lived with her mother and used a guide dog for mobility. Her hobbies were watching television and playing the guitar. Danielle rarely left her house.

When Danielle was first contacted by the TR specialist at the recreation center, she indicated that she was bored and that the center had little to offer. Eventually, Danielle accepted an invitation to a luncheon at the center. At the luncheon, Danielle appeared unkempt and displayed poor hygiene habits. After the luncheon, Danielle attended some of the programs at the center irregularly. Interviews with the activities coordinator revealed that Danielle had no goals or plans for her life. She seemed lost and unsure of her own identity. Danielle's hygiene habits remained a concern.

Archery for Danielle. After a few months, the TR specialist challenged Danielle to try archery, a sport that most consider impossible for people who are blind. Danielle agreed that it might be an interesting experience. After attending her first session of the archery program, Danielle did not miss one of the weekly sessions for the following year.

The archery intervention was organized at a local indoor archery range. The equipment used was standard recurve bows and wooden arrows with metal target tips. The target was a large outdoor target face, and the target support was placed at the five-meter range. At the first session, each participant was taken to the target and shown the target face by guiding their hands across the surface. Next, each participant was given a bow and allowed to inspect it for a period of approximately 5 minutes. Each participant was then shown how to hold the bow and draw the string. The draw lengths were measured and the appropriate length arrows were dispensed. The coach then instructed the group about the proper stance for shooting. The TR specialist and one assistant helped each archer discover the proper stance by moving and guiding the individuals. On the first day, each archer was permitted two rounds, or ends, of five shots each. In this first experience hand-on-hand guiding was used. After each participant had finished his or her shots, he or she was guided to the target and allowed to find where his or her arrows had scored. Danielle shot her second group without hand-on-hand assistance and was able to get all five arrows within the target face. Her excitement was very evident.

In weekly 90-minute sessions, the archers worked on form, stance, and release for the first four sessions. They were now shooting independently with an assistant giving them verbal cues for aiming. Danielle indicated that she had never been as excited about anything as she was about archery. Danielle demonstrated some leadership responsibility by requesting a target face to take home and returning with it the following week with tactile markings. These markings made it possible for her and the other archers to score themselves.

During the fifth week, an electronic scope was introduced. The scope consisted of a light sensor in the back of a 6-inch plastic tube 3/4 inch diameter. This scope had a volume control and an ear plug. The scope fastened to the bow just above the hand grip. A spotlight was mounted above the target. As the scope became more closely aligned with the light, the archer would hear a higher pitched sound from the scope. The archers now became more independent as they no longer needed others to give them sighting cues. Danielle became so involved that she started coming to the archery center several times per week to practice.

Danielle decided to train for open competition in archery. She needed her own equipment, which was somewhat costly. Her appearance suddenly changed, she came to the archery activity on the sixth week clean and neat. She created a job for herself teaching 12-string guitar and her life was changed in many positive ways, the most observable being her appearance and hygiene habits, and her activities outside her home. Her life had gained direction and she went on to compete in international archery competitions.

Summary

These case studies describe two individuals who have benefited from participation in organized sports activities. While Tim was able to regain independence and pursue his life goals after a spinal cord injury, Danielle overcame a general lack of interest in activities outside her home in addition to gaining independence and motivation. The benefits of sports participation generalized in other areas of both Tim and Danielle's lives. These examples illustrate a few of the potential benefits associated with participation in sports and recreation activities.

Intervention Implementation Exercises

When designing a sports program for people with disabilities a TR specialist can explore the various considerations involved in making adaptations. The following section includes four examples of considerations recommended for examination:

- Explore Adaptations of Sports
- Review Rules of Sports Designed for People with Disabilities
- Examine Adapted Equipment for Sports Participation
- Play a Sport with a Person with a Disability

Explore Adaptations of Sports

Sports programs for people with disabilities often require modifications of programs and materials. Often it is difficult to locate existing designs and adaptations. An understanding of the sport that is to be altered is necessary to know what adaptations should be made. Select several sports such as jogging, wrestling, and tennis and several disabilities including individuals with physical, sensory, and cognitive disabilities. Within a group, brainstorm ways to adapt a given sport for a specific disability.

Review Rules of Sports Designed for People with Disabilities

Obtain rules for a variety of sports for people with disabilities such as wheelchair tennis, or track events for people with visual impairments. Have each person from the class read rules to one sporting event and then summarize the rules for the other members of the class.

Examine Adapted Equipment for Sports Participation

Provide the class with several pieces of adapted sports equipment such as sports model wheelchair, soccer equipment used by soccer players with amputations, a hockey sled used by people with paraplegia, a beep baseball, and a bowling rail. Have the class examine the materials and practice using equipment that can be used in the existing setting.

Play a Sport with a Person with a Disability

Invite an athlete who has a disability to class. Arrange for necessary space and equipment to allow students to try the guest athlete's sport. This can be done with several of the wheelchair sports and with sports for people who are blind. Most sports will require a gymnasium or a ball field. This exercise can be modified to the level of observation through the use of videotapes of sports competitions.

Summary

The intervention implementation exercises found in this chapter are helpful when implementing sports programs for people with disabilities. The techniques of modifying existing programs and adapting sports equipment are starting points for understanding the possibilities of participation in sports by people with disabilities. Adaptations such as those described in previous sections of this chapter may require modifications to meet the unique needs of individual participants who may choose to actively pursue various sports and recreation options.

Conclusion

TR specialists can use sports as a therapeutic intervention when working with people with physical, sensory, and cognitive limitations. Sports engaged in by people with disabilities have been documented to influence participation incentives, physical functioning, and psychological well-being. When using sports as a therapeutic intervention, TR specialists are encouraged to conduct assessments, focus on sport skill development, provide resources, and facilitate community transition. Overall, sports can be an effective intervention for people with disabilities to encourage community involvement and promote leisure participation.

Discussion Questions

1. What are some major organizations devoted to promoting sports for people with disabilities?
2. What is one legislative act that has helped promote sports for people with disabilities?
3. What is one theory that helps explain the effects of sports participation on people with disabilities?
4. What are the three incentives that motivate behavior based on the theory of personal investment?
5. What are some incentives for people with disabilities to participate in sports?
6. What are some physical effects of sports on people with disabilities?
7. What are four physical limitations to consider when adapting basketball for people with disabilities?
8. What are six physical limitations to consider when adapting golf for people with disabilities?
9. What are three important areas to consider for making adaptations for tennis?

Resources

Archery

Wheelchair Archery Sports Section. 3595 E. Fountain Blvd., Suite L-1, Colorado Springs, CO 80910. (719) 574-1150.

American Wheelchair Archers. Road 2, Box 2043, West Sunbury, PA 16061. 612-520-0476

Basketball

Bankshot Basketball. Rabcan Associates, Inc. 485 Fifth Ave, New York, NY 10007.

Canadian Wheelchair Basketball Association. 2211 Riverside Drive, Suite B2 Ottawa, Ontario, K1H 7X5. (613) 260-1296 (or) 1-877-843-2922. http://www.cwba.ca

Dwarf Athletic Association of America (DAAA). 708 Gravenstein Hwy, North, #118, Sebastopol, CA 95472. 1-888-598-3222. http://www.daaa.org

International Wheelchair Basketball Federation. 181 Watson Street, #108 Winnipeg, Manitoba, Canada, R2P 2P8. 1-204-632-6475. http://www.iwbf.org

National Wheelchair Basketball Association. 6165 Lehman Drive, Suite 101 Colorado Springs, CO 80918. (719) 266-4082. http://www.nwba.org

National Amputee Golf Association. National Amputee Golf Association 11 Walnut Hill Rd., Amherst, NH 03031. http://www.nagagolf.org

United States of America Deaf Basketball Inc. PO Box 503, New York, NY 10022. http://www.usadb.org

USA Basketball. 5465 Mark Dabling Blvd., Colorado Springs, CO 80918-3842. (719) 590-4800. http://www.usabasketball.com/index.php

Wheelchair Basketball Education Resource. BT Paralympic World Cup. http://www.btparalympicworldcup.com/education/wheelchair_basketball.php

Bowling

American Wheelchair Bowling Association. AWBA P.O. Box 69, Clover, VA 24534. http://www.awba.org/

American Blind Bowling Association. James Benton, ABBA President: 1209 Somerset Road, Raleigh NC 27610. (919) 755-0700. http://www.abba1951.org

Canoeing

Cape Ability Outrigger Ohana Inc. http://www.adaptivecanoeing.org

United States Canoe Association. http://www.uscanoe.com/adaptive/index.html

Cycling

American Hand Cycle Association. 1744 Pepper Villa Dr., Elcalgin, CA 92021. (619) 596-1986.

Hand Crank Racing Association. Lake Redding Drive, Redding, CA 96003-3311. (530) 244-3577. http://www.shasta.com/geneva/CrankRace

International Wheelchair Roadracers Club Inc. 30 Meano Ln., Stanford, CT 06902. (203) 967-2231.

United States Handcycling Federation. (303) 459-4159. http://www.ushandcycling.org/

Golf

The Association of Disabled American Golfers. PO Box 280649, Lakewood, CO, 80228-0649. (303) 922-5228.

Challenge Golf (video). Motivation Media, 1245 Milwaukee Ave., Glenview, IL 60025. (708) 297-4740.

National Alliance for Accessible Golf. 12100 Sunset Hills Road, Suite 130, Reston, VA 20190. (703) 234-4136. http://www.accessgolf.org

National Amputee Golf Association (NAGA). 11 Walnut Hill Rd, Amherst, NH 03031. http://www.nagagolf.org

Never Say Never: Golf for the Physically Challenged (video). Kathy Corbin, 1309 E. Northern, Suite 308, Phoenix, AZ 85020. (602) 678-1832.

Physically Limited Golfers Association (PLGA). 2018 County Road 19 Maple Plain, MN 55359. (763) 479-6419. http://www.mngolf.org/allied_plga.cfm

United States Blind Golfers Association (USBGA). http://www.blindgolf.com

United States Golf Association. Modified Rules of Golf for Golfers with Disabilities, P.O. Box 708, Far Hills, NJ 07931-0708. (908) 234-2300. http://www.usga.org

Western Amputee Golf Association. 5980 Sun Valley Way, Sacramento, CA 95823. http://www.wagagolf.org

Hockey

American Amputee Hockey Association. http://www.usahockey.com/aaha/

American Sled Hockey Association. 21 Summerwood Court, Buffalo, NY 14223. (716) 876-7390. http://www.sledhockey.org

U.S. Electric Wheelchair Hockey Association. 7216 39th Ave. Minneapolis, MN 55427. (763) 535-4736. http://www.usewha.org

Quad Rugby

U.S. Quad Rugby Association. 330 Acoma St. #607, Denver, CO 80223. (303) 765-0288. http://www.usqra.com

Racquetball

National Racquetball Association. 1685 W Uintah St., Colorado Springs, CO 80904. (719) 635-5396. http://www.usra.org

Scuba Diving

Handicapped Scuba Association. 116 W. El Portal, Suite 104, San Clemente, CA 92672. (714) 498-6128. http://www.hsascuba.com

Shooting

NRA Adaptive Shooting. 11250 Waples Mill Road, Fairfax, VA 22030. (215) 663-0102.

National Wheelchair Shooting Federation. 102 Park Ave., Rockledge, PA 19111. (215) 379-2359.

Outdoor Buddies Hunting Program. PO Box 37283, Denver, CO 80237. (303) 771-8216. http://www.outbud.freeservers.com

Skiing

Adaptive Sports Center. PO Box 1639, Crested Butte, CO 81224. (866) 349-2296. http://www.adaptivesports.org/page.cfm?pageid=5131

American Blind Skiing Foundation. C/O Jim Hynan, Treasurer 8100 Foster Ln, #310, Niles, IL 60714-1159. http://www.absf.org/index.asp

Breckenridge Outdoor Education Center. PO Box 697 Breckenridge, CO 80424. (970) 453-6422. http://www.boec.org

Challenge Aspen. PO Box 6639 • Snowmass Village, CO 81615. (970) 923-0578. http://www.challengeaspen.org

Lounsbury Adaptive Ski Program. Holiday Valley Resort, P.O. Box 370, Ellicottville, NY 14731. (716) 699-3504. http://www.lounsburyadaptive.org/

Ski for Light. 1455 West Lake Street, Minneapolis, Minnesota 55408. (612) 827-3232. http://www.sfl.org/

United States Deaf Ski and Snowboard Association. http://www.usdssa.org

U.S. Disabled Ski Team. P.O. Box 100, Park City, UT 84060. (801) 649-9090. http://www.usskiteam.com

Soccer

American Amputee Soccer International. http://www.ampsoccer.org

United States Power Soccer Association. PO Box 1181, Carmel, IN 46032. http://www.powersoccerusa.net

USA Deaf Soccer Association. 3711 Sout State Route 157, Glen Carbon, IL 62034. http://www.usdeafsoccer.com

Softball

National Softball Association of the Deaf. http://www.nsad.org

National Wheelchair Softball Association. 13414 Paul Street, Omaha, NE 68154. (402) 305-5020. http://www.wheelchairsoftball.org

Sports Agencies & Directories

Access to Recreation Inc. (racket holder and grasp cuff). 8 Sandra Court, Newbury Park, CA, 91320. (800) 634-4351. http://www.accesstr.com/AMAZING/index.asp

Adaptive Information Resource Center. http://www.adaptiveirc.org/sportsN.html.

American Academy of Physical Medicine and Rehabilitation. Directory of Sports Organizations for Athletes with Disabilities. http://www.aapmr.org/condtreat/athletes3.htm

American Association of Adapted Sports Programs. 945 N. Indian Creek Drive, Clarkston, Georgia 30021. (404) 294–0070. http://www.adaptedsports.org

Blazesports. 280 Interstate North Circle, Suite 450, Atlanta, GA 30339. (770) 850-8199. http://www.blazesports.com

Deaf Olympics. http://www.deaflympics.com

Disabled Sports USA. http://www.dsusa.org

Disabled World. http://www.disabled-world.com/sports

International Paralympic Committee. Adenauerallee 212-214 53113 Bonn, Germany. http://www. paralympics.org

League of Fans. http://www.leagueoffans.org/sportsanddisabilities.html

Mobility-Advisor.com. Wheelchair Sports Activities. http://www.mobility-advisor. com/wheelchair-sports-activities.html

National Center on Accessibility. Indiana University Research Park, 501 North Morton St, Suite 109, Bloomington, IN 47404. (812) 856-4422. http://www.ncaonline.org

Special Olympics International. 1133 19th Street, N.W., Washington, DC 20036-3604. (202) 628-8298 (or) 1 (800) 700-8585. http://www.specialolympics.org

U.S. Association of Blind Athletes. 33 N. Institute Street, Colorado Springs, CO 80903. (719) 630-0422. http://www.usaba.org

U.S. Cerebral Palsy Athletic Association. 25 Independence Kingston, RI 02881. (401) 792-7130.

U.S. National Sports Center for the Disabled Page. Internet: http://www.mscd.org.

USA Deaf Sports Federation. PO Box 910338 Lexington, KY 40591-0338. TTY: (605) 367-5761; Voice: (605) 367-5760. http://www.usdeafsports.org

Wheelchairnet.org. http://www.wheelchairnet.org/WCN_Living/recreate.html

Wheelchair Sports, USA. 1236 Jungermann Rd, Suite A, St. Peters, MO 63376. (636) 614-6784. http://www.wsusa.org

Swimming

U.S. Wheelchair Swimming. 229 Miller St., Middleboro, MA 02346. (508) 946-1964.

Tennis

American Platform Tennis. 109 Wesport Drive, Pittsburgh, PA 15238. (888) 744-9490. http://www.platformtennis.org/

International Tennis Federation. Wheelchair Tennis Department, Bank Lane, Roehampton, London, SW15 5XZ, United Kingdom. Tel: +44 (0)20 8878 6464. http://www.itftennis.com/wheelchair

National Foundation of Wheelchair Tennis. 940 Calle Amancer, Suite B, San Clemente, CA 92672. (714) 361-6811. http://www.nfwt.org

United States Tennis Association. 70 West Red Oak Lane, White Plains, New York 10604. (914) 696-7000. http://www.usta.com/PlayNow/Wheelchair.aspx

U.S. Wheelchair Racquet Sports Association. P.O. Box 4673, Diamond Bar, CA 91765. (909) 861-7312.

Track and Field

Achilles Track Club. 42 West 38th Street, Suite 400, New York, NY 10018. (212) 354-0300. http://www.achillestrackclub.org

Volleyball

Disabled Volleyball. Disabled Sports USA, 451 Hungerford Drive, Suite 100 Rockville, MD 20850. (301) 217-0960.

References

Amateur Sports Act of 1978, Pub. L. No. 95-606, 92 Stat. 3045 (1980).

Americans with Disabilities Act of 1990, Pub. L. No. 101-336, 104 Stat. 328 (1991).

Arnett, J. B., Merriman, W. J., & Arnett, M. G. (1998). The effect of a swimming program on the cardiovascular fitness levels and basic water skills of blind and severe/profound mentally retarded adults. *Research Quarterly for Exercise and Sport, 69,* A-128.

Asken, M. J. (1991). The challenge of the physically challenged: Delivering sport psychology services to physically disabled athletes. *The Sports Psychologist, 5,* 370–381.

Association of Disabled American Golfers. (1995, Fall/Winter). *Making the turn.*

Association of Disabled American Golfers. (1996, Spring). *Making the turn.*

Atkinson, J. W. (1978). The mainsprings of achievement-oriented activity. In J. W. Atkinson & J. O. Raynor (Eds.), *Personality, motivation and achievement* (pp. 11–39). New York: Wiley.

Avery, B. (1996). Tee time. *Sports 'N Spokes, 1,* 40–44.

Blinde, E. M., & McClung, L. R. (1997). Enhancing the physical and social self through recreational activity. Accounts of individuals with physical disabilities. *Adapted Physical Activity Quarterly, 14,* 327–344.

Brazile, F. (1990). Wheelchair sports: A new perspective on integration. *Adapted Physical Activity Quarterly, 7*(1), 3–11.

Brazile, F., Kleiber, D., & Harnisch, D. (1991). Analysis of participation incentives among athletes with and without disabilities. *Therapeutic Recreation Journal, 25,* 18–33.

Brewer, B. W., Van Raalte, J. L., & Linder, D. E. (1993). Athletic identity: Hercules' muscles or Achilles heel. *International Journal of Sport Psychology, 24,* 237–254.

Brickey, M. (1984). Normalizing the Special Olympics. *Journal of Physical Education, Recreation and Dance, 55*(8), 28–29 & 75–76.

Campbell, E., & Jones, G. (1997). Pre-competition anxiety and self-confidence in elite and non-elite wheelchair sport participants. *Adapted Physical Activity Quarterly, 14,* 95–107.

Campbell, E., & Jones, G. (2002). Sources of stress experienced by elite male wheelchair basketball players. *Adapted Physical Activity Quarterly, 19,* 82–99.

Canabal, M. Y., (1988). C.I.V.I.T.A.N.-premier sponsor of the 1987 I.S.S.O.G. *Palaestra, 4,* 80.

Castagno, K. S. (2001). Special Olympics Unites Sports: Changes in male athletes during a basketball season. *Adapted Physical Activity Quarterly, 18,* 193–206.

Connor-Kuntz, F. J., Dummer, G. M., & Paciorek, N. J. (1995). Physical education and sports participation of children and youth with spina-bifida myelomenincele. *Adapted Physical Activity Quarterly, 12,* 228–238.

Dade, C. (1995, August 29). Disabled golfers are driving for greater access to courses. *The Wall Street Journal,* B1, B6.

Daquila, G., & Winnick, J. P. (1981). Athletic competition for the deaf. In J. P. Winnick and F. X. Short (Eds.), *Special athletic opportunities for individuals with handicapping conditions* (pp. 41–47). Brockport, NY: New York State University at Brockport.

DePauw, K. P., & Clarke, K. S. (1985). Sports for disabled U.S. citizenry: Influence of amateur sports act. In C. Sherrill (Ed.), *Sport and disabled athletes* (pp. 41–50). Champaign, IL: Human Kinetics.

Disabled World (n.d.). Retrieved June 24, 2009 from http://www.disabled-world.com/sports/wheelchair/basketball/

Draney, R. (1997). Quadriplegic tennis [Online]. Available: http://www.nfwt.org.

Dummer, G. M., Ewing, M. E., Habeck, R. V., & Overton, S. R. (1987). Attributions of athletes with cerebral palsy. *Adapted Physical Activity Quarterly, 4,* 278–292.

Education for all Handicapped Children Act of 1975, Pub. L. No. 94-142, 89 Stat. 773 (1977)

Farrell, R. J., Crocker, R. E., McDonough, M. H., & Sedgwick, W. A., (2004). The driving force: Motivation in Special Olympians. *Adapted Physical Activity Quarterly, 21, 153–166.*

Fiona M., Guy, E. J. Faulkner, J. A., & Kirsh, J. K., (2008). Physical activity and sport participation in youth with congenital heart disease: Perceptions of children and parents. *Adapted Physical Activity Quarterly, 25,* 49–70.

Furst, D. M., Ferr, T., & Megginson, N. (1993). Motivation of disabled athletes to participate in triathlons. *Psychological Reports, 72,* 403–406.

Gavron, S. (1989). Surviving the least restrictive environment. *Strategies, 2*(3), 5–6.

Goodwin, D., Johston, K., Gustafson, P., Elliot, M., Thurmeier, R., & Kuttai, H. (2009). It's okay to be a quad: Wheelchair rugby players' sense of community. *Adapted Physical Activity Quarterly, 26,* 102–117.

Goosey-Tolfrey, V. L. (2005). Physiological profiles of elite wheelchair basketball players in preparation for the 2000 Paralympic Games. *Adapted Physical Activity Quarterly, 22,* 57–66.

Greenwood, C. M., Dzewaltowski, D. A., & French, R. (1990) Self-efficacy and psychological well-being of wheelchair tennis participants and wheelchair non-participants. *Adapted Physical Activity Quarterly, 7,* 12–21.

Guttman, L. (1976). *Textbook of sport for the disabled.* Oxford, UK: H. M. & M. Publishers.

Harada, C. M., & Siperstein, G. N. (2009). The sport experience of athletes with intellectual disabilities: A national survey of Special Olympics athletes and their families. *Adapted Physical Activity Quarterly, 26,* 68–85.

Harter, S. (1982). The perceived competence scale for children. *Child Development, 53,* 87–97.

Hedrick, B., Byrnes, D., & Shaver, L. (1989). *Wheelchair basketball*. Washington, D.C.: Paralyzed Veterans of America.

Hedrick, B. N., & Broadbent, E. (1996). Predictors of physical activity among university graduates with physical disabilities. *Therapeutic Recreation Journal, 30,* 137–145.

History of Tennis. (n.d.). Retrieved June 19, 2009, from http://www.historyoftennis.net

Horton, R. S., & Mack, D. E. (2000). Athletic identity in marathon runners: Functional focus or dysfunctional commitment? *Journal of Sport Behavior, 23*(2), 101–120.

Hourcade, J. J. (1989). Special Olympics: A review and critical analysis. *Therapeutic Recreation Journal, 23,* 58–65.

International Paralympic Committee. (n.d.). Retrieved June 20, 2009, from http://www.paralympic.org/release/Main_Sections_Menu/index.html

Kegel, B., & Malchow, D. (1994). The incidence of injuries in amputees playing soccer. *Palaestra, 10,* 50–54.

Kennedy Foundation. (1978). *P.L.94-142: It's the law. Physical education and recreation for the handicapped*. Washington, DC: Special Olympics, Inc.

Kirkby, R. J. (1995). Wheelchair netball: Motives and attitudes of competitors with and without disabilities. *Australian Psychologist, 30,* 109–112.

Linton, R. (1936). *The study of man: an introduction*. New York: Appleton-Century.

Longo, P. (1989). Chair golf. *Sports 'N Spokes, 4,* 35–38.

Maehr, M. L., & Braskamp, L. A. (1986). *The motivation factor: A theory of personal investment*. Lexington, KY: D.C. Health.

Maiano, C., Ninot, G., Morin, J. S., & Bilard, J. (2007). Effects of sport participation on the basketball skills and physical self of adolescents with conduct disorders. *Adapted Physical Activity Quarterly, 24,* 178–196.

Martin, J. (2008). Multidimensional self-efficacy and affect in wheelchair basketball players. *Adapted Physical Activity Quarterly, 25,* 275–288.

Martin, J. J., Adams-Mushett, C. A., & Smith, K. L. (1995). Athletic identity and sport orientation of adolescent swimmers with disabilities. *Adapted Physical Activity Quarterly, 12,* 113–123.

Mastro, J. V., Sherrill, C., Gench, B., & French, R. (1987). Psychological characteristics of elite visually impaired athletes: The iceberg profile. *Journal of Sport Behavior, 10,* 39–46.

McGovern, J. N. (1991). The Americans with disabilities act: How this new law will change your parks and recreation agency. *Recreation and Park in Georgia, 20,* 22–23.

Mental Retardation Amendments of 1967, Pub. L. No. 90-170, 81 Stat. 527 (1968).

Nesbitt, J. (1986). *The international directory of recreation-oriented assistive device sources*. Marina Del Rey, CA: Lifeboat Press.

Nicholls, J. G. (1989). *The competitive ethos and democratic education*. Cambridge, MA: Harvard University Press.

Orelove, F. P., Wehman, P., & Wood, J. (1982). An evaluative review of Special Olympics: Implications for community integration. *Education and Training of the Mentally Retarded, 17,* 325–329.

Oxford University Press (n.d.). *Sport*. Retrieved June 19, 2009, from http://www.oup.com/oald-bin/web_getald7index1a.pl>

Paciorek, M. J. (2005). Adapted sports. In J. P. Winnick (Ed.), *Adapted Physical Education* (4th ed.) (pp. 39–54). Champaign, IL: Human Kinetics.

Paciorek, M. J., & Jones, J. (1994). *Sports and recreation for the disabled: A resource manual* (2nd Ed.). Indianapolis: Cooper Publishing Group.

Paciorek, M. J., Tetreault, P., & Jones, J. (1991). The integration of athletes with disabilities in amateur athletics: The 1991 U.S. Olympic Festival. *Palaestra, 8,* 30–33.

Parks, B. A. (1997). *Tennis in a wheelchair.* White Plains, NY: United States Tennis Association.

Pensgaard, A. M., & Sorensen, M. (2002). Empowerment through the sport context: A model to guide research for individuals with disability. *Adapted Physical Activity Quarterly, 19,* 48–67.

Pitetti, K. H., Jackson, J. A., Stubbs, N. B., Campbell, K. D., & Battar, S. S. (1989). Fitness levels of adult Special Olympic participants. *Adapted Physical Activity Quarterly, 6,* 354–370.

Poretta, D., Gillespie, M., & Jasma, P. (1996). Perceptions about Special Olympics from service delivery groups in the United States: A preliminary investigation. *Education and Training in Mental Retardation and Developmental Disabilities, 31*(1), 44–54.

Rehabilitation Act of 1973, Pub. L. No. 93-112, 87 Stat. 355 (1974).

Reina, R., Moreno, F., & Sanz, D. (2007). Visual behavior and motor responses of novice and experienced wheelchair tennis players relative to the service return. *Adapted Physical Activity Quarterly, 24,* 254–271.

Riggen, K., & Ulrich, D. (1993). The effects of sport participation on individuals with mental retardation. *Adapted Physical Activity Quarterly, 10,* 42–51.

Robb, G. (1994). Aiming for the birdie. *Sports 'N Spokes, 6,* 51–53.

Savage, M., & Winnick, J. P. (1981). Wheelchair sports. In J. P. Winnick & F. X. Short, *Special athletic opportunities for individuals with handicapping conditions* (pp.41–47). Brockport, NY: New York State University at Brockport.

Schaperclaus, G., de Greef, M., Rispens, P., de Calonne, D., Landsman, M., Lie, K. I., & Oudhof, J. (1997). Participation in sports groups for patients with cardiac problems: An experimental study. *Adapted Physical Activity Quarterly, 14,* 275–284.

Shapiro, D. R. (2003). Participation motives of Special Olympics athletes. *Adapted Physical Activity Quarterly, 20,* 150–165.

Shepherd Center Therapeutic Recreation Department (1995). *Wheelchair basketball information sheet* [Brochure]. Atlanta, GA: Author.

Sherrill, C., & Rainbolt, W. (1988). Self-actualization profiles of male able-bodied and elite cerebral palsied athletes. *Adapted Physical Activity Quarterly, 5,* 108–119.

Siperstein, G. N. (1980). *Instruments for measuring children's attitudes toward the handicapped.* Unpublished manuscript, University of Massachusetts, Boston.

Smith, R. (1993). Sport and physical activity for people with physical disabilities. *Parks and Recreation, 28,* 21–27.

Special Olympics International, Incorporated. (1992). *Special Olympics Basketball Sports Skills Guide.* Washington, DC: Joseph P. Kennedy, Jr. Foundation.

Special Olympics International. (n.d.). Retrieved June 11, 2009, from http://www.specialolympics.org/.

Stein, J. (1978). Accessible recreation: Can it be done? In P. Marx & P. Hall (Eds.), *Change strategies and disabled persons: Postsecondary education and beyond* (pp. 139–144). Washington, DC: U.S. Government.

Tasiemski, T., Kennedy, P., Gardner, B. P., & Blaikley, R. A., (2004). Athletic identity and sports participation in people with spinal cord injury. *Adapted Physical Activity Quarterly, 21,* 364-378.

United States Golf Association (2001). *A modification of the rules of golf for golfers with disabilities.* Far Hills, NJ: United States Golf Association.

United States Tennis Association (n.d.). Retrieved June 15, 2009, from http://www.usta.com/PlayNow/Wheelchair.aspx.

U.S. Department of Health and Human Services. (n.d.). *Healthy people 2010: Understanding and improving health.* Retrieved June 14, 2009, from http://www.health.gov/healthypeople

Vitello, P. (2008). *More Americans are giving up golf.* Retrieved June 22, 2009, from http://www.nytimes.com/

Wang, W., & DePauw, K. (1996). Early sports socialization of elite Chinese athletes with physical and sensory disabilities. *Palaestra, 11,* 40–46.

Wells, C., & Hooker, S. (1990). The spinal injured athlete. *Adapted Physical Activity Quarterly, 7,* 265–285.

World Golf (n.d.). Retrieved June 23, 2009, from http://www.worldgolf.com/courses/unitedstates/usa.html

Wu, S. K., & Williams, T. (2001). Factors influencing sport participation among athletes with spinal cord injury. *Medicine & Science in Sports & Exercise, 33*(2), 177–182.

Zigler, E. (1994). *Interim report on individual studies: Self-image, depression, and hopelessness in mildly retarded adolescents.* Unpublished manuscript, Yale University, New Haven, CT.

Zoerink, D. A., & Wilson, J. (1995). The competitive disposition: Views of athletes with mental retardation. *Adapted Physical Activity Quarterly, 12,* 34–42.

Chapter 19
Values Clarification

Alexis McKenney and John Dattilo

The aim of education is the knowledge not of fact, but of values.
—William Ralph Inge

Introduction

Each day, throughout the day, every person is confronted with decisions that require action. Every decision made and every action taken is based on a person's beliefs, attitudes, and values; however, people are not always clear about what they believe and value (Simon, Howe, & Kirschenbaum, 1995). Confusion about values is experienced in all areas of life, including leisure. To help participants clarify their leisure values, as well as seek out healthy and enjoyable leisure experiences, leisure professionals can use values clarification strategies (Johnson & Zoerink, 1977). Helping individuals clarify their values related to issues such as the use of free time, healthy lifestyle choices, leisure participation patterns, and barriers to participation can be a powerful in helping them to better understand themselves and society (Pinch, 2003).

This chapter introduces the reader to values clarification as a TR facilitation technique. After definitions associated with values clarification are presented, a description of values clarification as an intervention is described. Next, the theoretical foundation of values clarification is provided, followed by examples of studies that have investigated the effectiveness of values clarification strategies. A case study is then offered as an example of the potential effectiveness of values clarification strategies. Finally, lists of professional resources and references are provided.

Definitions

Values clarification, also referred to as values development, is a component of TR that helps people to answer some of the questions they may have about their goals, inspirations, interests and beliefs, and leisure. Values are expressed in everyday life through expressions of desire for justice, a cleaner environment, or world peace. In leisure, values might include criteria choosing, or even refraining from, activities of interest. For those who choose sport as leisure, for example, values:

> "might include not only criteria for success, such as winning or playing well, but also fair play, sportsmanship, friendship, and tolerance, which are concerned with the quality of interaction during the activity" (Lee, Whitehead, & Balchin, 2000).

To better understand values clarification as a component of TR, it is important to understand associated definitions. Therefore, this section of the chapter provides a critical examination of values clarification and examines the following definitions:

- Values
- The Valuing Process
- Value Indicators
- Values Clarification

Values

Values are defined as the "those aspects of our lives that are so important and pervasive that they include feelings, thoughts, and behaviors" (Simon et al., 1995, p. 10). Values vary in importance and serve as guiding principles in a person's life (Schwartz, 1994). According to Mosconi and Emmett (2003, p. 70), "Values provide standards for behavior, orient people to desired outcomes, and form the basis for goal setting." Values guide a person's behavior in all life situations (Lee et al., 2000). Raths and colleagues (1978, p. 26) stated that: "Our values show what we are likely to do with our limited time and energy." Simon and colleagues reported that a value has three components:

- Emotional
- Cognitive
- Behavioral

Emotional. The emotional component of a value reflects the idea that people care deeply about their values. According to Simon and colleagues, values are so important to people that they are often willing and at times eager to communicate them to other people.

Cognitive. The cognitive component of a value is seen in the careful process of thought that occurs when a person defines his or her values. The cognitive component includes the evaluation of pros and cons involved in choosing values.

Behavioral. The behavioral component involves action. Simon and colleagues stated that "We don't just say some things are important to us, but those beliefs or preferences are clearly and consistently discernible in how we live our lives" (p. 10). In other words, people demonstrate their values through their behaviors.

> For example, Noah expressed that he values football. In a discussion about football, Noah explained that he cares enough about football to set a goal of playing professional football (emotional). To play professional football, Noah considered the cons, such as the risk of incurring a serious injury, and the pros, such as experiencing the excitement of playing his favorite activity as a career (cognitive). Finally, Noah demonstrated that

he valued football by staying in top physical condition, lifting weights, and practicing football every day (behavioral).

The Valuing Process

The valuing process is the manner in which individuals clarify what they define to be a value. Raths and colleagues identified seven steps associated with the valuing process which were grouped into three major categories:

- Choosing
- Prizing
- Acting

Choosing. Individuals are able to attribute worth to objects and situations when they can identify personal values (Mosconi & Emmett, 2003). A lack of clarity, on the other hand, leads to dissatisfaction and poor decision-making (Brown & Crace, 1996). The first category, choosing, involves having participants explore their beliefs and behaviors. For the purposes of values clarification as a component of TR, choosing involves encouraging participants to explore their leisure-related options freely from alternatives, consider the possible consequences that may result from each of the alternatives, and choose from alternatives.

Prizing. The second category, prizing, involves having participants learn to cherish their beliefs and behaviors. Prizing involves encouraging participants to be happy with their choices, and willing to publicly affirm the choice. In other words, participants are willing to proudly share their choices with other people.

Acting. The third category, acting, involves having participants decide what they would be willing to do with their choice, and commit to regularly acting upon their values. To be considered a value, all seven of the criteria must be met (Raths et al., 1966).

> For example, Delaney participated in a values clarification facilitation technique in which she chose aerobics as a value from a list of exercises (choosing). Before choosing, Delaney considered the consequences of the alternatives such as that she lived on a highway without a sidewalk, so jogging or bicycling would be dangerous. After several weeks of engaging in a home video aerobics program, Delaney stated to the group that she had grown to cherish participating in aerobics as exercise (prizing). Finally, Delaney completed an aerobics schedule for 1 month and committed to making a new schedule each month (action).

Value Indicators

According to Raths and colleagues, a person is expressing a value indicator if all seven of the criteria are *not* met. These authors suggested that people often discuss things that indicate the presence of a value, but do not meet all of the criteria.

Therefore, these discussions contain value indicators rather than values. Examples of value indicators include goals, aspirations, attitudes, interests, feelings, beliefs, and worries. A person may express an interest in exercises, but not actually engage in an exercise activity. Simon and colleagues reported that value indicators can be elevated to values through the seven-step valuing process.

> For example, in a discussion with the TR specialist about writing, Emmitt mentioned that he once wrote a poem that was published in his school paper. Remembering Emmitt's proud appearance when he spoke of having his poem published, the TR specialist encouraged him to explore his interest in poetry through the values clarification intervention. After 4 weeks, Emmitt completed the valuing process resulting in Emmitt's renewed interest in poetry (value indicator) elevating it to a value.

Values Clarification

Simon and colleagues reported that the values clarification approach is a method used to help participants through the valuing process; that is, explore what is important to them and build their own value system. This approach helps participants to apply the valuing process to old and still emerging beliefs and behavior patterns. Emphasis is on how decisions affect an individual's future (Mosconi & Emmett, 2003). The values clarification approach typically uses one or a combination of three methods including the individual clarifying response, group discussions, and value sheets. These methods are elaborated in the following section.

Critical Examination

Although values clarification should be facilitated in such a way that encourages participants to examine potential consequences that may occur as a result of choosing a particular value, it requires that the TR specialist remain neutral when participants explore and declare their values. Educators have questioned how a facilitator can remain neutral when participants express values that are abhorrent (Lockwood, 1978). Lockwood questioned, for example, what it is a facilitator should do if a participant states that he or she believes racism is a good thing. Lickona (1991) provided the following example of what can happen as a result of using values clarification with a group of adolescents with emotional or behavioral problems:

> When we shared our lists, the four most popular activities listed by students were: sex, drugs, drinking, and skipping school. I asked why these were the most popular, and these are the things my students said: "I don't need this class to graduate, so why come?; School isn't important; Everyone drinks and smokes dope; Pot doesn't harm you; All my friends do it, so why can't I?; Sex is the best part of life; and sex, drugs, and rock and roll rule." (p. 237).

TR specialists working with children or adolescents with serious emotional or behavioral problems might consider using an alternative facilitation technique, such as Moral Discussions, as presented in this book.

Summary

Values clarification can be an important component of TR services; however, it is important to understand related definitions. Values are comprised of the feelings, thoughts, and behaviors that encompass a person's life. A person clarifies his or her values through the valuing process. Raths and colleagues specified that the valuing process involves choosing, prizing, and acting upon values.

A person, however, may not have met each criterion in the valuing process. In this case, what that person is stating may be a value indicator rather than a value. Value indicators may include a person's goals, aspirations, attitudes, interests, feelings, beliefs, and worries. Value indicators can be elevated to values with the use of the valuing process. According to Simon and colleagues, the values clarification approach is a tool designed to help participants through the valuing process. Nevertheless, caution is advised when working with children and youth with emotional or behavioral problems.

Descriptions

The values clarification approach is designed to help people build their own values systems. Strategies may involve helping individuals, families, or groups, to develop their own leisure value systems. TR specialists can help participants develop these leisure value systems with the use of three strategies developed by Raths and colleagues (1978):

- The Individual Clarifying Response
- Group Discussions
- Value Sheets

In this section, the strategies will be described followed by suggestions for implementing the values clarification strategies.

The Individual Clarifying Response

The individual clarifying response is a strategy used to encourage participants to think about something they said or did while interacting with other people. Interactions may occur in passing, during a group, or one-on-one with participants. The clarifying response is not planned; rather, it may be given in an informal dialogue with one participant as well as during a group discussion.

> For example, if Cedric tells a TR specialist that he is going camping over the weekend, the TR specialist might respond by saying, "That's great," or "Have fun." These responses, however,

are unlikely to provoke Cedric to think. The TR specialist might consider a response such as, "So, you're going camping, Cedric? Are you happy that you are going?" If Cedric responds by saying he would rather stay home and play with his friends, he would have developed more self-awareness. Cedric would have recognized that he is capable of doing things that he is not excited about; therefore, would have taken a step toward value clarity.

The effective clarifying response is one that encourages participants to think further about their ideas and beliefs. Similar to the argument provided above, the authors warn leaders that the clarifying response is not therapy; therefore, it should not be used with individuals with serious emotional or behavioral problems. Raths and colleagues presented guidelines for clarifying responses. According to the authors, it is helpful for leaders to understand that clarifying responses:

- Are not moralizing or criticizing
- Place responsibility on participants to decide what *they* want
- Are stimulating, but not insistent
- Help participants understand their ideas
- Do not result in an extended discussion
- Are individually tailored
- Are not made in response to everything said
- Do not provoke "right" answers
- Are used creatively

Are not moralizing or criticizing. The clarifying response is used in a manner that is not moralizing or criticizing, or made in a way that offers the facilitator's personal values, or evaluates participants' responses. According to Raths and colleagues, this excludes hints of what is good, correct, or acceptable as well as hints to what is not good, incorrect, or unacceptable.

> For example, if Monique, a 16-year-old participant, tells the TR specialist that she enjoys drinking alcohol as her favorite leisure activity, the TR specialist should not respond by saying, "Monique, that is not good for you," or "Monique, you are too young to drink."

Place responsibility on participants to decide what *they* want. Clarifying responses are made in a manner that places the responsibility on participants to decide what they want. Rather than the TR specialist leading participants toward a desirable answer, the TR specialist helps participants to think about their behaviors, ideas, or beliefs and decide for themselves what it is they want to do.

> For example, the TR specialist might ask Monique to consider if she enjoys other leisure activities, and how she decided upon drinking alcohol as her favorite leisure activity.

Are stimulating, but not insistent. Some participants may decide that they do not want to think more about their behaviors or ideas. Clarifying responses, therefore, are stimulating, but not insistent. The TR specialist expects that some participants will decline to answer when asked clarifying questions.

> For example, Monique may have never taken time to consider why she finds drinking alcohol to be her favorite activity; therefore, the TR specialist will not push Monique to immediately respond, but rather take time to consider possible reasons.

Help participants understand their ideas. The goal of clarifying responses is to help participants understand their ideas. Clarifying responses are not used in an interview format or to collect data about the participants. Instead, the responses help participants clarify their own ideas, beliefs, and lives if they chose to do so.

> For example, the TR specialist does not use clarifying responses to gather more information about Monique's interest in drinking alcohol, but rather uses them to encourage Monique to think about her belief that drinking is her favorite leisure activity.

Do not result in an extended discussion. Clarifying responses do not result in an extended discussion. Raths and colleagues suggested that participants have time to think that is often completed alone, without temptation to justify thoughts to an adult. When responding, the TR specialist can have two or three rounds of dialogue before a break in the conversation. The conversation can end with a noncommittal but honest phrase such as, "I understand what you were saying now."

> For example, Monique responded to the TR specialist about why she finds drinking alcohol to be her favorite activity by saying, "I don't know, I guess it's all I do with my friends." The TR specialist may respond by stating that she understands now and "it is easy to see how participating in one activity may lead to the belief that it is a favorite activity."

Are individually tailored. Clarifying responses are individually tailored. Values are personal things; therefore, one participant may need to clarify one topic, while another participant may need to clarify another topic. However, if a topic is of interest to a group, the TR specialist may choose to respond more generally.

> For example, if Monique is a member of a group receiving treatment for substance abuse, the TR specialist might temporarily open the discussion up to everyone, while responding specifically to Monique's comments.

Are not made in response to everything said. When responding, the TR specialist does not have to respond to everything said. Many things might be said in a group situation. When this is a problem, clarifying responses can be made to those who need them the most.

> For example, the TR specialist might first respond to Monique who states that she is only interested in drinking as a leisure activity, then to Eric who stated that he enjoys playing basketball.

Do not provoke "right" answers. In situations that involve feelings or beliefs, the clarifying response can be made in such a way that does not provoke *right* answers. It is not appropriate for clarifying responses to move a person toward a predetermined answer. In other words, the TR specialist does not have the answers.

> For example, the TR specialist does not respond to Monique by saying, "I think jogging would be a better answer than drinking. Don't you think so, Monique?"

Are used creatively. Clarifying responses are not derived from a formula, rather, they are be used creatively. The TR specialist uses his or her insights to respond while maintaining the purpose of the clarifying response. If the TR specialist responds in a manner that helps participants to clarify their thinking or behavior, the response is considered effective. Examples from Raths, Harmin, and Simon (1978) of clarifying responses include:

- Is this something you cherish?
- Are you happy about that?
- Have you felt this way for a while now?
- Was that something that you chose to do?
- What do you mean by . . . ?
- Are you saying that . . . ?
- What other possibilities are there?
- Is that a personal preference, or do you believe others should believe that?
- Is that very important to you?
- Do you value that?

> For example, the TR specialist might respond to Monique by asking "Are you happy with drinking as your favorite leisure activity?"

Group Discussions

To lead group discussions, Raths and colleagues stipulated that careful planning is important. The authors explained that discussions often evolve into private discussions, or result in participants becoming disinterested, and they suggested four steps that can be taken to encourage a reflective discussion if a TR specialist decides to use a large group discussion with a values focus. The four steps are:

- Select a topic.
- Encourage participants to think before speaking.
- Structure discussion to promote sharing.
- Help participants to learn.

Select a topic. The first step in promoting a values discussion involves selecting a topic for discussion. According to Raths and colleagues, topics may include issues that appear confusing to participants, or value-rich topics such as friendship and leisure. To initiate a discussion, a TR specialist may use quotations, pictures, a scene from a movie, or other sources that offer topics of interest.

> For example, the TR specialist may choose the topic of sports for persons with disabilities and show pictures of people with disabilities participating in a variety of sports to participants in a physical rehabilitation facility (see Figure 19.1).

Figure 19.1

Encourage participants to think before speaking. Raths and colleagues identified the second step in setting up a values discussion to be encouraging participants to think before speaking. A TR specialist can do this by asking participants to sit quietly and think about a question or issue for a few minutes before the discussion begins, or asking the participants to write down thoughts as they first react to the question or issue.

> For example, the TR specialist can ask the participants in the physical rehabilitation facility to think about whether they have participated in, or had an interest in, any of the sports represented in the pictures.

Structure discussion to promote sharing. Structuring the discussion to promote sharing is the third step in promoting a values discussion. Raths and colleagues suggested beginning discussions with statements such as, "The floor is open to comments by anyone. No need to raise your hand" (p. 134). A TR specialist might also place participants into groups of two, three, or four (see Figure 19.2). While in groups, participants may be asked to quickly go around the circle, allowing every participant a chance to make one initial comment about the issue.

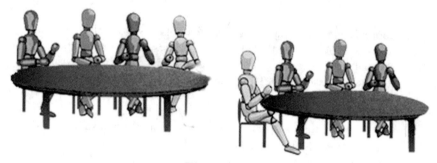

Figure 19.2

For example, after participants in the physical rehabilitation facility have taken time to think about the activities shown in the pictures, the TR specialist can ask them to discuss what they thought about with one or two other participants.

Help participants to learn. The final step involves helping participants to learn. Raths and colleagues suggested that to promote learning, participants should be asked to sit alone and consider what they learned from the activity. For example, after the participants have discussed the pictures with others in the group, they can be given a worksheet that encourages them to think about what they learned. Participants may be asked to complete sentences such as, "I learned that . . ." or "I never knew that . . . ."

Compared to the dialogue and writing strategies, Raths and colleagues offered only one suggestion for the discussion strategy to avoid subtle indoctrination. To do this, the TR specialists accept judgments they do not favor. Indoctrination may occur when the TR specialist restricts what participants can share in a value-clarifying discussion. Consequently, the participants may not learn to make decisions, or engage in their own valuing process.

For example, Carl may state that the activities shown are all "boring" or "ridiculous." The TR specialist can then seek to clarify why Carl feels that way, rather than responding by saying that he is "wrong" or "wouldn't know" because he has not participated in activities since acquiring his disability.

Value Sheets

Raths and colleagues suggested that a value sheet includes a provocative statement with questions, or simply a set of questions or fill-in-the-blank statements, designed to raise an issue among the participants. The questions are designed to guide the participants through the value-clarifying process. Participants are encouraged to individually complete the value sheet before engaging in a discussion.

The following is an example of a value sheet developed from a description of a leisure experience described by Kelly (1982, pp. 10–11):

> What are the most common reasons that people seek leisure opportunities and activity? If asked, most respond simply that "I like it." When questioned further as to why they "like it," common responses suggest some of the dimensions of why leisure is valued.
>
> "I like concentrating my mind, emotions, and body on the music," replies the young mother who plays Bach. Leisure integrates the self at the same time that it is expressive of it, especially when the activity requires the bringing together of attention and action. Further, the demonstration of mastery achieved through discipline and practice is found to be satisfying.
>
> 1. Why do you seek leisure opportunities and activity?
> 2. What can you find in your leisure (provide choice such as self-expression, friendship, health)?
> 3. What is important to you to do with your leisure?
> 4. What do you do, or what can you do to make this possible? How do you begin? What can you do today?

To produce reasonable values with the use of value sheets, a participant needs time to think and make clear decisions. Raths and colleagues suggested that the value sheets should not be used in a large group discussion. The authors argued that valuing is an individual process that may be difficult to engage in when several people are talking in the same room. Furthermore, group dynamics may alter the outcome of the valuing process. For example, participants may be motivated to adopt or verbalize a view in order to please the TR specialist or another participant. To create a beneficial value sheet activity, the authors recommended the following suggestions:

- Avoid "yes-no," "either-or," or "why" questions.
- Include "you" on the value sheets.
- Offer choices on every sheet.
- Create small groups for discussions.
- Have participants submit value sheets.
- Post selected writings.
- Provide comments in the margins.

Avoid "yes-no," "either-or," "why" questions. When creating value sheets, the TR specialist should avoid "yes-no," "either-or," or "why" questions because they potentially limit "value-related thinking." According to Raths and colleagues, "*why*" questions may push participants who lack reasons for their choices to create reasons to answer the question.

For example, when asked why he likes one activity more than another, Jacquez answered, "I don't know. I just do." An alternative question may be, "What alternatives did you consider before you arrived at your choice?" (Raths et al., 1978, p. 119).

Include "you" on the value sheets. The valuing process is individual. Each participant answers questions by describing how he or she feels about a particular issue; therefore, each value sheet includes "you." Questions are written in a way that asks each participant to consider what he or she believes.

> For example, participants can be asked the following question: "Do you feel leisure is an important part of a person's life?"

Offer choices on every sheet. In addition to having questions personally directed, the TR specialist offers choices on every sheet. Value sheets without choices are unlikely to promote value clarity. The authors suggested that participants consider the consequences of each choice as well.

> For example, a value sheet is designed to encourage Rebecca to think about exercise by offering a variety of options from which to consider. If Rebecca states that she does not value exercise, the TR specialist may encourage her to consider the consequences of not valuing exercise.

Create small groups for discussion. By creating small groups for discussion, the participants can share ideas without the TR specialist being present. Raths and colleagues argued that this lack of presence may encourage participants to think through issues without looking to the TR specialist for the right answers.

> For example, Pauline is typically quiet in large group discussions; however, she enjoys sharing her thoughts with two or three people. Consequently, Pauline is more likely to benefit from small group discussions rather than large group discussions.

Have participants submit value sheets. If the TR specialist decides to have participants submit value sheets, the TR specialist can read them later and select a few that raise interesting ideas or illuminate a particular issue. If this route is chosen, the TR specialist maintains writer anonymity, but allows the writer to claim credit deserved.

> For example, Maria wrote on a fitness value sheet that she values running because it helps her to keep her heart in good condition and maintain her body weight. Believing that the whole group would benefit from Maria's comments, the TR specialist may share her thoughts with the group.

Post selected writings. Another suggestion for using value sheets is to post selected writings. The TR specialist may choose to post writings on a bulletin board or another designated area. By posting selected writings, other participants, in or out of the group, may read the value sheets, thereby potentially stimulating individual thought or discussion among others.

> For example, if Champ thinks of something original, the TR specialist may post his value sheet for the rest of the group members to read.

Provide comments in the margins. The authors suggested that comments be provided in the margins. Comments are not written in a manner that evaluates a participant's comments, but rather in a way that stimulates thought. The TR specialist may ask further questions written in a way that encourages participants to rethink certain ideas, or consider alternatives.

> For example, the TR specialist may write such things as, "Interesting thought, David. Did you consider anything else when you made that decision?"

Summary

Values clarification strategies may be used to help participants develop their own leisure value systems. TR specialists can help participants develop these leisure value systems with the use of the clarifying response, group discussions, and value sheets. The clarifying response is a strategy used to encourage participants to think about something they said or did during any type of interaction. Group discussions involve four steps used to encourage a reflective discussion which include selecting a topic, encouraging participants to think before speaking, structuring the discussion to promote sharing, and helping participants to learn. Value sheets are designed to raise a value issue among the participants.

History

Since the 1950s, values have been an important area of inquiry in social sciences because they center on the standards and goals individuals and societies set for themselves (Lee, Whitehead, & Balchin, 2000). Values clarification was developed in the 1960s as a tool for American educators to use in character education programs. Lickona (1993) reviewed the history of values clarification and made the following conclusions.

Character education can be traced to the roots of education in America. In the nineteenth century, character education initially took the form of discipline, the teacher's example, and the Bible. In the mid-twentieth century, support for character education began to decline with the introduction of the philosophy of *positivism*. Supporters of positivism argued that compared to facts (which were objective truths), values were merely expressions of feelings, and therefore were private, not appropriate for schools.

The idea of *personalism* surfaced in the schools in the 1960s and it celebrated the worth, dignity, and autonomy of the individual, including the subjective self or inner life (Lickona, 1991). With personalism, people began to celebrate a freedom from responsibility and a love for individual freedom. Personalism was introduced into American schools in the 1970s with the advent of values clarification.

Although values clarification was designed as a tool for educators, in the 1970s recreation and leisure professionals adopted the values clarification as an approach to leisure counseling (Connolly, 1977). Values clarification activities began to appear in recreation articles and textbooks written to help recreation and leisure professionals in designing leisure counseling programs. Values clarification activities are presently abundant in leisure education workbooks such as those developed by Stumbo (1992; 1997; 2002).

Theoretical Foundations

The following theoretical premise for values clarification was described by Raths and colleagues (1978) and influenced by writers such as Maslow (1959), Rogers (1961), and Dewey (1939). Maslow and Rogers were humanistic writers who argued that individuals are responsible for discovering their values through honest self-examination and open-minded search for truths about life and Dewey believed that valuing occurs when the head and heart unite in the direction of action (Kinnier, 1995).

Life can present people with changes, choices, and opportunities that make it difficult for people to develop values. Values are what tend to give direction to life; therefore, without clear values, people may find it difficult to confront the changes, choices, and opportunities that confront them. The theory of values clarification was developed to help professionals devise programs that assist participants in confronting these challenges.

The theory of values clarification is based on the premise that many people face complicated decisions. Raths and colleagues suggested that some people flounder in confusion, apathy, or inconsistency. They do not get clear on their values and they cannot find life patterns that are purposeful and satisfying.

The theory of values clarification focuses on the belief that people can be helped to clarify their values, which in turn will result in a behavior change. In relation to leisure, according to the values clarification theory, if an individual becomes clear on his or her leisure values, then the person will experience a more purposeful and satisfying leisure lifestyle. Examples of behaviors that signal value difficulties include apathy (listlessness or a lack of interest in activities), uncertainty (difficulty making an activity decision), over-conforming (conforming to the dominant viewpoint), and over-dissenting (seeking to obtain an identity by disputing others).

Effectiveness

Although values clarification has not been examined in relation to leisure, it has been examined in school settings. This section of the chapter includes a summary of studies that have been conducted to investigate the effects of the values clarification strategies developed by Raths and colleagues (1966) on:

- Self-Concept
- Self-Esteem
- Value Awareness and Clarification

Self-Concept

Fitzpatrick (1977) examined effects of a 16-week values clarification program (1 x wk, 1-hr sessions) on the self-concept and reading comprehension of 288 female and 259 male seventh-grade students. The author administered a self-concept scale, personality test, and reading test before and after the intervention. Compared to the control group, the treatment group demonstrated significant increases in self-concept, personal adjustment, sense of personal feeling, feeling of belonging, reading comprehension, reading efficiency, and total reading achievement. The author concluded that values clarification had a significant effect on the self-concept and reading achievement of the seventh-grade students in the study.

To assess effects of an 11-week values clarification program on personal, social, and total adjustment, **Covault (1975)** implemented strategies (1 x wk, 1-hr sessions) with fifth-grade students. Participants were administered a self-concept scale before and after the intervention. Compared to the 48 participants in the control group, the 55 participants in the treatment group demonstrated significant improvement in self-concept, initiation in classroom activities, and attitudes toward learning. Participants were reported to be significantly less apathetic, flighty, uncertain, inconsistent, overconforming, and overdissenting after the intervention. The author concluded that positive changes in the treatment group support the argument that values clarification is an effective teaching strategy.

In a similar study, **Guziak (1975)** assessed effects of an 8-week values clarification program (1 x wk, 1-hr sessions) on the self-concept and classroom behavior of two fifth-grade classes. Effects were measured with a self-concept scale and a value-related behavior rating form. Compared to the 55 participants in the control group, the 51 participants in the treatment group demonstrated significant improvement in self-concept and initiation in classroom activities, in addition to apathetic, flighty, uncertain, inconsistent, drifting, overconforming, and overdissenting behaviors. The author concluded that values clarification appears to be an effective means for improving self-concept and the classroom behaviors of fifth graders.

Self-Esteem

DePetro (1975) implemented a values clarification program (40 hrs, 1 semester) with 60 senior high school students to examine effects on self-esteem and value priorities. Participants were assigned to a treatment or a control group and then administered a self-esteem inventory and value survey before and after the intervention. The author found small but significant gains in self-esteem scores; however, gains on participants' value priorities were not found. DePetro concluded that because the self-esteem scores were high before the intervention, the potential for higher scores to be found after the intervention was reduced. Furthermore, the author noted that the length of time used for the intervention may have been too limited to assess the effect of values clarification on self-esteem or value priority.

Value Awareness and Clarification

Ohlde and Vinitsky (1976) examined effects of values clarification on value awareness with 19 male and 41 female undergraduate students who had not yet decided on a field of study. Participants first completed a self-concept scale. The 30 participants with high self-concept scores were assigned to a high self-esteem group, and participants with low self-concept scores were assigned to a low self-esteem group. Fifteen participants of each group were randomly assigned to either a treatment or a control group. Participants then completed a value survey and participated in an occupational auction. After 5 weeks, the experimental group engaged in a 7-hour values clarification workshop, and the control group participated in an interpersonal-communication workshop. The treatment group demonstrated significantly greater gains in value awareness. Participants with low self-esteem scores demonstrated similar gains to those who scored high self-esteem. The authors concluded that values clarification strategies are useful in clarifying personal values of college students who were undecided on a college major and had low or high self-esteem.

Arguing that values clarification strategies were designed to help individuals *crystallize* their values rather than impact self-esteem or subject matter proficiency, **Tinsley, Benton, and Rollins (1984)** examined the strategies' effects on values clarification. Fifty-two female and fifty-one male middle school students engaged in values clarification activities that included information on career decision making, occupations, and leisure activities for 2 weeks. The eighth-grade participants experienced a significantly greater degree of confusion after participating in the intervention. Although the findings were not significant, the seventh-grade participants demonstrated a higher level of confusion as well. Tinsley and colleagues concluded that values clarification may help middle school participants begin the process of self-examination; however, the authors warned of the confusion that may be experienced as a result. The authors suggested that values clarification techniques may be used as part of a program, rather than as an entire program, designed to help participants to answer questions.

Summary

In summarizing literature reviewed in this section, there was limited research found examining effects of values clarification. Although existing research supports use of values clarification as an effective intervention, since this research lacked adequate rigor, values clarification cannot yet be identified as an empirically supported facilitation technique. This section of the chapter includes a summary of studies where the effects of the values clarification strategies on self-concept, self-esteem, value awareness have been positive, and effects on values clarification questionable.

Although positive results have been found, it is suggested that results of these studies be interpreted with caution. For example, Lockwood (1978) identified that the Covault (1975) and Guziak (1975) studies based their claims on teachers' judgments on rating sheets. Consequently, it is difficult to discern if the effect is a result of change in student behavior or if the teachers' experience with values clarification changed their criteria of judgment. Second, when values clarification strategies were used to examine effects on values clarification, results were negative (Tinsley et al., 1984). Nevertheless, Tinsley and colleagues provided the only study that examined effects of values clarification strategies on values clarification. It is worth noting that the studies were conducted between the years of 1975 and 1984. Values clarification studies were primarily conducted in the 1970s, a time when values clarification was a primary form of character education in American schools. Values clarification activities have since been used as one tool in character education programs (Kirschenbaum, 1995). However, recent studies have not examined values clarification specifically as a TR intervention.

Case Study

Karen

Upon completion of middle school, Karen, a 15-year-old adolescent, and her family moved to another state. Karen's father was promoted within his company resulting in the family moving to a new location. Karen had difficulty adjusting to the move, which became apparent once she began high school. Karen's parents reported that she withdrew from friends and family. Although Karen was reported as being somewhat shy in middle school, she did have friends with whom she socialized after school and on weekends. Karen, however, stopped socializing with friends when she began high school. Furthermore, although Karen played soccer in middle school, she refused to try out for the high-school team. Karen's parents brought her to a psychotherapist after the first 3 months of her freshman year at high school. After seeing the therapist for 2 months, Karen's parents and therapist decided Karen needed additional services. Karen was then admitted to an all-day psychiatric program.

One week after her admission to the program, Karen continued to appear depressed. Karen was quiet and withdrawn, making few attempts to speak with peers. Karen only spoke in group therapy when directly asked questions. Karen would not participate in unstructured recreation activities; however, she actively participated in structured TR activities when encouraged. When questioned, Karen explained that she was not interested in participating in the activities but participated because she felt that the only way to complete the entire treatment program was to consistently participate.

Values Clarification for Karen

During the first week, Karen completed the writing assignment, but did not engage in the related discussions. Karen declined when asked if she would like to share her answers. During the second week, the TR specialist asked Karen questions to encourage her to participate in the value sheet discussions. With encouragement from the TR specialist and Karen's peers, Karen discussed many of the answers she wrote on her value sheets. From her answers, the TR specialist identified to Karen the way in which her use of free time has changed since she moved. For example, after completing a *Pie of Life* worksheet, Karen discussed with the group how, compared to her present use of free time, she used to spend many hours after school and during the weekends playing soccer.

During the third week of the values clarification intervention, Karen participated in the *Leisure Values* and *Leisure Coat of Arms* activities (Stumbo & Thompson, 1986). From the *Leisure Values* exercise, Karen recognized that she continues to value playing soccer. Karen spoke to the group about wanting to play soccer again, but was afraid that it may be too late because of not trying out her freshman year of high school. The group communicated to Karen that if she played in recreation leagues or in neighborhood games, that she would probably feel more confident when try-out time arrives during her sophomore year. Karen agreed with the group and stated that she was going to start playing soccer again. From the *Leisure Coat of Arms* activity, Karen identified how soccer was an important part of her social life because many of her friends were teammates and opponents. Karen wrote on her value sheet that having friends is important to her. The TR specialist was aware that the issue of friends has been particularly difficult for Karen, so the TR specialist chose to encourage Karen to think about what she can do to maintain her friendships by asking thought-provoking questions on the value sheet rather than asking her questions in the group.

The last week of the intervention involved having Karen participate in the *Meet Your Values* and "Values Discussion" activities (Stumbo & Thompson, 1986; Stumbo, 1992). Although Karen chose to attend but not participate in the "Values Discussion," she did complete the *Meet Your Values* worksheet and share her thoughts with the group. Karen spoke, in particular, about the value of "love." She talked about "having picnics with her family" as the leisure activity she thought of when she thought of "love." Karen explained that when she feels closer to her family when they "go somewhere and do something" other than watching television. As a result, Karen was able to identify that she values her relationship with her family and cherishes the special times she spends with them.

Summary

Before participating in the values clarification intervention, Karen had withdrawn from her friends and family and quit playing soccer, an activity she had enjoyed throughout middle school. After participating in the intervention, Karen identified how important her friends, family, and soccer were to her. Karen stated that because moving to a new town was so difficult for her, she had forgotten what made her happy. As a result, Karen made a commitment to the TR specialist and the group to speak to and listen to family and friends as well as continue to participate in soccer.

Intervention Implementation Exercises

Values clarification activities can be found in a variety of resources; however, for this chapter, values clarification activities specifically designed for leisure education are compiled by Stumbo (1992) and Stumbo and Thompson (1986). The activities described include the following:

- Leisure Values
- Leisure Coat of Arms
- Meet Your Values
- Values Discussion

Leisure Values

"Leisure Values" involves having participants complete a value sheet that includes 16 word pairs separated by a seven-point scale, such as boring–interesting, empty–full, and bad–good. Participants are instructed to complete each of the scales by circling the point on the scale that best describes what leisure means to them. Participants are then asked to discuss what leisure experiences they thought of as they filled out the sheet. Finally, the TR specialist asks the participants to consider how negative and positive experiences influence future experiences, and how their values affect how much they enjoy leisure experiences.

Leisure Coat of Arms

For the "Leisure Coat of Arms" activity, participants are provided with a value sheet that includes a coat of arms with six numbered sections. Participants are asked to write or draw the answer to one question for each section of the coat of arms. Examples of questions include the following: (a) "What do you regard as your greatest personal achievement to date?" and (b) "What leisure activity do you enjoy most?" Upon completion of the value sheet, participants are asked to share their answers and explain why they chose their responses.

Meet Your Values

"Meet Your Values" involves having participants complete a value sheet that includes five values: beauty, love, friendship, truth, and peace. Next to each value, participants write down a leisure activity that represents the value and the reason why it was chosen. Upon completion of the value sheets, participants are instructed to share their responses with the group. Discussions center on reasons for choosing leisure activities and how the activities relate to the listed values.

Values Discussion

For the "Values Discussion" activity, participants are divided into groups of three or four. Each group is then instructed to review and choose one topic from a list of topics. Examples of topics include (a) "The best thing about today is . . . ."

and (b) "Say something about cigarettes." Participants are then asked to discuss the topic chosen for 5 to 10 minutes and listen for each participant's values as they speak. This process is repeated three to four more times before each group discusses the values they felt the other participants demonstrate. A closing discussion focuses on what each participant learned about his or her values and what others perceived to be their values.

Summary

The intervention implementation exercises presented in this chapter can be used to facilitate an initial understanding of the values clarification process. In this section, values clarification activities specifically related to leisure values were presented. As with other interventions, the values clarification activities can be modified to best meet the needs of participants.

Conclusion

Each day, people make decisions that are based on their beliefs, attitudes, and values (Simon et al., 1995). According to Simon and colleagues, people often experience confusion when deciding on personal values related to all areas of life. To help participants clarify their values related to leisure, TR specialists can use the values clarification approach (Johnson & Zoerink, 1977), which is a method used to help participants through the valuing process (Simon et al., 1995). The valuing process involves helping participants through a process of choosing, prizing, and acting upon their values (Raths et al., 1978). This chapter presents a description of values clarification as it relates to TR by providing relevant definitions, a description of the strategies, theoretical foundations, effectiveness studies, a case study, and professional resources and references.

Discussion Questions

1. What is a value indicator?
2. What are components of the valuing process?
3. What is the value clarifying response?
4. What are guidelines for making clarifying responses?
5. What can a TR specialist do to create a beneficial value sheet activity?
6. What are four steps involved in leading a values discussion?
7. With what philosophy was values clarification introduced into schools in the 1960s?
8. What were results of studies examining the relationship between values clarification and self-concept?
9. What were the results of the study that examined the relationship between values clarification and self-esteem?
10. What was the outcome of the values clarification intervention used with "Karen?"

Resources

Material Resources

Edginton, S. R., & Edginton, C. R. (1994). *Youth programs: Promoting quality services*. Champaign, IL: Sagamore.

Stumbo, N. J. (1992). *Leisure education II: More activities and resources*. State College, PA: Venture Publishing, Inc.

Stumbo, N. J., & Thompson, S. R. (1986). *Leisure education: A manual of activities and resources*. State College, PA: Venture Publishing, Inc.

Stumbo, N. J., (1997). *Leisure education III: More goal-oriented activities*. State College: PA: Venture Publishing, Inc.

Stumbo, N. J., (1998). *Leisure education IV: Activities for individuals with substance addictions*. State College: PA: Venture Publishing, Inc.

Websites

Therapeutic Recreation Directory: http://www.recreationtherapy.com/tx/txvalue.htm

References

Brown, D., & Crace, R. K. (1996). Values in life role choices and outcomes: A conceptual model. *The Career Development Quarterly, 44,* 211–223.

Connolly, M. L. (1977). Leisure counseling: A values clarification and assertiveness training approach. In A. Epperson, P. A. Witt, & G. Hitzhusen (Eds.), *Leisure counseling: An aspect of leisure education* (pp. 198–207). Springfield, IL: Charles C. Thomas.

Covault, T. (1973). *The application of value clarification teaching strategies with fifth grade students to investigate their influence on students' self-concept and related classroom coping and interacting behaviors*. Unpublished doctoral dissertation, Ohio State University, Columbus, OH.

DePetro, H. (1975). *Effects of utilizing values clarification strategies on self-esteem of secondary school students*. Unpublished doctoral dissertation, University of Northern Colorado, Greeley, CO.

Dewey, J. (1939). *Theory of valuation*. Chicago, IL: University of Chicago Press.

Fitzpatrick, K. (1977). Effects of values clarification on self-concept and reading achievement. *Reading Improvement, 14,* 233–238.

Guziak, S. (1975). *The use of values clarification strategies with fifth grade students to investigate influence on self-concept and values*. Unpublished doctoral dissertation, Ohio State University, Columbus, OH.

Johnson, L. P., & Zoerink, D. A. (1977). The development and implementation of a leisure counseling program with female psychiatric patients based on value clarification techniques. In A. Epperson, P. A. Witt, & G. Hitzhusen (Eds.), *Leisure counseling: An aspect of leisure education* (pp. 171–197). Springfield, IL: Charles C. Thomas.

Kelly, J. R. (1982). *Leisure*. Englewood Cliffs, NJ: Prentice-Hall.

Kinnier, R. T. (1995). A reconceptualization of values clarification: Values conflict resolution. *Journal of Counseling and Development, 74*, 18–24.

Kirschenbaum, H. (1995). *100 ways to enhance values and morality in schools and youth settings*. Boston: Allyn & Bacon.

Lee, M. J., Whitehead, J., & Balchin, N. (2000). *The measurement of values in youth sport: Development of the youth sport values questionnaire, 22*, 307–326.

Lickona, T. (1991). *Educating for character: How our schools can teach respect and responsibility*. New York: Bantam Books.

Lickona, T. (1993). The return of character education. *Educational Leadership, 51*, 6–11.

Lockwood, A. L. (1978). The effects of values clarification and moral development curricula on school-age subjects: A critical review of recent research. *Review of Educational Research, 48*, 325–364.

Maslow, A. H. (1959). *New knowledge in human value*. New York: Harper & Brothers.

Mosconi, J., & Emmett, J. (2003). Effects of a values clarification curriculum on high school students' definitions of success. *Professional School Counseling, 7*, 68–78.

Ohlde, C. D., & Vinitsky, M. H. (1976). Effect of values-clarification workshop on value awareness. *Journal of Counseling Psychology, 23*, 489–491.

Pinch, K. (2003). Surely you don't mean me? Leisure education and the park and recreation professional. *California Parks and Recreation Magazine, 59*, 36–39.

Raths, L. E., Harmin, M., & Simon, S. B. (1966). *Values and teaching: Working with values in the classroom*. Columbus, OH: Merrill Books.

Raths, L. E., Harmin, M., & Simon, S. B. (1978). *Values and teaching: Working with values in the classroom* (2nd ed.). Columbus, OH: Charles E. Merrill.

Rogers, C. R. (1961). *On becoming a person*. Boston: Houghton Mifflin.

Schwartz, S. H. (1994), Beyond individualism/collectivism: New cultural dimensions of values. In U. Kim, H. C. Triandis, C. Kagitcibasi, S. C. Choi, & G. Yoon (Eds.), *Individualism and collectivism: Theory, method, and application* (pp. 85–119). Thousand Oaks, CA: Sage.

Simon, S. B., Howe, L. W., & Kirschenbaum, H. (1995). *Values clarification: A handbook of practical strategies*. Chesterfield, MA: Values Press.

Stumbo, N. J. (1992). *Leisure education II: More activities and resources*. State College, PA: Venture Publishing, Inc.

Stumbo, N. J. (1997). *Leisure education III: More goal-oriented activities*. State College, PA: Venture Publishing, Inc.

Stumbo, N. J. (2002). *Leisure education I: A manual of activities and resources* (2nd ed.). State College, PA: Venture Publishing, Inc.

Stumbo, N. J., & Thompson, S. R. (1986). *Leisure education: A manual of activities and resources*. State College, PA: Venture Publishing, Inc.

Tinsley, H. E. A., Benton, B. L., & Rollins, J. A. (1984). The effects of values clarification exercises on the value structure of junior high school students. *The Vocational Guidance Quarterly, 32*, 160–167.

Other Books by Venture Publishing, Inc.

Health Promotion for Mind, Body, and Spirit
    by Suzanne Fitzsimmons and Linda L. Buettner
Inclusion: Including People With Disabilities in Parks and Recreation Opportunities
    by Lynn Anderson and Carla Brown Kress
Inclusive Leisure Services: Responding to the Rights of People with Disabilities, Second Edition
    by John Dattilo
Internships in Recreation and Leisure Services: A Practical Guide for Students, Fourth Edition
    by Edward E. Seagle, Jr. and Ralph W. Smith
Interpretation of Cultural and Natural Resources, Second Edition
    by Douglas M. Knudson, Ted T. Cable, and Larry Beck
Intervention Activities for At-Risk Youth
    by Norma J. Stumbo
Introduction to Outdoor Recreation: Providing and Managing Resource Based Opportunities
    by Roger L. Moore and B.L. Driver
Introduction to Recreation and Leisure Services, Eighth Edition
    by Karla A. Henderson, M. Deborah Bialeschki, John L. Hemingway, Jan S. Hodges,
    Beth D. Kivel, and H. Douglas Sessoms
Introduction to Therapeutic Recreation: U.S. and Canadian Perspectives
    by Kenneth Mobily and Lisa Ostiguy
Introduction to Writing Goals and Objectives
    by Suzanne Melcher
Leadership and Administration of Outdoor Pursuits, Third Edition
    by James Blanchard, Michael Strong, and Phyllis Ford
Leadership in Leisure Services: Making a Difference, Third Edition
    by Debra J. Jordan
Leisure and Leisure Services in the 21st Century: Toward Mid Century
    by Geoffrey Godbey
The Leisure Diagnostic Battery Computer Software (CD)
    by Peter A. Witt, Gary Ellis, and Mark A. Widmer
Leisure Education I: A Manual of Activities and Resources, Second Edition
    by Norma J. Stumbo
Leisure Education II: More Activities and Resources, Second Edition
    by Norma J. Stumbo
Leisure Education III: More Goal-Oriented Activities
    by Norma J. Stumbo
Leisure Education IV: Activities for Individuals with Substance Addictions
    by Norma J. Stumbo
Leisure Education Program Planning: A Systematic Approach, Third Edition
    by John Dattilo
Leisure for Canadians
    edited by Ron McCarville and Kelly MacKay
Leisure Studies: Prospects for the Twenty-First Century
    edited by Edgar L. Jackson and Thomas L. Burton
Leisure in Your Life: New Perspectives
    by Geoffrey Godbey
Making a Difference in Academic Life: A Handbook for Park, Recreation, and Tourism Educators
    and Graduate Students
    edited by Dan Dustin and Tom Goodale